A solid, hands-on, quick reference source for K9 officers to use as guidance in their normal day-to-day cases. Also, an excellent reference tool for state and district attorneys to use when researching case law. Truly exceptional!

Detective Jan Scofield, Master Trainer, North American Police Work Dog Association; National Instructor, National Narcotic Detector Dog Association

A must for all police and military law enforcement personnel and prosecutors. The book illustrates the fundamentals of working dogs on search for a scent that may be looking for a person or drugs. The book is very detailed in explaining the laws of search and seizure and how and what motivates the dog to work. I strongly recommend this book to all law enforcement officers, military police, and all county and state prosecutors. If you want to know how and why a dog works, here is the book. If you are a law enforcement officer you have to read this!

Detective Mike Drake, Kentucky State Trooper (Ret.), Pennyrile (Kentucky Regional) Narcotics Task Force (Former) (Renowned for Having Dismantled More Than 500 Meth Labs)

The most comprehensive summary of law enforcement K9 legal and scientific information I have ever seen. Every handler, prosecutor, and judge should read it. Providing K9 support in several homicides referenced in the book, it certainly brings to light many aspects of K9 issues of which everyone should be aware. Even with all the other support materials available for law enforcement K9, having faced one of the best K9 defense experts and coming out victorious as we did, our preparation would have been much easier for me and the prosecutor with a reference tool like *Police and Military Dogs*.

Corporal Jim DeCamp, Clermont County, Ohio, Sheriff's Department, K-9 Unit Supervisor

Police and Military Dogs

*Criminal Detection,
Forensic Evidence, and
Judicial Admissibility*

Police and Military Dogs

Criminal Detection, Forensic Evidence, and Judicial Admissibility

JOHN J. ENSMINGER

CRC Press
Taylor & Francis Group
Boca Raton London New York

CRC Press is an imprint of the
Taylor & Francis Group, an **informa** business

Any legal information in the book should not be construed as advice or writ; for legal advice and the such, please consult an attorney, and so forth.

CRC Press
Taylor & Francis Group
6000 Broken Sound Parkway NW, Suite 300
Boca Raton, FL 33487-2742

First issued in paperback 2019

© 2012 by Taylor & Francis Group, LLC
CRC Press is an imprint of Taylor & Francis Group, an Informa business

No claim to original U.S. Government works

ISBN-13: 978-0-4398-7239-0 (hbk)
ISBN-13: 978-0-367-86655-6 (pbk)

Library of Congress Cataloging-in-Publication Data

Ensminger, John J.
    Police and military dogs : criminal detection, forensic evidence, and judicial admissibility / author, John J. Ensminger.
        p. cm.
    Includes bibliographical references and index.
    ISBN 978-1-4398-7239-0 (hardcover : alk. paper)
    1. Police dogs--Law and legislation--United States. 2. Searches and seizures--United States. 3. Evidence, Criminal--United States. 4. Criminal investigation--United States. I. Title.

KF390.5.D6E57 2012
345.73'064--dc23   2011034137

Visit the Taylor & Francis Web site at
http://www.taylorandfrancis.com

and the CRC Press Web site at
http://www.crcpress.com

Contents

SECTION I Police and Military Dogs in the Twenty-First Century

SECTION II Tracking, Trailing, and Scent Identification

SECTION III   *Detection Functions*

SECTION IV   Apprehension and Rescue Functions

List of Figures

List of Tables

Author

John J. Ensminger is an attorney and a national consultant on canine legal issues involving skilled dogs and their handlers. His publications include: *Service and Therapy Dogs in American Society: Science, Law and the Evolution of Canine Caregivers* (Charles C Thomas, 2010); *Money Laundering, Terrorism, and Financial Institutions* (Civic Research Institute, 2003); the monthly *USA Patriot Act Monitor*; and contributions on canine legal issues to the *Journal of Animal Law*, *GP Solo: ABA General Practice*, and *Tax Notes*. Ensminger graduated from the University of California, Berkeley, where he majored in zoology, and was a member of the scientific team on an expedition of Stanford University's research vessel, *Te Vega*, to the Galapagos Islands. He earned his JD and LLM degrees from Hastings College of the Law and New York University School of Law, respectively, practices law in New York and is a member of the bar of the United States Supreme Court. He was chair of the Banking and Savings Institutions Committee of the American Bar Association Tax Section and was on the adjunct faculty of the Peter J. Tobin College of Business at St. John's University in New York, where he taught the taxation of complex financial transactions. Ensminger lives in Stone Ridge, New York, with his wife, Joan, and Chloe, a certified therapy dog. He reports on legal and scientific developments concerning dogs at: doglawreporter.blogspot.com.

Contributors

John G. Grubbs, president of United States Bomb Dogs, Inc., was a law enforcement officer for 20 years with the Explosives Detection Canine Unit of the U.S. Secret Service, in which capacity he guarded U.S. presidents, vice presidents, and world leaders.

Tadeusz Jezierski, Ph.D., head of the Department of Animal Behavior at the Institute of Genetics and Animal Breeding of the Polish Academy of Science, has published 65 scientific papers, including studies on canine scent detection.

L.E. Papet, Executive Director of K9 Resources, LLC, in Ohio, has developed 170 protocols for training, testing, and deploying canine units.

Introduction

This book describes police procedures, forensics studies, and the law that has been applied to evidence produced or affected by police canine work. It is my opinion that it is as artificial to separate these three aspects of dogs in law enforcement—indeed more artificial—than it is to combine them. A law enforcement canine handler should know how his work with a skilled police dog will affect the subsequent investigation and prosecution of the crime. A forensics scientist should be able to tell the handler how he and his dog can help solve the crime, and what procedures are optimal for finding and processing evidence. Similarly, the forensics specialist should understand the boundaries of admissibility of the evidence she produces, and in this way help the prosecutor. The prosecutor wants to be sure that the evidence provided by the police and forensics personnel will withstand challenges from the defense and skepticism from the courts. Defense counsel should be aware of the process by which evidence has been produced and should understand where that evidence might be sufficiently weak as to be excludable by a challenge. Finally, the judiciary—beginning with the trial judge but continuing up through the appellate system—must understand the value and limits of canine evidence.

It is with this continuum in mind that this book is written. The fact that many courts have made poor judgment calls as to certain types of canine evidence, such as with scent lineups, is not solely the fault of the judges. Police have often been able to dazzle lawyers and judges with stories about the perfection of their dogs, and far too many defense lawyers regard canine evidence as the least important element of the prosecution's case. This is most unfortunate given that many convictions have resulted almost exclusively from tracking or scent identification evidence, with supposed corroboration sometimes being almost fictional. The number of canine convictions where the defendant eventually argues ineffective assistance of counsel is disturbingly high. Many prisoners have lost years of their lives before finding exoneration, and one must believe that some never will.

It is also appropriate to say something about what this book does not attempt to do. This is not a training manual. Training issues are discussed where they have been the subject of research or judicial analysis and thus have received scientific scrutiny or legal attention, but I am not a trainer and defer to the many well-written books by highly experienced trainers that provide very detailed guidance. Since certification standards are sometimes used by courts in deciding on the admissibility of canine evidence, such standards will be discussed, but not with an eye to providing an ultimate "best practices" approach. Nor is this book a procedures guide. Again, where a handler's work is explained by police or military directives or policies that result in judicial scrutiny, the procedures and operations will be analyzed, but no set of guidelines will be categorized as optimal.

Many organizations that provide training guidelines and certification procedures will be mentioned here, but it is to be hoped that none of them have been favored. The standards provided by these organizations reflect the experience of their members, as well as the science and law at the time (or times) that the standards were drafted and instituted. These organizations provide useful resources, and Appendix A lists those whose officials or members have provided information to me, but the absence of a listing in a particular discussion (say, cadaver dogs) is not meant to indicate that the organization is inferior as to that issue. This too was a matter of conserving space in a manuscript that early on busted the bounds the publisher sought to impose on me, and I apologize to those officials whose efforts might not have received adequate recognition here.

I have placed certain boundaries on the topics covered here. Many areas of canine science and law can be seen as aspects of much larger subjects. The science of smell has filled many journals and books, but only studies directly relevant to canine police work will be reviewed here. Several sections of this book will discuss the qualification of a handler as an expert. This sometimes leads to questions about the scientific aspects of canine work. Although scientific issues will be discussed extensively, the broad question of the admission of scientific evidence in trials will only be described as this relates to canine work. Other areas of the law that will receive only brief mention include compensation of police canine handlers, which involves areas of employment and tax law that would be out of place in this context but ultimately may be necessary to understand for any lawyer representing either an employer or an employee where compensation for canine work is involved. Cases in which public officials have been sued because a dog performing official functions has bitten someone are often resolved not on the facts of the case but on concepts of immunity for public officials. Limitations of space have required that a broader discussion of immunity concepts be avoided. Any first-year law student has heard the law described as a seamless web. Just about any area of the law connects to many others, and the decision of how far afield to go in discussing a specific case or concept is, inevitably, somewhat arbitrary.

This book results from an effort that involved many people and I wish to credit those who helped at various stages. First, there are three contributors; one scientist, Tadeusz Jezierski; and two trainer-handlers, John Grubbs and L.E. Papet. Their biographies appear in the chapters they coauthored, but each of them is also responsible for many suggestions and corrections in other chapters. Gail K. McConnell, an assistant district attorney in Richmond, Texas, was kind enough to read and correct large portions of the manuscript. Gregory H. Keller, formerly Fire Chief of Salem, Oregon, provided a wonderful photo of himself and his arson dog, Charlotte, and read through the chapter on accelerant detection dogs. Professor Michael Perlin of New York Law School gave detailed notes regarding several papers that became the basis of chapters in this book. Professor Perlin's wide knowledge of constitutional law has undoubtedly saved me from many blunders as has been true in a friendship that goes back 35 years to when we worked together in the Department of the Public Advocate in New Jersey. J.J. Sullivan, official historian of the New York City Retired Transit Police Officers' Association, provided me with valuable leads on the history of police dogs in New York City. Jesse S. Mendez, a legend for his canine handling in Vietnam, was kind enough to provide me with an original photograph of himself jumping from a plane and forwarded useful materials on the history of military dogs. Ido Yitzhaki of DiagNose Consulting & Dectection Services in France, answered many questions on European matters, and supplied the image used for the cover.

More people than I could safely remember commented on drafts of articles and blogs that became fodder for this book, and I hope that it lives up to their expectations.

My wife, in addition to tolerating the two years I spent in my foxhole working on this manuscript, also helped prepare a number of the photographs and diagrams. I also wish to thank Rodney Miller, who cheerfully endured long descriptions of many sections of this book and for giving me scientific perspectives of great value. Finally, Mark Listewnik and Linda Leggio of Taylor & Francis/CRC Press gave many suggestions that helped shape the book and edited the manuscript with great skill. No author should be without such skilled editors as a final safety net.

Police dog work is not a static subject, and procedures, research, and the law continue to evolve. Although this means that subjects treated here will more often sooner than later be out of date, it is as good a time as any to take stock of this very large area of science and law. Our best friend continues to amaze all of us who work with dogs, and I and those who have contributed to this book hope you enjoy taking the journey with us.

Section I

Police and Military Dogs in the Twenty-First Century

Police dogs now perform a great many functions that they did not perform before 1970. A summary of the changes that have occurred in the last four decades will explain the focus of much of this book. Dogs have been used for behaviors that are explained by their evolution and their adaptation as the first domesticated animal. This unique relationship and their ability to communicate with and understand us have allowed us to take advantage of their astounding skills. A brief overview of these issues will be provided in the following two chapters.

1 Development of Police and Military Dog Functions

- Two men are killed in their sleeping bags in a cabin used by campers in the Sierra Nevada Mountains. The cabin can only be reached by hiking several miles from a highway. Shell casings at the door of the cabin are placed in a sterile glass jar and taken to a police station where a scent transfer unit, a specialized suction device, is used to transfer scent from the casings to a gauze pad. A bloodhound is brought from Sacramento, California, to the crime scene and scented on the gauze pad. The dog is commanded to track on the porch of the cabin. Within 10 feet the handler tells a fellow officer that the dog has found a trail, but it is not the path leading to the highway. The dog and the two officers follow the trail for 2 miles, going deeper into the woods until the trail disappears. The dog goes around the edge of a small lake to an open area where there is a tent and a fire that has recently been put out. Inside the tent the officers see a rifle that could have fired the shells found at the crime scene. When the camper returns the officers ask him to come with them for questioning.
- In Rotterdam, the Netherlands, a woman puts a gauze pad in front of a dog's nose and commands the dog to sniff. After the dog has sniffed for a few seconds she steps back and the dog walks toward an elevated platform on which are six metal tubes in a row. The dog has been trained to sniff each tube, and after doing so lies down in front of the third tube in the row. A person watching on a video camera notes which tube the dog alerted to. The dog has matched a scent from an object probably handled by the perpetrator at the crime scene to a scent of a suspect who is already in custody. The room is cleaned, new metal tubes are put in place, and another dog performs the same test. The second dog also alerts to a tube that was held by the same suspect, ignoring the tubes that had been held by foils. One more link in the evidence that will lead to a conviction has been made.
- A dog at a French airport is brought into a room with five stations, each station holding a small bottle that contains air extracted from a confined space. Two of the bottles contain air taken from inside the plastic wrapping around a large group of packages consolidated for an airfreight company. The dog sits down before one of the air stations, which happens to be one of the consolidated packages. The handler notifies an observer that this is a clear alert. The company that uses the canine scent detection system notifies the freight company that the explosives detection dog has alerted to air from a specific wrapped pallet. The packages in the pallet are deconsolidated and sniffed individually by another dog, this one provided by airport police. The dog alerts to a package labeled as containing printer cartridges. The package is opened and found to contain an explosive device that was set to go off when the plane reached 25,000 feet, which would have likely happened over the Atlantic Ocean.
- A woman's naked body is found in a ravine. The body has been ravaged by animals and is highly decomposed. There is an abandoned van at the top of the ravine. Examination of the license plates verifies that the van was reported stolen. A dog trained to smell decomposing human remains is brought to the vehicle and alerts inside the back of the van. The police learn that the man who had reported the van stolen had a tempestuous relationship with a young woman whose parents had reported her missing a month before. The cadaver dog

is taken to the man's house and alerts to another vehicle outside the garage. DNA analysis verifies that the body is that of the missing woman. The man becomes the prime suspect and the police continue to look for evidence.

- A fire in an abandoned building is ruled suspicious by the New York City Fire Department. An accelerant detection dog alerts to a location where a fire inspector says the burn pattern suggests that kerosene or another accelerant may have been poured. Laboratory analysis of items in the area where the dog alerted fails to confirm the presence of any accelerant, however, and the police investigation, while remaining open, stalls. The owner files a claim with an insurance company, which conducts its own investigation, including using another accelerant detection dog owned by an independent contractor. This dog, 2 weeks after the first dog, also alerts at several places in the rubble of the building, including the place where the police dog had alerted. The insurance company declines to pay on the policy after finding that the owner has twice filed claims on suspicious fires before. The owner sues on the policy and the court must decide whether to let the jury hear the evidence of the two accelerant detection dogs despite the absence of laboratory confirmation of the presence of an accelerant.

Only the first of these situations, adapted from parts of cases and studies, describes a canine function—tracking—that existed before 1970. Scientifically conducted scent lineups date from after 1990. Remote explosives detection systems using dogs have been studied with regard to landmines and have begun to be used for airfreight. The first dog devoted solely to finding cadavers was deployed in 1974, the first arson dog in 1986. Even the tracking situation described in the first scenario involves the use of a device, a scent transfer unit, which was patented in 1998.[1]

Police dogs today look much as they looked 50 years ago, though they now often travel in crates rather than in the backseats of squad cars, but it would be a mistake to think that there has not been a considerable amount of change in police work involving canines.

CATEGORIES OF CANINE FUNCTIONS

Police and military canine functions can be divided into four general categories: (1) tracking, trailing, and identification; (2) suspect apprehension and crowd control; (3) detection; and (4) rescue and protection. With modern scent lineup procedures, scent identification is increasingly separated from tracking and trailing functions, but since the same dogs sometimes do both tasks, particularly in the United States, they are grouped together here. Dogs trained in suspect apprehension are also often trackers or trailers, and the two responsibilities sometimes overlap in the same investigation with the same dog, yet the training regimens are considerably different. Detection functions are by far the largest category, both in terms of the broad range of scents detected and the number of dogs and handlers doing this type of work. This includes dogs trained to detect narcotics, explosives, and accelerants, as well as cadaver dogs. Detection work is also increasingly common in non-police work, such as with dogs trained to alert to bed bugs, termites, mold, or to detect illegal agricultural imports at borders. Almost all detection functions are relatively recent, most dating after 1970. The fourth category includes search and rescue dogs as well as military sentry dogs and dogs trained to protect diplomats and important political figures.

Many canine functions are the subject of intense research, and courts throughout the country are constantly being asked to rule on the admissibility of new types and variations of canine evidence. This book will discuss these developments in detail, chapter by chapter, but it is appropriate to begin with an overview and a discussion of issues common to all police dogs and the work they perform. Significant developments concerning police dogs are summarized in Table 1.1.

The number of police and military dogs in the United States is difficult to estimate, given the vast number of agencies that use dogs trained for police and military functions, the fluctuating nature of the needs of those agencies, and the increasing use of contract canine teams to perform certain

TABLE 1.1

Significant Developments in Canine Procedures, Forensics, and Law

Year	Development[2]
1893	Tracking evidence begins to be accepted by U.S. courts[3]; some judges express concern that raising bloodhounds to sell to police departments as tracking dogs will become a business activity for individuals looking for profit.[4]
1903	Crime in Germany solved by perhaps first scent lineup; suspect and foils asked to hold stones and put them on the ground; dog scented to knife from crime scene alerted to stone held by suspect; suspect confessed.[5]
1907	New York City begins use of police dogs (followed by New Haven, Connecticut, in 1910); male dogs preferred by most departments.[6]
1909	Otto Kalischer discovers that dogs can be trained to detect specific odors, even when mixed with other odors.[7]
1914–1918	Red Cross uses dogs on each side during World War I; dogs also work on battlefields as messengers and sentries[8]; 28,000 dogs requisitioned for use in the war.[9]
1917	Dogs follow a trail from the scene of the crime but do not encounter the perpetrator; later, such dogs sometimes alert to suspects in a police station; courts begin to admit such "station identifications" as evidence.[10]
1923	Scent lineups of humans enter U.S. trials; rejected as evidence by Iowa Supreme Court[11]; *Frye*, decided by the Court of Appeals for the District of Columbia, requires that scientific procedures have received "general acceptance in the particular field in which it belongs"[12]; *Frye* is still valid for much state law and is occasionally applied to canine evidence.
1942	Dogs for Defense created to train dogs for scout, tunnel, and mine detection; dogs were taught to discover buried metallic and nonmetallic mines, trip wires, and booby traps.[13]
1950	26th Infantry Platoon at Fort Riley, Kansas, trains dogs for Korean War; unit disbanded in 1953.[14]
1958	U.S. military dog training transferred from U.S. Army to Air Force, which assigns the function to the Patrol/Sentry Dog Training Branch, Department of Security Police Training, 327th Technical School at Lackland Military Training Center near San Antonio, Texas.[15]
1960	Scout, sentry, and mine detection dogs begin to be used in Vietnam; 1,100 trained dogs are with the troops by 1965, some of which are airborne.[16]
1970	Experimental narcotic detector dog training program begins at Lackland Air Force Base in San Antonio, eventually moving to the Canine Enforcement Training Center near Washington, D.C. (in 1980).[17] Los Angeles Police Department begins using narcotics detection dogs.[18]
1971	Air Force assumes responsibility for U.S. military working dogs.[19] Department of Defense obtains feasibility study on training dogs for explosives detection.[20]
1972	Transportation Security Administration Explosives Detection Canine Team Program begins.[21]
1973	Narcotics detection dog alerts begin to be admissible evidence in criminal prosecutions.[22]
1974	New York State Police deploy first cadaver dog.[23]
Late 1970s	Schools concerned about increasing drug problems implement sniffs of students, lockers, and school parking lots.[24]
1982	Scent match lineups begin to be introduced as evidence in U.S. courts; research indicates lineups often fail to take many variables into consideration.[25]
1983	U.S. Supreme Court decides *U.S. v. Place*[26]; opinion of Justice O'Connor describes canine sniff of luggage as *sui generis*, not constituting a search under the Fourth Amendment. Federal and state courts begin to extend reasoning of *Place* to other situations.
1986	Connecticut State Police deploy an arson dog. Iowa trainer begins training accelerant detection dogs in 1985.[27]
1990	Professor Taslitz examines scent lineup evidence in U.S. courts and concludes that such lineups fail to meet adequate evidentiary standards for criminal prosecutions.[28] While frequently cited in decisions, many courts accept such evidence anyway or declare that its admission by trial courts was harmless error.

—Continued

TABLE 1.1 (Continued)
Significant Developments in Canine Procedures, Forensics, and Law

Year	Development[2]
1993	*Daubert* decided by U.S. Supreme Court, rejecting *Frye* general acceptance standard.[29] Some states adopt *Daubert* standard while some retain *Frye* standard; *Daubert* sometimes applied to canine evidence.
1994	Schoon and de Bruin begin to describe scent lineups conducted with rigorous scientific standards[30]; police practice in Holland and Eastern Europe is heavily influenced by their protocol designs; FBI begins to adopt Schoon's protocols.
1998	Tolhurst and Harris patent the Scent Transfer Unit (STU 100)[31]; courts begin accepting scent identifications where dogs were scented to pads obtained from STUs.[32]
2000	U.S. Supreme Court disapproves of checkpoint in Indianapolis set up for general purpose of uncovering any illegal activity, including sniffing all cars stopped with narcotics detection dog[33]; temporary checkpoints subsequently focus on road safety and sobriety issues, but continue to involve drug detection dogs.
2001	Explosives detection, search and rescue, and therapy dogs work at the World Trade Center site after terrorist attack[34]; 9/11 increases demand for explosives detection dogs.[35]
2004	First complete genome sequence of a domestic dog is made public[36]; genome studies provide sophisticated analysis of canine olfactory receptor genes, including breed and individual variations.[37]
2005	U.S. Supreme Court decides *Caballes*, approving use of narcotics detection dogs during traffic stops[38]; other courts begin exploring the significance of the case to various types of sniffs. Search and rescue dogs work in the aftermath of Hurricane Katrina, sometimes assisting in rescuing pets as well as humans.[39]
2009	Dispute over largest working dog contract award by the military is resolved after litigation in Federal Claims Court and reviews by the Government Accountability Office; government Web site reports final contract was valued at over $44 million.[40]
2010	Handler of military working dogs in Iraq convicted of conspiracy and maltreatment of prisoners during interrogation at Abu Ghraib Prison, after years of press coverage of misuses of military working dogs.[41]

functions. One estimate in 2002 was that there were 7,000 police dogs in the United States, but this estimate seemed largely focused on federal dogs (not including military working dogs).[42]

THE RIGHT DOG FOR THE JOB

Deciding to train a puppy to perform a function for much of its adult life requires making an effort to find a dog that will have the right disposition for the work involved.[43] As with service dogs for individuals with physical and mental disabilities, training can be a long and expensive process, and constant reinforcement is required. Most types of police work require that dogs not be overly nervous or afraid, be lively and interested in their environment, willing to work long hours, and reasonably intelligent and quick to learn. Dogs must sometimes work off-lead.[44] Most functions require that the dog have a good searching drive and display an inclination to use their noses often.[45] Boldness has been correlated with success,[46] but too strong a prey drive may mean a dog will think too much about getting a reward.[47] One study found that dogs with a high probability of being certified as police dogs were, as puppies, willing to chase, catch, and fetch a tennis ball and follow a rag taken away from them; they did not show fear or run from a shovel striking a metal sewer lid, were willing to approach strangers, and passed obstacles at high speed with little hesitation.[48]

The first tracking dogs were often bloodhounds, but even at the end of the nineteenth century, many other breeds and mixed breeds were used for this function. European police dogs at the beginning of the twentieth century were generally from shepherd breeds, particularly those associated with the countries of the police departments.[49] Thus, Malinois and German shepherds were, and are, widely used. Large size may be a factor in the selection of breeds for a variety of functions, including tracking and suspect apprehension,[50] but detection dogs can be smaller since the olfactory abilities of the animal are paramount. German shepherds are often chosen in the United States because of their intimidating appearance, though other breeds have this quality as well. Some breeds known for aggressive appearance, such as pit bulls, may be avoided for reasons that are partly political. Breed preferences for specific assignments will be discussed in the following chapters.

TRAINING PHILOSOPHIES

Aversive training techniques preferred by many handlers 20 years ago have increasingly been replaced by techniques involving positive stimuli, such as treats, toys, and praise. This remains a matter of debate among trainers of police and military dogs as well as generally in the canine training industry. One Belgian and French team of researchers found that military working dogs trained with more aversive stimuli (such as yanking the leash and hanging dogs by their collars) performed less well than dogs that were trained with more positive stimuli (including stroking and petting). Handlers often used aversive stimuli when trying to get dogs to release a bite. "Hanging dogs by the collar to force them to release the sleeve is a rather 'reactive' training method: rather than forcing the dog to loosen its grip, this stimulus incites the dog to maintain this behaviour."[51] The researchers reaching this conclusion noted that improving dogs' attention (and reducing their level of distraction) could be influenced by using rewards, such as tug and retrieve games that require their concentration. Handlers often rewarded intermittently, even when the dog performed a task correctly, so the researchers recommended that trainers be taught to reward consistently.[52] Training handlers regularly was found to increase the use of positive stimuli and perhaps improved the welfare of the dogs.[53] Frequency of training sessions is also occasionally a matter of research. Training intensely may not be necessary, and may even be counterproductive. One study found that training dogs in a particular exercise—putting a paw on a mouse pad—was more effective if only done once a week than if done 5 days a week.[54]

Most police dogs are trained in several and sometimes many functions. Police officers and researchers debate whether an increasing number of functions means that a dog will perform some of them less well than others or less well than specialized dogs. Often the duties imposed on a canine team are a matter of economics for a police department. Having dogs that only do one thing may be too costly. There has been some research in this area, such as the finding that dogs trained to find both live persons in disaster sites and cadavers in those sites are less effective in finding survivors than dogs trained only to find survivors. In wilderness searches, where the missing person may be either alive or dead, a dog trained in both live and cadaver finding may be required.[55] Various professional organizations describe training standards and testing requirements for specific canine functions, which will be discussed separately in the following chapters.

Training is serious business. A trainer who sold dogs supposedly trained in explosives detection to the State Department, the Federal Reserve, and the Internal Revenue Service (IRS), was sentenced to more than 5 years in prison when the dogs turned out to have virtually no detection ability.[56] Training standards are provided by a number of national police dog organizations and courts have often looked to such standards in determining whether a dog is adequately trained.[57]

CANINE BEHAVIOR AND THE ALERT

Any study of skilled dogs requires frequent reference to canine behavior and, insofar as that behavior is interpreted, of human behavior. In analyzing the functions of police dogs, it must never be forgotten that the dogs and their handlers are teams, and their ability to work together depends on their ability to understand each other. Thus, studies about eye contact between humans and dogs and the ability of dogs to understand human pointing gestures are relevant to police dog functions.[58] The fact that dogs can understand pointing gestures when young, by 21 weeks of age, is important in designing training programs for police dogs.[59]

Most police dog functions involve an *alert*, a specific and simple behavior pattern by which the dog indicates to the handler that a target odor is present. Alerts can be active, such as growling and pawing the place where the odor is detected, or passive, such as sitting or lying down in front of the location of the odor. Alerts are taught for dogs trained in suspect identification and in all detection functions. Thus, dogs trained in scent identification, and in narcotics, explosives, and accelerant detection, as well as cadaver dogs and search and rescue dogs, are taught alerts. Whether the alert is active or passive may be partially the trainer's or handler's preference and partially the dog's inclination—what behavioral pattern emerges as most easy to reinforce during the training regimen—but may also be affected by the work the dog is being trained to perform. An aggressive alert, where the dog paws or bites the item from which the odor is emanating, is often preferred by narcotics dog handlers but can be dangerous where a dog is detecting hidden explosives or landmines. With accelerant detection and cadaver dog work, an aggressive alert can contaminate evidence. Search and rescue dogs may be taught to bark but not to growl, as this would frighten the person that the dog has found in the debris he is searching.

Alerts are not always clearly made by dogs in the field, and handlers should not call an alert where there is not a clear and specific behavior. A dog sniffing a row of airline luggage may "show interest" in one bag without alerting. The bag may contain food that the dog would like to get to, but may also contain such a small residue of drugs or explosives that the dog is uncertain whether she is detecting a target odor. A good many prosecutions hinge on the difference between alerting and showing interest, as the subsequent actions of the handler and the police may or may not be justified by an interest level. For instance, if a dog shows interest, without alerting, at the rear door of a car, is the officer justified in opening the car door so that the dog can sniff inside? Perhaps the dog will then alert to a bag in the backseat of the car and drugs will be found. It is doubtful that the officer's decision to open the car door without the passenger's consent can be justified on constitutional grounds even though drugs are found. An officer describing the dog's interest as an alert may have to argue against the evidence provided by the dashboard video camera of his patrol car, an increasingly common record of police work.[60] A discussion of alerts must recognize that there is something of a continuum in the dog's behavior, from lack of interest to mild interest to high interest to a weak alert to a strong alert. All these terms appear in the cases that will be discussed throughout this book under the various police dog functions.

THE SNIFF

The greatest growth aspect of police dog work in the United States concerns narcotics and explosives detection dogs, and this has come about in part because the U.S. Supreme Court, and other courts, have set boundaries that allow deploying dogs to perform sniffs in many situations without any advance judicial approval—that is, without a warrant. This has been held in sniffs of luggage compartments on planes, trains, and buses; sniffs of luggage being loaded and unloaded from carriers; sniffs of the exteriors of lawfully stopped vehicles; sniffs outside the sleeper compartments of trains or in the aisles of buses; sniffs in the common areas of commercial storage facilities, warehouses, and hallways where students have lockers; sniffs outside safe deposit boxes; and sniffs of packages being moved by the U.S. mail or commercial carriers. Not only may the sniff be performed without judicial approval, but in some cases, such as vehicle sniffs, a positive alert by the dog provides probable cause for an immediate search without a warrant.[61]

Sniffs of locations where some expectation of privacy applies, however, may be searches for Fourth Amendment purposes. This amendment provides that the "right of the people to be secure in their persons, houses, papers, and effects, against unreasonable searches and seizures, shall not be violated, and no Warrants shall issue, but upon probable cause, supported by Oath or affirmation, and particularly describing the place to be searched, and the persons or things to be seized." An expectation of privacy has been found to apply to sniffs in residences, in the property close to a house (within what is called in law "the curtilage"), inside private compartments of trains and vessels, and sniffs of the person.[62] In such cases, either a warrant or exigent circumstances may overcome a lack of consent to perform a search.[63] There are other exceptions to the warrant requirement, such as with a sniff incident to a lawful arrest, of a vehicle lawfully impounded, of items in plain view, or in a public emergency.[64]

In some situations where a warrant is not required courts may nevertheless specify that police canine work requires that there be a "reasonable suspicion" (sometimes a "reasonable, articulable suspicion") that criminal activity is taking place. This requirement has been applied to extending a traffic stop beyond the original reason the car was pulled over so that a drug dog could be brought to sniff the car, sniffs of luggage in possession of a suspect, and sniffs at the front door of a private residence. Here also, state and federal law sometimes diverge, and if the matter has not reached the U.S. Supreme Court, decisions by various federal courts may disagree as to what is permissible.

Not all states have followed the lead of the U.S. Supreme Court in some of these situations and have used language in state constitutions to provide protections—from a law enforcement perspective, barriers—to police conduct that do not apply under the U.S. Constitution. Thus, law enforcement agencies ideally should keep canine team officers familiar with situations where state law imposes additional requirements for sniffs and searches that do not apply for federal purposes.

LINEUPS IN POLICE DOG WORK

The canine alert is often used in a lineup setting, allowing the dog to choose between a number of items, only one of which will have prosecutorial significance. The procedure is similar to suspect lineups for visual identification by a victim or witness. In police dog work, lineups have been used with narcotics detection dogs sniffing a row of packages,[65] luggage,[66] and envelopes containing currency (where one of the envelopes contained cash taken from a suspected drug dealer).[67] Cadaver dogs have been used in lineups of vehicles, one of which was suspected of being used to transport a body.[68] In a California case involving a cadaver dog, a court imposed foundational requirements similar to those of basic tracking dog law—that the dog is trained, experienced, and proven reliable, that the lineup was properly and fairly conducted, and that the scent on the vehicle had not become stale. The tendency of courts to apply tracking dog requirements to nontracking situations will be discussed with regard to scent lineups.[69] Of course, narcotics and explosives detection dogs working at border checkpoints, airports, and other locations could be described as doing a sort of continual lineup work since they are being asked to identify a scent in a location containing a large number of objects that potentially could hold that scent.

DOG AND HANDLER AS A TEAM

A handler must learn many things about his or her dog's behavior in addition to its alerting behavior. The handler of a tracking or trailing dog must recognize when the dog is following the trail taken by the individual on whom the dog has been scented and must be able to tell when the dog has lost the trail. The handler must learn what motivates his dog best—generally treats, toys, praise, or some combination of these. The dog's assignment may limit which motivation may be used. Some trainers will not give treats or allow a toy before a tracking assignment is completed, as they believe this will give a new scent or distract the dog from the trail. The handler should sense when the dog is tired or becoming exhausted. Some agencies structure canine teamwork to take the dog's attention span into account. Police canine work requires that dogs be rested and willing to work with a common "duty cycle" being about an hour.[70] Data collected for the Federal Aviation Administration at Auburn University found that dogs can work between 91 and 120 minutes continuously and remain effective.[71]

The dog needs sleep more than the handler, but dogs have different sleep patterns from humans: about 16 to 20 minutes of sleep followed by a brief period of wakefulness, then sleep, then wakefulness, for hours on end. But dogs can indulge themselves in this pattern both day and night, making them much better for the swing and graveyard shifts than is often true of their handlers.[72] Dogs need more sleep as they get older so police dogs near the end of a career may, not surprisingly, be somewhat less available for work even if healthy.[73]

Both the dog and handler must have the correct qualities for police canine work. The handler must let the dog work on her own and must remain sensitive to what the dog is doing, not just what the handler wants the dog to be doing. Handlers must be patient. One hormonal study concluded that men can pass their frustrations at the loss of an agility competition onto dogs they were handling, with the dogs demonstrating increased cortisol levels associated with stress.[74] Maturity and calmness are therefore desirable in the handler. Nearly a century ago, Stephanitz described the relationship of dog and handler as an almost mystical connection:

> The success of all employment as an assistant of man depends in the first place on expert leadership, whereby the dog is always put in just the right place, and where the man is so well-acquainted with the peculiarities of the dog that he always knows how to interpret correctly the meaning of the dog's signs. A leader without expert knowledge and affection for the dog will achieve only very mediocre results with the best trained dog; while an expert dog-loving leader can achieve good results with a dog of only fair capacity. [In police dog work] the dog and his leader must know each other intimately. The leader must never disturb the dog in his work; he must never interfere, not even when he thinks that the dog is at fault, but he must always remain in closest interior rapport with the dog. He must be able to read the meaning of everything the dog reports to him in the manner of his work, by the play of features, and finally, by his success or his failure, which is often only apparent.[75]

The police dog is often a pet of the policeman's family while off duty.[76] One research team argued that a dog that lives and plays with its handler will be more obedient to the handler and generally a better police dog, and concluded that this is more important in achieving a good relationship than a long period of working together.[77]

CANINE EVIDENCE

The increasing breadth of police dog work has intensified research on the reliability of results obtained from their skills and has led courts into detailed consideration of the judicial limits of evidence acquired from their work. Police canine evidence is unique in that despite the high level of training now generally required of dogs and their trainers, the fact that the dog cannot speak and the inherent variability introduced by the animal's behavior must always be taken into consideration. A dog's alert to the outside of a vehicle or pawing the ground by a dog trained to recognize the smell of decomposing human tissue is not the same as taking an air sample from the same location that the dog is sniffing and running sophisticated tests to determine the chemical constituents, and particularly the suspicious constituents, inside the sample. It is because such procedures are sometimes less accurate than the dog's nose, and generally much more expensive and difficult to administer, that the dog has such high value in law enforcement. But the dog's nose comes with the potentially erratic behavior of the dog. The problem was well stated by Judge Stevan T. Northcutt of the Florida Second District Court of Appeal:

> Although we commonly refer to the "training" of dogs, manifestly they are not trained in the sense that human beings may be trained. It is not a process of imparting knowledge and skills that dogs want or need. However much we dog lovers may tend to anthropomorphize their behavior, the fact is that dogs are not motivated to acquire skills that will assist them in their chosen profession of detecting contraband. Rather, dogs are "conditioned," that is, they are induced to respond in particular ways to particular stimuli. For law enforcement purposes, the ideal conditioning would yield a dog who always responds to specified stimuli in a consistent and recognizable way, yet never responds in that manner absent the stimuli. But this does not happen. While dogs are not motivated in ways that humans are, neither can they be calibrated to achieve mechanically consistent results.[78]

Nevertheless, some dogs are more attentive and accurate than others. Countless factors can affect the performance of a dog, including temperature, humidity, diet, sleep, exercise, stress, the environment the dog is asked to work in, disease, and contact with other dogs.[79] Sometimes there is no explanation for a dog's failure to perform in certain circumstances. A dog may be effective in an assignment on one day but not on another.[80] The handler must know the limits of his or her dog. The skill of a dog will vary from day to day, even hour to hour. A witness in a narcotics case observed that "dogs are not unlike humans, dogs can have good and bad days just like we can. They can have headaches and stomach aches and everything else and just decide they don't feel like working."[81] It is important to recognize this variability in interpreting the dog's actions. The better each participant in the criminal justice system understands the strengths and weaknesses of canine evidence, the better and fairer that system will work. Canine evidence should not be dismissed as "junk science" despite its weaknesses. The failure to point out those weaknesses in trials that result in wrongful convictions has often been as much a fault of ineffective defense counsel as of overzealous police officers or sloppy forensics specialists.

The admissibility of canine evidence is not solely determined by the quality of the forensics work involved. Some states regard the possible prejudice of tracking and scent identification as so great that they decline to admit this evidence at all. Thus, in the chapters that follow, two pieces of evidence that seem from a forensics perspective, perhaps even from a common sense perspective, equally strong may not get the same reception depending on the court to which the evidence is presented, with one piece presented to the jury and the other excluded from its deliberations. Thus, police and forensics experts must be familiar with the vagaries of state law as interpreted by the courts to which the evidence may be presented. Sometimes this may influence prosecutorial decisions as to where and in which court system criminal charges may be filed.

Not All Canine Evidence Becomes Trial Evidence

Explosives detection has become more prevalent since 9/11, but not nearly as many cases have reached the courts, sometimes because, for security reasons, a matter was dealt with in a way as to limit public knowledge of the event. If no other evidence is found in a suspicious fire than a dog's alert, it may be accepted by the investigators that the alert was not to a chemical intentionally left at the location to start a fire but rather was the dog's recognition of a substance that was present in construction or carpeting materials at the site. If a body is found in a shallow grave after a cadaver dog alerts to a mound of earth, the body and the evidence gathered from it will likely make the dog's alert of only historical interest in a subsequent prosecution. There have, however, been instances where a body was not found and the dog's alert was crucial in establishing that a murder did occur. Thus, a dog's alert to the trunk of a suspect's car may be introduced to establish that a body was once in that trunk.

The attitudes of courts to specific types of evidence may evolve, often in response to research findings. Currency sniffs began as an aspect of narcotics detection, but when it was discovered that almost all $20 bills in the United States (and many other denominations) had trace levels of cocaine, many courts declined to accept a dog's alert as evidence that the person in possession of the currency was involved in narcotics trafficking. When research began to demonstrate that dogs do not alert to trace levels of cocaine that have been on the bills for very long, currency sniffs began to be accepted again, at least by some courts.[82]

LACK OF JUDICIAL UNIFORMITY

The United States Supreme Court has issued several landmark decisions involving police canine procedures. In the 1983 case of *U.S. v. Place*, Justice Sandra Day O'Connor held that temporarily detaining personal luggage for a sniff by a trained narcotics detection dog, where there is a reasonable suspicion that the luggage contains narcotics, did not violate the Fourth Amendment.[83] The opinion described the limited intrusiveness of a canine sniff as *sui generis*, unique. The detention in the case before it, which involved holding luggage over a weekend, was found to be unreasonable, but the Court clearly determined that a shorter detention could be reasonable. *Place* is probably the most cited canine police case ever decided, and hundreds of other courts have applied its logic to different sets of facts, or struggled to avoid its application when a court thought that the logic of the case could be stretched too far.

In the 2005 case of *Illinois v. Caballes*, Justice Stevens held that a canine sniff performed on the exterior of a car that was legally stopped for a traffic violation did not intrude on the driver's constitutional privacy expectations.[84] Justices Ginsburg and Souter separately dissented. Justice Souter discussed inaccuracies of detection dogs. Other courts, as with *Place*, have extended *Caballes* to situations involving a wide variety of facts.

Many other areas of canine evidentiary law have not received uniform treatment through either federal or state decisions. Some differences between decisions may be due to different applications of leading decisions such as *Place* and *Caballes*, but many decisions may be better understood as being driven by the unique set of facts under consideration. Such issues will receive detailed treatment in the various sections of this book describing different areas of police canine practice.

ECONOMICS OF CANINE WORK

A particularly significant economic issue for most police departments concerns the cost of developing and maintaining canine teams.[85] Unfortunately, this has led to the discontinuance of many programs.[86] Canine officers and police associations have been involved in litigation concerning the appropriate level of overtime for caring for a dog,[87] whether commuting time is covered,[88] whether overtime policies put a cap on compensation for canine maintenance,[89] and whether collective bargaining or other agreements limit an authority's liability.[90]

The cost of maintaining a police canine program has resulted in a curious revival of the original way tracking dogs were obtained before police departments owned dogs, that is, by using dogs trained and owned by private individuals and businesses,[91] or sometimes kept by prisons to track escaped convicts.[92] Private teams are becoming common in search and rescue efforts.[93]

DANGERS OF POLICE WORK

Police dogs do dangerous work, and many fall in the line of duty.[94] Injuring or killing a police dog is a crime[95] but may not be regarded as a serious one by some courts.[96] Other courts have imposed serious punishments, in one case up to 50 years for killing a police dog.[97] State laws often require that police dogs receive regular veterinary care.[98]

Police dogs can also be dangerous to the suspects they are apprehending, leading to serious injury and even death.[99] Excessive and deadly force arguments have received varying receptions in the courts, as will be discussed in a subsequent chapter. Generally, if an officer does not act in a way intended to harm a suspect who is not intending to harm him, the courts will find a way to excuse small excesses.

MILITARY APPLICATIONS

In World War II, the Korean War, and in Vietnam, military working dog units were created for combat assignments and disbanded once the wars were over. The American military now has permanent canine training and operational units. A good deal of training of both military and police dogs is done at military facilities, the nationally known "Dog School" at Lackland Air Force Base near San Antonio, Texas, being the most famous. Many training issues discussed in this book have their origins in military dog work.

Many police dog functions are also military dog functions. Mine detection was a military dog function as early as the World War II, well before dogs began to be deployed for explosives detection

FIGURE 1.1 Sergeant First Class Jesse Mendez parachuting with Army Scout Dog (PAL X296), Fort Benning, Georgia, April 17, 1969. (Courtesy of Jesse Mendez.)

assignments at civilian airports. Sentry work is a military dog function that is largely handled by private security outside of the military. Guard and protection work is provided both by private and public entities. Airborne dogs have been known since World War II,[100] and this approach may occasionally come in handy for police and fire departments deployed to remote areas. See Figure 1.1.

THE FUTURE

Forensics work with dogs involves a number of active areas of research. Protocols for conducting scent lineups continue to be improved, making possible increasing levels of reliability in identifying perpetrators. As new drugs and combinations of drugs enter the illegal markets, new explosives are developed, and arsonists change their preferences for accelerants, training programs adapt to teach dogs to alert to the new and modified materials. Research continues on what specific chemical components are detected by dogs sniffing people, bodies, drugs, explosives, and fire debris. Sometimes dogs alert to a chemical that is not in and of itself illegal, such as methyl benzoate, a compound found in street cocaine but also in some perfumes.[101] This has allowed for the development of training programs that do not depend on obtaining inventoried contraband or dangerous explosives. Sometimes the item detected is innocent, such as chemicals released by burnt carpet at a fire scene. As such research advances, we are better able to evaluate the significance of the dog's alert and determine whether canine forensic evidence should be presented to a jury.

Just as people must often worry whether their jobs will become obsolete because of machines, arguments are often made that artificial noses and other chemical sensing devices may sooner or later make detection dogs obsolete.[102] There will undoubtedly be developments that will allow dogs to be replaced in certain assignments. Thus, machines may someday conduct sniffs at U.S. borders. Even if this happens, however, dogs provide certain benefits that machines never will. In a traffic stop, the dog may not only alert to a car's trunk, but its presence may deter aggressive action on the part of a driver. As with humans, machines may replace certain skills, but it seems to the author that police dog functions will adjust rather than disappear.

It is safe to say that our best friend will remain our best helper in the criminal arena for a long time to come.

NOTES

1. The East German Ministry for State Security, commonly called the Stasi, began developing a "smell vacuum cleaner" as early as 1982. Macrakis (2008), 290, n. 29.
2. Dates that events reached courts are often a few years after the crimes occurred or the issue began to be part of police practice.
3. *Hodge v. Alabama*, 98 Ala. 10, 13 So. 385 (1893).
4. *Pedigo v. Kentucky*, 103 Ky. 41, 44 S.W. 143, 42 L.R.A. 432 (Ct. App. 1898) (Judge Guffy, concurring in part and dissenting in part).
5. Kaldenbach (1998), 89.
6. Strandberg (1997).
7. Kalischer (1909).
8. Lemish (1996), 11.
9. Stephanitz (1923), 346.
10. *Cranford v. Arkansas*, 130 Ark. 101, 197 S.W. 19 (1917). *West Virginia v. McKinney*, 88 W.Va. 400, 106 S.E. 894 (1921).
11. *Iowa v. Grba*, 196 Iowa 241, 194 N.W. 250 (1923).
12. *Frye v. U.S.*, 54 App.D.C. 46, 293 F. 1013 (1923).
13. Dogs were generally taught to alert by sitting one to four paces from the mine. Those dogs that survived were returned to the families that lent them to the Army. War Department Technical Bulletin TB 10-396-1, Mine Detection Dog (M-Dog) (1944). Dogs were not taught to alert to explosives but rather to recognize disturbances and objects in the ground. Lemish (1996), 97; but see Lloyd (1948) (describing dog sniffing mines, with a cartoon suggesting a kind of scent lineup of other smells was employed in training).
14. Murray (2005).
15. Ensminger (1977), 535.
16. ACTIV. 60th Infantry Platoon (Scout Dog; Mine/Tunnel Detector Dog) Final Report: Project No. ACG-65F (December 1969).
17. Customs and Border Protection, "The Canine Enforcement Training Center (CETC)," on CBP.gov (accessed September 1, 2010).
18. An episode of the television series *Dragnet*, that aired January 30, 1969 (Narcotics: DR-21) describes the training of a dog to recognize marijuana. An early part of the episode explains the value of using such dogs at the Los Angeles airport, though the plot involves finding marijuana in the apartment of two suspects being interrogated regarding sales of drugs to high school students.
19. Logistics: DOD Dog Program, Departments of the Air Force, Army, and Navy, AFR 400-8 (May 5, 1971).
20. Phillips (1971); Phillips et al. (1974).
21. Transportation Security Administration, National Explosives Detection Canine Team: Program History (www.tsa.gov/lawenforcement/programs/editorial_multi_image_0002.shtm).
22. *California v. Furman*, 30 Cal.App.3d 454, 106 Cal.Rptr. 366 (Ct. of Appeal, 4th Dist., Div. 1 1973).
23. Rebmann et al. (2000).
24. *Doe v. Renfrow*, 475 F.Supp. 1012 (N.D. Ind. 1979), rev'd on other grounds, 631 F.2d 91 (7th Cir. 1980), cert. denied 451 U.S. 1022, 101 S.Ct. 3015, 69 L.Ed.2d 395 (1981).
25. See *Epperly v. Virginia*, 224 Va. 214, 294 S.E.2d 882 (1982).
26. *U.S. v. Place*, 462 U.S. 696, 103 S.Ct. 2637, 77 L.Ed.2d 110 (1983).

27. Lilly and Puckett (1997). See also *Iowa v. Buller*, 517 N.W.2d (Sup. Ct. 1994) (describing Iowa trainer as beginning to train dog in accelerant detection in 1985).

28. Taslitz (1990).

29. *Daubert v. Merrell Dow Pharmaceuticals, Inc.,* 509 U.S. 579, 113 S.Ct. 2786, 125 L.Ed.2d 469 (1993).

30. Schoon and de Bruin (1994).

31. Tolhurst, W.D. and Harris, L.R., Scent Evidence Pad Holder, Patent D397051 (August 18, 1998); see Eckenrode et al. (2006).

32. See, for example, *Ochoa v. City of Buena Park*, 2008 WL 2003761 (C.D. Cal. 2008).

33. *City of Indianapolis v. Edmond*, 531 U.S. 32 148 L.Ed.2d 333, 121 S.Ct. 447 (2000).

34. The canine teams came from various agencies and volunteers including Urban Search and Rescue Response System of FEMA (www.fema.gov/emergency/usr/about.shtm).

35. *U.S. v. Ebersole*, 411 F.3d 517 (4th Cir. 2005), cert. denied, 126 S.Ct. 1142 (2006), on remand, 2007 WL 219969 (E.D.Va. 2007), aff'd, 189 Fed.Appx. 287 (4th Cir. 2006), motion to vacate denied, 2007 WL 750198 (E.D.Va. 2007) (fraud conviction for selling ineffective explosives detection dogs after 9/11 to the State Department, the Federal Reserve, and the IRS).

36. Lindblad-Toh et al. (2005) (first posted on Nature website for "in press" articles in 2004).

37. See, for example, Lesniak et al. (2008).

38. *Illinois v. Caballes*, 543 U.S. 405, 125 S.Ct. 834, 160 L.Ed.2d 842 (2005).

39. Schlegel (2005).

40. *EOD Technology, Inc. v. U.S.,* 82 Fed.Cl. 12 (Ct.Fed.Cls. 2008); GAO Protest B-400464.6 (May 5, 2009); Solicitation No. W91B4L-09-R-0025 (Award Date, December 11, 2009; dollar amount $44,775,558.79) (www.fbo.gov/index?s=opportunity&mode=form&tab=core&id=1faaec5ddbfbf28879b5b1255f6ac 02f).

41. *U.S. v. Smith*, 68 M.J. 316 (C.A.A.F. 2010). See also *CACI Premier Technology, Inc. v. Rhodes*, 536 F.3d 280 (4th Cir. 2008) ("Major General Taguba documented ... using unmuzzled military dogs to frighten, and in one case to bite, detainees"). Such misuses of dogs are not a focus in this book.

42. Hunter (2002), 90 (noting that another 10,000 dogs were to be recruited for the war on terror).

43. Wilsson and Sundgren (1997).

44. The American Working Dog Association specifies that obedience tests are to be conducted off-lead. For this organization, dogs must walk beside their handlers for 300 paces, mixing fast and slow pacing, with several turns and halts. Dogs must also do a sit-stay or down-stay while the handler moves 100 feet away. AWDA Web site (www.americanworkingdog.com/certification_standards.htm). The North American Police Work Dog Association also requires a 3-minute sit-stay or down-stay. NAPWDA Web site (www.napwda.com/pdflib/bylaws_cert_rules.pdf).

45. See Rooney et al. (2007).

46. Svartberg (2002).

47. Schoon and Haak (2002), at 86. See Gerritsen and Haak (2001), 106–109 (discussing the importance of search drive, tracking drive, prey drive, and "bring" drive in the context of tracking dogs).

48. Svobodova et al. (2008). See also Slabbert and Odendaal (1999) (retrieval at 8 weeks was factor indicting success in police dog work).

49. Stephanitz (1923), 337–339. ("Before the [First World] War, the German Police dog was the inspiring ideal; officials came from far and wide, and over the seas to glean information. They returned home with fully trained dogs and when there, they imitated our ways and methods, and to a large extent, went so far as to ask for German instructors.") German shepherds from Germany and Malinois from Belgium are still sought by many U.S. breeders and trainers.

50. High-speed running has been correlated with relatively stiff, brittle limb bones, whereas fighting requires bones with high resistance to failure. Kemp et al. (2005).

51. The North American Police Work Dog Association prohibits the use of sticks, whips, pinch collars, and electronic and ultrasonic devices. NAPWDA Web site (www.napwda.com/pdflib/bylaws_cert_rules.pdf).

52. Dogs do, on the other hand, learn differently, just as is true of people, and react differently to different rewards. Also, needless to say, different handlers have different skills in "reading" dogs.

53. Haverbeke et al. (2008).

54. Meyer and Ladewig (2008).

55. Lit and Crawford (2006).

56. *U.S. v. Ebersole*, 411 F.3d 517 (4th Cir. 2005).

57. See *Ohio v. Nguyen*, 157 Ohio App.3d 482, 811 N.E.2d 1180 (2004).

58. Miklosi et al. (1998).

59. Dorey et al. (2010).

60. *U.S. v. Prokupek*, 2009 WL 2634446 (D.Neb. 2009) (videotape showed dog's alert).
61. One court described the defendants' luggage as having been "sniff-searched." *U.S. v. Goldstein*, 635 F.2d 356 (5th Cir. 1981).
62. *U.S. v. Malone*, 886 F.2d 1162 (9th Cir. 1989) (sniff of person was conducted by consent; court rejected argument that consent was involuntary because suspect was afraid of dogs).
63. See *Washington v. Pleadwell*, 2010 WL 2994031 (Ct.App. 2010) (dog alerted near passenger door; when passenger got out, officer frisked her for weapons; finding an opaque bottle that he was concerned might contain a weapon, such as a razor blade, he opened the bottle, which contained Ecstasy; motion to suppress denied).
64. *Colorado v. Haley*, 41 P.3d 666 (Sup.Ct. 2001).
65. *U.S. v. Lyons*, 957 F.2d 615 (8th Cir. 1992) (suspicious package put in room with other packages; dog only alerted to suspicious package). See also *Colorado v. Boylan*, 854 P.2d 807 (1993); *Ohio v. Knight*, 82 Ohio Misc.2d 79, 679 N.E.2d 758, 759-760 (1997).
66. *U.S. v. Bronstein*, 521 F.2d 459 (2nd Cir. 1975) (dog sniffed 50 pieces of luggage on a conveyer belt); U.S. v. Ferguson, 935 F.2d 1518 (7th Cir. 1991) (two separate dogs alerted to suspect's luggage in lineup with three non-suspicious bags at DEA office in Union Station, Chicago).
67. *Hetmeyer v. Virginia*, 19 Va.App. 103, 448 S.E.2d 894 (Ct. App. 1994). The appellate court cited a tracking case, *Epperly v. Virginia*, 224 Va. 214, 294 S.E.2d 882 (1982), for designating the handler as an expert.
68. *New York v. Shulman*, 6 N.Y.3d 1, 843 N.E.2d 125, 809 N.Y.S.2d 485 (Ct. App. 2005); *California v. Rodrick*, 2001 WL 1422348 (Cal. App. 2001) (delay in bringing matter to trial partly due to conduct of "cadaver scent lineup," a procedure not otherwise described).
69. *Connecticut v. King*, 2004 WL 2012943 (Ct. App. 2004). For cadaver dogs, the staleness requirement makes limited sense since cadaver dogs are often able to recognize cadaver scent years after the body was present at a location.
70. Parmeter et al. (2000).
71. Institute for Biological Detection Systems, Auburn University, Duty Cycle of the Detector Dog, FAA Grant # 97-G-020 (April 2001) (finding that dogs could work effectively over 6 hours a day and noting "trainers and handlers can have a substantial impact on how long their dogs are willing and able to work effectively").
72. Adams and Johnson (1994a) (dog found about equally responsive to sounds while inactive as in quiet sleep, unlike humans, who are more responsive to auditory stimuli in rapid eye movement periods than in nonrapid eye movement sleep).
73. Zanghi et al. (2010) (noting senior dogs, between 11 and 14 years old, slept 75 more minutes during the day and 25 more minutes at night than the average dog).
74. In part because they seem to impart less stress to the dog and are more patient. For dealing with stress, agility is often incorporated into police dog training programs. See the certification procedures of the United States Police Canine Association (www.uspcak9.com/certification/USPCARulebook2010.pdf).
75. Stephanitz (1923), 334–335.
76. This will usually not mean that the family can treat the animal in all respects as a pet. The Model Policy on Law Enforcement Canines of the International Association of Chiefs of Police states that police canines "shall not be used for breeding, participation in shows, field trials, exhibitions or other demonstrations, or on- or off-duty employment unless authorized by the agency CEO."
77. Lefebvre et al. (2007). See *Audette v. Massachusetts*, 63 Mass.App.Ct. 727, 829 N.E.2d 248 (2005) (handler of dog explained that the dog lived with his family and regularly played with his children; summary judgment granted on excessive force claim where dog had never attacked anyone without orders before).
78. *Matheson v. Florida*, 870 So.2d 8, 13-14 (Ct. App. 2004). Judge Northcutt was once a journalist in the Washington, D.C., office of the *Chicago Tribune*.
79. Mesloh, Wolf, and Henych (2002).
80. Mesloh and James-Mesloh (2006) (noting that an area search dog would miss an unusual number of objects on some days, only to return several days later and be highly successful).
81. *U.S. v. Florez*, 871 F.Supp. 1411 (D.N.M. 1994).
82. See *U.S. v. $30,670*, 403 F.3d 448 (7th Cir. 2005). Trainers have advised the author that the amount of target material used in training will often influence the amount of target material to which dogs will alert to in the field.
83. *U.S. v. Place*, 462 U.S. 696, 103 S.Ct. 2637, 77 L.Ed.2d 110 (1983).
84. *Illinois v. Caballes*, 543 U.S. 405, 125 S.Ct. 834, 160 L.Ed.2d 842 (2005).

85. One official informally noted to the author that with the amount of time that an officer has to devote to training, usually weekly, and to caring for the dog, perhaps 1 hour per day, a police department may regard a canine team officer as working barely more than half time.

86. Because of the labor costs involved.

87. *Truslow v. Spotsylvania County Sheriff*, 993 F.2d 1539 (4th Cir. 1993) ($29,000 awarded for overtime); *Howard v. City of Springfield*, 274 F.3d 1141 (7th Cir. 2001); *Hellmers v. Town of Vestal*, 969 F. Supp. 837, 842 (N.D.N.Y. 1997) ("Time spent grooming, bathing, exercising, cleaning, and training the police dog is 'required by the employer and is pursued necessarily and primarily for the benefit of' the employer, and is thus 'work' under the FLSA."); *Karr v. City of Beaumont*, 950 F. Supp. 1317, 1322–1323 (E.D.Tex. 1997) (caring for and transporting dogs is compensable because integral and indispensable to police work, necessary for K-9 Division's business, and performed for benefit of police department); *Holzapfel v. Town of Newburgh*, 950 F. Supp. 1267, 1273 (S.D.N.Y. 1997) (basic level of care and attention is part of dog handler's work); *Andrews v. DuBois*, 888 F. Supp. 213, 216 (D.Mass. 1995) ("Feeding, grooming, and walking the dogs are therefore indispensable (albeit incidental) parts of maintaining the dogs as law enforcement tools; they are activities that are closely related to the work duties of a canine officer"); *Levering v. District of Columbia*, 869 F. Supp. 24, 26–27 (D.D.C. 1994) (feeding, exercising, and caring for dogs are integral and indispensable parts of dog handlers' work activities); *Truslow v. Spotsylvania County Sheriff*, 783 F. Supp. 274, 277–279 (E.D.Va. 1992) (home dog care activities are compensable under FLSA); *Reich v. New York City Transit Auth.*, 45 F.3d 646, 651 (2nd Cir. 1995) ("walking, feeding, training, grooming, and cleaning up are integral and indispensable parts of the handler's principal activities and are compensable as work"); *Albanese v. Bergen County*, 991 F.Supp. 410 (D.N.J. 1997); *Hellmers v. Town of Vestal*, 969 F.Supp. 837 (N.D.N.Y. 1997).

88. See *Graham v. City of Chicago*, 828 F.Supp. 576 (N.D.Ill. 1993); *Bolick v. Brevard City, Sheriff's Department*, 937 F.Supp. 1560 (M.D.Fla. 1996); *Aiken v. City of Memphis*, 190 F.3d 753 (6th Cir. 1999).

89. See *Holzapfel v. Town of Newburgh*, 145 F.3d 516 (2nd Cir. 1998).

90. See *Rudolph v. Metropolitan Airports Commission*, 103 F.3d 677 (8th Cir. 1996); *Brock v. City of Cincinnati*, 236 F.3d 793 (6th Cir. 2001).

91. *Fox v. Arkansas*, 156 Ark. 428, 246 S.W. 863 (1923) (officers "sent for a man in the neighborhood who owned what they termed a bloodhound—a dog trained and qualified to follow the human trail").

92. *Rolen v. Arkansas*, 191 Ark. 1120, 89 S.W.2d 614 (1936). See *North Carolina v. Dorsett*, 245 N.C. 47, 95 S.E.2d 90 (1956), for a relatively recent case where the services of a dog kept at a prison were used.

93. See Arkansas Code Annotated 5-54-126 defining "search and rescue dog" as owned by an independent handler or member of a search and rescue team).

94. See *Michigan v. Fortin*, 2002 WL 77184 (Ct. App. 2002) (police arrived to arrest defendant on felony warrant; defendant fled into woods, shot and killed police tracking dog; convicted of intentionally killing a police dog under Michigan Consolidated Laws 750.50c(2)).

95. See Arkansas Code Annotated 5-54-126 (purposefully killing or injuring a police dog or a search and rescue dog is guilty of a felony; interference or obstructing use of police dog or search and rescue dog is a misdemeanor; search and rescue dog may be owned by independent handler).

96. *Bass v. Florida*, 791 So.2d 1124 (Fla. App. 2000) (injuring police dog was not qualifying offense for Prison Releasee Reoffender sentence, overruling trial court's determination that police dogs receive same treatment as police officers). See Scheiner (1999) and (2001).

97. *Gilbert v. Franklin*, 2008 WL 781863 (E.D.Ok. 2008) (50-year sentence for killing one police dog and injuring another according to the prisoner "in order to escape from being caught").

98. See, for example, Massachusetts General Laws I.XIX.129.22A (dogs owned by police departments and law enforcement agencies to receive "routine veterinary care").

99. *Robinette v. Barnes*, 854 F.2d 909 (6th Cir. 1988) (burglary suspect died from bites).

100. Lemish (1996), 115–117.

101. Tetrahydrocannabinol (THC), the psychoactive component in marijuana, found in industrial hemp oil, is used in sun lotion and other products.

102. Nambayah and Quickenden (2004) (arguing that "a comparison between instrumental chemical analysis and the use of highly trained dogs for explosives detection suggests some advantages of the instrumental methods over those of canines"); Stubbs et al. (2005) (reporting "real-time molecular recognition of cocaine molecules").

2 Canine Biology and Behavior

All police dog functions derive from the unique survival skills that canines developed in their evolution. Wolves use their highly sophisticated noses to track prey over long distances, often in very cold climates. The prey may cross trails left by many other animals, but there is an advantage to wolves, and their descendants, dogs, in staying with the same scent of an animal that may soon need to rest. These skills were first helpful to humans in hunting, but have been adapted for tracking, scent identification, and detection work. Once prey is found, the dog must catch it. Large prey must be brought down. This skill has been adapted to suspect apprehension and crowd control. Dogs are pack animals, and their defense of the pack's food and territory becomes the basis of protection work.[1]

Adapting these inherent canine skills involves long periods of training, and this requires that police take advantage of the high level of interspecies communication unique between humans and canines.[2] Even species closer to humans from an evolutionary perspective, such as chimpanzees, are of considerably less use to us (and we to them, admittedly). The canine sense of smell explains the majority of their police functions, and their association with us in shared environments explains the rest. It is appropriate to survey aspects of canine biology that are relevant in understanding how their adaptation to us has been transformed in police work.

GENETICS

Odorant molecules bind to olfactory receptors in the canine's nasal epithelium, which send signals to the olfactory bulb and then to various areas of the cortex of the brain. The dog genome has at least 1,094 olfactory receptor genes.[3] One research group looked at just 16 olfactory receptor genes in 95 dogs of 20 breeds. The olfactory receptor genes were found to be highly polymorphic, and around 20% of the genes were pseudogenes, meaning they are not involved in protein production, but this percentage varies among breeds. More pseudogenes are found in boxers, which have a less acute sense of smell than some other breeds, than are found in poodles, thought to have a better sense of smell. This suggests that the choice of certain breeds for scent detection work may have a genetic explanation.[4] In 2008, a team of Polish scientists determined that variations in olfactory receptor genes "might affect the olfactory ability of service dogs in different fields of specific substance detection."[5]

Twin dogs with a specific allelic variant were found to significantly differ in the detection skills from dogs with other variants. Thus, it might soon be possible to predict, both for cancer sniffers and other detection dogs, whether a puppy is a good candidate for such work.

> Aside from the curiosities of this sensory modality, all of this ferment in the field of smell may ultimately provide translationally important advances in disease biomarkers, including early diagnosis of neurodegenerative and psychiatric diseases and the detection of specific disease states by changes in body odor.[6]

The canine sense of smell has already had medical applications.[7]

CANINE DNA AS EVIDENCE

Human DNA testing has been a major forensic tool since 1985, but animal DNA testing is now proving useful. The first use of DNA profiling on an animal that led to forensic evidence involved a cat. The police found a leather jacket spotted with a murder victim's blood on Prince Edward Island. There was no evidence linking the key suspect (the estranged common law husband of the victim) to the jacket, but numerous strands of cat hair were found on the jacket. Genotyping verified that it was hair from the cat that lived with the suspect. This was enough of a link to convict the suspect.[8] Dog hair led to a conviction in British Columbia in 1991.[9] A case decided in the state of Washington in 2003, however, rejected canine DNA evidence as not being sufficiently established as a scientific test for judicial purposes.[10] A Pennsylvania court was more accepting in 2009.[11]

CANINE OLFACTION

A great deal of research describes the anatomy of the dog's nose and brain.[12] The study of scent physiology has involved research at the highest level, including by Nobel Prize winners.[13] Detecting small molecules in the environment is a capacity of all living things, including both plants and animals.

> In animals, the chemical senses of smell and taste differ from the physical senses of vision, touch, and hearing in the diversity of possible stimuli that can be perceived to have a distinct taste or smell. Both small organic molecules and small proteins induce taste sensations. Volatile small molecule odorants as well as nonvolatile proteins and non-volatile hydrocarbons all can induce olfactory sensations, depending on the species.[14]

In 1938, two European scientists demonstrated that most air breathed in by a dog bypasses the olfactory epithelium, which is offset from the airway of the nasal cavity.[15] Soon after the Second World War, it was found that air passes into the olfactory region in expiration as well as inspiration, meaning that the dog's sense of smell could work even when it was breathing out.[16] Beginning in 1953, Walter Neuhaus designed experiments to detect the olfactory acuity of the dog. He found that a dog could detect 1 mg of butyric acid dispersed throughout 108 m^3 of air, that is, the volume of an entire town.[17] In 1958, Victor Negus noted that mammalian nostrils give direction to the inspired air.[18] In 1973, the long canine sniff was described.[19] In 1980, D.M. Stoddart found that the nasal swell body (alar fold) just inside the nostril controls the direction of the airflow into the nose.[20] In 1981, a study of 29 transverse sections of a beagle's nose revealed the elaborate turbinates.[21] In 2003, a research team looked at the external aerodynamics of sniffing.[22]

Dogs detect odors by sniffing, in which air is inhaled through the nostrils in short aspirations while the mouth often remains closed.[23] It has been argued that sniffing creates more turbulent gas flow in the air passage, which improves sensitivity as compared with even air flow. If the dog is panting, as it must to cool its body, most of the air passes through the mouth and causes a decrease in the sniffing rate.[24] Recent research has indicated that fluid dynamics in the canine nasal cavity occurs in a specific pattern while a dog is sniffing, and that these patterns contrast sharply with those of a human.[25] See Figure 2.1 for a cross-section of the canine nose.

ABILITY OF DOGS TO REMEMBER AND DISTINGUISH ODORS

One study found that dogs could be rather easily trained to detect 10 different odors and that the amount of time for training new odor discriminations tended to decrease as more odor discriminations were trained.[26] Dogs can remember different odors for months.[27] Dogs could distinguish the odors of 17 men, women, and children in a test that involved finding the handkerchief used by a specific person.[28] A study that looked at the ability of seven dogs to match scent samples with the people from whom they were taken found an 85% matching rate.[29]

Dogs have been shown to be capable of learning when only 9 days old.[30] Some trainers introduce target scents to future narcotics detecting canines that are only 10 days old,[31] though 9 to 10 weeks is probably more common. Prenatal chemosensory learning of the smell of aniseed during gestation has been demonstrated.[32]

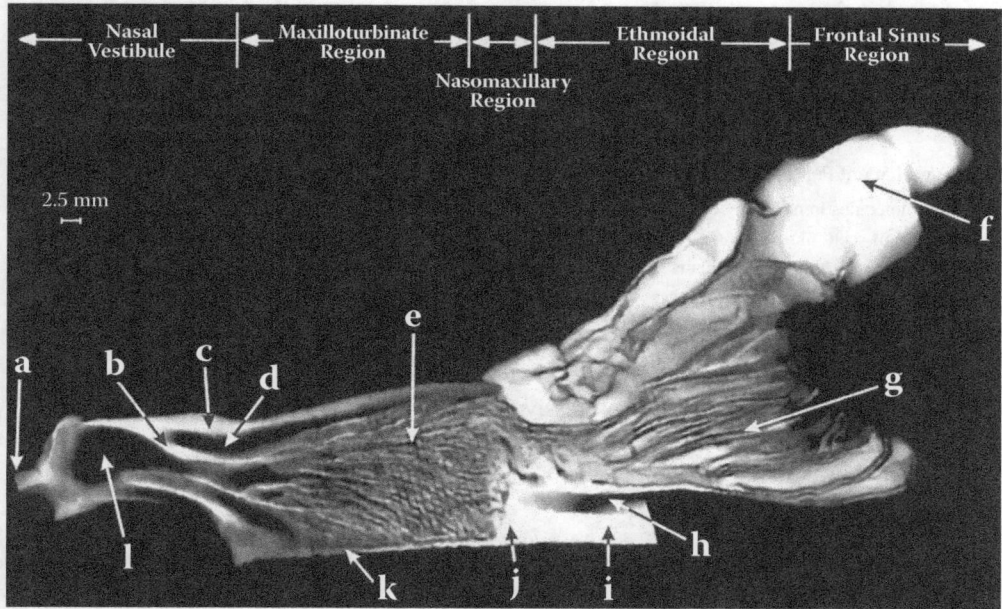

FIGURE 2.1 Sagittal section of canine nasal airway. This photograph was created by averaging multiple sagittal plane slices to represent the most prominent airway structures. Craven et al. (2007). (a) naris; (b) middle meatus; (c) dorsal meatus; (d) dorsal concha; (e) ventral concha (maxilloturbinate); (f) frontal sinus; (g) ethmoidal conchae (ethmoturbinates); (h) vomer; (i) nasopharygeal meatus; (j) nasomaxillary opening; (k) ventral meatus; (l) alar fold. (Courtesy of Brent A. Craven, Gas Dynamics Laboratory, Department of Mechanical and Nuclear Engineering, Pennsylvania State University, University Park, Pennsylvania.)

INTERFERENCE WITH SCENT PERCEPTION

A dog can have difficulty processing scent information at a number of stages. Table 2.1 summarizes where the processing of scent information can produce problems that might lead to misidentifications or no identification despite a positive match.[33] Thus, the procedures by which a dog ultimately identifies a suspect's scent as equal to that of the perpetrator must be conducted in a manner to reduce potential physiological and chemical limitations of the scent identification dogs used in a particular test.[34]

Diseases known to diminish olfactory function in dogs include canine distemper, canine parainfluenza, Cushing's disease, allergic rhinitis, hypothyroidism, seizure disorders, nasal tumors, head trauma, diabetes mellitus, and chronic renal failure.[35] Hormonal changes might also reduce a dog's functioning.[36]

CANINE–HUMAN COMMUNICATION

When Oliver Wendell Holmes said that "even a dog distinguishes between being stumbled over and being kicked,"[37] he probably had in mind something about a dog's eye contact. Dogs make more eye contact with us than any other species and look for us to give them directions.[38]

A study by researchers in Hungary looked at reactions of dogs selected from three breed groups: Belgian shepherds (Tervuerens and Groenendaels), retrievers (Golden and Labrador), and sled dogs (malamutes and huskies). The sled dog group and the retrievers continued to show friendly, tolerant behavior even when a stranger approached in a threatening manner, but half the Belgian shepherds responded to threatening behavior with their own aggressive and threatening behavior.[39] Even

TABLE 2.1
Possible Sources of Identification Errors Correlated with Stages of Scent Perception in Dogs

Stage of Scent Perception	Problems That May Cause Errors in Identification of Scent
Scent molecules in nasal cavity	Molecules cannot reach receptor
Reaction of scent molecules with receptors	No proper receptor available for certain kinds of molecules
Chemical reaction in sensory neuron	Sensory neuron does not react
Conduction of impulse through nerve	Nerve does not react
Processing of the impulse in the brain	Brain interprets the information incorrectly

those shepherds that did not respond aggressively did not ignore the threatening behavior. Thus, a threatening suspect might elicit different levels of responses from different breeds of police dogs.[40]

SLEEP PATTERNS

A study of domestic dogs in Perth, Australia, found a sleep cycle averaging 21 minutes, with about 16 minutes of sleep, beginning with quiet sleep and then active sleep, followed by spontaneous arousal and 5 minutes of waking time. Quiet sleep involved the dog lying still, except for breathing, with its eyes closed. Active sleep consisted of the dog

> lying with its head down and its neck muscles relaxed but showing rapid eye movement or spasmodic movements of its legs, paws, ears, tail, tongue or muzzle. Vocalisation by whining, yelping and muffled barking sometimes accompanied this pattern. During active sleep the dog was usually lying on its side. It finished this activity by spontaneously awakening either by raising its head and looking about, or by straightening all four legs which was usually accompanied by an audible sigh.

Unlike humans, who often do not do well when required to work at night and sleep during the day, the sleep patterns of working dogs appear largely the same, whether they are working at night or in the day. The ability of dogs to detect drugs has been found not to be adversely affected by which shift they work, which may not be the same for their handlers.[41]

NOTES

1. See Coppinger and Coppinger (2001) for a discussion of canine evolution and adaptation to human social environments. Handlers should understand pack behavior, as to the dog they should be pack leaders.
2. Miklósi (2007).
3. Quignon et al. (2005). Dogs only have a few hundred more receptor genes than humans, but many of the genes of humans are what are called *pseudogenes*, that is, genes that have accumulated small deletions and other problems that prevent the express of a function olfactory receptor protein. Humans have the most such pseudogenes of any known land animal (51%), much higher even than chimpanzees (41%), a close relative, and far higher than the 20% of defective genes in dogs. Differences between individuals of the same species, including both humans and dogs, have also been demonstrated. Lesniak et al. (2008).
4. Tacher et al. (2005).
5. Lesniak et al. (2008).
6. Buck and Axel (1991) (noting that "the advent of personal genome sequencing may make it feasible to correlate a given human's olfactory capacities with variations in her or his genome"; presumably the same could be said of dogs. Even more interesting [or frightening] is the possibility that the skills of a particular dog genome for detecting particular odors could even be selected for, or become aspects of a specific breeding program).
7. Ensminger (2010), Chapter 6.
8. Cassidy and Gonzales (2005).

9. Shutler et al. (1999).

10. *Washington v. Leuluahialii*, 118 Wash.App. 780, 77 P.3d 1192 (Ct. App. 2003), petition for review denied, 154 Wash.2d 1013 (2005); habeas corpus petition denied, *Leuluaialii v. Sinclair*, 2010 WL 891015 (W.D.Wash. 2010).

11. *Pennsylvania v. Treiber*, 582 Pa. 646, 874 A.2d 26 (Pa. Sup. Ct. 2005), 970 A.2d. 484 (Table, 2009).

12. For recent summaries, see Schoon and Haak (2002) and Gerritsen and Haak (2001).

13. Buck and Axel (1991). Linda Buck and Richard Axel shared the Nobel Prize in Medicine in 2004 for determining that odors stimulate the production of a chemical, cyclic adenosine monophosphate (cAMP), and reasoned that odorants would be detected by protein-coupled receptors in the olfactory epithelium that would couple odor binding to the production of cAMP.

14. Keller and Vosshall (2008).

15. Brueggemann and Jeckstadt (1938).

16. Dawes (1952). See also Becker and King (1957).

17. Neuhaus (1953), (1955), and (1981).

18. Negus (1958).

19. Zuschneid (1973).

20. Stoddart (1980).

21. Schreider and Raabe (1981) (comparing nasal structures of rats, rhesus monkeys, and beagles; a main difference was the greater complexity of the turbinate region of the dog).

22. Settles et al. (2003). See also Gerritsen and Haak (2001), 89–90, describing the 1973 thesis work of K. Zuschneid. Nostrils, even in humans, sample spatially distinct regions. See Porter et al. (2007).

23. See Zuschneid et al. (1976). Law enforcement personnel have sometimes been known to have keen senses of smell on their own. See *U.S. v. Gault*, 92 F.3d 990 (10th Cir. 1996) (DEA agent smelled ether, used to manufacture PCP, through zipper of nylon gym bag, justifying further actions leading to arrest of train passenger).

24. Israeli scientists have developed a device for the animal to wear so that someone in a remote location can determine if the animal is actually sniffing, or is panting and therefore may not detect an odor. Gazit et al. (2003).

25. Craven et al. (2010) (each nostril pulls in a separate odor sample, providing information on which direction to go in tracking).

26. Williams and Johnston (2002).

27. Williams et al. (1977).

28. Kalmus (1955).

29. Settle et al. (1994).

30. Bacon and Stanley (1968).

31. Julien (2009).

32. Wells and Hepper (2006).

33. Adapted from Schoon (1999).

34. See Furton and Myers (2001) (discussing physiological reasons that dogs may not perform well in detection assignments, particularly involving explosives detection).

35. See Furton and Myers (2001).

36. Schoon (1998).

37. The Common Law, Lecture 1. The full quote reads: "Vengeance imports a feeling of blame, and an opinion, however distorted by passion, that a wrong has been done. It can hardly go very far beyond the case of a harm intentionally inflicted: even a dog distinguishes between being stumbled over and being kicked."

38. Pongracz et al. (2001). See Ensminger (2010), 22–29.

39. Trainers note difficulties with getting certain breeds to release "suspects" in training. See Training Perspectives Q&A, *Police K-9 Magazine* (November/December 2010), 16–22.

40. Vas et al. (2005). A study by a Hungarian team found that police dogs could react to a threatening approach by fearfulness, aggressiveness, or ambivalence, which they described as "coping styles." The study involved sixty German shepherds, a single breed being used for comparing cortisol levels in different situations. Harvath et al. (2007).

41. Adams and Johnson (1994b); see also Adams and Johnson (1995).

Section II

Tracking, Trailing, and Scent Identification

Following the perpetrator of a crime from a crime scene or another location has been a function of dogs used in police work even from before dogs, in the United States, were owned by police departments. In early cases, where criminals often came to and left the crime scene on foot, the dogs could lead directly to the criminal, or his house, thereby identifying him or at least reducing the number of suspects to those people who were at the location where the dog stopped working. Tracking and trailing (which are distinguished by police dog handlers but not often by courts) are now sometimes separated from the more formal scent identification procedures, such as scent lineups, and dogs trained to track may not be trained to function in the confined space where scent lineups are conducted. Still, the overlap in history and practice argue for treating these functions together so that the discussion can focus on how they relate in police practice and in judicial analysis.

3 History and Judicial Acceptance of Tracking and Trailing Evidence

Tracking and trailing remain a major activity of police dogs, though now surpassed by detection functions. The Military Working Dog Program provides that about one in ten military patrol dogs should be trained in tracking.[1] Tracking and trailing classes are offered outside of police and military programs, and many law enforcement agencies retain private handlers and their dogs as incidents require.

Tracking and trailing should be distinguished, though many courts have not done so. In tracking, a dog is following disturbances to the ground surface, crushed vegetation, a person's body odor, and/or sweat coming through the person's shoes.[2] In trailing, a dog is thought to be following the odor of volatile substances that flow off human skin every minute containing organic compounds and bacteria, leaving a trail often described as a plume.[3]

STATES ACCEPTING TRACKING EVIDENCE

Thirty-six states accept tracking evidence, as does the District of Columbia, and probably two other states depending on one's interpretation of the judicial decisions. Not all courts have described the virtues and flaws in the same way, and some variations will be important to discuss. The states with cases accepting tracking evidence are as follows:

- Alabama
- Alaska[5]
- Arizona[6]
- Arkansas[7]
- California[8]
- Colorado[9]
- Connecticut[10]
- Delaware[11]
- District of Columbia[12]
- Florida[13]
- Georgia[14]
- Idaho[15]
- Iowa[16]

- Kansas[17]
- Kentucky[18]
- Louisiana[19]
- Maine[20]
- Maryland[21]
- Massachusetts[22]
- Michigan[23]
- Minnesota[24]
- Mississippi[25]
- Missouri[26]
- New Hampshire[27]
- New Jersey[28]
- New York[29]

- North Carolina[30]
- North Dakota[31]
- Ohio[32]
- Oklahoma[33]
- Oregon[34]
- Pennsylvania[35]
- South Carolina[36]
- Tennessee[37]
- Texas[38]
- Vermont[39]
- Virginia[40]
- Washington[41]
- West Virginia[42]

STATES REJECTING TRACKING EVIDENCE

Five states have rejected tracking evidence: Illinois,[43] Indiana,[44] Iowa,[45] Montana,[46] and Nebraska.[47] Iowa, however, specifically overruled the decision by which it had rejected dog tracking evidence, but in a case involving an accelerant detection dog.[48] A particularly useful decision from Maryland, *Terrell v. State*,[49] gathers most of the decisions from all states made prior to 1968. That court lists

New York in the column of states rejecting bloodhound testimony since *Terrell* was decided before *Centolella*.[50] The Maryland court interpreted dictum in an earlier New York case as a rejection of bloodhound testimony.[51]

FOUNDATIONAL REQUIREMENTS FOR TRACKING EVIDENCE

Courts have been concerned with dog tracking since such testimony began to be introduced by prosecutors in the late 19th century. Some courts likened the situation to allowing a dog to be a witness.

> There is no certainty in such evidence. *It is really the dog that is the witness*, and the evidence would seem to be hearsay in this view; and one court has vigorously maintained in a very recent case (*Brott v. State*[52] [Nebraska]) that such evidence is not admissible. But other courts have agreed that it is admissible under, and only under, substantially the following conditions: Even when it is shown that the dog is of pure blood, and of a stock characterized by acuteness of scent and power of discrimination, it must also be shown by preliminary evidence that the dog in question is possessed of these qualities, and has been trained or tested in their exercise in the tracking of human beings; and it must also appear that the dog so trained and tested was laid on the trail, whether visible or not, concerning which testimony has been admitted, at a point where the circumstances tend clearly to show that the guilty party had been, or upon a track which such circumstances indicate to have been made by him.[53]

A District of Columbia court in 1981 noted that a dog could not be cross-examined, but neither could photographs or exhibits.[54]

Foundational elements that have been required by U.S. courts include:

1. Qualification of the handler.[55]
2. Breed of dog.[56]
3. Training of dog in tracking or trailing.[57]
4. Reliability of dog.[58]
5. Dog placed on trail where perpetrator was likely to have been, or scented to an object likely to have been touched by the perpetrator.[59]
6. Dog put on scent and followed trail within the period of his reliability.[60]
7. Trail not contaminated.[61]
8. Circumstances regarding the tracking or trailing do not indicate evidence is not reliable.[62]

Courts have sometimes allowed relatively slight testimony to satisfy the tracking foundation:

> The foundational evidence need not be overwhelming or specific, but must be sufficient to indicate reliability of the evidence. ... Although Holladay did not testify to the dog's previous record in tracking human beings, such as how many times the dog had been used and the success rate of the dog, we believe the absence of testimony regarding the dog's "track record" goes to the weight of the evidence, not its admissibility.[63]

Corroboration is generally specifically required, as will be discussed later in this chapter.[64]

QUALIFICATIONS OF THE HANDLER

Handlers are generally required by courts to be shown to have training and experience in the use of a tracking dog.[65] Bloodhounds and handlers are sometimes borrowed from penitentiaries.[66] A handler in a 1956 tracking case from North Carolina was described as "a prisoner at the Taylorsville Prison Camp." Unfortunately, on finding the perpetrator, the dog was killed when the suspect stabbed the dog.[67]

Is the Handler an Expert?

A Colorado trial court concluded that the handler could testify concerning the qualifications and training of his dog as a lay witness, not as an expert, because "testimony about Yogi's training and performance could only be considered 'specialized knowledge … in the loosest sense of the term,' and would not support the 'gloss of expertise' under [Colorado Rules of Evidence] because no 'scientific method' had been offered to explain how dogs track a particular scent."[68] The Colorado Supreme Court agreed that the scientific basis of tracking was elusive but noted there are different types of expertise, finding that "Nichols focused on Yogi's training, reliability, track record, and performance in the case at hand—all matters based on specialized knowledge he obtained as Yogi's handler."

> Even a common eyewitness identification by way of lay testimony could involve "science" if one were to examine the scientific principles that underlie human vision and perception. The fact that some aspect of a witness' testimony can be *described* in scientific terms does not mean, *ipso facto,* that the jury must understand the science in order to find the testimony helpful. Instead, the courts should determine whether the opinion being offered either depends on scientific axioms, or is based on scientific theory, analysis, or experimentation.[69]

A South Carolina case from 2007 described a handler's testimony, in a case where a dog had tracked from an abandoned car to where a robber was hiding in the bushes, as that of an expert, but elaborated on what that meant:

> Gunter's testimony verified he had acquired, by training and experience, such knowledge and skill in the area of dog handling and tracking that rendered him better qualified than the jury to form an opinion on the particular subject of dog tracking. Furthermore, Gunter's testimony was based on his specialized knowledge, skill, and experience in the use of a scent-tracking dog, rather than on the validity of dog tracking as a scientific procedure. The nature of Gunter's testimony is analogous to that offered by a typical police officer who qualifies as an expert based on his experience with narcotics, not on his ability to explain the scientific theory behind his opinion.[70]

A New Jersey court stated that the handler must qualify as an expert:

> Thus, the handler of the dog must first qualify as an expert. It must be shown that the handler has sufficient skill, training, knowledge or experience to be able to evaluate the actions of the dog. Second, the handler, once qualified as an expert, must give testimony regarding the particular dog that he used and the facts. … [T]he testimony of the dog handler is not dispositive of the guilt or innocence of the defendant. It is, at best, circumstantial and corroborative evidence, which the jury may accept or reject. It is permitted to be offered because it is basically reliable and may be useful to the jury in assisting it in reaching a determination. Simply stated, it is this Court's function to determine the admissibility of the evidence. It is for the jury to determine the weight it is to be given.[71]

Professional Guidelines for Trainer Qualification

Most police working dog groups provide training standards for handlers as well as dogs.[72] Best practices proposed by the Scientific Working Group on Dog and Orthogonal Detector Guidelines (SWGDOG)[73] provide training and testing criteria that can be implemented by law enforcement agencies and private specialized dog trainers. SWGDOG's guidelines recommend that handler training is to involve human scent theory, relevant canine case law, and legal preparation, including court testimony. The handler is to learn how to recognize and articulate for others his dog's alert, which can be active or passive. Handler training may include learning to collect and store scented articles (in case a forensics team is unavailable).[74] One guideline deals with selection of handlers, including desirable personality traits.[75] Standards of certifying organizations will be discussed in other sections of the book.

BREEDS APPROPRIATE FOR TRACKING

Early cases often required that tracking be performed by bloodhounds or some restricted set of dogs seen as particularly effective in finding humans.[76] As early as 1896, an Ohio court referred to the "common knowledge" about the skills of bloodhounds:

> It is a matter of common knowledge, and therefore a matter of which courts will take notice, that the breed of dogs known as bloodhounds is possessed of a high degree of intelligence, and acuteness of scent, and may be trained to follow human tracks with considerable certainty and success, if put upon a recent trail.[77]

A Georgia court said dogs have to be "of a stock characterized by acuteness of scent and power of discrimination."[78]

PEDIGREE

Pedigree has sometimes been required.[79] A Missouri case from 1930 described dogs that tracked a chicken thief as being "of pure blood stock for six generations."[80] Breeds other than bloodhounds were sometimes accepted. An 1898 Kentucky case described "the bloodhound, foxhound, pointer, and setter" as being "remarkable for the acuteness of their sense of smell, and for their power of discrimination between the track they are first laid on and others which may cross it." This court acknowledged, however, that the term *bloodhound* is sometimes applied to dogs of different origins, describing, for instance, the Cuban bloodhound as a variety of mastiff.[81] A 1907 Ohio case saw pedigree as strengthening the evidence of a dog's reliability but apparently as not essential:

> [T]he reliability of the dog must be proved by a person or persons having personal knowledge thereof. This foundation may be strengthened by proof of pedigree, purity of blood, or the exalted standing of his breed in the performance of such peculiar work.[82]

A mixture of a bloodhound and a black-and-tan coonhound was praised as recently as 1981.[83] The faith in bloodhounds can still be found in the case law. A witness in a 2009 Texas case, described a bloodhound as "the Ferrari of the noses" compared to other breeds.[84] A 1985 New Hampshire case found that a foundation was deficient because it did not establish the dog's breed, the purity of his bloodline, or the virtues of the breed as trackers.[85] A 2003 California court said that the trial court record in a scent lineup case was devoid of any evidence to indicate that a Labrador retriever was "of a breed, stock or pedigree characterized by acute powers of scent and discrimination."[86] A 2009 South Carolina case described a tracking dog's extensive experience but also emphasized that "Aurie is a German shepherd that descended from a bloodline of known police and military working dogs."[87]

WORD OF HANDLER ON DOG'S ORIGINS

A 1928 capital case from Mississippi considered an attempt to assign error because written proof of pedigree was not provided.

> It seems to have been the theory of the appellant that it was not permissible to prove the breed of the dogs *viva voce* by the testimony of Gant, but that it should be done by written pedigree. We think it was competent to prove the breeding and training of the dogs by the oral testimony of their owner. Counsel have cited no authority which holds that a written pedigree is necessary, and we know of no statute

making it competent or exclusive evidence. We think it was competent to prove their training, breeding, and capacity by the method used in the present case.[88]

An Arkansas case from 1923 case contained the following description of a dog whose tracking evidence was admitted:

> The witness was asked the direct question whether or not the dog was a bloodhound, and he answered, in substance, that he did not know the pedigree of the dog, but that so-called bloodhounds had long ears and that this dog had that kind of ears. He said that the dog was not an ordinary hound and that he had had no trouble in training him to follow the human trail.[89]

KENNEL CLUB REGISTRATION

A 1936 Mississippi case considered AKC registration a factor in the qualification of a dog, but there were other matters of importance, including the kennel where the dogs were bred.

> Jenkins [the handler] testified that the two bloodhounds used by him on this trail were full-blooded English bloodhounds and registered by the American Kennel Club; that he had such registration papers; that one of the dogs he had owned for seven years and the other for not so long. He did not produce in court the registration papers of the dogs nor did he know the sire or dam of the dogs. He testified that he had been an expert trainer of bloodhounds to follow the trail of human beings for fifteen years; that the dogs were reliable and true on the trail, and that they had been permitted to trail no other animal; that once they started on a trail they would not leave it; and that he had tested them by running a thousand or more human beings, and that they had not failed in such trails. He stated that where a human being gets upon a train or into a car the dogs have failed to follow the trail. He further stated that these dogs were purchased from the Rookwood Kennel, a kennel recognized throughout the world for its bloodhounds.[90]

PEDIGREE SOMETIMES OF LITTLE IMPORTANCE

A California court stated that "[w]e simply cannot say all dogs can trail a human, or even that all dogs of specific breeds can do so." The court elaborated:

> [R]ather than attempt to identify certain specific criteria as being indicative of the ability of dogs, in general, to trail a human, we choose to require each particular dog's ability and reliability be shown on a case-by-case basis. We are not merely assuming a well-trained dog can trail a human; we say that this ability is a fact which, like other facts, may be proven by expert testimony. This testimony should come from a person sufficiently acquainted with the dog, his training, ability and past record of reliability. If the testimony comes from an expert in the area of training, trailing, and operational performance of such dogs, that expert is qualified to state an opinion as to the ability of that particular dog in question to trail a human.[91]

Looking to the specific dog, rather than the dog's breed, is the better approach and has become a critical issue in scent lineup identification procedures. A 1979 Vermont case, in which the state first accepted bloodhound evidence, responded to a challenge to the tracker's pedigree by stating:

> A pedigree must be shown in many jurisdictions, but the most recent cases have not stressed pedigree as a prerequisite for the admission of trailing evidence, reasoning in essence that a dog's reliability lies in performance, not papers. ... In any event, Winter testified without objection that West Virginia Red was a purebred bloodhound. Since no attempt was made to impugn her lineage at trial, the point will not be considered for the first time on appeal.[92]

As early as 1928, a Mississippi court found pedigree largely irrelevant. "Counsel [objecting to the introduction of tracking evidence] have cited no authority which holds that a written pedigree is necessary, and we know of no statute making it competent or exclusive evidence."[93]

Saying that a specific breed should not be required is not the same as saying that all dogs have the same noses. Scientists have argued that dogs with larger forenoses (in which the nostrils are situated) are capable of greater scent achievements.[94]

THE BLOODHOUND MYTH

A West Virginia judge writing an article in 1920 already knew that bloodhound accuracy was something of a myth and that even the term *bloodhound* was artificial. Writing of the shameful history of dogs tracking down escaped slaves, Judge McWhorter wrote:

> [T]he common fox hound was trained to trail the slaves, and for the purpose of keeping the slaves awed and intimidated, the reports were generally circulated that these dogs were bloodhounds, with great accent on the word "blood," and that they were infallible, and when put on the trail of a negro would never abandon it until the fugitive was run down and torn to shreds, and that there was no escape from such ferocious dogs. ...
>
> But by and by the slaves began to learn that these hounds were harmless, and that all the reports concerning their viciousness were false, and the "bloodhound" began to lose his terror. To offset this trouble, the common hound was then crossed with the Great Dane, or the Cuban Mastiff, both savage and vicious breeds of dogs, and a new strain produced called the "Cuban Bloodhound," and later and more appropriately called the "Nigger Hound." These dogs were vicious, and the former reports of the viciousness of the so-called "bloodhounds" were renewed and fully credited, not only by the negroes but by the whites of both North and South as well. The vivid stories about these dogs in "Uncle Tom's Cabin" had their counterparts in every slave-holding section of the country. These dogs could, with ease, track barefooted negroes through the swamps and low damp grounds of the South, and it was utterly immaterial whether the dog left an older trail for a fresher trail of another negro. Just so the dog "treed a nigger," the moral effect was the same. The slaves were kept intimidated, and these dogs were doing their work effectively, regardless of their accuracy.
>
> Thus this "common knowledge" of the work of the "bloodhounds" grew. These reports were exaggerated, and, without scruple, falsified and the sagacity, discriminating powers and deadly precision of these dogs magnified for the very purpose of keeping the slave terrified.

The judge effectively argued that slave-tracking bloodhounds were really mixed breeds, making the pedigree requirement a myth from the beginning.[95]

A VIABLE REQUIREMENT?

Often the first element in a list of foundational requirements, purebred status is now probably the least important. Although some breeds have been selected for traits that reduce nose size and restrict air passages, most dogs can be trained to follow tracks. The effectiveness of that training, and the handler's ability to work with the dog, are far more important issues.

SWGDOG guidelines emphasize the physical and temperament qualities of the particular animal that may be selected for search work. As to breeds, the guidelines only note that "sporting, herding, hound and working categories" have historically been selected for detection purposes.[96]

TRAINING

Courts accepting tracking evidence have always required evidence that the dog has been trained and proven reliable in tracking humans.[97] A dog's ability to track its own master may not be enough. A New York case involved tracking from the scene of a fire to a place where the defendant, a woman, was seen after the fire. The perpetrator had used boots that a farmer left in his field, but the stride of the person using the boots was much shorter than that of their owner, supporting the possibility that a woman had put them on. A significant part of the case rested on the tracking evidence, but the court delved into the prior experience of the dog and found it wanting.

In the case now under consideration the owner of the dog was called, and testified that the dog was what was known as a German police dog, that he had owned him for about three years, and since he was three months old, and that he had a registered pedigree, which was given, and then the witness was asked to detail what he had seen the dog do. He testified that at the Litchfield horse show he had taken a handkerchief of his own from which the dog could get the scent, and had then made a detour of a quarter of a mile, making several turns to the right and left and going through some pieces of woods and hid the handkerchief; that the dog was held by the judges in a position where he could not see the direction taken by the witness; that on his return the dog was let loose and told to go and get the article; that the dog immediately started over the course following the trail closely, and returned with the hand-kerchief. The witness said he had seen substantially this same feat performed many times, and that the dog immediately after being let loose followed the trail and never failed.[98]

The ability to make abrupt changes in direction, such as at right angles, is often tested by tracking organizations. The court continued:

This does not attempt to show that this particular dog had ever had any training in tracking human beings generally; it simply shows that he had been able to follow the fresh trail of his own master and to find a handkerchief which had been hidden a quarter of a mile away, a clever piece of work, perhaps, but hardly up to the standard required by the rule quoted. Many dogs are able to trace out their own masters, but to place him upon the trail of a stranger, and to have him follow up this trail, is quite another matter; and the witness admitted on cross-examination that there was a difference in following a trail by odor and following an article the dog had been allowed to smell of and then hidden away some place. The only other person whom it was claimed this particular dog had ever trailed was the wife of the witness. … He was an exhibition dog at the shows, and the mere fact that he did some surprising things in follow-ing the members of the witness' own family is not a proper foundation for the admission of the evidence complained of by the defendant. There is absolutely no evidence of the reliability of this dog in tracing strangers, no evidence that he had ever taken an old trail and followed it, and the mere conclusion of the witness that the dog could do this is worthless in establishing a foundation for the introduction of evidence as to the conduct of this dog when placed upon a trail five days old.[99]

The court developed a separate theory about whom the dog may have been tracking. The court sug-gested that the dog may not have been following the perpetrator at all but rather the investigators. The conviction was reversed and a new trial ordered.

Some dogs trained only in suspect apprehension may track for short distances.[100]

PROFESSIONAL GUIDELINES FOR TRACKING AND TRAILING DOG TRAINING

The Military Working Dog Program states that a skilled tracer dog may be able to follow a trail that is 12 hours old for 5 kilometers, but a minimum level of proficiency involves following a trail that is 1 hour old and takes several turns over varied terrain.[101]

For searches involving objects scented by the perpetrator (or "target" in training and testing situations), SWGDOG recommends using negative controls (sometimes called zero trials), where a scenting item does not relate to an odor trail so that the dog can demonstrate that it will not follow a trail when there is none matching the scent it has been given. For testing, one human target and two distracters are used to lay odor trails from 100 to 200 yards in length (in some instances as long as a mile), with most trails aged at least an hour before the dog is put on the scent (though one distracter may only be aged 30 minutes). Trials are to be performed blind to the handler,[102] and a dog must be at least 75% successful for certification. The alert on finding the target is to be described by the handler to the assessor before a trial is run, so that the assessor will know that the dog is alerting

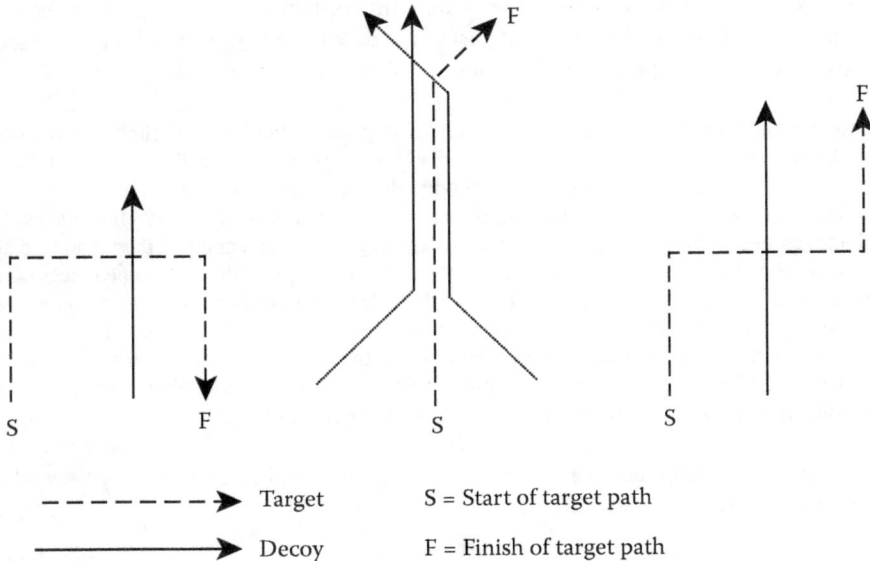

	→ Target	S = Start of target path
	→ Decoy	F = Finish of target path

FIGURE 3.1 Suggested trails for tracking or trailing people. (Data from SWGDOG SC 9—Human Scent Dogs: Tracking/Trailing People Based on Last Known Position [approved March 3, 2010]; Pre-Scented Canine—Aged Trail Search [posted for comment May 24, 2010].)

to the target independent of the handler's saying that this is what the dog's behavior indicates.[103] SWGDOG includes suggested track designs, as in Figure 3.1.[104] Tests are to be conducted on different surfaces.[105]

SWGDOG discusses recordkeeping and document management. Training records "may include," but are not limited to identifying information, date and time, location and environmental conditions, diagrams of trails, search results, and deficiencies and corrective measures. SWGDOG specifically states that records "may be discoverable in court proceedings and may become evidence of the canine team's reliability."[106]

RELIABILITY

Reliability has long been an essential foundation element for the admissibility of canine evidence. A Mississippi court said in 1926:

> One, and probably the only sure, test of the reliability of a bloodhound in tracking human beings is to put it repeatedly in a track known to have been made by a particular person, and see if it will track therefrom to that person. These tests should be so made as to demonstrate that the dog will continue to follow the same track and not leave it for another.[107]

Reliability is specific to the dogs used in a case. In a prosecution for a barn burning where part of the evidence against the defendant involved the tracking of bloodhounds, the defendant could not introduce evidence about other bloodhounds that had left a trail to attack sheep. The behavior of other bloodhounds that left a trail was not relevant.[108]

Older cases often relied on rather cursory descriptions of a dog's abilities. One 1904 Texas case described the bloodhound used to track a murderer as follows:

> W.D. Snodgrass was introduced as a witness for the state, and in substance stated that he was constable of Precinct No. 1 of Titus county, Tex., and when he heard of the homicide he went over to where it occurred, and carried Sam Porter's dog; that this dog was kept for the purpose of running people, and

was a bloodhound; that he had had experience with this dog, and it had been trained and was reliable; that if he was taken to a place, and put on the track, and he ever opened on the track, he would run that track to its destination, and he would run no other track except that particular track; that after he run said track to its destination he could be put on another track; that he was present when the dog was put on the track at the scene of the killing; that he kept up with him a part of the way, but he ran so fast he could not keep up all the way; that when he got to where appellant lived the dog was there.

The trial court overruled objections to the testimony.[109] Older cases sometimes allowed evidence concerning dogs that would likely not be satisfactory today. In a 1915 Arkansas case, a farmer whose hogs were stolen asked his local banker to wire for dogs from Tennessee. The banker was allowed to testify as to the dogs that came as a result of his wire.

Mr. Smith, the president of the bank, who telegraphed for the dogs, stated not only that he had heard a good deal about them running criminals down, that the reputation of the dogs for running criminals was good, but also that he got the dogs and had seen them trail some criminals one time from Wheatley to Cotton Plant, and that they did not catch them, because they took the train there; that he knew the dogs used in this case and they were the same ones.

This appears to be no more than unsubstantiated hearsay but the Arkansas Supreme Court held that this was "a sufficient showing of the qualification of the hounds."[110]

In a 1947 Georgia case, tracking evidence was admitted because an experienced handler "vouched for the breeding, accuracy, and reliability of the dogs."[111] In a 1979 Michigan case, the handler testified that "to his knowledge, Schultz had never made a mistake." The handler said that cases where the dog stopped tracking probably involved situations such as the defendant getting into a car.[112] Courts still sometimes spend little time verifying reliability, only noting that the dog's "responses had proved reliable in numerous other cases."[113] A District of Columbia case from 1980 allowed tracking evidence concerning a dog whose prior experience was described as tracking four or five escapees from a prison. The court cited testimony that the dog had shown no hesitation in following the trail from the scene of the crime to a vehicle where the suspect was found sleeping.[114] A 1937 Florida case admitted tracking evidence concerning a dog that had been "a man trailer for many months."[115] A 1983 New York case gushed with admiration of a handler who said his dog "has never been proven wrong."[116]

A federal court determined that a robbery and carjacking suspect could go forward with a false arrest suit against a California city partially because the dog's reliability had not been established. The dog had been scented on a baseball hat found in a stolen car, with the scent enhanced by a scent transfer unit (STU-100). The dog had passed by the plaintiff's house without showing interest, but on a later pass hit the door with her paw. The defendant officials did not introduce any evidence as to the tracking dog's reliability, and the plaintiff (suspect) pointed to several cases that called the dog's reliability into question. The district court concluded that the defendants had failed to demonstrate that the dog's alert supported probable cause for the suspect's arrest.[117] A Web site devoted to cases where defendants have been exonerated states that DNA evidence later established that another individual, who was apprehended, committed the crime in this case. The plaintiff served 10 months before the real perpetrator was found.[118]

Reliability should have to be established if a dog tracks to a vehicle or building and probable cause is necessary for a search.[119]

SUCCESS RATES

Reliability is sometimes established numerically. In a 1999 Colorado case, a handler testified that his dog had been unsuccessful in only 14 of 480 training sessions, which the witness attributed to handler error rather than to any failure of the dog.[120] Handlers often seem to exaggerate, but some are cautious about the accuracy of their dogs. A handler in a Connecticut case stated that dogs he trained had about an 80% success rate and that the dog in a particular case had about this success rate.[121]

Testimony concerning a dog that was described as having a 50% success rate was admitted in a North Carolina case where the dog had tracked from a location where the robber had been. The dog tracked to the defendant. Other dogs operating in the area were said to have success rates between 65% and 70%.[122] Despite this rather unimpressive success rate, the canine evidence was admitted. The court concluded that because the dog had accurately tracked from the automobile used in committing the crime to the service station that was robbed, it could to be trusted for tracking from a place where the robber had been to the defendant.[123] A 1997 case from Washington State found praise for a dog with a questionable record:

> Wieting argues that the reliability is undermined by the fact that in slightly over half of Ax's trackings, he was unable to track anyone. But we believe that the reliability of the dog in finding the correct person is enhanced, not undermined, by the dog's record of breaking off the track when the scent is lost. Better that the dog find no person than the wrong person.[124]

Handlers should keep records, including at least crude maps, of the tracks they teach and practice their dogs on. The record should include weather conditions, terrain, wind direction (with respect to the track), time of day, length of the track, time spent in tracking, and how the dog worked the track.[125] Records should not only be subject to discovery,[126] but should be maintained and to a reasonable degree verified by neutral organizations or government units. Further, the absence of such records should not be able to withstand defense objection.[127]

UNUSUALLY EFFECTIVE DOGS

An FBI publication described a case involving use of the mail to send bombs:

> On May 13, 2002, a U.S. mail carrier in Philadelphia discovered a package in a mailbox that appeared to be an improvised explosive device. The Philadelphia Police Bomb Squad responded and rendered the device safe. In a mailbox 1.5 miles away, a similar package was found the following day and rendered safe.
>
> Two days later, human scent was collected with the STU-100 from the remains of these two packages. Starting the dog at one of the mailboxes, a positive indication for scent was given, and the dog began to trail. After two days of car and pedestrian traffic, the bloodhound was able to follow the trail into a neighborhood where the trail ended. A second dog was started in the neighborhood and identified a house occupied by Preston Lit. The criminal investigation, conducted separately from the human-scent work, brought the police to the same location. ... Lit pleaded guilty and received a 16-month sentence in federal prison.[128]

Thus, two dogs successfully followed scent that was days old.[129]

Canine forensic specialists with the FBI have described a case where a dog was apparently able to track an individual from pipe bomb fragments 17 days after the explosion.

> In July 2002 a pipe bomb exploded inside a car in Washington, DC, and severely injured the driver, 21-year-old Wright Sigmund. Shortly after the bombing, Prescott W. Sigmund, the half-brother of the victim, disappeared. His car was found in a Metro parking garage with a suicide note. Seventeen days after the bombing, the Bureau of Alcohol, Tobacco, Firearms, and Explosives took the FBI's Human Scent Evidence Team to the entrance of an unknown neighborhood. With no prior knowledge of the whereabouts of Prescott Sigmund's residence, a Human Scent Evidence Team dog team, using scent collected from the pipe bomb fragments, trailed to Sigmund's house and alerted on the front door.

It gets better:

The team was then taken to the top level of the Vienna, Virginia Metro Station parking garage where Sigmund abandoned his car. Seventeen days after the car was abandoned, in nearly 100°F temperatures, the bloodhound immediately followed Sigmund's trail to the elevators and alerted on the elevator door. … On the ground level, the bloodhound ignored the other commuters and trailed to a bus stop kiosk where the trail ended. A check of the subway entrance was negative. It was the opinion of the dog team handler that Sigmund caught a bus or was picked up at the kiosk. Despite the high number of commuters that used this urban Metro station during the 17-day interval, the bloodhound had no difficulty differentiating the suspect's scent from that of thousands of riders.

After the suspect was arrested, he confirmed that he had taken a bus from the station out of town.[130] It is unlikely that, absent such an admission, evidence like this would be admitted by any U.S. court.

JURY DETERMINATION OF RELIABILITY

Some judges have left the determination of reliability to the jury, rather than treating the issue as a threshold that must be satisfied for the testimony to be admitted at all.

[T]he jury should be charged in substance that before they can consider the conduct of the dogs they must find that the dogs were accurate, certain, and reliable in following the trail of human footsteps, and that if they find this, then the evidence of the conduct of the dogs and its result may be considered, together with all the other evidence in the case, as a circumstance in determining the guilt or innocence of the defendant.[131]

Juries have sometimes been allowed to hear tracking testimony before the foundation for admission of such testimony is made.[132]

PERIOD OF RELIABILITY

Courts have been concerned whether dogs began tracking or trailing in the period of their reliability or efficiency. A 1985 New Hampshire decision found tracking evidence deficient because it was not shown that a dog had tracked inside its "period of efficiency." Certification documents, which were not presented, might have indicated a longer period of efficiency and allowed the canine evidence in.[133] One California appellate court found canine evidence not properly admissible (though it did not reverse because the error was harmless) because of "the absence of an adequate foundation from scientific or academic sources as to how long scent would remain at the location."[134]

Tracking that began 15 to 18 hours after the crime was allowed as evidence in a 1911 case, but there was also a confession.[135] A 1915 Illinois case rejected tracking evidence when the dogs followed a trail more than 30 hours after the crime. The trail "had been disturbed by hundreds of autos and buggies." Curiously, the statement of facts in the case suggests the possibility that the dogs may have been following a trail left in a rainstorm a week before the crime.[136] A 1976 Oregon case accepted tracking 45 hours after the crime.[137]

A 1990 Pennsylvania case involved the murder of a 10-year-old girl. The defendant was arrested after being identified by a 6-year-old boy who had been playing with the girl. Other witnesses identified the defendant's car. The girl's body was found with her throat slashed. Dogs tracked the victim's scent from the bridge where she began walking with the suspect to the scene of the killing. The dogs were also scented on clothing the suspect had worn and tracked to the building where he lived. This latter tracking was to verify that they could track the defendant. Finally, the dogs, scented on the suspect's clothes, tracked from the bridge where the girl began walking with the suspect to a point near the crime scene. All the tracking occurred 5 days after the murder. The conviction was affirmed.[138]

WEATHER CONDITIONS

Handlers often testify to environmental factors affecting a dog's ability to track. A handler in a 1936 Mississippi case testified that "a trail was harder for the dogs to follow in a 'dry spell' than in a 'wet,' and that on this occasion it was 'wet.'"[139] In a 1932 Missouri case, the handlers were described as testifying to the effect that "the scent is stronger on moist ground than dry, and on the occasion involved in the case the ground was dry."[140] A 1978 New Hampshire case, however, stated that "the night was particularly good for trailing because of the dew."[141]

RECORDS AND CERTIFICATION

In an Arizona case, a defendant objected that records of a dog's past failures were not described in its history. The Arizona Court of Appeals acknowledged that "a record of failures should be kept to substantiate the continued reliability of the dog," but determined that the defect alone did not make the foundation insufficient. The dog had been scented to footprints outside the home of the victim of an attack and led police to a nearby housing project, where it alerted to the defendant standing outside.[142] It is the opinion of the author that careful records should be kept and that tracking evidence should be excluded for failures to do so.[143] Records should not be manufactured at the time testimony is sought from the handler.

Certification has sometimes created a presumption of adequate training and reliability.[144] A Florida court complained in a case involving narcotics detection that "conditioning and certification programs vary widely in their methods, elements, and tolerances of failure."[145] One California court found canine evidence not properly admissible (though it did not reverse because the error was harmless) because of "the absence of an adequate foundation from scientific or academic sources as to ... the adequacy of the certification procedures for scent identifications."[146]

ACCURACY REQUIREMENTS IN PROFESSIONAL GUIDELINES

The certification requirements of Law Enforcement Training Specialists International Inc. require that for a canine felony tracking certification a team must successfully complete 80% of all tracks tested, including the following three tracks:

- Track #1 over a contaminated area such as a public park, schoolyard, and so forth. This track shall also be over average height grass and at some point go into, or through, a wooded area. Certification Official(s) shall use a distance of approximately one thousand (1,000) feet as a guideline, with a minimum of 2 turns on the track. An average time of one (1) hour shall be established as the age of the track.
- Track #2 in an urban environment (hard surface). Certification Official(s) shall use a distance of approximately three fourths (3/4 of a mile) as a guideline with a minimum of four (4) turns on the track. An average time of one (1) hour shall also be established as the age for this track.
- Track #3 is to be the same (similar) as either a #1 or #2 track, chosen according to the environment the team may commonly work. Certification Official(s) shall use typically encountered scenarios as the guidelines for establishing the requirements of the #3 track.[147]

A natural distraction—animals, people, vehicles, and so forth—is not to be considered a reason for a handler to terminate a track "for cause." At least one observer accompanies a team during a test to watch for traffic and to assure general safety. Objects may be dropped on the trail to simulate evidence, though failure to find such articles cannot be the sole basis for a failure.

Certification by the American Working Dog Association requires that dogs track in at least three separate terrains, which can include fields, gravel, leaves, creek beds, dirt, concrete, wooded areas, asphalt, and high grass. Tracks are to be at least 30 minutes old but not more than an hour old, at least 300 yards in length up to 1500 yards (for the highest level of tracker), with at least one cross-track laid. Teams are given 20 minutes to complete the tracking.[148]

SWGDOG suggests that certifications be valid for one year, and that certifying individuals are not to be routinely involved in the day-to-day training of a canine team that is evaluated. Certification can be denied for handler errors as well as canine errors. SWGDOG also describes maintenance training.[149]

Some states have their own certification procedures.[150]

CORROBORATION

Courts accepting scent-tracking evidence nevertheless often find it "too prejudicial where it is not corroborated by other independent evidence."[151] A 1978 Michigan case stated that "we note that no authority has been presented to us, nor have we found any, which indicates that tracking dog evidence, standing alone, can support a conviction."[152] A 1978 New Hampshire case instructed the jury that "while the evidence provided by the bloodhound is evidence which may be considered by you in your deliberations, it is not in and of itself evidence that a crime was actually committed."[153] The corroboration requirement generally appears in cases where the dogs' actions have been interpreted as identifying the perpetrator.[154]

EXAMPLES OF CORROBORATION

Corroboration can take the form of eyewitness identification.[155] Defendants have been known to confess when found by bloodhounds.[156] Knowing facts that the police had not made public was corroborative in a 1991 New Jersey case.[157] Scratches on the face of a rape suspect consistent with victim's description of what she did to defend herself was corroborative.[158] Sometimes the suspect's behavior is incriminating.[159] A New Hampshire case involved tracking a burglar for 45 minutes at night, at the end of which "Baron's actions indicated that they were nearing the person being tracked." These "actions" were not explained further, but the suspect suddenly "jumped from the brush and started to run."[160] A 1907 North Carolina case found corroboration when the tracks the dog had followed were consistent with a person who had one leg shorter than the other and the suspect, when found in a tree, had this characteristic.[161]

The evidence corroborated may actually arise from the tracking. In an 1893 Alabama case, footprints along the track that the dog followed were measured at several points and found to correspond to the shoes of the defendant. There was also evidence of threats the defendant had made against the murder victim. A shotgun of the sort used to kill the victim was found in the defendant's house.[162] Similarly, in a 1921 Arkansas case, a tracking dog that had been taken to a house that had burned down tracked to the suspect's house both at night and later in the day. Shoeprints were seen in the day near the path taken by the dog and found to have a peculiarity in the step, which was confirmed to be consistent with shoes worn by the suspect.[163] In a 1945 Georgia case, a dog tracked from the screen that was removed for the robber to get into a house, through fields, pastures, and "various other hazards, finally arriving at the porch of the defendant." Some of the corroborating evidence arose from the trail the dog followed:

> The defendant's shoes and the bottoms of his pants were wet. There was dew and dampness along the trail through which the dogs went sufficient to cause his shoes and pants to be damp. The defendant's tracks and tracks followed by the dogs, upon comparison, were found to be alike, his shoes having special identification marks which showed up in the tracks.[164]

Being found near items or clothing used in the crime has been held corroborative.[165] In a 1965 North Carolina case, corroboration was in the form of the denominations of bills found on the defendant after the dog tracked to him and the fact the defendant tried to keep the handler from seeing the bills.[166] In an Alabama case from 1913, a safe in a store was blown open during a burglary. Dogs tracked from the store into the woods, where some papers that had been in the safe were found. The dogs followed the trail to the house of Mary Smith, where more papers were found. She identified George Hawkins as the person leaving the items at her house on the night of the burglary. The dogs then led to the house of George Hawkins, where more items from the safe were found.[167]

FAILURE TO CORROBORATE

In a 1922 Kentucky case, the court noted that after the dogs tracked to the house of a suspect and the suspect came to the door, "one of the dogs went to him; but neither of them went to any other person in the house." Although this was presumably taken as an alert, the tracking evidence was not admitted because there was too little other evidence.[168] A 1990 California case involved a burglary where a dog arrived 25 minutes after an officer's call for backup and tracked into a vineyard, where a suspect was found hiding behind a berm. The dog alerted to the man, biting him. The case was reversed for lack of corroborating evidence. The court stated:

> [W]e emphasize that the corroborating evidence necessary to support dog-tracking evidence need not be evidence which independently links the defendant to the crime; it suffices if the evidence merely supports the accuracy of the dog tracking.[169]

A conviction in a case arising in Georgia was overturned when it could not be said that the dog was following the defendant. A prison official was called to help find some individuals who had abandoned a truck with bales of marijuana in it.

> Georgia prison officials were called, and a dog handler came with his bloodhound Clyde. Around 4:00 a.m. Clyde made a circle around the truck, and, according to the handler, picked up a scent and followed it without ever losing it. In the process officers had to swim two canals that were over their heads. Presumably Clyde picked up the scent on the other side each time. At some point, not described, the dog handler saw two sets of tracks (footprints) going along together. After some three to four hours, and three to four miles from where the GMC was found, Clyde and the officers found brother David and appellant asleep under a tree. They had with them one flashlight and two pair of gloves. When they were brought out of the woods the shirt of one of them was torn and both were wet and bore some scratches.
>
> *The dog handler was unable to testify, or give an opinion, whether Clyde was following the scent of one person found under the tree, or the other person, or both persons.*

Since it was not clear that the dog was tracking the defendant, and this was the only evidence connecting him with the conspiracy, the conviction was reversed.[170]

JURY INSTRUCTIONS

Jury instructions have been debated and described nearly from the beginning of tracking.[171] Juries have been seen, like corroboration, as something of a failsafe against the perceived difficulties of tracking evidence.[172] An Ohio court's instruction was succinct:

> Dog-trailing evidence must be viewed with the utmost of caution. It is of slight probative value. It must be considered in conjunction with all of the testimony in the case and does not warrant a conviction absent some other direct or circumstantial evidence of guilt.[173]

Standard California jury instructions specify that the jury must find that the tracking evidence corroborates other evidence.[174] A 1993 Kansas case reviewed a trial court's jury instruction:

"You are instructed that such evidence cannot be considered by you as proof of guilt ...; it may only be considered by you as some evidence that the Defendant was at the place where the crime was committed, and therefore, that he could have committed it." This instruction is erroneous, but the error operated in Wainwright's favor. The instruction should have read that "such evidence cannot be considered by you as the *sole* proof of guilt."

The defendant offered affidavits of a discussion between two jurors, one of whom had stated that since a dog followed the scent from the plastic bags to the defendant, he must be guilty.

The affidavits do not suggest the jury as a whole conspired to disregard the instruction on bloodhound evidence, nor do they indicate the jury used the bloodhound evidence as the sole proof of guilt. The verdict is not so contrary to the evidence that it suggests a conspiracy to disregard the instruction. Because there is no suggestion of a conscious conspiracy on the part of the jury, we find no abuse of discretion in the court's refusing to delve into the mental processes of the jury and no error in denying the motion for new trial.

The conviction was affirmed.[175]

Some cases have provided, or implied, that a cautionary instruction, along with a proper foundation, is necessary for a verdict and conviction to be affirmed.[176] Juries are to be instructed that dog tracking evidence is of slight probative value even without a request by defense counsel.[177] In a 2001 Georgia case, a tracking dog followed a track to where suspects were seen to be running. The jury was instructed that "the fact the dog has identified the charged defendant is not proof of guilt but merely some evidence that the party's track had been at the place where the crime was committed."[178]

APPELLATE REVIEW

Most of the cases we have discussed were decisions of appellate courts. A 1993 Kansas case considered the standard for appellate review of a trial court's decision to admit tracking evidence.

With regard to Wainwright's first complaint, no Kansas court has stated the standard for reviewing a trial court's decision to allow bloodhound tracking evidence. Because of its questionable nature and the process for admitting this evidence, we believe this type of evidence is akin to expert opinion. Admissibility of this type of evidence falls within the sound discretion of the trial court. ... We hold that the standard should be whether no reasonable person would agree with the trial court's decision to allow the evidence.[179]

The court determined that a trial court had not abused its discretion in declining to provide a defendant with funds to hire his own dog-tracking expert.

NOTES

1. MWD Pamphlet 190-12, § 3–26.
2. See the extensive discussion by Gerritsen and Haak (2001), 31–43.
3. Syrotuck argued that human skin flakes create the raft that dogs follow. Syrotuck (1972), 45–52. Others disagree with Syrotuck's raft theory. See Gerritsen and Haak (2001), 39. Courts sometimes still presume that a tracking dog is following a "skin flake" plume. See *North Carolina v. Cross*, 681 S.E.2d 566, 2009 WL 2177766 (Ct. App. 2009) ("The testimony of one canine handler indicated that the tracking dog could follow the scent of a person based on 'riffs,' or dead skin cells put off during high adrenaline situations."). One California court that explored the difference between tracking and trailing cited the testimony of an expert, Dr. Lawrence J. Myers, a professor at the College of Veterinary Medicine at Auburn University, to the effect that the distinction between tracking and trailing dogs may be artificial since they both detect and identify. *California v. Salcido*, GA052057, 11 (Los Angeles Super. Ct. 2005). One trainer stated:

"Air-scenting versus tracking is not really something I test for when evaluating dogs. Personally, I don't really care if the dog prefers to track or air-scent as long as he finds the bad guy." Training Perspectives Q&A, *Police K-9 Magazine* (November/December 2010), 25 (response of Ron Gurton).

4. *Little v. Alabama*, 145 Ala. 662, 39 So. 674 (1905); *Gallant v. Alabama*, 167 Ala. 60, 52 So. 739 (1910); *Loper v. Alabama*, 205 Ala. 216, 87 So. 92 (1920).

5. *Wilkie v. Alaska*, 715 P.2d 1199 (Ct. App. 1986).

6. *Arizona v. Coleman*, 122 Ariz. 130, 593 P.2d 684 (Ct. App. 1978); *Arizona v. Roscoe*, 145 Ariz. 212, 700 P.2d 1312 (1984), cert. denied, 471 U.S. 1094 (1985).

7. *Cranford v. Arkansas*, 130 Ark. 101, 197 S.W. 19 (Ark. Sup. Ct. 1917); *Adams v. Arkansas*, 149 Ark. 669, 235 S.W. 372 (1921).

8. *California v. Craig*, 86 Cal.App.3d 905, 150 Cal.Rptr. 676 (Ct. App. 1978); *California v. Malgren*, 139 Cal.App.3d 234, 188 Cal.Rptr. 569 (1983); *California v. Gonzales*, 218 Cal.App.3d 403, 267 Cal.Rptr. 138 (1990) (reversal for lack of corroborating evidence).

9. *Brooks v. Colorado*, 975 P.2d 1105, 81 A.L.R.5th 779 (1999).

10. *Connecticut v. Wilson*, 180 Conn. 481, 429 A.2d 931 (1980).

11. *Cook v. Delaware*, 374 A.2d 264 (1977).

12. *U.S. v. Smith*, 492 F.2d 650, 160 U.S.App.D.C. 384 (D.C.Cir. 1974).

13. *Edwards v. Florida*, 390 So.2d 1239 (Ct. App. 1980); *Green v. Florida*, 641 So.2d 391 (1994); McCray v. *Florida*, 915 So.2d 239 (Ct. App. 2005).

14. *Fife v. Georgia*, 16 Ga.App. 22, 84 S.E. 485 (Ct. App. 1915); *Aiken v. Georgia*, 16 Ga.App. 848, 86 S.E. 1076 (Ct. App. 1915); *Bogan v. Georgia*, 165 Ga.App. 851, 303 S.E.2d 48 (Ct. App. 1983).

15. *Idaho v. Streeper*, 113 Idaho 662, 747 P.2d 71 (1987).

16. *Iowa v. Buller*, 517 N.W.2d 711 (1994) (prior tracking rejection case specifically overruled in the context of an accelerant detection dog; language of overruling—"*Grba* is out of step with rules of evidence 403 and 702 and our present understanding of expert testimony"—sufficiently broad to cover tracking cases).

17. *Kansas v. Adams*, 85 Kan. 435, 116 P. 608 (1911); *Kansas v. Evans*, 115 Kan. 538, 224 P. 492 (1924); *Kansas v. Netherton*, 133 Kan. 685, 3 P.2d 495 (1931).

18. *Pedigo v. Kentucky*, 103 Ky. 41, 44 S.W. 143, 42 L.R.A. 432 (Ct. App. 1898); *Allen v. Kentucky*, 26 Ky.L.Rptr. 807, 82 S.W. 589 (Ct. App. 1904) (evidence was excluded because of lack of proper foundation; however, conversation of defendants concerning procuring Japanese oil to put on their shoes so dogs could not track them was properly admitted); *Debruler v. Kentucky*, 231 S.W.3d 752 (2007).

19. *Louisiana v. King*, 144 La. 430, 80 So. 615 (1919); *Louisiana v. Davis*, 149 La. 1009, 90 So. 385, 154 La. 295, 97 So. 449 (1923); *Louisiana v. Green*, 210 La. 157, 26 So.2d 487 (1946).

20. *Maine v. Cole*, 695 A.2d 1180 (1997).

21. *Terrell v. Maryland*, 3 Md.App. 340, 239 A.2d 128 (Ct. Spec. App. 1968); *Briscoe v. Maryland*, 40 Md.App. 120, 388 A.2d 153 (Ct. Spec. App. 1978).

22. *Massachusetts v. Smith*, 342 Mass. 180, 172 N.E.2d 597 (1961); *Massachusetts v. LePage*, 352 Mass. 403, 226 N.E.2d 200 (1967); *Massachusetts v. Smith*, 342 Mass. 180, 172 N.E.2d 597 (1961) (revocation of probation).

23. *Michigan v. Harper*, 43 Mich.App. 500, 204 N.W.2d 263 (Ct. App. 1973); *Michigan v. McMillen*, 126 Mich.App. 211, 336 N.W.2d 895 (Ct. App. 1983); *Michigan v. Baker*, 2007 WL 600584 (Ct. App. 2007); *Wade v. Sherry*, 2009 WL 5196166 (W.D. Mich. 2009) (habeas corpus).

24. *McDuffie v. Minnesota*, 482 N.W.2d 234 (Ct. App. 1992).

25. *Boatwright v. Mississippi*, 143 Miss. 676, 109 So. 710 (1926); *Fisher v. Mississippi*, 150 Miss. 206, 116 So. 746 (1928); *Prater v. Mississippi*, 18 So.3d 884 (Ct. App. 2009).

26. *Missouri v. Rasco*, 239 Mo. 535, 144 S.W. 449 (1912); *Missouri v. Long*, 336 Mo. 630, 80 S.W.2d 154 (Sup. Ct., Div.2 1935); *Missouri v. Fields*, 434 S.W.2d 507 (1968).

27. *New Hampshire v. Taylor*, 118 N.H. 855, 395 A.2d 505 (1978).

28. *New Jersey v. Parton*, 251 N.J.Super. 230, 597 A.2d 1088 (Ct. App. 1991); *New Jersey v. Wanczyk*, 196 N.J. Super. 397, 482 A.2d 964 (Super. Ct. 1984) ("A per se exclusion of bloodhound evidence is unreasonable. While it reflects a legitimate concern for the reliability of dog-tracking evidence, the majority rule of admitting the evidence, once a 'proper foundation' has been established, adequately safeguards against that concern.")

29. *New York v. Centolella*, 61 Misc.2d 726, 305 N.Y.S.2d 460 (Oneida Cty. Ct. 1969); *New York v. Muggelberg*, 132 A.D.2d 988, 518 N.Y.S.2d 285 (App. Div. 1987).

30. *North Carolina v. Freeman*, 146 N.C. 615, 60 S.E. 986 (1908); *North Carolina v. Davis*, 54 N.C. 596, 284 S.E.2d 139 (Ct. App. 1981); *North Carolina v. Styles*, 93 N.C.App. 596, 379 S.E.2d 255 (Ct. App. 1989). See *U.S. v. Carroll*, 710 F.2d 164 (4th Cir. 1983).
31. *North Dakota v. Iverson*, 187 N.W.2d 1 (1971) (station identification; dog lost the scent outside apartment).
32. *Baum v. Ohio,* 17 Ohio C.D. 569, 1904 WL 694 (Ohio Cir. 1904); *Ohio v. Dickerson*, 77 Ohio St. 34, 82 N.E. 969 (1907); *Ohio v. Pearson*, 2006 WL 3030787 (Ct. App. 2006).
33. *Buck v. Oklahoma*, 77 Okla.Crim. 17, 138 P.2d 115 (Ct. Crim. App. 1943).
34. *Oregon v. Harris*, 25 Or.App. 71, 547 P.2d 1394 (Ct. App. 1976).
35. *Pennsylvania v. Hoffman*, 52 Pa.Super. 272, 1912 WL 4825 (Super. Ct. 1912).
36. *South Carolina v. Brown*, 103 S.C. 437, 88 S.E. 21 (1916) (evidence not admitted because trail was not fresh and dogs pulled off trail at one point); *South Carolina v. Childs*, 299 S.C. 471, 385 S.E.2d 839 (1989); *South Carolina v. Johnson*, 306 S.C. 119, 410 S.E.2d 547 (1991); *South Carolina v. White*, 382 S.C. 265, 676 S.E.2d 684 (2009).
37. *Tennessee v. Brewer*, 875 S.W.2d 298 (Ct. Crim. App. 1994); *Tennessee v. Shepherd*, 902 S.W.2d 895 (1995).
38. *Parker v. Texas*, 46 Tex.Crim. 461, 80 S.W. 1008 (Ct. Crim. App. 1904). See *Trejos v. Texas*, 243 S.W.3d 30 (Ct. App. 2007) (tracking dog foundational elements adapted for cadaver dog evidence).
39. *Vermont v. Bourassa*, 137 Vt. 62, 399 A.2d 507 (1979).
40. *Epperly v. Virginia*, 224 Va. 214, 294 S.E.2d 882 (1982); *Pelletier v. Virginia*, 42 Va.App. 406, 592 S.E.2d 382 (Ct. App. 2004).
41. *Washington v. Loucks*, 98 Wash.2d 563, 656 P.2d 480 (1983); *Washington v. Welker*, 37 Wash.App. 628, 683 P.2d 1110 (Ct. App. 1984); *Washington v. Salazar-Rodriguez*, 1999 WL 780975 (App. Div. 1999); *Washington v. Lathim*, 2006 WL 1283758 (Wash.App., Div. 3 2006); *Washington v. Burnice*, 2006 WL 122198 (App., Div. 2006).
42. *West Virginia v. McKinney*, 88 W.Va. 400, 106 S.E. 894 (1921).
43. *Illinois v. Pfanschmidt*, 262 Ill. 411, 104 N.E. 804 (1914); *Illinois v. Cruz*, 162 Ill.2d 314, 643 N.E.2d 636 (1994); but see *Illinois v. Lefler*, 294 Ill.App.3d 305, 689 N.E.2d 1209, 228 Ill.Dec. 788 (Ct. App. 1998) (court reiterated inadmissibility of canine evidence, but held trial court's admission of such testimony to be harmless error based on other evidence for conviction).
44. *Ruse v. Indiana*, 186 Ind. 237, 115 N.E. 778 (1917); also see *Stout v. Indiana*, 174 Ind. 395, 92 N.E. 161 (1910) (exonerating bloodhound evidence not admissible); *Brafford v. Indiana,* 516 N.E.2d 45 (1987); *Indiana v. McDonald*, 322 Ill.App.3d 244, 749 N.E.2d 1066 (Ct. App. 2001) (directing jury to disregard bloodhound evidence cured error when jury heard references to tracking).
45. *McClurg v. Benton*, 123 Iowa 368, 65 L.R.A. 519, 98 N.W. 881 (1904); *Iowa v. Grba*, 196 Iowa 241, 194 N.W. 250 (Sup. Ct. 1923).
46. *Montana v. Storm*, 125 Mont. 346, 238 P.2d 1161 (1951) (handler and sheriff both interfered with trailing of two dogs, which the court criticized, but it did not confine its ruling to the facts; court determined to join those courts that reject bloodhound testimony).
47. *Brott v. Nebraska*, 63 L.R.A. 789, 70 Neb. 395, 97 N.W. 593 (1903).
48. *Iowa v. Buller*, 517 N.W.2d 711 (Sup. Ct. 1994).
49. *Terrell v. Maryland,* 3 Md.App. 340, 239 A.2d 128 (Ct. Spec. App. 1968).
50. *New York v. Centolella*, 61 Misc.2d 726, 305 N.Y.S.2d 460 (Oneida Cty. Ct. 1969).
51. *New York v. Whitlock*, 36 N.Y.Crim.R. 524, 183 A.D. 482, 171 N.Y.S. 109 (1918).
52. *Brott v. Nebraska*, 63 L.R.A. 789, 70 Neb. 395, 97 N.W. 593 (1903).
53. *Ohio v. Dickerson,* 77 Ohio St. 34, 82 N.E. 969 (1907) (emphasis added) (but accepting that "it is the human testimony that makes the trailing done by the animal competent, and its actions are described by human testimony, just as it would describe the operations of a piece of intricate machinery."); this language was quoted in *Pennsylvania v. Michaux*, 360 Pa.Super 452, 520 A.2d 1177 (Super. Ct. 1987).
54. *Starkes v. U.S.,* 427 A.2d 437 (D.C. App. 1981).
55. *California v. Gonzales*, 218 Cal.App.3d 403, 267 Cal.Rptr. 138 (Ct. App. 1990) ("handler was qualified by training and experience to use the dog").
56. *U.S. v. McNiece*, 558 F.Supp. 612, 12 Fed.R.Evid.Serv. 1870 (E.D.N.Y. 1983) ("of pure blood and of a stock characterized by acuteness of scent and power of discrimination, an in particular power of discrimination between individual human beings").
57. *U.S. v. McNiece* ("that the dog has been accustomed and trained to pursue the human track and to discriminate between individual human beings").
58. *Vermont v. Bourassa*, 137 Vt. 62, 399 A.2d 507 (1979) ("trained and accurate in tracking humans"); *U.S. v. McNiece* ("has been found by experience in actual cases to be reliable in such tracking and in such discrimination").

59. *U.S. v. McNiece* ("placed on the scent in a place where the scent of the alleged participant was present on the individual items sought to be identified"); *California v. Gonzales*, 218 Cal.App.3d 403, 267 Cal.Rptr. 138 (Ct. App. 1990) ("placed on the track where circumstances have shown the guilty party to have been").
60. *New Hampshire v. Maya*, 126 N.H. 590, 493 A.2d 1139 (1985); *U.S. v. McNiece* ("period of his efficiency").
61. *California v. Gonzales* ("whether or not the trail has become stale or contaminated").
62. *Terrell v. Maryland*, 3 Md.App. 340, 239 A.2d 128 (Ct. Spec. App. 1968) ("no interruptions in the tracking"); *Ohio v. Bridge*, 60 Ohio App.3d 76, 78, 573 N.E.2d 762 (Ct. App. 1989) ("circumstances surrounding the trailing must be shown"); *Michigan v. Laidlaw*, 169 Mich.App. 84, 96, 425 N.W.2d 738, 743 (Ct. App. 1988) (acknowledging dog had not tracked continuously because tracking was interrupted when handler learned suspect had been sighted elsewhere).
63. *Gavin v. Alabama*, 891 So.2d 907, 971–972 (Ct. Crim. App. 2003).
64. Canine evidence may sometimes be regarded as itself providing corroboration for other evidence more crucial to the conviction. See *Reyes v. Texas*, 1997 WL 196356 (Ct. App. 1997) (dog's alert to bags in motel room tended to support testimony of a witness connecting defendant with drugs, but since bags did not contain contraband, the corroboration was weak).
65. *California v. Gonzales*, 218 Cal.App.3d 403, 267 Cal.Rptr. 138 (Ct. App. 1990); *California v. Malgren*, 139 Cal.App.3d 234, 188 Cal.Rptr. 569 (Ct. App. 1983). Some police handlers may use their dogs primarily for suspect apprehension, and the training of the dog in tracking may be an aspect of that function. See *Illinois v. Griffin*, 48 Ill.App.2d 148, 198 N.E.2d 115 (Ct. App. 1964).
66. *North Carolina v. Hawley*, 54 N.C.App 293, 283 S.E.2d 387 (Ct. App. 1981).
67. *North Carolina v. Dorsett*, 245 N.C. 47, 95 S.E.2d 90 (1956).
68. *Brooks v. Colorado*, 975 P.2d 1105, 1108, 81 A.L.R.5th 779 (1999).
69. Ibid., 1112.
70. *South Carolina v. White*, 372 S.C. 364, 384, 642 S.E.2d 607, 617 (Ct. App. 2007) (the witness had qualified as an expert in other cases), aff'd in result, 382 S.C. 265, 676 S.E.2d 684 (2009).
71. *New Jersey v. Wanczyk*, 196 N.J. Super. 397, 482 A.2d 964 (Supr. Ct. 1984).
72. See Appendix A.
73. SWGDOG, according to its Web site, consists of federal, state, and local law enforcement agencies, international agencies, private vendors, and first responders. The membership is fixed at 55. See "About Us" at www.swgdog.org.
74. See SWGDOG SC 9—Human Scent Dogs: Tracking/Trailing People Based on Last Known Position (approved March 19, 2010, and posted under Approved Guidelines at www.swgdog.org).
75. SWGDOG SC 5—Selection of Handlers (approved October 2, 2006, and posted under Approved Guidelines at www.swgdog.org).
76. Faith in bloodhounds is well documented in England by the Middle Ages. See Jesse (1866), Chapter 52. Materials cited by Jesse show that English bloodhounds, even hundreds of years ago, were thought to be able to follow thieves and rustlers across difficult terrain, ignore other tracks, and attack the parties they were tracking even if they were in the midst of other people. A special tax was instituted in some areas of England in the reign of King James I to support bloodhounds to protect farmers from marauders. It was believed at the time that bloodhounds could track up to a day after a trail was laid.
77. *Ohio v. Hall*, 4 Ohio Dec. 147, 1896 WL 651 (Ct. Com. Pleas 1896). See also *Hodge v. Alabama*, 98 Ala. 10, 13, 13 So. 385, 386 (1893) ("It is common knowledge that dogs may be trained to follow the tracks of a human being with considerable certainty and accuracy"); *Pennsylvania v. Hoffman*, 52 Pa.Super. 272, 1912 WL 4825 (Super. Ct. 1912) ("It is a well-known fact that bloodhounds can be trained to follow or run the track of strangers. The gift or power or instinct being already inherent in the animal, he may be induced by special training to exercise it, under the persuasive influence and training of a skilled master. Being once accurately trained in this pursuit, we may presume that his exactness depends on the capacity bestowed upon him by nature, and developed by intelligent training").
78. *Fife v. Georgia*, 16 Ga.App. 22, 84 S.E. 485 (Ct. App.1915). See *Hays v. Kentucky*, 211 Ky. 716, 277 S.W. 1004 (Ct. App. 1925).
79. What documents might provide evidence of pedigree is not always clear. See *Louisiana v. Harrison*, 149 La. 83, 88 So. 696 (1921) (documents that were not certified copies of official records were inappropriately given to the jury before deliberation).
80. *Missouri v. Shawley*, 334 Mo. 352, 67 S.W.2d 74 (1933).
81. *Pedigo v. Kentucky*, 103 Ky. 41, 44 S.W. 143, 42 L.R.A. 432 (Ct. App.1898) (citing the *Encyclopedia Britannica* entry for "dog" regarding bloodhounds). See also *Davis v. Florida*, 46 Fla. 26, 36 So. 170 (1904) (admission of tracking evidence harmless since use of dogs was complete failure).

82. *Ohio v. Dickerson*, 77 Ohio St. 34, 82 N.E. 969 (Sup. Ct. 1907).
83. *North Carolina v. Hawley*, 54 N.C.App 293, 283 S.E.2d 387 (Ct. App. 1981) (Murf was said to have a 90% success rate in tracking humans and had followed a trail from where a perpetrator had thrown off a flip-flop to a trailer park where suspects were arrested); see also *North Carolina v. Green*, 76 N.C.App. 642, 334 S.E.2d 363 (Ct. App. 1985) (tracking by two dogs, a Doberman and a Rottweiler, admitted; court noted "a decreasing emphasis on the requirement that the tracking dog be a pureblood bloodhound" as long as training, experience, and proven ability were established).
84. *Perkins v. Texas*, 2009 WL 2837356 (Ct. App. 2009).
85. *New Hampshire v. Maya*, 126 N.H. 590, 493 A.2d 1139 (1985) (dog was Alsatian but this was not told to magistrate issuing warrant; apparently magistrate could have declined to issue warrant because of lack of evidence of purebred status).
86. *California v. Mitchell*, 110 Cal.App.4th 772, 2 Cal.Rptr.3d 49 (Ct. App. 2003).
87. *South Carolina v. White*, 382 S.C. 265, 676 S.E.2d 684 (2009).
88. *Fisher v. Mississippi*, 150 Miss. 206, 116 So. 746 (1928). See *Bullock v. Kentucky*, 249 Ky. 1, 60 S.W.2d 108 (Ct. App. 1933). See also *Denham v. Kentucky*, 27 Ky.L.Rptr. 171, 84 S.W. 538 (Ct. App. 1905) ("While the pedigrees of the dogs were not asked about, nor stated with particularity, we incline to the opinion that the testimony as a whole shows that they substantially possessed the breeding, qualities, and training required").
89. *Fox v. Arkansas*, 156 Ark. 428, 246 S.W. 863 (1923). See *North Carolina v. Porter*, 303 N.C. 680, 281 S.E.2d 377 (1981) ("sufficient if the dog's owner or handler identifies the dog as a bloodhound and the dog justifies this description by his performance"). See *Blair v. Kentucky*, 171 Ky. 319, 188 S.W. 390 (1916), after remand, 181 Ky. 218, 204 S.W. 67 (1918).
90. *Hinton v. Mississippi*, 175 Miss. 308, 166 So. 762 (1936).
91. *California v. Craig*, 86 Cal.App.3d 905, 150 Cal.Rptr. 676 (Ct. App. 1978).
92. *Vermont v. Bourassa*, 137 Vt. 62, 399 A.2d 507 (1979).
93. *Fisher v. Mississippi*, 150 Miss. 206, 116 So. 746 (Sup. Ct. 1928).
94. Gerritsen and Haak (2001), 18, citing Bodingbauer (1977).
95. McWhorter (1920).
96. SWGDOG SC 3—Selection of Serviceable Dogs (approved October 2, 2006, and posted under Approved Guidelines at www.swgdog.org). See *Gavin v. Alabama*, 891 So.2d 907, 971 (Ala.Crim.App. 2003) (handler preferred beagles).
97. *Davis v. Florida*, 46 Fla. 137, 35 So. 76 (1903). There can be too little evidence. See *Brummett v. Kentucky*, 263 Ky. 460, 92 S.W.2d 787 (Ct. App. 1936) (Answer "Yes, sir," to question about whether dog was skilled as tracker was insufficient since it was only evidence concerning dog's qualifications). Some courts have gone into detail on training procedures. See *Montana v. Storm*, 125 Mont. 346, 238 P.2d 1161 (Sup. Ct. 1951); *Iowa v. Grba*, 196 Iowa 241, 194 N.W. 250 (1923).
98. *New York v. Whitlock*, 36 N.Y.Crim.R. 524, 183 A.D. 482, 485–486, 171 N.Y.S. 109, 111 (1918).
99. 183 A.D. 482, 486–7, 171 N.Y.S. 112.
100. *California v. Lee*, 2003 WL 22100843 (Ct. App. 2003) (dog brought to scene of abandoned vehicle, about an hour after officers set up perimeter, went toward apartment building and found suspect lying under a bush in the backyard; dog had bitten suspect and not released, causing injuries requiring medical treatment).
101. MWD Pamphlet 90-12, § 3–26.
102. Some trials are to be performed blind to the assessor as well, since there is some concern that subtle movements of the assessor might cue the handler or the dog. See Miklosi et al. (2005).
103. SWGDOG SC 9—Human Scent Dogs: Pre-scented canine searches (approved August 15, 2007 and posted under Approved Guidelines at www.swgdog.org). Although the handler must be the one to recognize his dog's alert, there should be some recognizable behavior that could be described to someone else. An alert that consists of making eye contact with the handler would seem very hard to recognize, either for a handler or a third party. See *Michigan v. Jackson*, 2008 WL 2037805 (Ct. App. 2008) (testimony inconsistent with written report, but alert would have been hard to detect in any case).
104. From SWGDOG SC 9—Human Scent Dogs: Tracking/Trailing People Based on Last Known Position (approved March 3, 2010, and posted under Approved Guidelines at www.swgdog.org). S is the starting point for the human target and F is the finishing point. The black trails are those of distracters.
105. Under this guideline, some trails are to be at least 800 yards in rural environments and 300 yards in urban environments.
106. From SWGDOG SC 9—Human Scent Dogs: Tracking/Trailing People Based on Last Known Position.
107. *Harris v. Mississippi*, 143 Miss. 102, 108 So. 446, 447 (1926).
108. *Simpson v. Alabama*, 111 Ala. 6, 20 So. 572 (1896) (opinion of judge who wrote *Hodge*).

109. *Parker v. Texas*, 46 Tex.Crim. 461, 80 S.W. 1008, 100 Am.St.Rep. 1021 (Ct. Crim. App. 1904). One trial court, which fortunately was overruled, allowed a mayor and an insurance agent to testify concerning what they had heard about some dogs who had tracked from the location of a chicken theft to a neighbor. *McClurg v. Benton*, 123 Iowa 368, 65 L.R.A. 519, 98 N.W. 881 (1904).

110. *Holub v. Arkansas*, 116 Ark. 227, 172 S.W. 878 (1915).

111. *Mitchell v. Georgia*, 202 Ga. 247, 42 S.E.2d 767 (1947).

112. *Michigan v. Perryman*, 89 Mich.App. 516, 280 NW2d 579 (Ct. App. 1979).

113. *Pelletier v. Virginia*, 42 Va.App. 406, 421, 592 S.E.2d 382, 389 (Ct. App. 2004).

114. *Edwards v. District of Columbia*, 390 So.2d 1239 (D.C. App. 1980).

115. *Tomlinson v. Florida*, 129 Fla. 658, 176 So. 543 (1937).

116. *U.S. v. McNiece*, 558 F.Supp. 612 (E.D.N.Y. 1983).

117. *Ochoa v. City of Buena Park*, 2008 WL 2003761 (C.D.Cal. 2008).

118. Innocence Project: James Ochoa (retrieved December, 28, 2009, from www.innocenceproject.org/ Content/43.php).

119. *Connecticut v. Kelly*, 2009 WL 323481 (Super. Ct. 2009) (dog tracked to car in which perpetrator may have been; court found probable cause to let dog in the car for sniff, resulting in alert to driver's seat; argument built in part on analogy to probable cause arising from drug sniff of exterior of vehicle under *U.S. v. Place*, 462 U.S. 696 (1983)).

120. *Brooks v. Colorado*, 975 P.2d 1105 (1999).

121. *Connecticut v. Wilson*, 180 Conn. 481, 429 A.2d 931 (1980). See *Idaho v. Streeper*, 113 Idaho 662, 747 P.2d 71 (1987) (one dog had tracked in 50 cases with 80% success rate; other dog had tracked in over 100 cases with 75% success rate).

122. See *Connecticut v. St. John*, 282 Conn. 260, 919 A.2d 452 (2007) (completing training program with success rate of 70% satisfied tracking dog foundational requirement that dog be trained and accurate in tracking humans).

123. *North Carolina v. Davis*, 54 N.C. 596, 284 S.E.2d 139 (Ct. App. 1981).

124. *Washington v. Wieting*, 1997 WL 88957 (Ct. App. 1997).

125. Gerritsen and Haak (2001), 57.

126. See *Debruler v. Kentucky*, 231 S.W.3d 752 (2007) (failure to provide defense counsel with dog's training records was not reversible error because they had not been requested by such counsel and were not covered by defense counsel's request for "results or reports of physical or mental examinations, and of scientific tests or experiments made in connection with the particular case"; counsel was "well aware that the Commonwealth would be presenting evidence of dog tracking, but failed to request the desired documents prior to trial"; presumably records would have been discoverable if requested).

127. A defendant's ability to obtain training and field records of narcotics detection dogs in probable cause hearings has resulted in a variety of perspectives in federal and state courts. The South Dakota Supreme Court found three basic judicial perspectives: (1) courts that deem a dog's reliability established by a showing that it has been trained and certified; (2) courts deeming a dog's training and certification to be *prima facie* evidence the dog is reliable, but which can be challenged by other evidence; and (3) courts that allow or require a dog's field activity reports into evidence, along with evidence of training and certification. The court noted that many appellate courts defer to the trial court's ruling on the reliability of a dog. *South Dakota v. Nguyen*, 726 N.W.2d 871 (2007). See also *Ohio v. Nguyen*, 157 Ohio App.3d 482, 811 N.E.2d 1180 (2004).

128. Stockham et al. (2004a); see Meserve and King (2002).

129. See *Ohio v. Neeley*, No. B9705067 (1997) (defendant tracked successfully after 111 hours from the location of the victim's car, finding articles belonging to victim).

130. Stockham et al. (2004a).

131. *Fife v. Georgia*, 16 Ga.App. 22, 84 S.E. 485 (Ct. App. 1915).

132. *Harris v. Georgia*, 17 Ga.App. 723, 88 S.E. 121 (Ct. App. 1916). It was not clear that a subsequent failure to establish the foundation would have resulted in a reversal. A Kentucky case from 1904 admitted tracking testimony but directed the jury to disregard it when a proper foundation was not subsequently laid. The same court found admissible other testimony concerning a conversation the defendants had about getting Japanese oil to confuse the bloodhound, considering this to be distinguishable from the tracking evidence. *Allen v. Kentucky*, 26 Ky.L.Rptr. 807, 82 S.W. 589 (Ct. App. 1904). See also *Johnson v. Georgia*, 293 Ga.App. 32, 666 S.E.2d 452 (Ct. App. 2008).

133. *New Hampshire v. Maya*, 126 N.H. 590, 493 A.2d 1139 (1985).

134. *California v. Gutierrez*, 2004 WL 723161 (Ct. App. 2004).

135. *Kansas v. Adams*, 85 Kan. 435, 116 P. 608 (1911).
136. *Illinois v. Pfanschmidt*, 262 Ill. 411, 104 N.E. 804 (1914).
137. *Oregon v. Harris*, 25 Or.App. 71, 547 P.2d 1394 (Ct. App. 1976). See *Iowa v. Grba*, 196 Iowa 241, 194 N.W. 250 (1923) (handler testified dog would follow trail up to 40 hours old). One authority on trailing dogs wrote that they could often follow trails up to 16 hours old. Syrotuck (2002), 67–69.
138. *Virginia v. Patterson*, 392 Pa.Super. 331, 572 A.2d 1258 (Super. Ct. 1990).
139. *Hinton v. Mississippi*, 175 Miss. 308, 166 So. 762 (1936).
140. *Missouri v. Freyer*, 330 Mo. 62, 48 S.W.2d 894 (Sup. Ct. Div. 2 1932).
141. *New Hampshire v. Taylor*, 118 N.H. 855, 395 A.2d 505 (1978).
142. *Arizona v. Coleman*, 122 Ariz. 130, 593 P.2d 684 (Ct. App. 1978); see *Debruler v. Kentucky*, 231 S.W.3d 752 (2007).
143. See *Florida v. Foster*, 390 So.2d 469, 470 (Ct. App. 1980) (probable cause requires that the dog be trained, but the dog's "track record" is also important, with emphasis "placed on the amount of false alerts or mistakes the dog has furnished"; failure to produce track record resulted in determination that state had not met burden of establishing probable cause for search).
144. *U.S. v. Dix*, 2007 WL 3046347 (D.Neb. 2007) (noting concerning a drug dog's alert that "once the dog is found to be certified, he may be presumed to be well trained and reliable. … If the dog was not certified or otherwise had performance problems, that could be a circumstance for the court to consider").
145. *Matheson v. Florida*, 870 So.2d 8, 14 (Ct. App. 2004). See also *U.S. v. Howard,* No. 08-6143 (6th Cir. 2010) (finding defendant's "fixation on certification" to be misplaced. "Certification, much like a college or legal degree is, in the end, simply a statement by an institution that an individual has satisfactorily completed a particular course of study"; the court found the narcotics detection dog's training records more significant).
146. *California v. Gutierrez*, 2004 WL 723161 (Ct. App. 2004).
147. Law Enforcement Training Specialists International, Inc. Canine Felony Tracking Certification Requirements (posted at www.letsk9professionals.org/tracking.html).
148. AWDA Web site (www.americanworkingdog.com/certification_standards.htm).
149. SWGDOG SC 9—Human Scent Dogs: Tracking/Trailing People Based on Last Known Position (approved March 3, 2010, and posted under Approved Guidelines at www.swgdog.org).
150. See Washington State Criminal Justice Training Commission, K-9 Certification, www.isp.state.il.us/academy/localtraining.cfm (https://fortress.wa.gov/cjtc/www/K9/index.html); Illinois State Police K-9 Training (www.isp.state.il.us/academy/localtraining.cfm).
151. *Brooks v. Colorado*, 975 P.2d 1105, 1114 (1999). See *Kansas v. Fixley,* 118 Kan. 1, 233 P. 796 (1925) ("action of the dogs is practically the only evidence upon which the conviction of the defendant is based").
152. *Michigan v. McPherson*, 85 Mich.App. 341, 271 N.W.2d 228 (Ct. App. 1978); see *Michigan v. Jackson*, 2008 WL 2037805 (Ct. App. 2008). See *Michigan v. Laidlaw*, 169 Mich.App. 84, 96, 425 N.W.2d 738, 743 (Ct. App. 1988), stating: "Due to varying skills of dogs and their handlers, as well as the possibility that a jury may give more weight to dog-tracking evidence than it is entitled to, there must be other corroborating evidence presented before identification is sufficient to support a guilty verdict."
153. *New Hampshire v. Taylor*, 118 N.H. 855, 395 A.2d 505 (1978).
154. See *Meyers v. Kentucky*, 194 Ky. 523, 240 S.W. 71 (Ct. App. 1922); *Copley v. Tennessee*, 153 Tenn. 189, 281 S.W. 460 (1926); *Missouri v. Freyer*, 330 Mo. 62, 48 S.W.2d 894 (Sup. Ct. Div.2. 1932) (no one took the trouble to verify that any of the shoe tracks on the trail matched those of defendant; case was remanded in case new evidence could be found); *Short v. Kentucky*, 251 Ky. 819, 66 S.W.2d 33 (1933) (reversal of conviction because it rested "entirely on suspicion, surmise, and supposition"); *Missouri v. Long*, 336 Mo. 630, 80 S.W.2d 154 (Sup. Ct., Div.2 1935) ("This court has never sustained, and let us hope never will sustain, a conviction solely on what may be termed bloodhound evidence"); *North Carolina v. Lee*, 211 N.C. 326, 190 S.E. 234 (1937); *California v. Craig*, 86 Cal.App.3d 905, 150 Cal. Rptr. 676 (Ct. App. 1978); *Michigan v. Norwood*, 70 Mich.App. 53, 245 N.W.2d 170 (Ct. App. 1976); *Coleman v. U.S.,* 306 F.2d 751 (Ct. App. 1962) (dog followed a scent from scene to defendant, but no evidence connected him to the crime itself); *North Carolina v. Lanier*, 50 N.C.App. 383, 273 S.E.2d 746 (Ct. App. 1981); *Washington v. Loucks*, 98 Wash.2d 563, 656 P.2d 480 (1983).
155. *Michigan v. Harper,* 43 Mich.App. 500, 204 N.W.2d 263 (Ct. of Appeals, Div.2, 1973); *Hinton v. Mississippi,* 175 Miss. 308, 166 So. 762 (1936); *Terrell v. Maryland,* 3 Md.App. 340, 239 A.2d 128 (Ct. Spec. App. 1968).

156. *North Carolina v. Palmer*, 178 N.C. 822, 101 S.E. 506 (1919) (suspect offered bribe when dogs implicated him). But see *Daugherty v. Kentucky*, 293 Ky. 147, 168 S.W.2d 564 (Ct. App. 1943) (statement by defendant that bloodhounds would arrive in the morning was not clear admission of guilt to support conviction when only other evidence was tracking evidence).

157. *New Jersey v. Parton*, 251 N.J.Super. 230, 597 A.2d 1088 (Ct. App. 1991).

158. *Washington v. Nicholas*, 34 Wash.App. 775, 663 P.2d 1356 (Ct. App. 1983).

159. *Washington v. Ellis*, 48 Wash.App. 333, 738 P.2d 1085 (Ct. App. 1987) (dog tracked to man hiding under car).

160. *New Hampshire v. Taylor*, 118 N.H. 855, 395 A.2d 505 (1978).

161. *North Carolina v. Hunter*, 143 N.C. 607, 56 S.E. 547 (1907).

162. *Hodge v. Alabama*, 98 Ala. 10, 13 So. 385 (1893); described in VIII Law Notes 366 (October 1904).

163. *Adams v. Arkansas*, 149 Ark. 669, 235 S.W. 372 (1921). See also *Doyle v. Arkansas*, 166 Ark. 505, 266 S.W. 459 (1924) (shoeprints and statement by defendant that could be taken as a confession); *Kansas v. Schalansky*, 112 Kan. 87, 209 P. 816 (1922) (shoeprints found on tracking from first fire; horse tracks found on second).

164. *Schell v. Georgia*, 72 Ga.App. 804, 35 S.E.2d 325 (Ct. App. 1945).

165. *Michigan v. Stone*, 195 Mich.App. 600, 491 N.W.2d 628 (Ct. App. 1992); *South Carolina v. Bostick*, 253 S.C. 205, 169 S.E.2d 605 (1969) (rifle and cap found on trail corroborated confession defendant sought to retract).

166. *North Carolina v. Rowland*, 263 N.C. 353, 139 S.E.2d 661 (1965).

167. *Allen v. Alabama*, 8 Ala.App. 228, 62 So. 971 (1913).

168. *Meyers v. Kentucky*, 194 Ky. 523, 240 S.W. 71 (Ct. App. 1922).

169. *California v. Gonzales*, 218 Cal.App.3d 403, 267 Cal.Rptr. 138 (Ct. App. 1990).

170. *U.S. v. Rozen*, 600 F.2d 494 (5th Cir. 1979) (emphasis added).

171. *North Carolina v. Spivey*, 151 N.C. 676, 65 S.E. 995 (1909).

172. *Missouri v. Rasco*, 239 Mo. 535, 144 S.W. 449 (Sup.Ct. Div. 2 1912).

173. *Ohio v. DeWitt*, 2007 WL 1934335 (Ct. App. 2007). The case was also reviewed on a petition for writ of habeas corpus, which was denied. *DeWitt v. Jackson*, 2009 WL 948903 (S.D.Oh. 2009).

174. CALJIC [California Jury Instructions Criminal] 2.16. These jury instructions are issued by the Judicial Council of California. The instructions have been described as a synthesis of California tracking cases. *California v. Mitchell*, 110 Cal.App.4th 772, 2 Cal.Rptr.3d 49 (Ct. App. 2003).

175. *Kansas v. Wainwright*, 18 Kan.App.2d 449, 856 P.2d 163 (Ct. App. 1993).

176. *New York v. Muggelberg*, 132 A.D.2d 988, 518 N.Y.S.2d 285 (App. Div. 1987). See *New York v. Vandenbosch*, 216 A.D.2d 884 (App. Div. 1995) ("the [trial] court accorded minimal weight to the dog tracking evidence").

177. *Michigan v. Martin*, 2008 WL 108876 (Ct. App. 2008).

178. *Bacon v. Georgia*, 249 Ga.App. 347, 548 S.E.2d 78 (Ct. App. 2001) (emphasis in decision).

179. *Kansas v. Wainwright*, 18 Kan.App.2d 449, 856 P.2d 163 (Ct. App. 1993).

4 Scientific Analysis of Tracking, Trailing, and Scent Identification

John J. Ensminger and Tadeusz Jezierski[1]

Tracking and trailing evidence has been admitted by courts in the United States since the end of the 19th century, but the foundational requirements established at that time were not based on judicial standards regarding the admission of scientific evidence. Rather, courts accepted the long tradition, the "common knowledge," of the use of bloodhounds in finding fugitives and criminals, which in England goes back to the Middle Ages.[2] As forensics sciences developed, and courts began to expect that evidence with a scientific basis should be supported by the testimony of experts with appropriate credentials, canine testimony began to face new hurdles. This chapter focuses on the development of the research relevant to the use of dogs in finding and identifying criminals, and discusses the introduction of the findings of that research into criminal prosecutions.

Tracking, trailing, and identification presume that each human has an individual odor recognizable by a dog, that such odors are left along a path a person takes while walking and remain for some period of time,[3] that such odors are detectible by a dog on the trail, and that a dog can be trained to follow such an odor to the exclusion of others. Scent identification, in its most scientific application, presumes that an individual also leaves odor on objects he touches, and that this odor can be matched by a dog to an odor collected from the same individual on a specific object and placed in a row of identical or nearly identical objects.[4]

Scent lineup procedures have been accepted because a number of assumptions have guided police work with dogs in such procedures, including that individuals have unique odors,[5] such odors are stable over time,[6] dogs can differentiate between odors of individuals and can be taught to signal that two odors match and are produced by the same individual,[7] such signaling of identity will happen with approximately the same accuracy for any individual,[8] and that lineups can be designed to take advantage of these skills.[9] There is also an assumption that dogs will be relatively consistent in their abilities.[10]

HUMAN ODOR

Human scent can be described as a combination of various compounds differing in ratio from person to person along with some compounds that are specific to individuals. This combination of relative ratios may explain why each individual has a unique odor that a dog is able to detect.[11] A useful terminology lists three factors as contributing to human odor:

1. Primary odor—Odor constituents that are stable over time regardless of diet or environmental factors. These constituents are probably genetically determined.[12]
2. Secondary odor—Constituents present because of diet, environmental factors, disease, and medications.
3. Tertiary odor—Constituents present because of the influence of outside sources, such as lotions, soaps, perfumes, and so forth. These constituents will change as an individual's hygiene habits change.[13]

Material used for odor sampling and the place odor samples are taken may also add constituents.[14]

PRIMARY AND SECONDARY ODORS

A study of 197 adults from an Austrian village looked at the volatile compounds in their sweat, urine, and saliva, and concluded that the presence and proportion of some of these compounds produced a distinctive chemical signature for each individual.[15] Two researchers looking at volatile carboxylic acids secreted from axillary skin compared these odorant acids in 12 pairs of monozygotic twins. Variations were noted in the same subject if taken on different days, and this temporal difference was found to be only slightly lower than that between the identical twins. The researchers concluded that humans have a genetically determined body odor type that is at least partly composed of carboxylic acids.[16] Some changes in an individual's odor have been demonstrated to occur as a result of aging.[17]

One group of researchers noted that it is generally possible to control for tertiary odors, but dealing with secondary odors is more difficult. For example, women might be at different phases of menstrual cycles, which might provide differentiating odors for dogs, but this is difficult to obtain data on.[18]

EFFECTS OF TERTIARY ODORS

Animal-fat based soaps contain constituents that include compounds reported in humans.[19] One researcher found, nevertheless, that the external component of human odor related to cosmetics did not significantly affect a dog's ability to distinguish individuals. Dogs in the identification study were not confused by a "common" odor component related to the same cosmetics used by the scent donors. The researcher found a very low percentage of false alarms (1.92%) toward people who used the same cosmetics.[20] Other research has indicated that smoking cigarettes by scent donors does not influence the correctness of identifications.[21]

Because of the difficulty of knowing the effects of secondary and tertiary odors on dogs, such factors should be taken into consideration in lineups. The sex of individuals used in the lineup should be the same, age differences of donors should be kept to a minimum, and storage times of scent samples used in the lineup should not vary more than necessary. Thus, elderly people should not be tested in the same lineup with the samples from young people, and old samples should not be tested together with fresh samples.

ODORS OF THE TRAIL

Odors on a path a dog follows are not restricted to human odor and can include:

1. Artificial odors, including sausages, cheese, dog treats, and so forth.
2. Soil damage caused by walking, kicking, shuffling, and so on. Walking causes physical changes to the surface and brings out odors of plants (e.g., plant sap from crushing the plant, and subsequently bacteria growing on damaged areas of plants).
3. Odors of footwear (which vary according to the components of the shoe, such as rubber, leather, cloth, etc.), including shoe polish and items ground into the soles.
4. Individual human odor, as discussed earlier (including secretions of different glands and microbes present on human skin), and foot sweat.[22]

The front part of the foot leaves more odor than the back because the sole is thinner and this part of the foot contains the strongest smelling parts of our feet. Perspiration also comes out of the upper part of the shoe. The odors left by someone walking are also affected by such natural factors as:

- Instability of fatty acids (formic acid deteriorates quickly but most fatty acids do not).[23]
- Gaseous elements in the air (nitrogen, oxygen, carbon dioxide).
- Wind, temperature, and sunlight (causing evaporation and diffusion).

- Composition of surface on which a track is laid. For instance, asphalt contains chemicals that influence fatty acids.
- Water in the form of vapor, dew, rain, and snow. Although water can wash away scent, a foot depression that fills with water can create a reservoir holding the odor. Fatty acids evaporate faster at higher temperatures. The more humid the air, the slower the odor of the track evaporates.[24]

Ground contact seems to be important and some research has suggested that dogs will only follow a trail if there has been ground contact.[25] Ground contact probably does not require ground disturbance, as various studies have found that dogs can track on hard surfaces where there may be little if any ground disturbance.[26]

The individual odor source of scent sometimes presumes that dogs are detecting something about the epithelial cells we all shed into the environment:

> The surface of the skin contains about two billion cells, of which 1/30 are being shed daily (approximately 667 cells/sec). The average lifespan of an epithelial cell is approximately 36 h. Dead cells which are shed from the surface of the skin are sometimes referred to as "rafts" which are approximately 14 μ in size and weigh approximately 0.07 mg. The "raft" is composed of one or more dead cells, approximately four microbial bacteria, and body secretions, of which all three components are said to be characteristic to the individual. Each "raft" is also said to be surrounded by a vapor cloud, which results from bacterial action upon the cells. Studies conducted by the National Institute for Medical Research in London have shown that there is a current of warm air which surrounds the human body.[27] The air current is approximately one-third to one-half inch thick and it travels up and over the body at a rate of 125 feet per minute. Analysis of the air current on the surface of the human body showed that it contained four to five times as many "germs" as the air in the rest of the sampling room. The "germs" come from the bacteria that are shed off with dead skin cells, larger flakes of skin fall to the ground but smaller ones are drawn up into the current. These currents can also be visualized running along the outside of clothing. The warm air currents are said to carry the "rafts" from the body into the surrounding area allowing for the deposit of human scent in the environment.[28]

Thus, the "raft" air currents carry debris upward and away from the body, like a plume,[29] where it may deposit on the nearby area in a conically shaped pattern known as a scent trail.[30] Saturated with perspiration and skin oils, the raft is a breeding ground for bacteria normally found in the skin, and this bacterial activity may make up some part of what a dog detects in a human scent trail.[31] It has also been argued:

> The idea that human scent is produced through bacterial action on dead skin cells and secretions is the most common depiction of the creation of human odor. Other studies have suggested that odor is formed very quickly, supporting the idea that odor production is due to simple bond cleavage as opposed to a complex bacterial action.[32]

We cannot help laying trails that dogs can detect. Clothing designed to limit the ability of wildlife to smell an individual who is observing animals or hunting was shown to be almost useless in deterring a tracking dog.[33] However, another study found that when an individual wore a whole body suit, dogs were unable to follow the trail.[34]

COLLECTING SCENT AND SCENT ENHANCEMENT

The means by which scent is extracted from objects can have a considerable effect on what compounds are actually detectable in the extraction medium.[35] Human scent may be collected by four forensic applications:

1. Sampling the object (which can be difficult with small objects).
2. Wipe the object with absorbent material (which might destroy fingerprints or DNA).
3. Head space absorption, in which an absorber is placed in a container with the evidence (usually taking hours to days for a scent transfer).[36]
4. Dynamic head space concentration in which air is drawn from a sample object through a sampling tube holding a cotton gauze pad to trap scent on the pad. This speeds up the process of the previous approach by using airflow.

The first three categories have the disadvantage of possibly disturbing or contaminating trace evidence. The fourth category generally involves use of a scent transfer unit (STU), often used in tracking cases,[37] discussed later. One court accepted that it does not matter how the scent is deposited on an item to be collected by an STU.[38]

ITEMS USED TO SCENT DOGS

Items that have been used for scenting dogs in lineups include clothes,[39] weapons and shell casings,[40] cigarette filters,[41] plastic bags containing heroin,[42] a footprint at a place where the perpetrator had jumped off a roof,[43] a handkerchief tied over a victim's mouth with her blood,[44] and countless other items. Such items may be put directly before a dog's nose, or the dog may be exposed to a scent pad made by touching or rubbing an item or to a scent pad to which scent is added by use of a scent transfer unit.

SCENT PADS

Cloth and gauze have long been used to wipe items that cannot be moved and that the perpetrator may have touched.[45] Cotton, linen, gauze, and other fabrics absorb odors easily. Scent pads have been rubbed on seats and steering wheels of cars used in crimes.[46] A scent pad can be placed on a car seat with tongs and left there for 2 hours to allow for scent absorption. One police dog scenting expert recommends for absorption that the windows of the car should be open slightly in order to keep air circulating in the car. The pad is then returned to the sterile jar and kept until a suspect's odor is tested in a scent lineup.[47]

STORAGE OF SCENT SAMPLES

Scent samples from the crime scene must be stored until a suspect is found and there is reason to conduct a lineup, which can happen quickly or take years. A comparison of storage containers including glass, polyethylene, and aluminized pouches concluded that glass containers subject to minimal light exposure provide the most stable environment for stored human scent samples. The problem with polymer and aluminized containers is that compounds are transferred from them to cotton. Chinese specialists attempt to store scent samples at $-18°C$.[48]

SCENT TRANSFER UNITS

The fourth method of gathering scent listed earlier, dynamic head space absorption, has led to judicial controversy over whether the use of specialized equipment for gathering scent must meet a standard for admissibility of scientific evidence. Scent transfer units are often mentioned in recent scent lineup cases as the device by which scent was transferred from a crime scene item to a scent pad. The STU-100 is a portable, hand-held vacuum pump that pulls air through an inlet and across a sterile, surgical gauze pad (by Johnson & Johnson®) collecting primarily volatile or vaporized scent compounds. Scent transfer units have been described as modified dust busters.[49] Optimal airflow rates have been studied.[50] See Figure 4.1. The pad is removed after use of the device and usually double packaged in heat-sealed nylon envelopes.

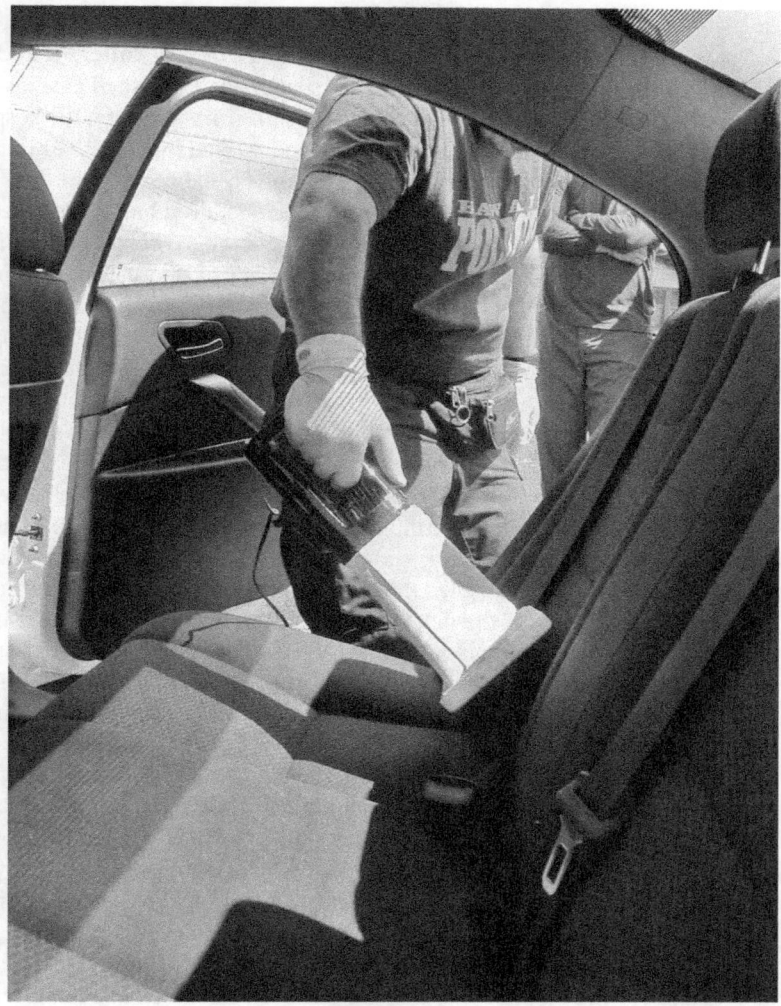

FIGURE 4.1   Scent transfer unit sweeping car seat. (Courtesy of Linda Dunn and Michael J. Craig, Big "T" LLC, www.stu100.com.)

To conduct a scent check with a trailing canine, the handler first acclimates the canine to the available volatiles profiles (scents and odors) at the start location and establishes a baseline for the canine. After harnessing, the handler opens the nylon envelope and places the pad in front of the canine's nose. If a matching odor is present at the trail start, the canine commences to follow the trail. If no matching odor is present, or the level of volatile organic compounds is below the detection capability of the canine, the canine is trained to respond by refusing to trail.[51]

In 2005, a California case stated that STUs were being used by 80 law enforcement agencies in 17 states as well as in the United Kingdom. The FBI has used STUs since 2001 as the exclusive means of retrieving scent off evidence.[52] Although the prosecution usually introduces STU evidence, there have been instances where a suspect was identified who was not prosecuted and defense counsel sought to introduce such evidence as exonerating.[53] Appellate courts have sometimes held that STU-related evidence should not have been admitted at trial, but affirmed the conviction in any case by finding that the admission of such evidence was harmless.[54]

Cases mention scent transfer units as having been used to take scent from car seats,[55] clothing,[56] shell casings,[57] a beer can,[58] a marijuana cigarette,[59] a cap,[60] and a bloody knife.[61] A 2003 California case involved the use of a scent transfer unit to prepare scent pads from shell casings found at the scene of a street gang murder. Scents were also collected from shirts worn by the suspects as well as the victim's shirt. Three control pads were made from chairs used by detectives in the homicide bureau who had not worked the case. A dog, having been given the scent from the shell casings, alerted to the scent taken from the shirt of a suspect the police believed had loaded the casings into the semiautomatic weapon used in the murder. The dog also alerted to scent collected from the victim's shirt, which the prosecution theorized happened as a result of the suspect turning the victim over after he was on the ground. The dog did not alert to scent pads taken from the clothing of any of the other suspects, which was explained as due to the probability that only one individual loaded the shells into the weapon. The trial court admitted the canine evidence. The appellate court found that scent transfer units had not been discussed in a *published* opinion and said that this was not a situation of a new device being used to conduct an established type of test nor of an established device being used to conduct a new type of test, but rather an STU was a "novel device used in furtherance of a new technique." Therefore, the admissibility of evidence obtained by such a device should have been subjected to a hearing to establish scientific acceptance of the device, proof that the witness testifying concerning it was a qualified expert, and proof that the device was used correctly.[62] The court noted that other people may have touched the bullets as well as the victim's shirt, and certainly other people had touched the chairs of the detectives from which the control pads were prepared. Although the dog's ability to isolate specific scent on objects containing multiple scents could be regarded as enhancing the value of the evidence, the court did not feel the matter was adequately considered by the trial court. The court found the admission of the evidence to be harmless error, however, and upheld the convictions.[63]

Procedures have been developed using STUs with dogs, which involve presenting a control to establish a negative response to trail from a virgin pad before the dog is scented with a pad scented by an STU from a crime scene item.[64] Although experts have testified to doubts about the use of STUs, forensic researchers have argued that the STU is a very useful tool,[65] and have noted that DNA profiles have been obtained from expended cartridge casings and bullets,[66] making it reasonable that human odor from such items could be extracted with an STU.[67] The length of time after the crime that a pad was prepared by an STU has sometimes been considered by courts.[68] The admissibility of evidence relying on the use of an STU has been discussed in a number of decisions, particularly in California.[69]

HOW LONG DOES SCENT LAST?

One researcher found no difference in identification accuracy as to samples collected after 15, 30, 45, and 60 minutes.[70] Other research has indicated that collecting scent from an object after 3 to 5 days is sufficient to allow a dog to make a correct identification.[71] The length of time that a scent will remain in a location is a matter of both research and dispute.

> In traditional bloodhound circles, the anecdotal information passed from trainer to student is that human scent is fragile and easily destroyed. Many dog handlers in the United States are taught that identifiable human scent disappears after 24 hours. European studies using properly trained scent-identification dogs showed acceptable performance levels with collected scent that was aged two weeks to six months.[72]

In 1972, William G. Syrotuck, looked at the physical and chemical phenomena of canine scenting and estimated that the detectable ground scent left by a human might last from 8 to 16 hours.[73] Gerritsen and Haak prepared a table showing "perception time" for dogs on various surfaces and under different weather conditions, adapted in Table 4.1.[74]

TABLE 4.1
Perception Time of Tracking Dogs on Various Surfaces under Different Weather Conditions

Surface	Weather	Wind Force	Temperature (C°)	Temperature (F°)	Humidity	Perception Time (hrs)
Grass	Cloudy	Calm	+17	63	Moist	18–36
	Bright	Gentle breeze	+22	72	Normal	12–24
	Rain	Near gale	+10	50	Moist	4–6
	Snow	Calm	–4	25	Moist	6–8
	Snow	Near gale	–8	17	Moist	2–4
Dirt field	Bright	Calm	+20	68	Moist	18–24
	Bright	Gentle breeze	+22	72	Normal	10–16
	Cloudy	Near gale	+17	63	Normal	6–8
	Rain	Moderate breeze	+25	77	Moist	3–5
	Bright	Light air	–5	23	Normal	10–12
	Snow	Fresh breeze	-8	17	Moist	4–6
Sand	Cloudy	Gentle breeze	+21	70	Normal	6–8
	Bright	Gentle breeze	+24	75	Dry	2–5
	Rain	Gale	+10	50	Moist	1–2
	Cloudy	Moderate breeze	–10	14	Normal	6–12
	Snow	Near gale	–5	23	Moist	3–4
Wooded area	Cloudy	Calm	+17	63	Moist	18–24
	Bright	Gentle breeze	+20	68	Normal	10–16
	Rain	Moderate breeze	+15	59	Dry	8–12
	Snow	Light air	–4	25	Moist	6–8
Concrete	Cloudy	Calm	+20	68	Normal	6–8
	Bright	Near gale	+25	77	Dry	2–4
	Rain	Fresh breeze	+11	52	Moist	1–2
	Snow	Light breeze	–5	23	Moist	4–6
Asphalt	Cloudy	Light air	+15	59	Moist	4–6
	Rain	Light breeze	+20	68	Moist	3–5
	Bright	Gentle breeze	+20	68	Normal	2–4
	Bright	Light air	+25	77	Dry	1–2
	Snow	Near gale	-6	21	Moist	3–4

Three researchers at Duke University lightly fingerprinted 1-by-3-inch glass slides, preparing one slide from each person for indoor storage and one for outdoor weathering. Indoor slides were stored in a cabinet. Outdoor slides were put in flat boxes and put on the laboratory roof. Environmental conditions were recorded. At 6, 12, 24, 48, 72, and 96 hours and at 1, 2, and 3 weeks, trays of equal age were taken from the cabinet and the roof. The same two dogs were used for trials. Slides were put in circles of five, four of which were blank for each trial. A fox terrier mix and a Weimaraner were taught to go around the circle off leash, sniff at each station, then sit when human odor was detected. A correct response was rewarded. At the end of 3 weeks, each dog could still detect indoor fingerprinted samples easily. By 8 weeks, performance was at chance levels (20% success). For weathered slides, the fox terrier reached chance levels at 2 weeks, but it took 3 weeks for the Weimaraner. The researchers found that slides exposed on dull, rainless days tended to be found more readily than slides exposed to the bright sun, but most weather data provided little correlation to results.[75]

In an experiment specifically designed to determine how aging of crime scene odors affects a dog's ability to match such an odor to a scent in a lineup, odors were collected by individuals handling metal or plastic tubes for a short while or putting cloth in their pockets for 10 minutes. In the trials, materials of the same sort as the scenting item were placed in glass jars in a circle, one of which, after a zero trial, contained the scent of the target while the others contained scents of foils. The trials were performed immediately after scenting all the items (time zero), then at 2, 4, 8, 12, 16, 20, and 24 weeks. Ten dogs were perfect at time zero, but recognition declined significantly even at 2 weeks, though more than half the dogs were correct up to 20 weeks. Dogs performed most poorly with plastic piping, though the type of material did not produce large differences overall. The author stated that scent discrimination has been displayed in some studies with scents up to 7 years old. She suggested that freezing the "crime scene item" or storing it at low temperatures might prevent the drop in performance, as is sometimes done in the United States.[76] This study demonstrates, that lineups occurring soon after the crime are more likely to be highly accurate.

Length of time in use of scent pads prepared with scent transfer units has been an issue in trials.[77]

CONTAMINATION

In Poland, police osmology experts have conducted experiments on the effects on the ability of dogs to identify evidential scent despite contamination by other scents. Contamination of the evidential scent by 10% vinegar did not prevent trained dogs from correctly identifying the perpetrators.[78] One researcher concluded that dogs are able to identify each of three persons who touched an object.[79]

Contamination cannot always be presumed because of contact. One study failed to establish that individual human odor molecules could be transferred from a person to an object indirectly by shaking hands with that other person and the other person then touching an object.[80]

TRANSFER OF SCENT THROUGH CLOTHES

Scenting techniques have sometimes been used to determine whether a suspect was sitting in a car and which seat he sat in.[81] A researcher in Warsaw has looked at some of the issues that arise with regard to scent transfers through clothing and found that if individual A puts on pants belonging to individual B and sits in a car belonging to individual D for an hour, three dogs could match the scent of B from the car to a comparative sample made by B. Thus B's scent transferred to the seat of the car even though B did not sit in the car. The same was not true of gloves of C, which were worn by A when he sat in the car. The substance of the clothing is significant in that hand odor was found not to go through leather gloves in the same way as body odor went through fatigues. Nor did it pass through rubber gloves in another experiment.[82]

The researcher from Warsaw concluded that a scent trace from a carrier may contain the individual scent of a person who has not had direct contact with it. Factors that could determine what a dog would alert to include:

* Duration of use of garment by owner.
* Duration of contact of garment with scent carriers.
* Surface of contact between the garment and the scent carrier.
* Elapsed time from when the scent trace originated to when it was secured.
* Rise in temperature at point of contact of garment with the carrier.

The researcher noted that individual scents of different people on an item producing a scent trace did not cancel each other out or create some new, different scent.[83]

Cases have described police as being able to define which seats in a car each suspect was sitting in during or around the time of a crime.[84] There may be a limited window as to how long the parties sat in the car. One researcher found that if two people sat in a car for 30 minutes and the scent samples were taken from the seats after no longer than 60 minutes, a dog could determine in a scent lineup which seat was occupied by each suspect. When the time from when the passengers left the car to when scent samples were collected was more than an hour, the identification could not be made. It did not matter if the passengers were wearing the same perfume.[85]

ABILITY OF DOGS TO DISTINGUISH AND REMEMBER ODORS

One study found that dogs could distinguish the odors of 17 men, women, and children, in a test that involved finding a handkerchief used by a specific person.[86] Yet another study looked at the ability of seven dogs to match scent samples with the people from whom they were taken. An 85% matching rate was found, but the dogs did not perform as well in the presence of observers.[87]

The question as to whether an object contains scent that the dog can distinguish and follow or use to identify a match goes to whether dogs can distinguish individual scents. Studies have confirmed that dogs generally can distinguish the scent of a specific individual and will generally not confuse it with the scent of another individual unless the other individual is an identical twin.[88] Dogs will be particularly confused by identical twins that live together, but will often distinguish identical twins that have lived apart, suggesting that environmental factors allow dogs even to distinguish identical twins.[89]

LENGTH OF THE SNIFF

Studies on tracking direction indicate that dogs only need a few seconds to determine the direction in which an individual is walking and only need five footsteps to do so.[90] Scenting dogs on items or scent pads for a scent lineup is usually restricted to a few seconds in experiments and in actual lineups.

SCENT FROM DIFFERENT PARTS OF THE BODY

Hand scent is of interest forensically since hands often hold weapons, stolen property, items the perpetrator touched but did not or could not move, and so forth.[91] Scent lineups usually involve collecting hand scent samples, often by wiping the suspect's hand with cotton or having the suspect hold a steel tube. A comparative study of hand scent forensics concluded that hand scent is more stable in the face of illness than scents from some other parts of the body:

> Hand odor is a combination of eccrine and sebaceous gland secretions without the involvement of the apocrine gland, which contributes immensely to the malodors generated from the armpit region. Alterations to portions of the odor of an individual may occur due to the influence of illness, the onset of puberty, the menstrual cycle in females, etc. Many of these factors directly affect the apocrine gland. The secretions obtained from the eccrine and sebaceous glands are less likely to be influenced by these changes, thereby more likely to produce the stable odor of an individual.[92]

Eccrine glands are found throughout the body but the highest densities are in the palms and the soles of the feet. These glands can secrete up to 2 to 4 liters of fluid each hour, about 98% of which is water. Sebaceous glands are usually located in body regions where hair is present. Sebaceous gland secretions, called sebum, consist of glycerides, free fatty acids, wax esters, squalene, and cholesterol. A person's diet can influence sebum.[93]

The uneven distribution of glands in the body raises the issue of whether each individual has distinguishable scents depending on from where on the body a scent sample is taken. If a criminal touches one item with his hand and another with the back of his arm, will the scent taken from the two items be the same? A study published in 1991 considered whether scent from different parts of the body are equally identifiable by dogs. The assumption of "folk wisdom," according to the authors, is that the same scent would be found in an individual's shirt, a handkerchief, socks, or a utensil the individual touched while eating. The researchers used three dogs that were trained to retrieve a dumbbell scented by the hand of the handler and placed on a pegboard near an identical but unscented dumbbell, which was wired to the board. The unscented dumbbell had been untouched by humans for at least 24 hours and had been stored on a tray open to the air for that period.[94] Dogs learned that the unscented dumbbell could not be retrieved because it was wired to the pegboard. After dogs learned to retrieve the scented dumbbell, the unscented dumbbell was also unwired. Dogs retrieving the wrong dumbbell had to repeat the process until the correct dumbbell was retrieved, at which time the dog was praised and allowed to stop. Gradually more identical dumbbells were added to the pegboard, some unscented, some scented by the hands of other people. The new scent objects were wired down at first but were unwired once the dogs learned to ignore them. The dog was directed to go forward and retrieve one of the items and bring it back to the handler.

Most dogs were highly accurate in telling their handler's hand from a dumbbell with no human scent[95] but less successful when elbow scent was compared to no human scent. Dogs were generally successful distinguishing between their handler's hand and a stranger's hand, but distinguishing between the handler's elbow and a stranger's hand produced results not statistically different from random. When choosing between the handler's hand and his elbow, dogs chose the hand scent 76.8% of the time, suggesting to the researchers that dogs had inadvertently been trained to identify a hand scent. The researchers concluded that there are body-part specific scents in addition to identifiable individual scents. The authors saw this as creating forensic problems.

> Particularly open to question, for example, would be the use of a piece of clothing from the upper part of the body (e.g., hat, gloves, shirt) as a reference scent article on the basis of which the dog is expected to select a track of human scent made by footsteps through the environment. Although it may indeed be possible to train individual dogs to perform such tasks, the results presented here make it clearly incumbent upon the individual dog trainer or handler to demonstrate that his or her dog can indeed perform the required scent identification tasks with an acceptable degree of statistical reliability, before evidence based on the performance of such a dog should be accepted in a court of law.[96]

This research was criticized in the same publication in which the study appeared as asking the dogs in the experiment an ambiguous question given that they were trained on hand odors, not elbow odors. The suggestion was made that training involving elbow odors would produce clearer results.[97] The authors of the original research replied to this argument by stating:

> We purposely introduced this ambiguity [asking dogs trained to discriminate hand odor from odors from different parts of the body] to determine whether trained dogs automatically generalize scents from one part of the body to other body parts, as a strict interpretation of the individual odor theory would suggest. Above all, many law enforcement authorities and courts of law would contend that such a task should not have been ambiguous, because the single individual odour associated with each human subject should have pervaded all scents regardless of the part of the body from which they were derived.[98]

The significance of this research is that dogs may not alert as correctly when the scenting item takes scent from another part of the body than the object in the lineup row took from the various suspects and foils who provided (often hand) scent for the lineup.

Two other researchers also looked at the hand–elbow distinction. They suggested that the inability of dogs to match smells collected from different body parts in the study just described "might well be a matter of training." The researchers used six police dogs trained in scent identification tasks. The experimental protocol used 10-cm stainless steel tubes that were cleaned with soap, boiled in tap water for at least half an hour, and handled with tongs thereafter. People scenting the tubes held them for 3 minutes and then replaced them in sterilized glass jars with twist-off tops. Most people scenting tubes were male and "suspects" were always male. Each trial scent consisted of three matches the dog had to make:

1. Matching elbow to hand—The sample tube the dog was given to smell had been scented in the crook of the elbow, while the six tubes in the row had been scented by hands.
2. Matching hand to elbow—The sample tube had been scented by hand, while the matching tube and two others in the row had been scented in the crook of the elbow, the other three by hand.
3. Matching pocket to hand—The sample tube had been scented in the pocket, while the six tubes in the row had been scented by hand.

The dog could choose between six tubes and a match was potentially possible in all trials, with a chance level of 16.7% for each trial. The dogs were 32% correct in the elbow-to-hand trials, and 32% correct in the hand-to-elbow trials. They were much better, 58%, in the pocket-to-hand trials. When the "suspect" was an employee of the Police Dog Training Center, the dogs were correct 73% of the time, but correct only 25% of the time when the "suspect" was a complete stranger. The researchers concluded that Dutch police dogs are capable of cross-matching scents collected from different body parts. The higher accuracy on tubes scented in a "suspect's" pocket may be due to the fact that pockets trap hand odor.[99]

Despite better results than the prior study, there must remain some concern as to how an item was handled at the crime scene by the perpetrator when that differs from how scent was imparted to objects used in the lineup. Problems will be reduced by having all items in the lineup scented in the same way, but it appears that this remains a weakness that cannot be fully overcome.

DISTINGUISHING GENDERS

Compounds present in male and female extracts have been shown to be qualitatively similar with minor quantitative differences.[100] One study concluded that the scent of a woman in a sequence of male scents is not attractive to dogs. When scented to a woman, they did not pick out another woman in a sequence that consisted otherwise of male scents.[101] Recent research has suggested that dogs are more attracted to the scents of women and may more easily distinguish one woman from another than one man from another.[102] The issue of scent attractiveness—when dogs appear to be attracted to a scent and may alert to it because of this characteristic—will be discussed in a subsequent chapter on scent lineups.

RESEARCH ON TRACKING AND TRAILING

A study carried out in Southern California compared dogs that were novices with less than 18 months of training against dogs that had more training. Scent pads were prepared from a number of men and women of different ages and ethnic groups. The subjects were given maps showing where they should walk in a regional park or a college campus. Each walked with a partner and about 50 feet from the end point of the trail, the trail layer and the partner split and hid behind nearby objects, such as trees. About 48 hours later, the trail layer and the partner came back and resumed these hiding positions and a dog was started out at the beginning of the trail. The overall result was that novice dogs had a 53.3% find rate and one false identification (picking a partner over the person to whom the dog had been scented). Veteran dogs, on the other hand, had a 96% find rate with no false identifications. Of 20 trails run, the veteran dogs ran 19 to completion. Of 20 trails run by the dogs with less than 18 months of training, 12 were run to completion. The results were considered good because heavy rains and winds occurred before some of the trailing. Two of the novice dogs were only 10 and 11 months old, respectively, but within 3 months were making their finds 100% of the time. The research confirms that highly experienced dogs have very high success rates in following trails, and seldom misidentify the correct party if that party separates from a decoy near the end of the trail.

Another identification experiment in the same study sought to determine whether dogs could distinguish the tracks of identical twins and other persons who were closely related, as well as individuals who were living together who might or not be related.[103] The experiments were conducted in a regional park and involved 13 bloodhounds. In the first test, the dog was given a scent of one person at the beginning of a track laid by another person, but that other person could have been a monozygotic twin of the person to whom the dog was scented, or could have been another relative or someone who lived with the person given the scent. The correct response was for the dog not to track since they had not been scented to the individual who laid the track. Monozygotic twins were the most difficult group for the bloodhounds to differentiate. No dogs were able to perform better than chance for twins that lived together. For twins that had lived apart for at least a year, only one dog out of nine performed better than chance. If the test involved related people living together (siblings or parent–child), 10 of 13 dogs performed significantly better than chance. If related pairs did not live together, all 12 bloodhounds used in the test performed better than chance. For nonrelated people living together, all 13 dogs performed a negative track significantly better than chance. This was also true of the 9 bloodhounds used to trail nonrelated people living apart.

In the second test, two individuals walked together for part of the time and then separated. The correct response was for the dog to follow the individual whose scent the dog had been given. An incorrect response was to follow the other trail layer. Only three bloodhounds performed better than chance when trailing monozygotic twins who lived together. Five out of nine dogs performed better than chance when trailing twins who lived apart. Of the 12 bloodhounds trailing related persons living together, 9 performed better than chance. When trailing related persons living apart, all 12 performed better than chance. Of the 13 dogs trailing nonrelated persons, 12 performed better than chance. The researchers concluded:

> The findings suggest that bloodhounds may use genetically derived odortype as its major source of scent while trailing. The more genetically similar two people are, the more difficult it is for the dogs to tell the difference. The similarities between two people may force the dog to rely on environmental cues for scent discrimination and trailing.

Odortype, according to the researchers, is not solely based on genetics, as environmental cues may affect a dog's performance. The authors observed that their study supported the use of bloodhound evidence in courts because it lent "credibility to the bloodhound's ability to trail and discriminate between various people using genetically derived odortype, as well as possible environmental signals."[104]

DIRECTION OF THE TRAIL

A good deal of research has indicated that dogs will tend to follow the trail in the direction that the perpetrator walked and that the dog will make this determination very quickly. Three Norwegian scientists studied the capacity of dogs to follow a trail in the direction the trail layer had walked. The scientists found three phases in the dogs' behavior:

1. Searching phase during which the dog found the trail.
2. Deciding phase when the dog determined the direction of the track.
3. Tracking phase when the dog followed the track.

During the searching phase, the dogs sniffed 10 to 20 times between each respiratory ventilation. The transition from the searching to the deciding phase was clear because the dogs halted for a moment when they detected the track. In the deciding phase, which lasted 3 to 5 seconds, the dogs stepped less often and had longer sniffing periods. They sniffed at two to five footprints, holding their noses close to the ground, about only a centimeter up when they were on concrete, though the distance was not clear on grass. In the tracking phase, the sniffing periods and walking frequency were similar to what was observed in the searching period. Sniffs averaged about six per second in all phases.[105]

Two other researchers had much less success in a similar study. They looked at whether trained tracking dogs would always go in the direction a track layer had taken when the dogs entered a 200 pace track at midpoint. A total of 66 tracks were run, but in only 60.6% of these (40 tracks) did the dogs track in the direction the track layer had walked. In 26 tracks, the dogs went in the wrong direction (backtracked).[106] As noted earlier, some dogs in field situations have tracked not in the direction the perpetrator left a crime scene, but the path he took to get to it. Some dogs have identified both the way the perpetrator left the crime scene as well as the way he came to it.

Research by Hepper and Wells concluded that dogs can determine directionality with only five steps available to sniff.[107] The research indicates that dogs can be put on the path of a perpetrator just about anywhere and that they will be able to determine the direction of that trail even if it is very short. See Figure 4.2.

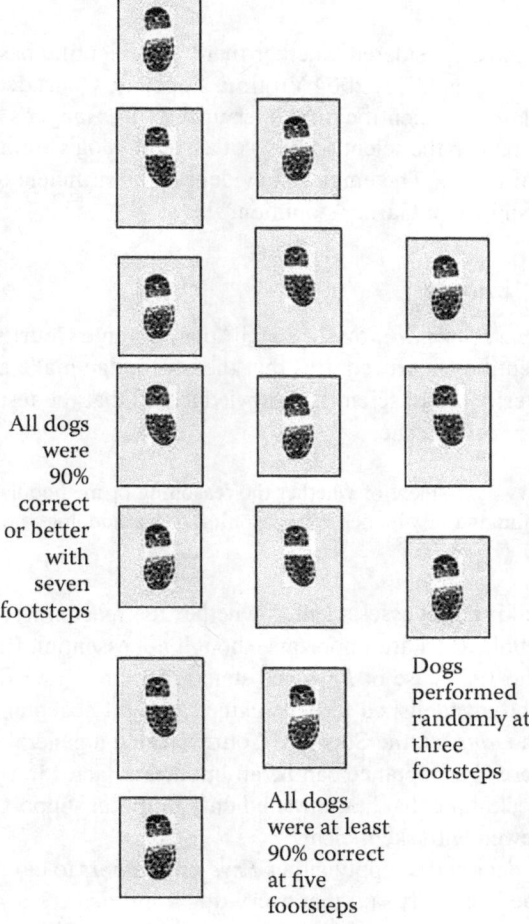

All dogs were 90% correct or better with seven footsteps

Dogs performed randomly at three footsteps

All dogs were at least 90% correct at five footsteps

FIGURE 4.2 Determination of tracking direction by ten dogs sniffing 7, 5, or 3 squares. (Created from data in Hepper, P.G. and Wells, D., How Many Footsteps Do Dogs Need to Determine the Direction of an Odour Trail? *Chemical Senses 30*, 291–298, 2005).

LENGTH OF THE TRAIL

It might be assumed that the longer the trail, the greater the risk of contamination, but there is some research that indicates that the dog's accuracy actually increases with distance. A 1967 thesis found the longer the distance before a trail splits between a target and two decoys, the more likely the dog will follow the target and not a decoy. When the trail split at 50 meters, dogs followed the correct trail only 45% of the time, but when trail split after 800 meters, dogs followed correct trail 75% to 85% of the time.[108]

JUDICIAL PERSPECTIVES ON SCIENTIFIC ASPECTS OF TRACKING

The Illinois Supreme Court, in rejecting dog-tracking evidence for the state in 1914, concluded that a jury could have no means

> of knowing why the dog does this thing or another in following in one direction instead of another. The information obtainable on this subject, scientific, legal or otherwise, is not of such a character as to furnish any satisfactory basis or reason for the admission of this class of evidence.[109]

Most U.S. courts that have considered whether there is a scientific basis of tracking or trailing have concluded that it is irrelevant.[110] A 2004 Virginia Appellate Court decision acknowledged that a handler "could not explain the scientific principles underlying Ranger's ability," but, in any case, he "was not required to establish the scientific basis of a trailing dog's ability to follow scent in order for his opinion to be admitted. ... The empirical evidence was sufficient to establish the reliability and, therefore, the admissibility of Garner's opinion."[111]

ADMISSION OF SCIENTIFIC EVIDENCE

In *Daubert v. Merrell Dow Pharmaceuticals, Inc.,*[112] the Supreme Court stated that the admission of the testimony of a scientific expert requires that the trial judge make a preliminary determination that the expert will testify as to scientific knowledge and that the testimony will help the jury understand or determine a fact in issue.

> This entails a preliminary assessment of whether the reasoning or methodology underlying the testimony is scientifically valid and of whether that reasoning or methodology properly can be applied to the facts in issue.

A key question for making this assessment is whether the reasoning or methodology has been tested. Peer review and publication are important, though not essential. Rate of error should "ordinarily" be considered. The 1923 case of *Frye* had stated that "the thing from which the deduction is made must be sufficiently established to have gained general acceptance in the particular field in which it belongs."[113] In *Daubert*, the Supreme Court rejected a general acceptance requirement, but did say that "[w]idespread acceptance can be an important factor in ruling particular evidence admissible," such that a technique that has attracted only minimal support in the scientific community "may properly be viewed with skepticism."

Courts have generally declined to apply either *Frye* or *Daubert* to canine evidence.[114] In a 1978 California case,[115] an appellate court said that every dog's abilities are different and the reliability of dog-tracking evidence was not subject to general scientific proof.[116] A Vermont case from 1979 held that foundational elements for admission of dog-tracking evidence were sufficient and did not need to be established by proof of its scientific principles.[117] An Arizona case from 1984 involved scent lineups of clothing and bicycles, but the Arizona Supreme Court said that the *Frye* test was inapplicable to dog tracking or scenting, requiring only basic foundational requirements.[118]

In a 1997 case where a dog was scented to a nylon mask used in a robbery and tracked to a location where the perpetrator may have entered a vehicle, a New York court stated:

> In our view, there is no scientific principle or procedure at issue here. The use of a trained canine is an investigative rather than a scientific procedure. ... Thus, a *Frye* hearing was unnecessary and all the People needed to do was lay a proper foundation for the admission of the dog-tracking evidence.[119]

Similar positions have been expressed with respect to *Daubert*.[120]

Courts that have considered the application of *Frye* and *Daubert* to tracking often contrast tracking with the "hard sciences."[121] This may be a valid distinction if tracking is considered as a whole, because tracking is a collection of behaviors and circumstances, and cannot be analogized to an experiment that determines whether a fingerprint is that of the defendant or the DNA of the victim. Rather, tracking consists of a series of forensic questions. Is there scent on an object a perpetrator may have touched? What path did he take in leaving the crime scene? Was an object found along the path connected with the crime in any way? Did the dog start working quickly enough that he will be able to continue on a number of surfaces? And so on. Each of these questions implicates both scientific issues and specific training and experiential issues regarding the dog. The only aspect of tracking that can fit easily into the mold of a laboratory experiment is the scent identification that occurs in a highly structured scent lineup.

One California court did find canine evidence not properly admissible (though it did not reverse because the error was harmless) because of "the absence of an adequate foundation from scientific or academic sources as to ... whether every person has a unique scent such as to permit an accurate basis for scent identification."[122]

EVIDENCE FROM SCENT TRANSFER UNITS

In California cases, *Frye* has been held applicable to the use of a scent transfer unit in the preparation of scent pads for use in a scent lineup.[123] California courts have not always been welcoming of scent transfer unit evidence.[124] Several California cases have suggested that dog scent lineups might require further analysis as to the admissibility of such evidence, but nevertheless affirmed convictions because of a finding that any error in admitting the scent identifications or procedures used in such identifications was deemed harmless.[125]

NOTES

1. Tadeusz Jezierski is Chair of the Department of Animal Behavior of the Polish Academy of Sciences, Institute of Genetics and Animal Breeding, Wolka Kosowska, Poland.
2. Jesse (1866), Chapter 52.
3. See, for example, Schoon and Haak (2002), 47.
4. For a summary of canine scent theory, see Ensminger, Jezierski, and McCulloch (unpublished manuscript 2010).
5. See, for example, Schoon and Haak (2002), 39 et seq.; Harvey et al. (2006) (arguing dogs may use a genetically derived odortype as the major source of scent while trailing, but can be confused more often by identical twins living together than identical twins living apart).
6. See, e.g., Schoon and Haak (2002), 47; see also Harvey et al. (2006) (longer related persons live apart, the more easily distinguishable they are by dogs).
7. See discussion of Schoon and Haak (2002), 48.
8. But see Jezierski et al. (2011) (dogs distinguished women better than men).
9. Too often—in fact, almost always—U.S. cases have assumed all the identification skills of the dogs used in a case and allowed the handler to provide a protocol for taking advantages of those skills in identifying a suspect as the perpetrator.

10. See *Risher v. Texas*, 227 S.W.3d 133 (Ct. App. 2006) (court overruled defense objection to admission of dog scent lineup because dog performing the lineup was on weight-loss medication at the time because handler testified he saw no decline in dog's ability, except that she was "a little slower").

11. Curran et al. (2006a). For additional discussion of possible biochemical bases of human odor, see Yamazaki et al. (1990, 1998, 2001).

12. Curran et al. (2007) (finding 63 human-produced compounds from the hands of 60 volunteers, and finding a high degree of variability, stating: "It is uncertain whether scent identity is distinguishable merely by ratios of the common compounds between individuals, the presence or absence of compounds which vary significantly between individuals, or if it is a combination of the two factors").

13. Curran et al. (2005a); Schoon et al. (2009).

14. Jezierski et al. (2003).

15. Phillips et al. (2000a, 2000b). Microflora resident on human skin participate in odor production. Korting et al. (1988).

16. Kuhn and Natsch (2008).

17. Phillips et al. (2000a, 2000b). Seasonal variation has also been described. See Zhang et al. (2005) ("emission behavior of human odors in the moist season varied from those taken in the dry season").

18. Jezierski et al. (2012).

19. Curran et al. (2005b).

20. Gawkowski (2000).

21. Schoon (1997b); Misiewicz (2000).

22. Gerritsen and Haak (2001), 33. These authors cite early work listing 12 different odor components to a track: general human odor, individual human odor, odor of the footwear, odor of the shoe polish, botanical odor, odor of the soil, added odors (manure, fertilizer), animal odors, blood trails of game, game tracks, artificial odors, and tracks of tires. Most (1926).

23. Some fatty acids may confuse dogs. See Uchida (1956).

24. Gerritsen and Haak (2001), 47–48, 100, 129–134.

25. Budget (1933); Syrotuck (1972), 101 (dogs were able to continue following track when mechanical foot left impressions in the ground but could not with no track at all).

26. Steen and Wilson (1990).

27. Citing Doyle (1970).

28. Curran et al. (2010b). "The fluid dynamics of plumes and how to follow them" is a part of sniffing. Settles (2005). The concept that dogs are picking up scent from a raft of skin flakes can be found in the case law. See *North Carolina v. Cross*, 681 S.E.2d 566, 2009 WL 2177766 (Ct. App. 2009) ("The testimony of one canine handler indicated that the tracking dog could follow the scent of a person based on 'riffs,' or dead skin cells put off during high adrenaline situations").

29. Craven and Settles (2006); Settles (2005).

30. Hunt (1999).

31. For a study of the aerodynamics of the wake of a walking human, see Edge et al. (2005).

32. Curran et al. (2010b), citing Zeng et al. (1991).

33. Shivik (2002) (subjects hid in boxes; dogs found subjects wearing odor-absorbing clothing in 95% of trials, and subjects wearing street clothes in 100% of trials).

34. Pearsall and Verbruggen (1982).

35. Lorenzo et al. (2004).

36. But see *Michigan v. Giles*, 2008 WL 2436529 (Ct. App. 2008) (gun put in plastic bag with sterile gauze pad for about 5 minutes).

37. *Ochoa v. City of Buena Park*, 2008 WL 2003761 (C.D.Cal. 2008); *California v. Barajas*, 2002 WL 1722329 (Ct. App. 2002); *California v. Rivera*, 2004 WL 2601335 (Ct. App. 2004); *California v. DeSantiago*, 2003 WL 21753766 (Ct. App. 2003).

38. *California v. Salcido*, GA052057 (Los Angeles Super. Ct., March 11, 2005).

39. *California v. Robinson*, 2004 WL 2418068 (Ct. App. 2004).

40. *California v. Barajas*, 2002 WL 1722329 (Ct. App. 2002).

41. Kaldenbach (1998), 120.

42. Ibid., 123.

43. Ibid., 125 (case thrown out because evidence tampered with unbeknownst to handler).

44. Ibid., 128.

45. Curran and Furton (2006) (noting it "has been shown that there is a measurable amount of human scent weight still present on gauze up to 84 days after a 15 minute scenting period").

46. See *California v. Aguilar*, 2004 WL 2051385 (Ct. App. 2004) (scent taken from car seat 15 days after impounding).
47. Kaldenbach (1998), 96. One California court accepted obtaining scent from a steering wheel using a paper towel found in the perpetrator's car by the handler, rejecting that this violated the foundational requirement that the trail not be contaminated). *California v. Sanders*, 2009 WL 3682460 (Ct. App. 2009).
48. Hudson et al. (2009).
49. See, for example, *California v. Mitchell*, 110 Cal.App.4th 772, 2 Cal.Rptr.3d 49 (2003).
50. Prada et al. (2007).
51. Eckenrode et al. (2006).
52. *California v. Salcido*, GA052057 (Los Angeles Super. Ct. 2005) (testimony of Rex Stockham, Supervisory Special Agent Hazardous Device Examiner, Explosives Unit, FBI Laboratory).
53. See *California v. Melara*, 2006 WL 164989 (Ct. App. 2006).
54. See *California v. Willis*, 115 Cal.App.4th 379, 9 Cal.Rptr. 3d 235 (Ct. App. 2004).
55. *California v. Chavez*, 2004 WL 1173075 (Ct. App. 2004); *California v. Aguilar*, 2004 WL 2051385 (Ct. App. 2004); *California v. Sandoval*, 2002 WL 519848 (Ct. App. 2002).
56. *California v. Aguilar*, 2004 WL 2051385 (Ct. App. 2004); *California v. DeSantiago*, 2003 WL 21753766 (Ct. App. 2003).
57. *California v. Alonzo*, 2008 WL 2248628 (Ct. App. 2008); *California v. Chavez*, 2004 WL 1173075 (Ct. App. 2004).
58. *California v. Barajas*, 2002 WL 1722329 (Ct. App. 2002).
59. *California v. Hackett*, 2003 WL 463976 (Ct. App. 2003).
60. *California v. Robinson*, 2004 WL 2418068 (Ct. App. 2004).
61. *California v. Salcido*, GA052057 (Super. Ct. 2005).
62. Citing *California v. Kelly*, 17 Cal.3d 24, 549 P.2d. 1240, 130 Cal.Rptr. 144 (1976).
63. *California v. Mitchell*, 110 Cal.App.4th 772, 2 Cal.Rptr.3d 49 (Ct. App. 2003).
64. Eckenrode et al. (2006).
65. Stockham et al. (2004a), discussing *California v. Willis*, 115 Cal.App.4th 379, 9 Cal.Rptr. 3d 235 (Ct. App. 2004).
66. See Wickenheiser (2002); Szakacs (2000). See Raymond et al. (2004).
67. Stockham et al. (2004a).
68. *California v. Aguilar*, 2004 WL 2051385 (Ct. App. 2004) (possibly 41 days); *California v. Alonzo*, 2008 WL 2248628 (Ct. App. 2008) (10 months); *U.S. v. McNiece*, 558 F.Supp. 612 (E.D.N.Y. 1983) (21 months). Scent samples from carefully preserved crime scene items have been used in European cases years after the crime. Rogowski (2001a).
69. See *California v. Melara*, 2006 WL 164989 (Ct. App. 2006) (trial court properly excluded exonerating evidence because of lack of proper foundation); *California v. Alonzo*, 2008 WL 2248628 (Ct. App. 2008) (lack of negative response test went to weight, not admissibility, of evidence); *California v. Craig*, 86 Cal.App.3d 905, 150 Cal.Rptr. 676 (Ct. App. 1978) ("The scent transfer unit is simply a device used to implement the obvious principle that scent travels in air. There is no novel scientific principle behind the use of suction to move air and the scent contained in it; it is the same principle at work in air filters in every home. *Kelly/Frye* does not require a foundational hearing on this principle in order to support the admission of testimony involving the use of the scent transfer unit."); *California v. DeSantiago*, 2003 WL 21753766 (Ct. App. 2003) (remand for hearing on scientific validity of STU); *California v. Mitchell*, 110 Cal.App.4th 772, 2 Cal.Rptr.3d 49 (Ct. App. 2003) (court was troubled that scent pads may have been prepared from items touched by individuals besides the defendant); *California v. Willis*, 115 Cal.App.4th 379, 9 Cal.Rptr. 3d 235 (Ct. App. 2004) (holding that it was "not obvious that a vacuum device can properly transfer scent to a gauze pad form an object," though other evidence was sufficient for jury to reach guilty verdict and error of admitting STU evidence was harmless); *California v. Salcido*, GA052057 (Super. Ct. 2005) (STU evidence admissible with corroboration). See *California v. Smith*, 2011 WL 1250762 (Ct. App. 2011) (trial court accepted *Salcido* findings in *Kelly/Frye* hearing).
70. Rogowski (2001b).
71. Rogowski (2001b); Zdanowicz and Kaminski (1998).
72. Stockham et al. (2004b).
73. Syrotuck (1972).
74. Gerritsen and Haak (2001), at 143.
75. King et al. (1964).
76. Schoon (2003).
77. *California v. DeSantiago*, 2003 WL 21753766 (Ct. App. 2003).

78. Dudek and Srebnik (2000).
79. Rogowski (2005).
80. Rogowski (2006).
81. *California v. Sandoval*, 2002 WL 519848 (Ct. App. 2002).
82. Rogowski, (2004). See Romanes (1887) (handler's dog followed boots of handler even when worn by stranger, but did not follow boots of stranger when worn by handler; nor did he follow new boots worn by handler).
83. Rogowski (2002).
84. *California v. Chavez*, 2004 WL 1173075 (Ct. App. 2004); *California v. Aguilar*, 2004 WL 2051385 (Ct. App. 2004); *California v. Sandoval*, 2002 WL 519848 (Ct. App. 2002).
85. Gawkowski (2001).
86. Kalmus (1955). It is perhaps worth noting that one study determined that dog owners could distinguish the smell of their own dog from that of other dogs. See Wells and Hepper (2000).
87. Settle et al. (1994).
88. Kalmus (1955).
89. Harvey et al. (2006); Hepper (1988, 1994).
90. Thesen et al. (1993); Hepper and Wells (2005). Recent research indicates that dogs' nostrils draw in separate odor samples, aiding in the determination of direction. Craven et al. (2010).
91. Curran et al. (2006b) (73% of human scent evidence collected in the U.S. comes from contact between objects and the hands of an individual). Tracking dogs are primarily following foot scent, particularly odor of the forefoot. Gerritsen and Haak (2001), 45–48.
92. Curran et al. (2010).
93. Curran et al. (2005a).
94. The assumption that scent would completely dissipate from lineup articles in 24 hours has not been made by other researchers. Steel tubes, under Dutch procedures for instance, are sterilized between uses in lineups.
95. The dogs distinguished objects scented by their handler's hand 93% but not 100% of the time from objects with no human scent. It seems implausible that those dogs were not able to sniff out the difference between no human scent and the scent of their handler. An explanation could be that this difference was not always interesting for the dogs, or that the dogs did not associate the handler's scent with the reward or were not sufficiently motivated to earn the reward.
96. Brisbin and Austad (1991).
97. Sommerville et al. (1993).
98. Brisbin and Austad (1993).
99. See Schoon and de Bruin (1994).
100. Curran et al. (2005b).
101. Rogowski (2003).
102. Jezierski et al. (2012). Attractiveness has been suspected as a factor in human visual lineups. See Wojcikiewicz et al. (1999); see Doob and Kirshenbaum (1973).
103. Dogs were trained under the method described for tracking dogs by Tolhurst (1991).
104. Harvey et al. (2006).
105. Thesen et al. (1993).
106. MacKenzie and Schultz (1987) (surveying substantial prior research providing inconsistent results).
107. Hepper and Wells (2005).
108. Honhon (1967).
109. *Illinois v. Pfanschmidt*, 262 Ill. 411, 461, 104 N.E. 804, 823 (1914).
110. As noted in the preceding chapter, although handlers and trainers distinguish tracking and trailing, courts seldom acknowledge, and perhaps do not always understand, the difference. See *California v. Sanders*, 2009 WL 3682460 (Ct. App. 2009) ("Officer Miller testified that dog 'tracking' and 'trailing' are slightly different skills and that Obe was trained to trail (but not track) scents. The relevant cases, as well as the parties on appeal, refer to dog-*tracking* evidence, but there is no suggestion that the relevant legal principles are not applicable to both tracking and trailing").
111. *Pelletier v. Virginia*, 42 Va.App. 406, 421, 592 S.E.2d 382, 389 (Ct. App. 2004).
112. 509 U.S. 579, 113 S.Ct. 2786, 125 L.Ed.2d 469 (1993).
113. *Frye v. U.S.*, 54 App.D.C. 46, 293 F. 1013 (D.C. App. 1923).
114. *Risher v. Texas*, 227 S.W.3d 133 (Ct. App. 2006); see *Connecticut v. Kelly*, 2009 WL 323481 (Super. Ct. 2009) (agreeing with "widespread belief that dog tracking evidence can be deemed reliable without a *Frye* or *Daubert* inquiry"; the court generally contrasted canine olfaction with the type of expertise

held by dog handlers and did not consider that other scientific aspects might be found in tracking evidence beyond olfaction; court also found that a scientific inquiry was "not required because it would be a superfluous confirmation of that which is already known"); *U.S. v. Outlaw*, 134 F.Supp.2d 807 (W.D.Tex. 2001). See *U.S. v. Berrelleza*, 90 Fed.Appx. 361, 365 (10th Cir. 2004) (relying on *Outlaw*); *U.S. v. Morales*, 489 F.Supp.2d 1250 (D.N.M. 2007) (drug dog jumped in open window of vehicle without assistance of agents and alerted, giving agents probable cause to search vehicle; *Daubert* hearing was "the wrong procedural vehicle through which to challenge the reliability of a canine alert"); *Brooks v. Colorado*, 975 P.2d 1105 (1999) (Supreme Court of Colorado admitted dog tracking evidence as expert testimony not subject to *Daubert* or *Frye* scientific valuation factors). See also *Michigan v. Giles*, 2008 WL 2436529 (Ct. App 2008) (Michigan appellate court was "not persuaded" that scent lineup evidence "was of such a 'scientific' nature as to necessitate application of *Daubert*"; defendant had not challenged methods and procedures used by handler at trial). For an argument applying *Frye* to scent lineups, see Taslitz (1990).

115. *California v. Craig*, 86 Cal.App.3d 905, 150 Cal.Rptr. 676 (Ct. App. 1978).
116. See also *California v. Sandoval*, 2002 WL 519848 (Ct. App. 2002) (following *Craig*).
117. *Vermont v. Bourassa*, 137 Vt. 62, 399 A.2d 507 (1979). See also *South Carolina v. White*, 372 S.C. 364, 642 S.E.2d 607 (Ct. App. 2007).
118. *Arizona v. Roscoe*, 145 Ariz. 212, 700 P.2d 1312 (1984) ("We hold, therefore, that dog tracking or identification evidence is admissible in Arizona upon a proper foundational showing that the breeding, training, performance and handling of the particular dog warrants that the results obtained from use of the dog are reliable").
119. *New York v. Roraback*, 242 A.D.2d 400, 405, 662 N.Y.S.2d 327 (App. Div. 1997).
120. *Debruler v. Kentucky*, 231 S.W. 752 (2007) ("Canine scent tracking is not a technique amenable to peer review or scientific standards and testing. Rather it concerns the behaviors of the dog and the meanings of those behaviors, a knowledge acquired through experience and training. For this reason, foundational evidence of the canine's scent tracking record; the qualifications of its handler, its training and history provide far more insight into the general reliability of the testimony than a *Daubert* analysis").
121. *Risher v. Texas*, 227 S.W.3d 133 (Ct. App. 2006); see *Connecticut v. Kelly*, 2009 WL 323481 (Super. Ct. 2009) (agreeing with "widespread belief that dog tracking evidence can be deemed reliable without a *Frye* or *Daubert* inquiry"; the court generally contrasted canine olfaction with the type of expertise held by dog handlers and did not consider that other scientific aspects might be found in tracking evidence beyond olfaction; court also found that a scientific inquiry was "not required because it would be a superfluous confirmation of that which is already known").
122. *California v. Gutierrez*, 2004 WL 723161 (Ct. App. 2004).
123. *California v. Salcido*, GA052057 (Superior Ct. 2005), considering the requirements of *California v. Kelly*, 17 Cal.3d 24, 130 Cal.Rptr. 144, 549 P.2d 1240 (1976); see also *California v. Alonzo*, 2008 WL 2248628 (Ct. App. 2008). The cases often describe *Kelly-Frye* hearings, referring to the leading California case adopting *Frye* for state purposes. *California v. Kelly*, 17 Cal.3d 24, 130 Cal.Rptr. 144, 549 P.2d 1240 (1976).
124. See, for example, *California v. Melara*, 2006 WL 164989 (Ct. App. 2006).
125. *California v. Hackett*, 2003 WL 463976 (Ct. App. 2003); *California v. Mitchell*, 110 Cal.App.4th 772, 2 Cal.Rptr.3d 49 (Ct. App. 2003).

5 Tracking and Trailing in Criminal Investigations and Prosecutions

Once the court has determined that the foundational elements of the training and skill of the dog have been established, the prosecution then presents the testimony that actually describes what the dog did on the trail.

DOGS AT THE CRIME SCENE

Dogs may be scented on a location within the crime scene,[1] an object touched by the perpetrator,[2] the victim's clothing, or a body that the perpetrator may have touched.[3] From early in the 20th century, courts have required proof that the trackers "were laid on a trail, whether visible or not, concerning which testimony has been admitted, and upon a track which circumstances indicate to have been made by the accused."[4]

SCENTING TO FOOTPRINTS

Sometimes tracking actually involves following footprints.[5] A 1904 Texas case involved a bloodhound that tracked from the scene of the murder to the house of the defendant.

> It is a matter of common knowledge and observation that trained animals of the hound species are capable of trailing and following tracks of human beings, and they have been used time out of mind for that purpose. Here, according to the testimony of the witness, the track assumed to be that of the supposed murderer, and which the circumstances in evidence tend to show was his track, was pointed out to the dog. He trailed this track from where it was pointed out to him to the residence of the defendant, some mile and a half; and the course of his pursuit of the track was followed by witnesses who testified in the case, and they show that the dog followed this track which they saw upon the ground, and which they described to the jury. We hold that this character of testimony is admissible.[6]

In a 1979 case, a dog was scented to blood and a footprint of a perpetrator who was shot trying to flee the house he had broken into. He was found a few blocks away with two bullets in his leg.[7]

SCENTING TO LOCATIONS

Dogs may be asked to pick up a scent from a position where a perpetrator is known to have been standing.[8] A 1923 Louisiana case describes dogs tracking from the place where smoke was seen after the victim was killed by gunshot.

> [The dogs] were laid on the trail at a certain spot in the pasture where the smoke was seen to come from behind a certain tree, which was pointed out to the witness Gant as the spot where the assassin had stood. This fact excludes the probability of their having been placed on a wrong trail, especially as no persons were permitted to go there until the dogs arrived.

The more convincing aspect of this case was that the dogs trailed to a defendant whose shoes were peculiar and fit the shoeprints found along the path they followed.[9]

A 1912 Pennsylvania case specified that there "must be an intelligent and truthful starting point, which will make an impression that the dog is able to recognize and distinguish from all other impressions." The starting point may have to be some distance from the scene of the crime, as explained in the case:

> The commonwealth offers to prove by this witness and other witnesses that upon the occasion referred to a bloodhound was procured and brought to the scene of the fire about half past eleven and within about an hour after the beginning of the fire. That the hound was placed within forty or fifty feet of the eastern side of the barn and as near to the barn as she could be placed by reason of the excessive heat. That the hound, then being in charge of its owner, Mr. Gregg, was laid upon the ground and took the track or trail at a point about fifty feet easterly from said barn and followed said track easterly some short distance to a rail fence and therefrom followed said track northerly and along said fence to the Bottom road, crossing the same, and from this point in a northwesterly direction of the defendant's lane and to a point near his house. That the hound upon reaching the premises of the defendant and while still upon and following said track encountered the defendant, smelled him, jumped upon him and manifested the same indications that the hound usually did when running and successfully locating the object of pursuit. That the hound followed said track, which was at intervals marked by the footsteps of a man recently made. ... This offer to be followed by evidence showing the presence of the defendant within a short distance of the barn burned immediately before the fire, and also by evidence showing that the defendant shortly before the fire left his home, and immediately after the fire was seen approaching his home in an excited, hasty manner, and when so seen was making substantially the same trail or track followed by said hound.[10]

A capital case from Mississippi in 1928 involved an appeal partially based on the lack of evidence concerning how the dogs were scented:

> It was competent to show that the dogs took the trail of some person at the place where Nicholas' body was found, as the public had been excluded therefrom until the arrival of the bloodhounds. Following this trail from the store to the house in which appellant lived tended to prove that he had recently been at the place of the homicide. It is an established law of the state that evidence of bloodhound's trailing a track from the scene of the homicide to the place where a person is found is admissible, where the evidence shows that the dogs were of the proper pedigree and breed, and that they had been properly trained and were reliable in trailing such tracks.

Thus putting the dogs in the place of the crime was sufficient to indicate that they were properly scented, provided other foundational elements were satisfied.[11]

In a 1926 Mississippi case, dogs tracked from the scene of a gunfight. Officers had learned that whiskey might be thrown from a train and staked out the location. When two kegs were thrown from the "negro coach," someone near the tracks carried one of the kegs away. The officers moved closer and when the suspect moved in to pick up the second keg, the officers shined flashlights, and a gunfight began. No one was hurt. Dogs tracked to the house of a suspect's mother, about a block and a half from where this suspect was living. The Mississippi Supreme Court held the value of the evidence was for the jury to determine and affirmed the conviction.[12]

In a 1909 Kentucky case, the court criticized the handler for how he scented the dogs and for other things:

> Several of appellant's witnesses testified that when Mullen, the owner of the bloodhounds, arrived at Cooper's with them, he did not keep their heads up or hold them in hand to prevent their getting the scent of persons who had walked about the premises and up and down the road, and that no effort was made by Cooper [the victim whose house was burned] to keep persons from passing over and contiguous to the ground upon which the house had stood. These witnesses further testified that in starting the dogs to trailing no object or point was selected as indicating where the supposed incendiary had

been, nor were they taken to any place where the fire was thought to have started; that in proceeding to appellant's house the dogs kept their noses much of the time in the air, and would only put them to the ground when hissed or urged on by Mullen, who with quite a crowd accompanied them on the way.

The dogs were followed by a crowd. When the crowd reached the defendant's house, it is not clear that they had a chance to alert.

The door was opened by a sister of appellant, and the party accompanying the dogs with them entered the house and discovered appellant standing near the fireplace. Mullen, the owner of the dogs, then pointed to appellant, and said to a deputy sheriff present, "There is the man who burned Cooper's house." Whereupon appellant declared the dogs had made a mistake; that he was at home all night, and the dogs had tracked the wrong man. When appellant made this declaration, Mullen became angry, cursed him for disputing the work of his dogs, and demanded of the deputy sheriff his gun that he might shoot appellant.

Fortunately, the Kentucky Court of Appeals determined that such bloodhound evidence could not go to the jury.[13]

A 1979 Vermont case involved an objection to the scenting of a tracking dog, which the Vermont Supreme Court described:

Nor do we find any basis in the appellant's distinction that the dog should have been placed on the culprit's scent with an object that the men had abandoned on the roof rather than with the patch of grass where they landed after they leaped from the roof. The grass was a sufficient starting point to link the accused with the scene of the crime.[14]

TRAILING TO WHERE THE PERPETRATOR WAS BEFORE THE CRIME

In a 1981 case from the District of Columbia, a woman who was raped was able to identify her assailant from mug shots. The suspect's location before the rape was determined by a tracking dog that followed a scent from the scene of the crime to a restaurant and to a chair in a restaurant. No one was in the chair but witnesses later identified the defendant as having been sitting in the chair some time before the crime.[15]

DOGS PUT ON THE TRAIL TOO FAR FROM THE CRIME SCENE

In a 1970 North Carolina case, a dog picked up a trail about 50 feet from the front door of the furniture store that had been burglarized and tracked along railroad tracks for 2 miles to where the defendants were found in a sweaty and exhausted condition. The evidence was deemed admissible.[16] A 1974 North Carolina case resulted in a reversal when the bloodhounds were put on a trail that began 300 feet from the house. The defendants were found about 2 miles away. The court reversed the convictions because there was no reason to believe the dogs had been put on the trail of the perpetrators.[17]

DOGS SCENTED TO OBJECTS

Dogs may be scented to an object left by the perpetrator near the scene of the crime and begin tracking from there.[18] In a case arising in North Carolina, a dog trailed from the gun the suspect dropped while running from police to the police car where the suspect was being held.[19] In a 1985 California case, the dog did not track from the crime scene but from a location where an anonymous caller told police a woman's body could be found. The police scented the dog to clothing of a missing person, which led to panties and then to the body.[20]

Dogs Tracking Not to Find the Perpetrator But to Find Other Evidence

Tracking dogs are sometimes used not to find the perpetrator, who may have already been arrested on other evidence, but to find items that the perpetrator may have lost or disposed of along the path he took.[21] Tracking dogs may lead handlers to bodies.[22] In a 1981 Tennessee case, clothing items were obtained from the defendants who were in jail and used to scent a bloodhound at the site of the burglary. The dog led to a cache of items taken from the house in the woods behind it.[23]

TRACKING FROM SECONDARY LOCATIONS

Tracking sometimes occurs after a suspect abandons a vehicle and flees on foot.[24] In a 1983 case involving theft of a jewelry store, the court described the tracking:

> [T]he detective stated that, while he and the dog were at the scene of the theft, he received a call that a man matching the description of the suspect had been seen running a short distance from the scene. Browning immediately transported the dog to the new area where the dog picked up a trail and led Browning to a spot where he observed and arrested appellant.[25]

In a 1987 Idaho burglary case, a dog tracked from a car in a field near where a suspect was seen running to the feed store that had been broken into. A jacket was found in the car and the dog was scented to it and tracked to a house where a wrecking bar with blood on it was found and the suspect was in the basement.[26]

In order to put a dog on the trail of a fleeing suspect who had been chased for a time by a police officer, a dog handler carried a dog to a point where only the suspect was laying a trail.

> Holladay [the handler] had Investigator Smith show him the exact spot he had stopped the pursuit so that the dog would not track Investigator Smith's trail from the roadway but would track the trail of the person who had entered the woods. Holladay testified that he then carried his dog to that spot and put him down. Holladay said that the dog immediately picked up a scent and tracked it into the woods to a creek. Holladay testified that he saw a man, whom he positively identified at trial as Gavin, standing in the creek under a bush, and that when Gavin saw him, Gavin attempted to flee. Holladay stated that he ordered Gavin to stop, but that Gavin did not stop until Holladay fired a shot over Gavin's shoulder.[27]

A case from Missouri asked whether tracking evidence could convict a defendant about whom the only other evidence was that he had been seen in the store 2 hours before the robbery and had left the home of one of the other suspects (who was arrested at the scene of the robbery) about 3 hours before the robbery. The tracking evidence consisted of the dog tracking from a car used in the robbery to a street where the defendant was seen walking. There is no mention of the dog alerting to the defendant but he did stop at the point where the defendant was seen. The court determined there was insufficient evidence for conviction.[28]

Tracking Where the Suspect Lives

A research case involving an FBI workshop involved tracking in a location a target had not been in for a considerable time.

> In May 2003 the FBI hosted a bloodhound research workshop at its Academy in Quantico, Virginia. One of the blind tests conducted during this workshop evaluated the viability of aged human scent in a heavily populated residential area after a long scent-build-up period. The test was designed to determine if targets' scent would build up at their primary residence and remain detectable after a long absence.
>
> After living in a Stafford, Virginia, house for 7 years, the test subject moved to Albuquerque, New Mexico. Six months after her departure, a bloodhound team was started at an intersection several houses away [from her former home in Virginia]. Using scent collected from a letter mailed from the

former occupant, the bloodhound indicated matching human scent, trailed to, and identified the house in question. Not incidentally, the letter used in this test was mailed from Albuquerque, New Mexico, to Stafford, Virginia, through the U.S. Postal system. Upon arriving in Virginia, the letter was irradiated at the U.S. Army Medical Research Institute of Infectious Diseases, Fort Detrick, Maryland, with Cobalt 60 at an average rate of 39.5–40.7 kGy for 59 minutes. Thus, in spite of an irradiated and heavily contaminated-scent article, and a residence unoccupied by the scent target for 6 months, the dog performed successfully in this blind exercise.[29]

These facts would probably not be admitted in an actual case given "period of reliability" issues.

SCENTING TO ITEMS OR LOCATIONS WITH ODORS OF MULTIPLE INDIVIDUALS

Some cases indicate that police or courts may overlook the possibility that an area or item might have multiple scents. In a 1927 Kentucky case, a woman was bludgeoned to death. Bloodhounds were placed at a point indicated by the victim's husband, but they only trailed to a well, and then back to the house and into the room where the husband was standing. He was charged and convicted. There was other evidence concerning the defendant to support the conviction but it must be questioned whether the dogs would have trailed to the husband in any case as his scent was inevitably in the area.[30]

MISSING MEMBER

If an object may have been touched by other individuals besides the perpetrators, an effort is often made to exclude these scents. In a 2009 Texas case, items in a burglarized house from which scent pads were collected were probably also touched by members of the household, so the bloodhound was taken to the scene to sniff members of the household with the hope that the dog would then try to find the "missing member"—the individual whom he has yet to sniff.[31] An experienced handler has said of this procedure:

> My experience with the missing member approach is extensive yet inconclusive. I have found it to be a necessary tool with a contaminated scene, yet it is not wholly reliable. Regardless, I have found success with this method, and I believe it should be practiced when scent articles are seriously contaminated.[32]

In tracking or trailing, a dog is expected to isolate one scent. If the dog follows a different scent, it is brought back to the beginning point and scented again.[33]

CIRCUMSTANCES OF THE TRAIL

Courts sometimes require that the circumstances regarding the trailing itself be explained.[34] If dogs lose a track, perhaps at a point the suspect entered a vehicle and drove away,[35] courts have required separate proof that the vehicle was at the particular location where the dogs lost the track.[36] An Arkansas case from 1921 allowed evidence that a dog tracked from the location a young woman was assaulted to a location along a train line where other evidence had indicated that the defendant may have boarded a car.[37]

Losing the scent does not necessarily make tracking evidence irrelevant. In a 2001 Maryland case, a dog tracked from the scene of a rape to a parking lot. Although the dog did not track to a car nearby, officers were suspicious of the car and obtained a warrant. A shotgun was found in the trailer behind the car, which fit the description of a weapon used in the rape. The Maryland Court of Special Appeals affirmed the conviction.[38] In a 1935 Kentucky case, a handler testified that he could not take his dog closer to the defendant's house than the gate because "two big dogs" met his bloodhound. He nevertheless testified that the house was where the bloodhound was leading. The court concluded that the evidence was insufficient to support a conviction and the matter was remanded for a new trial.[39]

In an Alabama case from 1906, testimony indicated that dogs trailing a murderer left the trail several times. In the words of the Alabama Supreme Court:

> [D]efendant's counsel proved, on cross-examination by the state's witness, that the dogs left the trail in the woods and went out into a field, and that the witness called them back and put them again on the track, and that the trail was several times lost. Thereupon the solicitor asked the witness on redirect examination, "Why did the dogs quit and leave the trail and go out into the field?" The defendant interposed an objection to the question upon the ground, among others, that it called for the conclusion of the witness. The trial judge sustained the objection, but only conditionally; for he remarked "that the witness could not testify as to why they did so, unless the witness was thoroughly acquainted with their habits and training." Thereupon the witness answered: "From what I know of these dogs, I would say that the reason the dogs quit the trail and went out into the field was because there was a body of men out in the front, and the dogs expected to find the person they had been trailing."

The court said that the defendant's motion to exclude this testimony should have been granted as the reason dogs abandon a trail can be a matter of inference only. If the witness could speak of facts from which the jury could infer the reason the dogs left the trail, that would have been admissible, but here the witness was substituting himself for the jury. The conviction was reversed, and the defendant had at least another chance to avoid the sentence of hanging that had been imposed at the first trial.[40]

Some courts allow a certain deviation from the track.

> Mr. Overcash stated that the dog became confused while on the track and that it was necessary to work the dog around another house in the neighborhood before the dog picked up the scent again and followed it to the service station. The relative locations (as depicted in the aerial photograph) of the house where the dog became confused, the Hipp house, the Wood house and the service station were such that one could reasonably infer the guilty party took a side trip beginning at the house where Snoopy became confused to the Hipp house and back before returning to the service station.[41]

It should be noted that just because a dog stops sniffing does not mean it has lost the trail. Dogs may need to remove their noses from the track to avoid tiredness or "nose fatigue," which will reduce their performance.[42]

In a 1997 case from Washington, the court accepted the handler's decision to move the dog off the trail.

> Wieting argues that while this original placement may have complied, the dog was twice moved off track by Worthington. But the evidence shows that taking Ax off track did not disrupt the integrity of the tracking. Worthington testified that Ax has been trained using decoys who cross the track. Worthington further testified that when Ax finds a new scent, he becomes hesitant; whereas when he is on the same scent he remains high-spirited. Finally, Worthington testified that when he moved Ax off the track to a new point where a person, whom he believed to be the suspect, had been, the dog did not show the hesitancy typical of finding a new scent.[43]

Handlers have been known to take dogs off a track to see if they will return to it.[44]

Physical obstructions may require that a dog be taken off a trail. In a 1999 Colorado case involving a burglary that occurred in 1993, a burglar ran from the house as police arrived on the scene. A bloodhound arrived soon after and was taken to footprints left by the suspect and began following the trail. The trail was interrupted at one point:

During the chase, when Yogi would reach a fence, Officer Nichols would pull him from the trail, move the dog to the other side, and allow him to continue tracking. (On one occasion, Officer Nichols and Yogi were unable to locate the other side of one of these fences due to the layout of the neighborhood and the cul-de-sacs in the area. When this happened, Nichols and Yogi were driven to another location where they could more easily access and continue to follow the trail.) As the officers and Yogi approached one such fence, a man fitting the general description of the suspect aired earlier jumped from some shrubbery on the other side and ran.

The dog eventually led his handler to another private residence in the subdivision. Officers who had been following the suspect's footprints also arrived. The dog began sniffing around a pickup truck inside the garage. An officer's flashlight discovered someone hiding beneath the vehicle. The suspect fit the general description of the perpetrator. An informal scent lineup was then conducted and the dog alerted to the suspect.[45]

In a wrongful arrest suit that received national attention,[46] a dog tracked from the body of the deceased to the defendant's residence, even though this required that the dog track for a period in which the defendant must have been in a car. The defendant dog handler in the civil suit attempted to introduce an FBI article stating that tracking an individual who is in a car is possible because vehicles recycle air in their ventilation systems, putting internal air with a subject's scent into the atmosphere and laying a trail. There was also a scent lineup, not described in detail, which the court said "supposedly" identified the defendant. The court determined that sufficient factual issues had been presented for the wrongful arrest action not to be dismissed.[47]

DOGS TRACKING TO MULTIPLE ITEMS OR SUSPECTS

Dogs sometimes seem to move from one perpetrator to another. In a 1923 Arkansas case, a dog tracked from the cash register opened in a burglary to one defendant's house, and then onto a second defendant's house. Evidence indicated that the second defendant had spent the night at the first defendant's house before going to his own house.[48] A victim in a North Carolina case was shot by two assailants but lived long enough to name them. Bloodhounds were used to corroborate his dying declaration.

Bloodhounds were brought from Tennessee, and after being put on the tracks, which had been carefully guarded, around the chestnut log they trailed until they came to the home of the prisoner Wiggins and marked him while he stood in the yard. They then followed the track and met the deputy sheriff, who had Miller in custody, whereupon the dogs who were trailing the track ran up to Miller and marked him also.

The court found the trailing evidence admissible.[49]

In a 1917 Arkansas case, a dog tracked to a suspect's home, then went to a drawer inside the home where there were spent cartridges of the sort used in the attempted murder, then looked under the bed where a shotgun was found. Finally, the dogs were taken to the building where the defendant had previously been put under arrest and went to him in the office where he was being held. The court's description of the facts is worth quoting:

Immediately after O'Kelly was shot, on the morning of September 1, 1916, guards were placed at the scene of the shooting to prevent anyone from walking over the trail. O'Kelly was removed to Bauxite, and Bob King, owner of the bloodhounds, was brought to Bauxite from Conway, arriving at the scene of shooting about 10 o'clock on the same day. The dogs took up a hot trail at a hickory tree about 20 yards from where O'Kelly was shot. The trail was not lost by the dogs until they arrived at appellant's house. The dogs were let in the house, and went to a drawer of a dresser and scratched on it. The drawer was opened, and five No. 12-gauge cartridges were found. The dogs then went to the north room in which a 12-gauge double-barrel shotgun was found under the bed. The right barrel had been recently fired. The dogs were then carried in an automobile to Bauxite, where they again took up the trail, and located appellant in the office where he was under arrest. The dogs were of a pure strain of blood, registered, and the oldest one was a graduate of a training school for bloodhounds. Both dogs were experienced in trailing offenders of the law. The testimony showed that they were accurate, certain, and reliable.[50]

The identification of the defendant in the police station can be described as something of a precursor to a scent lineup. In a case arising in Florida, a dog following tracks of suspects on a beach alerted to four suspects who had been arrested and taken onto a patrol boat. The dog sniffed no one else on the boat, which was taken as identification of the individuals leaving the tracks.[51]

RETRACING THE TRACK

In a state of Washington case from 1981, the victim was struck from behind and her assailant began to drag her from the scene, but a motorist stopped and chased him. A motel owner called the police, who arrived almost immediately. A police canine unit was called and Officer Seth and his dog, Justice, tracked down two streets, lost the track for a time when they passed a van, then picked it up 50 to 100 yards further on. Officer Seth brought Justice back to the van and this time Justice alerted to it. The defendant was found inside the van in a sleeping bag. The question was why the dog had not alerted to the van the first time he passed it. "Officer Seth further testified that the suspect could not have been in the van more than 10 or 15 minutes when Justice first passed by or Justice would have detected the scent."[52] The tracking evidence was properly admitted.

DOG'S ATTENTION FOCUSED ON POINTS ALONG A TRAIL

Just because a dog stops along the trail does not mean that it has lost the trail.

> The trail led into a wooded area along a path to a bluff, then to flat ground and the water's edge. Garner described an area of "pool scent" [a large amount of scent] at this location and testified that the dog's body language indicated that "something had happened here."[53]

Another case refers to a dog having three lengthy pauses, which the handler interpreted as meaning that the person tracked had lingered at these points.[54]

TAKING THE DOG OFF THE TRAIL AND FORCING THE TRAIL

Handlers sometimes encounter serious difficulties in keeping dogs on a trail. In a Montana case, the handler kept the dogs from going into a "cat tail bog." The Montana Supreme Court was critical of the fact the dogs had not been permitted to trail without interference:

> While some courts have admitted "bloodhound testimony" yet none have accepted it where, as here, after being given their initial scent and after running a portion of their course, the dogs were deliberately dragged off the scent by their handler, — taken down the state highway to a spot in a country lane and there given a fresh start and headed toward the trailer house of the accused wherein the sheriff was patiently awaiting the arrival of the captive dogs.

The court did not, however, confine itself to the facts at hand, but rather decided to join Nebraska as a state that would not accept bloodhound-tracking evidence.[55]

Courts have sometimes excluded evidence where a handler prevented dogs from trailing on their own.[56]

FOLLOWING ANIMAL TRAILS

A 1915 Illinois case declined to admit testimony about a tracking dog, a Russian bloodhound, that may have been tracking a horse rather than a suspect, though the horse may have been pulling a buggy used by the suspect.

> Evidence of the trailing of an *animal* by a bloodhound, so far as we are advised, has never been admitted by any court or sanctioned by any standard legal authority in this or any other country.[57]

In an Arkansas case of 1915, a hole was torn in the fence of a hog farmer. The farmer kept anyone from getting near the fence and had the president of the local bank wire to Tennessee for bloodhounds to be brought. The bloodhounds tracked by a circuitous route to the house of the defendant. Testimony disagreed as to whether either of the dogs alerted to the defendant. There was other evidence, including the fact that seven hogs' heads were found in the defendant's smokehouse. It was not clear if the dogs were tracking the man or the hogs, but the conviction was affirmed.[58]

In a 1923 Kansas case, the dog tracked the same defendant after two different crimes, but one time the defendant left the scene on foot while the other time he rode a horse.[59] In an Oklahoma case, the owner of a barn woke to find his barn was on fire. He telephoned the sheriff of Okmulgee County and requested that he bring bloodhounds. Two men came from the penitentiary with two bloodhounds. The dogs took up a trail and followed it to where a horse had been tied to a tree. The dogs continued to a gate near the defendant's house. They found the horse wet with sweat and verified that it had one hoof that made the peculiar track. Most of the evidence against the defendant was circumstantial. One witness said that the defendant had once said it would be funny to burn Reavis's buildings to the ground. The court concluded that despite the circumstantial nature of the evidence, the jury was entitled to consider the tracking and affirmed the conviction. Some of the tracking appeared to be of the defendant while riding a horse.[60]

It has been argued that if the ventilation system of a car is on, it is possible that a scent trail may be laid.[61]

SCENTING FIRST TO SUSPECT

A dog might be scented to a suspect to see if it alerts to anything at the crime scene or picks up a trail from the location.[62] As stated by three canine forensic experts:

> Assuming that the scent article being used contains a viable amount of scent, a negative response during a location check provides strong evidence to eliminate the suspect from the investigation.[63]

A 2004 California case involved scenting a dog at the scene of a crime to a scent pad prepared by wiping the hands of a suspect. The dog trailed from the scene of the crime to a location where other testimony indicated the defendant had been picked up by a car. The appellate court determined that the trailing evidence should have been excluded but found its admission to be harmless error.[64] In a 1994 case, a dog scented on a scent pad trailed from the scene of a crime to a building but did not alert to any apartment in the building.[65] In a 1993 Kansas case, marijuana wrapped in plastic bags was found near a highway. An individual found nearby claimed to have gone to sleep beside the road. Dogs tracked from the bags to where the suspect said he had been sleeping and then alerted to the suspect.[66]

CONTAMINATION OF THE TRAIL

To limit contamination of the trail, a tracking or trailing dog should precede a search party or other officers accompanying the handler.[67] This is a major problem in that officers first on a scene should protect the area when they know a canine team is on the way but too often do not. Timeliness in beginning tracking or trailing work is also important in limiting contamination.

The Nebraska Supreme Court in 1903 described how a trail can become so weak or contaminated that the scent the dog is following is likely something besides what was left by the perpetrator. The opinion is worth quoting at length for showing what a judge, writing a century ago, thought tracking was.

> The burglary was committed on the morning of July 5th, before daylight. The trailing did not commence until about 5 in the afternoon. In the meantime the trail, near the scene of the crime, had been walked over, closely paralleled, and crossed, directly and obliquely, perhaps, a hundred times. And the sun had been shining on it steadily for more than 12 hours. The situation the dogs had to deal with was an exceptionally difficult one, and it was, we think, reversible error to accept their conclusion as legal evidence of defendant's guilt. To get a nearer and clearer view of the nature of the evidence erroneously admitted, let us consider closely what trailing is. The path of every human being through the world, at every step, from the cradle to the grave, is strewn with the putrescent excretions of his body. This waste matter is in process of decomposition. It is being resolved into its constituent elements, and its power to make an impression on the olfactory nerves of a dog or other animal becomes fainter and fainter with lapse of time. Under favorable conditions, such as free exposure to air and sun, every compound particle is rapidly separated into its original parts, and when the dissolution is complete its characteristic scent is gone. The bloodhound is endowed with a remarkably keen scent. He has great ability for differentiating smells. His method of trailing is simple and well understood. Particles of waste matter given off by a particular individual fall to the ground, and while undergoing chemical change come in contact with the olfactory nerves of the dog, and produce an impression which he is able to recognize, as distinct and different from all other impressions. Hence for a short time a man may be easily trailed in the woods or in the open country by the effluvia in his wake. But in a city, and after the lapse of considerable time, the trailing is obviously more difficult, and often manifestly impossible. But difficulties do not deter the bloodhound from pursuing his business. He trails as best he can. He always follows some scent, and he goes somewhere. Undoubtedly nice and delicate questions are time and again presented to him for decision. But the considerations that induced him in a particular case to adopt one conclusion rather than another cannot go to the jury. The jury cannot know whether the reasons on which he acted were good or bad; whether they were all on one side, or evenly balanced; nor whether his faith in the identity of the scent which he followed was strong or weak. In attempting to separate one smell from ten, twenty, fifty, or a hundred similar smells with which it is intermixed and commingled, it is highly probable, if not quite certain, that the bloodhound undertakes a task altogether beyond his capacity. Like other dogs, he has his limitations, and they must be recognized in courts of justice, if not elsewhere.[68]

This type of concern was soon distilled into a requirement that the trail not have become stale or contaminated.[69] A 1921 Minnesota Supreme Court case found that dogs may have been laid on tracks of bystanders who had come to watch a barn burn, the tracking had begun about 18 hours after the fire began, and most of the places the dogs went while tracking had nothing to do with the defendants. There was insufficient evidence even to justify a new trial.[70] In a habeas corpus proceeding in Virginia, a petitioner argued unsuccessfully that both the scent object and the trail were contaminated.[71]

A dog's behavior may provide sufficient evidence that a trail was not contaminated:

> Sergeant [the dog] followed the trail from the rear door of the house to the area of the tire tracks without hesitation or difficulty. ... The defendant hypothesizes that the trail belonged to a police officer investigating the crime scene who walked from the backyard to the spot where the tire tracks were found. ... No evidence supports the hypothesis that an investigating police officer searched from the backyard to the sandy area near the intersection of Howard Drive and Paradise Avenue on foot and then departed from that spot by vehicle or other means. In light of all these circumstances, we conclude that the trial court properly admitted the tracking evidence.[72]

The time of day when the dog began tracking may affect whether a court finds contamination likely or not:

> Although the dog was unable to follow the scent of a particular individual, the early morning hours of the robbery indicated that there was little likelihood that anyone other than the perpetrator had established a more recent trail away from the crime scene. Circumstances indicated that cigarettes had been stored in trash bags and taken from the Food Center. The dog followed the scent of trash bags to the defendant's vehicle. The engine was still warm upon their arrival. Similar generic cigarette butts were found near the hole made at the rear of the store and in the ashtray of the defendant's car.[73]

Securing the scene of the crime against other parties is an important forensic precaution for limiting contamination of scent.[74] As early as 1907, the Ohio Supreme Court described the place where the body was found:

> It seems true that, the day before these dogs arrived, very many people, young and old, had trodden upon and over this scene, and some had experimented with the pressure of the two saplings by placing their own necks where, as supposed, the neck of Mrs. Hughes had been found. This fact goes to the weight of such evidence, rather than its competency, if it be otherwise competent.[75]

Preserving evidence in a way that it does not become contaminated is also sometimes an issue.[76]

CONTAMINATION IS DIFFERENT FOR TRACKING AND TRAILING DOGS

The scene of an apartment fire was described by one officer as being "as big a mess as I've seen" with "a lot of traffic in and out." The handler argued that this would not affect his trailing dog as much as a tracking dog:

> Crawford testified that Cassie is not a tracking dog, which is trained to detect a person's path from crushed vegetation, but rather is a trailing dog, which is trained to follow a person's scent. Although workers' activity at the site would interfere with a tracking dog's ability to detect a path from crushed vegetation, Crawford testified that Cassie was able to detect a particular individual's scent across an area where other persons had passed through, so the presence of other workers would not necessarily contaminate the trail.

The conviction was affirmed.[77]

PURPOSEFUL CONTAMINATION BY THE PERPETRATOR

Case descriptions involve instances where perpetrators may have tried to confuse dogs. In a 1921 North Carolina case, the prosecution alleged that a defendant put dead birds in his yard in an effort to provide a reason for the dogs going there.[78]

CONTAMINATION NEGATING IDENTIFICATION

A dog's alert to a person may be negated as an identification when there is evidence that onlookers contaminated the trail after the crime. In a 1901 North Carolina case, several individuals were arrested based on a dog's alert:

> [S]ome time during the next day Brinson arrived from Kinston with his dog, and carried him to the window, where he smelt in a basket, and was then carried inside, where he smelt at the window, and around the counters, and when he reached the meat block he barked, and then went to the back door, and smelt the steps, and went to the creek, 18 or 20 feet away, and barked and came back, and then trailed

about the door and steps and up the street, going into divers places, and finally went up to Dixon, one of the defendants, and bayed him, and then trailed about, and afterwards went up to defendant Moore, and bayed him. It was also in evidence that said Moore and Dixon were present all the while in the crowd while the dog was trailing, and frequently near the dog, and that the other two defendants Jesse and Joseph Edwards were also there in the crowd near the dog at the time.

The North Carolina Supreme Court determined that the evidence should not have been admitted since a number of the parties had been in the area in any case and there was no reason to think the dog had identified the perpetrators of the burglary.[79]

IDENTIFICATIONS

When a dog finds objects along the track, those objects may provide some connection between a suspect and the crime, but this is to be distinguished from the situation where the dog leads to the suspect and alerts to him, which has often been taken as a direct identification. Dogs have sometimes led to clothing that a suspect may have discarded,[80] but may also alert to clothing found near the suspect, which may be taken as a type of direct identification.[81] Scent identification may occur when the tracking or trailing dog follows the path of the perpetrator and alerts to an individual at the end of that path.[82] Dogs may also alert to a suspect who has already been placed in a police car or taken to a station.[83] Such station identifications have been described in an FBI publication as follows:

> Investigators may bring a suspect into a police station for questioning or in custody. The suspect is taken to a room and the route documented. A dog team is then started on the suspect's trail using scent evidence from the crime. The dog team is blind to the suspect's trail and room location. A scent match produces a trail into the building, along the route traveled by the suspect, ending with a dog identification of the suspect. A no-scent match produces a negative indication, and the dog refuses to trail. Station identifications should be performed with discretion due to building ventilation, other areas in the building the suspect may have walked, and the potential for cross-contamination with scent from investigators or crime scene personnel.[84]

Tracking more often led from the scene of the crime to the defendant in the early days of tracking jurisprudence than is the case today.[85] Some tracking identifications are particularly troubling. In an Alaska case, a dog was scented at the vehicle of the victim of a rape three times.

> The police responded immediately [after the rape], calling in Officer Robert W. Jones and his dog Kai. Kai was placed next to the driver's side of S.C.'s vehicle to begin tracking. Kai began traveling towards the domestic terminal. Officer Jones stopped Kai and took him back to the driver's side of the car. This time Kai went to the back of the vehicle and signaled an alert. Again Jones started Kai, this time Kai started towards the international terminal. Jones encouraged Kai by shouting "good boy."
> Before reaching the international terminal, Kai abruptly turned and circled a red pickup truck. Jones determined that no one was in the truck and returned with Kai to his original track. Kai then went straight to the international terminal, entered, went to the Japan Airlines counter and jumped up on the counter. Seconds later, Jeffrey Wilkie, who was on the phone "popped up" from behind the counter.

Wilkie was arrested and convicted despite contested physical evidence, failure of the victim to pick him out of a lineup, and the exclusion of potentially exonerating polygraph testimony. The Alaska Court of Appeals did not discuss the fact the dog was started three times and affirmed the conviction.[86] Even more disturbing is an Arkansas decision of 1910. The victim was sitting by the fire in his home when he was shot. Witnesses saw men either leaving the house or in the vicinity, and bloodhounds were brought.

The dogs were tracking a human being from the point where the man stood who shot Worthington to the west side of town, where the trail was lost. After they lost that trail, they were taken back to the starting point. They then went in a northeasterly direction, different from the one they first followed. When they were put on the trail the second time, they trailed up to the steps of one or more houses. The dogs lost the trail so badly that the party in charge took them off, rested them awhile, and washed out their mouths and noses. It rained some before they arrived at Padgett's house. The ground was very muddy. The dogs led the party to Padgett's house. There were two men in the house when the party arrived at Padgett's. The dogs barked some while they were on the west trail, and also while they were on the last trail that led to Padgett's house. The sheriff went in ahead of the dogs and arrested Padgett, placing handcuffs upon him. He seemed to be excited. The sheriff took charge of the trousers which were exhibited, and which Padgett had on the night of the killing. They did not have much mud on them. His shoes and trousers were dry. The sheriff also took charge of the coat and a cap which Padgett was supposed to have had on that night.

The sheriff testified, on cross-examination, that he knew where he was going; that he was at Padgett's; and that he went ahead of the dogs and got him, asked for the suit that he wore the night before, and the corduroy suit described was presented to him. His shoes were not near so muddy as witness expected to find them. In going out the sheriff and posse got their clothes covered with mud. They found in Padgett's house a No. 12 shotgun; found a shell or two in his coat pocket, but those shells were loaded with small shot, and not buckshot. Padgett complained of being sick.

Other witnesses testified as to the manner in which the dogs trailed that night; that they got on trails and went to other houses also, and last went to Padgett's house. One of the witnesses who was in the crowd following the dogs stated that when the dogs stopped and went into another man's house witness remarked, "We know where we have started, and we had just as well go down there and get him." This witness stated that when they reached Padgett's house Padgett was in bed; he complained of being sick. They called for his clothes, and they were promptly furnished. They found nothing unusual about them. There was nothing on his shoes or clothes to indicate that he had come over the trail that the dogs followed. The dog, when he went into Padgett's house and walked up to Padgett, seemed to be perfectly satisfied, but he did not bark and whine nor attempt to jump on or bite Padgett.

Thus, there seems to have been no alert, and the clothing was hardly corroborative. A private detective was placed in the jail with the prisoner and testified that Padgett admitted to the shooting, but a physician testified that he had seen Padgett early in the evening of the crime and that Padgett was very sick, too sick to have left his house. There was also testimony of several witnesses that Padgett stayed in bed that night. Despite these weaknesses in the prosecution's case, a jury convicted and the Arkansas Supreme Court affirmed.[87]

The Illinois Supreme Court, in rejecting dog tracking evidence for the state in 1914, noted that a dog could "be used to track down a known fugitive from justice," such as an escaped convict, and that if the dog does find the fugitive, "there can be no mistake as to whether or not he is the party sought."[88] Thus, tracking was deemed useful if the identity of the individual sought is known to begin with.[89] Where the perpetrator was not known, however, the Illinois court said other evidence must identify him.

ALERT AS IDENTIFICATION

Identification of a suspect by a dog's alert has sometimes been rather casually described. A 1908 Mississippi case said no more than that the bloodhounds that had tracked an arsonist "identified him in their peculiar way."[90] A 1919 Missouri case described a dog tracking from the scene of the murder where the victim was shot through a window to a house where the defendant was staying. The bloodhound was described as having "pointed him out as the one who had dropped the cartridge and made the tracks along beside the porch where deceased was killed."[91]

Some cases describe dogs as refusing to track any further, which is taken as indicating they have found the person they were tracking.[92]

Lack of Alert

Dogs do not always show clear alerts, but "showing interest" should not be sufficient to be considered an identification.[93] The lack of an alert or any kind of demonstration on encountering a defendant was noted in the reversal of a murder conviction in a 1928 Kentucky case. The dogs did sit down and look at a co-defendant, but as to the defendant the Court of Appeals described itself as "wholly at a loss to account for the verdict of guilty and the punishment fixed by the jury in this case where the testimony is not sufficient to create a real suspicion much less afford evidence of guilt of appellant." The case was remanded for a new trial.[94] A lack of an alert did not result in a conviction being overturned where bloodhounds trailed to the house where the defendant lived with other men. Although the dog did not identify the defendant, the victim of the rape did.[95]

In a 1933 Missouri case, dogs tracked from the house where a murder occurred to a place where automobile tracks were found, perhaps indicating that the perpetrator had left from that point in a car. Later the dogs were in the home where the murder occurred but they did not alert to the defendant, who was also there. This may have been explained by the following sentence describing the handler's testimony: "And the houndmaster said, by sprinkling red pepper on one's clothes, or by the use of witch hazel, the human or personal scent could be destroyed." The court described the bloodhound testimony as "very unsatisfactory" but, because of ballistics evidence, the conviction was affirmed. It appeared that the lack of an alert might arguably have been exonerating, though this was not stated and may not have been argued.[96]

Exonerating Identifications

Some tracking cases have involved the admissibility of potentially exonerating tracking evidence.[97] A 1917 Missouri rape case admitted evidence concerning dogs that had tracked to someone other than the defendant. The dog trailed to a man in a shed, but the victim said he was not the man that raped her. The man who was later arrested was permitted to introduce this evidence as exonerating, but he was convicted in any case.[98]

Is Trailing More Successful Than Identification?

It might be presumed that a dog trailing a perpetrator and reaching several individuals at the end of the trail would be almost certain to alert to the perpetrator and not one of the foils with him. There is, however, at least one study where this was found not to be the case. Dogs in staged car bomb and improvised explosive device (IED) tests in Arizona were scented to the steering wheel of the car used in the car bombing and alligator clips from the devices. Scent pads were created from the remnants using a scent transfer unit and the dogs began trailing 3 to 4 hours after the targets walked away from the blast sites. Most targets walked into buildings about half a mile from the blast sites.

In dogs following targets from the car bomb, 12 of 12 dogs followed the correct odor trail, ignoring decoys and cross-tracks of camera personnel, but only 8 of 12 dogs correctly identified the target at the end of the trail. In dogs following targets who handled the improvised explosive device, there were two separate starting points for the tracking, one beside the device and another at a remote location. All but one dog followed the correct trail and all but that dog made the correct identification, meaning that in this part of the test, 91.7% of the teams followed the correct trail and the same percent correctly identified the target. In the second part of the IED experiment, 10 of 11 teams correctly trailed the target, but only six teams identified a correct target. Two teams that trailed correctly alerted falsely to decoys. Thus, dogs in the IED tests were 91% correct on trailing but only 54.5% in tracking.

Summing all the results, 33 of 35 dogs trailed correctly, giving an overall success rate of 94.3%, but dogs correctly alerted to a target in only 73.5% of cases. Although there were only two false alerts (some dogs did not alert when reaching the end of a trail), the results of the experiment suggest that dogs are more accurate in trailing than in identifying, even when the scent of the perpetrator has been with them during the entire period of the trailing.[99]

STATION IDENTIFICATIONS

Many cases describe dogs alerting to suspects they have previously been tracking,[100] often in police stations. In a 1917 Arkansas case, dogs tracked to the suspect's house and even to a drawer where spent cartridges similar to those used in the attempted murder were found, and to a bed under which was found the possible murder weapon. The dogs were then taken to the police station and went to the defendant in the office where he was being held.[101] In a 1936 Mississippi case, dogs picked up the trail of a suspect outside the county courthouse and followed it to the cell where the suspect had been placed after his arrest on other evidence.[102] In a 1996 New York case, a dog scented on the victim's car alerted to the defendant in the sheriff's office. The court held this use of the dog was not a search under the Fourth Amendment.[103]

In a 1971 North Dakota case, a dog's actions in helping find the murderer are described by the North Dakota Supreme Court where testimony indicated:

> Rye was given a scent from a pillowcase in Carol's apartment; that Rye twice followed a trail that ended in the alley outside Carol's apartment; that she and Rye, along with the pillowcase, were taken to the Grand Forks Police Department, where Rye was once again given a scent from the pillowcase; that he then followed a trail into and through the police station to the place where Iverson was seated; and that he then smelled Iverson and wagged his tail and looked toward her, which is the sign that Rye had identified the source of the scent found on the pillowcase.

The court was satisfied that a proper foundation was laid for the evidence "notwithstanding that the bloodhound was put on the trail 24 to 48 hours after the victims had been murdered." This is actually a tracking case where the dog was scented on a path the officers knew the suspect had walked when going into the police station.[104]

A 2004 California case resulted in alerts to three separate individuals apparently involved in a crime and also involved tracking from the scene of the crime. An individual got out of a car and shot several people, murdering one. Officers arrived a few minutes later and found an expended bullet and nineteen 9-mm shell casings. A dog was scented to the casings, and to the driver's and passenger's seats. The dog tracked to a house and the inhabitants were arrested and taken to a police station. What happened at the police station is then described by the court:

> After the suspects arrived at the police station, Hamm [the handler] used two bloodhounds, Scarlet and Knight, to perform three identifications. First, Hamm provided Scarlet the scent taken from the Corolla's passenger seat. Scarlet began at an alley near the police station and led Hamm to an interview room inside the police station, where she identified Trigueros. Hamm then gave Knight the scent taken from one of the shell casings. Knight began at the alley near the police station, went to an interview room in the police station, and identified Trigueros. Finally, Hamm gave Scarlet the scent taken from the Corolla's driver's seat. Scarlet began at a parking structure near the police station and led Hamm to an interview room inside the station, where she identified Chavez.[105]

Defendants have sometimes sought to introduce evidence of station identifications where the dog identified someone besides a defendant, making the alert exonerating.[106]

Sometimes lineups in the United States have been conducted near the scene of the crime or near the terminal point to which a dog has tracked.[107] Scent lineups will be discussed in the following chapters.

NOTES

1. *Aiken v. Georgia*, 16 Ga.App. 848, 86 S.E. 1076 (Ct. App. 1915) (dog scented at window where thief left a house and led to one house, but scented again led to another house, which may have meant the dog tracked from the place the thief came from and the place he went to after the burglary; conviction was reversed because of erroneous admission of other testimony); *New York v. Tunstall*, 278 A.D.2d 585, 717 N.Y.S.2d 685 (App.Div. 2000) (fact that dog tracked from crime scene to area where defendant was apprehended "constituted independent relevant evidence ... serving to confirm defendant's identity as the intruder").
2. *Fisher v. Mississippi*, 150 Miss. 206, 116 So. 746 (1928) (dogs placed beside safe in store tracked to house of defendant).
3. *North Carolina v. Taylor*, 337 N.C. 597, 447 S.E.2d 360 (1994).
4. *Fife v. Georgia*, 16 Ga.App. 22, 84 S.E. 485 (Ct. App. 1915). See *Kelly v. Kentucky*, 259 Ky. 770, 83 S.W.2d 489 (Ct. App. 1935) (dogs tracked from spot where shotgun was fired); *Scott v. Mississippi*, 108 Miss. 464, 66 So.973 (1915) (nothing in record showed bloodhounds were put on scent at scene of the crime).
5. See *Arizona v. Bible*, 175 Ariz. 549, 858 P.2d 1152 (1993); *Bible v. Schriro*, 497 F.Supp.2d 991 (D.C.Az. 2007) (handler that put his dog in vehicle after high-speed chase did not know if dog was tracking the perpetrator or the victim who had been in the car, though the dog led officers to the perpetrator who was hiding under branches and debris).
6. *Parker v. Texas*, 46 Tex.Crim. 461, 80 S.W. 1008, 100 Am.St.Rep. 1021 (Ct. Crim. App. 1904) (reversed for errors on other matters). See Jesse (1866), Chapter 52, for use of bloodhounds (*Canis sagax sanguinarius*) to track thieves and marauders from at least the 16th century.
7. *Michigan v. Perryman*, 89 Mich.App. 516, 280 NW2d 579 (Ct. App. 1979).
8. See SWGDOG SC 9—Human Scent Dogs: Tracking/Trailing People Based on Last Known Position (approved March 3, 2010, and posted on www.swgdog.org under "Approved Guidelines").
9. *Louisiana v. Davis*, 149 La. 1009, 90 So. 385, 154 La. 295, 97 So. 449 (1923).
10. *Pennsylvania v. Hoffman*, 52 Pa.Super. 272, 1912 WL 4825 (Super. Ct. 1912). See *Alsept v. Kentucky*, 240 Ky. 395, 42 S.W.2d 517 (Ct. App. 1931) (trail led from scene of suspicious fire to homes of defendants). See *South Carolina v. Jordan*, 258 S.C. 340, 188 S.E.2d 780 (1972) (defendant alleged he had not been at the spot where dogs were put on trail, but tracking evidence was admitted because other evidence linked defendant with the location).
11. *Fisher v. Mississippi*, 150 Miss. 206, 116 So. 746 (1928), citing *Harris v. Mississippi*, 143 Miss. 102, 108 So. 446 (1926). See *Troup v. Georgia*, 26 Ga.App. 623, 107 S.E. 75 (Ct. App. 1921) (dog did not pick up trail until about 300 yards from place of shooting, trailed at night and lost the trail at least once, may or may not have alerted to defendant, but handler's testimony was admitted).
12. *Boatwright v. Mississippi*, 143 Miss. 676, 109 So. 710 (1926).
13. *Sprouse v. Kentucky*, 132 Ky. 269, 116 S.W. 344 (Ct. App. 1909).
14. *Vermont v. Bourassa*, 137 Vt. 62, 399 A.2d 507 (Sup. Ct. 1979).
15. *Starkes v. U.S.*, 427 A.2d 437 (D.C. App. 1981).
16. *North Carolina v. Bines*, 8 N.C.App. 1, 173 S.E.2d 605 (Ct. App. 1970).
17. *North Carolina v. Marze*, 22 N.C.App. 628, 207 S.E.2d 359 (Ct. App. 1974).
18. For suggested standards regarding searches using such objects, see SWGDOG SC 9—Human Scent Dogs: Pre-scented canine searches (approved August 15, 2007, and posted on the SWGDOG Web site, www.swgdog.org under "Approved Guidelines").
19. *U.S. v. Cofield*, 391 F.3d 334 (4th Cir. 2007).
20. *California v. Brown*, 709 P.2d 440, 220 Cal.Rptr. 637 (1985). See also *North Carolina v. Taylor*, 337 N.C. 597, 447 S.E.2d 360 (1994) (dog scented from victim's body, led from bottom of embankment where body was found to Pathfinder, which was then connected to defendant).
21. See *North Carolina v. Walston*, 193 N.C.App., 666 S.E.2d 872 (Ct. App. 2008) (dog was used "to quickly locate the item Officer Quagliarello observed defendant throw in the gulley"); *Michigan v. Hill*, 2010 WL 1873105 (Ct. App. 2010) (dog found purse, some money, and a checkbook); *Connecticut v. Wallace*, 181 Conn. 237, 435 A.2d 20 (1980) (dog scented on dropped glove led handler to white knit cap and pair of socks, which contained fibers identical to those of defendant's coat); *U.S. v. Batts*, 21 F.3d 425, 1994 WL 83385 (4th Cir. 1994) (officer saw perpetrator throw gun away, handler and dog trained in article searches found gun soon after). See SWGDOG SC 9—Human Scent Dogs: Article Search (approved March 12, 2007, and posted under Approved Guidelines at www.swgdog.org), stating that this "discipline is used for searching areas, usually

near crime scenes, for human-scented articles that were thrown away or left behind." A dog must be able to locate at least 75% of planted articles. Items used in article searches by the North American Police Work Dog Association include a plastic credit card, a matchbook, a shotgun shell, a leather wallet, a screwdriver, a crumpled cigarette package, and empty metal handgun, and an empty pop gun. NAPWDA Web site (www.napwda.com/pdflib/bylaws_cert_rules.pdf).

22. See *Moore v. Howes*, 2010 WL 1494764 (E.D. Mich. 2010).
23. *Tennessee v. Barger*, 612 S.W.2d 485 (Ct. Crim. App. 1981).
24. See *U.S. v. Mondello,* 927 F.2d 1463 (9th Cir. 1991); *California v. Craig*, 86 Cal.App.3d 905, 150 Cal. Rptr. 676 (1978).
25. *Johnson v. Georgia*, 165 Ga.App. 146, 299 S.E.2d 740 (Ct. App. 1983).
26. *Idaho v. Streeper*, 113 Idaho 662, 747 P.2d 71 (1987).
27. *Gavin v. Alabama*, 891 So.2d 907, 966 (Ct. Crim. App. 2003).
28. *Missouri v. Cheatham*, 458 S.W.2d 336 (1970).
29. Stockham et al. (2004).
30. *Stidham v. Kentucky*, 221 Ky. 49, 297 S.W. 929 (Ct. App. 1927). See *Kansas v. Netherton*, 133 Kan. 685, 3 P.2d 495 (1931) (dogs tracked from basement where woman was murdered to her husband).
31. *Perkins v. Texas*, 2009 WL 2837356 (Ct. App. 2009) (gauze pads were rubbed over objects possibly touched by burglars; dogs sniffed members of burglarized household so dogs could isolate scent of missing member in scent lineup).
32. Schettler (2010), 35, 38.
33. See, for example, *Cranford v. Arkansas*, 130 Ark. 101, 197 S.W. 19 (1917). A cross track on a trail is somewhat different than another scent on a scenting item. With a cross track, the dog has been given the target's scent and encounters other scents as it follows the trail. See *North Carolina v. Yates*, 159 N.C.App. 231, 582 S.E.2d 725 (Ct. App. 2003) (dog "trained to stay on the initial track and to ignore any 'cross tracks' on his path"; handler testified dog had performed various kinds of "disturbance tracks" in training); *California v. Beverford*, 2008 WL 1799763 (Ct. App. 2008) ("Officer Shalhoob testified that Oscar's training included cross-tracking in which the trainer intentionally tried to throw the dog off a scent by laying a different scent to cross track or divert the dog. If there were five individuals in an area, Oscar was trained to pick up their scents and the scent of the sixth person, i.e., the suspect. If Oscar was diverted by someone else's scent, the dog was trained to go back to the start point and track the scent again. Officer Shalhoob stated that Oscar exhibited no crosstracking problems and that it took less than a minute to track the scent on the gloves to the sliding glass door"); *Green v. Florida*, 975 So.2d 1090 (2008) (evidence indicated that dog had not been misled by cross tracks in training settings).
34. *Terrell v. Maryland*, 3 Md.App. 340, 239 A.2d 128 (Ct. Spec. App. 1968); *Michigan v. Norwood*, 70 Mich. App. 53, 245 N.W.2d 170 (Ct. App. 1976) (dog became distracted by other dogs). See *Trejos v. Texas*, 243 S.W.3d 30 (Ct. App. 2007) (adapting foundational requirements of tracking to use of cadaver dogs; method of search involved dogs working independently, using a grid search, working off-lead, etc.).
35. Dogs may also lose scent where a perpetrator crosses water. See *Arizona v. Navarrete*, 2008 WL 4287066 (App. Div. 2008) (dog lost scent on canal bank, which perpetrator apparently crossed since he was later found on opposite bank dripping wet).
36. *Massachusetts v. LePage*, 352 Mass. 403, 226 N.E.2d 200 (1967) (other evidence indicated defendants had entered cab where dog stopped trailing). See *Aaron v. Alabama,* 271 Ala. 70, 122 So.2d 360 (1960) (handler should not have been permitted to speculate that dogs stopped trailing because the perpetrator "got off the ground there, he rode off or something").
37. *West v. Arkansas*, 150 Ark. 555, 234 S.W. 997 (1921).
38. *Briscoe v. Maryland*, 40 Md.App. 120, 388 A.2d 153 (Ct. Spec. App. 1978).
39. *Crabtree v. Kentucky*, 260 Ky. 575, 86 S.W.2d 301 (Ct. App. 1935).
40. *Richardson v. Alabama*, 145 Ala. 46, 41 So. 82 (1906).
41. *North Carolina v. Irick*, 291 N.C. 480, 231 S.E.2d 833 (1977). See also *Missouri v. Rasco*, 239 Mo. 535, 144 S.W. 449 (1912) (accepting that even though dogs were taken off trail and taken to another point, they would not have resumed tracking had they not picked up the same scent); *Brooks v. Colorado*, 975 P.2d 1105, 81 A.L.R.5th 779 (1999) ("Yogi had been trained to 'drop-trail.' That is , he had the ability to continue following a scent even after being pulled off the original trail for a period of time"); *Youngblood v. Conway*, 426 F.Supp.2d 107 (W.D.N.Y. 2006) (dog lost track, but police went in direction given by witness and dog picked up scent again).
42. Gerritsen and Haak (2001), 30.
43. *Washington v. Wieting*, 1997 WL 88957 (Ct. App. 1997).

44. *Crabtree v. Kentucky*, 260 Ky. 575, 86 S.W.2d 301 (Ct. App. 1935).

45. *Brooks v. Colorado*, 975 P.2d 1105, 81 A.L.R.5th 779 (1999).

46. Schwartz (2009).

47. *Buchanek v. City of Victoria*, 2009 WL 500564 (S.D.Tex. 2009).

48. *Fox v. Arkansas*, 156 Ark. 428, 246 S.W. 863 (1923).

49. *North Carolina v. Wiggins*, 171 N.C. 813, 89 S.E. 58 (1916). See *Meyers v. Kentucky*, 194 Ky. 523, 240 S.W. 71 (Ct. App.1922) (tracking to two suspects in a barn burning).

50. *Cranford v. Arkansas*, 130 Ark. 101, 197 S.W. 19 (1917).

51. *U.S. v. Lavado*, 750 F.2d 1527 (11th Cir. 1985).

52. *Washington v. Socolof*, 28 Wash.App. 407, 623 P.2d 733 (Ct. App. 1981) (reversed on other grounds).

53. *Pelletier v. Virginia*, 42 Va.App. 406, 592 S.E.2d 382 (Ct. App. 2004).

54. *Epperly v. Virginia*, 224 Va. 214, 294 S.E.2d 882 (1982).

55. *Montana v. Storm*, 125 Mont. 346, 238 P.2d 1161 (1951).

56. *Minnesota v. Scharmer*, 501 N.W.2d 620 (1993) (instead of allowing dog to follow a secondary track, handler took the dog to a nearby grain elevator where the defendant was found; evidence held insufficient to support conviction).

57. *Illinois v. Pfanschmidt*, 262 Ill. 411, 104 N.E. 804 (1914) (emphasis added) (the dogs were also taken off the trail many times and may have been forced along a path the defendant would not likely have taken). Some studies have indicated that dogs could not track suspects riding bicycles or suspended from a cable apparatus. Gerritsen and Haak (2001), 84–85, 138 (recommending against letting a dog follow a bicycle track if the foot track ends); but see Steen and Wilsson (1990) (dogs followed bicycle tracks on grass and asphalt, but choice of direction was not significantly different from random, unlike dogs following walking tracks).

58. *Holub v. Arkansas*, 116 Ark. 227, 172 S.W. 878 (1915).

59. *Kansas v. Schalansky*, 112 Kan. 87, 209 P. 816 (1922).

60. *Buck v. Oklahoma*, 77 Okla.Crim. 17, 138 P.2d 115 (Ct. Crim. App. 1943).

61. Stockham et al. (2004a). The article discusses testimony in the trial court that resulted in a California appellate court decision, *California v. Willis*, 115 Cal.App.4th 379, 9 Cal.Rptr. 3d 235 (Ct. App. 2004). This article was referenced by a handler in a wrongful arrest action to explain how his dogs had tracked over 5 miles from the location where the victim's body had been found to the house in which she had lived, going along several roads and highways. *Buchanek v. City of Victoria*, 2009 WL 500564 (S.D.Tex. 2009), 2009 WL 1268069 (S.D.Tex 2010).

62. Described by SWGDOG as a "location check." See SWGDOG SC 9—Human Scent Dogs: Pre-Scented Canines—Location Check (posted March 12, 2007, at www.swgdog.com; a proposed revision, with considerable expansion, is posted as of this writing under Documents for Public Comment). See *Cowans v. Bagley*, 2002 WL 31370475 (S.D.Oh. 2002) (dog scented to suspect's shirt tracked from victim's home through wooded area to edge of suspect's property line).

63. Stockham et al. (2004b).

64. *California v. Gutierrez*, 2004 WL 723161 (Ct. App. 2004).

65. *Grant v. City of Long Beach*, 315 F.3d 1081 (9th Cir. 2002) ("scent pad created at the crime scene").

66. *Kansas v. Wainwright*, 18 Kan.App.2d 449, 856 P.2d 163 (Ct. App. 1993).

67. MWD Pamphlet 190-12, § 2–16.

68. *Brott v. Nebraska*, 63 L.R.A. 789, 70 Neb. 395, 97 N.W. 593 (1903). The Nebraska Supreme Court, in rejecting bloodhound testimony, seemed to reject the notion of individual scent, noting that if such testimony were accepted "some citizen be deprived of his property, his liberty, or his life, because, forsooth, within 24 or 40 hours after the commission of a crime, a certain dog indicated by his conduct that he believed the scent of some microscopic particles supposed to have been dropped by the perpetrator of the crime was identical with, or closely resembled, the scent of the person who had been accused and put upon trial." See also *Aiken v. Georgia*, 16 Ga.App. 848, 86 S.E. 1076 (Ct. App. 1915) (also noting that a dog might have to distinguish between "ten, fifty or a hundred" other scents).

69. *Fife v. Georgia*, 16 Ga.App. 22, 84 S.E. 485 (Ct. App. 1915). For more recent statements, see *California v. Gonzales*, 218 Cal.App.3d 403, 267 Cal.Rptr. 138 (1990); *California v. Malgren*, 139 Cal.App.3d 234, 188 Cal.Rptr. 569 (1983); *Idaho v. Streeper*, 113 Idaho 662, 747 P.2d 71 (1987); *Connecticut v. Kelly*, 2009 WL 323481 (Super. Ct. 2009).

70. *Crosby v. Moriarity*, 148 Minn. 201, 181 N.W. 199 (1921). Convictions have stood even though not all tracking foundation requirements were met when the other evidence for conviction was overwhelming. *Michigan v. Sands*, 280 N.W.2d 579 (Ct. App. 1979).

71. *Epperly v. Booker*, 235 Va. 35, 366 S.E.2d 62 (1988) (petitioner failed to carry burden).

72. *Connecticut v. Esposito*, 235 Conn. 802, 670 A.2d 301 (1995). See also *Connecticut v. St. John*, 282 Conn. 260, 919 A.2d 452 (2007) (trail not contaminated even where environment is permeated with automobile exhaust because dog continued to follow scent of perpetrator).

73. *Tennessee v. Brewer*, 875 S.W.2d 298 (Ct. Crim. App. 1994).

74. *Green v. Florida*, 641 So.2d 391 (1994).

75. *Ohio v. Dickerson*, 77 Ohio St. 34, 82 N.E. 969 (1907).

76. *Epperly v. Booker*, 997 F.2d 1 (4th Cir. 1993) (officer put scenting underwear in paper bag against preservation protocol and kept this with him for 9 or 10 hours, but did not touch scent item; handler testified that if the officer had contaminated the item, the dog would have nuzzled him; also dog followed trail that officer had not been on, indicating violation of protocol did not result in contamination; ineffective assistance of counsel claim rejected).

77. *Michigan v. Garcia*, 2006 WL 1009017 (Ct. App. 2006).

78. *North Carolina v. Robinson*, 181 N.C. 516, 106 S.E. 155 (1921). See *Allen v. Kentucky*, 26 Ky.L.Rptr. 807, 82 S.W. 589 (Ct. App. 1904) (defendants discussed procuring Japanese oil to put on their shoes so dogs could not track them; description of conversation was properly admitted).

79. *North Carolina v. Moore*, 55 L.R.A. 96, 129 N.C. 494, 39 S.E. 626 (1901).

80. *Holcombe v. Alabama*, 437 So.2d 663 (Ct. Crim. App. 1983).

81. *North Carolina v. McIver*, 176 N.C. 718, 96 S.E. 902 (1918).

82. *U.S. v. Carroll*, 710 F.2d 164 (4th Cir. 1983).

83. *Cranford v. Arkansas*, 130 Ark. 101, 197 S.W. 19 (1917).

84. Stockham et al. (2004a).

85. *Aiken v. Georgia*, 16 Ga.App. 848, 86 S.E. 1076, 1078 (1915).

86. *Wilkie v. Alaska*, 715 P.2d 1199 (Ct. App. 1986).

87. *Padgett v. Arkansas*, 125 Ark. 471, 188 S.W. 1158 (1916).

88. *Illinois v. Pfanschmidt*, 262 Ill. 411, 461, 104 N.E. 804, 823 (Ill.Sup.Ct. 1914).

89. See *Pedigo v. Kentucky*, 103 Ky. 41, 44 S.W. 143, 42 L.R.A. 432 (Ct. App. 1898) (Judge Guffy, concurring in part and dissenting in part, accepted use of dogs where "the object sought was the arrest or capture of known fugitives." His concern was that "[i]t is now proposed to use the hound, not to capture a fugitive, but to ascertain or furnish evidence to convict some citizen of crime." Judge Guffy also expresses concern that raising bloodhounds will become a business activity for individuals wishing to profit from their use by police departments).

90. *Spears v. Mississippi*, 92 Miss. 613, 46 So. 166 (1908).

91. *Missouri v. Dooms*, 280 Mo. 84, 217 S.W. 43 (1919) (failure to object at trail waived any incompetency of the evidence on appeal).

92. *Denham v. Kentucky*, 27 Ky.L.Rptr. 171, 84 S.W. 538 (Ct. App. 1905).

93. *California v. Willis*, 115 Cal.App.4th 379, 9 Cal.Rptr. 3d 235 (Ct. App. 2004).

94. *Keaton v. Kentucky*, 223 Ky 645, 4 S.W.2d 675 (Ct. App. 1928).

95. *Missouri v. Barnes*, 289 S.W. 562 (Sup. Ct. Div. 2 1926).

96. *Missouri v. Shawley*, 334 Mo. 352, 67 S.W.2d 74 (1933).

97. *Indiana v. Stout*, 174 Ind. 395, 92 N.E. 161 (1910); *Michigan v. Warriner*, 461 Mich. 885, 601 N.W.2d 378 (1999).

98. *Missouri v. White*, 195 S.W. 994 (Sup. Ct., Div. 2 1917). See *North Carolina v. McLeod*, 196 N.C. 542, 146 S.E. 409 (1929), 198 N.C. 649, 152 S.E. 895 (1930). See also *Washington v. Lord*, 128 Wash.App. 216, 114 P.3d 1241 (Ct. App. 2005) (failure of dog to alert was noted by dissent; defense argued that potentially exonerating dog-tracking evidence had not been provided in discovery, but court disagreed that the evidence would have been useful).

99. Curran et al. (2010).

100. See *U.S. v. Cofield*, 254 Fed.Appx. 971, 2007 WL 3083542 (4th Cir. 2007) (tracking dog sniffed gun near flight path of perpetrator and followed path to police car where defendant was under arrest); *California v. Sanders*, 2009 WL 3682460 (Ct. App. 2009) (trailing dog scented to paper towel that wiped steering wheel led to batting glove, later alerted to car in which suspect was sitting; court rejected defense argument that paper towel may have been contaminated because officer did not know if anyone else may have touched it).

101. *Cranford v. Arkansas*, 130 Ark. 101, 197 S.W. 19 (1917).

102. *Hinton v. Mississippi*, 175 Miss. 308, 166 So. 762 (1936).

103. *New York v. Gangler*, 227 A.D.2d 946, 643 N.Y.S.2d 839 (App. Div. 1996).

104. *North Dakota v. Iverson*, 187 N.W.2d 1 (1971); see also *California v. Salcido*, GA052057 (Super. Ct. 2005) (dog alerted to suspect in room with two other individuals); *California v. Willis*, 115 Cal.App.4th 379, 9 Cal.Rptr. 3d 235 (Ct. App. 2004) (dog showed interest in locations where suspects were thought to have been but did not alert; later put her head on suspect's lap in police station, which was considered an ambiguous alert; appellate court found admission of the canine evidence clear error, in part because of doubts about scent transfer unit, but affirmed because error was harmless).

105. *California v. Chavez*, 2004 WL 1173075 (Ct. App. 2004); see also *California v. Sandoval*, 2002 WL 519848 (Ct. App. 2002) (dog scented to scent pads created with scent transfer unit from seats of car used in street gang murder tracked to cells of three suspects in police station, thereby arguably identifying where each suspect sat in the vehicle); *California v. Alonzo*, 2008 WL 2248628 (Ct. App. 2008) (dog scented on pad with scent of shell casings followed path suspect had previously taken in police station to room where suspect was seated and put his head on suspect's lap, not the dog's usual alert, perhaps explained by dog's age); *California v. Demirdjian*, 2003 WL 1963204 (Ct. App 2003), *Demirdjian v. Sullivan*, 2009 WL 2767673 (C.D.Cal. 2009) (also involving Hamm and Scarlet; dog tracked from crime scene to house of defendant's parents, and next day identified defendant in interview room when there were about 30 people in the police station; there was also a scent matching conducted later by a different team).

106. *California v. Robinson*, 2004 WL 2418068 (Ct. App. 2004) (dog did not alert to suspect that was in patrol car but later alerted to that suspect's cell in police station; evidence not admitted because of lack of proper foundation regarding scent transfer unit used to prepare scent pads as scenting items for the dog); *California v. Melara*, 2006 WL 164989 (Ct. App. 2006) (dog alerted to suspect not charged; handler was not "professional scientist" who could qualify admission of evidence based on creating scent pads with scent transfer unit).

107. *U.S. v. Carroll*, 710 F.2d 164 (4th Cir. 1983); *Buchanek v. City of Victoria*, 2009 WL 500564 (S.D.Tex. 2009), 2009 WL 1268069 (S.D.Tex 2010).

6 Judicial Admissibility of Scent Lineup Evidence

Scent identification procedures, particularly scent lineups, differ from narcotics or explosives detection work in that the dog must match an odor on an item believed to have been touched by the perpetrator at a crime scene to an item touched by a suspect in that crime, such as a metal tube in an row of tubes, the rest of which have been touched by other individuals having nothing to do with the crime. The items not touched by the suspect are called foils. Either that, or particularly in older cases, the dog matched the odor on the crime scene item to a row of individuals, one of whom was the suspect. This is closer to the traditional sight lineup used for witnesses and victims of a crime. Variations of both these approaches can be found in U.S. cases.

One Texas case found tracking and scent lineups to be so similar that scent lineup evidence could be admitted with the same foundation.

> For purposes of judging the reliability of evidence based on a dog's ability to distinguish between scents, we believe there is little distinction between a scent lineup and a situation where a dog is required to track an individual's scent over an area traversed by multiple persons. ... Accordingly, we conclude that the use of scent lineups is a legitimate field of expertise.[1]

Dogs have often been expected to function both as trackers and as identifiers for scent lineups. One handler in a Texas case testified that only after a dog demonstrated consistency in running trails did he teach it to do lineups.[2] A Maryland court suggested that tracking is sometimes similar to a scent lineup in that the dog traverses ground crossed by individuals other than the one the dog is tracking.[3]

As with tracking cases, handlers have too often been able to qualify the competence of themselves and their dogs in scent lineups, and as with tracking cases, courts, and even defense counsel, have also too often been reluctant to question such assurances by a handler. A Texas court dismissed an objection that a dog was medicated at the time of a scent lineup, noting that there was no evidence this affected her performance, rather than requiring evidence that the medication did not affect performance.[4]

More recent cases considering scent identification procedures have been inclined to recognize that a distinction should be made between tracking and identification, and that different foundational requirements should apply.[5] For instance, in a 2004 California case involving a dog picking out a suspect from among five police officers, the court felt that more was required than the traditional tracking elements.

> The prosecution cannot rely solely on anecdotes regarding the dog's capabilities. Instead, a foundation must be laid from academic or scientific sources regarding (a) how long scent remains on an object or at a location; (b) whether every person has a scent that is so unique that it provides an accurate basis for scent identification, such that it can be analogized to human DNA; (c) whether a particular breed of dog is characterized by acute powers of scent and discrimination; and (d) the adequacy of the certification procedures for scent identifications.[6]

A great deal of foundational testimony, both in tracking and scent lineup cases, could be described as anecdotal. The court did not reverse, however, finding other evidence so overwhelming that another jury would not likely reach a different verdict. Table 6.1 lists a number of differences between tracking and trailing and scent lineups.[7]

Suspects have been held not to have a right to counsel present during the conduct of a scent lineup.[8] One case described an agreement between prosecution and defense counsel under which the prosecution would not attempt to introduce evidence of a scent lineup if the defense would not object to the admission of tracking evidence.[9]

BREEDS FOR SCENT LINEUP WORK

Scent lineup cases relying on traditional tracking foundational requirements have sometimes insisted on aspects of those requirements that are largely outdated. A 2003 California court said that the trial court record in a scent lineup case was devoid of any evidence to indicate that a Labrador retriever was "of a breed, stock or pedigree characterized by acute powers of scent and discrimination."[12]

TRAINING

Dogs used in scent identification lineups in the United States are sometimes trained in other police dog functions. In the Netherlands, Poland, Germany, and other European countries, dogs are specifically trained for scent identification procedures and often may work in no other capacity. Recently, the FBI has begun to train dogs according to European procedures and it can be expected, or at least hoped, that some larger U.S. law enforcement agencies will have dogs devoted primarily if not exclusively to scent identification work.

TRAINING IN HOLLAND

Lineup procedures of the Canine Unit of the Netherlands National Police force are rigorous.[13] Odors in scent lineups are put on stainless steel tubes 10 cm long and 2 × 2 cm wide. Between trials, tubes are washed in a dishwasher at the highest temperature for an hour. A tube is scented by asking the suspect or foil to open a jar, take a tube out, and hold it for about a minute. The person then returns the tube to the jar and closes the lid. The jar is airtight. Participants who touch the tubes all wash their hands with the same soap and dry their hands with the same type of clean towel.[14] Tubes are placed on wooded platforms coated with a nonslip surface. Platforms are 5.5 m × 1 m, and steel plates in the middle are designed to hold the tubes. Tubes can be released by a mechanism underneath the platform controlled by a switchbox. Each testing room has two platforms. Kaldenbach notes that when being moved to a new step, dogs may not perform well and some allowance must be made to simplify the task or move back to a prior step for a brief time.[15] The six-step training regimen used in the Netherlands is described in Figure 6.1.[16]

HANDLER'S QUALIFICATIONS

As with tracking cases discussed earlier, the issue of the handler's expertise has arisen in scent lineups. To testify concerning the conduct of the lineup and how procedures are designed to limit erroneous identifications, a handler with sufficient training could be adequate, though some of this testimony might be based on scientific results the handler could not testify concerning.[17] In a 2002 Texas case,[18] the defense moved to exclude the testimony of a handler who had performed a scent lineup where the dog had alerted to the defendant's scent. The Texas Court of Appeals concluded:

> [W]hen addressing fields that are based upon experience or training as opposed to scientific methods, the appropriate questions for assessing reliability are (1) whether the field of expertise is a legitimate

TABLE 6.1
Differences between Tracking and Trailing and Scent Lineups

Tracking and Trailing	Scent Lineup
Dogs trained to follow tracks or trails of targets usually on long, loose leads	Dogs trained in procedures designed to emphasize matching of scents correctly; dogs in modern procedures more often work off-lead
Dogs may be trained in other police dog functions or may be tracking specialists	Dogs may be trained in other police dog functions but are generally specialists in European procedures and in the most reliable protocols
Dog ideally scented to object touched by perpetrator but sometimes scented to area where perpetrator likely to have been present; dogs occasionally scented to pads	Dog scented to object likely to have scent of perpetrator or to scent pad created from object perpetrator may have touched
Scent occasionally extracted and enhanced by scent transfer unit	Scent on items from crime scene and scents in stations of lineup frequently extracted and enhanced by scent transfer unit
Dogs more often follow foot scent as individual human odor	Dogs more often scented to objects touched by perpetrators' hands
Scent source may have been touched by multiple individuals ("missing member" may be performed to eliminate nonsuspects); track may have been crossed by multiple individuals	Multiple individuals may have touched scent source; lineup design generally precludes scents from individuals other than the suspect and foils in the lineup stations
Dogs must ignore cross tracks laid at different times generally by unknown individuals	Dogs must choose between objects on which, ideally, scent is placed at same time and by individuals of same gender, age, and ethnicity of suspect; lineup stations are usually identical
Dog need not choose any individual but may lead to suspect	Dogs can choose between a number of objects scented by target and decoys (in zero trials, no choice is correct)
Dogs may work in tandem or in groups	Dogs work alone; when trials involve using multiple dogs, equipment must be carefully cleaned between each trial
Object of work is to find path taken by perpetrator, find objects perpetrator may have left, and possibly find perpetrator	Object of trial is to determine if suspect's scent can be linked to crime scene or objects related to the offense
Handler may have to know facts about perpetrator in case he encounters him or her while tracking (particularly if perpetrator may be armed and dangerous)	The handler and anyone within the dog's vision during a trial should be blind as to the correct location of the target; handler should not be able to see experimenter or other individual who knows correct station during the trial
Environment of tracking generally cannot be controlled beyond limiting the interference of other investigators or bystanders	Environment should be highly controlled to avoid contamination and cueing
Trail may be followed by more than one team, though this should not occur at the same time	Equipment must be cleaned between trials as dogs may leave saliva or exhaled particles at scenting stations
Trail cannot be followed after scent disappears	Test can be performed as long as scents are preserved
Procedure may produce additional evidence (e.g., items dropped or abandoned by perpetrator, locations where perpetrator may have been)	Procedure does not produce additional evidence
Dogs track in diverse environments; may track to a building or vehicle, implicating privacy interests[10]	Procedure generally conducted in police station or other facility
Procedure rarely videotaped[11]	Videotaping increasingly common and often required
Tracking foundational requirements directly apply	Tracking foundational requirements require adaptation or ignoring (e.g., putting on track where perpetrator likely to have been; tracking continuously)
Cueing the dog generally only possible if suspect is encountered; cases sometimes describe dogs being forced to follow a path against their inclination	Cueing the dog possible if the handler knows suspect is in the lineup or where the scent of the suspect is located
Dog may have to be rescented if it loses trail or becomes distracted	In optimal protocols, dog will not be rescented during trial

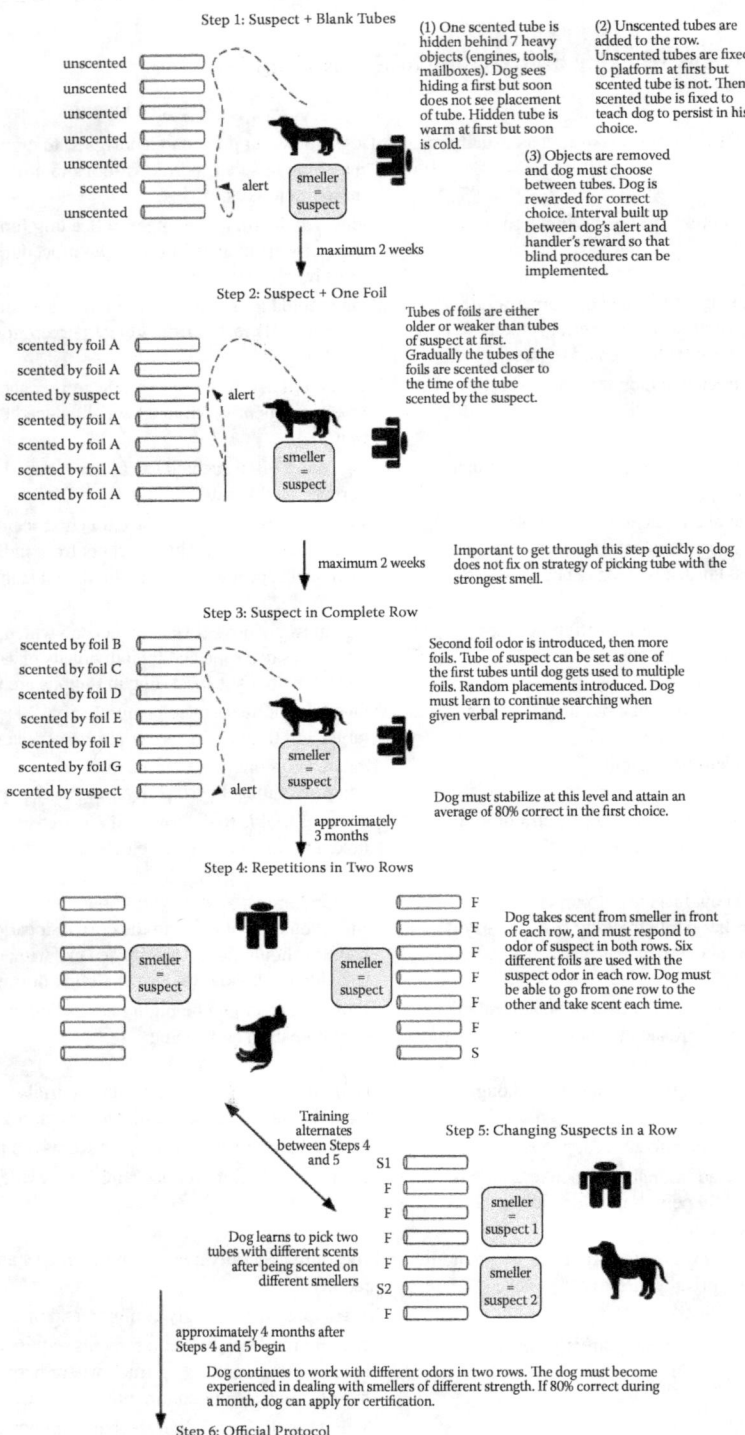

FIGURE 6.1 Dutch scent identification training procedures. The "smeller" is the scent item. (Graphic created from Schoon, G.A.A. and Haak, R., 2002, *K-9 Suspect Discrimination*, Calgary, Alberta, Canada, Detselig Enterprises.)

one, (2) whether the subject matter of the expert's testimony is within the scope of the field, and (3) whether the expert's testimony properly relies upon or utilizes the principles involved in the field.[19]

The court said that "a dog's reaction to a scent lineup is based upon training and experience, and not scientific method," making the more rigorous requirements for admission of scientific testimony inapplicable.[20] As to the first prong of the three-part test, the court concluded that dog scent lineups were a legitimate field of expertise. This conclusion was reached based on a number of observations:

- Many types of dog-related evidence are admitted, including tracking, explosives detection, and drug detection; 37 states and the District of Columbia admit scent-tracking evidence, and only 4 do not.
- Prior cases have acknowledged that dogs can distinguish humans by scent.[21]
- The FBI had recognized the specific handler's help in solving in identifying a serial killer.

As to whether the expert's testimony properly relied on the principles of the field, the court held that this determination required an analysis of three factors: (1) the qualifications of the particular trainer, (2) the qualifications of the particular dog, and (3) the objectivity of the particular lineup. The court accepted that the credentials of the handler testifying were sufficient. As to the qualifications of the dog, the court determined that this referred to the requirements of tracking cases that (1) the dog be of a breed characterized by acuteness of scent and power of discrimination, (2) the dog had been trained to discriminate between human beings by their scent, (3) the dog has been reliable, (4) the dog was scented to an item that had the scent of a participant in the crime, and (5) the scent was given to the dog within the period of its efficiency.[22] Thus, the traditional tracking factors were once again applied. The dogs used in the case were bloodhounds, and the testimony concerning the breed appears to have come only from the handler. The handler testified that the dogs were taught in trailing prior to being taught to perform scent lineups, and that he had run over 1,000 trails with the dogs. The handler also testified that his dogs had never trailed a false scent and had never misidentified a scent in a scent lineup. The dogs were scented on an item believed to have been moved by a perpetrator. The court did not discuss the dog's period of efficiency but did state that the scent lineup took place a day after a scent sample was obtained from the suspect (though the other samples in the lineup may have been obtained earlier). The court held that the foundational requirements for the admission of the handler's expert testimony had been met.[23]

In a 2003 California case,[24] the California Court of Appeals felt the distinction between tracking and scent lineups could go to the admission of expert testimony and praised the trial court for declining to admit the testimony of an expert whose sole experience was in tracking and trailing.[25] The trial court was criticized, however, for allowing two handlers to testify as to how long scent could remain on an object (2 to 4 months), but "no effort was made to present information from any academic or scientific sources, let along peer review journals, regarding these testimonial assertions."[26] The court also noted that the handlers, who did not have scientific backgrounds, were unable to cite any scientific data supporting the notion that each individual has a unique scent. The court found that the dog performing the scent identification "analogous to a machine that [the handler] can calibrate and read." Therefore, scientific standards under Kelly[27] "should have been applied to this evidence." In the very next paragraph, however, the court seems to consider that modifying the foundational requirements in scent identification cases might obviate the need for a Kelly/Frye type of analysis.

We further conclude that, even if Kelly were not deemed to apply to scent identification evidence in general, a greater foundation than the one provided here is needed for its admission. In tracking and trailing, there is a history of canine performance which provides the basis for [the requirement that] the dog was put on a fresh trail. For scent identification to be relevant, there must be some basis for assumptions made about degradation and contamination of scent, both before and during collection, as well as the uniqueness of each person's odor, beyond the mere experiences of one trainer and one dog.[28]

This at least demonstrates a healthy recognition that scent lineups should not be admitted solely on the foundational elements that have been applied historically in tracking cases.

Defendants may be as impressed as courts often are with scent lineups. In one 2003 Texas case, a defendant was told the results of a lineup, after which she began negotiating a plea.[29]

ACCURACY RATES

A 2006 Texas case cited a handler's testimony that one dog had performed 760 scent lineups, identifying the wrong subject only twice.[30] A handler in a Connecticut tracking case was somewhat more reasonable, stating that dogs he trained had about an 80% success rate and that the dog in a particular case had about this success rate.[31]

Although the handler's interpretation of a dog's actions as a positive alert is seldom questioned, objections have occasionally been raised concerning different reactions of a dog being interpreted as positive alerts.[32] In a 2009 California case, a defense expert was unable to interpret the handler's training logs and stated that he could not therefore assess the dog's reliability. Nevertheless, the handler testified he was not aware that his dog had made any mistakes in 171 lineups and the court found the handler's testimony sufficient to qualify the dog and admit the evidence concerning the lineup.[33]

CORROBORATION

In cases where scent lineups have been admitted, appellate courts have often followed tracking cases with regard to the corroboration requirement. A federal district court in New York found that the other evidence must be sufficient to establish a defendant's guilt by clear and convincing evidence. That combined with the scent lineup evidence would then have to be in total convincing beyond a reasonable doubt.[34]

European courts have also considered corroboration important.[35] A survey of judges in Poland found that only 22% of 41 judges presiding over criminal trials regarded scent lineups as sufficient to convict a defendant where the lineup results were the only evidence for conviction.[36] A scientist and a lawyer in Holland have argued that scent lineup evidence should only be admitted as corroborative of other evidence.[37]

Corroborating evidence has sometimes seemed fairly weak. In a 2009 Texas case, the corroborating evidence consisted of the defendant saying something incriminating to a cellmate and referring to himself as the "number one suspect" at a time when he was not suspected. On the other hand, although dogs alerted to another suspect in the case, no charges were brought against her because there seems to have been no other evidence implicating her.[38]

JURY INSTRUCTIONS

An early scent lineup case quoted an instruction admonishing the jury not to put too much weight on the evidence from a scent lineup, alluding to the "who is the witness" issue:

> Evidence has been presented in this case that law enforcement authorities conducted portions of their investigation with the aid of a trained dog. Because it is of course not possible for the dog to communicate its findings to us directly, we must rely on the interpretation of the dog's actions provided by the testimony of its trainer. ... Because of the nature of this evidence, you are instructed to receive it with caution and not to give it undue weight. It is to be considered as a part of, and along with, all the other evidence in the case in your deliberations.[39]

In 1983, a New York federal district court concluded that a jury could consider scent lineup evidence but that the jury must:

1. Determine *beyond a reasonable doubt* that the dog, based on his previous lineup record, has demonstrated the ability to identify reliably and discriminate among "odors."
2. Use the dog identification evidence to convict defendant only if the other evidence in the case establishes defendant's guilt by *clear and convincing evidence*.[40]

Thus, the court put the determination of corroboration on the jury, with different proof standards for first finding the evidence usable in the case and then for using it to convict the defendant. Cautionary instructions such as these have been common through more than a century of tracking cases.[41]

JUDICIAL PERSPECTIVES ON SCIENTIFIC RELIABILITY OF SCENT IDENTIFICATIONS

In the 1983 federal case discussed in the preceding section, the court concluded, citing only three scientific sources,[42] that "scientific data clearly demonstrate that a properly trained dog can distinguish among the 'odors' of different persons and can detect the 'odor' of a particular person on an object." The court also concluded that "the nonlikelihood that two individuals would have similar or identical 'scents' or 'odor' characteristics has not been established in the scientific community." The court held that this did not require the exclusion of canine evidence.

> Unlike a precise, mechanical instrument such as the spectrograph, which jurors may view as incapable of error, a dog may be seen as more "human-like" and therefore subject to lapses in judgment and perception. Thus, because of the lesser potential prejudicial impact that evidence resulting from a dog's identification may have on the jury, courts need not apply as strict a standard when considering the admissibility of such evidence as they are required to apply when considering the admissibility of the seemingly flawless evidence produced by a mechanical instrument.

The federal district court held that before the canine evidence could be given any consideration or weight, it must find that the dog "has previous actual case lineup experience and that his record in such cases is sufficient to conclude, beyond a reasonable doubt, that his powers of discrimination and identification are reliable." Then also, as discussed earlier, the jury must also find that all the other evidence establishes the defendant's guilt by clear and convincing evidence.[43]

An Arizona case from 1984 involved scent lineups of clothing and bicycles, but the Arizona Supreme Court said that the *Frye* test was inapplicable to dog tracking or scenting, requiring only the foundational requirements of tracking.[44] Florida has required that admission of scent lineup evidence involve a demonstration that:

> (1) this type of lineup evidence is reliable; (2) the specific lineup is conducted in a fair, objective manner; and (3) the dog used has been properly trained and found by experience to be reliable in this type of identification.

The court said that more evidence was required than the testimony of a dog handler and a police officer, but it is not clear what would establish the reliability of lineup evidence.[45]

In a 2001 decision of a Texas federal district court,[46] the court had determined, in a narcotics case, that a *Daubert* hearing was "the wrong procedural vehicle through which to challenge the reliability of a canine alert."[47] In a 2006 Texas case involving a scent lineup of an African American and five Caucasian police officers, the handler rejected contentions of the defendant that the lineup was defective because it should have only used scent pads, not people standing in a line. The handler also deflected criticism that the lineup should have only used people of the same race, and the fact the defendant was the only person in the lineup wearing handcuffs (meaning in effect that the lineup could not have been blind). Despite these flaws, the appellate court determined that the trial court did not abuse its discretion in admitting testimony regarding the lineup. The trial court had held a hearing to determine if the handler's testimony in a scent lineup would be admitted, and referred to this hearing as a *Daubert* hearing. The court concluded that *Daubert* and *Frye* factors ("(1) whether the theory or technique can be or has been tested, (2) whether the theory or technique has been subjected to peer review or publication, (3) the known or potential rate of error, and (4) general acceptance within the relevant scientific community") do not necessarily apply outside of the "hard sciences," looking only to the foundational elements of the qualifications of the trainer, the dog, and the objectivity of the particular lineup.[48] The court also noted the defense objection that the dog was on medication at the time of the lineups but found no evidence that this affected her performance, except perhaps to make her a little slower. The medication was apparently for weight loss.[49]

Another 2006 Texas case, concerning the same crime discussed in the preceding paragraph, but different defendants, also followed *Nenno*.[50] This court found the lineup objective despite the fact that the procedure was not double-blind (only the defendants were handcuffed), and of the two line-ups, only the defendants were different as the other participants were the same three officers.[51]

One prominent legal scholar argued strongly in 1990 that courts should not admit scent lineups because they do not meet *Frye* standards.[52] In 1999, a Polish professor of forensic science, summarizing European research, found this argument to be valid still.[53]

FOREIGN JUDICIAL PERSPECTIVES ON SCENT IDENTIFICATION

The Netherlands Supreme Court has been accepting scent lineups since 2001.[54] German courts have shown more caution, admitting scent lineups only as circumstantial evidence.[55] Polish courts also recognized scent lineups as circumstantial and of limited probative value,[56] but in 1999, Poland's Supreme Court provided specific requirements for the admissibility of scent identification evidence.[57] This court specified that an expert in the area of scent examination should be appointed not to provide an opinion on the correctness of scent lineups carried out by the police, but rather to conduct scent lineups using relevant specialists to collect scent samples and dog handlers for the lineups.[58] Polish courts require (1) two separate lineups, (2) proof that the dog has been shown reliable, (3) a demonstration that appropriate foils were selected, and (4) placing items in the lineup was done blind, without the dog or handler present.[59]

Tomaszewski and Girdwoyn note that the acceptance of scent lineups in Poland has changed dramatically in that such evidence was initially circumstantial, but then began to be regarded as expert testimony, and that sometimes it was accepted as the only incriminating evidence sufficient to prove the defendant guilty.[60] Then some notorious cases somewhat lessened the value courts were willing to give to scent lineups, which began to emphasize again that these were only circumstantial evidence and would have to be evaluated in relation to the totality of the evidence presented.[61] A 2003 decision of the Supreme Court of Poland stated:

> So far, scent evidence has not provided such certainty as can be derived, for instance, from fingerprint or DNA examinations, and hence the need of preserving a high dose of precaution in judicial decisions when basing sentences exclusively on scent evidence. While avoiding disapproval, this type of evidence should be subject to a penetrating and comprehensive analysis with due respect to other evidential material.[62]

Tomaszewski and Girdwoyn describe an increasing skepticism.

In Lithuania and the Ukraine, dog scent lineups are used as investigative tools but not as evidence in court.[63]

NOTES

1. *Winston v. Texas*, 78 S.W.3d 522 (Ct. App. 2002) (concluding, at 527-528, that a dog is qualified if "it (1) is of a breed characterized by acuteness of scent and power of discrimination, (2) has been trained to discriminate between human beings by their scent, (3) has been found by experience to be reliable, (4) was given a scent known to be that of the alleged participant of the crime, and (5) was given the scent within the period of its efficiency"). See also *Risher v. Texas*, 227 S.W.3d 133 (Ct. App. 2006) (adopting *Winston* factors and discussing reliability in particular).
2. *Robinson v. Texas*, 2009 WL 5205361 (Ct.App. 2009).
3. *Roberts v. Maryland*, 53 Md.App. 257, 452 A.2d 1271 (Ct. Spec. App. 1982), aff'd, 298 Md. 261, 469 A.2d 442 (Ct. App. 1983).
4. *Martinez v. Texas*, 2006 WL 3720136 (Ct. App. 2006); *Risher v. Texas*, 227 S.W.3d 133 (Ct. App. 2006).
5. *California v. Mitchell*, 110 Cal.App.4th 772, 2 Cal.Rptr.3d 49 (Ct. App. 2003) (noting that "a greater foundation" than the basic tracking foundation should be required for a scent lineup, and additional scientific expertise beyond that of a typical handler is necessary to establish the basis for assumptions about the degradation and contamination of scent, as well as "the uniqueness of each person's odor, beyond the mere experiences of one trainer and one dog").
6. *California v. Willis*, 115 Cal.App.4th 379, 9 Cal.Rptr. 3d 235 (Ct. App. 2004).
7. Tracking dogs are also to be distinguished from dogs trained to locate individuals who are nervous or scared and thereby emit an enhanced scent. *California v. Espinoza*, 2008 WL 2908718 (Ct. App. 2008). In a case involving a dog that was trained to distinguish between normal scents emitted by humans and fear scents, the court found that this training did not satisfy the foundational requirement for tracking humans, though the error was considered harmless. *California v. Searcy*, 2006 WL 689135 (Ct. App. 2006).
8. *Jennings v. Texas*, 2009 WL 167858 (Ct. App. 2009) (lineup was not "critical stage" of proceedings; objection that commenter on video was within hearing range of handler while video was made was held harmless error, if error at all; court noted that video demonstrated that one dog missed the suspect's scent on the first pass, but ignored fact lineup was not blind).
9. *California v. Rivera*, 2004 WL 2601335 (Ct. App. 2004).
10. *Connecticut v. Kelly*, 2009 WL 323481 (Super. Ct. 2009) (dog tracked to car in which perpetrator may have been; court found probable cause to let dog in car for sniff, resulting in alert to driver's seat).
11. A curious case involved introduction of a videotape not of the tracking but of a recreation of the tracking. The Ohio Supreme Court had upheld the trial judge's decision to admit the videotape despite the facts that (1) a dog walking a trail is not the same as a dog following a trail, (2) the dog lost the scent at least twice while trailing but this was not depicted in the video, and (3) the route in the video was not identical with that in the actual trailing. The video was offered "for purposes of illustration," and the Supreme Court found it not to be so prejudicial as to be an abuse of discretion. *Ohio v. Cowans*, 1999 WL 699870 (Ct. App. 1999); 87 Ohio St. 68, 717 N.E.2d 298 (1999); habeas, *Cowans v. Bagley*, 2002 WL 31370475 (S.D. Ohio 2002).
12. *California v. Mitchell*, 110 Cal.App.4th 772, 2 Cal.Rptr.3d 49 (Ct. App. 2003).
13. Schoon (2001); Schoon and Haak (2002).
14. Kaldenbach (1998), 99–100.
15. Ibid., 99–100.
16. Ibid., 97, describes a similar training regimen taking at least 8 months. It specifies that training begins with the dog on a leash.
17. Courts sometimes seem to depict the scientific basis of scent identification as only involving a discussion of the dog's nose. See *Connecticut v. Kelly*, 2009 WL 323481 (Super. Ct. 2009) ("the fallibility of canine olfaction is common knowledge … jurors can be made aware of the conditions impacting accuracy during cross, and jurors are free to use their common sense in attributing what weight to accord his type of evidence. The court is persuaded that a juror does not require a scientific explanation of canine olfaction to appreciate that dogs, like all animals, also have flaws and can be influenced by the events taking place around them, both of which can impact their ability to successfully complete the tasks for which they were trained"). Particularly in scent lineups, accuracy rates from controlled lineups can inform whether a particular procedure is sufficiently likely to be reliable for admission with adequate corroborating evidence.
18. *Winston v. Texas*, 78 S.W.3d 522 (Ct. App. 2002).
19. Ibid., citing *Nenno v. Texas*, 970 S.W.2d 549 (Ct. Crim. App. 1998) and describing this as the *Nenno* test. The court noted that, in *Brooks v. Colorado*, 975 P.2d 1105, 1106 (1999), the Colorado Supreme Court had held that canine scent tracking evidence may be based on scientific axioms, but was not science per se and was not subject to the *Daubert* scientific evidence factors.

20. The defense had argued that the court should exclude the handler's testimony under *Kelly v. Texas*, 824 S.W.2d 568, 573 (Ct. Crim. App. 1992), in which the Texas Court of Criminal Appeals had rejected the *Frye* standard, but required that "evidence derived from a scientific theory, to be considered reliable, must satisfy three criteria in any particular case: (a) the underlying scientific theory must be valid; (b) the technique applying the theory must be valid; and (c) the technique must have been properly applied on the occasion in question."

21. *Winston*, 78 S.W.3d at 527, citing *Arizona v. Roscoe*, 145 Ariz. 212, 700 P.2d 1312, 1319–1320, n. 2 (1984); *Roberts v. Maryland*, 298 Md. 261, 469 A.2d 442, 447, n. 5 (1983); *New York v. Price*, 54 N.Y.2d 557, 446 N.Y.S.2d 906, 431 N.E.2d 267, 269 (1981).

22. *Winston*, 78 S.W.3d at 527-28, citing *U.S. v. Gates*, 680 F.2d 1117, 1119 (6th Cir. 1982) and *Brooks*, 975 P.2d at 1114.

23. See *Robinson v. Texas*, 2006 WL 3438076 (Ct. App. 2006), stating: "Our research has turned up nothing since *Winston* calling scent-tracking evidence or scent identification lineups into question. We find that human scent identification evidence involving the use of trained dogs to be a legitimate field of expertise." (footnote omitted)

24. *California v. Mitchell*, 110 Cal.App.4th 772, 2 Cal.Rptr.3d 49 (2003).

25. The court noted, for instance, that the requirement of tracking cases that the trail not be stale required a "dramatic revision" for application to scent lineups.

26. See also *California v. Gutierrez*, 2004 WL 723161 (Ct. App. 2004) ("In the absence of an adequate foundation from scientific or academic sources on how long the scent would remain at the location, whether every person has a unique scent such as to permit an accurate basis for scent identification, the powers of the dog as to scent and discrimination, and the adequacy of the certification procedures for scent identifications …, the evidence was erroneously admitted in this case." Nevertheless, the court found the admission of the evidence to be harmless error.)

27. *California v. Kelly*, 17 Cal.3d 24, 549 P.2d. 1240, 130 Cal.Rptr. 144 (1976) (adopting *Frye* standard in California).

28. 110 Cal.App.4th 793–794.

29. *Drake v. Texas*, 123 S.W.3d 596 (2003) (no description of scent lineup in published opinion).

30. *Robinson v. Texas*, 2006 WL 3438076 (Ct. App. 2006).

31. *Connecticut v. Wilson*, 180 Conn. 481, 429 A.2d 931 (1980). See *Idaho v. Streeper*, 113 Idaho 662, 747 P.2d 71 (1987) (one dog had tracked in 50 cases with 80% success rate; other dog had tracked in over 100 cases with 75% success rate. For tracking purposes, Connecticut cases have found 70% success rates adequate for satisfying the tracking foundational requirement that the dog be trained and accurate in tracking humans. *Connecticut v. St. John*, 282 Conn. 260, 919 A.2d 452 (2007); *Connecticut v. Kelly*, 2009 WL 323481 (Super. Ct. 2009).

32. *Arizona v. Roscoe*, 145 Ariz. 212, 700 P.2d 1312 (1984) (different alert responses detracted from reliability of handler's interpretations). See *U.S. v. Clarkson*, 551 F.3d 1196 (10th Cir. 2009), on remand, 2009 WL 1651043 (D.Utah 2009) (narcotics detection dog's alert could not support probable cause for search of vehicle when dog's alerts varied outside and inside the car and a video of the traffic stop was inconsistent with the handler's description of the dog's alerts; a defense expert opined that the handler may have cued the dog to alert in any case; the defense expert doubted the dog was adequately trained given that the handler was considering changing the dog's alert from a passive alert to an active alert).

33. *California v. White*, 2009 WL 3111677 (Ct. App. 2009).

34. *U.S. v. McNiece*, 558 F.Supp. 612 (E.D.N.Y 1983).

35. Kaldenbach (1998), 130 (evidence corroborated by scent lineups includes statements made by the defendant to others indicating knowledge of the crime because facts in the statements had not been made public). See LJN AO03222 Court of Appeals—Hertogenbosch (February 9. 2004), summarized by Broeders (2006), 159 (knife with suspect's scent dropped as evidence in retrial after DNA evidence obtained).

36. Wojcikiewicz (2000). See also Oliver et al. (2006).

37. Frijters and Boksem (2004) (describing scent lineups as being almost like Russian roulette). Frijters has argued that the methodology of scent lineups used in Holland is sufficiently defective that they should no longer be used. Frijters (2006).

38. *Winfrey v. Texas*, 291 S.W.3d 68 (Ct. App. 2009), rev'd 323 S.W.3d 875 (Ct. Crim. App. 2010) (female suspect may have picked up defendant's scent through significant physical contact with him). The conviction was reversed by the Texas Court of Criminal Appeals, which noted that no eyewitnesses put the defendant at the crime scene, the state was unable to match the defendant to a fingerprint and footprints found at the crime scene, and the defendant did not match the DNA profile obtained from the crime scene.

The court said the defendant's referring to himself as the number one suspect when he was not and the testimony of a cellmate to whom the defendant told things he had heard about the crime without admitting any involvement in it was "legally insufficient to support a conviction of murder beyond a reasonable doubt." The court cited other state courts that had held that dog-scent evidence was insufficient, standing alone, to support a conviction, and cited Taslitz (42 Hastings Law Journal 15 (1990)) in holding that scent-discrimination lineups were to be regarded as "separate and distinct from dog-scent tracking evidence." The court said that the scent lineup evidence could raise a "strong suspicion" of the defendant's guilt but could not convict him. A judgment of acquittal was entered.

39. *U.S. v. Gates*, 680 F.2d 1117 (6th Cir. 1982). See also *Michigan v. Giles*, 2008 WL 2436529 (Ct. App. 2008) (scent matching evidence was described as "tracking dog" evidence that jury was cautioned had "little value as proof").
40. *U.S. v. McNiece*, 558 F.Supp. 612, 616–17 (E.D.N.Y. 1983) (emphasis added).
41. See, for example, *North Carolina v. Spivey*, 151 N.C. 676, 65 S.E. 995 (1909); *Missouri v. Rasco*, 239 Mo. 535, 144 S.W. 449 (1912); *Ohio v. DeWitt*, 2007 WL 1934335 (Ct. App. 2007).
42. *U.S. v. McNiece*, 558 F.Supp. at 614, citing Davis (1974); Hafez (1969), at 380–381; Kalmus (1955).
43. *U.S. v. McNiece*, 558 F.Supp. 612 (E.D.N.Y. 1983).
44. *Arizona v. Roscoe*, 145 Ariz. 212, 700 P.2d 1312 (1984) ("We hold, therefore, that dog tracking or identification evidence is admissible in Arizona upon a proper foundational showing that the breeding, training, performance and handling of the particular dog warrants that the results obtained from use of the dog are reliable").
45. *Ramos v. Florida*, 496 So.2d 121 (1986).
46. *U.S. v. Outlaw*, 134 F.Supp.2d 807 (W.D. Tex 2001). See also *U.S. v. Berrelleza*, 90 Fed.Appx. 361, 365 (10th Cir. 2004) (relying on *U.S. v. Outlaw*); *U.S. v. Morales*, 489 F.Supp.2d 1250 (D.N.M. 2007) (drug dog jumped in open window of vehicle without assistance of agents and alerted, giving agents probable cause to search vehicle).
47. See also *Brooks v. Colorado*, 975 P.2d 1105 (1999) (Supreme Court of Colorado admitted dog tracking evidence as expert testimony not subject to *Daubert* or *Frye* scientific valuation factors). See *Michigan v. Giles*, 2008 WL 2436529 (Mich.App. 2008) (Michigan appellate court was "not persuaded" that scent lineup evidence "was of such a 'scientific' nature as to necessitate application of *Daubert*"; defendant had not challenged methods and procedures used by handler at trial).
48. *Risher v. Texas*, 227 S.W.3d 133 (Ct. App. 2006); see *Connecticut v. Kelly*, 2009 WL 323481 (Conn. Super. 2009) (agreeing with "widespread belief that dog tracking evidence can be deemed reliable without a *Frye* or *Daubert* inquiry"; the court generally contrasted canine olfaction with the type of expertise held by dog handlers and did not consider that other scientific aspects might be found in tracking evidence beyond olfaction; court also found that a scientific inquiry was "not required because it would be a superfluous confirmation of that which is already known").
49. *Risher v. Texas*, 227 S.W.3d 133 (Ct. App. 2006).
50. *Nenno v. Texas*, 970 S.W.2d 549 (Ct. Crim. App. 1998).
51. *Martinez v. Texas*, 2006 WL 3720136 (Ct. App. 2006).
52. Taslitz (1990). Excessive faith in the abilities of dogs may make acceptance of bloodhound testimony dangerous for the defendant, but there have been times where excessive doubt may have negated valid evidence. One police dog expert described a murder where press suspicions of a dog's abilities may have influenced both public and judicial opinion. Kaldenbach (1998), at 132–139.
53. Wojcikiewicz (1999).
54. Tomaszewski and Girdwoyn (2006), 192 and 195, n. 4, citing AD5148 No. 01327/01 (November 21, 2001); AE8856, No. 01707/01 (November 5, 2002) (scent recovered from firearms matched to scent collected from suspect); AF5388, No. 01890/02 (March 25, 2003) (dog alerted to samples of suspect in two lineups).
55. Tomaszewski and Girdwoyn (2006), 192 and 195, n. 5.
56. Ibid., 192 and 195, ns. 9, 10.
57. Ibid., 192 and 195, n. 11, citing 05.11.1999 Supreme Court sentence V KKN 440/99 OSNKW 1999/11-12/76 (November 5, 1999); II KKN 467/99 LEX No. 53895 (May 7, 2002).
58. Ibid., 192 and 195, n. 12, citing IV KKN 269/99 LEX No. 51139 (January 12, 2000).
59. Ibid., 192 and 195, n. 13, 14.
60. Ibid., 192 and 195, n. 16, citing SN III KKN 333/98 LEX No. 52013 (February 5, 2001).
61. Ibid., 192 and 195, n. 17, citing 2002.05.29 sentence of Court of Appeal II Aka 94/02 KZS 2002/9/14 Cracow (September 14, 2002); SN V KKN 283/01 LEX No. 56843 (October 21, 2002).
62. The author has modified the translation reproduced by Tomaszewski and Girdwoyn (2006), 192.
63. Wojcikiewicz (1999). For European academic legal perspectives also doubting scent lineups as valid evidence, see Jaworski (1999); Widacki (1999, 2000); Frijters (2006); and Frijters and Boksem (2004, 2006).

7 Scent Lineups in Criminal Investigations and Prosecutions

John J. Ensminger and Tadeusz Jezierski

Scent lineups have been used in European countries since the beginning of the 20th century and are a common part of police practice in the Netherlands, Poland, Germany, Russia, and other Eastern European countries. In the United States, scent lineups as formal procedures have been used by some law enforcement agencies since the 1970s,[1] but U.S. courts have largely seen scent lineups as an extension of tracking cases, and lineups probably began in the United States from station identifications that occurred after a tracking dog's field assignment was completed. Although dogs in modern scent lineups may be "scented to" an item from a crime scene in the same way as tracking and trailing dogs are scented before they begin following a path, scent identification dogs do not follow footsteps or a plume, but rather are presented with (usually) five to seven objects that individuals including a suspect have handled and must choose the object that has a similar scent on it, or some of the same components to the scent, as the item taken from the crime scene.

Scent lineups are a significant forensic and evidentiary tool, though they are sometimes dismissed as "junk science."[2] With the resources available to many U.S. law enforcement agencies, it is arguable that lineups should remain as part of the investigative process as the procedures used will not assure sufficiently low error rates for a positive identification to be admitted as evidence in a criminal prosecution. The procedures that would make scent lineup evidence admissible are sufficiently rare in the United States that the Federal Bureau of Investigation (FBI) may be one of the few agencies with facilities adequate to produce such evidence. Many state and local police departments are struggling against budget cuts and can only afford one or two canine teams, and the dogs must be generalists, trained to apprehend fleeing suspects and detect narcotics, and perhaps to fulfill other police dog functions.[3] Some law enforcement agencies depend on independent contractors, but few of these have dedicated scent identification dogs. Few U.S. handlers have received the level of training that might assure that their results could withstand a rigorous scrutiny by the experts in this area and perhaps none have facilities adequate to conduct rigorous testing. In contrast, by the late 1990s Poland had as many as 117 certified police scent dogs, performing from 1,600 to 1,800 scent procedures annually. Training procedures are rigorous and forensic lineups are carefully controlled.[4]

BEGINNING OF FORMAL IDENTIFICATION PROCEDURES

Scent identification has some similarity to tracking and trailing, but in those activities the animal follows the path an individual took going to or from a crime scene, the path itself continually reinforcing the odor the dog began with.[5] This may lead to identification of a suspect if the dog actually comes to the individual it has been following and alerts to that individual, but quite often the trail will end at the door of a building the suspect went into or at a place on a road where the suspect entered a vehicle and drove away. In formal scent identifications, the dog is in a confined area, a room or an open space, and deals only in scents, not generally in tracks left on a surface (except sometimes in station identifications and perhaps in live lineups).

It was not in the United States that scent lineups were first severed from tracking as separate procedures, but in Europe. Procedures with elements of the modern scent identification lineup began to be used in the Netherlands and Germany in the early 1900s. The first formal scent lineup, according to a Dutch police officer, may date from 1903:

> The first person to demonstrate suspect discrimination in practical police work was inspector Bussenius from Braunsweich, Germany, in 1903. At the time, he was a policeman/dog handler working with his dog Harras von der Polizei on a murder case. He worked with pebbles—six people were asked to hold pebbles in their hand. One of the six was Duwe von Hagenhof, who was suspected of murdering a maid. The six people were asked to put their stones on the ground. The dog was given the knife found at the scene to smell, then searched and picked out the stone held by Duwe. He confessed after that.[6]

Stones were used in an early experiment on scent identification. Six people standing near each other threw stones onto a gravel surface. A dog was allowed to smell one of their hands and directed to find that person's stone. The dog brought back the right stone.[7]

An early case from the Netherlands concerned a court official who began to receive anonymous letters from someone who must have hated him. The police told him to collect objects from neighbors and other suspects. A German shepherd trained in tracking was brought to the town and smelled the obscene letter before being set loose to sniff the objects that had been collected. The dog retrieved a hat belonging to a neighbor of the court official. She was convicted, despite her persistent denials.[8] An unusual case from the Netherlands involved distinguishing manure from different locations, connecting manure from the barn where the crime was committed to manure found on the shoe of one of the perpetrators. This was thus not a match of the scent of the individual.[9]

In the 1980s, the East German secret police, the Stasi, obtained large numbers of scent samples of political suspects on dust cloths and stored them in jam jars, occasionally attempting to use scent matching to identify people involved in the printing and distribution of anti-government pamphlets. People involved in printing and distributing such pamphlets had become cautious and seldom left fingerprints. The Stasi's efforts to use police dogs for "smell traces comparison" were largely unsuccessful but most records were destroyed or made unavailable.[10]

SCENT LINEUPS OF PEOPLE

Older cases, following tracking experience or visual lineups of suspects before an eyewitness, allowed the dog to choose from a line of individuals, one of whom was generally a suspect while the others were foils. More recently, perhaps partially in response to research and protocols in European and FBI scent lineups, dogs have usually had to choose between a number of similar or identical objects, one of which was scented by a suspect while the others were scented by foils (a procedure sometimes referred to as "scent matching").

In a 1923 Iowa case, a taxi driver arrived home and an explosion of dynamite at the side door of his house injured him so badly that he soon died. The police cordoned off the area and kept car lights on it to avoid anyone leaving additional footprints or handling objects. It appeared that the defendant had attempted to buy explosive materials in the days before the murder, and that prior to that he had begun an affair with the victim's wife. About 2 P.M. the next day, two bloodhounds were taken to the end of the wires that led from the step under which the explosive device had been placed to a field where someone had apparently laid in wait for the victim. They took a scent. The circumstances at the jail are described in more detail in the handler's own words:

> I took my dogs into the sheriff's office and the sheriff says, "We will have the men walk by the dogs," and he says, "I want you to see if you can pick the man that we have and see if we have the right man

or not if the dogs know." I did not know who the man was. He was a perfect stranger to me, and I didn't know what kind of a looking man he was. There was quite a few fellows came in the sheriff's office and came by and the dogs stood at leisure right side of me. I didn't have no strings on them or nothing. There was probably five or six men went by and then there was three men came in and started by. When they came up by us both dogs turned and begun to kind of swing their heads and went over to this one man. They smelled of him, and he kind of held his hands up like this. One dog was smelling of his shoes, and the other kind of smelling around here on him.

The Iowa Supreme Court did not admit the evidence, joining those states that rejected bloodhound testimony.[11] This was one of the earliest U.S. cases that could be called a scent lineup though it was unusual in that the suspect and the foils walked past the dog rather than the dog encountering these persons in a structured lineup.

Courts have seldom made much of a distinction between such human lineups and scent matching or object lineups, but in one Sixth Circuit decision a concurring judge noted that the handler had described the dog's training as involving scent lineups of objects, but the lineup admitted in evidence in the case involved the actual suspect and an unstated number of human foils. Although finding this a defect, the judge nevertheless felt there was enough other evidence for the conviction to stand.[12]

In a Maryland case from 1982,[13] a tracking dog was scented on a cap that the perpetrator wore during a rape that was left at the crime scene. The dog tracked to a road and then lost the trail where tire tracks were found. Three hours later, the dog was scented on the cap again and placed across from a line of police officers standing about approximately 5 feet 7 inches tall and of stocky build, but the races of the foils were not stated, though the dog was familiar with all of them. The court found this familiarity with the foils irrelevant but did not remark on the fact that the lineup was obviously not blind. The dog alerted to the defendant in two lineups, which seem only to have differed in the configuration of the suspect and the foils. The court stated:

> We have also surveyed to some extent the general literature concerning tracking dogs and find no indication that a trained and reliable tracking dog will signal a find because the person found is the only one unfamiliar to the dog from among a group of persons. To the contrary, so far as we can determine from the literature, the purpose of training a tracking dog is to keep it focused on the given scent and undistracted by other scents.

Thus, the purpose of training was determined to be the result produced. The court noted that tracking involves a sort of lineup whenever the dog tracks over an area traversed by one or more human beings other than the subject.

In *Martinez v. Texas*[14] and *Risher v. Texas*,[15] both involving the same crime and decided in 2006, the codefendants led police on a high-speed chase during which they threw cocaine bricks out of the car. The bricks were recovered and scent was taken by putting gauze pads beside them in an evidence bag. The defense objected to the introduction of the lineup evidence because the lineup was not blind (i.e., the handler knew who the defendant was in each lineup), the same officers participated as foils in both lineups, and the defendants were handcuffed during the lineups while the officers were not (which would have made it obvious who was the suspect even if the handler had not been told). Also, Risher was African American and was thus easily distinguishable in a lineup of five Caucasian officers. The court in *Martinez*, however, found that enough precautions had been taken to legitimate the lineup:

> Officer Oglesby took affirmative steps to administer the scent lineup objectively by: (1) keeping the officers that handled the cocaine out of the lineup; (2) having two scent lineups, one for the appellant and one for the co-defendant; (3) having the officers stand in a similar fashion as the appellant, with their hands behind their back; and (4) repositioning the officers and the lineup location between each lineup. Moreover, Officer Oglesby testified he used both the manual from the National Police Bloodhound Association and his training with other dog handlers in his practice of scent identification.

The appellate court determined that the defendant had failed to demonstrate that the trial court erred in admitting the dog scent lineup testimony. The court in *Risher* concluded that scientific standards for such a procedure were not the same as might be required of the "hard sciences."[16]

Suspect lineups have long been disapproved of in Europe. In 1936, one classic of dog research stated:

> It is still more dangerous to let a dog choose a person out of a row of people on the score of the odour of an object offered to the dog. Even if the trainer knows nothing about the test, and has himself no suspicion of anybody, there still remains the possibility, by no means a light one, that the dog may respond to the faintest movement of one of those persons.[17]

Scent lineups with real people also have the disadvantage of allowing the dog to interact with the subjects, making it difficult to interpret a dog's reactions. Common defects found in human lineups include using other police officers familiar to the handler and the dog as foils,[18] having the defendant handcuffed during the lineup,[19] and having foils all of a different race from the suspect in the lineup.[20]

CUEING

A particular problem with any situation where a dog may alert, which may occur in tracking or in a lineup, concerns the handler cueing the dog to identify a suspect or a scent as that of the perpetrator.[21] This phenomenon can be unconscious and is sometimes called the *Clever Hans effect*, a term coming from a horse that tapped a hoof to answer mathematical questions.[22] This effect is particularly likely to emerge where there is a strong and long-lasting emotional bond between the dog and the handler.[23]

SCENT MATCHES

In a scent match, a dog is scented on an object thought to have been touched by the perpetrator, then given a choice of objects, such as scent pads, stones, or tubes, one of which is scented by the suspect and the others scented by foils. A scent match is sometimes distinguished from a scent lineup but is generally categorized as a type of scent lineup.[24] Dogs are sometimes scented to an object while at the crime scene.[25]

Scent lineups of objects, just as with scent lineups of humans, can involve scenting the dog to a wide range of items, including an electrical cord used to tie up a victim,[26] and even legal documents the suspect may not have handled for a considerable time.[27] Scent pads are sometimes rubbed against objects touched by the perpetrator at a crime scene to provide scent for a lineup.[28] Shell casings can be used to place scent on gauze pads through scent transfer units, as described in a previous chapter.[29] Seats and steering wheels of vehicles have also provided scent,[30] sometimes through use of scent transfer units.[31]

A lineup may include an object found at the crime scene or taken from the victim and similar objects, such as clothing,[32] towels,[33] sheets,[34] tools,[35] the butt of a marijuana cigarette,[36] that the perpetrator is assumed to have contacted.[37] In some cases, the lineup may be used to determine if the victim contacted an object. Vehicles have been lineup objects.[38] A Virginia case involved scenting a dog to a towel the victim had likely touched, to which the dog alerted. This was taken as evidence that the victim had been transported in the suspect's car.[39] Bicycles have also been lineup objects.[40]

Lineup objects should be as similar as possible. A lineup is suspect if only the target object has blood, which may make the item attractive to the dog.[41] A lineup of sheets where one was from the victim and four were from prisoners should have also been questioned based on the timing of collection of the foils and the means by which they were selected.[42] One case involving a lineup of scent pads included one obtained by swabbing the arms of suspects. Foils consisted of scent pads obtained from individuals of the same ethnic background, but these samples appeared to be part of the handler's inventory for conducting scent lineups and there was no showing that they had been obtained in the same manner as the pads from the suspects or that scent was taken at the same time as the pad from the suspect.[43]

Time has sometimes been considered by courts in analyzing scent-matching lineups. A conviction involving a scent lineup occurring at least 3 months after the crime was reversed, though primarily based on the exclusion of the testimony of a defense expert.[44] Results of an object lineup occurring 21 months after a burglary were admitted, with the possible staleness of the evidence going only to its weight, not its admissibility.[45]

SCENT-MATCHING MATERIALS

When identical items are put in a lineup, distinguished only by having been handled by different people, police practice varies from country to country as to which material is best for such a test. This also has been the subject of research. One study found that in the particular testing system used, dogs were more accurate at matching scents to scents on steel tubes than to scents of cloths in jars, with 85% accuracy in the former and 80% accuracy in the latter.[46] Also, training dogs using steel tubes took less time than using glass jars. The researchers noted that some dogs clearly had more aptitude for this kind of work than others. They thought it likely that with appropriate training, many breeds of dogs selected for tracking and retrieval could achieve high and dependable success rates.

> However, variations do occur in the individual aptitude of dogs and even a good dog may sometimes perform badly, so it is essential to subject each dog to several trials when a suspect is being identified. If this is done, selected dogs should provide a valuable resource in criminal investigation and security operations.[47]

U.S. courts have too readily accepted scent lineups in which dogs performed only one trial, and controls are seldom mentioned and not likely performed very often. For a dog alerting in a scientific scent lineup procedure, see Figure 7.1.

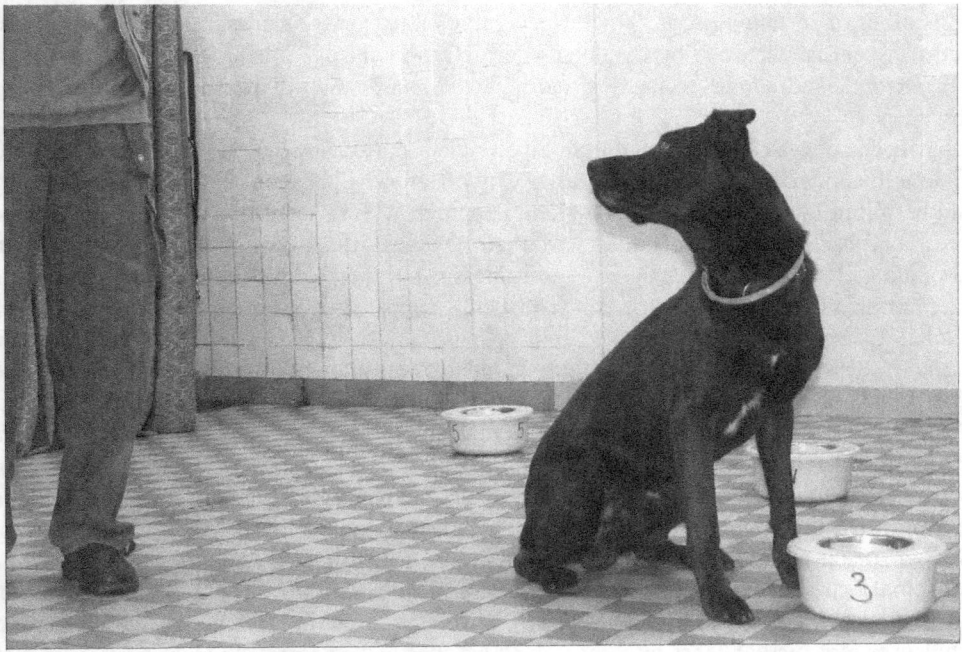

FIGURE 7.1 Dog alerting in scent lineup. This dog at the Polish Academy of Sciences was trained to alert by sitting before the indicated sample and looking at the handler. (Courtesy of Tadeusz Jezierski.)

SELECTING FOILS

In a lineup, a dog has to select from a row of scent samples, usually obtained from different people. The suspect is usually but not always one of the samples, but the others are foils, different people often with characteristics similar to those of the suspect to the extent such characteristics can be identified. One Dutch detective described how money that had been taken from a victim in a robbery had to be used to identify the suspect. Since the woman had touched the money, other women were used to scent tubes for the lineup. It was learned the woman was menstruating, so an officer went through the halls of the headquarters announcing that he needed such a person. A volunteer came forward.[48]

NUMBER OF STATIONS IN A LINEUP

The number of stations in a lineup varies in both research and police practice, generally being from five to seven. The higher number of stations and the lower number of targets in the lineup, the lower the probability that a dog will indicate correctly by chance. In the canine identification procedure applied by Polish police, the most typical lineup has five stations of which one is the target station.[49] In the Netherlands, police usually use two parallel scent lineups of six or seven stations.[50] It is important that the dog sniff all stations in the lineup since omitting some stations increases the probability that the sample may have been indicated correctly only by chance.[51]

SCENT ATTRACTIVENESS

Results of a lineup may be less accurate if dogs sometimes select matching items because of some attraction to an odor rather than because of an actual match to the scenting item. Schoon and de Bruin found that dogs were much more often correct when alerting to a "suspect" they knew than one not known to them.[52] This may not only be familiarity, however. The scent of particular persons may be attractive to particular dogs, which means that dogs may tend to make false-positive identifications of certain persons, which is a significant reason for using decoys in control trials. If a control's scent is alerted to by the dogs incorrectly in controls, it can be assumed that this particular person is "attractive" to the dog and reliable identification in an evidential lineup becomes impossible.

It has been suggested that a dog might be attracted to a scent because it is different from other odors in a lineup, and that this is one reason why differences between scent providers for a lineup should be minimized. To avoid this problem, people providing scent should be of the same sex,[53] similar racial background, and should wash their hands with non-perfumed soap prior to scenting tubes or cloths.[54] The phenomenon of attractiveness is not merely an issue with forensic scent lineups; its has also been observed in a study of scent lineups in which dogs were trained to identify individual tigers from scat.[55]

Attractiveness has been measured by the number of false alerts toward decoys in experimental lineups. In a study using scent of 186 persons, only 19.3% of persons examined had a "non-attractive" scent to the dogs (0% of false alerts). The majority of persons (76.3%) had a scent that was of low attractiveness to the dogs (>0% to 25%) of false alerts) and only 1.1% of persons were of higher attractiveness to the dogs (50% to 75% of false alerts).[56] It is not clear that this attraction will always be apparent during the control trials.[57] Thus, attractiveness could sometimes be difficult to distinguish from an alert that is false for other reasons.

What makes the scent of a person more attractive to the dogs is not clear, although one researcher has argued that the "scent attractiveness" may be related to the interference of the scent memory, which causes a particular scent to be perceived by dogs as "pleasant."[58] Odor samples were taken from the vulva of a female dog during heat, placed in one stand in the lineup amid human scents, did not result in false alerts toward this scent, but the attractiveness of the odor was demonstrated by a much longer sniffing duration.[59] Curiously, the longer a dog sniffs, research has indicated that the less likely it is to give a correct response. This could mean that when a dog searches too long, it could forget the scent it was supposed to match.[60]

There is recent evidence that dogs more easily distinguish women than men. Analysis of 3,675 trials with lineups consisting of exclusively male scents (2,523 trials) or exclusively female scents (1,152 trials) showed that dogs made significantly more correct choices (66.8%) when they had to find a matching female scent samples than when they had to find matching male scent samples (63.4%). Additionally, the dogs made nonsignificantly fewer false alarms toward female scents than toward male scents, and significantly fewer misses in relation to female scents.[61] This may indicate that scent lineups will be more reliable when the target scent is female.

SCIENTIFICALLY CONDUCTED SCENT LINEUPS

The official protocol in the Netherlands used by trained dogs is a five-step procedure depicted in Figure 7.2.[62] Data from dogs trained under this regimen, along with other dogs trained in similar regimens indicated that dogs identified the correct person who touched an object between 60% and 90% of the time. Dogs used for the statistics alerted to no tube between 9% and 35% of the time. This was a false negative: a correct choice could have been made but in fact no choice was made.

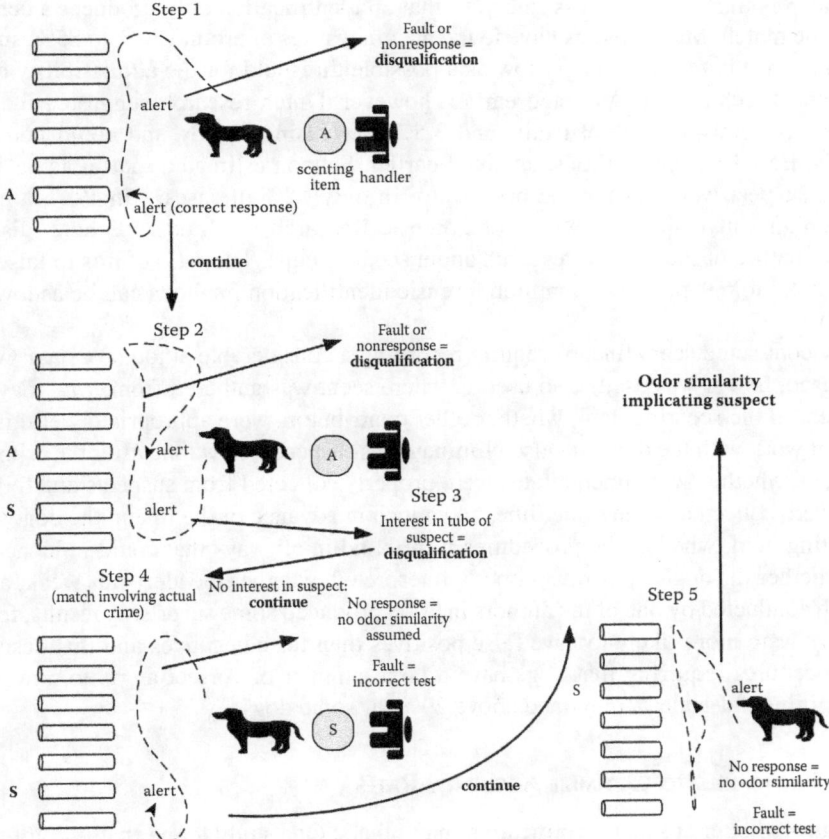

FIGURE 7.2 Dutch protocol for scent identification lineups since 1997. (Adapted from Schoon, G.A.A., Scent Identification Line-Ups Using Trained Dogs in the Netherlands, *Problems in Forensic Sciences, 47,* 175–183, 2001.)

Finally, dogs pointed to foils between 1% and 5% of the time. This was a false positive: a correct choice could have been made but an incorrect choice was made.

Similarly, using data from the same sources, where the scenting item was not touched by anyone who touched a lineup tube, but one of the lineup tubes was touched by a suspect, dogs identified the suspect between 0.5% and 4% of the time, but chose no one between 75% and 97% of the time. The latter was the correct response. However, dogs alerted to a foil between 2.5% and 20% of the time. This also was incorrect.[63]

In analyzing data from actual cases, Schoon noted that only 3.5% of dogs were disqualified in control trials in the protocol, meaning that certified dogs alerted correctly in 96.5% in control trials.[64] When asked to compare scent samples from crime scenes with scent samples of suspects and foils, the dogs alerted in 43% of cases. Schoon found that false negatives occurred in about 6.8% of these actual results, and thereby concluded that false positives must have occurred with 1.1% of the alerts. She concluded that scent lineups are now "a useful tool in criminal investigation and evidence collection."[65] Schoon and Haak argued that such error rates are sufficiently low that canine scent identification can be considered as more accurate than a number of widely received evidentiary techniques, including paint analysis, glass analysis, fiber analysis, and hair analysis (not DNA).[66]

Success Rates of Scent Lineup Procedures

A scent lineup is like an eyewitness lineup in that an identification only produces a certain likelihood of a true match. Many studies have found accuracy rates of around 80% to 85%, substantially better than chance but a disturbingly low as a possible threshold for the admissibility of evidence from a forensic technique.[67] As noted earlier, however, Dutch research suggested that 96.5% of dogs alerted correctly in control trials, and 3.5% alerted incorrectly and could not be used in actual trials. Based on probabilities, as noted earlier, Schoon estimated that in actual trials dogs alerted to a suspect who was not the perpetrator in only 1.1% of cases.[68] In 1999, a professor at the Jagiellonian University & Institute of Forensic Research in Krakow, Poland, discussed the inconclusive nature of the limited research about scent lineups. The ratio of hits to false alerts has ranged from 4.3 to 6.9, but other common forensic identification methods can be as low as 3 or as high as 160.[69]

Properly conducted scent lineups require recording a considerable amount of data: what equipment was used, how it was used, who used it, where scent was gathered from, who may have contributed scent to the scenting item, whether other contributors were appropriately eliminated from further scent work with the dog (and also eliminated as suspects), how long after the crime the scent was collected, whether scent lineup items were properly collected from suspects and foils, whether the scents were collected at the same time, how much in advance of the lineup the dog was scented to the scenting item, whether the procedures were blind in all ways that could influence the dog's decision, whether the dog's alert was properly interpreted, whether the alert was weak, and so on.

Research conducted by one of the authors in 2008 produced some surprising results, for one finding that dogs were more likely to have false positives than false negatives and that despite precise training procedures requiring that dogs have a large number of correct alerts to move to further stages of training, false alerts remained above 20% for some dogs.[70]

Designing Protocols to Optimize Accuracy Rates

Certain dogs are better at scent identification than others. One study found that in 4,100 trials with six dogs, the best dog performed correctly 72.7% of the time, whereas the worst was correct in only 32.1% of the trials. The percentage of false alerts for the best dog was 15.6% and for the worst 52.8%.[71] Dutch research reached similar results with the best dog giving 65% correct indications and the worst 26%, the best dog having 22% false alerts and the worst 59%.[72]

To reach a sufficient level of forensic reliability to justify the admission of scent lineup evidence in criminal prosecutions, the effort must be to conduct lineups in such a way as to keep errors of individual dogs to a minimum. One way is to provide for trials that eliminate dogs that are not working well on a particular day and to check for the possibility of attractiveness to a particular scent. Another is to increase the number of dogs. Both approaches have been used, often in conjunction, and can be shown to reduce error rates to a level to bring scent lineup evidence within the accuracy rates of some other accepted forensic techniques used as evidence.[73]

COMPARISON WITH VISUAL LINEUPS

False identification of innocent suspects (not foils) in eyewitness lineups may be the most frequent cause of wrongful convictions in the United States.[74] An analysis of actual police lineups in the Greater London area in 1992 found that witnesses picked foils almost 20% of the time. Foils were selected by the police and known not to be involved in the crimes under investigation, but the results also mean that witnesses could have misidentified suspects who were not involved as the perpetrators.[75] All in all, scent lineups are as accurate as visual lineups.[76]

FBI USE OF DUTCH PROCEDURES

The U.S. Federal Bureau of Investigation has adapted Dutch training methods and protocols. The FBI procedures include the following:

1. Evidence that can hold a scent is collected from the crime scene. This could be a piece of clothing or even a shotgun shell. Gloves are used at the crime scene in an effort to prevent adding scent to an object. The evidence is placed in a sterilized glass jar or in a heat-sealed, tamper-proof bag. The evidence is stored under chain-of-custody guidelines.
2. Six 5-inch steel pipes are boiled in water or cleaned in a pressurized steam-cleaning machine, then placed in separate glass containers, each with a different colored lid. Besides the suspect, five other individuals, ideally of the same race and sex as the suspect are selected. All participants, including the suspect, wash their hands with a neutral soap in an effort to eliminate any foreign odor.[77] Each member of the lineup stands behind a glass jar, which officers have placed on the floor in the lineup room. Each person opens the jar in front of him, takes out the steel pipe, and holds it for 5 minutes. Then he places the pipe back in the container. The police personnel retrieve the pipes and place them on the floor in the lineup room, about 20 inches apart. The handler of each pipe is carefully recorded. The dog enters the room with its handler after everything but the pipes is removed.
3. An investigator brings the evidence from the crime scene into the room and the handler holds it with forceps before the dog's nose. The handler then leaves the room. The dog sniffs the pipes. It either picks up the one that matches the crime scene evidence or sits next to this pipe and barks.
4. As a control, agents sometimes use a second set of pipes that does not contain a pipe handled by the suspect. In this lineup, the dog should not pick up or identify any of the pipes.[78]

Sometimes additional controls are added, such as requiring the dog to overlook familiar smells when selecting from a lineup.[79]

Three authors, one of whom is with the FBI, described a number of best practices for scent identification procedures. They state the importance of negative controls:

Periodically throughout an investigation, blind-negative controls should be introduced to the dog-handler team. This negative control should contain a human scent that is not present at the location being checked. The inclusion of a negative control offers a measure of surety that the dog is not providing a false-positive alert. Failure to properly respond to a negative control during an investigation should preclude the dog-handler team from conducting any further work until training and blind-proficiency testing demonstrate the dog's renewed reliability to differentiate between positive and negative trails.

The authors also state that positive responses should be verified by at least one other canine team.[80] All verifications should be blind. A second scent article is recommended, if available. The chain of custody of scent evidence must be maintained, and if used with multiple dogs, each dog should be listed on the chain-of-custody form. Evidence storage documentation must also be maintained.[81]

GUIDELINES OF PROFESSIONAL ORGANIZATIONS

The Scientific Working Group on Dog and Orthogonal Detector Guidelines (SWGDOG) has issued procedures for scent identification lineups, specifying that maintenance training should involve at least 16 hours a month.[82] Training records are to include the name of the handler and the dog, the names of those assisting, and the time, date, location, and environmental conditions. The records should also specify if an exercise was nonblind or blind, and who was blind in each trial. Names or descriptions of individuals contributing scents to the lineup are to be recorded. The article used for prescenting is to be described, how it was stored, and the duration of contact with the individual providing the scent. Results are to be described, along with any deficiencies or corrective measures implemented.

SWGDOG provides detailed procedures for assessing canine teams on odor recognition and other skills, and recommends standards for certification and documentation procedures. Certification is valid for 1 year and is dependent on the dog's passing a comprehensive assessment, somewhat more complicated than the odor recognition assessment described earlier. A double-blind assessment may also be required in which no one in the room with the dog during the lineup procedure may know where the target sample is located. Certification records include the certifying authority, the names of the individuals awarding certification, and a description of the certification tests. Digital records are preferred in general. Records are presumed to be discoverable by court proceedings and may be evidence of the team's reliability.

NOTES

1. The first cases specifically conducted as lineups date from the early 1980s. See *Epperly v. Virginia*, 224 Va. 214, 294 S.E.2d 882 (1982).
2. See Dog Scent Lineups: A Junk Science Injustice, report of the Innocence Project of Texas (September 21, 2009) (posted at www.innocenceprojectoftexas.org/pdf/junk-science-2009.pdf) (stating that three men suspected in part by one handler's testimony have been exonerated); Scent Lineups and Unvalidated Science, *Innocence Blog* (June 30, 2009).
3. See *U.S. v. Lambert*, 834 F.Supp. 1318 (D.Kan. 1993) ("multi-purpose dog" certified in obedience, agility, narcotics detection, explosives detection, cadaver detection, article search, area search, tracking, building search, and aggression control); *Byrom v. Mississippi*, 863 So.2d 836 (2003) (dog trained in narcotics, tracking, and apprehension); *Tariq-Madyun v. Alabama*, 2010 WL 2160290 (Ct. Crim. App. 2010) (handler described his canine partner as a "dual purpose canine" that worked as a narcotics detector but also worked as a tracker and performed building searches, area searches, and article searches; dog led to shirt that was found to contain DNA of suspect). Some functions merge in specific cases. See *Illinois v. Griffin*, 48 Ill.App.2d 148, 198 N.E.2d 115 (Ct. App. 1964) (dog released to apprehend suspect in building followed scent to suspect); *Michigan v. Laidlaw*, 169 Mich.App. 84, 425 N.W.2d 738 (Ct. App. 1988) (dog following location scent was put in car after suspect was sighted and taken to that location, where he caught up with suspect; handler interpreted dog's "signs" as indicating he had found the source of the scent he had previously been following); *Illinois v. Holmes*, 397 Ill.App.3d 737, 922 N.E.2d 1179, 337 Ill.Dec. 602 (Ct. App. 2010) (dog brought to do article search finds drugs; dog was trained in both tracking and narcotics detection). Cross-training is not always desirable. The National Narcotic Detector Dog Association will not dual certify in narcotics and explosives, for instance. NNDDA Narcotic Detection Standards and Explosive Detection Certification (www.nndda.org/docman/cat_view/86-training-a-certification-documents).

4. Jezierski (2010); Ensminger, Jezierski, and McCulloch (2010).
5. Curran et al. (2010a); Honhon (1967).
6. Kaldenbach (1998), 89.
7. Buytendijk (1936), 97–98.
8. Schoon and Haak (2002), 20. For the early history of scent identification, see also Schoon and Massop (1995).
9. Schoon and Haak (2002), 27.
10. See Macrakis (2008), 281 (chapter on "Smell Science").
11. *Iowa v. Grba*, 196 Iowa 241, 194 N.W. 250 (1923).
12. *U.S. v. Gates*, 680 F.2d 1117 (6th Cir. 1982) (concurrence of Judge Cornelia Kennedy).
13. *Roberts v. Maryland*, 53 Md.App. 257, 452 A.2d 1271 (Ct. Spec. App. 1982), aff'd, 298 Md. 261, 469 A.2d 442 (Ct. App. 1983).
14. *Martinez v. Texas*, 2006 WL 3720136 (Ct. App. 2006).
15. *Risher v. Texas*, 227 S.W.3d 133 (Ct. App. 2006).
16. See also *California v. Schoppe-Rico*, 140 Cal.App.4th 1370 (Ct. App. 2006) (no final determination on admissibility of lineup of defendant and "three randomly selected deputy sheriffs" needed to be made because jury's verdict would not likely have been different in any case).
17. Buytendijk (1936), 100.
18. *Roberts v. Maryland*, 53 Md.App. 257, 452 A.2d 1271 (Ct. Spec. App. 1982), aff'd, 298 Md. 261, 469 A.2d 442 (Ct. App. 1983).
19. *Martinez v. Texas*, 2006 WL 3720136 (Ct. App. 2006).
20. *Risher v. Texas*, 227 S.W.3d 133 (Ct. App. 2006).
21. Cueing has also been suggested by defense experts in various times of canine cases. See *South Dakota v. Nguyen*, 726 N.W.2d 871 (2007) (expert testified that repeated use of German word "gift" while leading narcotics detection dog around vehicle suggested cueing).
22. See Miklosi et al. (2005). In an experiment where handlers were to follow trails with dogs scented to car bomb fragments, two dogs alerted to decoys. Reviews of videotapes convinced researchers that this was due to handler error in that the handlers had cued the dogs to alert to the wrong person. From the description of the methodology, the handlers were certainly not supposed to cue the dogs and presumably did so unconsciously. Curran et al. (2010). If this can happen in a controlled research environment, where handlers know they are being videotaped, the ease with which such cueing can happen indicates how risky field identifications may be.
23. Gawkowski (2000).
24. A somewhat different procedure, sometimes called a reverse and check, involves scenting the dog to the suspect and then matching this scent to *corpus delicti* placed in the lineup. For an American example, see *U.S. v. McNiece*, 558 F.Supp. 612 (E.D.N.Y. 1983).
25. *Connecticut v. Kelly*, 2009 WL 323481 (Super. Ct. 2009) (dog scented to cash register knocked off counter during armed robbery, tracked down street to hat, which he picked up and thrashed, which handler interpreted as having the same scent the dog was following; dog then led to car in which two men were sitting and alerted, which handler interpreted as indicating car also had same scent; after men left car, dog jumped through open window and alerted to driver's seat, which handler interpreted as meaning the scent from the cash register was also on the driver's seat; case also determined that letting dog in car to sniff driver's seat was not violation of privacy).
26. *Robinson v. Texas*, 2006 WL 3438076 (Ct. App. 2006) (conviction for aggravated robbery), after remand, 2009 WL 5205361 (Ct. App. 2009) (conviction for capital murder; scent pads made from clothing of the deceased and clothing of defendant, also wallet from which perpetrator extracted cash; though a ranger testified there was no indication the wallet of the deceased had been handled by the defendant).
27. *Buchanek v. City of Victoria*, 2009 WL 500564 (S.D.Tex. 2009), 2010 WL 1268069 (S.D.Tex. 2010) (suit for wrongful search, seizure, and investigation).
28. *Winston v. Texas*, 78 SW3d 522 (Ct. App. 2002) (scent pad taken from microwave moved during burglary); *Thomas v. Texas*, 297 S.W.3d 458 (Ct. App. 2009) (scent on currency taken from robbery suspect matched to scent of victim; procedure not specified).
29. *California v. Mitchell*, 110 Cal.App.4th 772, 2 Cal.Rptr.3d 49 (2003).
30. *Isler v. Texas*, 2010 WL 724172 (Ct. App. 2010) (scent pad rubbed on seat where defendant sat in one car supposedly matched in lineup of six paint cans to scent pad rubbed on seat where defendant sat in another car; foil scents taken directly from prisoners at a different time from target scent).

31. *California v. Aguilar*, 2004 WL 2051385 (Ct. App. 2004) (scent pads prepared from passenger seat of Volkswagen where shooter had been seated according to witnesses; handler had said scent would last on car seat for 5 days, but car had not been impounded until 15 days after the crime; trial court had admitted evidence but appellate court held its admission harmless error given testimony of three eyewitnesses); see also Aguilar v. Woodford, 2009 WL 509127 (C.D.Cal. 2009) (habeas corpus action); *California v. Sanders*, 2009 WL 3682460 (Ct. App. 2009) (swab of steering wheel used to scent dog, which found batting glove in bushes after about 45 minutes of trailing; dog later alerted to car in which defendant had been placed).

32. *Arizona v. Roscoe*, 145 Ariz. 212, 700 P.2d 1312 (1984) (dog scented to clothing of suspect for lineup of five articles of clothing, one of which had been worn by the murdered victim; alert taken as evidence suspect had touched victim's clothing); *Ramos v. Florida*, 496 So.2d 121 (1986) (lineup of five shirts, four belonging to one foil, one worn by victim during assault and murder and the only one with blood on it).

33. *Epperly v. Virginia*, 224 Va. 214, 294 S.E.2d 882 (1982).

34. *Dedge v. Florida*, 442 So.2d 429 (Ct. App. 1983) (dog scented to paper towels used by suspect alerted to victim's sheets in lineup of 5 sheets, but only on second pass in lineup; foil sheets were supplied by other prisoners).

35. *U.S. v. McNiece*, 558 F.Supp. 612 (E.D.N.Y. 1983) (dog scented to sock worn by suspect and given an array of tools, including bolt cutters used in break-in at postal station; lineup occurred 21 days after crime).

36. *California v. Hackett*, 2003 WL 463976 (Ct. App. 2003) (as well as glove left at crime scene, both scents enhanced by scent transfer unit; court did not decide on defense objections, finding admission harmless error).

37. *Perkins v. Texas*, 2009 WL 2837356 (Ct. App. 2009) (scent pads rubbed against objects in room where burglar had taken items).

38. See *Arizona v. Roscoe*, 145 Ariz. 212, 700 P.2d 1312 (1984) (dog scented to clothing of murder victim, alerted to suspect's car in lineup of four other cars; taken as evidence victim had been in car).

39. *Epperly v. Virginia*, 224 Va. 214, 294 S.E.2d 882 (1982) ("numerous" cars were in lot; procedure took place 14 days after suspect's disappearance; dog subsequently went into police station and alerted to suspect, who said three times, "That's a damn good dog"; court accepted handler's testimony that dog had followed trails as old as 21 days).

40. *Arizona v. Roscoe*, 145 Ariz. 212, 700 P.2d 1312 (1984) (lineup of five bicycles, including victim's, alert taken as evidence suspect had touched bicycle victim was riding during period of her disappearance).

41. *Ramos v. Texas*, 496 So.2d 121 (1986) (in lineup of five shirts, only one shirt, the victim's had blood on it; also lineup of five knives, only one of which, that found in victim, had blood on it; dog licked the knife with blood, suggesting attractiveness may have trumped scent identification); *Epperly v. Virginia*, 224 Va. 214, 294 S.E.2d 882 (1982) (towel found along trail and used in lineup may have had blood).

42. *Dedge v. Florida*, 442 So.2d 429 (Ct. App. 1983).

43. *Perkins v. Texas*, 2009 WL 2837356 (Ct. App. 2009) (scent pads rubbed against objects in room where burglar had taken items); see also *Buchanek v. City of Victoria*, 2009 WL 500564 (S.D.Tex. 2009), 2010 WL 1268069 (S.D.Tex. 2010) (same handler, Keith Pikett).

44. *Dedge v. Florida*, 442 So.2d 429 (Ct. App. 1983) (defendant was again convicted in a second trial, but exonerating DNA evidence resulted in defendant's release in 2004).

45. *U.S. v. McNiece*, 558 F.Supp. 612 (E.D.N.Y. 1983).

46. Steel tubes have the advantage of being both objects to sniff and rewards because dogs can play with them. Some dogs, however, are reluctant to retrieve hard metallic objects. Steel tubes cannot be used a second time after retrieval because the dog's saliva is left on the tube, which may be a cue for the dog during the next search. Cloths are placed in jars, which prevent the dog from touching them and they do not need to be replaced during a series of trials.

47. Settle et al. (1994).

48. Kaldenbach (1998), 147.

49. Gawkowski (2000).

50. Schoon (1996, 1997a, 1998) (suggesting new paradigm that has not been adopted).

51. Jezierski et al. (2003).

52. Schoon and de Bruin (1994) (dogs responded correctly in 75% of trials toward scent samples of people who were well known to the dogs; there were 67% correct responses towards people whose scents were frequently used in tests, and only 25% of correct indications of people who were completely unknown to the dogs; only three dogs were used in the experiments).

53. As noted previously, one study found that female scent was not in and of itself attractive to dogs. Rogowski (2003). But see Jezierski et al. (2012) (dogs more accurate in distinguishing women).

54. Schoon (1998).
55. Kerley and Salkina (2007).
56. Jezierski et al. (2003).
57. Schoon explained a dog's disqualification in one set of trials as due to the "interest" the dog had in the suspect. Schoon (2001).
58. Gawkowski (2001). Scent repulsiveness is also possible, whereby a dog might not want to pick a scent the dog does not like.
59. Jezierski (2002).
60. Jezierski et al. (2008). One study of olfaction in rats determined the ability of the subjects to recognize odors by the length of time a scent was investigated. A rat would spend less time sniffing when the scent was more familiar. Ables et al. (2007).
61. Jezierski et al. (2011). See Schoon (1997b).
62. Kaldenbach (1998), 93, describing similar procedures, says that the same dog may not do a discrimination for the same suspect within 14 days. This, according to Kaldenbach, gives the dog enough time to "forget" the odor. He also says that the dog may not be rewarded in any way during the procedures. In Schoon's description, the dog is rewarded if it alerts to the correct tube by the release of the tube and a short period to play with the tube.
63. Schoon and Haak (2002), 118.
64. Negative controls are also now emphasized in U.S. scent lineup practice. Stockham et al. (2004a).
65. Schoon (2001), 182. Regulations for conduct of scent lineups in Germany, Poland, and the Netherlands, are translated in an appendix to Schoon and Haak (2002).
66. Schoon and Haak (2002), 119.
67. See, for example, Harvey and Harvey (2003) (96% find rate in trailing tests for experienced dogs, but 53.3% for novice dogs); Harvey et al. (2006) (dogs performed better than chance in distinguishing trails of individuals related or living together provided the relationship was not that of identical twins); Schoon (2003) (dogs 100% correct in matching item touched immediately before test to station in lineup, but accuracy declined significantly even in 2 weeks); Settle et al. (1994) (85% matching rate with lineup involving steel tubes, 80% with cloth); Curran et al. (2010) (82.2% correct identification of targets after trailing from detonation sites of car bombs and improvised explosive devices; dogs only alerted to decoys twice, correctly identifying 25 targets, so most errors were misses).
68. Schoon and Haak (2002).
69. Wojcikiewicz (1999).
70. Jezierski et al. (2008).
71. Jezierski (2002).
72. Schoon (1996).
73. Ensminger, Jezierski, and McCulloch (2010).
74. Huff et al. (2000); Scheck et al. (2000); See also Rattner (1988) (52% of 205 cases of proven wrongful convictions were due to mistaken eyewitness identifications).
75. Wright and McDaid (1996).
76. For additional comparisons, see Ensminger, Jezierski, and McCulloch (2010).
77. The choice of soap may be important as the presence of compounds in some animal-fat based soaps contain substances similar to constituents of human scent. Curran et al. (2005b).
78. Hargreaves (1996).
79. See Schoon (1998).
80. This is preferable to using the same dog twice as the dog may be attracted to a particular scent.
81. Stockham et al. (2004a).
82. SWGDOG SC 9—Human Scent Dogs: Scent Identification Lineups, issued for public comment until March 19, 2010 (posted at www.swgdog.org).

Section III

Detection Functions

A group of scientists from Florida International University assembled a list of 30 types of detector dogs that have been trained and used (Lorenzo et al., 2004). Some of the types of dogs on their list will be covered in detail here, including accelerant detection dogs, cadaver dogs, explosives detection dogs (which the scientists distinguished from chemical weapons detection dogs as well as from gun/ammunition detection dogs and landmine trip wire detection dogs), narcotics detection dogs (which were distinguished from currency detection dogs), concealed person detection dogs, search and rescue dogs, tracking dogs (including fleeing suspect detection dogs), and scent lineup dogs. Even such a comprehensive list is probably not exhaustive as new detection functions are constantly being researched and developed, just as new explosives and drugs are developed in military and criminal cultures.

8 Judicial Admissibility of Canine Detection Evidence

Scent odors from narcotics drift with air currents and may seep out through gaps in a container such as a motor vehicle. In a period of 9 months in 1988 and 1989, 12 drug-sniffing dogs at the U.S. Border Patrol Station in El Paso, Texas, detected $100 million in narcotics and $1 million in drug-contaminated cash. Drug smugglers have been known to try to kill certain dogs, including one that assisted in the detection of $64 million in narcotics.[1] Drug-sniffing dogs are not just used by law enforcement units and governments. Many businesses and industry use drug-sniffing dogs on a routine basis. Many segments of the energy industry use narcotics detection dogs,[2] and nightclub owners have used drug detection dogs to deter the use of drugs in their establishments.

Probable cause may be challenged on various grounds, among the most common of which are that the dog and handler had no reason to conduct the sniff, that the dog was not sufficiently qualified for an alert to justify a subsequent search, or that the handler cued the dog to alert on the item sniffed. Although something of a geography of judicial probable-cause perspectives has been attempted by two courts,[3] it is questionable if jurisdictions can be put into clean categories, such as those that accept canine evidence with a mere statement of the handler, those that will accept contradictory evidence to the handler's statement, and those that require evidence concerning a dog's training and field records before establishing probable cause. Decisions are often highly fact specific, with different kinds of items containing drugs or explosives, some of which involve vehicle searches that had to be conducted in relatively limited time frames, and many of which involve different types and levels of corroborating evidence. Nevertheless, there is something of a trend toward allowing defendants to delve into a dog's training and performance history, which is appropriate since Fourth Amendment issues are often raised. Also, it can be expected that as more courts face arguments based on cases that allow an examination of a dog's reliability, additional nuance will appear in some jurisdictions that might at present be seen as accepting handler's statements in a knee-jerk fashion.

A California case from 1973 contains one of the first judicial references to a narcotics dog:

> Although we are aware of no reported cases involving the use of dogs as marijuana detectors, their use in tracking fugitives has long been admissible in evidence to show an accused was the doer of a criminal act.

Thus, a court considering the evidence of a narcotics detection dog for the first time found support for this function in tracking dog history. The handler testified that the dog alerted to objects containing marijuana or hashish. The dog had alerted to a suitcase.[4]

BREED PREFERENCES

Narcotics detection work has placed much less emphasis on breed preferences than was true in the early days of tracking evidence. There is, however, some scientific support for the use of specific breeds in detection functions. A study that surveyed handlers and trainers found that English springer spaniels and Border collies scored significantly closer to ideal levels in detection dog functions compared to Labrador retrievers and cross breeds. Border collies had less of a tendency to be distracted than other breeds and cross breeds. Spaniels rated highest in stamina. The comparison was limited to the three breeds and cross breeds because relatively few breeds are used for detection work in England. The survey also concluded that male and female dogs are equally suitable, though male dogs were sometimes more aggressive toward other dogs than was considered desirable.[5] It is not likely that such findings will result in spaniels becoming common police dogs, as the intimidation factor is not present.

TRAINING

To issue a warrant for a search after a dog has alerted, the Eighth Circuit in 1991 stated that an affidavit in support of a warrant did not need to go into the educational background of the dog.[6] A reference to training in narcotics detection was sufficient.[7] In a 1999 Georgia case, an officer pulled over a car and smelled burnt marijuana when the car window was opened. The officer retrieved his drug dog, which alerted. The officer then had the dog search the interior of the car, where it alerted to a briefcase found to contain marijuana and cocaine. The defendant argued that the drug dog was not shown to be reliable and its actions, therefore, did not support probable cause for the vehicle search. The court noted that the dog's alert corroborated the officer's smell of marijuana. The court accepted that training and reliability would have to be established were it the only basis for probable cause, but that was not the case here where the dog was used to confirm the officer's suspicion arising from his own senses. Nevertheless, training records were introduced, which indicated generally good performance on the dog's part:

> Officer Albritton [the handler] testified that he and the dog, Jessica, had been trained together in drug detection at the Global Training Academy in Texas. Albritton and Jessica received a score of 97% on a performance test involving searches of buildings, vehicles, and luggage. They received a certificate of training on August 1, 1996, indicating the successful completion of 120 hours of training. The State introduced Jessica's training records from the academy, indicating that she successfully located hidden drugs on 95 out of 99 occasions. … [D]uring the months of August and September 1996, Jessica successfully located narcotics on 49 occasions during training without a single false alert. [In the same two-month period], Jessica performed 92 vehicle searches. On 58 occasions she located contraband, and on 22 occasions she alerted but no contraband was found.[8]

Alerts to vehicles where no contraband is found are not uncommon, and may mean that contraband was in the vehicle previously but had been removed by the time of the sniff. Thus, such false alerts are to residual odors and do not negate a dog's training records. The Supreme Court of Virginia held in 2006 that training and experience were sufficient to establish reliability where the police department did not perform "backward checks" to quantify the number of times a dog correctly alerted in the field.

> We hold that a positive alert from a narcotics detection dog establishes probable cause to conduct a search of a vehicle and that evidence seized during the search is admissible after a proper foundation has been laid to show that the dog was sufficiently trained to be reliable in detecting narcotics. The narcotics detection dog's reliability can be established from its training and experience, as well as a proven track record of previous alerts to the existence of illegal narcotics. Specific certifications and the results of field testing are not required to establish a sufficient foundation. However, if the dog's qualifications are challenged, the trial court may consider any relevant evidence in determining whether the Commonwealth has established the dog's reliability in detecting narcotics.[9]

Some courts have acknowledged that more may sometimes be required than a cursory description of the dog's training and certification.[10] Some courts have stated that records of a dog's history, including training and performance, should be admissible or discoverable.[11]

LACK OF TRAINING RESULTING IN EXCLUSION

Lack of training can be fatal to a prosecution. In a 2009 Tenth Circuit case,[12] the fact that the dog had not completed narcotics detection training and had not been certified meant that other evidence would have to establish its qualifications. Since other evidence did not establish that the dog was a qualified narcotics detection dog, the alerts of the dog did not provide probable cause for a search of a vehicle. The dog's alerts seemed to be different outside the car and inside the car, and a video of the traffic stop was inconsistent with the handler's description of the dog's alert at the stop. A defense expert argued that the lack of a consistent alert, and the fact the handler had been thinking of changing from a passive to an active alert, indicated that the dog had not been fully trained. The defense expert also expressed an opinion that the handler may have cued the dog to alert, an issue that has been discussed already in tracking and scent identification and that will be discussed in detection work later in this chapter. On remand, the federal district court held that the dog was not qualified and its alert did not provide probable cause for the search of the vehicle.[13]

Insufficient evidence of training may be overcome by a test in preparation for trial. A Texas federal district court noted that evidence had not been presented on a dog's training or success in past searches, and suggested that a "sterile run" to test the dog's ability to detect currency taken from a financial institution would have been appropriate.[14]

TRAINING CONSIDERED WITH OTHER FACTORS

A Tennessee case from 2000 stated:

> [T]he trial court, in making the reliability determination may consider such factors as: the canine's training and the canine's "track record," with emphasis on the amount of false negatives and false positives the dog has furnished. The trial court should also consider the officer's training and experience with this particular canine.[15]

A Florida appellate court in 2004 referred to "the inherent variables in the training endeavor."

> Razor and his handler had undergone just one initial 30-day training course and one week-long annual recertification course. In neither course was Razor conditioned to refrain from alerting to residual odors. Whereas the Customs Service will certify only dogs who achieve and maintain a perfect record, Razor's certification program accepted a seventy percent proficiency. These disparities demonstrate that simply characterizing a dog as "trained" and "certified" imparts scant information about what the dog has been conditioned to do or not to do, or how successfully. ... Given the "language barrier" between humans and canines—thus, for example, preventing the officer from questioning the dog further for corroborative details, as he might a human informant—the most telling indicator of what the dog's behavior means is the dog's past performance in the field. Here, the State did not present any evidence of Razor's track record. Accordingly, we conclude that the State did not meet its burden to establish that the deputies had probable cause to search Matheson's car.[16]

A case arising in Michigan in 1994 analogized a court's analysis of the training of a dog to consideration of the qualifications of an expert. A dog's alert had been used to obtain a warrant to search the defendant's car, which was parked at an airport.

> Courts have not definitively addressed the issue of the quality or quantity of evidence necessary to establish a drug detection dog's training and reliability. We look to analogous principles of evidence law for guidance on this issue. As with evidence generally, trial judges have broad discretion in determining the admissibility of expert evidence. ... Similarly, an expert's qualification is a question that lies within the trial judge's discretion. ... The court considers the proffered expert's education and experience in determining if he is qualified. ... Formal education is not always necessary to qualify an expert; practical skill and experience may suffice. ...

We find these principles to be useful guides in evaluating the training and reliability of a drug detection dog for the purpose of determining if probable cause exists based on the results of the dog's sniff. When the evidence presented, whether testimony from the dog's trainer or records of the dog's training, establishes that the dog is generally certified as a drug detection dog, any other evidence, including the testimony of other experts, that may detract from the reliability of the dog's performance properly goes to the "credibility" of the dog. Lack of additional evidence, such as documentation of the exact course of training, similarly would affect the dog's reliability. As with the admissibility of evidence generally, the admissibility of evidence regarding a dog's training and reliability is committed to the trial court's sound discretion.[17]

Low accuracy rates may sometimes be correlated with poor training regimens. In an Arizona case, a dog's performance records showed that illegal drugs were only found in 42% of the cases where the dog alerted positively to the odor of illegal drugs.

[T]he [trial] court noted that Aros' "training procedure was apparently not designed in the manner best suited to detect and, if necessary, correct any cueing problem." In fact, Deputy Shrum testified that he placed the drugs in the training vehicle himself. Further, Mr. Nicely testified about the possibility of a cueing problem and the training that may be done to correct this problem, but had not been done here. Both the State's and Appellee's expert witnesses testified about the absence of important details in Aros' training records, including the quantity of drugs used, the height and location of where the drugs were hidden, and the weather conditions. Deputy Shrum even testified that there was essentially no training program in place in Yavapai County.

The Arizona appellate court therefore determined that the trial court properly granted the motion to suppress the canine evidence.[18] The case demonstrates the importance of the defense obtaining its own expert where canine evidence is significant and not relying solely on attacking the prosecution's witnesses to limit the damage of a canine alert.

Training Aids

Obtaining samples of heroin, cocaine, and marijuana requires registration with the Drug Enforcement Administration. Maximum amounts that may be procured by military trainers are generally 20 grams of heroin, 20 grams of cocaine, 20 grams of hashish, and 200 grams of marijuana.[19] Pseudococaine and pseudoheroin substances have been prohibited under a number of standards as training aids, though some trainers still use them, perhaps to avoid registration with the Drug Enforcement Administration.

The use of pseudo-drugs to train detector dogs can be compared to the problem created when a dog that is trained to detect marihuana is assumed to be able to detect hashish. Although both substances contain tetrahydrocannabinol (THC), the THC exists in different concentrations. A dog trained to detect marihuana may not respond on hashish because of this difference. A properly trained dog is therefore trained to detect and respond on both marihuana and hashish.[20]

The National Tactical Police Dog Association also specifies that certification requires the use of "real narcotic samples only."[21]

Handler's Training

References to the training of the handler are much less common than those that concern the training of the dog,[22] and it is probably correct to observe that "courts frequently neglect examination of the dog's handler."[23] To some extent this is understandable in that the handler and the trainer usually go through training and testing programs together, and the time spent by one is time spent by the other.[24]

CERTIFICATION

Once a dog has been trained, various organizations provide a certification that it has passed a proficiency test, or a series of tests. To be certified by the National Tactical Police Dog Association, a dog is allowed one false alert (alerting where there are no narcotics) or one miss (failing to alert where there are), but a passing percentage of 90% or greater is required. For that organization, two samples of marijuana, cocaine, heroin, and methamphetamines are placed in separate areas, with four blank areas also used. Substances are to be hidden from ground level to 4 feet high. The dog "must alert to and the handler must indicate to the evaluator the general location of the narcotic."[25] The American Working Dog Association requires three types of searches for a narcotics detection certification: a vehicle search, a building or residential search, and a parcel search (which can be luggage or packages). Test hides for this organization are to weigh at least 5 grams, but some large amounts should be used if possible.[26] Some states have developed their own certification procedures.[27]

Certification has sometimes been seen as a threshold for admissibility by courts, and sometimes as sufficient by itself to justify admission of evidence concerning a dog's alert.[28] The Tenth Circuit took a results-oriented approach in responding to a defendant's motion for pretrial production of "training records, veterinary records, false-positive/false-negative alert records and all other records establishing the dog's ability to smell." The handler had testified that the dog had never false-alerted in 3 years of service. The circuit court found the records irrelevant because the dog was certified on the day in question and properly alerted to presence of contraband.

> Defendant contends she made the requisite showing for pretrial production. We disagree. First, we do not believe the documents were relevant because the dog was certified on the day in question and because the dog properly alerted to the presence of contraband. … Indeed, had the dog's records indicated it had false-alerted in the past, defendant's ability to cross-examine would not have been enhanced because there is no doubt it correctly alerted in this instance. Moreover, based on defense counsel's extensive cross-examination of Agent Pena at the suppression hearing, we simply cannot say the defendant was precluded from either preparing for the suppression hearing or from exploring the issue of dog reliability. Thus, we affirm the district court's denial of defendant's motion for pretrial production because the ruling was not "arbitrary, capricious, whimsical, or manifestly unreasonable."

The court noted that the dog had briefly lost its certification because of a broken leg and a long bout of infection, but had recently been recertified and may still have been using some medication.[29]

In a South Dakota case, a dog whose certification had lapsed alerted to the presence of narcotics during a traffic stop. The dog had been trained and had previously been certified. It had passed a recertification test but the paperwork had not been properly completed. The South Dakota Supreme Court held that, given the dog's passing of the test, no purpose would be served by suppression.[30]

In a 2004 Sixth Circuit case, a dog alerted to the defendant's pocket but no drugs were found on him, though drugs were found nearby. The matter did not come to trial for several years, during which time the dog died.

> On cross-examination, Boxley asked Officer Anderson whether he had any documentation, such as "search find sheets," to verify the dog's prior history and accuracy. Anderson stated that the department did not keep accuracy records for drug dogs, but that Cuffs was certified as a drug dog after a two-month training program. Anderson also explained that Cuffs's record on the department's computer database was deleted after Cuffs passed away, more than two years before Boxley's trial. When asked whether Cuffs had alerted in the past to a finding of no drugs, as he did in this case, Anderson acknowledged that Cuffs had done so one other time in his prior sixty to seventy searches. Anderson also stated that no dog can be "one hundred percent accurate." On appeal, Boxley claimed that the district court abused its discretion in allowing Anderson's testimony because Cuffs's qualifications could not be documented or verified.

The court said that testimony about a dog's record was sufficient. The police records of the dog had been deleted after its death. The court held that it was not necessary to provide the dog's training and performance records.

> We also determined that it is not necessary for the government to show that the dog is accurate one hundred percent of the time, because "a very low percentage of false positives is not necessarily fatal to a finding that a drug detection dog is properly trained and certified." ... In this case, Officer Anderson testified that Cuffs was certified as a drug detection dog after a two-month training program. Because Cuffs was certified, the district court properly admitted Anderson's testimony.

The conviction was affirmed.[31]

Narcotics detection dogs are sometimes trained and certified in firearms detection.[32]

IS CERTIFICATION SUFFICIENT WHEN SECURITY REASONS PRECLUDE DISCOVERY OF FIELD RECORDS?

A case arising in New Mexico involved an attempt to discover the records of a Border Patrol dog. The court found that there were valid security reasons for limiting such discovery:

> Mr. Devaney [Canine Training Coordinator with the Customs and Border Protection Office and Training Development National Canine Facility in El Paso, Texas] testified that the National Canine Facility maintains records documenting such confidential or sensitive information as how its dog/handler teams are trained; where they are trained; what they are trained to detect; and how they are rated (*i.e.,* average, excellent, etc.).
>
> Criminal organizations involved in smuggling undocumented persons and/or controlled substances have an obvious interest in the information contained in the National Canine Facility's records because an organization in possession of such information could then attempt to coordinate its illicit activities in such a way as to minimize its chances of being apprehended.
>
> If the records maintained on the dog/handler teams were redacted to prevent disclosure of the confidential or sensitive information described above, then the substantive portions of the remaining information would merely duplicate what already appears on the certification ... and in the testimony of the handler.

The court described the certification procedures of the National Canine Facility. The dog and handler must perform 14 searches in a variety of environments, many of which will involve distractions, such as food and toys. A team may miss no more than 2 of 15 finds. The environments include vehicle exteriors and interiors, residences, businesses, factories, and luggage. At least one search must be conducted "in limited light conditions, using only a flashlight." The handler is scored on every search performed. Handlers must score at least 80% on a final examination that takes about 4 hours to complete. On completion of the training, the team receives a letter stating that it has participated in the United States Border Patrol Detection Dog Certification program. The certification is valid for 12 months. After certification, the team must attend 16 hours of regular, monthly continuing education. The motion to suppress the canine evidence was denied.[33]

RELIABILITY

As with training, descriptions of reliability are often extremely unspecific, such as a statement that a dog "has proven reliable in detecting drugs and narcotics on prior occasions."[34] A large number of cases accept minimal reference to a dog's training and certification as adequate to satisfy probable cause requirements.[35] A 1995 Fifth Circuit case held that a showing of reliability of a dog is not necessary as a preliminary matter to obtaining a search warrant and is not necessary "if probable cause is developed on site as a result of a dog sniff of a vehicle."[36] Probable cause may be provided by an alert for both a search and an arrest.[37]

Courts often refer to success rates, but many require little support beyond a handler's testimony.[38] Appellate courts often display considerable deference to the trial court's analysis of a dog's reliability.[39] Some courts refer to failure rates but still accept the evidence despite obvious weaknesses.[40] A Tennessee case criticized the prosecution for not establishing the reliability of a dog:

> For reasons that do not appear on the record, the government did not obtain testimony from the dog's handler or anyone else familiar with the performance or reliability of the dog. Therefore, there is no indication in the record as to the trustworthiness of this particular dog. This fact distinguishes this case from [other cases], where testimony established the reliability of the dogs.[41]

One court allowed a courtroom demonstration in cross-examination of a dog's ability to sniff out drugs as a means of establishing reliability.[42]

ACCURACY RATES

In an early narcotics sniff case from 1973, the handler testified that the dog had achieved 90% accuracy at the detection school in San Antonio and had only made two mistakes in his marijuana-sniffing career. He had never made, to the handler's knowledge, a false-positive alert.[43] In a sniff at the Los Angeles airport (followed by an arrest in Buffalo, New York), the narcotics detection dog was described as follows:

> Frog was trained to detect the presence of cocaine, heroin or marihuana; he was rated 100% effective by the Los Angeles police, having indicated the presence of drugs 705 times in 705 opportunities to do so.[44]

The accuracy of the dog is often established through testimony of the handler.[45]

A Seventh Circuit case where a dog had alerted to packages containing both methamphetamine and currency described the dog's accuracy as follows:

> According to the record, 62% of Wendy's alerts were followed by the discovery of drugs; another 31% signaled the presence of currency. Some alerts to currency may have been false positives, but a considerable number likely resulted from currency with unusually high concentrations of drug residue, a telltale sign of money sent between drug dealers to pay for inventory.... Only 7% of Wendy's "hits" are unambiguous false positives, according to this record.... Wendy has been right 62% of the time, enough to prevail on a preponderance of the evidence, and "probable cause" is something less than a preponderance.[46]

Thus, to one court a 62% accuracy rate was enough to meet the judicial standard of preponderance and thus probable cause. In a 1998 Nebraska case, 60% reliability, and an analogy to baseball statistics, also supported probable cause:

> I can summarize Castor's drug-detection record by saying that his reliability as to when he alerts to drugs and drugs that are actually found is about 60-percent correct. (Although a batting average for a baseball player of .600 would be spectacular, the evidence leaves me, and the trial judge, to our own devices in trying to figure out whether Castor's record shows that he is an "all-star" or a "bum" as a drug-detection dog.) O'Callaghan conceded that Castor was not perfect, but maintained that he was reliable. However, no evidence was offered as to how Castor's record compares with the best or the worst drug-detection dog. There was evidence that a dog can alert to the odor of drugs, i.e., from an odor in the fabric of a couch, when there are no drugs present. Thus, there are explanations for Castor's record when we remember that the dog reacts to the odor of drugs—not the presence of drugs. This odor can be present without there being drugs present.
>
> However, the evidence on Castor's use and training record really goes to whether Castor is qualified as an "expert witness." I say this because that is in essence what a drug-detection dog does. The dog provides an expert opinion by its actions, which are interpreted and testified to by its handler, that the odor of drugs is or is not present. The records introduced by Yum's counsel go more to Castor's

"qualifications," not to whether Castor was right or wrong on the particular night in question. On the night in question, if Castor alerted, he was unquestionably correct. And, according to O'Callaghan, Castor indicated at the rear of the truck, and Castor can be seen on the videotape jumping up on the bumper to the rear door and heard barking vigorously.

I see evidence on the videotape that Castor was behaving in the way that the testimony indicates a dog would behave if he were detecting the odor of drugs. I, of course, cannot use the fact that drugs were found in the truck to "boot strap" Castor into being a better drug-detection dog than his history indicates or to prove that probable cause was indeed present by virtue of his alert. However, the evidentiary record contains the testimony of O'Callaghan that Castor alerted, plus there is clear evidence on the videotape of the dog acting in a fashion which has been described as an "alert." There is no evidence that Castor did not alert while sniffing exterior of the truck.

The alert, though questioned by the trial court, was held to have provided probable cause to search the interior of the truck.[47]

Rather than analogizing a dog's alert to expert testimony, a federal district court in New Mexico compared an alert to an informant's tip:

A dog alert, like an informant's tip, relays information which may be sufficient to establish "a fair probability that contraband or evidence of a crime will be found in a particular place."[48]

As with an informant's tip, police cannot be certain that a dog's alert will lead to drugs in a subsequent search. Presumably the court expected that a full record of an informant's history could be required to establish his reliability because the absence of complete recordkeeping of the dog involved and the absence of other corroborating evidence in the case resulted in the exclusion of the drugs found in the search following the dog's alert.

In a 1997 case arising in New Mexico, the court criticized a handler's recordkeeping as being "shoddy at best," but accepted that a 70% to 80% success rate was sufficient for probable cause when there was also an informant's tip.[49] In a 2002 Georgia case, the handler provided training records but acknowledged he did not keep records of the dog's work in the field, saying only that he had never seen his dog give a false alert on a car door. This was sufficient to deny a motion to suppress.[50] In a 1996 Kansas case, a federal district court analyzed a number of cases where the issue of a dog's history had been raised by the defense and concluded:

That trained and certified dogs may occasionally make false alerts is a fact, which in this court's opinion, does not detract from the accepted notion that a certified dog's alert creates a "fair probability" of contraband being present. Both Tenth Circuit [*U.S v. Ludwig*[51]] and Fifth Circuit [*U.S. v. Williams*[52]] precedent recognize that a probable cause showing must at a minimum prove that the dog is trained and currently certified. There may be circumstances where a more complete investigation is required, because the reliability presumed from certification and training is subject to question. These may include that the dog's training or certification was substandard, that the health of the dog was such as to possibly affect reliability, and that the circumstances of the particular search raise issues regarding the dog's reliability.

The court held that in the case before it, the defense had shown that the dog had committed errors, but this did not suggest any reasonable grounds for questioning the dog's reliability. The court determined that not all records needed to be produced and those the government had agreed to produce were all that were needed.[53]

In a 2005 forfeiture that was upheld by the Seventh Circuit, the trial court received detailed testimony regarding a drug dog's experience:

Bax is a certified narcotic detector dog, having received his certification in November 1997 upon completion of 400 hours of training with his handler, Officer Arrigo. Bax's diploma indicates that he was qualified to detect marijuana, cocaine, and heroin; in 1999, Bax underwent recertification at which time he was certified to detect methamphetamine. During the performance of his duties in the years after certification, Bax racked up an impressive record. Drugs or currency were found after 97.6% of his alerts. Drugs were found after 70.1% of his alerts. Only five of Bax's alerts (the remaining 2.4%) were unambiguous false positives, and none of those took place in the two years prior to the seizure of Calhoun's cash hoard. These facts are reflected in the record and set forth in the government's statement of material facts, and Calhoun disputed none of these facts in his opposition to summary judgment.[54]

In a 2008 decision of the South Dakota Supreme Court, records of a dog's history indicated to a defense expert that in 183 searches based on a drug dog's alerts, controlled substances were found in only 84 instances, about 46% of the time. The defendant did not dispute that the dog was trained and certified but argued that the reports reflected unreliability. The court noted that many of the individual reports stated that no drugs were found but the suspect was a known user or admitted to being a user. The dog's training records demonstrated consistently passing scores. There was some question as to whether the dog performed its standard alert to the trunk area of the car, but the trial court accepted the prosecution's evidence that the dog had alerted. The appellate court concluded that it could not say this finding was clearly erroneous. The defense also claimed that the handler cued the dog to alert, but again the appellate court found nothing to justify overturning the trial court's conclusion that there had been no cueing.[55]

In a 2010 Eleventh Circuit case, the defendant argued that police lacked probable cause despite a drug dog's alert. The defendant argued that the dog was trained to detect the odor of drugs, not their presence, and that in 44.9% of searches by the canine team involved, no measurable amounts of contraband were discovered. The court held that the training of the dog alone was sufficient proof of reliability, citing a Fifth Circuit case to the effect that a dog's past performance is not required for a finding of reliability. The circuit court held that even if the canine team only had a 55% accuracy rate, this was sufficient to establish probable cause.[56]

A case arising in Tennessee involved a challenge to the reliability of a narcotics detection dog where the handler, named Whitlock, "did not know exactly what training he was actually required to perform with Spanky as his handler," and had failed to keep records of false alerts. It was the handler's supervisor, who was also the dog's trainer, who saved the day:

[A]fter reviewing the record we are not left with a firm and definite conviction that a mistake has been made regarding the district court's finding that Spanky was trained and reliable. Testimony from Lieutenant Mark Robinson indicated that he had been the supervisor of the canine unit for the past eight years and was a certified canine trainer. Lieutenant Robinson testified that he trained both Deputy Whitlock to be a canine handler and Spanky to be a drug detection dog. Lieutenant Robinson described the extensive procedures under which Spanky was trained, and stated that Spanky passed each level of the extensive training such that Spanky was a certified drug detection dog. In addition, Lieutenant Robinson testified that Spanky passed post-certification training as well. Finally, Lieutenant Robinson stated that he had reviewed the training and performance records kept by the Shelby County Sheriff's Department on Spanky and other drug detection dogs, and in his professional opinion, Spanky was reliable.

The conviction was affirmed.[57]

In a case decided in Massachusetts in 1998 that involved the same trainer, probable cause was affirmed, even though the search had produced no drugs and the dog had previously failed certification tests, because the dog was certified at the time of the stop. The dog had alerted while officers were waiting for the results of a vehicle registration check. The car was searched and the officers found various firearms including an Uzi, as well as $16,000 in cash, but no drugs or drug residue. The defendant objected to the fruit of the dog's alert since no drugs were found, but the court determined that the alert had given probable cause for a search. An expert testified that Torque had failed two certification tests and was unreliable. The government responded:

Mark Robertson, the training supervisor for the Shelby County Sheriff's drug interdiction team, ... offered explanations for Torque's [the narcotics detection dog's] failure in the certification tests. Robertson claimed responsibility for Torque's first failure, stating that he had prematurely entered the then newly trained dog in a national test against top dogs. He attributed Torque's second failure to handler error. He also emphasized that *Torque was certified at the time of the Tennessee stop*. In the end, Robertson testified that Torque was an extremely reliable dog, and that Torque and his handler were among the best. Torque's handler, Carrole Owen, also testified for the government, and opined that Torque's reliability was excellent. The district court ultimately credited the government's testimony and determined that Torque was sufficiently reliable to support a finding of probable cause. With due deference to the district court's greater ability to gauge the demeanor and credibility of the witnesses, we cannot say that the court's finding was clearly erroneous.

The convictions were affirmed.[58] As will be discussed in more detail later, cases have held probable cause was established when a dog alerted to drugs it was not trained to recognize. An unclear or atypical alert may also undermine an argument for probable cause.[59]

It is difficult to summarize these diverse opinions and results. Police should keep accurate records, including both training and field records, and police administrators should see that this is being done. In addition to raw data, records should include accuracy percentages, and independent evaluators should periodically assess whether records are being maintained appropriately. Nevertheless, depending on the court and the corroborating evidence, a failure to keep complete records may be overcome.

DISCOVERY OF RELIABILITY

In a Ninth Circuit case, the defendant was arrested at the Mexican border when a narcotics detection dog alerted to his gas tank. Defense counsel sought discovery of the dog's performance records including the handler's log, all training records and score sheets, certification records, and training standards and manuals. The district court reviewed the training records *in camera* but declined to compel their release to defense counsel. The Ninth Circuit disagreed, holding that the material should have been disclosed.

[T]he handler testified that the dog had been certified several times and had achieved a much-better-than-passing score on the certification tests. We can see no reason why the certification documents, the production of which had been requested and about which the handler testified, should not have been disclosed. Moreover, the dog's training materials and records ... were not made in connection with investigating or prosecuting this or any other case, and most of them (with the possible exception of the training log) are not statements by prospective government witnesses.

The circuit court held, however, that the error was harmless as the defendant would have been convicted on the evidence in any case.[60]

DEFENDANT'S RIGHT TO AN EXPERT ON RELIABILITY

A federal district court in Tennessee considered a defense request for an expert who would question the dog's reliability in a vehicle sniff.

Defendant is seeking $4,300, pursuant to 18 U.S.C. § 3006A(e), to cover the services and expenses of Mr. Robert Gonzalez, an expert whose "experience with detection canines is extensive and includes five years of service as the Branch Manager of the 37th Security Forces on Lackland Air Force Base in Texas." ... Defendant asserts he is in need of an expert to aid in analyzing the records and training of the drug detection dog Titan ("Titan") and Titan's handler, Detective Eduardo Choate of the Bradley County, Tennessee Sheriff's Office. ... In light of the particular facts of this case, the specific expertise of the named expert, and the general nature of the request here, the Court is not persuaded the services of Mr. Gonzalez are necessary or would be helpful in the probable cause determination by the judicial official called upon to make the probable cause determination. The Court is concerned that if it approved this request based on the general arguments advanced by Defendant, the Court would be required to approve this request in every case involving an alert by a drug-detection dog. Such a requirement would be unduly burdensome given the frequency with which dog alerts are used as a basis for probable cause. It is conceivable the facts surrounding a particular dog alert would warrant the services of an expert, but no such facts have been identified here.[61]

The case began as a traffic stop of a Volkswagen Passat. After a search, which was not in issue in the case, 5 kilograms of cocaine and two cell phones were found. When one cell phone rang, the police told the caller that the Passat had been wrecked and gave a detective's phone number as the contact for the wrecking service. Later that day, the driver's girlfriend, Amy, called the detective's phone and said she would drive with her stepfather to pick up the Passat. At the wrecking company, a policeman, pretending to be a wrecking company employee, tried to get Amy to bribe him for $500 not to reveal a secret compartment. She told him she did not know what he was talking about, but he arrested her anyway. The stepfather was also arrested and a drug-detection dog brought to sniff the car, a Suburban, they had driven in. The dog, Titan, alerted to the Suburban. A search yielded approximately $100,000 in cash. The defendant moved to suppress the search. The defendant's argument for the necessity of an expert was summarized as follows:

Defendant's supporting memorandum argues expert services are necessary for several reasons: "to determine if the [National Narcotic Detector Dog Association ("NNDDA")] utilizes acceptable methods in its certification process"; to determine the meaning of the dog's performance and training records; and because "[w]ithout access to its own expert with respect to the capabilities of these dogs, their training, and the type of skills which the animal must acquire in order to render reliable 'alerts' on contraband, the defense will not be able to properly challenge the admissibility of evidence with respect to contraband located by Titan.".

The court held that the dog's certification was sufficient to support probable cause.

Questions about the quality of the dog's training, the dog's performance in the field, and other issues go to credibility and not the admissibility of the evidence.[62] … A trier of fact may find the credibility of the testimony relating to the dog's training and reliability sufficiently questionable so as to determine the dog's alert was unreliable even though the dog had been properly certified. While Diaz[63] addressed the quality and quantity of evidence necessary to establish the minimum standard of training and reliability for admissibility of evidence of a positive alert, no case to date in the Sixth Circuit has answered the question of the quality and quantity of evidence sufficient to undermine the credibility of a dog and its handler once certification is established.

Since Titan, the dog in the case, was certified, the court did not think that the expert that the defense wanted funded would be particularly useful, even if he did challenge the certifying organization:

Defendant's argument here is akin to someone wanting to challenge the testimony of a properly licensed medical doctor by attempting to show the licensing agency failed to ask the proper questions.

As to the scientific basis of scent detection, the court adapted the "common knowledge" language of earlier cases and referred to law review articles summarizing the olfactory abilities of dogs.[64] The court conceded that a dog without proper training could not function as a narcotics detection dog.[65] The motion for appointment of an expert was denied.[66]

THE HANDLER AS AN EXPERT

A Virginia case held that a handler of a dog that had alerted to currency in a lineup was an "expert in the area of dog handling as a [*sic*] interpreter of his dog, Doc." The handler had used the dog in a lineup of envelopes, one of which contained currency from a motel room where the defendant had been arrested. The dog had alerted to the envelope with the currency.[67]

ALERTING

Narcotics detection dogs may be trained to alert passively (sit, sit and stay, lie down, point), or to alert aggressively (scratch, snarl, bark, whine, paw, attack).[68] As explained in a federal district court case of 2006 from Tennessee, when dogs sniff an item there are four possible results:

> Every dog sniff has four possible results: true positive, true negative, false positive, or false negative. ... An alert with drug scent particles present is a true positive, whereas an alert with no drug scent particles present is a false positive. ... Failure to alert when no drug scent particles are present is a true negative, and failure to alert when drug scent particles are present is a false negative. ... Statistical analysis of reliability must take into account the type of alert category being measured and each category's unique potential for error. In controlled training environments where the location of drug scents is known in advance by trainers, negative alerts are easily categorized as true or false. In the field, however, they are often impossible to quantify because, in the absence of other factors establishing probable cause, a negative alert does not lead to a search and the presence or absence of drugs remains undetermined. Moreover, a positive alert where no drugs are found does not mean the dog did not detect drug scent particles. Drugs may well have been present but removed by the time the dog alerted leaving the scent particles behind.
>
> Overlaying all of this is the issue of communication on the part of the handler. The handler must interpret the dog's action correctly. For example, if the dog in fact detects drug scent particles and alerts, and the handler fails to interpret the action as an alert, then this would erroneously be categorized as a false negative.[69]

The court noted that whether the dog has alerted or has not alerted generally depends on the handler's interpretation of his dog's actions. "Because the handler is the only witness who can speak to the subjective interaction during a particular dog alert, it is necessary to defer to his testimony if it is found to be credible." A case from the District of Columbia involved a dog that had been trained to perform an aggressive alert, but had developed the habit of alerting in a different manner:

> It is argued that Ben II, who had been trained to exhibit aggressive behavior on detecting drugs, instead froze and pointed at the compartment as would a bird dog. Officer Buss explained, however, that Ben II alerted in that fashion "on a majority of occasions" and had alerted correctly (finding drugs) in 58 out of 60 alerts. That Ben II's behavior is idiosyncratic (perhaps a triumph of genetics for a Golden Retriever) does not diminish its reliability so long as the dog's peculiar brand of alert is a trustworthy method of communicating the presence of drugs.[70]

Often the dog's alert in a specific case is not described at all.[71]

STRONG ALERTS

As in tracking, drug dogs have different alerts.[72] A case in Maine concerned a dog that alerted to a Gap bag, pulled out some clothing, then pulled out a bag with a white substance that the dog threw into the air.[73] A Border Patrol dog near Alamagordo alerted by perking her ears and tail and increasing her respiration. The court distinguished an alert from "an indication."

An "alert" is defined as a change in body posture and an increase in respiration when a dog first encounters an odor it has been trained to detect. The manner by which a dog alerts is "dog-specific" and could include such hallmarks as twitching an ear or wagging the tail. A handler is trained to recognize his or her particular dog's unique manner of alert. ... An "indication" is defined as trained behavior by the dog that pinpoints the source of odor. There are two types of indications. The first type is an "aggressive" (or "positive" or "active") indication, during which the dog will scratch or bite at the source of the odor. The second type is a "passive" indication, during which the dog will sit down or point. All United States Border Patrol dogs are trained in passive indication.[74]

Courts have sometimes emphasized the strength of an alert in determining whether police actions were appropriate.

The dog's *strong alert* to the two crates, when turned loose in a warehouse containing some 300 crates, was enough to give agent Murphy, who had worked with the dog since 1971, reason to believe the crates held contraband. We do not, of course, suggest that any dog's excited behavior could, by itself, be adequate proof that a controlled substance was present, but here the Government laid a strong foundation of canine reliability and handler expertise. Murphy testified that the dog had undergone intensive training in detecting drugs in 1971, that he had had at least four hours a week of follow-up training since then, as well as work experience, and that the strong reaction he had had to the crates was one that in the past had invariably indicated the presence of marijuana, hashish, heroin or cocaine. The DEA agents were entitled to rely on Murphy's experience and special expertise in judging the dog's reaction and they were aware that the crates had been sent from a border state, Arizona, and that they weighed 270 pounds, facts that were consistent with the dog's reaction.[75]

ALERT EFFECTIVELY BECOMING A SEARCH

A federal case arising in Minnesota involved a package that a Northwest Airlines employee in Minneapolis deemed suspicious. Police recognized the recipient as someone suspected of being in the drug trade. They brought a narcotics detection dog into a room with other packages, to which he showed no interest, but he became agitated at the suspicious package and tore it in two, spewing its contents onto the floor. The dog had to be treated to counteract the effect of cocaine he may have eaten. The Eighth Circuit considered whether the dog's tearing of the package turned the sniff into a search.

The magistrate and district court found that the dog tore the package without prompting, and the evidence supports this finding. There was testimony that tearing a package would be a normal part of Grady's response to the presence of drugs, but the police testified that in this case the entire event happened in seconds, so quickly that police had no chance to stop Grady from tearing the package. ... Given the certainty that the course of action the police were pursuing at the time of the alleged "search" would have led to discovery of the same evidence forthwith by unquestionably legal means, there is no reason to penalize the police for this accident by excluding evidence.[76]

Dogs with aggressive alerts may not be appropriate for sniffing people. In a case arising in Puerto Rico, there was a 45-minute delay to obtain a drug dog with a passive alert because the only dog at the airport was considered too dangerous for use on a human subject.[77]

DOG TAUGHT TWO SEPARATE ALERTS

One case arising in a military court describes a dog as having two alerts, one for a location where drugs were formerly present but have been removed, and one for the actual presence of drugs.

The dog had two kinds of alert. One was called a "dead" alert, which meant marijuana had been present but removed, leaving only a residual odor to which the dog responded but as to which he could not fix an exact location. The second alert was characterized as a "true" alert because the dog's response indicated the physical presence of marijuana at a pinpointed location. Colonel Latham's instruction was that a search was to be made "if the dog alerts," without qualification as to the kind of alert.[78]

It must be questioned if dogs can be trained to alert specifically to a location where drugs were but are no longer. It is more likely the dogs were showing interest in cases where drug odors were weak and a full alert where the odors were stronger. Most trainers the author has spoken with question the advisability of two-alert programs.

SPECIFICITY OF ALERT

Cases have noted that dogs sometimes alert to more than one location outside a vehicle.[79] A dog's alert to the driver's-side door during a walk-around was held sufficient to justify a search of the car's trunk. The Fourth Circuit summarized its reasoning:

> The government argues that the K-9 drug dog's "alerting" on the driver side of the car gave Mooney probable cause to search the *entire* vehicle: including the trunk and the suitcase. We think that over-states the matter. Because probable cause must be tailored to specific compartments and containers within an automobile, the key is whether the dog "alerted" in the precise vicinity of the trunk. That is a question of fact that the district court resolved in favor of the government, finding that the dog's "alert-ing" was sufficiently close to the trunk to give Officer Mooney probable cause to believe it contained contraband. We review the district court's [Eastern District of North Carolina] findings of fact in a suppression hearing only for clear error. ... And it was not clearly erroneous for the district court to conclude that the dog's "alerting" was prompted by the contents of the trunk.[80]

An Ohio court has held, however, that a dog's alert gives probable cause to search the entire vehicle. The court argued that "many factors may prevent the dog from getting to [the odor's] source," and "the only practical rule is to permit a thorough search of the vehicle."[81] This is the bet-ter reasoning at least as to cars and smaller vehicles.

SHOWING INTEREST WITHOUT A CLEAR ALERT

Cases have sometimes focused on behavior that suggests the dog has some degree of interest in an item but has not made an unambiguous alert.

> At the suppression hearing, Hubert explained at length the distinction between a drug-detection canine's "alert" to the presence of contraband and a canine's "indication" to the location of the same. Specifically, he testified that a properly trained canine will "alert" to *the presence* of contraband when it *first* encounters a known odor by changing its body posture and by increasing its respiration. By con-trast, the same dog will "indicate" *the precise location* of that contraband through some other change in behavior, such as by staring, sitting, scratching, biting, or barking. Such an "indication" is generally given at the point where the odor of the contraband is at its strongest. Hubert also stated that the canine used in this case was trained as a "passive indicator," meaning that she would generally sit or stare where an odor she was trained to detect was at its strongest, rather than scratch, bite, or bark as an "aggressive indicator" would do.[82]

A case in the Eighth Circuit considered the significance of a dog's show of interest in a FedEx package without any alert to it. An officer in Arizona notified officers in Iowa about a suspicious FedEx package.

> At the Federal Express office, six to eight packages, including the package addressed to the defendant, were isolated in a room. The police then brought in a drug dog, "Turbo," to conduct a canine sniff. "Turbo" examined all of the packages and showed an interest in the defendant's package by pushing it

around with his nose and scratching it twice. This action did not amount to an official "alert," however, so the dog's handler was not sure that the package contained drugs. Officer Henderson, a Task Force member at the Federal Express office, called Brotherton in the magistrate judge's chambers to relay this information. He told Brotherton that "the dog had showed an interest in the package, but had not given a full alert to the package." ... Brotherton then typed on the warrant application that "the Johnson County Drug Dog, 'Turbo' was presented with 8 different packages including the package being sent to Ron Jacobs. The Canine exhibited an interest in only that particular package addressed to Ron Jacobs." ...

After Henderson's call, the police requested that a second dog examine the package. This dog failed to alert or show an interest in the defendant's package. In a second phone call to Brotherton, Officer Henderson learned that the warrant had already been issued. Henderson informed Brotherton that a second dog had arrived, and that the team was going to wait for this dog to conduct a sniff before executing the warrant. Neither the magistrate judge or, apparently, Officer Brotherton was informed of the results of the second sniff.

After receiving the search warrant, the Task Force, despite the results of the second sniff, decided to open the package. Upon opening the package, the police discovered cocaine. They then rewrapped the package and delivered it to the defendant's residence. Approximately fifteen minutes after this delivery, the police executed a second search warrant at the defendant's residence. There, the police found the Federal Express package, additional quantities of drugs, several guns, drug paraphernalia, and a large sum of money.

The defendant argued that by not advising the magistrate that Turbo had not alerted, vital information had not been made available for the determination of probable cause. Also, the magistrate did not know about the second dog's failure to alert. The Eighth Circuit agreed:

In this case, if the warrant application were reworked to include the omitted phrase, it would read something like this: "The dog had showed an interest in the [defendant's] package, but had not given a full alert to the package." ... We hold that such an application, on its face, would not support probable cause. The evidence in support of probable cause would be limited to the information that Officer Brotherton received from Officer Billingsley in Phoenix, plus the fact that the dog had shown an interest in the package, but had not alerted to it. *Without an alert, the police clearly lacked the probable cause necessary to open the package.* While the information received from Officer Billingsley, plus the fact that the dog showed an interest in the package, might have provided reasonable suspicion that it contained contraband, more is needed to overcome the defendant's Fourth Amendment right to privacy in its contents. In this case, the failure to inform the magistrate judge that the dog had not given its trained response when confronted with a package containing drugs, coupled with the dog handler's admission that he could not say with certainty that drugs were in the package, causes us to hold that the warrant would not have been supported by probable cause, if the omitted material had been included.

Thus, showing interest may support reasonable suspicion, but did not support probable cause. The judgment of the district court was reversed and the cause remanded.[83]

In the inspection of a truck and trailer at the Los Indios port of entry, a dog did not alert but was described as "casting" several times. A witness defined this as follows:

The phrase of "casting" is in a sense the dog maybe feels not a strong alert, but something that temporarily stops him and deters his attention at that point. And although he doesn't pursue as aggressive alert, he does stop and give it minute attention and continues with his duties by continuing his examination.

The court then considered whether this casting created probable cause for a search:

We hold that, in this case, the government has not met its burden. The government has not provided sufficient evidence that casting should always be deemed equivalent to an alert as a matter of law. It did not put on any expert testimony on what casting means, or what weight we should give it. The Customs official testified that he sought out the dog handler for his opinion as to why the dog had cast the vehicle, but defense counsel properly objected to his answer on the ground of hearsay. The government did not attempt to cure this lapse in its evidence by putting on the dog handler. In fact, the only evidence the government can rely on is the lay testimony by the Customs official that the difference between an alert and a cast is the difference between scratching and biting at an object, and temporarily stopping, giving part of the object "minute attention" and continuing with the inspection. If anything, this evidence suggests that casting is too distantly related to an alert to create reasonable suspicion on its own as a matter of law. We thus conclude that in this case, the government has not satisfied its burden of proving it had a reasonable suspicion when the dog's cast at Rivas' vehicle. We thus grant Rivas' motion to suppress, and exclude all evidence obtained from the border search.

All the evidence obtained from the search after the cast was therefore excluded and the convictions were reversed.[84] In another case, a motion to suppress was denied when a dog alerted to cash the defendant was carrying but did not alert to his suitcase. The affidavit in support of the warrant mentioned the alert to the cash but did not mention the failure to alert to the suitcase. The warrant was issued, the suitcase was opened, and 10 kilograms of cocaine were found inside. The Third Circuit affirmed the denial of the motion to suppress and affirmed the conviction.[85]

A Tenth Circuit case involved taking a dog into the hallway outside an apartment where the landlord had been smelling marijuana. The dog, according to the affidavit in support of a warrant, "had a slight change in behavior that ... was consistent with the odor of illegal narcotics, [but this] change ... is not conclusive to the fact that the odor is emitting from inside of apartment #230." The Tenth Circuit determined that regardless of the ambiguities of the dog's response, there was enough other evidence to support the warrant.[86]

In a 1980 case arising in Maryland, a show of interest of a narcotics dog was sufficient, with other factors, such as the nervousness of the passengers, to give probable cause for a search warrant. The bag alerted to was found to contain PCP, a drug in which the dog had received training, but on which it had not been certified.[87] There are many reasons why a dog may receive training without being certified, some of which may not be due to any failure on the dog's part. These include that the testing authority may not have been asked to certify the dog as to a specific drug, the drug may not have been available for testing, or the drug may not be appearing on the street enough to make it a priority for a law enforcement unit.

In a 1983 case arising in California, mild alerts to cargo containers by two narcotics detection canines in a customs offload area of a harbor were sufficient to justify another sniff of the contents of the containers 2 days later. The initial alerts justified the second sniff even though one dog had alerted falsely in 61 alerts, and the other had alerted falsely in 4 of 6 alerts.[88]

QUESTIONING WHETHER A DOG ACTUALLY ALERTED

In a 1993 Kansas case, a "checklane" project on Interstate 70 resulted in an officer smelling alcohol on a driver's breath. A drug dog was walked around the car while the driver was taking the breath test, which found that the amount of alcohol in the air sample was below the legal limit. The dog alerted and a search of the car uncovered marijuana. A white substance was found in the driver's pocket. The driver argued that probable cause did not exist for the search. In affirming the suppression of the evidence, the Kansas Supreme Court said that "there must be some evidence that the dog's behavior reliably indicated the likely presence of a controlled substance."[89] There must be an alert and there must be some evidence that the alert was reliable.[90]

A case arising in Nebraska resulted in a dispute as to whether a dog had alerted. The trooper who took his dog around the car he had stopped testified that the dog had alerted.

Trooper Duis testified that in this case Robbie "alerted" to the presence of drugs by sniffing more intensely around certain areas of the car, but he acknowledged that such "alert" behavior was subtle and might only be recognized by himself or another person who was familiar with Robbie's tendencies.

Although Robbie was trained to "indicate" (by scratching) when he located the strongest source of the drug odor, he did not do so in this case. Defendants' experts testified that the "alert" behavior described by Trooper Duis could easily be attributed to his "cueing" of the animal, either intentionally or unintentionally, by changing the leash from one hand to the other, by stopping, by blocking the way, or by other actions. They saw nothing on the videotape to indicate that Robbie had detected the presence of drugs.

The court said that "there must be an objectively observable 'indication' by the dog of the presence of drugs."[91]

In a currency sniff case arising in Florida, witnesses 3 years after the alert disagreed as to whether the dog had a passive or aggressive alert, but the trial court was satisfied that the dog had alerted in any case.[92] A dog's failure to alert does not mean that probable cause cannot arise from other circumstances.[93]

REWARDING FOR ALERT

Cases rarely mention the dog after it alerts, but one New Mexico case noted that after a dog named Bobo alerted to a suitcase on a train, he was rewarded with his red ball for the positive alert. When it was decided to conduct a second sniff, the ball was taken away from him until he completed that sweep and again alerted.[94]

ALERT RECOGNIZED BY SOMEONE OTHER THAN THE HANDLER

Although handlers are usually the witnesses confirming a dog's alert, one Tennessee court seemed disturbed that other parties were not certain that the dog had alerted:

> In fact, there is little probative evidence in the record that the dog actually alerted to Easterly's property. Camp and Moore both testified that they did not know that the dog had alerted until the handler told them so. According to Moore, the dog sat down after sniffing. Camp could not recall how the dog reacted.[95]

ALERTS TO RESIDUAL ODOR

Dogs may falsely alert, but they may also alert to the odor of a substance that is no longer present, such as to drugs that have likely been removed.[96] In a 2004 Maryland case, the driver was pulled over for tailgating and the trooper called for assistance. While still completing the paperwork for the stop, a K-9 unit arrived and the dog alerted. The vehicle was searched and $178,840 was found in a hidden compartment, along with three compressed pellets of heroin. The driver attacked probable cause, arguing that the dog may have alerted to a stale odor of contraband. The court noted that a dog might alert to drugs that are no longer present because of a residual odor.

> He has confused probable cause with proof beyond a reasonable doubt. If a trained drug dog has the ability to detect the presence of drugs that are no longer physically present in the vehicle or container, but were present perhaps as long as 72 hours prior to the alert, such an ability serves to strengthen the argument that the dog has a superior sense of smell on which to rely to support a finding of probable cause. The possibility that the contraband may no longer be present in the vehicle does not compel the finding that there is no probable cause; for purposes of the probable cause analysis, we are concerned with probability, not certainty.[97]

One court described residual odor as "the lowest scent threshold," but it is not clear why this would necessarily be the case.[98] Certain training regimens presume that dogs can recognize a place where a substance has been but is no longer and follow it to the source.[99]

ALERTS TO ITEMS NOT TRAINED TO RECOGNIZE

Dogs have been known to alert to items that contained illegal substances but not substances they have been trained to recognize, and this has been found to provide probable cause.[100] In a 1993 case from Maine, a narcotics detection dog alerted to a package in a post office that was found to contain LSD on blotter paper. The dog was not trained to recognize LSD, but rather to find marijuana, cocaine, hashish, and heroin. This could mean that the person who packaged the LSD had been using one of these substances but no theory was advanced by the court for the alert.[101] An alert of a dog at a UPS distribution center resulted in warrants to open two packages. The packages did not contain drugs but rather Rolex watches, Apple iPods, Sony camcorders, and other electronic items. It was determined that the items were purchased with stolen credit card information. The Fourth Circuit declined to overturn the district court's denial of the motion to suppress. The dog's accuracy level was not impugned by the fact it had alerted to packages that contained electronic items, not drugs.[102] Another dog alerted to a lockbox that turned out to have many sexually explicit photographs of "very, very young girls having sex" with the defendant.[103]

Delta Airlines informed the Charlotte, North Carolina, narcotics squad of a suspicious looking package at the company's airfreight terminal. Officer Harkey took a trained narcotics detection dog named Cajun to the terminal. The dog, wandering among the packages stored in the terminal, bit into the package and brought it to Harkey. A search warrant was obtained and the package was opened and found to contain Talwin and tripelennamine, known on the street as "T and Blues," two drugs sold as a pair. A similar package arrived a week later but Cajun did not alert to it, though after obtaining a warrant, it was found to contain the same substances. The manager of a drug store was indicted.[104]

> It developed at trial that "Cajun" was not trained to detect either Talwin or Tripelennamine, but would "alert" to packages that had been handled by individuals who had been handling marijuana, cocaine, or heroin.

The dog may therefore have alerted to scent left on the package by someone who had used one of the three drugs it could detect.

> The only contention advanced by [the defendant] on appeal is that the narcotics detection dog, "Cajun," while trained to detect marijuana and cocaine, was not trained to detect Talwin or Tripelennamine. She argues that since the dog was not trained to detect these specific substances, probable cause was not established when the dog "alerted" the package which she had mailed. There is no merit to this argument. The detection of narcotics by a trained dog is generally sufficient to establish probable cause. … Although "Cajun" was trained to detect other narcotics, he was also trained to "alert" to packages which had been in the possession of individuals who had handled marijuana, cocaine, or heroin. His initial detection, therefore, was sufficient to establish probable cause for a search for controlled substances—the fact that a different controlled substance was actually discovered does not vitiate the legality of the search.

The convictions were affirmed.[105]

An explosives detection dog that had not received drug detection training nevertheless seemed to have the ability to detect drugs and alerted to drugs at the Tulsa airport.[106] Dogs have been known to alert to precursors of the drugs they are trained to recognize. In a Wyoming case, a dog alerted to ephedrine, a precursor to methamphetamine.[107]

Falsely Stating That Dog Had Alerted

Telling a suspect that a dog had alerted to her luggage nullified her consent to the search. No sniff had been conducted and the officer lied to the suspect. A motion to suppress was granted and affirmed by the Eighth Circuit.[108]

Cueing

Cueing was discussed under scent identification, and the handler's conscious or unconscious belief in the presence of narcotics or explosives may result in a dog alerting in a detection situation. In a case arising in Michigan, a defense witness, a former drug detection dog trainer, testified that when a dog had alerted to a car parked at the airport, the handler may have unconsciously cued her dog to alert. The court concluded that "a very low percentage of false positives is not necessarily fatal to a finding that a drug detection dog is properly trained and certified."[109] The court noted that the handler had run the dog around a test car "to avoid unduly suggesting to the dog a specific place to indicate; and that Dingo indicated on [the defendant's] car but not on the test car." This meant that the chance of an incorrect cueing was reduced. The court felt the handler's testimony, although faulted by a better known expert, was adequate to establish the dog's reliability.[110]

In a South Dakota case involving a dog's alert to a vehicle, the defense expert claimed that the handler had cued the dog to alert to the trunk area. The handler used the German word *gift* while leading the dog around the vehicle. The court explained:

> Pronounced "geeft," the word "gift" is German for poison or venom. According to Sergeant Huntimer, when the trooper uses the word "gift" he was telling Kaz to look for the odor, find the odor he is trained to detect. The dog associates the word "gift" with the toy it is rewarded with when it is successful in locating the source of a target drug odor.

The defense expert said the use of the word was cueing and should not occur in the field. That expert also thought there may have been a hand signal, but the prosecution's expert said it was merely a guiding motion. The appellate court could find no reason to overturn the trial court's conclusion that there had been no cueing.[111]

A 2005 South Dakota case appeared to involve such an effort to get a dog to alert that it seems likely the handler was forcing the behavior.

> Trooper Swets decided to check the car with Crockett. ... The trooper led Crockett around the vehicle twice. On the second time around, Crockett alerted at the crease of the passenger side door. His sniffing intensified, his body lowered to smell either the bottom crease of the passenger's door or under the car, and he spent roughly ten seconds on that side of the vehicle. The dog, however, did not exhibit any behavior, such as jumping or scratching on the car. Trooper Swets then directed him around the front end and started back down the driver's side of the car.
>
> On the driver's side, Crockett again caught an odor and sniffed at the seam of the door. The dog remained on the driver's side for roughly five seconds. His sniff was more intense around the seam of the door, and his body turned to an almost perpendicular position in relation to the vehicle. Again, however, Crockett did not show scratching or jumping behavior. Nonetheless, when Trooper Swets tried to pull the dog away from the scent, it resisted and the trooper pulled again, telling him, "I saw that."
>
> Trooper Swets guided Crockett to the trunk area. The dog sniffed at the trunk. Then, telling the dog to "get up there" and "get after it," the trooper encouraged Crockett to jump up onto the trunk. Crockett jumped, pawed, and thus "indicated" at the trunk of the Chrysler. With the dog's purported detection of an illicit substance, the troopers acquired the requisite probable cause to conduct a warrantless search of the defendants' vehicle.[112]

The officers found 17 pounds of marijuana. On appeal, the court reviewed and included much of the trial transcript concerning the dog's behavior as well as the testimony of a defense witness, an animal behaviorist, who argued that the dog had been cued. The South Dakota Supreme Court concluded that the trial court should be deferred to because its rulings on the dog's alerting behavior were not clearly erroneous. The conviction was affirmed. Two justices, concurring in part and dissenting in part, stated:

> Drug dogs are not 100% accurate and are fallible. We should, at least, require the state to present evidence of the dog's clear indication of smelling drugs before approving of the search. In other situations, we require an accurate calibration of technical devices in detecting alcohol or illegal substances. Similarly, we should also require the necessity of a clear indication from a drug dog before finding probable cause to search.[113]

Courts have sometimes noted that there was no indication that a dog was cued to alert by the handler, as if anticipating an objection of this sort.[114]

HUMAN SENSE OF SMELL CAN SUPPORT PROBABLE CAUSE

A DEA agent was able to obtain a warrant based on his own sense of smell, which the Eleventh Circuit was willing to acknowledge as rather out of the ordinary: "Zeke, Rocky, Bodger and Nebuchadnezzar, and the drug dogs of the southeast had best beware. [DEA Agent Paul] Markonni's sensitive proboscis may soon put them in the dog pound."[115]

TYPES OF NARCOTICS SNIFFS

Narcotics detection dogs perform sniffs in a wide variety of environments. The majority of U.S. case law concerning canine evidence arises from such sniffs. The legality of the sniff depends on what is sniffed (car, luggage, door of house, etc.), the reason for conducting the sniff (reasonable suspicion or probable cause that narcotics, explosives, or accelerants are present), and a vast number of circumstances that may tip the scales for or against legality in the use of the dog (consent, suspicious items in plain view, etc.).[116] In a traffic stop, as long as the car is lawfully seized for the traffic violation, no reasonable suspicion is necessary for a sniff prior to the completion of the original reason for the stop.[117] Reasonable suspicion may sometimes be found in the general circumstances of the sniff, such as from knowledge that buses coming across borders often contain mules—people who are carrying drugs—justifying a sniff of a luggage compartment or taking a dog down the aisle of the passenger cabin. Setting up a roadblock along a freeway on the likelihood that some cars will contain drugs, however, is not a sufficiently particularized suspicion to make the police activity legal.[118] Table 8.1 lists the most common types of sniffs, the legal requirements for conducting the sniff, and some of the more important issues that may affect the legality of the sniff.

TABLE 8.1

Levels of Legal Certainty Required for Conducting Common Types of Sniffs and Obtaining Warrants

Sniff Location	Level of Certainty Required to Conduct Sniff	Issues Affecting Result
Vehicle stopped for traffic violation before traffic issue is resolved	None under *Caballes*, as long as car was lawfully seized for traffic violation,[119] but different results possible under constitutions of some states[120]	Reason for traffic stop must be adequate
Vehicle stopped for traffic violation after traffic issue resolved	Reasonable suspicion[121] or consent[122]	Grounds for suspicion must be adequate for the length of time the stop is extended;[123] diligence in obtaining dog may be relevant[124]
Inside vehicle that dog entered by jumping through window	None if part of external sniff and officer did not encourage or facilitate dog's action[125]	Officer seeing suspicious items inside car may also help avoid exclusion of evidence[126]
Inside vehicle after dog alerts outside vehicle	Outside alert provides probable cause for search inside[127]	Alert outside may justify more than one sniff or search[128]
Sniff of occupant of car after dog alerts outside car	Outside alert may not provide probable cause for sniff of occupants[129]	Detention of passengers to obtain warrant may be proper with reasonable suspicion
Sniffs at checkpoints, roadblocks, weight stations, prison entrances; inventory searches	Generally approved if checkpoint is appropriate, but specific purpose or function required[130]	Consent may extend permissible detention period;[131] nature and operation of the checkpoint can bring in many additional factors
Sniffs of parked vehicles	External sniff generally permitted of vehicles parked where there is no expectation of privacy[132]	Approval of motel owner may reinforce appropriateness of allowing dogs in the area;[133] surveillance of driver may justify sniff after driver leaves car[134]
Sniffs of luggage (general)	Federal law provides for screening of all passengers and property, including checked baggage;[135] reasonable suspicion justifies temporary detention;[136] federal law requires checked baggage to be subjected to manual or other type of search[137]	Holding luggage too long may be unreasonable;[138] some state courts have held that luggage detentions are searches under state constitutional law;[139] reason for holding luggage for sniff must be adequate;[140] length of delay may preclude introducing evidence of alert[141]
Sniffs of carry-on luggage	Carry-on luggage subject to screening[142]	Being told to remove luggage from bus has been considered an unlawful order;[143] involuntary abandonment may make seizure unlawful;[144] unlawful detention of passenger may make sniff of carry-on luggage fruit of poisonous tree[145]
Sniffs of baggage cars and luggage docks	No reasonable suspicion required[146]	Manipulation of luggage may result in suppression of evidence, but cases are inconsistent[147]
Sniffs of abandoned luggage	No reasonable suspicion required, but abandonment must be actual, not forced[148]	Abandonment generally must be established by prosecution[149]
Sniffs outside sleeping compartments of trains	No reasonable suspicion required[150]	Dog going into compartment on its own may be analogous to jumping in car window[151]

—Continued

TABLE 8.1 (Continued)
Levels of Legal Certainty Required for Conducting Common Types of Sniffs and Obtaining Warrants

Sniff Location	Level of Certainty Required to Conduct Sniff	Issues Affecting Result
Sniffs inside compartments (roomettes) after alert	Exigent circumstances may allow search without warrant;[152] leaving door to roomette open may negate expectation of privacy[153]	Consent may also allow search of compartment[154]
Sniffs outside room in hallway of hotel or motel	No expectation of privacy in public airspace of hotel[155]	Fact suspect was under suspicion might increase reasons for surveillance[156]
Sniffs inside hotel room	A search warrant is necessary absent consent exigent circumstances[157]	Search incident to lawful arrest could include hotel room suspect was leaving[158]
Sniffs of packages in custody of postal service or common carrier	Reasonable suspicion justifies detention of package to subject it to a sniff[159]	Positive alert will generally require obtaining a warrant to open the package;[160] substantial delays have been justified with diligence[161]
Sniffs of storage areas, common areas outside safe deposit boxes, areas around cargo containers	Sniffs in public areas of storage places have been held not to be searches;[162] some courts have required reasonable suspicion;[163] state constitutional law sometimes declares such sniffs to be searches[164]	Approval of owner of storage facility has been deemed significant[165]
Sniffs in common areas of apartment buildings	Sniffs in common areas have been deemed not to be searches;[166] but a reasonable suspicion should exist;[167] some states require probable cause[168]	Circumstances providing reasonable suspicion can be highly variable
Sniffs in yards of houses	Some courts have said that expectation of privacy does not extend to yard, at least beyond curtilage[169]	Some states do not apply curtilage concept in sniff cases
Sniffs inside a residence	Probable cause and warrant required absent exigent circumstances[170]	Probable cause may be supplied by sniff at door[171]
Sniffs in classrooms	Sniffs in classrooms have been approved on reasonable suspicion of drug activity among the student body;[172] other courts have not approved classroom sniffs without individualized suspicion;[173] cases generally involve sniffs conducted by school authorities or their agents[174]	Many inner city schools now conduct searches at entrances, looking for arms as well as drugs
Sniffs of lockers and school parking lots	Sniffs in public areas, including outside lockers have been held not to be searches[175]	Sniffs may be conducted as school inspections rather than law enforcement operations[176]
Currency sniffs	Drug sniffs of any sort may lead to the discovery of currency, with or without drugs being present;[177] sometimes a drug dog is brought solely to sniff currency where it is already known that no drugs are present[178]	Courts look to the totality of factors to determine if a forfeiture is to be upheld because of a probable connection to drug trafficking[179]
Sniffs of the person	Probable cause required for search of person;[180] threat passenger may be armed justifies pat-down;[181] searches of persons and effects at border entrances do not require reasonable suspicion, probable cause, or warrant[182]	Airline passengers regularly subjected to inspections;[183] dog's interest without alert to person may justify detention to obtain warrant;[184] unintentional sniff of person may not implicate Fourth Amendment[185]

Note: Citations are exemplary; discussions in subsequent chapters will discuss case law in more detail.

NOTES

1. Lilly and Puckett (1997).
2. L.E. Papet (personal communication, December 28, 2010).
3. *South Dakota v. Nguyen*, 726 N.W.2d 871 (2007); *Ohio v. Nguyen*, 157 Ohio App.3d 482, 811 N.E.2d 1180 (2004).
4. *California v. Furman*, 30 Cal.App.3d 454, 106 Cal.Rptr. 366 (Ct. App. 1973). An episode of a television series, *Dragnet*, shown on January 30, 1969 (Narcotics: DR-21) depicts the Los Angeles Police Department as investigating marijuana-sniffing dogs for use at the Los Angeles airport.
5. Rooney and Bradshaw (2004). See Maejima et al. (2007).
6. *U.S. v. Maejia*, 928 F.2d 810 (8th Cir. 1991) ("there is no legal requirement that the affidavit specify the number of times the dog previously has sniffed out drugs").
7. *U.S. v. Berry*, 90 F.3d 148 (6th Cir. 1996); *U.S. v. Delaney*, 52 F.3d 182 (8th Cir. 1995) (statement that dog had alerted 50 times sufficient to support warrant). See *U.S. v. Fernandez*, 772 F2d 495 (9th Cir. 1985) (mere fact dog alerted does not provide probable cause without establishing reliability); *U.S. v. McGlothen*, 2008 WL 4533971 (D.Neb. 2008) ("at least some discovery" to be allowed on issue of dog's reliability); *U.S. v. Venema*, 563 F.2d 1003 (10th Cir. 1977) (affidavit in support of a search warrant need not describe drug detection dog's education background and general qualifications with specificity to establish probable cause); *U.S. v. Daniel*, 982 F.2d 146 (5th Cir. 1993) (affidavit need not show how reliable drug detection dog was in past to establish probable cause); *Dawson v. Georgia*, 238 Ga.App. 263, 518 S.E.2d 477 (Ga.App. 1999) ("evidence that the dog has been trained and certified as a drug detection dog constitutes prima facie evidence of its reliability for purposes of probable cause determination").
8. *Dawson v. Georgia*, 238 Ga.App. 263, 267-8, 518 S.E.2d 477, 480-1 (Ct. App. 1999).
9. *Jones v. Virginia*, 277 Va. 171, 181, 670 S.E.2d 727, 733 (2009).
10. *U.S. v. Wood*, 915 F.Supp. 1126 (D. Kan. 1996), rev'd on other grounds, 106 F.3d 942 (10th Cir. 1997) ("There may be circumstances where a more complete investigation is required, because the reliability presumed from certification and training is subject to question"; not all records need be produced, however): *U.S. v. Lingenfelter*, 997 F.2d 632 (9th Cir. 1993) (defense offer to show that dog alerted in past when no drugs were present was rejected because claim was based on other cases and case law); *U.S. v. Ludwig*, 10 F.3d 1523, 1528 (10th Cir. 1994) ("A dog alert might not give probable cause if the particular dog had a poor accuracy record, but the evidence shows that the dog in this case has never falsely alerted"); *Ohio v. Knight*, 83 Ohio Misc.2d 79, 679 N.E.2d 758 (Ct. Com. Pleas 1997) ("The presumption of reliability obtained from the training and certification evidence may be thereafter attacked by evidence focused upon the training procedures, certification standards, or other factors, such as the health of the dog, which relate to the issue of reliability").
11. *Florida v. Laveroni*, 910 So.2d 333 (Ct. App. 2005) ("Neither the motion to suppress, nor the argument presented by defendant at the evidentiary hearing, raised the qualifications of the narcotics dog. Because the state was not on notice that this was an issue until the court raised it, the court should have granted the state's request to call witnesses to qualify the dog"; citing *Florida v. Foster*, 390 So.2d 469 (Ct. App. 1980) as correctly requiring production of dog's performance history); *U.S. v. Florez*, 871 F.Supp. 1411 (D.N.M. 1994) (lack of corroborating evidence and "indicia of reliability," along with indications of unreliability, meant probable cause for warrantless search of suitcases did not exist); *Kansas v. Barker*, 252 Kan. 949, 850 P.2d 885 (1993) ("to establish probable cause for the search of the vehicle, some foundation testimony is necessary to establish that the 'alert' of the dog provided probable cause for the search of the vehicle. On a proper showing, a narcotics dog's reaction to a vehicle may supply the probable cause necessary to justify a search of the vehicle, but there must be some evidence that the dog's behavior reliably indicated the likely presence of a controlled substance").
12. *U.S. v. Clarkson*, 551 F.3d 1196 (10th Cir. 2009).
13. *U.S. v. Clarkson*, 2009 WL 1651043 (D.Utah 2009) (on remand). See also *$217,590 in U.S. Currency v. Texas*, 54 S.W.3d 914 (Ct. App. 2001) (expert testified that handler's methods for maintaining dog's proficiency were insufficient to eliminate false alerts and records were inadequate; handler testified that in some cases of apparent false alerts, he had smelled marijuana; appellate court deferred to trial court's factual determination and admission of evidence of alert); *Florida v. Laveroni*, 910 So.2d 333 (Ct. App. 2005) ("Neither the motion to suppress, nor the argument presented by defendant at the evidentiary hearing, raised the qualifications of the narcotics dog. Because the state was not on notice that this was an issue until the court raised it, the court should have granted the state's request to call witnesses to qualify the dog"; appellate court cited *Florida v. Foster*, 390 So.2d 469 (Ct. App. 1980) as correctly requiring production of dog's performance history).
14. *U.S. v. $80,760*, 781 F.Supp. 462 (N.D.Tex. 1991).

15. *Tennessee v. England*, 19 S.W.3d 762, 768 (2000) (handler testified concerning dog's training and that it had given positive alerts in between 50 and 100 situations where narcotics were found).
16. *Matheson v. Florida*, 870 So.2d 8, 13–14 (Ct. App. 2004). The case was decided before *Caballes*.
17. *U.S. v. Diaz,* 25 F.3d 392 (6th Cir. 1994).
18. *Arizona v. Wright*, 2009 WL 2411298 (Ct. App. 2009) (training and certification not sufficient to establish dog's reliability when "real world" records indicated serious deficiencies); see also *U.S. v. Donnelly*, 475 F.3d 946 (8th Cir. 2007) (accuracy rate of 54%, along with numerous other factors, were sufficient to provide probable cause for search).
19. MWD Pamphlet 190-12, § 4-2. See 21 CFR Part 1301.
20. MWD Pamphlet 190-12, § 4-9. Well-trained marijuana detection dogs will generally alert to hashish.
21. NTPDA Web site (www.tacticalcanine.com/certification.htm).
22. *U.S. v. Delaney*, 52 F.3d 182 (8th Cir. 1995), cert. denied 116 S.Ct. 209 (1995) (affidavit stated handler was certified drug canine handler who had received 76 hours of training in handling drug dogs; that and the fact dog was certified in detecting cocaine and other drugs and had alerted 50 times where drugs were located was enough to establish reliability).
23. Bird (1997), 421. See *Washington v. Gross*, 57 Wash.App. 549, 552 789 P.2d 317, 319 (Ct. App. 1990), overruled on other grounds, *Washington v. Thein*, 138 Wash.2d 133, 977 P.2d 582 (1999) ("canine officer presumably had at least 180 hours of training in how properly to use the dog").
24. See, for example, *U.S. v. Diaz*, 25 F.3d 392, 394 (6th Cir. 1994) ("Wayne County Deputy Sheriff Kris Dennard, Dingo's trainer and handler, testified that she and Dingo successfully attended an 8-week training school in which both learned techniques for the detection of controlled substances, including marijuana, cocaine, and heroin; that as part of the training, Dingo was subjected to 'live' search tests (in which drugs were present) and 'dead' search tests (in which drugs were not present, but plastic bags and live animals sometimes were)"); *U.S. v. Lingenfelter*, 997 F.2d 632, 639 (9th Cir. 1993) ("expertise statement stated that Carlos and Officer Fleet have participated in approximately 300 hours of training searches, and that Carlos has never given a false alert or failed to detect the drug and narcotic training aids that Carlos was asked to find"; offer of proof that dog had alerted in cases where no drugs were found was rejected by trial court and affirmed by circuit court because offer was not based on actual statements of potential witness but on "other cases and case law"); *U.S. v. Carroll*, 710 F.2d 164, 168 (4th Cir. 1983) ("Officer Hickman testified that he and Damian successfully had completed a 10-day detection and tracking training course, that he and Damian practiced tracking at least three times a week, that he and Damian previously had worked on about 17 to 25 cases, and that Damian successfully had tracked objects and people on hundreds of prior occasions in training sessions and in actual police work. That testimony established a proper foundation for the evidence").
25. NTPDA Web site (www.tacticalcanine.com/certification.htm).
26. AWDA Web site (www.americanworkingdog.com/certification_standards.htm).
27. *U.S. v. Gastelo-Armenta*, 2010 WL 1440451 (D.Neb. 2010) (describing Nebraska's certification procedure requiring 14 different searches for hidden narcotics).
28. *U.S. v. Lopez*, 380 F.3d 538 (1st Cir. 2004). See also *U.S. v. Shayesteh,* 161 F.3d 19, 1998 WL 694500 (10th Cir. 1998) ("As there is no question the dog used in this case was certified, there was probable cause for the search of the bag and its contents"), 54 Fed.Appx. 916, 2003 WL 42509 (10th Cir. 2003) (second appeal; prisoner not denied effective assistance of counsel including with respect to canine evidence); *Emory v. Maryland*, 101 Md.App. 585, 647 A.2d 1243 (Ct. Spec. App. 1994) (statement in affidavit that dog was trained and certified as a marijuana-sniffing dog was sufficient to issue warrant); *Fitzgerald v. Maryland*, 153 Md.App. 601, 837 A.2d 989 (Ct. Spec. App. 2003), aff'd 384 Md. 484, 864 A.2d 1006 (2004) (certified dog's alert could support probable cause for search and arrest).
29. *U.S. v. Gonzalez-Acosta*, 989 F.2d 384 (10th Cir. 1993). See also *U.S. v. Klinginsmith*, 25 F.3d 1507 (10th Cir. 1994); *U.S. v. Rosborough*, 366 F.3d 1145 (10th Cir. 2004).
30. *South Dakota v. Guerra*, 772 N.W.2d 907 (2009) (two justices dissented on the certification issue).
31. *U.S. v. Boxley*, 373 F.3d 759 (6th Cir. 2004).
32. *Bastible v. Weyerhouser Co.,* 427 F.3d 999 (10th Cir. 2006) (security company dogs sniffed cars in parking lot of Weyerhouser Co., alerting to cars of employees who had violated company rules and brought firearms to work).
33. *U.S. v. Morales*, 489 F.Supp.2d 1250 (D.N.M. 2007).
34. *U.S. v. Klein*, 626 F.2d 22 (7th Cir. 1980) (quoting without analysis affidavit in support of search warrant).
35. *U.S. v. Race*, 529 F.2d 12 (1st Cir. 1976) (dog had undergone "intensive training in detecting drugs … had a least 4 hours a week of follow-up training since then, as well as work experience, and … strong reaction he had to crates was one that in the past had invariably indicated the presence of marijuana,

hashish, heroin or cocaine"); *U.S. v. Massac*, 867 F.2d 174, 176 (3rd Cir. 1989) (alert gave probable cause because of "the demonstrated fact that trained dogs can detect the presence of concealed narcotics with almost unerring accuracy and the finding of the district court that this particular dog met the training and reliability requirements"); *U.S. v. Berry*, 90 F.3d 148 (6th Cir. 1996) (affidavit stating dog and handler "have both been trained, qualified in the processes and procedures required to properly conduct such [narcotics] investigations" was "sufficient to establish training and reliability of the drug-detecting dog"; "affidavit's references to the dog as a 'drug sniffing or drug detecting dog' reasonably implied that the dog was a 'trained narcotics dog'"); *U.S. v. Sundby*, 186 F.3d 873 (8th Cir. 1999) (affidavit supporting warrant stated dog was trained and certified, but district court granted suppression motion because affidavit did not establish dog was reliable; circuit court reversed and remanded for further suppression proceedings); *U.S. v. Venema*, 563 F.2d 1003 (10th Cir. 1977) (affidavit in support of a search warrant need not describe drug detection dog's education background and general qualifications with specificity to establish probable cause); *U.S. v. $175,260*, 741 F.Supp. 45 (E.D.N.Y. 1990) ("DEA agent Mark Thornton testified to the reliability and accuracy of the dog, Zoom"); *U.S. v. Garcia*, 52 F.Supp.2d 1239 (D.Kan. 1999) (alert gave probable cause for arrest of occupants of two vehicles in apparent convoy); *U.S. v. Patty*, 96 F.Supp. 703 (E.D.Mich. 2000) (recitation of dog's certification by United States Police Canine Association and North American Police Work Dog Association was sufficient to establish dog's reliability despite defense expert's criticism of techniques used in dog's training); *U.S. v. Trayer*, 701 F.Supp. 250, 256 (D.D.C. 1988) ("dog's *curriculum vitae* unnecessary in the context of ordinary warrant applications"); *Washington v. Gross*, 57 Wash.App. 549, 552 789 P.2d 317, 319 (1990), overruled on other grounds, *Washington v. Thein*, 138 Wash.2d 133, 977 P.2d 582 (1999) (telephone transcript in support of warrant stated dog was trained, certified by the Washington State Police Canine Association and the Washington State Criminal Justice Training Commission, had been used in narcotics detection, and qualified by both federal and local courts was "more than sufficient"); *In re Montrail M.*, 87 Md.App. 420, 589 A.2d 1318 (Ct. Spec. App. 1991), aff'd 325 Md. 527, 601 A.2d 1102 (1992) (stop of juveniles driving car was based on reasonable articulable suspicion; no additional Fourth Amendment rights implicated in canine sniff during stop of car); *Timmons v. Maryland*, 114 Md.App. 410, 690 A.2d 530 (Ct. Spec. App. 1997) (once dog alerted, officer had probable cause to detain passenger and search vehicle); *Dawson v. Georgia*, 238 Ga.App. 263, 518 S.E.2d 477 (Ct. App. 1999) ("evidence that the dog has been trained and certified as a drug detection dog constitutes prima facie evidence of its reliability for purposes of probable cause determination").

36. *U.S. v. Williams*, 69 F.3d 27 (5th Cir. 1995).
37. *Carter v. Maryland*, 143 Md.App. 670, 795 A.2d 790 (Ct. App. 2002), cert. denied 369 Md. 571, 801 A.2d 1032 (2002) (dog's alert provided probable cause for warrantless search, which revealed marijuana, which supplied probable cause for warrantless arrest); *Florida v. Foster*, 390 So.2d 469 (Ct. App. 1980).
38. *U.S. v. Waltzer*, 682 F.2d 370 (2nd Cir. 1982), cert. denied 463 U.S. 1210 (1983) ("Kane was capable of determining whether a particular piece of luggage contained narcotics and of alerting agents to the presence of drugs by biting and gnawing at the luggage. Kane had a perfect record—on each occasion his alerting of agents to a particular bag had led to the discovery of narcotics. Kane alerted the agents to the luggage described by Sheriff Carl"; dog's alert established probable cause for arrest); *U.S. v. Delaney*, 52 F.3d 182 (8th Cir. 1995) (statement that dog had alerted 50 times sufficient to support warrant); *U.S. v. Maejia*, 928 F.2d 810 (8th Cir. 1991) ("there is no legal requirement that the affidavit specify the number of times the dog previously has sniffed out drugs"); *U.S. v. Kennedy*, 131 F.3d 1371 (10th Cir. 1997) (handler's training and recordkeeping "shoddy at best"; certified with passing rate of 96%; 70%–80% success rate sufficient for probable cause); *U.S. v. Limares*, 269 F.3d 794 (7th Cir. 2001) ("Wendy has been right 62% of the time, enough to prevail on a preponderance of the evidence, and "probable cause" is something less than a preponderance."); *U.S. v. Trayer*, 898 F.2d 805, 283 U.S.App.D.C. 208 (D.C. Cir. 1990) (handler testified that dog had alerted by pointing on majority of occasions and had alerted correctly in 58 out of 60 times).
39. See *Idaho v. Braendle*, 124 Idaho 173, 997 P.2d 634 (Ct. App. 2000) (evidence that dog had alerted to alerting to residual odor, or odor on clothing; appellate court deferred to trial court).
40. *U.S. v. Spetz*, 721 F.2d 1457 (9th Cir. 1983) (mild alerts to cargo containers by 2 narcotics detection canines in a customs offload area of a harbor were sufficient to justify another sniff of the contents of the containers 2 days later; initial alerts justified the second sniff even though one dog had alerted falsely in 61 alerts, and the other had alerted falsely in 4 of 6 alerts); *Ohio v. Crowder*, 2000 WL 874681 (Ct. App. 2000) (probable cause satisfied where dog had completed training 2 months before traffic stop, had 40 sniffs with 6 alerts but only 3 produced drugs).
41. *U.S. v. $67,220*, 957 F.2d 280 (6th Cir. 1992).

42. *U.S. v. Rackley*, 742 F.2d 1266 (11th Cir. 1984).

43. *California v. Furman*, 30 Cal.App.3d 454, 106 Cal.Rptr. 366 (Ct. App. 1973).

44. *New York v. Price*, 54 N.Y.2d 557, 431 N.E.2d 267, 446 N.Y.S.2d 906 (1981).

45. *California v. Sommer*, 12 Cal.App.4th 1642, 16 Cal.Rptr.2d 165 (Ct. App. 1993).

46. *U.S. v. Limares*, 269 F.3d 794 (7th Cir. 2001).

47. *Nebraska v. Yum*, 1998 WL 19484 (Ct. App. 1998).

48. *U.S. v. Florez*, 871 F.Supp. 1411 (D.N.M. 1994). But see *U.S. v. Gonzalez-Acosta*, 989 F.2d 384 (10th Cir. 1993) (circuit court found training documents not relevant because dog was certified on the day in question and properly alerted to presence of contraband). See also *U.S. v. Ludwig*, 10 F.3d 1523, 1528 (10th Cir. 1994) ("A dog alert might not give probable cause if the particular dog had a poor accuracy record, but the evidence shows that the dog in this case has never falsely alerted"); *U.S. v. Washburn*, 383 F.3d 638 (7th Cir. 2004) (suspect's history and statements were corroborated by dog's alert).

49. *U.S. v. Kennedy*, 131 F.3d 1371 (10th Cir. 1997).

50. *Warren v. Georgia*, 254 Ga.App. 52, 561 S.E.2d 190 (Ga.App. 2002).

51. *U.S. v. Ludwig*, 10 F.3d 1523 (10th Cir. 1993).

52. *U.S. v. Williams*, 69 F.3d 27, 28 (5th Cir. 1995).

53. *U.S. v. Wood*, 915 F.Supp. 1126 (D. Kan. 1996), rev'd on other grounds, 106 F.3d 942 (10th Cir. 1997); see also *Ohio v. Knight*, 83 Ohio Misc.2d 79, 679 N.E.2d 758 (Ct. Com. Pleas 1997) ("reliability is initially proven by evidence of training and certification. The presumption of reliability obtained from the training and certification evidence may be thereafter attacked by evidence focused upon the training procedures, certification standards, or other factors, such as the health of the dog, which relate to the issue of reliability").

54. *U.S. v. $30,670*, 403 F.3d 448 (7th Cir. 2005). See also *U.S. v. Johnson*, 323 F.3d 566 (7th Cir. 2003) (dog alert among other reasons for search after controlled drug buy).

55. *South Dakota v. Nguyen*, 726 N.W.2d 871 (2007). See *U.S. v. Ludwig*, 2011 WL 1533520 (10th Cir. 2011) (dog "identifies 'seizable' quantities of drugs only 58% of time").

56. *U.S. v. Anderson*, 2010 WL 597230 (11th Cir. 2010), citing *U.S. v. Williams*, 69 F.3d 27, 28 (5th Cir. 1995).

57. *U.S. v. Hill*, 195 F.3d 258 (6th Cir. 1999).

58. *U.S. v. Owens*, 167 F.3d 739 (1st Cir. 1998) (emphasis added).

59. *U.S. v. Heir*, 107 F.Supp.2d 1088 (D.Neb. 2000) (officer stated that dog had alerted though not by scratching, his usual alert, but by more intense sniffing than usual; magistrate held, and district court agreed, that dog had not positively indicated the presence of drugs and may have been cued by the handler in any case).

60. *U.S. v. Cedano-Arellano*, 332 F.3d 568 (9th Cir. 2003).

61. *U.S. v. Howard*, 448 F.Supp.2d 889 (E.D.Tenn. 2006).

62. Citing *U.S. v. Boxley*, 373 F.3d 762 (6th Cir. 2004); *U.S. v. Hill*, 195 F.3d 258 (6th Cir. 1999).

63. *U.S. v. Diaz*, 25 F.3d 392 (6th Cir. 1994).

64. Specifically, Bird (1997); Taslitz (1990); Myers (2006a, 2006b).

65. Citing *U.S. v. Outlaw*, 134 F.Supp. 807 (W.D.Tex. 2001).

66. *U.S. v. Howard*, 448 F.Supp.2d 889 (E.D.Tenn. 2006).

67. *Hetmeyer v. Virginia*, 19 Va.App. 103, 448 S.E.2d 894 (Ct. App. 1994). The appellate court cited a tracking case, *Epperly v. Virginia*, 224 Va. 214, 294 S.E.2d 882 (1982), for labeling the handler as an expert.

68. *U.S. v. Spetz*, 721 F.2d 1457 (9th Cir. 1983). See *U.S. v. Johnson*, 323 F.3d 566 (7th Cir. 2003), quoting Sandy Bryson, Police Dog Tactics, 257 (2nd ed., 2000): "Typically the dog is trained to signal a find in one of two ways: the aggressive alert or the passive alert. Either style requires a dog with strong search drives that reacts reliably when he detects drugs. The dog trained to alert aggressively tries to contact the scent source (biting, scratching, penetrating, attempting to retrieve), while the dog that alerts passively does not try to contact the scent source but instead performs trained behavior (sitting, looking at the source, sniffing toward the source, looking at the handler)."

69. *U.S. v. Howard*, 448 F.Supp.2d 889 (E.D.Tenn. 2006).

70. *U.S. v. Trayer*, 898 F.2d 805, 808, 283 U.S.App.D.C. 208, 211 (D.C.Cir. 1990) (footnote omitted).

71. *U.S. v. Attardi*, 796 F.2d 257 (9th Cir. 1986) (sniff by dog led officer to reasonable belief luggage contained narcotics).

72. *U.S. v. Lerebours*, 87 F.3d 582 (1st Cir. 1996) (biting and scratching mattress revealed crack cocaine under it).

73. *U.S. v. Esquilin*, 208 F.3d 315 (1st Cir. 2000). See also *U.S. v. Waltzer*, 682 F.2d 370 (2nd Cir. 1982), cert. denied 463 U.S. 1210 (1983) ("Kane was capable of determining whether a particular piece of luggage contained narcotics and of alerting agents to the presence of drugs by biting and gnawing at the luggage. Kane had a perfect record—on each occasion his alerting of agents to a particular bag had led to the discovery of narcotics. Kane alerted the agents to the luggage described by Sheriff Carl").

74. *U.S. v. Morales*, 489 F.Supp.2d 1250 (D.N.M. 2007).

75. *U.S. v. Race*, 529 F.2d 12 (1st Cir. 1976) (emphasis added); see also *U.S. v. Colon*, 845 F.Supp. 923 (D.Puerto Rico 1994) (referring to a "strong alert").

76. *U.S. v. Lyons*, 957 F.2d 615 (8th Cir. 1992).

77. *U.S. v. Nunez*, 19 F.3d 719 (1st Cir. 1994).

78. *U.S. v. Unrue*, 1973 WL 14783 (CMA), 47 C.M.R. 556, 22 USCMA 466 (1973).

79. *U.S. v. Hogan*, 539 F.3d 916 (8th Cir. 2008).

80. *U.S. v. Carter*, 300 F.3d 415 (4th Cir. 2002).

81. *Ohio v. Bolding*, 1999 WL 334494 (Ct. App. 1999). See *U.S. v. Hammons*, 152 F.3d 1025 (8th Cir. 1998) (consent given by person renting vehicle included consent to search container in vehicle).

82. *U.S. v. Forbes*, 528 F.3d 1273 (10th Cir. 2008).

83. *U.S. v. Jacobs*, 986 F.2d 1231 (8th Cir. 1993) (emphasis added). See *Lippman v. City of Miami*, 2010 WL 2836713 (S.D.Fla. 2010) (bomb dog's showing of interest on parked vehicle insufficient to provide probable cause for search without warrant).

84. *U.S. v. Rivas*, 157 F.3d 364 (5th Cir. 1998).

85. *U.S. v. Frost*, 999 F.2d 737 (3rd Cir. 1993).

86. *U.S. v. Garcia-Zambrano*, 530 F.3d 1249 (10th Cir. 2008).

87. *U.S. v. Sullivan*, 625 F.2d 9 (4th Cir. 1980) (dog was proficient in detecting marijuana, heroin, and cocaine). See *Hillman v. Beightler*, 2010 WL 2232640 (N.D.Oh. 2010) (dog did not have strong reaction and handler suspected drugs were not in car but rather with passengers; consent to physical search confirmed this).

88. *U.S. v. Spetz*, 721 F.2d 1457 (9th Cir. 1983).

89. *Kansas v. Barker*, 252 Kan. 949, 850 P.2d 885 (1993) (citing *Doe v. Renfrow*, 475 F.Supp. 1012 (N.D. Ind. 1979)).

90. *Kansas v. Barker* (case was remanded to determine these issues and thereby determine if probable cause existed).

91. *U.S. v. Heir*, 107 F.Supp.2d 1088 (D.Neb. 2000).

92. *U.S. v. $242,484*, 389 F.3d 1149 (11th Cir. 2004).

93. *Ohio v. Alexander*, 141 Ohio App.3d 590, 784 N.E.2d 1225 (Ct. App. 2003) (defendant fit within drug courier profile); *McKay v. Maryland*, 149 Md.App. 176, 814 A.2d 592 (Ct. Spec. App. 2002) (dog had been sick and should not have been working but failed to alert; absence of alert did not negate probable cause but was factor to consider in determining if probable cause existed); *Colorado v. Ortega*, 34 P.3d 986 (2001) (dog did not alert but luggage had strong chemical smell and was very expensive, also lacked identification other than claim check).

94. *U.S. v. Florez*, 871 F.Supp. 1411 (D.N.M. 1994).

95. *U.S. v. $67,220*, 957 F.2d 280 (6th Cir. 1992).

96. See *U.S. v. Salas-Torres*, 60 F.3d 837, 1995 WL 406937 (10th Cir. 1995) (search after alert revealed soap powder spread throughout trunk and blocks of wood in the springs. "Testimony at trial indicated that smugglers commonly use soap powder to mask the odor of marijuana and will place blocks in the springs of a heavily-laden car to keep it from riding conspicuously low"; when released from checkpoint, officers followed the driver because he drove in the direction from which he had come; the driver met someone pulling a motor home on a frontage road; search of the motor home revealed 82 pounds of marijuana; trial court found reasonable suspicion and probable cause; appellate court affirmed). See also *U.S. v. Salamasina*, No.09-2188 (8th Cir. 2010).

97. *Maryland v. Cabral*, 159 Md.App. 354, 381, 859 A.2d 285 (Ct. App. 2004).

98. *U.S. v. Florez*, 871 F.Supp. 1411 (D.N.M. 1994).

99. See Auburn University's Vapor Wake Detection Program for specialized explosives detection dogs (diagrams at www.vetmed.auburn.edu/cdri/vapor-wake-detection/vapor-wake-scenting-concepts). Trailing studies discussed in the second section of this book indicate dogs can determine directionality of tracks.

100. *U.S. v. Robinson*, 707 F.2d 811 (4th Cir. 1983) ("Although 'Cajun' was trained to detect other narcotics, he was also trained to 'alert' to packages which had been in the possession of individuals who had handled marijuana, cocaine, or heroin."); *U.S. v. Lovell*, 849 F.2d 910 (5th Cir. 1988) (dog not trained to react to quaaludes alerted to bags containing them; probable cause was satisfied by training of dog); *U.S. v. Viera*, 644 F.2d 509 (5th Cir. 1981).
101. *U.S. v. Allen*, 990 F.2d 667 (1st Cir. 1993).
102. *U.S. v. Koon Chung Wu*, 217 Fed.Appx. 240, 2007 WL 412169 (4th Cir. 2007).
103. *U.S. v. Smith*, 459 F.3d 1276 (11th Cir. 2006).
104. This does not necessarily mean that the dog was performing well. The amounts and packing may have differed between the packages.
105. *U.S. v. Robinson*, 707 F.2d 811 (4th Cir. 1983).
106. *U.S. v. McCranie*, 703 F.2d 1213 (10th Cir. 1983). Cross-contamination in training is a concern that many trainers describe as perhaps resulting in dogs alerting to substances that they are not being specifically trained to recognize.
107. *U.S. v. Patten*, 183 F.3d 1190 (10th Cir. 1999).
108. *U.S. v. Escobar*, 389 F.3d 781 (8th Cir. 2004).
109. *U.S. v. Diaz*, 25 F.3d 392 (6th Cir. 1994) (citing *U.S. v. Alvarado*, No. 90-6058, 1991 WL 119265 (6th Cir. 1991) (95% accuracy), and *U.S. v. Spetz*, 721 F.2d 1457 (9th Cir. 1983)).
110. *U.S. v. Diaz*, 25 F.3d 392 (6th Cir. 1994). See also *Arizona v. Wright*, 2009 WL 2411298 (Ct. App. 2009) ("certification process did not eliminate inadvertent or unconscious 'cueing' by the dog's handler").
111. *South Dakota v. Nguyen*, 726 N.W.2d 871, 883 (2007).
112. *South Dakota v. Lockstedt*, 695 N.W.2d 718, 720-1 (2005) (footnotes omitted). See also *U.S. v. Rodriguez*, 2008 WL 2401494 (D.Neb. 2008) (dog circled car three times but seemed to show no more than interest, though handler said the dog had alerted, though this was no clear on the videotape; "vague statement that Alex exhibited 'significant behavior changes' is insufficient to establish probable cause"). *U.S. v. Glinton*, 154 F.3d 1245 (11th Cir. 1998) (dog went around car twice before alerting, establishing probable cause).
113. *South Dakota v. Lockstedt*, 695 N.W.2d 718, 730.
114. *U.S. v. Trayer*, 898 F.2d 805, 283 U.S.App.D.C. 208 (D.C.Cir. 1990).
115. *U.S. v. Sentovich*, 677 F.2d 834 (11th Cir. 1982); *U.S. v. Nielsen*, 9 F.3d 1487 (10th Cir. 1993) (human sniffer requires additional evidence to establish probable cause but a "dog would have no reason to make a false alert").
116. See *U.S. v. Steed*, 548 F.3d 961 (11th Cir. 2008) ("As long as Gonzalez was authorized to conduct the administrative inspection, no level of suspicion was required for him to request the canine unit during the course of that inspection").
117. *Illinois v. Caballes*, 543 U.S. 405, 125 S.Ct. 834, 160 L.Ed.2d 842 (2005).
118. *City of Indianapolis v. Edmond*, 531 U.S. 32, 121 S.Ct. 447, 148 L.Ed.2d 333 (2000). Three justices—Rehnquist, Thomas, and Scalia—dissented.
119. *Illinois v. Caballes*, 543 U.S. 405, 125 S.Ct. 834, 160 L.Ed.2d 842 (2005).
120. *Montana v. Tackitt*, 315 Mont. 59, 69-70, 67 P.3d 295, 302-3 (Sup.Ct. 2003).
121. *Bain v. Florida*, 839 So2d 739 (Ct. App. 2003).
122. *U.S. v. White*, 42 F.3d 457 (8th Cir. 1994); U.S. v. Hornbecker, 316 F.3d 40 (1st Cir. 2003).
123. *U.S. v. Bell, III,* 555 F.3d 535 (6th Cir. 2009).
124. *U.S. v. Branch*, 537 F.3d 328 (4th Cir. 2008); *U.S. v. Bloomfield*, 40 F.3d 910 (8th Cir. 1994) (officer radioed for canine assistance 6 minutes after stop).
125. *U.S. v. Stone*, 866 F.2d 359 (10th Cir. 1989).
126. *U.S. v. Hutchinson*, 471 F.Supp. 497 (M.D.Pa. 2007).
127. *Wisconsin v. Miller*, 256 Wis.2d 80, 647 N.W.2d 348 (Ct. App. 2002).
128. *U.S. v. Farrior*, 535 F.3d 210 (4th Cir. 2008). See U.S. v. Eura, 440 F.3d 625 (4th Cir. 2006).
129. *Maryland v. Wallace*, 372 Md. 137, 142-3, 812 A.2d 291, 294 (Ct. App. 2003), cert. denied 540 U.S. 1140, 124 S.Ct. 1036, 157 L.Ed.2d 951 (2004) (noting that if the dog had separately sniffed the defendant, a nonowner, nondriver, and alerted to him, probable cause for the search and a subsequent arrest might have existed). See also *Illinois v. Fondja*, 317 Ill.App.3d 966, 251 Ill.Dec. 553, 740 N.E.2d 839 (Ct. App. 2000).
130. *City of Indianapolis v. Edmond*, 531 U.S. 32, 121 S.Ct. 447, 148 L.Ed.2d 333 (2000). Three justices—Rehnquist, Thomas, and Scalia—dissented.
131. *U.S. v. Chavira*, 9 F.3d 888 (10th Cir. 1993). See *U.S. v. Pinedo-Montoya*, 966 F.2d 591 (10th Cir. 1992).
132. *U.S. v. Ludwig*, 10 F.3d 1523 (10th Cir. 1994).
133. Ibid.

134. *U.S. v. de Soto*, 885 F.2d 354 (7th Cir. 1989).

135. 49 U.S.C. 44901(a), (c).

136. *U.S. v. Place*, 462 U.S. 696, 103 S.Ct. 2637, 77 L.Ed.2d 110 (1983).

137. 49 U.S.C. 44901(a), (e); 49 CFR 1546.205(g)(2) (screening of cargo loaded inside the U.S.)

138. Ibid.

139. *Montana v. Scheetz*, 286 Mont. 41, 950 P.2d 722 (1997).

140. *U.S. v. Williams*, 356 F.3d 1268 (10th Cir. 2004).

141. *U.S. v. Jodoin*, 672 F.2d 232 (1st Cir. 1982).

142. 49 U.S. 44901(a).

143. *U.S. v. Garzon*, 119 F.3d 1446 (10th Cir. 1997).

144. *U.S. v. Stephens*, 206 F.3d 914 (9th Cir. 2000).

145. *U.S. v. $90,000 in United States Currency*, 2009 WL 6327469 (D.Minn. 2009).

146. *U.S. v. Garcia*, 42 F.3d 719 (10th Cir. 1994).

147. *U.S. v. Gwinn*, 191 F.3d 874 (8th Cir. 2000). See U.S. v. Nicholson, 144 F.3d 632 (10th Cir. 1998).

148. *U.S. v. Stephens*, 206 F.3d 914 (9th Cir. 2000).

149. *U.S. v. Tugwell*, 125 F.3d 600 (8th Cir. 1997).

150. *U.S. v. Colyer*, 878 F.2d 469, 278 U.S.App. D.C. 367 (D.C.Cir. 1989).

151. *U.S. v. Liberto*, 660 F.Supp. 889 (DC D.C. 1987).

152. *U.S. v. Tartaglia*, 864 F.2d 837, 275 U.S.App.D.C. 15 (D.C.Cir. 1989)

153. *U.S. v. Liberto*, 660 F.Supp. 889 (DC D.C. 1987).

154. *U.S. v. Whitehead*, 849 F.2d 849 (4th Cir. 1988).

155. *Wilson v. Texas*, 98 SW3d 265 (Ct. App. 2002); *Nelson v. Florida*, 867 So.2d 534 (Ct. App. 2004).

156. *U.S. v. Roby,* 122 F.3d 1120 (8th Cir. 1997). See also *U.S. v. Riley*, 927 F.2d 1045 (8th Cir. 1991) (sniff occurred while baggage handlers were still unloading luggage from flight).

157. *U.S. v. Roby*, 122 F.3d 1120 (8th Cir. 1997).

158. *U.S. v. Burns*, 624 F.2d 95 (10th Cir. 1980) (citing *U.S. v. Pollard,* 466 F.2d 1 (10th Cir. 1972) ["limited warrantless search of a motel room incident to the lawful arrest of its occupants is permissible"]).

159. See also *North Dakota v. Kesler*, 396 N.W.2d 729 (1986) (reasonable suspicion package contained drugs justified delay in delivery).

160. *New York v. Offen*, 78 N.Y.2d 1089, 585 N.E.2d 370, 578 N.Y.S.2d 121 (1991).

161. *U.S. v. Lafrance*, 879 F.2d 1 (1st Cir. 1989).

162. *Oregon v. Smith*, 327 Or. 366, 963 P.2d 642 (1998) (padlocking of storage unit was unlawful but was irrelevant because evidence would have been obtained regardless).

163. *Pennsylvania v. Johnston*, 515 Pa. 454, 530 A.2d 74 (1987).

164. *Minnesota v. Carter*, 697 N.W.2d 199 (2005).

165. Ibid.

166. *Stabler v. Florida*, 990 So.2d 1258, 1262 (Ct. App. 2008).

167. *Nebraska v. Ortiz*, 257 Neb. 784, 600 N.W.2d 805 (1999).

168. *New York v. Dunn*, 77 N.Y.2d 19, 564 N.E.2d 1054, 563 N.Y.S.2d 388 (1990), cert. den. 501 U.S. 1219, 111 S.Ct. 2830, 115 L.Ed.2d 1000 (1991) (raising the "Orwellian" spectre of "police roaming indiscriminately through the corridors of public housing projects with trained dogs in search of drugs"). See also *New Hampshire v. Pellicci*, 133 N.H. 523, 580 A.2d 710 (1990).

169. *U.S. v. Hayes*, 551 F.3d 138 (2nd Cir. 2008).

170. *Florida v. Rabb*, 920 So.2d 1175 (Ct. App. 2006), cert. denied, 549 U.S. 1052 (2006).

171. *Rodriguez v. Texas*, 106 S.W.3d 224 (Ct. App. 2003).

172. *Doe v. Renfrow*, 475 F.Supp. 1012 (N.D. Ind. 1979), rev'd on other grounds, 631 F.2d 91 (7th Cir. 1980), cert denied 451 U.S. 1022, 101 S.Ct. 3015, 69 L.Ed.2d 395 (1981).

173. *Jones v. Latexo Independent School District*, 499 F.Supp. 223 (E.D.Tex. 1980).

174. *New Jersey v. T.L.O.*, 469 U.S. 325, 105 S.Ct. 733, 83 L.Ed2d 720 (1985).

175. *Horton v. Goose Creek Independent School District*, 690 F.2d 470 (5th Cir. 1982), on motion for rehearing, *Horton v. Goose Creek Independent School District*, 693 F.2d 524 (5th Cir. 1982), cert. denied 463 U.S. 1207 (1983).

176. *Zamora v. Pomeroy*, 639 F.2d 662 (10th Cir. 1981).

177. *U.S. v. Garcia*, 496 F.3d 495 (6th Cir. 2007).

178. *U.S. v. $144,770*, 157 F.3d 600 (8th Cir. 1998).

179. *U.S. v. $42,500*, 283 F.3d 977 (9th Cir. 2002). See also *U.S. v. $215,300*, 882 F.2d 417 (9th Cir. 1989) (confiscated money was placed in desk to which dog alerted; forfeiture affirmed).

180. *U.S. v. $53,082*, 985 F.2d 245 (6th Cir. 1993). See U.S. v. Pinkard, 125 F.3d 863 (10th Cir. 1997). See *Kaniff v. U.S.*, 351 F.3d 780 (7th Cir. 2003); *Saffell v. Crews*, 183 F.3d 655 (7th Cir. 1999).

181. *U.S. v. Jackson*, 390 F.3d 393 (5th Cir. 2004).

182. *U.S. v. Montoya de Hernandez*, 473 U.S. 531, 105 S.Ct. 3304, 87 L.Ed.2d 381 (1985).

183. *Kaniff v. U.S.*, 351 F.3d 780 (7th Cir. 2003). See *Saffell v. Crews*, 183 F.3d 655 (7th Cir. 1999) (dog's alert to luggage leads to strip search).

184. *U.S. v. Munoz-Nava*, 524 F.3d 1137 (10th Cir. 2008) (defendant was wearing overly large boots that bulged and had no luggage).

185. *U.S. v. Reyes*, 349 F.3d 219 (5th Cir. 2003).

9 Scientific Issues in Detection Functions

It has been known for more than a century that dogs can be taught to alert to very specific scents and chemicals,[1] yet it was only in the 1970s, with narcotics and explosives detection dogs, that this skill began to have forensic applications.[2] Because of the high value of specific substance detection for law enforcement, this canine skill and its potential applications have received a great deal of scientific and forensic study and will undoubtedly continue to be a major area of forensics research.

RECOGNITION OF ILLEGAL SUBSTANCES AND SECONDARY CHEMICALS

Narcotics detection dogs are commonly trained to alert to marijuana, cocaine, crack cocaine, heroin, and methamphetamine. Scientific studies have demonstrated that dogs are sometimes detecting something with which the drug has been treated or packaged with rather than the drug itself. A number of studies have shown that even when dogs alert to the drug, they may actually be detecting volatile odor chemicals associated with a drug rather than the parent drug itself.[3] A study by two Alabama scientists found that dogs could be trained rather easily to detect 10 different odors and that the amount of time for training new odor discriminations tended to decrease as more odor discriminations were trained.[4]

COCAINE

One research team looked at the amount of cocaine odor that was necessary for a narcotics detection dog to successfully find the substance.[5] The researchers noted that with illegal drugs, including cocaine, there are many constituents besides the drug itself. These substances may be by-products of refinement or contaminants from processing or packaging. Methyl benzoate is a consistent constituent in illegal cocaine and may come as a compound extracted with the cocaine from coca leaves, as a decomposition by-product from excessive use of hydrochloric acid in isolating cocaine hydrochloride, and as a product of the hydrolysis of cocaine. Dogs were taught to recognize both cocaine hydrochloride and methyl benzoate.

The experiments involved the dog being placed in a chamber. The dog learned to insert his head into a large hole on hearing a beeping tone. There were two levers on either side of the hole where the dog put its head. The dog was taught to press the left lever when the air in the chamber was clean, but to press the right level when an odor was present. Food was given for correct responses and a blackout of the chamber for an incorrect response. Testing began when a dog's accuracy in discriminating clean air from air with a target odor was consistently high. A typical session lasted about 55 minutes and involved about 65 clean air trials and 65 odor trials. Seven dogs were trained and tested on vapor from methyl benzoate. Six were trained and tested on vapor from pharmaceutical and illicit cocaine hydrochloride. Five of the dogs trained with methyl benzoate were also trained to press a middle lever on trials when vapor from a nontarget odor was presented in the chamber.[6]

The pharmaceutical cocaine was more than 99% pure, while the illicit cocaine was approximately 93% pure. The research team found that in detecting pharmaceutical cocaine, the dogs could detect only very high concentrations of the vapor generated. The dogs were much better at detecting illicit cocaine, in other words, cocaine with contaminants including methyl benzoate. Four dogs were successful at rates between 80% and 90% with concentrations of the illegal drug above 0.1 ppb, but success rates fell rapidly below 0.05 ppb. The researchers concluded that "when dogs are trained to detect cocaine in the field, their discriminations probably depend on one or more constituents in the vapor sample in addition to cocaine HCl." They suggested that "methyl benzoate may be one of the constituents of the illicit cocaine odor signature for dogs," but it is apparently not the only one.

The same team looked at the effects of extraneous odors on canine detection.[7] These tests were performed because criminals sometimes put other odors, masking agents, in shipments of contraband to thwart canine detection efforts, and dogs must sometimes work in environments where there is automobile exhaust and other smells. The researchers were surprised to find that "detection performance changed little in the presence of all but the very highest extraneous odor concentrations." Thus, it appears almost impossible to impede a dog's ability to smell a target odor.

NUMBER OF TARGET ODORS THAT DOGS CAN RETAIN

One study trained dogs to alert to 10 different odors and not to alert to other odors. The dogs were trained to alert to specific odors until they had a correct response rate of 94%.[8] It was found that the dogs retained the ability to recognize the target odors for periods up to 120 days.

DETECTION OF COCAINE ON CURRENCY

Currency may become contaminated with drugs, particularly cocaine.[9] In a 1994 case from the Ninth Circuit,[10] the court cited reports that 75% to 90% of all circulated currency in Los Angeles is contaminated with cocaine residue. Other researchers found almost all $20 bills in circulation have cocaine residue.[11] Although this would suggest that dogs would alert on large amounts of currency, this has been shown not to be the case. Presumably the drug odor dissipates over time, leaving trace amounts on currency that can only be detected in the laboratory.

The simplest form of standardized currency sniff test is called the one room–six position design. In this approach, there are six identical envelopes with an equal number of bills. Five of the envelopes contain money samples from general circulation, while the sixth contains suspected drug money. The handler is not informed of which envelope contains the "dirty money" when he directs the dog to search the room for drugs. In the scratch-box design, on the other hand, the target odor is placed in one of six positions in a box, requiring the dog to search and eliminate five compartments, while alerting on the sixth position. Airholes at the top allow transfer of narcotic odor for the dog to sample, but dividers on the bottom prevent the odor from traveling lengthwise from compartment to compartment. See Figure 9.1.

Researchers at the International Forensic Research Institute at Florida International University determined that although U.S. currency often demonstrates the presence of cocaine, this is usually not at levels where it can be easily removed other than by solvent washing. No other drugs besides cocaine have been shown to be widely found as contaminants of U.S. currency, though diacetylmorphine and tretrahydrocannabinol have been reported. Reviewing prior studies, the researchers found that U.S. currency shows an average amount of 14.5 μg cocaine per bill. The researchers sought "to confirm the identity and quantity of the unique volatile odor chemical (or chemicals) of illicit cocaine that dogs use to detect cocaine employing solid-phase microextraction (SPME) combined with gas chromatography (GC), including the optimization of controllable variables such as fiber chemistry, extraction time, and desorption time."

> The purities of cocaine base and cocaine hydrochloride from the production of illicit cocaine are typically 80–95% and 80–97%, respectively. Pharmaceutical-grade cocaine may contain more than 99.5% cocaine, but it also has some coca-related impurities. ...The quantity and quality of the impurities in illicit cocaine (i.e., benzoic acid, anhydroecgonine methyl ester, anhydroecgonine, *trans*-cinnamic acid, ecgonine methyl ester, ecgonine, pseudoecgonine, tropacocaine, benzoylecgonine, norcocaine, beta-truxinic

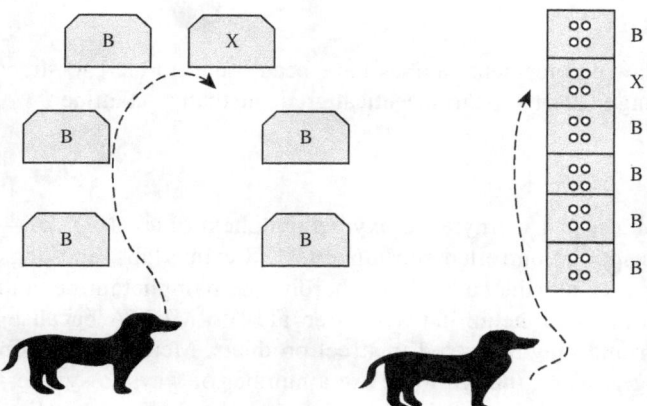

FIGURE 9.1 Two ways of testing currency for significant drug residue. On the left, equal amounts of currency are placed in envelopes. The dog alerts to crime-related currency (X), while not alerting to envelopes with bank currency (B). On the right, currency is placed in boxes with airholes. (Created from data in Mesloh, C., Henych, M., and Wolf, R., Sniff Test: Utilization of the Law Enforcement Canine in the Seizure of Paper Currency, *Journal of Forensic Identification*, *52*(6), 704, 2002.)

acid, alpha-truxillic acid, *cis*-cinnamoyl ecgonine methyl ester, *trans*-cinnamoyl ecogonine methyl ester, and *N*-formylcocaine) are different from sample to sample and batch to batch. We have also found *methyl benzoate* to be commonly present, which was not analyzed for in previous studies.[12]

Solutions containing different amounts of cocaine and by-products were prepared in chloroform and applied to $1 denominations of U.S. currency at least 20 minutes before testing. This allowed time for the chloroform to evaporate completely without significantly reducing the odor chemicals present. Successively increasing amounts of pharmaceutical grade cocaine, street cocaine, and cocaine by-products were spiked onto the currency. Currency was placed in precleaned and oven-dried 9-inch-round steel boxes with six small holes in the top. Negative control boxes were also used. Dog handlers were blind to the target boxes and were simply told to sweep the test field for controlled substances and determine to which boxes the dogs alerted. The researchers found that the only chemical that elicited a consistent response was methyl benzoate (in a training product called Sigma Pseudo Cocaine). Pharmaceutical grade cocaine did not elicit responses from most dogs tested. The researchers found that the effective dose for 50% of the animals tested was approximately 1 µg of methyl benzoate.

None of the dogs tested alerted to byproducts other than methyl benzoate, and the majority did not alert to pharmaceutical-grade cocaine even at the highest levels tested of 1 g. Because this level is some 100,000 times greater than that reported on circulated currency, *it is not plausible that innocently contaminated U.S. currency contains sufficient enough quantities of cocaine and associated volatile chemicals to signal an alert from a properly trained drug detector dog.*[13]

In a case arising in Ohio, the defendant attempted to argue that the officers involved in his arrest had smeared pseudococaine on the door of his car so that a dog would alert to it. He was unable to persuade the court of this, however.[14]

Currency may be found in a vehicle search. If there is suspicion that those handling the money recently also handled drugs, the currency should be secured by a "money officer" who has not handled any illicit substances in the previous 24-hour period and who can maintain the chain of evidence. A control officer should collect money from general circulation to act as a control. This officer also should not have handled illicit substances within the previous 24 hours. If strict protocols are maintained, it may be verified that the currency was handled by individuals who also handled drugs.[15]

METHAMPHETAMINE

As with cocaine, law enforcement canines have been found to alert to street methamphetamine samples while failing to alert to pharmaceutical grade methamphetamine.[16]

ECSTASY

Ecstasy—to chemists, 3,4-methylenedioxymethamphetamine (MDMA)—is the fifth most common nonprescription controlled substance in U.S crime labs, and dogs have been trained to alert to it along with marijuana, cocaine, heroin, methamphetamine, and other drugs. Dogs trained to alert to methamphetamine will often alert to MDMA because the substances are chemically similar and may be mixed in street products. Methamphetamine may also be part of the synthesizing process, though there are a number of ways to synthesize MDMA. Merck first synthesized it in 1914 from safrole, which can be obtained by distilling sassafras oil. Because of the different synthesizing routes, dogs should be tested on MDMA from different sources. Where different characteristics are detected in seizures of MDMA, narcotics investigators may sometimes be able to identify the laboratory or criminal organization behind a particular catch.[17]

Recent research has demonstrated that a number of chemicals that are found in an MDMA tablet will not be found in a headspace extraction technique.[18] This indicates that where simulated odor must be used, it is important to verify that the artificial odor includes compounds the dog is actually going to smell when it encounters the real narcotic. This becomes more difficult when it is realized that the compounds may differ depending on the synthesizing process used to create MDMA. The dominant odor signature chemical in MDMA has been shown to be piperonal, and a "pseudo" MDMA containing this compound was found to be very effective in obtaining alerts from dogs trained to recognize MDMA.[19]

DOGS COMPARED TO OTHER TECHNOLOGIES

Comparing dogs to other technologies for detecting chemicals, one report argued: "[D]rug-sniffing dogs tend to have lower purchase costs than most technology-based trace detection systems, but they can have higher maintenance costs related to training."[20] The report notes, however, that there "is always a tradeoff between the number of drugs or other substances the dog can detect and the proficiency with which the dog detects on particular substance."[21] A comparison of the advantages of technology-based drug detectors and drug dogs is shown in Table 9.1.

TABLE 9.1
Comparing Canine and Technology-Based Drug Detection

	Technology	Canine
Work period	24 hours/day (in principle)	1–2 hours before rest
Mobility	Poor to good	Excellent
Follows scent to source	No	Yes
Molecule detected	Drug of interest, or adduct or fragment	Uncertain in most cases (though research is progressing)
Purchase cost	Moderate to high	Low
Maintenance costs	Low to moderate	High (including training and handler)
Best application	Checkpoint screening	Search

SCIENTIFIC STANDARDS AND DETECTION EVIDENCE

The treatment of canine evidence under judicial standards for admissibility of scientific evidence has already been discussed concerning scent identification, and will be discussed later as to various types of canine detection work. A common perspective has been that canine scent detection is outside of strict scientific realms. As stated by one California appellate court:

> Training for narcotics detection work may be more sophisticated and thus a proper subject of expert testimony than training a dog to sit, fetch a ball or stay out of the garbage, but the average juror has some basis in his or her own experiences to muster a healthy skepticism for the expert's testimony on such matters. Most jurors have never seen a polygraph, voiceprint or breathalyzer. Many, however, have everyday contact with dogs. The average juror has had sufficient experience with the subject matter to be able to evaluate the evidence concerning a dog's training, performance, and behavior that the application of the *Kelly/ Frye* test to such evidence is unnecessary.[22]

Some cases have avoided scientific threshold issues on procedural grounds.[23]

NOTES

1. Kalischer (1909).
2. *California v. Furman*, 30 Cal.App.3d 454, 106 Cal.Rptr. 366 (Ct. App. 1973).
3. Lorenzo et al. (2004).
4. Williams and Johnston (2002).
5. Waggoner et al. (1997).
6. For a detailed description of the operation of the chamber, see Johnston et al. (1994).
7. Waggoner et al. (1998).
8. Williams et al. (1997). For a discussion of how cotton fibers may hold trace amounts of cocaine and other chemicals, see Sleeman et al. (2000).
9. Mesloh, Henych, and Wolf (2002).
10. *U.S. v. $30,060*, 39 F.3d 1039, 1042 (9th Cir. 1994).
11. Negrusz et al. (1998). Aware of this defense, the government usually provides facts that bolster a dog's alert to currency, but not always. See *Muhuammed v. DEA, Asset Forfeiture Unit*, 92 F.3d 648 (8th Cir. 1996) (government chastised for "lamely" pointing to arrest of defendant during a later incident).
12. Furton et al. (2002) (emphasis of methyl benzoate added).
13. Furton et al. (2002) (March 2002) (emphasis added); See also Furton et al. (1997a) (finding "majority of the canines did not alert to pharmaceutical grade cocaine even at levels as high as 1 g").
14. *U.S. v. Navarro-Camacho*, 186 F.3d 701 (6th Cir. 1999).
15. Mesloh, Henych, and Wolf (2002a).
16. Lorenzo et al. (2004).
17. Ibid.
18. Solid-phase microextraction (SPME)/gas chromatography-mass spectrometry (GC-MS).
19. Lorenzo et al. (2004); see also Macias et al. (2010).
20. Parmeter et al. (2000).
21. Gazit et al. (2005) (noting that the ability to find odors decreased as the chances of encountering the odor by the dog decreased).
22. *California v. Sommer*, 16 Cal.Rptr.2d 165 (Ct. App. 1993).
23. *California v. Schoppe-Rico*, 140 Cal.App.4th 1370 (Ct. App. 2006) (failure to conduct *Frye* hearing on admission of dog evidence was not prejudicial as it was not reasonably likely jury would have reached a different verdict had dog scent evidence been excluded); *California v. Chavez*, 2004 WL 1173075 (Ct. App. 2004) (court accepted evidence but noted laxity in raising issue); *California v. Loaiza*, 2005 WL 237258 (Ct. App. 2005) (failure to object at trial means issue is not preserved on appeal even though law may have been changing at the time); *California v. Melara*, 2006 WL 164989 (Ct. App. 2005) (defense sought to introduce exonerating scent evidence obtained in part from scent transfer unit, but failed to produce proper expert, only dog handlers); *California v. Adams*, 2008 WL 21153557 (Ct. App. 2008) (objection based on *Frye* not made at trial); *Aguilar v. Woodford*, 2009 WL 509127 (C.D. Cal. 2009) (not reasonably probable result would have been different even if dog scent evidence had been excluded).

10 Automobile Sniffs

The majority of narcotics sniffs in the case law occur near or inside automobiles. Cars and trucks allow for fast movement and permit a reasonably careful criminal to remain anonymous through most of a short or long journey. On the other hand, police patrol highways used by drug traffickers, and many police units travel with narcotics detection dogs or can summon one in short order. This is one area where the Supreme Court has provided basic uniformity for the federal judicial system and to a somewhat lesser degree for state courts.

ILLINOIS v. CABALLES

Roy Caballes was arrested for speeding. A member of the Illinois State Police Drug Interdiction Team was nearby and overheard a transmission of the arrest and brought his drug dog to the location. The dog alerted to the trunk of the car and a search revealed marijuana. The trial court determined that the dog's alert was sufficiently reliable to give probable cause for a search. A state appellate court affirmed but the Illinois Supreme Court reversed, finding the canine sniff had been performed without "specific and articulable facts" to suggest drug activity, so that the use of the dog unjustifiably enlarged the scope of a routine traffic stop into an investigation.[1]

The U.S. Supreme Court granted certiorari on the question of whether "the Fourth Amendment requires reasonable, articulable suspicion to justify using a drug-detection dog to sniff a vehicle during a legitimate traffic stop." Justice John Paul Stevens, writing for the majority, noted that the reasonableness of the search was critical.

> [A] seizure that is lawful at its inception can violate the Fourth Amendment if its manner of execution unreasonably infringes interests protected by the Constitution.[2] ... A seizure that is justified solely by the interest in issuing a warning ticket to the driver can become unlawful if it is prolonged beyond the time reasonably required to complete that mission. In an earlier case involving a dog sniff that occurred during an unreasonably prolonged traffic stop, the Illinois Supreme Court held that use of the dog and the subsequent discovery of contraband were the product of an unconstitutional seizure.[3] ... We may assume that a similar result would be warranted in this case if the dog sniff had been conducted while respondent was being unlawfully detained.

In *Caballes*, however, the Illinois Supreme Court had concluded that the duration of the stop was entirely justified by the traffic offense and the ordinary inquiries incident to such a stop. That court said that the seizure became unlawful solely because of the canine sniff outside the car. Justice Stevens stated that the state court concluded that "the use of the dog converted the citizen–police encounter from a lawful traffic stop into a drug investigation, and because the shift in purpose was not supported by any reasonable suspicion that respondent possessed narcotics, it was unlawful." Justice Stevens, writing for the U.S. Supreme Court, disagreed, saying that the dog sniff was performed on the exterior of the car while the driver "was lawfully seized for a traffic violation. Any intrusion on respondent's privacy expectations does not rise to the level of a constitutionally cognizable infringement." More emphatically:

> A dog sniff conducted during a concededly lawful traffic stop that reveals no information other than the location of a substance that no individual has any right to possess does not violate the Fourth Amendment.

The judgment of the Illinois Supreme Court was vacated, and the case remanded.[4]

Justices Ginsburg and Souter separately dissented. Justice Ginsburg noted that Caballes had been driving 71 miles per hour in a 65 mile per hour zone. As will be discussed later, the most minor offenses have justified stops that have led to drug busts. She also noted that the state trooper had not requested any assistance but the officer with the drug dog showed up anyway. The trooper was in the process of writing Caballes a warning ticket when the dog alerted at the trunk of the car. Justice Ginsburg argued that the decision to which she was dissenting "clears the way for suspicionless, dog-accompanied drug sweeps of parked cars along sidewalks and in parking lots. ... Nor would motorists have constitutional grounds for complaint should police with dogs, stationed at long traffic lights, circle cars waiting for the red signal to turn green."[5]

Justice Souter, also dissenting, was concerned with the inaccuracies of detection dogs.

> The infallible dog, however, is a creature of legal fiction. Although the Supreme Court of Illinois did not get into the sniffing averages of drug dogs, their supposed infallibility is belied by judicial opinions describing well-trained animals sniffing and alerting with less than perfect accuracy, whether owing to errors by their handlers, the limitations of the dogs themselves, or even the pervasive contamination of currency by cocaine.

Justice Souter cited cases referring to accuracy rates of drug dogs,[6] a currency sniff case referring to drug residues on currency,[7] and a study finding that dogs may make false alerts up to 60% of the time.[8] Justice Souter concluded that in "practical terms, the evidence is clear that the dog that alerts hundreds of times will be wrong dozens of times."

Decisions based on state constitutional law may, at least in some jurisdictions, require reasonable suspicion before a sniff of a car may be conducted. In a 2002 Montana case, a confidential informer told a drug task force that the defendant was dealing in large amounts of marijuana. An officer had a canine team sniff the exterior of the defendant's vehicle. The dog alerted, a warrant was obtained, and drugs were found in the trunk of the car. The Montana Supreme Court held that the defendant had a reasonable expectation of privacy as to the trunk of his vehicle and the canine sniff of the vehicle was a search under the Montana Constitution. However, a warrantless search is not unreasonable if there is particularized suspicion that criminal activity is currently taking place.

> [W]hen a person maintains control of a container in which he has a reasonable expectation of privacy, but where the odors from that container are freely exposed to the public, particularized suspicion is required for the use of a canine to detect those odors.[9]

The Montana Supreme Court held that the effectively anonymous tip, a prior conviction for possession of paraphernalia, and records mentioning the defendant's name in connection with drug activity did not provide sufficient particularized suspicion. It is not difficult to imagine other courts taking the opposite perspective.

ALERTS DURING THE INITIAL REASON FOR THE STOP

Vehicle sniffs often occur during or following police stops for traffic violations,[10] as happened in *Caballes*. Stops that have justified subsequent sniffs have included cases involving dangerous driving,[11] tailgating,[12] speeding,[13] driving too slowly,[14] violating a left-lane law by passing too slowly,[15] having an overweight axle,[16] running a stop sign,[17] driving on the shoulder of the road,[18] changing lanes without signaling,[19] driving over traffic lines illegally,[20] drifting over the fogline twice,[21] apparent road rage,[22] following another vehicle too closely,[23] failure to use a seat belt,[24] having a broken headlight,[25] having broken tail lamps,[26] having a broken license plate light,[27] not having a visible license plate,[28] having a license plate registered to a different vehicle,[29] having a broken windshield,[30] having windows tinted too dark,[31] merely being stopped at a border checkpoint,[32] being at a location under a stakeout for drug activity,[33] picking up someone at a bus station when an informant had indicated drugs would arrive on the bus,[34] and having a license plate violation in an area of high drug activity.[35]

EXTENDING THE STOP

Once a driver is stopped, circumstances may require additional investigation or provide suspicion justifying a longer stop than might otherwise be the case, such as the discovery that the driver has a suspended license, which was held to justify an hour-and-a-half detention before a drug dog arrived.[36] Also in this category have been food wrappers on the floor,[37] a strong odor of air freshener,[38] metal shavings on the front floorboard,[39] acting nervous after a stop,[40] sweating profusely,[41] refusing to make eye contact,[42] a criminal record of a passenger,[43] a vehicle registered in a state where neither the driver nor the passenger lived,[44] passengers giving conflicting accounts of where they were going or the purpose of their trip,[45] an outstanding warrant,[46] a walkie-talkie (sometimes used by drug dealers to keep in contact with each other while transporting drugs),[47] cigar smoke (which may mask marijuana smoke, but not to a dog),[48] smell of marijuana,[49] having well-manicured hands but claiming to be a mechanic,[50] appearing glassy eyed with pinpoint pupils,[51] a driver saying he was not in a hurry but then when questioned about contraband saying he was in a hurry,[52] traveling expensively but claiming to be unemployed,[53] and an informant's report.[54] In a case arising in Oregon, an officer thought he smelled drugs but wanted a dog to confirm his suspicions, resulting in a find of methamphetamine.[55] In a case arising in Florida, an officer offered to fill a gas can for the defendant whose car had run out of gas. The defendant said he would rather wait for a tow truck, providing enough suspicion for the officer to call for a canine unit.[56]

It can be argued that stronger grounds for suspicion justify longer periods for questioning and detention. A dog sniff that occurs while an officer is still working on the purpose of the initial stop generally cannot be found to involve an improper extension of the stop.[57] In a case arising in Maine, the First Circuit stated:

> Perhaps if Steadman had had only very weak grounds for suspicion, he should, as the court below suggested, have dismissed Quinn and Streifel after one or two questions. But Steadman had not only *reasonable* grounds, he had very *strong* grounds, approaching probable cause, for suspicion.[58]

The "very *strong* grounds" included an informant's tip, another party coming from the same location was found to have marijuana, and suspects were at the property being watched very late without persuasive explanations for their activities. In a Sixth Circuit case, detention beyond 13 minutes was illegal because that was the point where the officer's questions ceased being necessitated by the suspected traffic violation.[59]

Many decisions are driven by facts and the importance that courts attach to those facts. Reasonable suspicion must be more than a hunch. In an Eighth Circuit case, use of a rental vehicle, traveling from California, not having luggage in the passenger compartment, and the fact the driver was looking for a job in a distant location were not sufficient for continued detention after an oral warning.[60] A sniff occurring an hour after a traffic stop has been held not to be an unreasonable period.[61] Telling an officer he did not have anything illegal in his vehicle was not a reason for extending a traffic stop in a 2004 Arkansas case.[62] Denial of an officer's request to search a vehicle does not provide reasonable suspicion to prolong a traffic stop.[63]

DILIGENCE AND CONSENT

Longer periods will be permitted if there is consent.[64] Diligence in attempting to get a narcotics dog has been recognized as significant in the determination of whether a delay was too long.[65] If the police already had probable cause to search a vehicle even without a dog sniff, then waiting for a drug dog did not violate the defendant's rights in a Third Circuit case.[66]

REQUEST TO OPEN VENTS PRIOR TO SNIFF

At a stop in Wyoming, officers requested that prior to a dog sniff of the exterior of a vehicle, the passengers roll up the windows, open the vents, and get out of the vehicle. The case was remanded for consideration of whether these requests changed the nature of the exterior sniff and made it something more than a *Caballes* situation.[67] The Illinois Supreme Court found no Fourth Amendment violation in this procedure.[68]

JUMPING INTO A VEHICLE

Dogs performing external sniffs sometimes jump into a vehicle through an open window or door. See Figure 10.1. Although this may result in finding drugs inside the vehicle, this does not always happen.[69] In a federal case arising in New Mexico, Border Patrol agents stopped a van they thought might be carrying illegal aliens. The driver and his passenger produced papers indicating they were legally in the United States and the driver, Winningham, consented to a search. Finding no one inside, the agent left the door open and told Winningham that he had information the van was

FIGURE 10.1   A dog jumping into a car. Dogs sometimes jump in open windows or through open doors of vehicles trying to get at the source of a narcotics or explosives scent. This dog was trained to enter a vehicle in apprehension situations when a suspect refused to exit a vehicle. (Courtesy of Tonna Marek, Nampa [Idaho] Police Department, May 2005.)

carrying narcotics. The agent asked permission to run the dog on the vehicle. Winningham agreed but the agents did not have a dog. After 5 or 6 minutes, a dog arrived with other agents. The dog did not clearly alert outside the van, though the officer said that he observed a noticeable difference in the dog's behavior near the van. The officer opened a door and the dog jumped inside the van, where it alerted at a rear vent. Inside the vent, the agents found 50 kilograms of marijuana. The district court found that there was no voluntary consent for the dog to enter the cabin of the van and suppressed the evidence. The Tenth Circuit affirmed the district court's grant of the motion to suppress.[70]

Cases have gone against defendants who were themselves responsible, directly or indirectly, for a dog entering a vehicle. An officer at a traffic stop smelled crystal methadrine in the defendant's car and attempted to get a warrant but the magistrate refused to issue one and released the driver, Stone. The officer then called the Albuquerque police and suggested they pull Stone over and subject the car to a sniff. Stone was pulled over for speeding and engaged in conversation.

> Within a few more minutes another police officer arrived with the dog. The dog circled the car, showed interest underneath the rear area of the car and at the passenger door, and then jumped in the open hatchback where he "keyed" on a duffel bag. ... The police then searched the entire car and the duffel bag. ... The bag contained approximately 33,000 methaqualone tablets.

The trial court found that the dog's leap into the car "did not vitiate the seizure, regardless of whether or not it was a search." The defendant had voluntarily opened the hatchback to get a citation requested by the officer. The Tenth Circuit held that the external sniff was not a search under *Place*,[71] a Supreme Court case discussed later concerning a luggage sniff (the case was pre-*Caballes*). The Tenth Circuit was troubled by the dog entering the car. "People have a reasonable expectation of privacy in the interiors of their automobiles; police may not search an automobile unless they have probable cause to believe it contains contraband." The circuit court emphasized that until the dog alerted inside the car, the police had only reasonable suspicion that narcotics might be found. The alert gave probable cause. The court held that the fact the dog jumped in on its own was significant.

> There is no evidence, nor does Stone contend, that the police asked Stone to open the hatchback so the dog could jump in. Nor is there any evidence the police handler encouraged the dog to jump in the car. ... In these circumstances, we think the police remained within the range of activities they may permissibly engage in when they have reasonable suspicion to believe an automobile contains narcotics.

The conviction was affirmed.[72]

In an Idaho case, a narcotics detection dog that jumped in the trunk of an impounded car during an inventory search alerted to a black briefcase. A warrant was obtained and the briefcase was found to contain $34,000. The impounding was proper and justified an inventory search. The court held that the dog's disobeying of a command and jumping into the vehicle did not make the inventory search invalid. There was no Fourth Amendment violation and the forfeiture was proper.[73]

Another federal case arising in New Mexico also focused on placing or helping a dog get inside a vehicle being sniffed.

> [T]he credible and undisputed suppression-hearing testimony disclosed that Laika began to alert as she approached the driver-side door of Defendant's vehicle and was on alert as she jumped into the vehicle through the open driver-side window. No evidence was presented to support a conclusion that Agent Hubert or anyone else placed or helped Laika into the vehicle. To the contrary, Laika's entry into Defendant's car appears to have been wholly instinctive.

A motion to suppress was denied.[74]

A federal district court case arising in Pennsylvania involved two factors that tipped the scale. After a traffic stop, the officer saw what he believed to be some marijuana debris on the front seat of the car. During a walk around the car, the dog jumped into the car and alerted to a duffel bag in the back seat.

> Zeus did not so much conduct an exterior sniff of the Grand Am, but instead apparently entered into the car via an open window prior to alerting to the duffel bag on the back seat. Because *Edmond* and *Caballes* appear to be limited to declaring that external canine sniffs may be conducted during traffic stops even absent reasonable suspicion that the vehicle contains contraband, it is not clear that these decisions would support a dog sniff that moves from the exterior of an automobile to the interior of the car. … Although the Court has not identified any binding authority on the point, the consensus among the courts that have addressed this question appears to be that a canine sniff that migrates from outside a car or other container to the interior does not constitute a violation of the Fourth Amendment, *provided that the canine makes entry into the suspect vehicle of its own initiative and is neither encouraged into nor placed in the vehicle by a law enforcement officer.*

The court discussed prior cases on the issue[75] and concluded:

> [T]he majority of federal courts that have confronted questions similar to that presented in this case have concluded that canine sniffs of the interior of a vehicle or other container are lawful, but suggest that such interior sniffs may become constitutionally infirm in the event that the interior sniff is accomplished or facilitated by the officer-handler.

The court then discussed the plain view doctrine and its extension, the plain smell doctrine,[76] and held that the alert to the duffel bag gave probable cause to justify a search.[77]

ALERT OUTSIDE A CAR PROVIDING PROBABLE CAUSE FOR A SEARCH INSIDE

An alert outside a car has been held to provide probable cause for a search inside the car, and it has also been held to provide probable cause to allow the dog to sniff inside the car.[78] A car stopped at the permanent Border Patrol checkpoint near Alamagordo, New Mexico, came under suspicion because the car had only a temporary license tag, common among smugglers. The agent asked for permission to walk a dog around the car, which the defendant gave. The Border Patrol agent asked the defendant to move the car to the secondary inspection area, where the agent took a narcotics detection dog from a kennel. The dog alerted to the car. Admitted to the car, the dog sniffed along the top of the back seat and again alerted. A subsequent search revealed bundles of marijuana hidden behind the rear portion of the back seat. The defendant argued that the search inside the car was unlawful. The trial court had found that the alert outside the car provided probable cause for the dog to search further. The circuit court held that "the search of the car interior was supported by probable cause based on the dog's behavior outside the car."[79]

The Fifth Circuit has stated that a dog sniff "does not constitute a search whether it occurs at the primary checkpoint or at the secondary checkpoint."[80]

ALERT JUSTIFIES TWO SEARCHES

An Eighth Circuit case involved a dog alerting to a truck after a traffic stop, followed by a search that revealed nothing. The officers then moved the truck to a nearby wrecker service where a more complete search revealed 5,000 grams of cocaine hidden under the windshield. The court held this was not an unreasonable extension of the traffic stop.[81]

The fact that a physical search of a car did not find anything does not preclude a subsequent dog sniff and another search.[82]

USE OF MORE THAN ONE DOG

Some sniffs involve more than one dog. In a case arising in Texas, one dog was startled by a truck's refrigeration sounds but a second alerted, resulting in a search that revealed cocaine.[83]

In a case arising in Michigan, a canine team circled a car and the dog showed some interest in the rear hatch area but did not alert. The defendant should have been released at that point but the police called for an additional team, which arrived an hour and 20 minutes later. This dog definitely did alert. A warrant was obtained and $706,000 was found in boxes. The district court found no Fourth Amendment violations. The Sixth Circuit held, however, that the police lacked reasonable suspicion of drug-trafficking activity after the first dog failed to alert.

> Once the drug-sniffing dog was brought to the scene and failed to alert positively to the presence of narcotics in the vehicle, the officers' suspicions that Davis was in possession of narcotics were dispelled. Drug-sniffing dogs are highly trained to detect the presence of narcotics, and the dog Rocky did not detect any narcotics in the car. Officer Craigin, Rocky's handler, noted during the suppression hearing that Rocky was a qualified, trained, and certified dog. Rocky had been in service as a drug-sniffing dog for approximately three years prior to Davis's stop and underwent training on a continual basis. Officer Craigin testified that Rocky's success rate at accurately identifying the presence of narcotics was over ninety percent. Based upon this information, there were no grounds for the police to continue to believe that the vehicle contained narcotics after Rocky failed to alert.[84]

BODY SNIFFS OF PASSENGERS

An alert outside a vehicle may provide probable cause to search the vehicle without providing probable cause to search a particular occupant.

> Officer Nelson advised Officer Hertik, who was still in the process of writing tickets, that Bosco had made a positive alert on the vehicle. While Officer Nelson returned Bosco to her patrol car, Officer Hertik approached the Buick to speak with the driver. She informed the driver that she suspected that the vehicle contained drugs and asked the occupants to exit the vehicle so the police could search them.
>
> The occupants were taken out of the car one at a time and searched while the others remained in the car. The other officers watched the occupants of the car while the searches were being conducted. Officer Jonathan Supko, one of the officers who had arrived at the scene, searched the three males. Officer Supko testified that his actions were not a mere "frisk" or "pat down" but were intended to discover anything suspicious, for "anything apparent ... [w]eapons and what not." Officer Supko first searched the driver and then he searched the front seat passenger.

The court concluded that the alert gave probable cause to search the car but not without more evidence to search every occupant.[85]

DRUGS NO LONGER PRESENT

A positive alert by a narcotics dog may be admitted even if drugs are not found in a subsequent search. A dog's alert to a nylon bag in a car was admitted even though the bag contained no contraband. A search of the defendant revealed a cocaine-sniffing spoon on his keychain. The defendant was also connected to drugs found in a co-conspirator's car, and his conviction for conspiracy to import cocaine and marijuana was affirmed.[86]

ALERTS AFTER INITIAL REASON FOR STOP IS COMPLETED

Different considerations come into play when the initial reason for the stop has been completed and no reasonable suspicion for extending it has arisen.[87] A driver was stopped at a permanent checkpoint near the Mexican border where agents were checking for illegal aliens changed focus when the agents noticed that the driver was becoming increasingly nervous. A brief detention beyond the check for aliens to take a narcotics detection dog around the car was held by the Ninth Circuit not to be a violation of the Fourth Amendment.[88] The shorter the detention, the less likely the defendant will be able to avoid conviction.[89]

In a federal case arising in Arkansas, a driver was pulled over for tailgating. After giving the driver back his license and issuing a verbal warning, the officer told the driver he was free to go. Then the officer began asking if the driver had weapons or drugs. The driver initially denied having anything illegal. The officer asked if he could search the car. The driver asked what would happen if he declined to allow the search. The officer asked the driver to get out of the car and told him that a drug dog would soon arrive and circle around the car. The driver then admitted to having methamphetamine in his briefcase. The Eighth Circuit concluded that the totality of the circumstances failed to produce a reasonable suspicion that could justify the continued, or renewed, detention, and held the seizure unlawful.

> The consensual nature of the encounter between Officer Taylor and Beck continued until Beck asked what would happen if he refused to permit a search of his automobile. At that point Officer Taylor informed Beck that if he refused to consent to a search, Officer Beck would have a canine unit conduct a drug sniff of his automobile. Because a consensual encounter can become an investigatory detention as a result of police conduct, ... we do not believe a person in Beck's situation, who had been present when a canine unit had been summoned to the scene and was then told by Officer Taylor that he was going to have a canine unit conduct a drug sniff of Beck's car, would reasonably have felt free to leave. ...
>
> Furthermore, any doubts that Beck had that he was free to drive away were extinguished when, after refusing consent to a search of his automobile, Officer Taylor ordered Beck to get out of his automobile and to stand on the side of the road. At that point, having been ordered out of his vehicle in order to permit a drug dog sniff, a reasonable person in Beck's situation would not have felt free to leave.

The conviction was reversed.[90]

Courts have sometimes specified that an officer must have reasonable suspicion for calling in a canine unit after the initial reason for the stop was concluded.

> To establish an unreasonably prolonged detention, the defendant must show that the officer detained him beyond the amount of time otherwise justified by the purpose of the stop and did so without reasonable suspicion.[91]

A 1996 Georgia case found that reasonable suspicion could not support a sniff after the initial stop had been completed merely because (1) the driver and his passenger appeared nervous, (2) the vehicle was rented and the rental agreement was in the driver's wife's name, and (3) the passenger was the driver's girlfriend. In the absence of reasonable suspicion, the officers should have obtained the defendant's consent for the sniff. The case was remanded to determine if consent was obtained.[92] An officer's skill in obtaining consent is often critical in judicial analysis of marginal cases.

DOG ALERTS BUT NOT DURING SNIFF

In a 1990 case arising in Texas, a dog that had not been commanded to conduct a sniff nevertheless alerted. The Fifth Circuit determined that this provided probable cause for a search. Agents discovered 330 pounds of marijuana in a compartment behind a trap door under the diesel tank. The conviction was affirmed.[93]

ALERTS AT SECONDARY LOCATIONS

Many reasons, including dangerous traffic situations, may justify moving a stop to a secondary location, but results are often specific to the facts. A traffic stop for driving on the shoulder could be extended when the driver agreed to follow a deputy sheriff to a checkpoint 30 miles away where a dog alerted to the vehicle. The gas tank was removed and found to contain 195 pounds of marijuana. The conviction was affirmed, though the move was consensual.[94]

OFFICERS MOVE A VEHICLE TO AID IN SNIFF

When a car was stopped near some puddles and the police had reason to believe the driver was involved in drug dealing, an officer moved the car 5 feet so the dog would not have to walk through puddles. The Seventh Circuit concluded that moving the car was probably illegal, but it did not produce any items in and of itself so the subsequent alert and search were deemed valid.[95] Moving a vehicle to a gas station to open a spare tire to which the dog had alerted was approved by the same circuit court when the defendant had consented to the move. The tire was found to contain marijuana.[96] Moving a car and luggage to a Drug Enforcement Administration (DEA) garage for a sniff was found not to be illegal where the defendant had been involved in a high-speed chase along with another car. Drugs were found in both cars and in the luggage.[97] In a case heard in the Eighth Circuit, the vehicle was moved to a separate location because the driver needed to use a bathroom but did not want to use the facility at a police station.[98]

In a case arising in Missouri, the defendant was arrested and taken to jail for a traffic violation. His truck was towed, but no suspicions had arisen regarding the possibility of drugs in the car. In jail, the defendant called his brother, whose phone was being tapped by the Federal Bureau of Investigation (FBI). In the conversation the defendant mentioned that his truck was "dirty." Based on this, a narcotics dog sniffed the impounded truck and alerted. A warrant was obtained, and cocaine and weapons were found.[99]

A case arising in Iowa involved a traffic stop where the defendant consented to a search of his vehicle, and the ensuing search yielded suspicious items but no contraband. After the search, the defendant said he wanted to leave, but the officer detained the vehicle until a drug dog could arrive. The dog alerted to the presence of narcotics, and the officer took the vehicle to a nearby truck stop to search. The officer again did not find any contraband, but the defendant had left the scene and the vehicle could not be returned. The following day, one-and-a-half pounds of methamphetamine was found in the vehicle after a search pursuant to a warrant.[100]

ARREST BEFORE MOVING A VEHICLE TO A SECONDARY LOCATION

In a 2007 Eleventh Circuit decision, an individual who was not a suspect in a drug investigation had contact with a suspect of the investigation, then drove his car to a service station, where officers began to speak to him. Fearing that a suspect might see them talking to this individual, the officers placed the individual in one of their cars and handcuffed him, though they did not formally arrest him. When a drug dog did not arrive, one of the officers drove the individual's car to another location where a narcotics detection dog sniffed the car and alerted to the trunk. The trunk was opened and drugs were found. The individual, already handcuffed and in the back of a police car, was now formally arrested.

> The seizure here was unreasonable absent probable cause because of its scope and intrusiveness. While not unduly lengthy, the seizure was accomplished by the taking of Virden's vehicle to a new location for the purposes of investigation. We have frowned upon the movement of individuals for such purposes. ... Furthermore, to effectuate this seizure the officers handcuffed Virden, and without formally arresting him, drove him to another location.

The Eleventh Circuit determined that the district court properly suppressed the evidence.[101]

SNIFFS AT CHECKPOINTS, ROADBLOCKS, AND PRISON ENTRANCES

A good many disputes have arisen where sniffs occurred at places where traffic was being funneled through a checkpoint, either temporary or permanent.

TEMPORARY CHECKPOINTS

In 2000, the Supreme Court considered dog sniffs at checkpoints in *City of Indianapolis v. Edmond*.[102] About 30 officers were at each checkpoint, where drivers were asked to produce a license and registration. The primary purpose of the checkpoints was narcotics interdiction. Officers looked for signs of impairment and walked a narcotics detection dog around each stopped vehicle. Citing *Place*, the Supreme Court, in another opinion of Justice O'Connor, stated that "an exterior sniff of an automobile does not require entry into the car and is not designed to disclose any information other than the presence or absence of narcotics." The Court said that it had approved checkpoints at border stations and to ensure roadway safety (e.g., sobriety checkpoints), but because "the primary purpose of the Indianapolis narcotics checkpoint program is to uncover evidence of ordinary criminal wrongdoing, the program contravenes the Fourth Amendment." The Court felt it could not approve a regime of suspicionless stops and felt the primary purpose of the Indianapolis program was "ultimately indistinguishable from the general interest in crime control."[103] Such a general crime control purpose could "only be justified by some quantum of individualized suspicion," which was not present here.[104] Justice Rehnquist dissented, joined by Justice Thomas, and as to part of his dissent by Justice Scalia, noting that there was nothing in the record to indicate that the dog sniffs involved lengthened the stops. The checkpoints resulted in 49 arrests unrelated to drugs, including drunk driving, vehicle registration, and lack of proper licenses.

It would appear that a checkpoint focused on driver impairment could involve a drug detection dog without contravening the restrictions of *City of Indianapolis v. Edmond*.

BORDER CHECKPOINTS

Many canine sniff cases arise at border checkpoints where a dog has a chance to sniff a car for the presence of hidden illegal aliens or drugs.[105] The Supreme Court has held that

> the Fourth Amendment's balance of reasonableness is qualitatively different at the international border than in the interior. Routine searches of the persons and effects of entrants are not subject to any requirement of reasonable suspicion, probable cause, or warrant. ... We hold that the detention of a traveler at the border, beyond the scope of a routine customs search and inspection, is justified at its inception if customs agents, considering all the facts surrounding the traveler and her trip, reasonably suspect that the traveler is smuggling contraband in her alimentary canal.[106]

The fact that the primary purpose of a checkpoint was to find illegal aliens did not preclude the use of drug detection dogs.[107] If a dog sniff does not lengthen the period of the stop beyond what is necessary to determine that the travelers are U.S. citizens, it does not violate the Fourth Amendment.[108]

Individuals walking across the Mexican border are sometimes subjected to canine sniffs. In a case arising in Texas in 2002, a dog alerted to a pedestrian at an entry point, and then alerted in a room to which the individual was taken. The search uncovered Rohypnol and Valium pills, and the conviction was affirmed.[109]

Consent to a dog sniff extends the permissible detention period at a border checkpoint.[110] Buses may be subjected to canine sniffs at border checkpoints.[111] Although most border checkpoint cases occur near the Mexican border, an increasing number of sniffs have been occurring near the Canadian border.[112]

It should not be assumed that border checkpoints only involve looking for items entering the United States. The Treasury Department reported that a shipment of appliances going south at

Laredo was brought to a secondary location, where a dog alerted to a mattress. An imaging system indicated anomalies in the mattress, which was found to contain $1,000,035 in currency. The driver, who was enrolled in a trusted shipper program, was arrested.[113]

EXITING EARLY TO AVOID CHECKPOINTS

Seeming to exit early to avoid a posted checkpoint has been considered grounds for suspicion.[114] In a case arising in Missouri, officers set up a sign "Drug Enforcement Checkpoint Ahead, One Fourth Mile: Drug Dogs in Use," but the sign was a ruse to see which drivers would try to get off at the preceding exit, where the checkpoint actually was. A driver exited with his tractor-trailer, but the area was one where big rigs seldom exited. Cocaine was found in a duffel bag.[115] On the other hand, the Sixth Circuit disapproved of a checkpoint ruse of this sort as being intrusive and unreasonable under the Fourth Amendment.[116]

SEARCHES AT WEIGH STATIONS

Suspiciously high weight for an 18-wheeler that did not have a trailer or a load justified a 10-minute detention for a narcotics dog to arrive after the driver declined to permit a search. The dog alerted and 2,398 pounds of marijuana were found.[117]

PRISON ENTRANCES AND MILITARY FACILITIES

Canine sniffs of visitors to prisons have been determined to be reasonable. In a case arising in Alabama, a visitor coming to see a prison inmate realized her car would be sniffed and asked to leave. When told it was too late, she admitted to having a revolver in her purse; but drug detection dogs also found a crack pipe, crack cocaine, and $23,000.[118]

At a roadblock on the access road to a prison in Oklahoma, a dog alerted to a woman who was coming to visit a prisoner. The Tenth Circuit held that ordering Ms. Romo to open her car doors, if done for traditional law enforcement purposes, would have presumptively required probable cause. There were, however, special issues due to the location.

> [A]lthough the opening of the vehicle's doors and trunk was an invasion of Ms. Romo's protected privacy interest in her car, the officers did not physically search through the car or trunk; rather, opening the door and trunk merely facilitated the dog's sweep of the vehicle. Given plaintiffs' reduced expectation in privacy, this was reasonable when balanced against the government's strong interest in keeping narcotics out of the prison.

Visitors to prisons have a lower expectation of privacy because of the location.[119]

Dog sniffs at entrances to military bases have been approved.[120]

SNIFFS OF PARKED VEHICLES

A case arising in California involved a parked tractor-trailer that an informant had said held about a ton of marijuana. Customs officials took marijuana-sniffing dogs to the trailer and both alerted. The district court had granted a motion to suppress. The circuit court's analysis, pre-*Place*, took inspiration from the property law concept of curtilage:

> The dogs' intrusion such as it was into the air space open to the public in the vicinity of the trailer appears to us reasonably tolerable in our society. There was no invasion of the "curtilage" the trailer. No sophisticated mechanical or electronic devices were used. The investigation was not indiscriminate, but solely directed to the particular contraband. There was an expectation that the odor would emanate from the trailer. Efforts made to mask it were visible. The method used by the officers

was inoffensive. There was no embarrassment to or search of the person. The target was a physical fact indicative of possible crime, not protected communications. We hold that the use of the dogs was not unreasonable under the circumstances and therefore was not a prohibited search under the fourth amendment.

The granting of the motion to suppress was reversed and the case remanded for trial.[121]

In a case beginning in Truth or Consequences, New Mexico, in 1992, a motel manager had been permitting sniffs of the parking lot of a Super 8 Motel by Border Patrol agents with narcotics dogs. The case had troubled Justice Ginsburg in her dissent in *Caballes*, but the result would not be different because of that case. A dog alerted to a guest's Chevy Impala, which the agents then put under surveillance. When Ludwig came for his car the next morning, agents requested permission to search the car, which Ludwig denied. The dog again alerted to the trunk. When Ludwig again refused, the agent took the keys from the ignition, opened the trunk, and found several large bags of marijuana. The trial court granted a motion to suppress on the grounds that there were no exigent circumstances justifying the warrantless search. As to the dog sniff, the Tenth Circuit noted that the parking lot was not fenced or private in any way and no signs restricted entry to it. Ludwig's parking space was open to the street and he had no more expectation of privacy in the particular parking space than he or the motel owner had in the lot generally.

> Ludwig also suggests that the dog sniffs of his car were unreasonable searches because the agents had no reason to suspect that there were drugs in his car. Although the Border Patrol generally knew that the motel was a staging area for smugglers, [the agent] initially did not have any reasonable suspicion that Ludwig's car contained drugs. He entered the lot with the narcotics dog routinely to sniff all the cars in the lot, without any particular suspicion. This case thus presents the previously unanswered question whether random dog sniffing of vehicles and other objects without prior lawful detention or reasonable suspicion violates the Fourth Amendment. ... We hold that even such random and suspicionless dog sniffs are not searches subject to the Fourth Amendment.

The dog alert, according to the circuit court, gave the agents probable cause to search Ludwig's trunk.[122]

> Probable cause means that "there is a fair probability that contraband or evidence of a crime will be found in a particular place." ... Although Ludwig cites several cases of mistaken dog alerts, a dog alert usually is at least as reliable as many other sources of probable cause and is certainly reliable enough to create a "fair probability" that there is contraband. We therefore have held in several cases that a dog alert without more gave probable cause for searches and seizures. ... A dog alert might not give probable cause if the particular dog had a poor accuracy record, but the evidence shows that the dog in this case has never falsely alerted.

One of the Border Patrol agents did not know how detection dogs alert, but the differences between his testimony and that of the dog's handler did not amount to proof that the dog did not alert. The court also noted that if "police have probable cause to search a car, they need not get a search warrant first even if they have time and opportunity."[123] The Tenth Circuit reversed the district court's denial of the motion to reconsider its suppression order and remanded for further proceedings.[124]

A sniff of a parking lot of a motel in Wisconsin was held not to be a search. Officers went to the room of the owner of the vehicle and were invited inside, where they found drugs in the room. There was held to be no expectation of privacy in a parking lot, where the sniff was conducted.[125] In a case arising in Texas in 2007, post-*Caballes*, a sniff and alert of a parked trailer was followed by surveillance of the trailer until a tractor came to pick it up. As the tractor-trailer began to move, it was stopped and a second sniff resulted in an alert. The trailer was searched and 264 packages of cocaine were found. The search was upheld but the case was reversed on another issue having to do with a confidential informant.[126]

Cars have sometimes been sniffed because their drivers came to buildings under surveillance,[127] or the cars were parked outside buildings that were being searched.[128] Sometimes officers become suspicious of an arriving passenger and find it easier to take the dogs to the passenger's car than to sniff his luggage.[129] Being in the parking lot of a probation department and admitting that the car had been used to transport drugs (by someone who had borrowed it from the driver) was enough that the sniff was held not to be a search.[130]

INVENTORY SEARCH AFTER AN ARREST

A driver was pulled over for making an illegal U-turn and a computer check revealed that the driver's license had been revoked. The driver was arrested and the car was towed. Seeing that the bed of the truck had five large duffel bags, the arresting officer called for canine officer assistance.

Canine officer Roegge arrived and Krider instructed him to use the dog to assist in the inventory of the bed of the truck. While Krider filled out the automobile inventory paperwork, Roegge walked his canine around the truck. The dog became very excited when it came to the rear portion of the truck. Roegge opened the bed's topper and allowed the canine to jump up into the bed. Once in the bed, the canine "alerted" to one of the duffel bags. Roegge removed the duffel bag from the bed and unzipped it. The bag contained clothing and "several large bricks of gray duct-tape," which Roegge believed to be some kind of narcotic. Roegge then removed the remaining duffel bags from the truck, placed them on the sidewalk, and let the canine conduct another sniff search. The canine "alerted" to another bag. Roegge opened the bag, which revealed more bricks covered with gray duct-tape. Roegge then put all five duffel bags back into the truck and called the vice unit.

The truck was found to contain 182.3 kilograms of marijuana. Because the district court did not commit clear error in finding that the inventory search conformed to Peoria Police Department procedures, the circuit court affirmed the district court's denial of Lozano's motion to suppress.[131]

A sniff of bags that were removed from a car that was being impounded was approved under the "inevitable discovery" theory, which allows evidence seized unlawfully to be admitted if it would inevitably have been discovered in a subsequent inventory search.[132]

CONSENT IN VEHICLE SEARCHES

People who are detained often see sniffs as less intrusive than searches, and many cases describe an individual refusing to consent to a physical search of an item but allowing a canine sniff.[133] Courts must often decide on conflicting evidence whether a driver or other occupants of a vehicle consented to a dog sniff or search inside a vehicle. In a case arising in Florida, the court determined that there was consent to let a dog sniff inside the vehicle, where it alerted to a stuffed rabbit. The alert to the rabbit justified squeezing it, revealing a pouch with cocaine.[134]

In a case arising in Hawaii, consent to a search was not vitiated by the threat of bringing a dog aboard a yacht because the officer had reasonable suspicion that justified boarding the vessel in any case.[135] Consent was not involuntarily given despite the fact that an officer's drug detection dog began to howl during an encounter.[136]

In a 1999 case arising in Texas, a driver was pulled over for tailgating and consented to the search of his trunk. No drugs were found. The officers told the driver he was free to leave but said they would detain the car until a dog could search it. A computer check was completed but the driver was not told he was free to go. About 20 minutes after the initial stop, the canine unit arrived and the dog alerted to the driver's side door and seat, but the search still uncovered no contraband. The canine officer said that the drugs might be on the driver and a third pat down found a baggie in the driver's crotch area that contained 137.5 grams of cocaine. The court concluded that after the computer check had been completed, the seizure became unlawful. Therefore, any "probable cause established as a result of the canine search was subsequent to the unlawful seizure." The court reversed and remanded for a judgment of acquittal.[137]

NOTES

1. *Illinois v. Caballes*, 207 Ill.2d 504, 802 N.E.2d 202 (2003).
2. Citing *U.S. v. Jacobsen*, 466 U.S. 109, 124 (1984).
3. Citing *Illinois v. Cox*, 202 Ill. 2d 462, 782 N. E. 2d 275 (2002), cert. denied 539 U.S. 937, 123 S.Ct. 2574, 156 L.Ed.2d 622 (2003).
4. *Illinois v. Caballes*, 543 U.S. 405, 125 S.Ct. 834, 160 L.Ed.2d 842 (2005). See also *U.S. v. Chadwick*, 433 U.S. 1, 97 S.Ct. 2476, 53 L.Ed.2d 538 (1977), in which the Supreme Court found a warrantless search following a canine alert to a footlocker to be an illegal search. The use of the dog was not questioned, but rather the timing of the warrantless search. Given the arrest of the defendants, it would have been easy to obtain a warrant. A number of lower courts had earlier reached the same result as the Supreme Court in *Caballes*. See, for example, *Gama v. Nevada*, 112 Nev. 833, 920 P.2d 1010 (1996); *Massachusetts v. Feyenord*, 62 Mass.App.Ct. 200, 815 N.E.2d 628 (Ct. App. 2004); *Bradshaw v. Indiana*, 759 N.E.2d 271 (Ct. App. 2001); *Idaho v. Parkinson*, 135 Idaho 357, 17 P.3d 301 (Ct. App. 2000).
5. This may overstate the case. In *U.S. v. Ludwig*, 10 F.3d 1523 (10th Cir. 1993), a sniff of cars in a motel parking lot was approved despite the lack of particular suspicion), but in *City of Indianapolis v. Edmond*, 531 U.S. 32 148 L.Ed.2d 333, 121 S.Ct. 447 (2000), random checkpoints for general criminal activity were held to violate the Fourth Amendment. In *U.S. v. Friend*, 50 F.3d 548 (8th Cir. 1995), taking a drug dog around cars parked outside a motorcycle clubhouse in Omaha was approved as fitting under the guidelines of *U.S. v. Place*, 462 U.S. 696, 707, 103 S.Ct. 2637, 2644, 77 L.Ed.2d 110 (1983), an earlier U.S. Supreme Court decision regarding a luggage sniff discussed in the next chapter.
6. *U.S. v. Kennedy*, 131 F.3d 1371 (10th Cir 1997) (71% accuracy rate); *U.S. v. Scarborough*, 128 F.3d 1373 (10th Cir. 1997) (a Postal Service dog alerted falsely four times out of 19 while working for the Postal Service and 8% of the time over its entire career); *U.S. v. Limares*, 269 F.3d 794, 797 (7th Cir. 2001) (dog gave false positives between 7% and 38% of the time); *Laime v. Arkansas*, 347 Ark. 142, 60 S.W. 3d 464 (2001) (dog had made between 10 and 50 errors).
7. *U.S. v. $242,484.00*, 351 F.3d 499, 511 (11th Cir. 2003).
8. Garner et al. (2001).
9. *Montana v. Tackitt*, 315 Mont. 59, 69-70, 67 P.3d 295, 302-3 (Sup.Ct. 2003).
10. *Ohio v. Rusnak*, 120 Ohio App.3d 24, 696 N.E.2d 633 (Ct. App. 1997) (extending traffic stop to get defendant's driving record, during which sniff occurred, was permissible).
11. *U.S. v. Jensen*, 425 F.3d 698 (9th Cir. 2005).
12. *U.S. v. Beck*, 140 F.3d 1129 (8th Cir. 1998); U.S. v. Gregory, 302 F.3d 805 (8th Cir. 2002); *U.S. v. Linkous*, 285 F.3d 716 (8th Cir. 2002).
13. *U.S. v. Finke*, 85 F.3d 1275 (7th Cir. 1996); Conrad v. Davis, 120 F.3d 92 (8th Cir. 1997); *U.S. v. Castro*, 166 F.3d 728 (5th Cir. 1999); *U.S. v. Blaylock*, 421 F.3d 758 (8th Cir. 2005).
14. *U.S. v. Cuellar*, 478 F.3d 282 (5th Cir. 2007).
15. *Laime v. Arkansas*, 347 Ark. 142, 60 SW3d 464 (Sup. Ct. 2001).
16. *U.S. v. Munroe*, 143 F.3d 1113 (8th Cir. 1998).
17. *U.S. v. $30,060*, 39 F.3d 1039 (9th Cir. 1994).
18. *U.S. v. Sanchez-Pina*, 336 F.3d 431 (5th Cir. 2003).
19. *U.S. v. Bloomfield*, 40 F.3d 910 (8th Cir. 1994); *U.S. v. Fiala*, 929 F.2d 285 (7th Cir. 1991).
20. *U.S. v. Hunnicutt*, 135 F.3d 1345 (10th Cir. 1998).
21. *U.S. v. Pulliam*, 265 F.3d 736 (8th Cir. 2001).
22. *U.S. v. Rodriguez-Morales*, 929 F.2d. 780 (1st Cir. 1991).
23. *U.S. v. Gregory*, 302 F.3d 805 (8th Cir. 2002).
24. *U.S. v. Villa-Chaparro*, 115 F.3d 797 (10th Cir. 1997); *U.S. v. Castro*, 166 F.3d 728 (5th Cir. 1999); *U.S. v. Williams*, 403 F.3d 1203 (10th Cir. 2005).
25. *U.S. v. Jeffus*, 22 F.3d 554 (4th Cir. 1994).
26. *U.S. v. Seals*, 987 F.2d 1102 (5th Cir. 1993). See *U.S. v. Duffaut*, 314 F.3d 203 (5th Cir. 2002); *U.S. v. Martin*, 411 F.3d 998 (8th Cir. 2005).
27. *U.S. v. Holloman*, 113 F.3d 192 (11th Cir. 1997); *Illinois v. Cox*, 318 Ill.App.3d 161, 739 N.E.2d 1066, 251 Ill.Dec. 133 (App. Ct., 5th Dist. 2000) ("rear registration light").

28. *U.S. v. Peralez*, 526 F.3d 1115 (8th Cir. 2008). See also *U.S. v. Olivera-Mendez*, 484 F.3d 505 (8th Cir. 2007); *U.S. v. Herrera-Martinez*, 354 F.3d 932 (8th Cir. 2004).

29. *Miller v. Clark County*, 340 F.3d 959 (9th Cir. 2003).

30. *U.S. v. Jeffus*, 22 F.3d 554 (4th Cir. 1994).

31. *U.S. v. Palacios-Suarez*, 149 F.3d 770 (8th Cir. 1998) (though there was no violation because the Iowa law only applied to vehicles registered in Iowa, which this one was not); but see *U.S. v. Johnson*, 256 F.3d 214 (4th Cir. 2001) (officer did not have reasonable suspicion vehicle was in violation of South Carolina sunscreen law so stop was invalid and drugs found during subsequent search had to be suppressed).

32. *U.S. v. Dovali-Avila*, 895 F.2d 206 (5th Cir. 1990); *U.S. v. Resio-Trejo*, 45 F.3d 907 (5th Cir. 1995).

33. *U.S. v. Tamari*, 454 F.3d 1259 (11th Cir. 2006). This was a case where the initial search found nothing, but a dog's alert justified a second search. See also *U.S. v. Watts*, 329 F.3d 1282 (11th Cir. 2003) (first dog alerts to Mustang, but no drugs are found; second dog also alerts, but then alerts to area of console inside and drugs are found).

34. *U.S. v. Brown*, 500 F.3d 48 (1st Cir. 2007).

35. *Iowa v. Bergmann, III*, 633 N.W.2d 328 (2001).

36. *U.S. v. Fiala*, 929 F.2d 285 (7th Cir. 1991).

37. *U.S. v. Finke*, 85 F.3d 1275 (7th Cir. 1996) (drug dog arrives while officer was giving defendant ticket for running red light).

38. *U.S. v. Patterson*, 65 F.3d 68 (7th Cir. 1995); U.S. v. Foley, 206 F.3d 802 (8th Cir. 2000).

39. *U.S. v. Williams*, 69 F.3d 27 (5th Cir. 1995).

40. *U.S. v. Taylor*, 934 F.2d 218 (9th Cir. 1991).

41. *U.S. v. Perez*, 37 F.3d 510 (9th Cir. 1994); *U.S. v. Lebrun*, 261 F.3d 731 (8th Cir. 2001) (sweating profusely despite cold weather, along with nervousness, wrappers on the floor, and vague answers).

42. *U.S. v. Perez*, 37 F.3d 510 (9th Cir. 1994); *Louisiana v. Kalie*, 699 So.2d 879 (1997).

43. *U.S. v. Finke*, 85 F.3d 1275 (7th Cir. 1996) (drug dog arrives while officer was giving defendant ticket for running red light).

44. *Resendez v. Miller*, 203 F.3d 902 (5th Cir. 2000).

45. *U.S. v. Owens*, 167 F.3d 739 (1st Cir. 1998); *Conrad v. Davis*, 120 F.3d 92 (8th Cir. 1997); *U.S. v. Mendoza*, 468 F.3d 1256 (10th Cir. 2006); *U.S. v. Lyons*, 486 F.3d 367 (8th Cir. 2007) (31-minute wait for drug dog not unreasonable). See also *U.S. v. Valle Cruz*, 452 F.3d 698 (8th Cir. 2006) (dog sniff of both car stopped by police and second car that pulled over because drivers were traveling together but gave inconsistent stories).

46. *U.S. v. Hill*, 386 F.3d 855 (8th Cir. 2004) (since arrest for outstanding warrant preceded sniff, officers did not need justification for holding car pending canine inspection); *U.S. v. Garcia*, 205 F.3d 1182 (9th Cir. 1999).

47. *U.S. v. Williams*, 271 F.3d 1262 (10th Cir. 2001). See *U.S. v. Cervine*, 347 F.3d 865 (10th Cir. 2003) (warning of DEA agents and driving erratically gave police reasonable cause to detain 30 to 50 minutes for canine sniff); *U.S. v. Foreman*, 369 F.3d 776 (continued detention past traffic stop was supported by reasonable articulable suspicion, following reasoning of *Williams*).

48. *U.S. v. Morgan*, 270 F.3d 625 (8th Cir. 2001).

49. *Cole v. Georgia*, 254 Ga.App. 424, 562 S.E.2d 720 (Ct. App. 2002).

50. *U.S. v. Perez*, 37 F.3d 510 (9th Cir. 1994).

51. *U.S. v. Bizier*, 111 F.3d 214 (1st Cir. 1997).

52. *U.S. v. Suitt*, 569 F.3d 867 (8th Cir. 2009) (alert to bed of pickup revealed 32 bales of marijuana).

53. *U.S. v. Wood*, 105 F.3d 942 (10th Cir. 1997).

54. *U.S. v. Maddox*, 2010 WL 4352210 (D.C. Cir. 2010).

55. *U.S. v. Ibarra*, 345 F.3d 711 (9th Cir. 2003).

56. *Bain v. Florida*, 839 So2d 739 (Ct. App. 2003).

57. *U.S. v. Bell, III*, 555 F.3d 535 (6th Cir. 2009) ("Once Trooper Roberts received the results of the license and warrant checks, on his second return to the patrol car, he decided to issue a warning and then almost immediately walked back to Bell's car and began writing the warning and discussing it with Bell. It was during this discussion that the dog alerted. At no time did the actions of the officers improperly extend the length of the stop."); *U.S. v. Vazquez*, 555 F.3d 923 (10th Cir. 2009) ("while the dog sniff was being conducted, Malcom and Mr. Vazquez were locating the phone number of Mr. Vazquez's girlfriend in his cell phone's memory so that the officers could confirm her ownership of the car and his right to be driving it").

58. *U.S. v. Quinn*, 815 F.2d 153, 158 (1st Cir. 1987) (emphasis in original).

59. *U.S. v. Ellis*, 497 F.3d 606 (6th Cir. 2007).

60. *U.S. v. Beck*, 140 F.3d 1129 (8th Cir. 1998).

61. *U.S. v. Bloomfield*, 40 F.3d 910 (8th Cir. 1994). See also *U.S. v. Fuse*, 391 F.3d 924 (8th Cir. 2005) (drug dog, Butkus, sniffed car approximately 15 minutes from initial stop).

62. *Sims v. Arkansas*, 356 Ark. 507, 157 S.W.3d 530 (2004).

63. *Colorado v. Haley*, 41 P.3d 666 (2001) (relying on the Colorado state constitution; driver's consent to sniff luggage but not car did not create reasonable suspicion).

64. *U.S. v. White*, 42 F.3d 457 (8th Cir. 1994); *U.S. v. Hornbecker*, 316 F.3d 40 (1st Cir. 2003) (defendant signed consent form approximately 23 minutes after stop).

65. *U.S. v. Branch*, 537 F.3d 328 (4th Cir. 2008); *U.S. v. Bloomfield*, 40 F.3d 910 (8th Cir. 1994) (officer radioed for canine assistance 6 minutes after stop).

66. *U.S. v. Burton*, 288 F.3d 91 (3rd Cir. 2002).

67. *U.S. v. Ladeaux*, 454 F.3d 1107 (10th Cir. 2006).

68. *Illinois v. Bartelt*, 384 Ill.App.3d 1028, 894 N.E.2d 482, 323 Ill.Dec. 715 (Ct. App. 2008), aff'd 2011 WL 1049788 (2011) (officer told driver to roll up windows and turn vents "on high" to blow out air; dog alerted; court said the request was nonintrusive as doors and windows remained closed and found no Fourth Amendment violation).

69. *Karnes v. Skrutski*, 62 F.3d 485 (3rd Cir. 1995) (dog jumped through open driver's window twice, but no drugs were found; driver brought action for violation of his rights; Third Circuit remanded as triable issues remained).

70. *U.S. v. Winningham*, 140 F.3d 1328 (10th Cir. 1998).

71. *U.S. v. Place*, 462 U.S. 696, 103 S.Ct. 2637, 77 L.Ed.2d 110 (1983).

72. *U.S. v. Stone*, 866 F.2d 359 (10th Cir. 1989). See *U.S. v. Watson*, 783 F.Supp. 258 (E.D.Va. 1992); *U.S. v. Lewis*, 2005 USDist LEXIS 38142 (W.D.Mich. 2005); *U.S. v Vazquez*, 555 F.3d 923, 930 (10th Cir. 2009) (citing *Stone* that sniff was legal where "dog's leap into the car was instinctual rather than orchestrated and (2) the officers did not ask the driver to open the point of entry"); *U.S. v. Pierce*, Docket No. 1-08-cr-00126-001 (3rd Cir. 2010) (dog alerted to narcotics found in Pierce's glove box; dog jumped through an open door and alerted to the front passenger seat and glove box area, and in so doing acted instinctively and without facilitation by his handler); *Ohio v. Palicki*, 97 Ohio App.3d 175, 646 N.E.2d 494 (Ct. App. 1994) (dog alerted outside car and officer then put dog in car where it alerted to marijuana; alert outside produced probable cause for sniff inside); *California v. Terrill*, 2002 WL 1308297 (Ct. App. 2002) (dog jumped inside car that was missing a window and alerted aggressively).

73. *Idaho Department of Law Enforcement v. $34,000*, 121 Idaho 211, 824 P.2d 142 (Ct. App. 1992).

74. *U.S. v. Morales*, 489 F.Supp.2d 1250 (D.N.M. 2007). See also *U.S. v. Neatherlin*, 66 F.Supp.2d 1157 (D.Mont. 1999) (dog jumped into vehicle, ignored officer's command to exit vehicle, and alerted; motion to suppress denied); but see *New Mexico v. Warsaw*, 125 N.M. 8, 956 P.2d 139 (Ct. App. 1998) (officers removed carpet and encourage dog to jump in trunk of car damaged in accident; conviction reversed); *Kansas v. Freel*, 29 Kan.App.2d 852, 32 P.3d 1219 (Ct. App. 2001) (officer encouraged dog to go through open window where dog alerted to floor board; video confirmed officer's encouragement; evidence should have been suppressed).

75. *U.S. v. Stone*, 866 F.2d 359 (10th Cir. 1989); *U.S. v. Watson*, 783 F.Supp. 258 (E.D.Va. 1992); *U.S. v. Reed*, 141 F.3d 644 (6th Cir. 1998); *U.S. v. Reed*, 141 F.3d 644 (6th Cir. 1998); *U.S. v. Lyons*, 957 F.2d 615 (8th Cir. 1992).

76. See *Horton v. Goose Creek Independent School District*, 690 F.2d 470 (5th Cir. 1982) ("the sniffing of a dog is 'no different [from an officer smelling an odor],' or that the dog's olfactory sense merely 'enhances' that of the police officer in the same way that a flashlight enhances the officer's sight"); *U.S. v. Reed*, 141 F.3d 644, 649 (6th Cir.1998) ("Just as the sniffing of contraband by trained canines does not constitute an unlawful search, neither does the viewing by humans of contraband in plain sight amount to an unlawful search. As long as the observing person or the sniffing canine are legally present at their vantage when their respective senses are aroused by obviously incriminating evidence, a search within the meaning of the Fourth Amendment has not occurred"). See also *Arizona v. Morrow*, 128 Ariz. 310, 625 P.2d 898 (1981).

77. *U.S. v. Hutchinson*, 471 F.Supp.2d 497 (M.D.Pa. 2007) (emphasis added). See also *U.S. v. Meindl*, 83 F.Supp.2d 1207 (D.Kan. 1999) (plain smell exception applied in residence).

78. *Wisconsin v. Miller*, 256 Wis.2d 80, 647 N.W.2d 348 (Ct. App. 2002).

79. *U.S. v. Sukiz-Grado*, 22 F.3d 1006 (10th Cir. 1994). See also *U.S. v. Singh*, 363 F.3d 347 (4th Cir. 2004).

80. *U.S. v. Dovali-Avila*, 895 F.2d 206 (5th Cir. 1990).

81. *U.S. v. Rivera*, 570 F.3d 1009 (8th Cir. 2009). See also *U.S. v. White*, 584 F.3d 935 (10th Cir. 2009) (defendant was allowed to move his vehicle to secondary location to facilitate dog sniff; "Trooper Dean's actions in directing White to drive to the KDOT office in order to expedite the dog sniff were reasonably

related in scope to detaining White and Richardson until the trooper was able to confirm or dispel his suspicions that Defendants were involved in ongoing criminal activity"; motion to suppress denied); *U.S. v. Carbajal-Iriarte*, 586 F.3d 795 (10th Cir. 2009) (consent to moving vehicle to secondary location to connect with drug dog was voluntary and extended permissible duration of stop); *U.S. v. Oliver*, 363 F.3d 1061 (10th Cir. 2004) (defendant, car, and package found in car were transported to police station where dog alerted to package, which was opened without a search warrant and found to contain methamphetamine; officers had probable cause justifying warrantless search).

82. *U.S. v. Farrior*, 535 F.3d 210 (4th Cir. 2008). See *U.S. v. Eura*, 440 F.3d 625 (4th Cir. 2006).

83. *U.S. v. Gonzalez-Basulto*, 898 F.2d 1011 (5th Cir. 1990). *U.S. v. Carrazco*, 91 F.3d 65 (8th Cir. 1996) (two dogs brought to traffic stop; first did not clearly alert to exterior of truck but second did; search found marijuana). See *U.S. v. DeLuca*, 269 F.3d 1128 (10th Cir. 2001) (two dogs separately alerted to vehicle).

84. *U.S. v. Davis*, 430 F.3d 345 (6th Cir. 2005).

85. *Maryland v. Wallace*, 372 Md. 137, 142-3, 812 A.2d 291, 294 (Ct. App. 2003), cert. denied 540 U.S. 1140, 124 S.Ct. 1036, 157 L.Ed.2d 951 (2004) (noting that if the dog had separately sniffed the defendant, a nonowner, nondriver, and alerted to him, probable cause for the search and a subsequent arrest might have existed). See also *Illinois v. Fondja*, 317 Ill.App.3d 966, 251 Ill.Dec. 553, 740 N.E.2d 839 (Ct. App. 2000).

86. *U.S. v. Guerrera*, 554 F.2d 987 (9th Cir. 1977). See also *Ohio v. Carlson*, 102 Ohio App.3d 585, 657 N.E.2d 591 (Ct. App. 1995) (alert to residual odor did not vitiate probable cause).

87. See *U.S. v. Campbell*, 920 F.2d 973 (11th Cir. 1991) (reasonable suspicion dissipated after initial search revealed no narcotics).

88. *U.S. v. Taylor*, 934 F.2d 218 (9th Cir. 1991). See also *U.S. v. Ramirez,* 473 F.3d 1026 (9th Cir. 2006); *U.S. v. Hernandez*, 314 F.3d 430 (9th Cir. 2002).

89. *U.S. v. Moore*, 329 F.3d 399 (5th Cir. 2003) (dog sniff within 10 minutes of traffic stop was reasonable); *Arizona v. Box*, 205 Ariz. 492, 73 P.3d 623 (Ct. App. 2003) (brief extension for drug dog to arrive).

90. *U.S. v. Beck*, 140 F.3d 1129 (8th Cir. 1998). See also *U.S. v. Alexander*, 448 F.3d 1014 (8th Cir. 2006) (dog sniff 4 minutes after conclusion of traffic stop was a *de minimis* extension of the stop and not unreasonable); *U.S. v. Gray*, 369 F.3d 1024 (8th Cir. 2004) (drug dog "Rudy" alerted to forward area of Camaro, leading to find of 17.5 pounds of cocaine; consent not required for dog sniff of exterior of vehicle).

91. *U.S. v. Donnelly*, 475 F.3d 946, 951-2 (8th Cir. 2007). For an analysis of the issue of probable cause being vitiated by a prolonged detention, see *Wilkes v. Maryland*, 364 Md. 554, 774 A.2d 420 (Ct. App. 2000); *Colorado v. Reyes*, 956 P.2d 1254 (1998) (police had reasonable suspicion to stop truck because of informant's tip that driver was dealing drugs; dog's alert to truck and reasonable suspicion for stop provided probable cause for search of interior where dog alerted to package containing cocaine); *U.S. v. Page*, 154 F.Supp. 1320 (M.D.Tenn. 2001) ("because the purposes of the initial stop were concluded, and the officers lacked any reasonable suspicion of criminal activity at the time of the drug sniff, the defendant's continued detention and drug sniff were unreasonable for the purposes of the Fourth Amendment"); *U.S. v. Buchanon*, 72 F.3d 1217 (6th Cir. 1995) (seizure before sniff made sniff illegal; but the case was pre-*Caballes* and a different result might be possible based on the facts if *Caballes* were considered).

92. *Simmons v. Georgia*, 223 Ga.App. 781, 479 S.E.2d 123 (Ct. App. 1996); see also *U.S. v. Mesa*, 62 F.3d 159 (6th Cir. 1995) ("Although there is always a temptation in cases of this nature when a substantial quantity of drugs and firearms are found to let the end justify the means, it must be remembered that the courts only see cases in which the conduct of the officer resulted in contraband being found. If the officers had found no drugs in the defendant's car, obviously we would not even know that this traffic stop had ever occurred. Therefore, we must accept that courts will always be 'thwarting' what some may view as a good piece of police work when a motion to suppress is granted in cases of this nature." Nervousness was not sufficient to provide reasonable suspicion for continued detention after traffic stop was completed.); *U.S. v. Smith*, 263 F.3d 571 (6th Cir. 2001) (nervousness was primary reason for continued detention after initial traffic stop, but all factors were not sufficient to provide reasonable articulable suspicion).

93. *U.S. v. Dovali-Avila*, 895 F.2d 206 (5th Cir. 1990). See also *U.S. v. Martin*, 422 F.3d 597 (7th Cir. 2005) (dog sniff 2 minutes after conclusion of traffic stop not unreasonable); *U.S. v. Rogers*, 387 F.3d 925 (7th Cir. 2004); *U.S. v. $404,905 in U.S. Currency,* 182 F.3d 643 (8th Cir. 1999) (sniff 30 seconds to 2 minutes after conclusion of traffic stop was not unconstitutional detention); *U.S. v. Suitt*, 569 F.3d 867 (8th Cir. 2009) (walking drug dog around vehicle 3 minutes after traffic stop ended was *de minimis* extension of stop with no Fourth Amendment violation).

94. *U.S. v. Sanchez-Pina*, 336 F.3d 431 (5th Cir. 2003).

95. *U.S. v. Jones*, 275 F.3d 648 (7th Cir. 2001).

96. *U.S. v. Moralez*, 964 F.2d 677 (7th Cir. 1992).

97. *U.S. v. Rivera*, 825 F.2d 152 (7th Cir. 1987).
98. *U.S. v. Bloomfield*, 40 F.3d 910 (8th Cir. 1994).
99. *U.S. v. Adams*, 110 F.3d 31 (8th Cir. 1997).
100. *U.S. v. Yang*, 345 F.3d 650 (8th Cir. 2003). See *U.S. v. Rodriguez-Morales*, 929 F.2d. 780 (1st Cir. 1991). See *The City of Blue Ash v. Kavanagh*, 113 Ohio St.3d 67 (Ct. App. 2007) (car with expired tags could not be driven away, so sniff while waiting for tow truck was timely).
101. *U.S. v. Virden*, 488 F.3d 1317 (11th Cir. 2007) (also finding stop exceeded permissible police activity under *Terry v. Ohio*, 392 U.S. 1, 88 S.Ct. 1868, 20 L.Ed.2d 889 (1968)). See *U.S. v. Hardy*, 855 F.2d 753 (11th Cir. 1988) (detention for 50 minutes until drug dog could be obtained was reasonable; distinguished from *Place* because police could not have anticipated stop of defendant; *Ohio v. Serrano*, 2004 WL 628970 (Ct. App. 2004) (probable cause not required when driver was asked to move car one mile down road to be next to vehicle officers reasonably believed was traveling in tandem with suspect vehicle).
102. *City of Indianapolis v. Edmond*, 531 U.S. 32, 121 S.Ct. 447, 148 L.Ed.2d 333 (2000). Three justices—Rehnquist, Thomas, and Scalia—dissented.
103. 531 U.S. at 45. See *Merrett v. Moore*, 58 F.3d 1547 (11th Cir. 1995) (vehicle citation rate of 4.6% justified dog sniff during check of license and registration).
104. *City of Indianapolis v. Edmond*, 531 U.S. at 47.
105. See *U.S. v. Taylor*, 934 F.2d 218 (9th Cir. 1991); *U.S. v. Dovali-Avila*, 895 F.2d 206 (5th Cir. 1990); *U.S. v. Moreno-Vargas*, 315 F.3d 489 (5th Cir. 2002).
106. *U.S. v. Montoya de Hernandez*, 473 U.S. 531, 105 S.Ct. 3304, 87 L.Ed.2d 381 (1985).
107. *Merrett v. Moore*, 58 F.3d 1547 (11th Cir. 1995) (Florida roadblocks to check drivers' licenses and registrations could add slightly to delays for dog sniffs); *U.S. v. Moreno-Vargas*, 315 F.3d 489 (5th Cir. 2002). See *U.S. v. Gonzalez-Basulto*, 898 F.2d 1011 (5th Cir. 1990) (driver consented to search at immigration checkpoint; first dog was startled by refrigeration sounds, but second alerted to boxes which turned out to have cocaine; alert gave probable cause for search).
108. *U.S. v. Machuca-Barrera*, 261 F.3d 425 (5th Cir. 2001); *U.S. v. Holloman*, 113 F.3d 192 (11th Cir. 1997). See *California v. Valenzuala*, 28 Cal.Rptr.4th 817, 33 Cal.Rptr.2d 802 (Ct. App. 1994) (declining to give green card back to driver at agricultural checkpoint until driver agreed to allow dog sniff outside and inside vehicle negated fruits of search; drug did not alert outside vehicle but alerted passively inside; officers took apart dashboard before finding drugs).
109. *U.S. v. Kelly*, 302 F.3d 291 (5th Cir. 2002).
110. *U.S. v. Chavira*, 9 F.3d 888 (10th Cir. 1993). See also *U.S. v. Pinedo-Montoya*, 966 F.2d 591 (10th Cir. 1992).
111. *U.S. v. Garcia-Garcia*, 319 F.3d 726 (5th Cir. 2003). See also *U.S. v. Cagle*, 849 F.2d 924 (5th Cir. 1988) (dog sniff in baggage area); *U.S. v. Outlaw*, 134 F.Supp.2d 807 (2001), aff'd 319 F.3d 701 (5th Cir. 2003) (dog not trained to alert to PCP but PCP was found in suitcase).
112. *U.S. v. Maltais*, 403 F.3d 550 (8th Cir. 2005) (also holding that 3-hour delay allowing a drug dog to reach the remote location of the investigation acceptable when officers "acted with diligence and pursued the quickest and least intrusive means of investigation reasonably available to confirm or dispel ... suspicions [defendant] was engaged in drug trafficking").
113. Treasury Officer of Inspector General, CBP Officers Seize $1 Million in Undeclared Outbound Currency from FAST Driver at World Trade Bridge (April 13, 2009), Audit of the Department of the Treasury Forfeiture Fund's Fiscal Years 2009 and 2008 Financial Statements (November 24, 2009), 7.
114. *U.S. v. Klinginsmith*, 25 F.3d 1507 (10th Cir. 1994); U.S. v. Carpenter, 462 F.3d 891 (8th Cir. 2006). See Low (2010).
115. *U.S. v. Martinez*, 358 F.3d 1005 (8th Cir. 2004).
116. *U.S. v. Huguenin*, 154 F.3d 547 (6th Cir. 1998).
117. *U.S. v. Munroe*, 143 F.3d 1113 (8th Cir. 1998). See also *U.S. v. Williams*, 429 F.3d 767 (8th Cir. 2005).
118. *U.S. v. Prevo*, 435 F.3d 1343 (11th Cir. 2006).
119. *U.S. v. Romo*, 46 F.3d 1013 (10th Cir. 1995) (fact dog briefly touched defendant's daughter did not vitiate constitutionality of sniff inside vehicle).
120. *U.S. v. Rotramel*, 1 M.J. 559 (U.S. Air Force Court of Military Review 1975) (search conducted by security police guard was not made in accordance with the rules set by the commander for administrative searches, which were to be conducted by a narcotic detection dog team).
121. *U.S. v. Solis*, 393 F.Supp. 325 (C.D.Cal. 1975), 536 F.2d 880 (9th Cir. 1976). For other cases considering the concept of curtilage, see *U.S. v. Tarazon-Silva*, 166 F.3d 341, 1998 WL 912178 (5th Cir. 1998) ("dog-sniff of the outer edge of the garage and the dryer vent on the exterior wall of the house did not occur on protected curtilage; Tarazon had no reasonable expectation of privacy in those areas"); *U.S. v. Hayes*, 551 F.3d 138 (2nd Cir. 2008).

122. Regarding an alert at a car's trunk, see also *Millsap v. Mississippi*, 767 So.2d 286 (Ct. App. 2000) (dog alert at trunk provided probable cause to search entire vehicle).

123. Citing *U.S. v. Crabb*, 952 F2d 1245 (10th Cir. 1991), cert. denied, 504 U.S. 925 (1992).

124. *U.S. v. Ludwig*, 10 F.3d 1523 (10th Cir. 1993).

125. *Wisconsin v. Garcia*, 195 Wis.2d 68, 535 N.W.2d 124 (Ct. App. 1995); see also *U.S. v. Jacob*, 377 F.3d 573 (6th Cir. 2004) (alert in parking lot led officers to think car had hidden compartment; car was later stopped after officers "believed their surveillance had been compromised," leading to a second alert after which cocaine was found in a duffel bag in the trunk; officers had reasonable suspicion to conduct investigatory stop).

126. *U.S. v. Ibarra*, 493 F.3d 526 (5th Cir. 2007).

127. *U.S. v. de Soto*, 885 F.2d 354 (7th Cir. 1989).

128. *U.S. v. Berry*, 90 F.3d 148 (6th Cir. 1996).

129. *U.S. v. Teslim*, 869 F.2d 316 (7th Cir. 1989).

130. *U.S. v. Brown*, 24 F.3d 1223 (10th Cir. 1994).

131. *U.S. v. Lozano*, 171 F.3d 1129 (7th Cir. 1999).

132. *U.S. v. Blaze*, 143 F.3d 585 (10th Cir. 1998); *U.S. v. Marrocco*, 578 F.3d 627, 640 (7th Cir. 2009) ("the officers certainly would have subjected the briefcase to a dog-sniff test even absent the illegal search. After the test was performed, the officers would have known (1) that Mr. Fallon fit a drug-courier profile; (2) that Mr. Fallon had admitted that the briefcase contained a large sum of money; and (3) that the dog-sniff test indicated that the briefcase carried the odor of drugs. It would be unreasonable to conclude that, after discovering all of this information, the officers would have failed to seek a warrant").

133. *U.S. v. Thame*, 846 F.2d 200 (3rd Cir. 1988). For the reverse situation, see *New Mexico v. Van Cleave*, 131 N.M. 82, 33 P.3d 633 (2001) (consent to search trunk included consent to bring dog to sniff trunk).

134. *U.S. v. Dunkley*, 911 F.2d 522 (11th Cir. 1990).

135. *U.S. v. Todhunter*, 297 F.3d 886 (9th Cir. 2002).

136. *U.S. v. Manjarrez*, 348 F.3d 881 (10th Cir. 2003).

137. *U.S. v. Dortch*, 199 F.3d 193 (5th Cir. 1999).

11 Sniffs of Luggage, Transportation Facilities, and Hotels

Before there was *Caballes* for vehicles, there was *Place* for luggage, the case to be discussed next and probably the best reasoned Supreme Court opinion regarding canine police law.[1]

U.S. v. PLACE

In 1983, the Supreme Court dealt expansively on luggage sniffs in a decision written by Justice Sandra Day O'Connor that continues to reverberate through drug search cases generally. In *Place*,[2] a passenger consented to a search of his luggage at the Miami International Airport after he had already checked the two bags. Because the flight was about to leave, officers decided not to search the bags but instead called Drug Enforcement Administration (DEA) authorities in New York, who met the passenger at La Guardia Airport, where he was again asked to allow a search of his luggage. This time he declined, but the DEA officers took the luggage to Kennedy Airport where it was subjected to a "sniff test" by a trained narcotics detection dog. When the dog reacted positively to one suitcase, the DEA agents obtained a warrant and opened it and found cocaine. The defendant pled guilty to the charge of possession but reserved the right to appeal the denial of his motion to suppress the evidence. The Second Circuit reversed on the motion, holding that the prolonged seizure of respondent's luggage exceeded the limits of the type of investigative stop permitted by *Terry v. Ohio*.[3]

Justice O'Connor wrote the opinion for the Court, which accepted the appeal. The Court stated the problem as follows:

> This case presents the issue whether the Fourth Amendment prohibits law enforcement authorities from temporarily detaining personal luggage for exposure to a trained narcotics detection dog on the basis of reasonable suspicion that the luggage contains narcotics. Given the enforcement problems associated with the detection of narcotics trafficking and the minimal intrusion that a properly limited detention would entail, we conclude that the Fourth Amendment does not prohibit such a detention.

This answered a question, but did not determine the result, because, on the facts of the case, the Court held that "the police conduct exceeded the bounds of a permissible investigative detention of the luggage." Justice O'Connor noted that after the sniff test on Friday afternoon, the agents had to wait until Monday morning to get a search warrant. As to the sniff, the Court said:

> A "canine sniff" by a well-trained narcotics detection dog, however, does not require opening the luggage. It does not expose noncontraband items that otherwise would remain hidden from public view, as does, for example, an officer's rummaging through the contents of the luggage. Thus, the manner in which information is obtained through this investigative technique is much less intrusive than a typical search. Moreover, the sniff discloses only the presence or absence of narcotics, a contraband item. Thus, despite the fact that the sniff tells the authorities something about the contents of the luggage, the information obtained is limited. This limited disclosure also ensures that the owner of the property is not subjected to the embarrassment and inconvenience entailed in less discriminate and more intrusive investigative methods.

The Court described the canine sniff as *sui generis*, unique because it was limited in the information obtained, which did not constitute a "search" for Fourth Amendment purposes. The Court found the 90-minute detention to subject the luggage to a narcotics dog was unreasonable and that this was exacerbated by continuing to hold the luggage over the weekend.[4]

Justice Brennan, joined by Justice Marshall, concurred in *Place* because he believed that the seizure involved was more prolonged than the kind of limited investigative stop the Supreme Court had approved 15 years earlier in *Terry v. Ohio*.[5] Justice Brennan argued that the Fourth Amendment protects two different interests of the citizen: the interest in retaining possession of property and the interest in maintaining personal privacy. A seizure threatens the former while a search threatens the latter.[6] Justice Brennan argued that a reasonable suspicion could in limited situations justify a search, but probable cause was needed for a seizure, at least independent of the seizure of the person. Justice Brennan did not think the Court should have addressed the issue of whether the exposure of the luggage to a narcotics detection dog was a search, noting the matter had not been briefed or argued. Justice Blackmun, in a separate concurrence also joined by Justice Marshall, disagreed with "the Court's haste to resolve the dog-sniff issue."

Place was decided in 1983. A year later, another search case, *Jacobsen*,[7] concerned a package from which a white powder had leaked. *Jacobsen* did not involve a dog but a dissent by Justice Brennan, again joined in by Justice Marshall, foreshadowed the same concern Justice Ginsburg would express in *Caballes* over 20 years later. Justice Brennan noted that under *Place* and *Jacobsen* "law enforcement officers could release a trained cocaine-sensitive dog to paraphrase the California Court of Appeal, a 'canine cocaine connoisseur'—to roam the streets at random, alerting the officers to people carrying cocaine."[8]

Four years after *Place*, the federal district court of Kansas analogized the use of drug detection dogs to the use of metal detectors and x-ray screening of luggage at airports, and said that *Place* meant that a reasonable suspicion was not needed to subject luggage to canine screening provided the luggage "(1) is not taken from the immediate possession of the traveler or from an area in which he has a legitimate privacy interest; and (2) the delay involved is brief and does not interfere with the traveler's plans." The court said that under these circumstances no search or seizure of the luggage has occurred and "no legitimate privacy interests of the traveler have been violated."[9]

Place was not the only time that the Supreme Court considered a dog involved in checking luggage. Justice Rehnquist, in a 1989 decision, analyzed the concept of reasonable suspicion for a warrant to search luggage, noting that reasonable suspicion cannot be reduced to a neat set of legal rules. A dog's alert was one of the factors in the case but was not specifically discussed.[10]

STATE CONSTITUTIONS AND *PLACE* SITUATIONS

Prior to *Place*, a number of courts held that luggage sniffs were not searches under the Fourth Amendment.[11] After *Place*, some courts determined that state constitutional law would follow federal in regard to luggage sniffs.[12] The Alaska Court of Appeals held, however, that a luggage sniff is a search, distinguishing Alaskan constitutional law from U.S. constitutional law as articulated in *Place*. The case involved two dog sniffs, one at the San Francisco International Airport, where an agent of the California Department of Justice, Bureau of Narcotic Enforcement, became suspicious of a boarding passenger and subjected his luggage (unbeknownst to the passenger) to a canine sniff. When the dog alerted, the agent notified Alaska authorities at the flight's destination in Anchorage. There, another narcotics detection dog alerted to the luggage and a warrant was obtained, revealing 11 pounds of marijuana. The court held that based on the call from San Francisco, Alaskan officers had reasonable suspicion that the defendant was carrying contraband and that this suspicion justified the limited seizure of the suitcases at the Anchorage Airport to subject them to a dog sniff. The court stated:

Even assuming that more protection is afforded in Alaska, however, this does not compel the conclusion that a sniff of luggage is a "search" in the traditional sense. As Justice Blackmun wrote [concurring] in *Place,* "a dog sniff may be a search, but a minimally intrusive one that could be justified in this situation under *Terry* upon mere reasonable suspicion."

Thus, even though the Alaskan court distinguished the state constitutional position from the federal constitutional position enunciated by the U.S. Supreme Court, the difference was not that great in practice and seems to follow a concurrence in *Place.* The conviction was affirmed. The court did consider that the agent in San Francisco may have violated the defendant's Fourth Amendment rights when he manipulated the luggage, pressing it in order to try to determine what was inside, but the court found that this was not enough to taint the warrant in Alaska.[13]

REASONS FOR INVESTIGATORY STOPS

As with vehicle sniffs, reasons for further investigation at transportation facilities can involve relatively benign behavior on the part of a passenger, including nervousness,[14] scanning other passengers in a way that suggests a passenger is trying to determine if anyone is watching him,[15] nervously watching a security guard,[16] avoiding eye contact,[17] seeming to be with another passenger and then pretending not to be with that passenger,[18] walking fast,[19] taking a circuitous route through the airport and providing an inadequate explanation of this behavior,[20] purchasing tickets just prior to departure,[21] waiting outside the terminal while someone else buys the ticket with cash and gives it to the passenger,[22] denying having arrived on a flight from Miami,[23] lying about the city from which one flew,[24] having expensive Delci bags with airtight seals preferred by high-end drug couriers,[25] having a Fu Manchu-type mustache,[26] having luggage that seems heavy,[27] using a duffel bag,[28] arousing an agent's suspicions during flight while sitting next to him and talking to him,[29] having inconsistencies in answers to questions posed by officers,[30] having a history of being refused entry to airline cabins because airline personnel believed the passenger was under the influence of drugs,[31] paying for a ticket with cash,[32] purchasing a one-way ticket with cash,[33] purchasing a ticket with cash very close to departure,[34] providing ticket agents with a false or nonworking telephone contact number,[35] using false names,[36] using tickets issued to other people, being angry,[37] staring at an officer,[38] staring straight ahead,[39] looking over one's shoulder,[40] scanning the entrance before buying a ticket with cash,[41] making a phone call without putting one's ear to the receiver,[42] entering restroom then exiting 15 seconds later,[43] avoiding other passengers and sitting in one's compartment until departure,[44] changing rooms during a trip,[45] flicking one's nostrils (said to be a habit among cocaine users),[46] wearing sweatpants,[47] having gym bags instead of standard luggage,[48] denying having packed the bags one was carrying,[49] providing inconsistent information in response to questions of agents,[50] and attempting to run away after being approached by a narcotics detection dog.[51]

Courts sometimes find a reason insufficient. In a case beginning at O'Hare Airport, agents stopped a passenger but had no reason for this beyond the fact that he flew from Tampa and may have looked around the terminal when he entered it. The federal district court granted a motion to suppress.[52] The fact a passenger used a duffel bag instead of some other type of luggage was found insufficient as reasonable suspicion by the Fourth Circuit.[53] Eccentricity alone has sometimes not been enough, as noted by one Texas court:

The behavior upon which the investigating officers here relied may have seemed odd to them. But that is not the issue. Appellant's demeanor must have been indicative of drug trafficking in particular, not merely of eccentricity. It must have been of such character as to justify an involuntary investigative detention of all persons exhibiting it. Without some evidence tending specifically to show a significantly higher incidence of such behavior among drug traffickers than in the general population, a well-founded, reasonable suspicion of criminal wrongdoing simply was not objectively justified in this case.

This Texas case resulted in a reversal of a conviction even though the luggage was found to contain marijuana.[54]

Informant evidence is often important in determining whether an officer had reasonable suspicion for conducting the investigatory stop.[55]

TRAINING EXERCISES

At the Luis Munoz Marin International Airport in Puerto Rico, a training session involving a drug-sniffing dog, Hershel, was being conducted. Hershel was to pick out "dummy" luggage with narcotics, which would be placed against other suitcases awaiting departure. Hershel alerted to bags that were not dummies. An x-ray revealed the bags contained loaf-shaped packages. A warrant was obtained and drugs were discovered in the bags. The First Circuit determined that the dog's alert provided probable cause and even though the x-ray was unconstitutional, it was overcome by the consent of the defendant. The conviction was affirmed.[56]

CONDUCT OF THE SNIFF

Luggage sniffs are next most common to vehicle sniffs, and many unique circumstances occur. Luggage sniffs are now, however, often explosives detection sniffs, though narcotics sniffs continue to be used.

OFFICER DID NOT NEED TO DO A BACKGROUND CHECK ON A DOG THAT THE DEA SUPPLIED

An officer using a dog inside a train at Washington's Union Station had reasonable suspicion for an investigative detention once the dog alerted to a passenger's luggage. The officer could rely on the dog that the DEA supplied the dog and did not need to perform a background and reliability check on the dog to determine if its alert gave rise to reasonable suspicion.[57]

CHECKED LUGGAGE

Passengers sometimes check luggage on buses but do not travel with the luggage to the destination city. They use some other means of getting to the destination and only pick up the luggage at that point when they are satisfied that the bag is not being watched. The Seventh Circuit found, in such a situation, that the detention of such a bag for a sniff at an intermediary stop "did not implicate the concerns that the Supreme Court had addressed in *Place*." Rather, this was more like a piece of freight being transported by a common carrier, so the detention did not interfere with the owner's possessory interests until the time for delivery had come and gone.[58]

In a pre-*Place* 1974 case arising in the District of Columbia, an employee at a Greyhound Bus Terminal in Yuma, Arizona, told the city's drug task force that three hippies were sending two footlockers to Washington, D.C. A U.S. Customs Service marijuana-sniffing dog was brought to the station and allowed to sniff in the luggage area. The footlockers were found to contain marijuana. Some of the marijuana was removed but some was left in the bags, which were sent on their way. The conviction was affirmed.[59]

In a case arising in Oklahoma, a couple had picked up luggage at the baggage claim area of an airport when officers asked to speak to them. They consented to having the luggage sniffed by a drug dog, but the dog alerted to one of the passengers. An officer put his hands on a bulge in the defendant's waistband. The court held that the dog's alert gave probable cause to make an arrest, which in turn meant there was probable cause for a pat-down search. The court affirmed the denial of the motion to suppress.[60]

CARRY-ON LUGGAGE

Transportation Security Administration (TSA) inspectors were not satisfied with a passenger's answers to questions about his travel and moved him to a separate security room. The passenger had a record of financial fraud and there was an outstanding arrest warrant, but the officers did not act on the warrant. Although officials said that they had informed the passenger he was free to go, this was disputed and a federal magistrate determined that a reasonable person would not have believed he was free to go. A sniff of the passenger's carry-on luggage violated his Fourth Amendment rights when the seizure of the luggage was without either probable cause or a reasonable articulable suspicion. The physical inspection of the luggage revealed three large bags of cash. Before the narcotics dog alerted to the cash, which the passenger did not contest, the seizure had already become illegal and the court did not consider the significance of the canine sniff in connecting the cash to possible narcotics activity. The sniff was part of the fruit of the poisonous tree.[61] It would appear that if the sniff had been conducted during the initial search of the luggage, it would have been legal.[62]

BAGGAGE CARS

A drug detection dog was taken through the baggage car of an Amtrak train at the Albuquerque station. The dog alerted to two bags that were found to contain 53 pounds of marijuana. The defendant argued that *U.S. v. Place*,[63] involving a dog sniff in a public area of an airport, did not apply because the baggage car was a nonpublic area. The circuit court stated that the defendant, when he checked his bags, had a reasonable expectation that the contents of the bags would not be exposed in the absence of consent or a legally obtained warrant, but this expectation did not extend to the air surrounding the luggage.

> The entry by the police into the car was authorized by Amtrak and therefore was legal. ... The police access to the baggage car and subsequent dog sniff did not invade defendant's home or bodily integrity, and did not subject defendant to any inconvenience or annoyance. ... The dog sniff of luggage in the train's baggage car without reasonable suspicion did not violate defendant's Fourth Amendment right to be free from unreasonable search and seizure.[64]

MOVING LUGGAGE SO THAT THE DOG CAN SNIFF

In a 1992 case that arose in Arkansas, a narcotics dog alerted by lifting his head, an indication that the dog detected something in the overhead baggage area of a bus. Bags in the area of the initial alert were put on the floor of the passenger cabin, and the dog alerted to two bags. The Eight Circuit, following *Place*, held that the sniff was not a search because the officers had only moved the luggage from one public area to another, and that the temporary removal from the overhead compartment in and of itself caused no delay in the passenger's travel. The circuit court affirmed the district court's denial of the motion to suppress the sniff.[65] In another case, moving bags from the overhead compartment to the seats below to enable a dog sniff was held to involve "no meaningful interference with the defendant's possessory interest in the bag." The passengers had previously exited the bus.

> The bag was moved only a short distance (from an open overhead compartment to the seat below), for a short time (just long enough for the dog to walk up and down the aisle), and the movement occurred at a time when defendant had left the bag unattended, so his access to it was never impaired. Finally, had the dog not indicated that the bag contained drugs, defendant would have been able to travel uninterrupted to the next stop with his bag. Because there was no meaningful interference with defendant's possessory interest in his bag, there was no seizure.[66]

In airport situations, bags are frequently subjected to canine sniffs more than once.[67]

Manipulating a Bag to Feel or Smell What Is Inside

A case arising in Memphis began when officers positioned a narcotics detection dog outside a bus. Passengers were asked if a dog could sniff their luggage. Guzman put his bag down for the dog to sniff. The dog showed interest but did not sit down, which was the dog's way of alerting. After the passengers were off, officers entered the empty bus. An officer felt Guzman's bag in the overhead compartment and felt what he thought were bricks of drugs. The officers asked Guzman if they could search the bag but he declined to allow this. The officers asked Guzman to get off the bus and Guzman then consented to a dog sniffing the bag. Both dogs alerted. A search warrant was obtained and 6,000 grams of cocaine were found. The magistrate concluded that the officers did not have authority to touch Guzman's bag and recommended that the evidence be suppressed, though the district court did not adopt this position. The circuit court concluded that since the "defendant had no reasonable expectation of privacy in the exterior of his bag when it was on the open luggage rack of a commercial bus, we hold that Hoing's initial touch of the exterior of defendant's bag was not an unreasonable search in violation of the Fourth Amendment." The circuit court affirmed the district court's denial of the motion to suppress.[68]

Manipulation of a bag to force air out so an officer could smell marijuana has, however, been held to make an otherwise permissible search impermissible.[69]

Requiring Passengers to Remove Luggage

At a layover in Denver, an officer asked the passengers to take their carry-on items with them past a trained narcotics detection dog. The defendant left his backpacks on the bus. The bus driver had advised passengers before they arrived in Denver that continuing passengers could leave their bags on the bus.

> [W]hen the bus arrived in Denver at approximately 1:15 p.m., it was met by DEA agents Charlie Olachea and Vinnie Sanchez, along with Denver Police officers David Kechter and Jerry Snow and a trained narcotics detection dog, Sintha. Agent Olachea boarded the bus and, after welcoming the passengers to Denver, stated that Denver police were conducting drug interdiction activities at the terminal. Olachea informed the passengers that a trained narcotics detection dog was waiting outside the bus and said: "I would appreciate it if you would hold your carry-on luggage in your right hand as you walk past the narcotics-trained dog." Olachea then told the passengers that all carry-on luggage would need to be removed so that the bus could be "cleared" before going on to Chicago. Several passengers inquired whether they were required to remove their baggage from the bus, and Olachea responded via the intercom that they were so required. All of the passengers then left the bus. As he left the bus, Garzon carried a blue backpack. Officer Kechter noted that Garzon held his bag high on his left side, away from the dog; this made Kechter suspicious, and he thus asked another officer to keep an eye on Garzon.

Some bags that had not been taken from the cabin were removed by officers and put with the baggage from the compartment underneath the bus for Sintha to sniff. Sintha alerted to a backpack, which was found to contain cocaine. The defendant moved to suppress the warrantless search, which the court denied from the bench. The district court ruled that the bags had not been abandoned but that the defendant had no reasonable expectation of privacy when he ignored the request to remove the bags. The Tenth Circuit determined that the order to remove personal belongings from the cabin was an unlawful order and could not be justified on safety concerns or otherwise. Therefore, the fruits of the search had to be suppressed unless the defendant abandoned his backpack. The circuit court determined that the defendant had not abandoned his backpack.[70]

ABANDONMENT OF LUGGAGE

Searches have been upheld when trial courts have determined that the luggage was abandoned.[71] However, denial of ownership of a bag does not necessarily mean that an individual does not have standing to challenge a search.[72] Two narcotics officers observed a passenger as he was waiting to reboard a bus in Sacramento. The officers saw him take a bag onto the bus and put it in an overhead compartment. When they asked him if he had any carry-on luggage, he said he did not. The bag was taken off the bus and a narcotics detection dog alerted to it. The bag contained cocaine. The district court determined that the bag had been abandoned, which the Ninth Circuit found not clearly erroneous. The Ninth Circuit, however, determined that the passenger involuntarily abandoned his bag as a result of an unlawful seizure.

> Here, the STING officers advised passengers that they were "free to leave" the bus. They did not tell passengers that they were free to remain on the bus and terminate the encounter by declining to answer their questions. The instructions given over the Greyhound public address system conveyed to passengers that they had two choices: stay on the bus and consent to the search, or get off the bus. This was a Hobson's choice because by getting off the bus, a passenger ran the risk of giving the STING officers reasonable suspicion to stop him.

The Ninth Circuit reversed the district court's denial of the defendant's motion to suppress.[73]

INTEREST WITHOUT ALERTING

In a 1983 case, a dog in Miami gave a rather weak alert to the luggage of a passenger who had come under suspicion ("not a strong reaction"). When the plane arrived in Detroit, a second dog gave a strong alert, a warrant was obtained and the bag was found to contain a large amount of cocaine.[74] A dog did not fully alert to the boots of a passenger getting off a bus in Albuquerque but later did alert at the DEA office. In a 2008 decision, the Tenth Circuit determined that the narcotics dog's interest in the shoes, though not a full alert, was sufficient with other evidence to provide probable cause for the detention of the defendant to obtain a warrant.[75]

ALERT IN ONE JURISDICTION SUPPORTING WARRANT IN ANOTHER

An alert in one location may support a warrant in another.[76] An alert at the Los Angeles airport supported a warrant that was executed when the flight landed in Buffalo.[77] An alert in one state may also lead to a sniff and alert in another.[78]

DOG ALERTS BUT OTHER CONTRABAND IS FOUND

A previous section on canine alerts noted that dogs sometimes alert to items or substances they have not been trained to recognize. The item or substance may nevertheless be illegal. A dog sniff of luggage arriving on a flight into Los Angeles produced weapons but no drugs.[79] A lockbox was opened based on a dog's alert, but instead of finding drugs the officers found thousands of illegal child pornography pictures.[80] A dog that was trained to alert to heroin, hashish, marijuana and related drugs alerted to a bag at a bus station. The bag was found to contain Quaaludes, an unrelated narcotic.

> The only question for a reviewing court evaluating the propriety of a search warrant is whether the magistrate had sufficient material before him to permit an independent judgment that there was probable cause to justify a search. Assuming the warrant was properly authorized, anything the government agents found in their search of the suitcases was admissible under the "plain view" doctrine. "An example of the applicability of the 'plain view' doctrine is the situation in which the police have a

warrant to search a given area for specified objects, and in the course of the search come across some other article of incriminating character."[81]

The defendants also objected to the officer's "prepping" of the bag, pressing it to release some air and scent, but the Fifth Circuit affirmed the conviction.[82] In another 2003 case arising in Texas, agents were conducting a routine citizenship status check of the passengers on a bus while an agent took a narcotics detection dog to sniff the luggage in the bin under the bus.[83] The dog alerted to a suitcase. The passenger who owned the bag was asked to step off the bus and agreed to a search. The bag contained phencyclidine (PCP), a drug the dog was not trained to detect. The denial of the motion to suppress was affirmed.[84] Another court held that probable cause had been found where an explosives-sniffing dog had alerted to a suitcase found to contain narcotics.[85]

RAILROAD POLICE

Railroad police work for private industry but are not security guards. They have authority to enforce federal laws and the laws of the states through which the tracks pass.[86] Because their responsibilities include finding trespassers to buildings and trains, they use dogs. Burlington Northern Santa Fe Railroad reimburses police for reasonable expenses, including officers in canine teams.[87] Separate canine units for railway police date from soon after the beginning of formal police dog programs in Europe at the beginning of the 20th century.[88]

BUSES AT IMMIGRATION CHECKPOINTS

As with cars at borders, buses may be searched at immigration checkpoints. In a 2003 case arising in Texas, agents conducted an immigration inspect of a northbound bus at a permanent checkpoint north of Laredo. The dog alerted beside the undercarriage of the bus, but it was determined that the dog was not alerting to any luggage there. The handler suspected that drugs might be hidden in the bathroom of the bus, but the dog alerted beside the seat of a passenger. The dog put its nose against the defendant. Apparently the alert was not quite normal for the dog, though the court accepted that this was due to the confined space in the aisle of the bus.

> Zelmer asked Garcia "what he had"; Garcia lifted his shirt to reveal packages taped to his body. Zelmer told Gutierrez, and Garcia lifted his shirt to show Gutierrez the packages. The agents removed Garcia from the bus; when Garcia was exiting, the dog again alerted to him. Zelmer led the dog back into the bus, where a full inspection triggered no additional alerts. Garcia was subsequently searched at the secondary checkpoint complex; additional packages were found taped to his lower legs, and all of the packages contained marijuana.

The court determined that the sniff did not exceed the scope and limits of immigration checkpoint activity. The alert provided reasonable suspicion that the passenger possessed drugs. The momentary contact of the dog's nose to the defendant was purely incidental and did not make the otherwise reasonable search unconstitutional.[89] The denial of the motion to suppress was affirmed.[90]

Sometimes the dog's first alert does not produce drugs, but a second may do so. In a 2003 Texas case, a dog alerted to a bag in the cargo compartment of a bus at a Border Patrol checkpoint. The passenger consented to a search of his bag, but it turned out to contain no drugs. The passenger admitted to having smoked marijuana earlier but the dog did not alert to him at that time. The Border Patrol agent and the dog handler asked the bus company to have the passengers exit the cabin. The dog stood four to five feet from the exiting passengers and followed two of them, to whom he alerted. One of the two was the person who the dog had already sniffed. He had no drugs but the other passenger ran and was caught. A search revealed cocaine taped to his body. The court noted that Border Patrol policy was to have passengers exit the passenger compartment before commencing a search. The court considered whether a sniff that touches a person is a search. Looking at cases that involved school sniffs of students,[91] the court noted that a dog sniffing close to a person is offensive and is more likely to be a search than sniffing other items. Here, however, the dog was farther away.

> [D]efendant and his companion were approximately four to five feet away from the dog when they exited the bus and the dog alerted to an odor. Because the dog was not in close proximity to the defendant at the time he alerted, the dog's sniff was only minimally intrusive. Moreover, there is no evidence that Agent Morales intended to search the passengers exiting the bus or to have the dog sniff them. He testified that he intended "[t]o wait for everybody to get off ... and then put the dog inside the bus." Considering that the sniff was unintentional and that the dog was approximately four to five feet away from the defendant at the time the sniff occurred, we conclude that the sniff does not constitute a search with the meaning of the Fourth Amendment.

The Fifth Circuit affirmed the district court's denial of the motion to suppress.[92]

LUGGAGE LINEUPS

As with suspects, luggage lineups are sometimes used as a means of verifying that a dog is alerting to a particular bag. A passenger arriving at Union Station in Chicago was questioned by detectives who were suspicious because the passenger was constantly looking around and appeared nervous. When the passenger declined to consent to a search, the detectives informed him they would detain his luggage because the passenger was transporting narcotics. The bags were taken to a DEA office and put in a line of three nonsuspect bags. Two separate narcotics dogs sniffed the line of bags and alerted to the passenger's bags. This took place within 40 minutes of the interview of the passenger, who had since left. The court held that the trial court had properly denied the motion to suppress.[93]

Dogs called in for sniffs often sniff all the checked baggage on a flight or bus.[94] A dog sniffing 50 pieces of luggage on a conveyer belt alerted to two of them, which were found to contain marijuana. The dog failed to alert to two other bags of the suspects, which also contained drugs, but the Second Circuit noted that this mistake—a false negative—favored the suspects. In a pre-*Place* decision, the court found no search or seizure had violated the Fourth Amendment and that there was ample probable cause for the arrest. [95]

DELAYS FOR SNIFFS

As with vehicle sniffs, delays become a factor, particularly when they affect a passenger's ability to get to his or her destination on time. A sniff occurring while luggage is being uploaded for a flight will generally be acceptable to a court.[96] A sniff that occurred 1 hour and 15 minutes after the defendant's luggage was seized and she left the terminal was found to be reasonable by the Seventh Circuit.[97] A 15-minute detention of luggage of an Amtrak passenger satisfied the dictates of *Place*. The Seventh Circuit emphasized that the defendant's conduct had created reasonable suspicion for the temporary detention, and the officers acted diligently.[98] Even a delay of 4 days before a warrant was obtained and cocaine discovered, 3 days after a detector dog had failed to alert to a suitcase, was held legal when probable cause existed on substantial other information available to DEA agents.

> We [the First Circuit] also believe that these facts as set forth in a DEA agent's affidavit warrant the magistrate's later decision to issue a search warrant. Although a drug detecting dog did not react when it sniffed the suitcase, the agents pointed out that, according to dog handlers, "the dogs are not foolproof," they "are less accurate on hot muggy days," and drug traffickers have found ways "to mask the odors of contraband to fool detection efforts." The dog's failure to react does not, in our view, destroy the "probable cause" that would otherwise exist. It is just another element to be considered by the magistrate.

The owner of the suitcase had been permitted to leave the airport and had done so after about 20 minutes from the initial questioning when a drug dog was not produced.[99]

A 20-minute detention of luggage in which the defendant missed his train was not considered too long by the Seventh Circuit. As to arguments that the officers could have avoided this delay and inconvenience by calling ahead and had a dog at the next stop, or taking the dog on the train and had it sniff while the train was in motion, the court said:

> So we must consider whether the police in this case might have conducted a further investigation of the defendant that would not have entailed delaying his trip by 24 hours. They could have brought the sniffer dog onto the train with them or let the defendant and his luggage continue to the next station but call ahead and have a dog waiting there. However, these would not have been satisfactory alternatives to seizing the luggage. A sniffer dog might not do his stuff in the unfamiliar setting of a train's interior. And apparently there aren't enough of these highly trained dogs to have one tethered at every bus station, train station, and airport in Chicago. As for the officers' calling ahead, the defendant could have dumped the incriminating contents of his luggage out of the window of his compartment between Chicago and the train's next stop. And there is no suggestion that the police deliberately delayed [allowing the defendant to board] until the last minute so that he would miss his train. They got there as soon as they could—for remember that the defendant had bought his ticket only an hour before the train was to leave.

The court said that the officers could have offered to give the passenger a receipt for his luggage and let him go, but acknowledged that not many travelers will want to be separated from their luggage. The Seventh Circuit emphasized that the defendant's purchase of a ticket with cash just before the train's departure and other behaviors of the defendant gave rise to reasonable suspicion allowing the police to hold the luggage for the sniff.[100]

A delay of 3 hours from the time when a passenger's shoulder bag was seized to the time when it was subjected to a sniff at another terminal in the airport was too long. The court noted that since the officers were stationed at the airport to investigate transportation of illicit drugs, it was reasonable to expect that they would arrange to have a drug dog readily available.[101] The Sixth Circuit has labeled a detention of over 3 hours excessive in duration.[102] A passenger was questioned for 45 minutes to an hour and permitted to leave without his luggage. Since no dog was available, his bags were kept for 13½ hours. The Sixth Circuit concluded that no probable cause existed when the bags were seized.[103]

A New Mexico case resulted in the Tenth Circuit holding that a motion to suppress should have been granted because of the length of the delay but also because officers did not tell an Amtrak passenger where they were taking his luggage or how long they would hold it. There, agents boarded a westbound Amtrak train in Albuquerque and searched the defendant's duffel bag but he would not consent to their opening two packages in the bag. They did not think they had enough for an arrest and left the train. In checking out the defendant's criminal history, they found that he had lied about not having a record for drugs. They drove to the next stop of the train in Las Vegas, New Mexico, and gave the defendant a receipt for his luggage, but the train had started moving and they could not get off. They were told that there were problems with the plumbing and two shoeboxes had been found in the bathroom trash. The agents finally got off the train in Raton, New Mexico, and subjected the suitcases to a sniff, but this involved driving to the state penitentiary in Santa Fe. The dogs alerted about 7 hours after the luggage was seized. The agents then obtained a warrant and discovered cocaine inside the suitcase. The district court had concluded that the alert of the dogs gave probable cause for the subsequent search, but the circuit court noted other factors:

> [A]s in *Place*, the intrusion here "was exacerbated by the failure of the agents to accurately inform [Scales] of the place to which they were transporting the luggage, of the length of time he might be dispossessed, and of what arrangements would be made for return of the luggage if the investigation dispelled the suspicion." ... All Agent Small did was to give Scales a receipt which contained Agent

Small's name, agency, phone number, the date, Quinton Scales' name, and the case number. ... We conclude under *Place* that the seizure of Scales' suitcase exceeded the DEA agents' narrow authority to detain the suitcase briefly for investigative purposes.

Therefore, the circuit court determined that the district court erred in denying the motion to suppress.[104]

The Eleventh Circuit found a 140-minute delay too long. The passenger arrived at Atlanta's Hartsfield International Airport and piqued an agent's interest, apparently by staring at him. Because of inconsistencies in the passenger's answers, the agent told the passenger that he was detaining his luggage for a dog sniff. The passenger's plane left with the passenger, but unexpectedly returned, and the passenger got in line for another flight, where he was arrested.

The 140 minutes, combined with the intrusiveness on Puglisi's right to the possession of the bag, rendered this seizure unreasonable under the standards set forth in *Terry* and *Place*. We therefore hold that the cocaine found in Puglisi's bag should have been suppressed.

The court noted that the agent could have phoned ahead and had agents in Las Vegas meet the flight with a detector dog, though in the case before it the flight never reached Las Vegas.[105]

No Requirement for Having a Dog Immediately Available

A passenger aroused suspicions at the airport in Miami, where he refused a search of his suitcase. The agents let him board but called agents at Logan Airport in Boston. No dog was available so the agents told the passenger that he could board his flight for Burlington but they were going to hold his suitcase until a dog arrived. He boarded his flight. The dog arrived and alerted to the suitcase, which after a warrant was obtained was found to have 20 ounces of cocaine.

West argues that the officers were not diligent because they did not have a dog waiting at the gate when he arrived. While, as the district court found, the agents could have avoided alerting the suspect to the fact that he was under surveillance by concealing the dog and its handler in a non-public area near the gate ..., we do not believe the agents acted unreasonably in not bringing a dog to the immediate vicinity before West's plane arrived. Given the frequent delays in air traffic, an absolute requirement that DEA agents have a dog waiting near the gate whenever a sniff test of a known suspect's baggage is either probable or possible would seem excessively burdensome. If dogs are to be used at all, the government must have some flexibility, bearing in mind there are practical limits to the number of dogs and handlers the government can maintain at one airport. In the present case West's flight was over 50 minutes late, and thus the dog and handler would have been forced to wait uselessly for over an hour near the gate before detention of West's luggage for sniffing.

The court seemed to suggest that a 90-minute delay, as in *Place*, would have been too long, but noted that there is no "talismanic time period." The First Circuit concluded that the seizure and detention comported with the standards of *Place*.[106]

In a North Carolina case, passengers left their luggage at the airport because an agent had determined that the men fit a drug courier profile and told them a briefcase would be subjected to a sniff. No dog was available at the airport and the briefcase was taken to a police academy where a dog alerted to it. The Fourth Circuit found that it might have been possible to conduct the sniff before the defendants' flight departed, but concluded that the duration of the detention was not unnecessarily prolonged. The court said that it could not impose a rule that "police keep their narcotics dogs at the airport whenever they are observing incoming flights for drug couriers."[107]

The Eleventh Circuit approved a 35-minute delay despite the fact that the luggage had been removed from a plane after the defendant boarded a plane from Miami to Richmond. A DEA agent had called a DEA agent in Richmond to try to get a drug detection dog to meet the flight, but the Richmond agent doubted he could get a dog to the airport in time. After the dog alerted, the luggage was opened and cocaine was found. The Eleventh Circuit held that it was unwilling to hold that police must have a dog on site at an airport at all times.[108] Looking at other cases, the 35-minute delay for the sniff was found not to be too long.[109] The circuit court reversed the district court's judgment of acquittal as to the passenger.[110]

SEARCHES OF PASSENGER COMPARTMENTS OF TRAINS

Having been alerted to a suspicious passenger, officers arrived at Union Station where the train was scheduled to be stopped for 25 minutes. The dog alerted to the roomette where the passenger opened the door but said no to a request to speak to him. An officer told the defendant he was searching the compartment based on the dog's alert. A knapsack was found to contain cocaine. The D.C. Circuit Court concluded that exigent circumstances justified the search without a warrant.[111]

After receiving a call from agents at the Miami Amtrak station, agents boarded a train at Baltimore and brought two dogs into a passenger's compartment, where one alerted to one piece of luggage and the other alerted to both. The police obtained a warrant to open the luggage and discovered 3 kilograms of cocaine.

> Whitehead [the defendant] on appeal concedes, as he must, that the exposure of luggage located in a public place to a trained canine is not a "search" for fourth amendment purposes [citing *Place*]. He contends, however, that his luggage was not located in a "public place," but in a train compartment that was the functional equivalent of a temporary home similar to a hotel room.[112] … Based on this reasoning, he argues that the police could not bring their trained canines into his compartment without a warrant, or at the least, probable cause. We disagree. Like the trial court, we reject the contention that a passenger train sleeping compartment is a "temporary home" for fourth amendment purposes. While occupants of train roomettes may properly expect some degree of privacy, it is less than the reasonable expectations that individuals rightfully possess in their homes or their hotel rooms.[113]

The Fourth Circuit also determined that the defendant had consented to the search, albeit reluctantly. The conviction was affirmed.[114]

Dog Escaping a Handler's Control

As with vehicle sniffs, dogs sometimes elude a handler's control and alert in areas where the handler has not sent them. In a case arising in Washington, D.C., in 1987, a police officer handling a trained narcotics detection dog entered a railroad car while it was standing in Union Station. When the dog came to the defendant's roomette, it twice lunged through the opening of the curtain and was pulled back, but the third time the handler failed to restrain it and it jumped onto a seat in the roomette and sniffed toward the defendant's suitcase, which was on a rack above the dog's head. The case was decided after *Place*, and the court determined that by leaving the door to the roomette open and the curtains parted, the defendant "was not relying on any increased expectation of privacy afforded by a separate compartment." The dog's alert gave the officers probable cause to believe the luggage contained illicit drugs. The court said that obtaining a warrant was not a reasonable expectation under the circumstances that the train had stopped to change engines. The defendant's motion to suppress was therefore denied.[115]

CONSENT TO LUGGAGE SEARCHES

Consent to a search obviates the need to determine whether a dog's alert provided probable cause to search a bag.[116] Consent to search a bag is consent to search the containers inside it.

> [L]uggage of a typical traveler is likely to include numerous containers, such as those in which health and hygiene products are packaged. A reasonable person who consents to a search of one of his bags would not expect the officer to repeat his request for consent before examining each new item encountered in the bag.[117]

Passengers sometimes consent to a search because they have been informed that luggage will be detained for a dog sniff. A consent was nullified by the Eighth Circuit where there was no reasonable articulable suspicion of criminal activity and the officer threatened a dog sniff to pressure an airline passenger to allow a search. The court reversed the district court's denial of the motion to suppress and reversed the conviction.[118] On nearly indistinguishable facts, the Eighth Circuit found a search to be consensual.[119]

A 2006 Seventh Circuit decision involved a passenger who declined to consent until he was told that his luggage would be detained for a dog sniff. After the luggage had been opened and Ecstasy found inside, the officers closed the luggage again and subjected it to a sniff. The dog alerted. Although the delay was only 20 minutes, the passenger had to wait 24 hours for another train to his destination. The conviction was affirmed.[120]

SNIFFS LEADING TO BODY SEARCHES

In a 1993 case arising in Michigan, DEA agents became suspicious of men carrying gym bags. The men agreed to a search of their bags. The men had $45,000 in the socks they were wearing, which the agents said would be subjected to a dog sniff. The dog alerted and the U.S. government instituted a forfeiture action. The Sixth Circuit noted that the men were not given any choice regarding the sniff and described it as more intrusive than a luggage search because it involved their persons. The court determined that probable cause requires less than a *prima facie* case but more than mere suspicion. Here, there was only mere suspicion. The circuit court affirmed the district court's grant of summary judgment to the claimants.[121]

In a 2004 case arising in Louisiana, officers advised passengers that a narcotics detection dog was going to be brought aboard a bus. The officers told the passengers that they could disembark during the procedure, but they did not have to. The dog alerted to an empty seat and two bags above the seat. The alert to the seat suggested to the officers that a passenger was carrying drugs on his body. Because of a passenger's nervousness, an officer patted down the defendant. He said he was wearing a back brace but when officers raised the passenger's shirt they found bags taped to his chest that contained powder. The court concluded that the pat down was permissible given the threat that a narcotics carrier might be armed.[122]

A passenger returning from Jamaica was subjected to a body cavity search and an x-ray of her abdomen because a drug dog standing on the jetway alerted to her. Nothing was found in her luggage, so a pat-down search followed, then the body cavity and x-ray. The Seventh Circuit stated that the trial transcripts supported the government's argument that the dog alerted, though the handler apparently stopped the dog from performing a full alert:

> Upon further questioning by the district court, the dog handler testified that he did not allow the dog to finish his alert by sitting down because the handler was not in a position immediately to verify the source of the narcotics odor and did not want to reward the dog for a potential false alert. The district court, however, found nothing equivocal in the dog's alert, which it was entitled to do based on this testimony.

The court concluded that the customs inspectors had reasonable suspicion of drug smuggling for their actions.[123]

HOTELS AND MOTELS

Courts have generally held that there is no expectation of privacy in the airspace outside a hotel room.[124] Allowing a dog to sniff inside a motel room has been held not to be a search when the occupant consented.[125]

Hotel searches sometimes occur because there was not time to perform a sniff on baggage. In a case arising in Arkansas, Little Rock police officers were notified of suspicious passenger who would be flying from Los Angeles to Little Rock. The officers met the passenger and asked to search his luggage, but he declined. He took a taxi to his hotel, where in the lobby an officer again requested to search the passenger's luggage and again was denied. The passenger went to his room. A narcotics dog was walked up and down the hallway and alerted several times to the door of the passenger's room. A search warrant was obtained and 10 pounds of cocaine were found in the passenger's briefcase. The government conceded at oral argument that the lobby encounter was impermissible but the court concluded that the sniff in the corridor of the hotel did not violate the passenger's expectation of privacy. The denial of the motion to suppress, and hence the conviction, was affirmed.[126]

When suspects were arrested on leaving a motel room, officers took a dog into the motel room after the arrest and the dog alerted to a briefcase and a suitcase. A warrant was obtained to open the luggage, which yielded cocaine and a large amount of cash. The court found the sniff did not offend constitutional guarantees.[127]

SEARCH OF A HOTEL ROOM LEADS TO SNIFF OF A CAR

A defendant paid for his room each day, often later than hotel policy permitted, but one day the hotel sold out and determined not to let him pay for another day. The hotel began to inventory the items in the room and found a large wad of bills in the occupant's clothing. The hotel called the Alexandria police, who conducted a cursory search and found some cocaine. This did not involve the dog but after the defendant was arrested, an officer asked the canine officer to search the defendant's car, which was in the entry area with the driver's door open.

> The drug-sniffing dog proceeded to climb into the car where he "started biting on the passenger seat, indicating that he hit on some type of narcotic smell, either on that seat or underneath it." ... Officer Duquette then popped the trunk lever located next to the driver's seat. ... The dog jumped in the trunk and bit on a plastic foam food container. . Officer Duquette opened the container and found roughly $16,000 in bundled cash. ...
>
> After the canine officer finished with the search of Mr. Watson's car, he proceeded up to room 827. Once there, he exposed the canine to the luggage cart. The luggage cart contained two clothes hampers, three large green trash bags, and two brown briefcases. ... The dog failed to alert to the luggage cart. The officers proceeded to search the items on the luggage cart until they found approximately 237 grams of cocaine and $12,600 in cash. The cocaine was found inside two ziplock bags, which were inside a brown paper bag, which was inside one of the large green trash bags.

The court granted the motion to suppress the search of the hotel room and its luggage as the defendant had not abandoned the room and the items were not in plain view. The motion to suppress the search of the automobile, however, was denied. Therefore, a prosecution could proceed as to the cash found in the car, perhaps a forfeiture proceeding.[128]

CRUISE SHIPS

A case beginning in the Virgin Islands described how a narcotics detection dog prepared for a visit to a cruise ship:

> On the morning of September 25, 2004, the Adventure of the Seas cruise ship, which can carry up to 3,838 passengers and 1,185 crew, arrived from the foreign port of St. Maarten and docked in St. Thomas, United States Virgin Islands. Prior to the ship's arrival, United States Customs and Border Protection officers gathered to prepare to board the ship and conduct enforcement actions. Canine Enforcement Officer Ralph Dasant was on duty that morning, and, after retrieving his drug-sniffing dog

from its kennel, he used the Treasury Enforcement Communications System ("TECS"), a computerized database, to access the list of vessels arriving from a foreign port. He then used the database to access the manifest of crew and passengers aboard the Adventure of the Seas. Based on TECS information generated through this search, he selected approximately ten of the ship's staterooms (out of a total of 1,557) to be looked at upon boarding the ship.

One of the passengers of interest was the defendant.

A team of customs officers, including Dasant and the drug-sniffing dog, boarded the ship and proceeded directly to the chief of security of the ship. Together, they went to the deck of the ship where Whitted's cabin was located. After the officers knocked on the door to the cabin and ascertained that Whitted was not there, the chief of security unlocked the door and the officers began to prepare the room for canine screening. The dog did not alert in the hallway or at the door to the cabin. However, immediately after the cabin was prepped, the dog bolted into the room without being given a command and alerted to a bag. Dasant called him off and indicated the bag to the other officers. Customs officers Gail Fraser and Norman Ramirez then entered the room and searched through the bag, where they found "ladies' shoes, men's sandals, perfume bottles and a shaving cream container." ... After ascertaining from the chief of security that no woman was assigned to the room and noting that the shaving cream container seemed strange, they set aside those items found in the bag for further examination. The chief of security offered them the use of the ship's x-ray machine. While x-raying the items, officers Fraser and Gloria Lambert noticed what appeared to be "pebbles" inside.

The pebbles were heroin. As to preparing the cabin for the dog, a footnote explains:

These preparations consisted of ensuring that no sharp objects, food, or anything else that might harm or distract the dog were in the cabin, moving bags from under the bed into the center of the room, and pressing the surface of the bags to expel any air inside. No bags were opened at this time.

Whitted filed a motion to suppress, which was denied by the district court. The circuit court noted that the dog had not alerted outside the cabin. However, there were other reasons that raised suspicions and the court affirmed the denial of the motion to suppress.[129]

A dog's alert inside a cabin was not suppressed when owners of the vessel had consented to a search of the vessel, the seaman's roommate had pointed out the seaman's belongings, and the dog alerted to the shoes. The court held these factors were sufficient to provide reasonable suspicion, which was all that was needed for the search of a seaman's cabin. The insoles were found to contain cocaine hydrochloride.[130]

PRIVATE VESSELS

Customs officers in an aircraft illuminated a vessel and saw the crew dumping bales into the water. The bales were later found to contain cocaine. When a Customs vessel arrived, the suspect vessel tried to outrun it and was rammed astern by the Customs vessel. The dog's alert to the vessel corroborated the testimony concerning the crew dumping bales over the side.[131]

PRIVATE AIRPLANES

A district court's granting of the government's forfeiture motion was reversed by the Ninth Circuit when the narcotics dog sniff occurred 6 days after the seizure of a Cessna. The plane was first observed flying into U.S. airspace near Mexicali. It did not stop in Calexico, California, the required airport of entry, but proceeded to Hemet-Ryan Airport. It left that airport 3 minutes later, without the pilot contacting anyone. The plane made numerous turns and course changes in the Banning Pass area. The plane eventually crossed back into Mexico. The plane flew back into U.S. airspace about 2 hours later, stopping briefly at the Holtville Airport for 15 minutes. It then landed at Desert Air Sky Ranch where it was blocked by a Customs aircraft. No debris or narcotics were found. It fit the profile of a drug plane:

> [T]he plane was equipped with some advanced equipment, including: state-of-the-art programmable ground to air radios and a ham radio with an "omnidirectional" antenna. Also, the plane had been fitted with an "after-market" nose fuel tank and additional fuel tanks in the wings. The fuel tanks increased the Cessna's flying time by some two and one half hours—about a 50% gain.

Officials then flew it to the North Island Naval Air Station. Six days after it was seized, Brutus, a narcotics detection dog, alerted to a section of the carpet that was unrolled in the cargo area, but no drug or debris was found.

> Brutus' handler also testified at trial. He stated that, based on his dog's alert, in his opinion a large quantity—up to 50 pounds—of marijuana had been in the plane in the prior two weeks. He also testified that he did not believe that any drugs were actually then present in the plane. He did not know who had been in the plane during the six-day period between the initial seizure and the dog search. He argued that as far as he knew, anyone who had the scent of marijuana on them could have been in the plane during that period, thus causing Brutus to alert. He also testified that the carpet was not rolled up in the back of the plane but had been laid flat.

The court found that "the probative value of the alert must be rejected." Customs officials testified that they did not know who had been in the plane during the 6-day period. Someone with marijuana smell could have entered the plane during that period and caused the dog to alert, and there was evidence of tampering with the contents of the plane. A carpet, which had been rolled up in the back of the plane when it was seized, had been unrolled by the time the handler arrived with Brutus. The Ninth Circuit reversed the district court's grant of the forfeiture motion.[132]

CONSENT TO A PRIVATE PLANE SEARCH

A pilot agreed to a search of his personal effects aboard a private airplane he was flying. A dog brought aboard alerted to a package wrapped as a Christmas present (3 weeks after Christmas). The dog was pulled away from the package to prevent the animal from tearing it apart. The package was opened and found to contain marijuana. A search of the plane disclosed evidence that it had been used to transport drugs from Mexico. The conviction of the pilot was affirmed.[133]

NOTES

1. Many Supreme Court cases that do not concern police dogs nevertheless affect police dog work, such as the requirement "that the officer did not violate the Fourth Amendment in arriving at the place from which the evidence could be plainly viewed." *Horton v. California*, 496 U.S. 128, 110 S.Ct. 2301, 110 L.Ed.2d 112 (1990). What the officer can plainly view, the dog may plainly smell.
2. *U.S. v. Place*, 462 U.S. 696, 103 S.Ct. 2637, 77 L.Ed.2d 110 (1983).
3. *Terry v. Ohio*, 392 U.S. 1, 88 S.Ct. 1868, 88 S.Ct. 1868, 20 L.Ed.2d 889 (1968).
4. See *U.S. v. Lambert*, 834 F.Supp. 1318 (D.Kan. 1993) (reviewing cases in 10 years after *Place*).
5. *Terry v. Ohio* (1968). See also *Florida v. Royer*, 460 U.S. 491, 103 S.Ct. 1319, 75 L.Ed.2d 229 (1983) (noting in a case that did not involve dogs that their presence would have allowed limiting an investigative detention). Justice Blackmun concurred as well in *Place*, and Marshall joined this concurrence as well.
6. Citing Justice Stevens concurring in *Texas v. Brown*, 460 U.S. 730, 103 S.Ct. 1535, 1546, 75 L.Ed.2d 502 (1983).
7. *U.S. v. Jacobsen*, 466 U.S. 109, 104 S.Ct. 1652, 80 L.Ed.2d 85 (1984).
8. Citing *California v. Evans*, 65 Cal.App.3d 924, 932, 134 Cal.Rptr. 436, 440 (1977). The Second Circuit had used the phrase "canine cannabis connoisseur" in 1975. *U.S. v. Bronstein*, 521 F.2d 459 (2nd Cir. 1975), in describing a dog's sniff of a row of about 50 pieces of luggage.

9. *U.S. v. Germosen-Garcia*, 712 F.Supp. 862 (D.Kan. 1989). See also *U.S. v. Maldonado-Espinosa*, 767 F.Supp. 1176 (D.Puerto Rico 1991) (random sniffing of airport luggage in areas not frequented by the public containing both domestic and international luggage was legal).

10. *U.S. v. Sokolow*, 490 U.S. 1, 109 S.Ct. 1581, 104 L.Ed.2d 1 (1989).

11. *U.S. v. Goldstein*, 635 F.2d 356 (5th Cir. 1981); *U.S. v. Johnson*, 660 F.2d 21 (2nd Cir. 1981) (probable cause from alert not negated by fact odor might have been residual); *Cavaluzzi v. Florida*, 409 So.2d 1108 (Ct. App. 1982); *U.S. v. Lewis*, 708 F.2d 1078 (6th Cir. 1983).

12. See, e.g., *Montana v. Scheetz*, 286 Mont. 41, 950 P.2d 722 (1997).

13. *Pooley v. Alaska*, 705 P.2d 1293 (Ct. App. 1985).

14. *U.S. v. Large*, 729 F.2d 636 (8th Cir. 1984); *U.S. v. Thomas*, 87 F.3d 909 (7th Cir. 1996) (so nervous as to almost spill coffee); *U.S. v. Ferguson*, 935 F.2d 1518 (7th Cir. 1991); *U.S. v. Carter*, 985 F.2d 1095, 300 U.S.App.D.C. 36 (D.C.Cir. 1993).

15. *U.S. v. Erwin*, 803 F.2d 1505 (9th Cir. 1986).

16. *U.S. v. Withers*, 972 F.2d 837 (7th Cir. 1992).

17. *U.S. v. Low*, 887 F.3d 232 (9th Cir. 1989).

18. *U.S. v. Williams*, 726 F.2d 661 (10th Cir. 1984).

19. *U.S. v. Large*, 729 F.2d 636 (8th Cir. 1984).

20. *U.S. v. Erwin*, 803 F.2d 1505 (9th Cir. 1986).

21. *U.S. v. Houston*, 21 F.3d 1035 (10th Cir. 1994).

22. *U.S. v. Butler*, 988 F.2d 537 (5th Cir. 1993).

23. *U.S. v. Pantazis*, 816 F.2d 361 (8th Cir. 1987).

24. *U.S. v. Carhee*, 27 F.3d 1493 (10th Cir. 1994).

25. *U.S. v. Bloom*, 975 F.2d 1447 (10th Cir. 1992).

26. *U.S. v. Borys*, 766 F.2d 304 (7th Cir. 1985).

27. *U.S. v. Hall*, 978 F.2d 616 (10th Cir. 1992) (officers tried to smell luggage when dog did not arrive).

28. *U.S. v. Moore*, 22 F.3d 241 (10th Cir. 1994). But see *U.S. v. Torres*, 65 F.3d 1241 (4th Cir. 1995).

29. *U.S. v. MacDonald*, 670 F.2d 910 (10th Cir. 1982).

30. *U.S. v. Valles*, 292 F.3d 678 (10th Cir. 2002).

31. *U.S. v. Ayarza*, 874 F.2d 647 (9th Cir. 1989).

32. *U.S. v. Smith*, 492 F.2d 650, 160 U.S.App.D.C. 384 (D.C.Cir. 1974); *U.S. v. Massac*, 867 F.2d 174 (3rd Cir. 1989); *U.S. v. Cooper*, 873 F.2d 269 (11th Cir. 1989); *U.S. v. $639,558*, 955 F.2d 712, 293 U.S.App.D.C. 384 (1992); *U.S. v. Johnson*, 990 F.2d 1129 (9th Cir. 1993).

33. *U.S. v. Puglisi*, 723 F.2d 779 (11th Cir. 1984).

34. *U.S. v. Goodwin*, 449 F.3d 766 (7th Cir. 2006).

35. *U.S. v. Smith*, 492 F.2d 650, 160 U.S.App.D.C. 384 (D.C. Cir. 1974); *U.S. v. Massac*, 867 F.2d 174 (3rd Cir. 1989).

36. *U.S. v. Cooper*, 873 F.2d 269 (11th Cir. 1989); *U.S. v. McCarthur*, 6 F.3d 1270 (7th Cir. 1993).

37. *U.S. v. Glover*, 957 F.2d 1004 (8th Cir. 1992).

38. *U.S. v. Ferguson*, 935 F.2d 1518 (7th Cir. 1991); *U.S. v. Puglisi*, 723 F.2d 779 (11th Cir. 1984).

39. *U.S. v. Avery*, 137 F.3d 343 (6th Cir. 1997).

40. *U.S. v. Sterling*, 909 F.2d 1078 (7th Cir. 1978).

41. *U.S. v. Whitehead*, 849 F.2d 849 (4th Cir. 1988).

42. *U.S. v. Sullivan*, 903 F.2d 1093 (7th Cir. 1990).

43. *U.S. v. Frost*, 999 F.2d 737 (3rd Cir. 1993).

44. *U.S. v. Kennedy*, 131 F.3d 1371 (10th Cir. 1997).

45. *U.S. v. $639,558*, 955F.2d 712, 293 U.S.App.D.C. 384 (1992).

46. *U.S. v. McCarthur*, 6 F.3d 1270 (7th Cir. 1993).

47. *U.S. v. Avery*, 137 F.3d 343 (6th Cir. 1997); *U.S. v. O'Neal*, 17 F.3d 239 (8th Cir. 1994) (wearing a Chicago Bulls Starter jacket and walking briskly; but court held that these and other factors would not have supported the warrant were it not that a later confession by the defendant provided sufficient evidence for the warrant).

48. *U.S. v. $53,082*, 773 F.Supp. 26 (1991), 985 F.2d 245 (6th Cir. 1993).

49. *U.S. v. Kennedy*, 131 F.3d 1371 (10th Cir. 1997).

50. *U.S. v. McCarthur*, 6 F.3d 1270 (7th Cir. 1993).

51. *U.S. v. Williams*, 356 F.3d 1268 (10th Cir. 2004).

52. *U.S. v. Freymuller*, 571 F.Supp. 61 (N.D.Ill. 1983).

53. *U.S. v. Torres*, 65 F.3d 1241 (4th Cir. 1995) (80-minute delay; suspicion may have only been based on duffel bag).

54. *Crockett v. Texas*, 1991 Westlaw 11999, 803 S.W.2d 308 (Ct. Crim. App. 1991).
55. *U.S. v. McGauley*, 786 F.2d 888 (8th Cir. 1986) (informant was defendant's wife).
56. *U.S. v. Maldonado-Espinosa*, 968 F.2d 101 (1st Cir. 1992). See also *U.S. v. de Los Santos Ferrer*, 999 F.2d 7 (1st Cir. 1993) (almost identical facts to Maldonado-Espinosa, including x-ray).
57. *U.S. v. Battista,* 876 F.2d 201, 278 U.S.App.D.C. 16 (D.C.Cir. 1989). See *U.S. v. Carrasquillo*, 877 F.2d 73, 278 U.S.App.D.C. 128 (D.C.Cir. 1989) (dog alerted after bag removed to train platform).
58. *U.S. v. Ward*, 144 F.3d 1024 (7th Cir. 1998).
59. *U.S. v. Fulero*, 498 F.2d 748, 162 U.S.App.D.C. 206 (D.C.Cir. 1974).
60. *U.S. v. Pinkard,* 125 F.3d 863 (10th Cir. 1997).
61. *U.S. v. $90,000 in United States Currency*, 2009 WL 6327469 (D.Minn. 2009).
62. See, for example, *U.S. v. Martell*, 654 F.2d 1356 (9th Cir. 1981) (passengers detained 20 minutes for narcotics detection dog to sniff their luggage caused them to miss their flight; dog's alert gave probable cause for search; conviction affirmed).
63. *U.S. v. Place*, 462 U.S. 696 (10th Cir. 1983).
64. *U.S. v. Garcia*, 42 F.3d 719 (10th Cir. 1994). Compare to *U.S. v. Ward*, 961 F.2d 1526 (10th Cir. 1992) (defendant reasonably believed he could not leave his compartment and was not advised he could terminate interview, so initial detention violated Fourth Amendment rights and subsequent dog sniff was fruit of poisonous tree).
65. *U.S. v. Harvey*, 961 F.2d 1361 (8th Cir. 1992). See *U.S. v. Graham*, 982 F2d 273 (8th Cir. 1992) (another case where Judd alerted to a suitcase on a bus; motion to suppress denied).
66. *U.S. v. Gant*, 112 F.3d 239 (6th Cir. 1997).
67. *Shqeirat v. U.S. Airways Group, Inc.*, 645 F.Supp.2d 765 (D.Minn. 2009).
68. *U.S. v. Guzman*, 75 F.3d 1090 (6th Cir. 1996).
69. *U.S. v. Gwinn*, 191 F.3d 874 (8th Cir. 2000). See *U.S. v. Nicholson*, 144 F.3d 632 (10th Cir. 1998).
70. *U.S. v. Garzon,* 119 F.3d 1446 (10th Cir. 1997).
71. *U.S. v. Tugwell*, 125 F.3d 600 (8th Cir. 1997); *U.S. v. Hernandez*, 7 F.3d 944 (10th Cir. 1993).
72. *U.S. v. Fernandez*, 772 F2d 495 (9th Cir. 1985).
73. *U.S. v. Stephens*, 206 F.3d 914 (9th Cir. 2000).
74. *U.S. v. Lewis,* 708 F.2d 1078 (6th Cir. 1983).
75. *U.S. v. Munoz-Nava*, 524 F.3d 1137 (10th Cir. 2008) (defendant was wearing overly large boots that bulged, had no luggage).
76. *Washington v. Wolohan*, 24 Wash.App. 813, 698 P.2d 421 (Ct. App. 1979).
77. *New York v. Price*, 54 N.Y.2d 557, 431 N.E.2d 267, 446 N.Y.S.2d 906 (Ct. of Appeals 1981).
78. *Neuhoff v. Indiana*, 708 N.E.2d 889 (Ct. App. 1999) (alert in Texas resulted in notifying Indian postal inspector, which led to a second alert).
79. *U.S. v. Brown*, 731 F.2d 1491 (11th Cir. 1974), modified at 742 F.2d 1505 (11th Cir. 1984). See also *U.S. v. Williams*, 365 F.3d 399 (5th Cir. 2004); *U.S. v. Grogg*, 534 F.3d 807 (7th Cir. 2008).
80. *U.S. v. Smith*, 459 F.3d 1276 (11th Cir. 2006).
81. Citing *Coolidge v. New Hampshire*, 403 U.S. 443, 465, 91 S.Ct. 2022, 2037, 29 L.Ed.2d 564 (1971).
82. *U.S. v. Viera*, 644 F.2d 509 (5th Cir. 1981). See also *U.S. v. Lovell*, 849 F.2d 910 (5th Cir. 1988).
83. One case described a passenger's testimony as being thankful that a dog only sniffed the luggage hold. Bowline would later testify that she narrowly escaped detection when the bus was stopped en route and its luggage compartment inspected by a drug-detecting dog. Had the dog been brought onto the bus, it surely would have alerted to Bowline, who testified that she reeked of marijuana. *U.S. v. Adams*, No. 08-4205 (7th Cir. 2010).
84. *U.S. v. Outlaw*, 134 F.Supp.2d 807 (2001), aff'd 319 F.3d 701 (5th Cir. 2003).
85. *U.S. v. McCranie*, 703 F.2d 1213 (10th Cir.1983).
86. Under section 1704 of the U.S. Crime Control Act of 1990: "A railroad police officer who is certified or commissioned as a police officer under the laws of any one state shall, in accordance with the regulations issued by the U. S. Secretary of Transportation, be authorized to enforce the laws of any other state in which the rail carrier owns property." See 49 U.S.C. 28101. Some state grant general peace officer authority to railroad police, while other states restrict the authority of railroad police to railroad property.
87. DeFranco (1999). BNSF dogs work at finding trespassers but also as bomb detection dogs. "BNSF Competes in Railroad Police K9 Trials" (May 24, 2007) (www.bnsf.com).
88. Stephanitz (1923), 341–342. Stephanitz also describes postal workers using trained protection dogs at the time.
89. Citing *Romo v. Champion*, 46 F.3d 1013 (10th Cir. 1995).

90. *U.S. v. Garcia-Garcia*, 319 F.3d 726 (5th Cir. 2003). See also *U.S. v. Cagle*, 849 F.2d 924 (5th Cir. 1988) (dog sniff in baggage area).

91. *Horton v. Goose Creek Independent School District*, 690 F.2d 470 (5th Cir. 1982); *B.C. v. Plumas Unified School District*, 192 F.3d 1260, 1266 (9th Cir.1999).

92. *U.S. v. Reyes*, 349 F.3d 219 (5th Cir. 2003).

93. *U.S. v. Ferguson*, 935 F.2d 1518 (7th Cir. 1991). See also *U.S. v. Edwards*, 898 F.2d 1273 (7th Cir. 1990) (dog alerted at Amtrak office in Chicago).

94. *U.S. v. Massac*, 867 F.2d 174 (3rd Cir. 1989).

95. *U.S. v. Bronstein*, 521 F.2d 459 (2nd Cir. 1975).

96. See *U.S. v. Riley*, 927 F.2d 1045 (8th Cir. 1991).

97. *U.S. v. Sterling*, 909 F.2d 1078 (7th Cir. 1978).

98. *U.S. v. Edwards*, 898 F.2d 1273 (7th Cir. 1990). See also *U.S. v. Nurse*, 916 F.2d 20, 286 U.S.App.D.C. 303 (D.C.Cir. 1990) (20-minute delay approved).

99. *U.S. v. Jodoin*, 672 F.2d 232 (1st Cir. 1982).

100. *U.S. v. Goodwin*, 449 F.3d 766 (7th Cir. 2006).

101. *Moya v. U.S.*, 761 F.2d 322 (7th Cir. 1985). Not having a narcotics detection dog available does not mean that other means, even more intrusive ones, are necessarily unreasonable. *U.S. v. Hooper*, 935 F.2d 484 (2nd Cir. 1991).

102. *U.S. v. Sanders*, 719 F.2d 882 (6th Cir. 1983). A 40-minute delay was not unreasonable in *U.S. v. Orsolini*, 300 F.3d 724 (6th Cir. 2002).

103. *U.S. v. Saperstein*, 723 F.2d 1221 (6th Cir. 1983).

104. *U.S. v. Scales*, 903 F.2d 765 (10th Cir. 1990).

105. *U.S. v. Puglisi*, 723 F.2d 779 (11th Cir. 1984).

106. *U.S. v. West*, 731 F.2d 90 (1st Cir. 1984).

107. *U.S. v. Alpert*, 816 F.2d 958 (4th Cir. 1987).

108. Citing cases from the First, Fourth, and Seventh Circuits: *U.S. v. Alpert*, 816 F.2d 958 (4th Cir.1987), *U.S. v. Borys*, 766 F.2d 304, 314 (7th Cir.1985); *U.S. v. West*, 731 F.2d 90 (1st Cir.1984).

109. Citing *U.S. v. Borys*, 766 F.2d 304, 314 (7th Cir.1985) (75-minute delay not too long); *U.S. v. Hardy*, 855 F.2d 753 (11th Cir.1988) cert. denied 109 S.Ct. 1137, 103 L.Ed.2d 198 (1989) (50 minutes not too long).

110. *U.S. v. Cooper*, 873 F.2d 269 (11th Cir. 1989).

111. *U.S. v. Tartaglia*, 864 F.2d 837, 275 U.S.App.D.C. 15 (D.C.Cir. 1989). See *U.S. v. Colyer*, 878 F.2d 469, 278 U.S.App. D.C. 367 (D.C.Cir. 1989) (alert outside sleeper compartment; dog sniff outside compartment was not Fourth Amendment search).

112. Citing *Stoner v. California*, 376 U.S. 483, 490, 84 S.Ct. 889, 893-94, 11 L.Ed.2d 856 (1964) (according full Fourth Amendment protection to hotel room guests).

113. Also citing *U.S. v. Liberto*, 660 F.Supp. 889 (D.D.C. 1987), aff'd 838 F.2d 571 (D.C.Cir.1988) (holding lunge of narcotics dog sniffing in a public passageway outside the defendant's train compartment into roomette and alert at suitcase was not a Fourth Amendment search).

114. *U.S. v. Whitehead*, 849 F.2d 849 (4th Cir. 1988).

115. *U.S. v. Liberto*, 660 F.Supp. 889 (DC D.C. 1987).

116. *U.S. v. Knox*, 839 F.2d 285 (6th Cir. 1988).

117. *U.S. v. Gant*, 112 F.3d 239 (6th Cir. 1997), citing *U.S. v. Battista*, 876 F.2d 201 (D.C.Cir.1989) (consent to search luggage included consent to search plastic bags inside and stating that the court refuses to turn such searches into games of "Mother-may-I") and *Florida v. Jimeno*, 500 U.S. 248, 111 S.Ct. 1801, 114 L.Ed.2d 297 (1991).

118. *U.S. v. Green*, 52 F.3d 194 (8th Cir. 1995).

119. *U.S. v. Robinson*, 984 F.2d 911 (8th Cir. 1993).

120. *U.S. v. Goodwin*, 449 F.3d 766 (7th Cir. 2006).

121. *U.S. v. $53,082*, 773 F.Supp. 26 (E.D.Mich. 1991), aff'd 985 F.2d 245 (6th Cir. 1993).

122. *U.S. v. Jackson*, 390 F.3d 393 (5th Cir. 2004).

123. *Kaniff v. U.S.*, 351 F.3d 780 (7th Cir. 2003). See *Saffell v. Crews*, 183 F.3d 655 (7th Cir. 1999) (dog's alert to luggage leads to strip search).

124. *Wilson v. Texas*, 98 SW3d 265 (Ct. App. 2002); *Nelson v. Florida*, 867 So.2d 534 (Ct. App. 2004).

125. *U.S. v. Esquilin*, 208 F.3d 315 (1st Cir. 2000) (trial court had held sniff inside motel room was, under *Place*, not a search by a dog on a 6-foot leash while the handler spoke with the occupant and occupant consented in any case).

126. *U.S. v. Roby*, 122 F.3d 1120 (8th Cir. 1997). See also *U.S. v. Riley*, 927 F.2d 1045 (8th Cir. 1991) (sniff occurred while baggage handlers were still unloading luggage from flight).

127. *U.S. v. Burns*, 624 F.2d 95 (10th Cir. 1980) (citing *U.S. v. Pollard*, 466 F.2d 1 (10th Cir. 1972) that a "limited warrantless search of a motel room incident to the lawful arrest of its occupants is permissible").
128. *U.S. v. Watson*, 783 F.Supp. 258 (E.D.Va. 1992). See also *Reyes v. Texas*, 1997 WL 196356 (Ct. App. 1997) (dog pawed bags in hotel room but no drugs were found, then alerted to trunk of car revealing heroin and cocaine).
129. *U.S. v. Whitted*, 541 F.3d 480 (3rd Cir. 2008).
130. *U.S. v. Cunningham*, 1996 WL 665747 (E.D.La. 1996). See *U.S. v. Meyer*, 536 F.2d 963 (1st Cir. 1976).
131. *U.S. v. Rosario-Peralta*, 199 F.3d 552 (1st Cir. 1999).
132. *U.S. v. Dickerson v. One Cessna 421B Aircraft*, 873 F.2d 1181 (9th Cir. 1989).
133. *U.S. v. Richards,* 500 F.2d 1025 (9th Cir. 1974).

12 Mail and Package Sniffs

Mail and package sniffs are often regarded as similar to luggage sniffs, and when luggage is checked through to a destination independent of the route of the passenger, there is no difference.

REASONS FOR INVESTIGATION OF PACKAGES

Reasons that a package may be suspicious to postal authorities and inspectors are varied, and have included an excessive amount of tape,[1] being larger than most private packages,[2] paying in cash,[3] sending a package in an expensive way when a cheaper alternative seems appropriate,[4] giving the appearance of trying to avoid security cameras,[5] having misspellings on labels,[6] having handwritten labels,[7] arriving at a facility in a rental car,[8] smelling of masking agents such as coffee,[9] and being sent from a bad neighborhood.[10] Packages coming from a narcotics source city often adds to other suspicions, but it seems that any city or state near a border can fit this classification.[11] Going to a narcotics destination city can be equally broad in law enforcement perspectives.[12] FedEx packages without telephone numbers have been called suspicious.[13]

In a pre-*Place* decision in Ohio, a sniff of a package on an American Airlines flight was held to be a search and analogized to attaching a device to the outside of a phone booth:

> [T]he first issue is whether the sniffing of the air around the package by the dog constitutes a search. That question must be answered in the affirmative. By the use of a sophisticated device, albeit flesh and blood, the user perceived something entirely hidden from human senses, enhanced or unenhanced. As conceded in the *Solis* case by the government, no real distinction can be drawn between the use of specially trained dogs with superior olfactory powers than use of an electronic instrument which registers a smell which a human cannot perceive. In this respect the case is comparable to that of [an] electronic device attached to the outside of the enclosed telephone booth constituted a search even though there was no physical intrusion of the enclosure.

However, the court determined that the search was not unreasonable.[14]

POSTAL INSPECTIONS

In a case tried in a federal court in Kansas, an element in the conviction was a canine alert, though this was not specifically contested. The case is worth consideration, however, because it describes postal procedures regarding profiling of packages:

> In addition to these elements, [postal] inspectors also pay close attention to the city of origination and to the addressee's name (e.g., if multiple packages are sent to a single address but each package is addressed to a different individual). If a package matches one or more of the elements of the profile, the package is detained and subjected to a canine sniff. If the dog alerts to the package, the package is sent to its destination city under controlled conditions. Upon arrival, the package is once again subjected to a canine sniff. If the dog alerts to the package, the postal inspector obtains a search warrant. The package is then searched pursuant to a warrant. If illegal drugs are found, the inspector generally obtains authorization for a signaling device to be placed in the package. After the package is delivered to the addressee (or to the person to whom the addressee delivers the package), a search warrant for the residence is obtained and executed.
>
> In the case at bar, the package addressed to defendant Lux and delivered by her to defendant Hill was detained at the Los Angeles Airport (LAX) on October 14, 1988, along with seventeen other

packages matching various criteria of the Drug Package Profile. Of the eighteen packages detained, the dog alerted to nine, including the package at issue in this case. Of those nine packages, three were eventually found to contain cocaine, including the package addressed to defendant Lux and delivered by her to defendant Hill. The package at issue in this case was detained at LAX because it met three of the Drug Package Profile criteria and because it originated in a city known to be a source for illegal drugs—Los Angeles. Specifically, the package at issue had a handwritten label, the return addressee was fictitious, and the package's destination was Kansas City, a known destination city for illegal drugs.

The court noted that not all the packages that the dogs alerted to in fact contained drugs. One package had steroids, while others had videotapes and clothes, but the court noted that the dog's alert might mean that the person packaging the items had narcotics on his hands at the time. The motion to suppress was denied.[15]

In a federal case arising in Alaska, a postal inspector became suspicious of a package that arrived in Juneau. He submitted the package to a canine sniff and the dog alerted. A warrant was obtained and methamphetamine was found inside the package. Law enforcement personnel obtained a "beeper warrant" and placed a beeper inside the package. When the beeper went off, law enforcement arrested the recipient. The Ninth Circuit determined that the use of the narcotics detection dog did not implicate legitimate privacy interests.[16] The Seventh Circuit followed *Place* in holding that subjecting a package that fit a narcotics package profile to a dog sniff was not a search. A warrant was obtained to open the package, revealing about a pound of cocaine.[17] Probable cause has generally been found in such alert cases for opening a package.[18]

A dog sniff of a package in North Dakota followed contact between an Arizona postal inspector and a Minnesota postal inspector about a package that the Arizona inspector suspected of containing drugs. A dog alerted at the Minneapolis airport and a warrant was issued. The package contained methamphetamine. The district court granted a defense suppression motion because the affidavit in support of the warrant did not show the dog to be reliable or the authorities to have a reasonable suspicion that the package contained drugs. The Eighth Circuit reversed, but remanded for further suppression hearings to determine if the postal inspector really had reasonable suspicion. The remand thus gave the government the opportunity to cure any defects, and establish that the dog was reliable.[19]

A 1991 New York case held that subjecting a package to a dog sniff, resulting in an alert, was not illegal if supported by a reasonable suspicion, and the alert justified issuance of a warrant to search the package, the defendant's residence, and his car.[20] Subjecting a package to two dog sniffs did not mean that the first alert had not provided reasonable suspicion.[21] An informant's tip can provide reasonable suspicion to conduct a sniff of a package.[22]

PACKAGE LINEUPS

Postal package sniffs, as luggage sniffs, are sometimes conducted as lineups.[23] A dog sniff of a package at a Federal Express office was held to be a search under Colorado constitutional law, but the police had "specific and articulable facts which, when taken together with the reasonable inferences from these facts," gave rise to a reasonable suspicion that the package contained contraband. The dog had alerted to the package in an array of five packages several times.[24]

Drug interdiction officers were training at a UPS office in West Sacramento where a suspicious package was noticed. The sender had only a first name and all the openings were heavily taped with clear tape.

Special Agent Rowden took the package to a parking lot off UPS property and set the package on the ground with four other controlled packages that were placed about three feet apart and placed a plastic milk crate over each package. Special Agent Rowden then directed a narcotics dog, Clause, to sniff the packages. Clause positively alerted to the package that had been targeted. ... Due to the way Clause alerted to the package, Special Agent Rowden was certain the package contained narcotics. Special

Agent Rowden returned the package to Detective Sloan and advised him that he wanted to hold the package to write an application for a search warrant based on the probable cause of the narcotics dog alert.

Following the alert, a UPS employee was not told to open the package, but comments were made that led her to believe there would be no problem if she did. Eventually she took this as encouragement (which it was) and she opened the package. It turned out to contain methamphetamine. The district court held, and the circuit court affirmed, that the search of the package violated the Fourth Amendment, but the inevitable discovery exception applied to bar exclusion of the evidence.[25]

LENGTH OF DETENTION

The Sixth Circuit held in 2004 that a brief detention of a few hours in order to obtain a dog sniff was justified on the basis of reasonable suspicion, not probable cause.[26] The case cited decisions to the same effect from the Fifth,[27] Sixth,[28] Seventh,[29] Eighth,[30] and Eleventh Circuits.[31] Detention of a package for 2 days in order to have a dog sniff a package from which a brown substance leaked when it was accidentally torn was approved by the Seventh Circuit in a 1989 case.[32] A 4-day delay was held not to be unreasonable in a 2003 decision.[33] A 5-hour delay for a warrant after a 15-minute delay for a dog sniff was not excessive.[34] A 90-minute delay was easily found not to be unreasonable.[35]

When a package in Alaska had to be sent 700 miles to Anchorage for a dog sniff, this was held to be an acceptable fact of life in Alaska, justifying a detention of 3 days.[36] A recipient of a package was misled about the reason for the delay in the delivery of a package but the defendant was not misled by the officers involved. Rather, the FedEx employees were responsible for this deception. The officers had been diligent, so there was no reason to grant the motion to suppress.[37]

MULTIPLE SNIFFS

Postal employees in Utah became suspicious of packages being delivered to a post office box and subjected one of the packages to a dog sniff. The dog did not alert and the package was returned to the mail stream. Suspicions continued, however, and another package was detained and when opened was found to have methamphetamine. The defendant argued that the package should have been subjected to a dog sniff and returned to the mail stream if there was no alert. The court noted that "drug-detecting dogs have not supplanted the neutral and detached magistrate as the arbiter of probable cause." Also, some contraband is not detectable by drug dogs because of careful packaging.[38] In a Wyoming case, a package was subjected to a sniff but the dog did not alert. Because the postal inspector was not satisfied, he sent it to Denver where two dogs did alert. The court determined that the defendant did not have a right to have the package returned to the mail stream for good once the first dog failed to alert.[39]

An Eighth Circuit case held that two negative sniffs did not dissipate reasonable suspicion. A postal inspector delivered a package accompanied by plain-clothes deputies from the Maricopa County Sheriff's Department. Inside the package was a *People Magazine* with $4,000 between the pages and another $3,000 in an envelope. Arizona officials communicated with Minnesota officials where the brother of the Arizona suspect lived. Later a package arrived from Arizona, but a narcotics dog did not alert to it. A Minnesota inspector discounted this sniff and arranged for another, but this also was negative. A third sniff was, however, positive. A warrant was obtained and methamphetamine was found inside a doll. The defendants argued that reasonable suspicion was dissipated by the two dog sniffs.

[W]e do not find that the second negative dog sniff dissipated Nichols's reasonable suspicion. Officer Meyer explained why Mindy may have failed to alert on the package the first time. Meyer stated that his home had vaulted ceilings, and the package was placed in a very large area, thus making it "difficult for the dog to be able to pick up odors that may be coming off the package. ..." Therefore, Meyer put the package in a contained area "to take what little odor is coming off the package and restricting it down to a small area." ... After this was done, Mindy alerted on the package for the presence of a controlled substance. We find no error in the district court's determination that this positive dog sniff was enough to establish probable cause for a search warrant.

The third sniff provided probable cause for a warrant.[40] The issue of cueing might arise when the result is arguably determined in advance.

NOTES

1. *U.S. v. Gomez*, 312 F.3d 290 (8th Cir. 2002).
2. Ibid.
3. *U.S. v. Walker*, 324 F.3d 1032 (8th Cir. 2003); *U.S. v. Smith*, 383 F.3d 700 (8th Cir. 2004).
4. *U.S. v. Daniel*, 982 F.2d 146 (5th Cir. 1993).
5. *U.S. v. Gill*, 280 F.3d 923 (9th Cir. 2002).
6. Ibid.
7. *U.S. v. Robinson*, 390 F.3d 853 (6th Cir. 2004); *U.S. v. Morones*, 355 F.3d 1108 (8th Cir. 2004).
8. *U.S. v. Walker*, 324 F.3d 1032 (8th Cir. 2003).
9. *U.S. v. Quoc Viet Hoang*, 486 F.3d 1156 (9th Cir. 2007).
10. *U.S. v. Terriques*, 319 F.3d 1051 (8th Cir. 2003).
11. *U.S. v. Gomez*, 312 F.3d 290 (8th Cir. 2002).
12. *U.S. v. Logan*, 362 F.3d 530 (8th Cir. 2004) (Los Angeles was source city, St. Louis was destination city).
13. *U.S. v. Quoc Viet Hoang*, 486 F.3d 1156 (9th Cir. 2007).
14. *Ohio v. Elkins*, 47 Oh.App. 307, 354 N.E.2d 716 (Ct. App. 1976), referring to *U.S. v. Solis*, 393 F.Supp 325 (C.D. Cal, 1975), rev'd 536 F.2d 880 (9th Civ. 1976); see *Ohio v. Riley*, 88 Ohio App.3d 468, 624 N.E.2d 302 (1993), holding *Elkins* no longer law on drug sniff after *Place*; *Ohio v. Palicki*, 97 Ohio App.3d 175, 646 N.E.2d 494 (Ct. App. 1994) (use of dog to sniff interior of car "no more intrusive than the use of the dog to sniff the outside of the car, since the dog was still able to smell the presence of contraband without disturbing possessions of appellant").
15. *U.S. v. Hill*, 701 F.Supp. 1522 (D.Kan. 1988). The other party in this scheme, Laurena Ann Lux, fared no better. U.S. v. Lux, 905 F.2d 1379 (10th Cir. 1990).
16. *U.S. v. Jefferson*, 566 F.3d 928 (9th Cir. 2009).
17. *U.S. v. Dennis*, 115 F.3d 524 (7th Cir. 1997).
18. *U.S. v. Banks*, 3 F.3d 399 (11th Cir. 1993); *U.S. v. DeMoss*, 279 F.3d 632 (8th Cir. 2002). See also *North Dakota v. Kesler*, 396 N.W.2d 729 (1986) (reasonable suspicion package contained drugs justified delay in delivery).
19. *U.S. v. Sundby*, 186 F.3d 873 (8th Cir. 1999). See also *U.S. v. Vasquez*, 213 F.3d 425 (8th Cir. 2000) (dog's alert while package was still in stream of mail provided sufficient basis to hold package and district court properly denied motion to suppress evidence of methamphetamines found after package opened). See *Laime v. Arkansas*, 347 Ark. 142, 60 SW3d 464 (2001) for an analysis of *Sundby* by the Arkansas Supreme Court.
20. *New York v. Offen*, 78 N.Y.2d 1089, 585 N.E.2d 370, 578 N.Y.S.2d 121 (1991).
21. *U.S. v. Zacher*, 465 F.3d 336 (8th Cir. 2006).
22. *Washington v. Stanphill*, 53 Wash.App. 623, 769 P.2d 861 (Ct. App. 1989).
23. *U.S. v. Lyons*, 957 F.2d 615 (8th Cir. 1992) (suspicious package put in room with other packages; dog only alerted to suspicious package); *Ohio v. Knight*, 82 Ohio Misc.2d 79, 679 N.E.2d 758, 759-760 (Ct. Com. Pleas 1997) ("Six boxes were laid on the floor and only one was a suspicious box from Oregon. The dog alerted to the Oregon package. Another controlled search was conducted with five boxes that were different from the first test and the other package from Oregon. Again Chelsea alerted to the other suspicious package from Oregon.").
24. *Colorado v. Boylan*, 854 P.2d 807 (1993).
25. *U.S. v. Souza*, 223 F.3d 1197 (10th Cir. 2000).
26. *U.S. v. Robinson*, 390 F.3d 853 (6th Cir. 2004).
27. *U.S. v. Daniel*, 982 F.2d 146 (5th Cir. 1993).
28. *U.S. v. Underwood*, 97 F.3d 1453, 1996 WL 536796, at *3 (6th Cir. 1996); *U.S. v. Reid*, 67 F.3d 300, 1995 WL 579436, at *1–*2 (6th Cir. September 28, 1995).

29. *U.S. v. Dennis*, 115 F.3d 524, 531–32 (7th Cir.1997).

30. *U.S. v. Terriques*, 319 F.3d 1051, 1056 (8th Cir.2003).

31. *U.S. v. Banks*, 3 F.3d 399, 401–02 (11th Cir.1993).

32. *U.S. v. Mayomi*, 873 F.2d 1049 (7th Cir. 1989). See *U.S. v. Bell*, 892 F.2d 959 (10th Cir. 1989).

33. *U.S. v. Ganser*, 315 F.3d 819 (7th Cir. 2003).

34. *U.S. v. Reid*, 67 F.3d 300 (6th Cir. 1995).

35. *U.S. v. Longbehn*, 898 F.2d 635 (8th Cir. 1990).

36. *U.S. v. Aldaz*, 921 F.2d 227 (9th Cir. 1990). See *U.S. v. Lozano*, No. 09-20151 (9th Cir. 2010) (delay of 22 hours for package to be shipped to where dog could sniff it was not unreasonable; also package had defendant's P.O. box but wrong name and defendant had asked postal employees about whether drug dogs were used).

37. *U.S. v. Lafrance*, 879 F.2d 1 (1st Cir. 1989). For additional cases on delays, see *Georgetown Law Journal*, Annual Review of Criminal Procedure: Warrantless Searches and Seizures (2008).

38. *U.S. v. Glover*, 104 F.3d 1570 (10th Cir. 1997).

39. *U.S. v. Ramirez*, 342 F.3d 1210 (10th Cir. 2003).

40. *U.S. v. Lakoskey*, 462 F.3d 965 (8th Cir. 2006).

13 Sniffs of Storage Areas, Cargo, and Commercial Spaces

As with luggage and package sniffs, sniffs of some locations, such as the common areas around storage lockers, have justified a degree of intrusion that would not apply to a residence.

WAREHOUSE AND STORAGE LOCKER SNIFFS

Users of warehouses have been held to have no legitimate expectation that a narcotics canine would not detect the odor of marijuana in the warehouse.[1] Similarly, a sniff in the walkway of a public storage facility was held not to be a search under federal or Colorado constitutional law.[2] The Oregon Supreme Court reached the same result, finding that dog sniffs conducted in public places are not searches.[3] A Pennsylvania case saw the sniff of a storage facility, conducted in the corridors of the building with the permission of a representative of the facility, as similar to the situation in *Place*.

> Although *Place* does not concern a canine sniff carried out on private property and directed at the closed door of a private area, we believe that the majority view of the United States Supreme Court would be that the canine sniff in the present case would not constitute a search. We reach this conclusion because of the importance the federal court attaches to the lack of intrusiveness of a canine sniff; because the disclosure of information as a result of the sniff is extremely limited; because the consequent embarrassment and inconvenience is minimal; and because although the appellant's parcels were not located in a public place, they were located near enough a public hallway that a trained dog, standing in that hallway could identify the odor of marijuana.

That did not resolve all issues, however, since there was also the question of Pennsylvania state constitutional law. The court held that the dog could be deployed under the facts of the case if (1) the police are able to articulate reasonable grounds for believing that drugs may be present in the place they seek to test; and (2) the police are lawfully present in the place where the canine sniff is conducted.[4]

A warrant to search a storage unit has been found to include a truck at the unit.[5] Where a sniff was conducted outside a storage locker based on prior knowledge of police of the suspect's involvement in cocaine trafficking, a court did not find certification of the dog a prerequisite to the issuance of a warrant.[6]

TRAINING EXERCISE RESULTS IN REAL ALERT

A case in Oregon involved a sniff of a warehouse, not because of any suspicion as to any locker, but rather because a canine handler requested that the facility allow him to conduct a training exercise inside it. The handler had placed a bag of marijuana in an unused locker in the facility. When Breaker was released to find the marijuana planted by Fillmore, he unexpectedly alerted, or signaled, the presence of marijuana at a locker. Fillmore contacted Deputy Kennedy, a narcotics investigator, who went to the facility. The officers walked Breaker through the facility, and the dog again alerted at the same locker. Kennedy then got down on his hands and knees and sniffed at the door of the locker. He detected a distinct odor of marijuana. The following day, he obtained a warrant to search the locker. The ensuing search disclosed the marijuana. On appeal to the Oregon

Supreme Court, the defendant argued that the training was a pretext. The Supreme Court noted that the odor was even detectible by an officer.

> [T]he officer (and Breaker) were in a place where they had a right to be when Breaker unexpectedly alerted to defendant's locker. Breaker's discovery was not the result of a purposive intrusion into defendant's privacy—the officer hoped and expected that Breaker would find marijuana in another locker, not in defendant's. There being no purposive intrusion into a protected area, there was no search by Breaker.

The Supreme Court affirmed and the conviction stood.[7]

STATE CONSTITUTIONAL LAW

State constitutional law has sometimes recognized canine sniffs outside buildings to be searches. A canine sniff outside a warehouse was a search under the Alaska Constitution, according to the Alaska Court of Appeals, but only reasonable suspicion was required. The search revealed marijuana growing equipment and the conviction was affirmed.[8] The Court of Appeals cited its earlier decision holding that luggage sniff was a search, distinguishing Alaskan constitutional law from U.S. constitutional law in *Place*.[9]

The Minnesota Supreme Court agreed with the Alaskan and Pennsylvania approaches.

> We are persuaded by the decisions of the courts in Alaska and Pennsylvania and our own Minnesota constitutional precedents that there are good reasons to guard against a police officer's random use of a drug-detection dog to sniff in the area immediately outside of a person's storage unit, absent some level of suspicion of drug-related activity. We reach this conclusion by considering the strength of the expectation of privacy in a self-storage unit and the degree of intrusiveness of a drug-detection dog sniff in the area immediately outside that unit.
>
> We conclude that a person's expectation of privacy in a self-storage unit is greater for the purpose of the Minnesota Constitution than it has been determined to be under the Fourth Amendment. This is particularly true of storage units like appellant's that are equivalent in size to a garage and are large enough to contain a significant number of personal items and even to conduct some personal activities. Unlike an automobile or luggage, the dominant purpose for such a unit is to store personal effects in a fixed location.
>
> We are mindful that a person's expectation of privacy in a self-storage unit does not extend to that which can be plainly seen or smelled from the area immediately outside the unit. But we consider the smell of that area to be "plain" only if a person is capable of detecting it. Stated another way, a renter of such a unit must expect that other people will lawfully be in the area outside the unit and will be able to smell plain odors emanating from the unit. But the renter need not expect that police will be able to bring to that area drug-detecting dogs that can detect odors that no person could detect. Such dogs do not enable a police officer to smell the odor, but instead … provide information to the police officer that was "previously * * * unknowable without physical intrusion."[10]
>
> We conclude that the sniff of a drug-detection dog outside appellant's storage unit was a search for purposes of the Minnesota Constitution.

The Minnesota Supreme Court held that an articulable reasonable suspicion would have been necessary to deploy the narcotics detection dog.

> Because police did not articulate reasonable suspicion that drugs were present in appellant's storage unit, we hold that the deployment of a drug-detection dog was an unreasonable search under the Minnesota Constitution; that the evidence resulting from the dog sniff was unlawfully obtained and must be suppressed; that the application for a warrant to search the storage unit was not otherwise supported by probable cause; and that, accordingly, the evidence seized during the search of the storage unit was unlawfully obtained and must be suppressed. Because the error in admitting the seized evidence was prejudicial to appellant, we reverse his conviction and remand for a new trial.

The court accepted that the expectation of privacy as to a storage unit was less than a home, but might be more than a car. The Minnesota Bureau of Criminal Activity had observed suspicious activity at the facility about 4 weeks before the dog sniff. The delay in bringing the dog to the facility might have worked against the argument for an articulable reasonable suspicion.[11]

SAFE DEPOSIT BOXES

Officers brought a narcotics dog into a bank for a sniff of safe deposit boxes, and though it was not clear if the manager consented initially, he apparently did so later. The dog could not isolate particular boxes but alerted to a specific group of boxes. A search warrant was obtained because the bank did not keep duplicate keys for the boxes. The court concluded that the sniff in the aisle in front of the boxes did not constitute a search under the Fourth Amendment since the defendant could not have a legitimate expectation of privacy as to the aisle, which the court described as a semipublic area.[12]

CARGO CONTAINERS

Members of the U.S. Customs Special Contraband and Narcotics Interdiction Team took narcotics dogs to a cargo terminal at the Los Angeles harbor, where the dogs "mildly" alerted to two containers. Two days later the dogs alerted to a Van-Pak that had been taken from the container to which they alerted earlier. From these alerts, a search warrant was issued and 1440 pounds of marijuana were found inside the Van-Pak. The Ninth Circuit held that harbor authorities properly admitted the dogs to the customs area where goods were offloaded from ships. The second sniff was justified by the positive alerts, mild though they might be, from the first sweep of the area. The second sniff gave rise to a founded or articulable suspicion that the Van-Pak contained illegal drugs. Thus, the warrant was properly obtained and the convictions were affirmed.[13] Figure 13.1 shows a dog performing a remote sniff at a cargo facility.

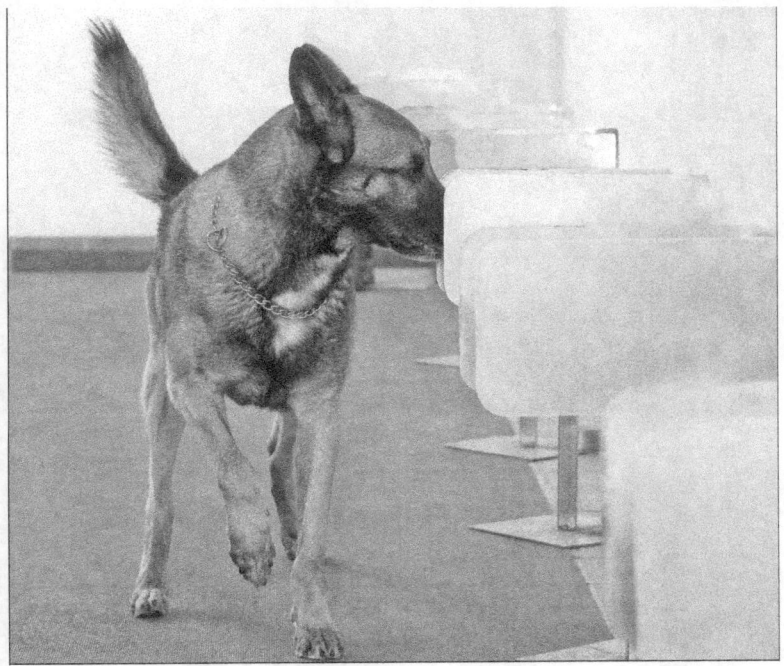

FIGURE 13.1 Remote scent detection at a cargo facility. (Courtesy of Ido Yitzhaki, DiagNose®.)

NOTES

1. *U.S. v. Venema*, 563 F.2d 1003 (10th Cir. 1977) (also stating that an affidavit in support of a search warrant need not describe drug detection dog's education background and general qualifications with specificity to establish probable cause); *U.S. v. Lingenfelter*, 997 F.2d 632 (9th Cir. 1993); *U.S. v. Mahler*, 141 F.3d 811 (8th Cir. 1998); *Pennsylvania v. Johnston*, 515 Pa. 454, 530 A.2d 74 (1987).
2. *Colorado v. Wieser*, 796 P.2d 982 (1990) (reversing trial court's grant of motion to suppress).
3. *Oregon v. Smith*, 327 Or. 366, 963 P.2d 642 (1998) (padlocking of storage unit was unlawful but was irrelevant because evidence would have been obtained regardless).
4. *Pennsylvania v. Johnston*, 515 Pa. 454, 530 A.2d 74 (1987).
5. *U.S. v. Ortega-Jiminez*, 232 F.3d 1325 (10th Cir. 2000).
6. *Miles v. Texas*, 2009 WL 4358959 (Ct. App. 2009).
7. *Oregon v. Slowikowski*, 307 Or. 19, 761 P2d 1315 (1988).
8. *McGahan v. Alaska*, 807 P.2d 506 (Ct. App. 1991).
9. See *Pooley v. Alaska*, 705 P.2d 1293 (Ct. App. 1985).
10. Quoting *U.S. v. Kyllo*, 533 U.S. 27, 121 S.Ct. 2038, 150 L.Ed.2d 94 (2001).
11. *Minnesota v. Carter*, 697 N.W.2d 199 (2005).
12. *Strout v. Texas*, 688 SW2d 188 (Ct. App. 1985); *Washington v. Boyce*, 44 Wash.App. 724, 723 P.2d 28 (Ct. App. 1986) (no expectation of privacy for sniff in general vault area).
13. *U.S. v. Spetz*, 721 F.2d 1457 (9th Cir. 1983).

14 Residential Sniffs

Entry into a person's living space generally requires a warrant. When an entry by police officers into an apartment is found to be illegal, a subsequent alert by a dog brought in by the officers has to be suppressed.[1] The boundaries of a person's residence are, however, not always obvious. A sniff without a warrant at a side door may be illegal, but a sniff outside a garage door, for instance, was held constitutional under federal and Texas state law and supported an affidavit for a warrant.[2]

SNIFFS IN COMMON AREAS OF APARTMENT BUILDINGS

In a case arising in Indiana,[3] the defendant had a locked bedroom inside of a house. A dog alerted outside the bedroom and a warrant was issued, resulting in finding cocaine and other drugs. The court found no expectation of privacy given that the police were present in the common areas of the shared home with the consent of the defendant's roommate.

In a decision issued in 2011, the Florida Supreme Court considered (1) whether a sniff conducted at the front door of a private residence is a search under the Fourth Amendment, and (2) if it is a search, whether a canine officer must have reasonable suspicion or probable cause to conduct it. The court noted that the situation involved in the case was not merely a single canine handler taking his dog to the front door of the defendant's home:

> On the scene, the procedure involved multiple police vehicles, multiple law enforcement personnel, including narcotics detectives and other officers, and an experienced dog handler and trained drug detection dog engaged in a vigorous search effort on the front porch of the residence. Tactical law enforcement personnel from various government agencies, both state and federal, were on the scene for surveillance and backup purposes. The entire on-the-scene government activity—i.e., the preparation for the "sniff test," the test itself, and the aftermath, which culminated in the full-blown search of Jardines' home—lasted for hours. The "sniff test" apparently took place in plain view of the general public. There was no anonymity for the resident.

Such a spectacle, according to the court, invariably entailed public opprobrium, humiliation, and embarrassment and amounted to an official accusation of crime. The court was concerned that approval of such a procedure would mean that any citizen could be subjected to the same practice. The court concluded that there was a search, and that probable cause was required.[4]

In 1999, the Nebraska Supreme Court held that taking a drug dog to the threshold of a dwelling required at least a reasonable, articulable suspicion. After an anonymous "concerned citizen" called police and said the defendant was dealing drugs, police took a drug dog to his apartment building and the dog alerted. A warrant was obtained for the apartment and various drugs were found. The court concluded that the anonymous phone call did not suffice to provide a reasonable suspicion.[5]

In a case before the New York Court of Appeals in 1985, a narcotics detection dog was taken to the common hallway and alerted at the door to the suspect's apartment. The court found *Place* controlling as to federal law, but held that it did was not the proper reasoning for the New York State Constitution.

> [T]he use of the trained canine outside defendant's apartment constituted a search. By resorting to this investigative technique, the police were able to obtain information regarding the contents of a place that has traditionally been accorded a heightened expectation of privacy.

The court concluded that under state constitutional law there had been a search. The state court said that given the "uniquely discriminate and nonintrusive nature" of a canine sniff, "it may be used without a warrant or probable cause, provided that the police have a reasonable suspicion that a residence contains illicit contraband." Thus, though there was a search, it was not unconstitutional under state law. The conviction was affirmed.[6] In another federal case arising in New York, a dog's alert could support a search of an apartment when other evidence was available.[7]

YARDS OF HOUSES

Police accompanying paramedics to a house where there had been a possible cocaine overdose were given permission by the defendant's girlfriend to search the house. Small amounts of marijuana were found. An officer returned with a narcotics dog.

> As Officer Dewey awaited the warrant, he decided to let Kilo out of the car because the dog had been confined in the police cruiser for four to five hours at that point. Once outside the car, which was parked in front of the house, Officer Dewey began to play with Kilo, using a frisbee. He threw the frisbee into Hayes's front yard in a trajectory "parallel to Marble Island Road." Kilo chased after the frisbee for a short distance, stopped and pointed its nose in the air as if it were alerted to something. At that point, Officer Dewey asked Kilo: "Whatta ya got?" According to Dewey, this was a verbal signal to encourage the dog to continue investigating.

Kilo moved around the house and went into some brush, finding a black bag, which the dog brought to the handler. Officer Dewey opened the bag and found plastic baggies with white powder later identified as cocaine. The defendant argued that Kilo had trespassed on the curtilage in the path he took to the black bag. The circuit court disagreed. "The sanctuary of the home simply does not extend to the front yard of Hayes's property, where the initial sniff occurred." The court said that even if the dog had temporarily crossed through the curtilage, this "transient trespass does not implicate the Fourth Amendment where the incriminating evidence is discovered outside the curtilage." The conviction was affirmed.[8]

SNIFFS AT FRONT DOORS OF HOUSES

In a 2002, a Texas appellate court determined that a dog sniff outside the defendant's house was legitimate as there is no reasonable expectation of privacy in possessing illegal drugs.[9] In a 2008 Michigan case, an informant told the police that a man previously convicted of marijuana possession was dealing in the drug so they took a narcotics detection dog to the man's house, where the dog alerted. The appellate court held that there was no reasonable expectation of privacy as to a front porch.

> The record contains no evidence that the canine team crossed any obstructions, such as a gate or fence, in order to reach the front door, or that the property contained any signs forbidding people from entering the property.[10]

In a case arising in Indiana, the court held that a dog sniff at the front door of a house was not a search, but held that a reasonable suspicion is needed to conduct a dog sniff of a private residence.[11]

In a case arising in Florida, a search of a residence followed on the Broward County Sheriff's Office submitting an affidavit that the defendant was growing marijuana. The defendant's car was stopped for a lane change violation and a drug dog alerted to the exterior of the vehicle. The dog was then placed inside the car and alerted to the ashtray, where a marijuana cigarette was found. The defendant was arrested. About an hour later, the dog was taken to the defendant's residence and alerted at the front door. The officers said they could smell marijuana at the door. A search warrant was issued, and various drugs were found inside. The court considered the Fourth Amendment's protection of a house and found a strong analogy in a case where the Supreme Court had disapproved of the use of a heat-sensing device to determine that there might be halide lamps for growing marijuana plants.[12] Therefore, the dog sniff at the front door was an illegal search.[13]

The resident of the upper flat of a double house in Mansfield, Ohio, heard a thump and an alarm going off. The alarm stopped about 20 minutes later, then soon went on again after the sound of glass breaking. Police officers arrived, found a broken window and a door ajar and called for a canine team to sweep the building for trapped intruders. Deputy James Sweat arrived with Cheddy and released the dog in the apartment with the command to "find them." Cheddy, also trained as a drug dog, alerted for drugs at several areas during the search. Cheddy was trained to bark at intruders, and to scratch, dig, or bite at an object containing drugs. In the bedroom, the dog apparently knocked an open drawer off its runners. A bag of cocaine was in plain view. Other drugs and paraphernalia were found and Reed was placed under arrest. The defendant argued this was a warrantless search of his home.

> Here, the canine team was lawfully present in Reed's flat, either due to the pursuit of a burglar, or Reed's consent. Any contraband seen by Sweat, or sniffed by Cheddy, therefore, fell within the "plain-view" doctrine or the "canine-sniff" rule.

The court said that the instinctive acts of trained dogs, such as a dog jumping into a car, do not violate the Fourth Amendment.[14] The conviction was affirmed.[15]

An unusual 1986 case from Colorado involved the sniff of a safe that had been stolen from the home of the defendant and recovered by the police. The thieves had taken the safe because they believed it to contain drugs. A dog alerted to the safe at the police station and a warrant was obtaining yielding cocaine and marijuana. The Colorado Supreme Court determined that the sniff was a search (despite *Place*) because the defendant had a reasonable expectation of privacy as to the contents of a safe in his home. Therefore, a reasonable suspicion was a prerequisite for this sniff search, but such a suspicion did exist and the conviction was affirmed.[16]

SNIFFS ON MILITARY BASES

Military courts have affirmed the authority of base commanders to conduct sniffs of lockers of military personnel.[17] As noted earlier in the chapter on vehicle sniffs, roadblock systems to find drugs in vehicles have been approved.[18] Use of a drug detection dog in the common area outside a service member's room has been held not to be a search for Fourth Amendment purposes.[19]

NOTES

1. *U.S. v. DiCisare*, 765 F.2d 890 (9th Cir. 1985).
2. *Smith v. Texas*, 2004 WL 213395, 2004 Tex.App. LEXIS 1121 (Ct. App. 2004), cert. denied 544 U.S. 961, 125 S.Ct. 1726, 161 L.Ed.2d 602 (2005). See also *U.S. v. Vasquez*, 909 F.2d 235 (7th Cir. 1990).
3. *U.S. v. Brock*, 417 F.3d 692 (3rd Cir. 2005). See also *U.S. v. Cota-Lopez*, 358 F.Supp. 2d 579 (W.D.Tex. 2002), *U.S. v. Scott*, 610 F.3d 1009 (8th Cir. 2010).
4. *Jardines v. Florida*, 2011 WL 1405080 (2011).
5. *Nebraska v. Ortiz*, 257 Neb. 784, 600 N.W.2d 805 (1999); *U.S. v. Jackson*, 2004 WL 1784756 (S.D.Ind. 2004) (dog sniff could not be supported by a generalized suspicion of wrongdoing insufficient to provide probable cause or even to be a reasonable suspicion). See *Illinois v. Yarber*, 279 Ill.App.3d 519, 663 N.E.2d 1131 (Ct. App. 1996) (anonymous tip led to luggage sniff, but reasonable suspicion was lacking when only innocent details could be verified).
6. *New York v. Dunn*, 77 N.Y.2d 19, 564 N.E.2d 1054, 563 N.Y.S.2d 388 (1990), cert. den. 501 U.S. 1219, 111 S.Ct. 2830, 115 L.Ed.2d 1000 (1991) (raising the "Orwellian" specter of "police roaming indiscriminately through the corridors of public housing projects with trained dogs in search of drugs"). See also *New Hampshire v. Pellicci*, 133 N.H. 523, 580 A.2d 710 (1990).

7. *U.S. v. Young*, 745 F.2d 733 (2d Cir.1984), cert. denied 470 U.S. 1084, 105 S.Ct. 1842, 85 L.Ed.2d 142 (1985). But see *U.S. v. Thomas*, 757 F.2d 1359, 1367 (2nd Cir. 1985), cert. denied sub nom. *Wheelings v. U.S.*, 474 U.S. 819, 106 S.Ct. 67, 88 L.Ed.2d 54 (1985) (use of trained dog to sniff for narcotics outside apartment door was a search: "a practice that is not intrusive in a public airport may be intrusive when employed at a person's home"). See Lunney (2009) (arguing that Thomas was correctly decided and deploring fact that other federal circuits had rejected the Second Circuit's reasoning); Smith (2009). See also *U.S. v. Broadway*, 580 F.Supp.2d 1179 (O.C. D.C. 2008) (sniff outside apartment was not search within meaning of Fourth Amendment).

8. *U.S. v. Hayes*, 551 F.3d 138 (2nd Cir. 2008).

9. *Porter v. Texas*, 93 S.W.3d 342 (Ct. App. 2002). See also *Rodriguez v. Texas*, 106 S.W.3d 224 (Ct. App. 2003) (dog's sniff at door of house was not an investigative method that could reveal illegal information about the interior of a home but only the existence of illegal items); *Romo v. Texas*, 315 S.W.3d 565 (Ct. App. 2010) ("Rocky's sniffs of the garage door and the backyard fence were not searches under the Fourth Amendment or the Texas constitution because he sniffed areas that were not protected from observation by passersby and because Romo had no reasonable expectation of privacy in the odor of marihuana coming from his backyard."); *Texas v. $27,877.00*, 2010 WL 5187608 (Ct. App. 2010) (sniff at front door justified warrant).

10. *Michigan v. Jones*, 279 Mich.App. 86, 95, 755 N.W.2d 224, 229 (Ct. App. 2008).

11. *Hoop v. Indiana*, 909 N.E.2d 463 (Ct. App. 2009).

12. Referring to *Kyllo v. U.S.*, 533 U.S. 27, 121 S.Ct. 2038, 150 L.Ed.2d 94 (2001). See *U.S. v. Esparza*, No. CF-07-14-S-BLW (D. Id. 2007) (use of explosives detection dog analogized to *Kyllo* rather than *Caballes* because "explosives detection dog, like the thermal-imaging device at issue in Kyllo, detects both contraband and non-contraband items. … The explosives detection dog should not be used as a general criminal investigative technique"; reasoning of the order must be questioned because narcotics detection dogs may also detect noncontraband items; court found officers lacked probable cause to search the vehicle; reliability of dog was not considered).

13. *Florida v. Rabb*, 920 So.2d 1175 (Ct. App. 2006), cert. denied, 549 U.S. 1052 (2006). See *Washington v. Dearman*, 92 Wash.App. 630, 962 P.2d 850 (Ct. App. 1998) (police had to obtain search warrant before they conducted sniff at defendant's door).

14. Citing *U.S. v. Stone*, 866 F.2d 359, 364 (10th Cir. 1989) and *U.S. v. Lyons*, 957 F.2d 615, 617 (8th Cir. 1992).

15. *U.S. v. Reed*, 141 F.3d 644 (6th Cir. 1998).

16. *Colorado v. Unruh*, 713 P.2d 370 (1986).

17. *U.S. v. Thomas*, 1975 WL 15554 (NCMR), 40 C.M.R. 114 (U.S. Navy Court of Military Review 1975) (dog pulled package containing marijuana from locker left open).

18. *U.S. v. Unrue*, 1973 WL 14783 (CMA), 47 C.M.R. 556, 22 USCMA 466 (U.S. Court of Military Appeals 1973).

19. *U.S. v. Alexander*, 34 M.J. 121 (U.S. Court of Military Appeals).

15 Currency Sniffs

Alerts to currency in luggage and other locations are very common. Dogs sometimes alert to cars that turn out to have large amounts of currency.[1] Testimony concerning one dog indicated that 62% of her alerts were to drugs, 31% were to currency, much of it likely held by drug dealers, and only 7% were described as "unambiguous false positives."[2] As with other searches involving narcotics, police officers may also be able to detect drug odors on currency, particularly marijuana.[3] Gas chromatography can also detect drug residues on currency.[4]

UNREASONABLY LONG SEIZURES

As with other searches, a seizure of currency for a dog sniff can reach a point of being unreasonably long. A case arising in California in 1994 concerned a passenger who claimed $191,910 he was carrying was for buying gems. On boarding a plane in San Diego, he had told a baggage scanner that the sheets inside his luggage were pamphlets, but she could see they were bills and notified the San Diego Harbor Police. The passenger told the police he was a gemologist. The flight departed for Oakland, California, along with the luggage, and the San Diego police notified the San Francisco International Airport Drug Task Force, where agents tried to get a narcotics dog to meet them at the flight's arrival in Oakland. The dog did not arrive but the passenger permitted the agents to search his luggage, where they saw the currency. The agents told the passenger they would hold his bags for a dog sniff and gave him a receipt. Two hours later a sniff was conducted at the Oakland airport and the dog alerted. The Ninth Circuit agreed with the district court that the detention was too long, providing a hypothetical:

> [I]f an unforeseeable canine virus suddenly afflicted all of the drug-sniffing dogs in Hawaii, leaving them out of commission for a 24-hour period, government agents in Hawaii would not be justified in detaining a traveller's bags for the entire period on a mere reasonable suspicion. Regardless of the government's good faith and exercise of due care, the Fourth Amendment would not allow such an extensive impingement of the traveller's liberty without probable cause.

The circuit court said that when a seizure becomes unreasonably long is hard to define, but noted that it will generally fall somewhere short of 90 minutes, the time period before the sniff occurred in *U.S. v. Place*. The court noted that the authorities should not be expected to keep drug dogs available at all times, but that there had been plenty of notice here. The court found that there were only three suspicious items regarding the suspect: his understatement of the amount of money he was carrying, discrepancies in stories he told various agents, and the x-ray images in San Diego. The circuit court said that these were not sufficiently probative of wrongdoing and even less so of drug activity.[5]

A seizure of currency has sometimes been described as tantamount to a seizure of the holder's person. In a case arising at the Detroit Metropolitan Airport, a seizure of cash a suspect was carrying lacked probable cause at the time it occurred and was effectively a seizure of the individual since remaining with the money required that he miss his plane. The individual was convicted of cocaine possession and conspiracy based on substantial other evidence, and the admission of evidence about the currency was considered harmless error.[6]

EVIDENTIARY VALUE OF A DOG'S ALERT

Because of the amount of cocaine residue on U.S. currency, many courts have considered an alert to currency as of little probative value. The Eleventh Circuit, in affirming a forfeiture judgment of the district court, nevertheless disagreed with the district court, which had described the evidentiary value of the dog's alert as weak but relevant. The circuit court did not characterize the alert as strong evidence, but held that it was "yet another fact weighting in favor of probable cause." [7]

A 1993 case from Tennessee described a dog's alert to currency as of "extremely little probative weight," observing:

> The presence of trace narcotics on currency does not yield any relevant information whatsoever about the currency's history. A bill may be contaminated by proximity to a large quantity of cocaine, by its passage through the contaminated sorting machines at the Federal Reserve Banks, or by contact with other contaminated bills in the wallet or at the bank.

The district court criticized other courts for continuing to accept such evidence, and determined that the dog's alert did not provide probable cause for instituting the forfeiture action.[8]

In a 1994 case arising in California, a driver was pulled over for running a stop sign. The officers noticed a bag full of money beside the driver, who said he got it from working at a café he was found never to have worked at. A narcotics detection dog alerted to the money, but no drugs were found in the car. The district court dismissed the forfeiture action, stating that there was insufficient evidence to support a forfeiture on the grounds that the money was drug money, though the court said a narcotics dog's alert was strong evidence in a probable cause determination, though "not enough on its own, however." The court held that the aggregate of the facts must demonstrate the money's connection to drugs.[9]

Courts have acknowledged the limits of canine alerts to currency, yet held an alert shifted the burden to the holder to establish that the currency was *not* involved in drug trafficking. In a 1989 case arising in New Jersey, a search of a car resulted in finding $87,375 in cash in a pillowcase.

> Officer Eichmann [the handler] was asked to have Coco [a narcotics detection dog] examine the trooper's locker room at the Woodstown barracks for the presence or odor of a controlled substance. Officer Eichmann first took Coco on a "control run" or a "sterile run" of the locker room by leading her around the perimeter and past the lockers and chests of drawers. On the "control run," Coco did not alert to anything. Officer Eichmann and Coco then left the locker room, and the pillowcase with the currency which was found in Mr. Camacho's car was hidden in a locker room chest of drawers. Upon her return to the locker room, Coco alerted almost instantly to the presence or odor of a controlled substance in the chest of drawers containing the pillowcase and currency. A similar search was conducted in Mr. Camacho's car and Coco alerted to the presence or odor of a controlled substance on the back seat, where the suitcase had been.

The dog's alerts were supportive of the government's claim that the currency had been furnished in exchange for illegal drugs. The claimants failed to introduce sufficient credible evidence, to show by a preponderance of the evidence, that the currency was not involved in illegal drug activity. Therefore, the government's motion to forfeit was granted.[10]

In a Virginia case, drugs were found in a motel room as well as money. At the police station, a lineup was conducted:

> Thompson retained possession of the cash and, upon arrival at police headquarters, arranged with Officer George Ball, a "narcotics dog handler," to provide a "drug dog ... to come up ... to run on the money." Detective Tosloskie agreed to assist in this procedure and Thompson passed him the "bundle." Tosloskie, as instructed by Ball, obtained five new interdepartmental envelopes, "stuffed paper towels in four envelopes," placed the money in the fifth, and "laid them [all] in the hallway." Ball then entered

the hall with his dog, Doc, who, after walking past "at least three of the envelopes ... immediately upon reaching the envelope with the money in it ... attacked it with his paws and ... teeth."

The dog's handler testified that the majority of his investigations with the dog in recent years had involved "currency runs." The trial court accepted the handler as an "expert in the area of dog handling [and an] interpreter of his dog, Doc." The defendant objected at trial that the other envelopes did not contain odors like those used in making cocaine but the trial judge held that this went to the weight of the evidence, not its admissibility. The conviction was affirmed.[11]

Other factors besides drugs may work against the person on whom currency is found. In a 2001 federal case arising in Arizona where an airline passenger had more than $22,000 under his clothing, a forfeiture action was upheld despite the fact that a dog alerted to the passenger's luggage but no contraband was found after the passenger consented to a search of the luggage. The dog did not alert to the clothing the passenger was wearing, but did alert to the currency. The Ninth Circuit noted that Phoenix, the destination city of the passenger's flight from Dallas, was a known source city for drugs. The passenger had a previous cocaine conviction. There were inconsistencies in the stories told by the passenger and witnesses on his behalf. The government presented evidence that the dog would not have alerted to the currency had it not recently been in the proximity of cocaine. Defense counsel did not dispute this evidence. The court held that the burden had shifted to the passenger to produce evidence indicating that there was an innocent source for the currency. This burden had not been met and the circuit court affirmed the district court's grant of summary judgment of forfeiture to the government.[12]

METHOD OF CONCEALMENT

Cases have held that extreme efforts to hide cash provide evidence that the cash must have been derived from illegal activities.[13] In a case arising in Nebraska, a patrolman stopped a Toyota camper and smelled the heavy odor of fabric softener sheets when he spoke to the driver. The owner agreed to a search of the camper. In the ceiling of the camper they found $141,770 in Ziploc bags. At the police station, a drug dog named Nero searched an empty room and did not alert. Then money collected from various troopers was placed in the room. Nero did not alert. Finally, one of the Ziploc bags was placed in the room and Nero did alert. The court found the method of concealment significant.

> Had the money simply been concealed above the ceiling, Moreno could reasonably argue that its connection to drug trafficking was not immediately apparent. But where, as here, large sums of currency are not only stowed above the ceiling panel, but also wrapped in scented fabric softener sheets and sealed in three layers of zip-lock bags, the connection to drug trafficking cannot reasonably be disputed. The only conceivable reason for packaging money in this manner is to conceal the scent of illegal narcotics.

The court also noted the widespread use of scented dryer sheets to mask the smell of illegal narcotics.[14]

A passenger boarding an aircraft in San Diego agreed to a search of her luggage but said that a duffel bag was packed by someone else and her own bag was inside it. The search revealed $42,500. She signed a "Disclaimer of Ownership of Currency" form. A dog alerted to the money, and the handler stated that the dog did not alert to cocaine but rather to a by-product of cocaine that does not linger on currency very long. The court also noted that the currency was wrapped in cellophane, which is impermeable to gas and commonly used to disguise drug smells. The district court, as affirmed by the Ninth Circuit, concluded that the totality of factors supported probable cause of the currency being drug money, and the forfeiture motion was granted.[15]

Currency may be found in body searches.[16]

INABILITY TO EXPLAIN PRESENCE OR AMOUNT OF CURRENCY

A holder's inability to explain the amount of currency he is carrying, or offering inconsistent explanations, has been taken as evidence that the currency may be drug connected. In a 2002 case arising in Florida, a dog alerted to a passenger's backpack after she arrived on a flight from New York. The passenger was found to be carrying a large amount of currency. The handler stated that the dog was trained to detect cocaine, marijuana, heroin, and methamphetamine.

> Not being a "cash hound," Rambo does not alert to the scent of untainted currency, but only to the scent of one of those four drugs. The backpack with the money was placed with four or five other bags while Rambo and his handler were out of the room. Rambo was brought in, and he alerted to Stanford's backpack, "indicat[ing] positive to the presence of a controlled substance in that bag."

The defendant argued that most currency in the country is tainted with cocaine residue, but the court concluded that other evidence, such as the defendant's shifting explanations, were also of evidentiary value and that the government had probable cause to believe the cash came from illegal drug transactions.[17]

Testimony by a passenger that currency was new was inconsistent with the fact that a drug dog alerted to it and evidence that the passenger was connected with a heroin ring.[18]

ALERTS AS MONEY LAUNDERING EVIDENCE

The Eleventh Circuit in a 1986 case arising in Florida allowed evidence of alerts of narcotics dogs in a prosecution for money laundering. The court held that the evidence did not need to be "conclusive of a material issue in order to be admitted," but could be admitted if it assisted the jury in determining that the laundered money represented drug proceeds. Defects in the quality of the evidence only went to its weight, not its admissibility.[19]

In a 1993 California case, a narcotics detection dog alerted to cash deposits made by a suspect on four separate dates. Later the dog took part in a search of the suspect's apartment and alerted to currency in a nightstand drawer as well as to currency packages under her bed. No drugs were found in the search of the home. There was considerable testimony as to the past reliability of the dog.

> Star's handler said that there was one incident where Star alerted but no narcotics were found. In that incident, in which a search revealed a large amount of cut cocaine, Star also alerted to a hamper filled with the suspect's dirty clothes. The handler assumed that Star had alerted to the hamper because there was a narcotic smell on the suspect's clothes, and that the amount of narcotics in the hamper was not an amount detectable by human devices.

Although one expert discussed the fact that currency in general circulation often contains cocaine residue, the expert testified that in her experience dogs did not false alert on general circulation currency. The conviction was affirmed.[20]

In a 2007 case arising in Texas, the defendant was stopped for driving 40 miles per hour in a 70 mile-per-hour zone and seemed very nervous. A dog alerted to money in the defendant's pocket and to the back of the car, where $83,000 was found wrapped in bundles of plastic bags wrapped in duct tape and concealed in a compartment underneath the floorboard. Goat hair had been placed in the area of the concealed cash, a common way that criminals try to distract drug sniffing dogs. The appellate court determined that the jury could properly conclude that the cash was being hidden because it represented illegal drug proceeds. The conviction for international money laundering was affirmed.[21]

CURRENCY WITH VISIBLE LEVELS OF COCAINE

In a 1995 case from Rhode Island, the head of a criminal organization was convicted of racketeering, money laundering, and other crimes. Part of the money laundering conviction was based on deposits of cash made by some of the defendant's underlings to which narcotics detection dogs alerted. The court concluded that the trial court had not abused its discretion in admitting the canine sniff evidence.

> Even though widespread contamination of currency plainly lessens the impact of dog sniff evidence, a trained dog's alert still retains some probative value. Ordinary experience suggests that currency used to purchase narcotics is more likely than other currency to have come into contact with drugs. Here, moreover, the evidence supports an inference that Bosco's frenzied reaction was caused by more than a mere trace of contamination.
>
> The record contains corroboration of Bosco's olfactory evidence. Several witnesses testified that ordinary human senses could detect something unusual about the money that appellant's associates brought to the banks. One teller testified that he occasionally noticed that the money felt "dusty ... almost floury from pizza dough, that type of feeling."[22] Another teller reported that she noticed an odor or fragrance, akin to that of an orchid. This evidence, along with Conley's testimony that the dog did not react in other areas of the banks, buttressed the lower court's belief that the dog sniff evidence had probative force.

The fact that Bosco did not alert in other areas of the bank may have been significant if he was close to currency in many areas.[23]

CURRENCY IN MAIL PACKAGES

A case involving suspicious parcels began in Fort Wayne, Indiana. Inspectors subjected a suspicious parcel to a drug detection dog, which alerted. The package was opened and found to contain $18,000 in currency, then sent on its way to Fresno. The next day a package arrived from Fresno bound for Fort Wayne. The dog alerted again and a second warrant was obtained. The package contained methamphetamine. The defendant argued that the dog was unreliable and had falsely alerted to the package containing currency, so a warrant should not have issued on the second alert. The court found no defect in the warrants.[24]

RELIABILITY OF DOG QUESTIONED

A forfeiture action in Texas in 1999 failed where the government could not do more than show the passenger fit a drug courier's profile and a drug dog had alerted to the currency.

> Reliability problems arise when the dog receives poor training, has an inconsistent record, searches for narcotics in conditions without reliability controls or receives cues from its handler. Here, the available evidence indicates that the agents placed the currency in a drawer and "U.S. Customs Inspector Abelardo Santibanez, utilizing K-9 'Jack' (C-453) searched the area. K-9 'Jack' located the currency, alerting for a positive scent to narcotics on the currency." The Court was not told of Jack's training and success in past searches. Nor does it appear that the agents verified Jack's alert by conducting a "sterile run," placing the currency in a different location, substituting a different material (preferably used cash withdrawn from a banking institution) or conducting a second search with a different dog. Verification, supported by testimony of the dog's handler, is an essential prerequisite to consideration of the evidence.[25]

In a 2001 case arising in Delaware, defendants stopped for a traffic violation near Wilmington agreed to a search of the trunk of their car, where currency was found wrapped inside layers of blue plastic bags. One of the men was found to have murder charges pending. A dog alerted to the currency and an ion scan analysis indicated high levels of cocaine residue. The court rejected the evidence because the government had not presented any evidence concerning the particular dog's past training and its degree of accuracy in detecting narcotics on currency. The decree of forfeiture was reversed and remanded.[26]

SNIFFS WHERE CONNECTION TO DRUG TRAFFICKING WAS NOT ESTABLISHED

Before evidence began to accumulate that dogs do not usually alert to currency unless it has recently been in contact with narcotics, despite the amount of U.S. currency with cocaine residue, courts were more inclined to accept that a narcotics dog alert was not particularly meaningful. In a 1992 case from the District of Columbia, a dog alerted to an Amtrak passenger's luggage and it was found to contain a large amount of currency. The cash was washed in a vat at the DEA offices and cocaine was recovered from the wash. Witnesses for both sides agreed that a high proportion of U.S. currency has cocaine residue, and a witness testified that bills in general circulation "may contain as little as a millionth of a gram of cocaine, but that is many times more cocaine than is needed for a dog to alert." The motion to suppress was granted by the district court, and affirmed by the circuit court.[27]

The government must sometimes show more than that the money was hidden or wrapped in a suspicious manner. The absence of drugs does not mean, however, that there might not be other evidence connecting the currency with drug activity.[28] There must be some showing of a likely connection with illegal activity. In a 1997 case arising in Illinois, an informant told police about fencing stolen property at a pizzeria. A search of the pizzeria uncovered unregistered guns and $500,000 in a barrel wrapped in plastic bags. A drug dog alerted to the currency. Besides referring to the tainted currency argument, the court noted that the government had not been able to show a narcotics nexus between the currency and any drug activities. The Seventh Circuit remanded with instructions that the money should be returned to the owners of the pizzeria.[29]

An anonymous tip to a Continental Airlines operator in Tampa said a drug courier would be on a flight to Cleveland. The courier was described as a black male, 5 feet 10 inches tall. When the flight arrived, agents saw a 6-foot 4-inch black male and pulled him aside for questioning. He consented to a search of his bags and $9,750 was found, along with $5,000 in his jacket. A narcotics detection dog alerted to the cash. The Sixth Circuit found the anonymous tip devoid of probative weight, given the height difference between the subject of the tip and the person investigated. The court also noted that much cash in circulation is tainted by cocaine and the forfeiture was reversed.[30]

A curious case from Utah involved a car that was found to have $102,000 hidden in a gas tank. A drug dog alerted to the cash. The court noted that forfeiture under state law required that the currency be associated with a drug transaction in Utah.

> It is not enough that the currency may have been generated in a drug transaction which took place outside of Utah. In that case, there would be no violation of the Utah act. It is only when the Utah act is violated that drug proceeds are subject to forfeiture. … Here, no attempt was made by the State to prove that the money came from or was intended to be used in a drug transaction in this state. No controlled substances were found in the van or on the person of any of the occupants. No criminal charges were filed against any of them. The van was merely passing through Utah on an interstate highway.

Therefore, the currency was held not to be subject to forfeiture.[31]

FITTING A COURIER PROFILE IS NOT ENOUGH

In a 1997 case arising in California, an airline passenger had $2,000 strapped under his pants and $49,576 in a checked bag. The passenger also fit a drug-courier profile. Although the district court held that the seizure of the currency was proper, the Ninth Circuit reversed, noting the widespread contamination of currency with drug residue in the Los Angeles area.[32]

CURRENCY SNIFFS COME BACK INTO FAVOR

In a Seventh Circuit case that arose from an incident at Chicago's Midway Airport on September 5, 2000, agents confiscated $30,670 in cash to which a drug dog had alerted. The money was put in an empty suitcase among many other empty cases in the DEA office in the airport and the handler was not told which suitcase contained the cash. The dog alerted to the suitcase containing the bundles of cash by scratching and biting. The government conceded that its forfeiture case turned on the dog alert evidence. Because of the scientific and legal debate over the issue of the probity of a dog's alert to currency, the trial court "invited" the parties to supplement their arguments with "publicly available empirical information" on the question. The trial court delved into the research, noting first that dogs probably alert not to cocaine but rather to methyl benzoate, which is "volatile enough to evaporate from the currency within a short period."[33] The court cited research arguing that dog sniffs are reliable despite currency tainting by narcotics because dogs do not alert to trace amounts of drug odor after a period of dissipation. That period may be relatively short as one study found that 90% of methyl benzoate evaporates from the surface of currency in 2 hours. Indeed, one researcher was cited as stating that dogs would not alert to by-products other than methyl benzoate and would not alert to pure cocaine unless methyl benzoate was added.[34]

> Dr. Furton and Dr. Rose undertook some 200 field and laboratory trials and ultimately concluded that dogs do not alert to innocently tainted currency in general circulation because the amount of cocaine and methyl benzoate is too small for detection. ... ("[A] positive alert to U.S. currency by a properly trained ... canine indicates that the currency had recently ... been in close or actual proximity to a significant amount of narcotics, and is not the result of any alleged innocent environmental contamination of circulated U.S. currency by microscopic traces of cocaine.") The research indicated that, in contrast to the levels found on general circulation currency, the "threshold level of cocaine and methyl benzoate required for a canine to signal an alert was substantial and reproducible [FN: methyl benzoate is always associated to some degree with cocaine]."[35] ... Calculation from the amount of methyl benzoate required for a reliable detector dog alert (>85% [detection success] at 10 [micrograms]), the amount of methyl benzoate observed in street cocaine sample[s], ... and the diffusion rates of methyl benzoate from individual bills (ca. 10% remaining after 2 hours) indicate a required amount of recently contaminated cocaine residue of ca. 500 [milligrams] cocaine (initially) ... This required amount is "50,000 higher than the amount reported on circulated currency (ca. 10 micrograms/bill)." ... Therefore, generously assuming that *all* bills in general circulation are tainted by 10 micrograms of cocaine, it would take at least fifty thousand bills to generate enough methyl benzoate to trigger a dog alert. And, as Dr. Furton and Dr. Rose point out, "the odor produced by contaminated bills stacked together does not increase proportionally to the number of bills, but rather is a function of the available surface area" of the bills. ... This indicates that stacked or bundled bills, which obviously have less contaminated surface area exposed to the air, would exude a correspondingly smaller odor signature and the 50,000 figure therefore may be too small by orders of magnitude when tainted bills are bundled together (although stacked bills do retain the methyl benzoate for longer periods).[36]

A researcher was quoted as describing as "alarming" that courts had been accepting the cocaine residue argument. Of particular focus in the case was the Ninth Circuit's decision in *U.S. v. $30,060*.[37] The court then summed up the science by saying that "it is likely that trained cocaine detection dogs will alert to currency only if it has been exposed to large amounts of illicit cocaine within the very recent past." After reviewing the alerting dog's record, the court affirmed the forfeiture.[38]

NOTES

1. *U.S. v. Garcia*, 496 F.3d 495 (6th Cir. 2007).
2. *U.S. v. Limares*, 269 F.3d 794 (7th Cir. 2001).
3. *U.S. v. $252,300*, 484 F.3d 1271 (10th Cir. 2007).

4. Zuo et al. (2008) (using gas chromatography, finding presence of cocaine more common on $5, $10, $20, and $50 bills than on $1 and $100 bills).
5. *U.S. v. $191,910*, 16 F.3d 1051 (9th Cir. 1994).
6. *U.S. v. Baro*, 15 F.3d 563 (6th Cir. 1994).
7. *U.S. v. $242,484*, 389 F.3d 1149 (11th Cir. 2004).
8. *Jones v. U.S. Drug Enforcement Administration*, 819 F.Supp. 698 (M.D.Tenn. 1993).
9. *U.S. v. $30,060*, 39 F.3d 1039 (9th Cir. 1994).
10. *U.S. v. $87,375*, 727 F.Supp. 155 (D.N.J. 1989). See also *U.S. v. $124,700*, 458 F.3d 822 (8th Cir. 2006) (driver unable to identify party he said was going to help him buy refrigerated truck for business); *U.S. v. $84,615*, 379 F.3d 496 (8th Cir. 2004) (dog given chance to sniff currency from vehicle and stack of bills from the officers present and alerted only to currency from vehicle).
11. *Hetmeyer v. Virginia*, 19 Va.App. 103, 448 S.E.2d 894 (Ct. App. 1994).
12. *U.S. v. $22,474*, 246 F.3d 1212 (9th Cir. 2001).
13. *U.S. v. Cuellar*, 478 F.3d 282 (5th Cir. 2007).
14. *U.S. v. $144,770*, 157 F.3d 600 (8th Cir. 1998).
15. *U.S. v. $42,500*, 283 F.3d 977 (9th Cir. 2002). See also *U.S. v. $215,300*, 882 F.2d 417 (9th Cir. 1989) (confiscated money was placed in desk to which dog alerted; forfeiture affirmed).
16. *U.S. v. $53,082*, 773 F.Supp. 26 (E.D.Mich. 1991), 985 F.2d 245 (6th Cir. 1993).
17. *U.S. v. $242,484*, 389 F.3d 1149 (11th Cir. 2004).
18. *U.S. v. $183,791*, 2010 WL 30961 (11th Cir. 2010).
19. *U.S. v. Ospina*, 798 F.2d 1570 (11th Cir. 1986).
20. *California v. Sommer*, 12 Cal.App.4th 1642, 16 Cal.Rptr.2d 165 (Ct. App. 1993) (testimony admitted that a dog is more sensitive than a machine in detecting explosives, though the case concerned narcotics).
21. *U.S. v. Cuellar*, 478 F.3d 282 (5th Cir. 2007) (conviction under 18 U.S.C. 1956(a)(2)).
22. See *U.S. v. Golb*, 69 F.3d 1417 (9th Cir. 1995) (money was coated as if with "flour in a bakery shop").
23. *U.S. v. Saccoccia*, 58 F.3d. 754 (1st Cir. 1995).
24. *U.S. v. Limares*, 269 F.3d 794 (7th Cir. 2001).
25. *U.S. v. $80,760*, 781 F.Supp. 462 (N.D.Tex. 1991) (footnote omitted). See *U.S. v. $100,000*, 761 F.Supp. 672 (E.D.Mo. 1991) (claiming money was won in bingo game, then that it was thrown from car and picked up by person from whom it was seized, did not meet burden; forfeiture granted).
26. *U.S. v. $10,700*, 258 F.3d 215 (3rd Cir. 2001).
27. *U.S. v. $639,558*, 955 F.2d 712, 293 U.S.App.D.C. 384 (D.C. Cir.1992). See *U.S. v. Trayer*, 898 F.2d 805, 283 U.S.App.D.C. 208 (D.C.Cir. 1990) (dog, Ben II, had been trained to exhibit aggressive behavior on detecting drugs; dog alerted at defendant's roomette then at briefcase removed from roomette; handler testified that dog had alerted by pointing on majority of occasions and had alerted correctly in 58 out of 60 times; evidence did not indicate that dog was cued at target roomette; dog's alert provided probable cause to search roomette).
28. *U.S. v. Cardona-Usquiano*, 25 F.3d 1194 (3rd Cir. 1994).
29. *U.S. v. $506,231*, 125 F.3d 442 (7th Cir. 1997).
30. *U.S. v. $5,000*, 40 F.3d 846 (6th Cir. 1994).
31. In re $102,000, 823 P.2d 468 (9th Cir. 1992).
32. *U.S. v. $49,576*, 116 F.3d 425 (9th Cir.1997).
33. *U.S. v. $30,670*, 403 F.3d 448 (7th Cir. 2005).
34. Furton et al. (1999).
35. Citing Furton et al. (1997b).
36. Ibid.
37. *U.S. v. $30,060*, 39 F.3d 1039 (9th Cir. 1994).
38. Citing Mesloh, Henych, and Wolf (2002).

16 School Sniffs

John J. Ensminger and L.E. Papet[1]

In the late 1970s through the 1980s, school officials sought to stem the increasing presence of illegal drugs in schools by conducting schoolwide sniffs of virtually all students. Some schools confined sniffs to locker and parking lot areas. This led to a great deal of legal activity, often actions by parents against school systems. School sniffs are also conducted using explosives detection dogs when bomb threats are received.[2]

The Supreme Court has held that the Fourth and Fourteenth Amendments limit the actions of school officials. The Court has found that the student's expectation of privacy must be balanced against "the substantial interest of teachers and administrators in maintaining discipline in the classroom and on school grounds." Disorder has increased because of drug use and violent crime in the schools, creating "major social problems."

> How, then, should we strike the balance between the schoolchild's legitimate expectations of privacy and the school's equally legitimate need to maintain an environment in which learning can take place? It is evident that the school setting requires some easing of the restrictions to which searches by public authorities are ordinarily subject. The warrant requirement, in particular, is unsuited to the school environment: requiring a teacher to obtain a warrant before searching a child suspected of an infraction of school rules (or of the criminal law) would unduly interfere with the maintenance of the swift and informal disciplinary procedures needed in the schools.[3]

Justice Byron White, writing for the Court, said that the "school setting also requires some modification of the level of suspicion of illicit activity needed to justify a search." The Supreme Court joined other courts

> in concluding that the accommodation of the privacy interests of schoolchildren with the substantial need of teachers and administrators for freedom to maintain order in the schools does not require strict adherence to the requirement that searches be based on probable cause to believe that the subject of the search has violated or is violating the law. Rather, the legality of a search of a student should depend simply on the reasonableness, under all the circumstances, of the search.[4]

For the analysis here, this means that school sniffs are distinguishable from other uses of dogs. Justice White made clear that the actions at issue were conducted by school authorities, not the police.[5] A case that involved significant police involvement, though school officials "continued to act under the color of their statutory school authority," held that "the standard of probable cause for an actual arrest" had to be met to justify a strip search.[6]

It is worth noting that dogs that enter schools to look for drugs are not necessarily perceived negatively by the students. One canine team created cards to give to the students, who often want to interact with the dog. The police handler was reported to have given out more than 15,000 cards to children.[7]

SNIFFS OF STUDENTS

On March 23, 1979, the Highland School System in Indiana, using dogs of the Highland Police Department as well as volunteer canine units trained in marijuana detection, conducted sniffs throughout its junior and senior high schools during the first period of the day. Students were instructed to keep their hands on their desks while a handler and dog went up and down the aisles.[8] Students wishing to go to a bathroom had to go with an escort. Almost 3,000 students were sniffed by 14 dogs, leading to about 50 alerts. Seventeen students were suspended and four had to remove their clothing in a nurse's station. One student, given the pseudonym Diane Doe because of her age, was strip searched and found to have nothing. It was later learned that she had a dog that was in heat and may have been attractive for that scent to the drug detection dog.

The district court concluded that the entry of the officials into the classrooms was not a search and no warrant was necessary. The court empathized with the school system's efforts to stop drug use among students and said that the action was justified because there was a "reasonable cause to believe" that drugs were present among the students. When a dog alerted, however, the district court held that this provided reasonable cause to believe a student was concealing narcotics. Thus, the pocket search of Diane Doe did not violate her Fourth Amendment rights. A nude search, however, was another matter. The court held that the dog's alert did not provide reasonable cause for such an intrusive search because the odor may have only been present on Diane Doe's clothing from inadvertent contact. The Supreme Court declined to grant a writ of certiorari, but Justice Brennan dissented, arguing that the Supreme Court should have reviewed the case because the search was unconstitutional.[9] The generality of the sniff was arguably as broad as the checkpoint sniffs that the Supreme Court disapproved in *Indianapolis v. Edmond,* so it is not clear how the Supreme Court would dispose of such a matter now.[10]

In a 1982 case from Texas, the Fifth Circuit held:

[T]he dogs' sniffing of cars and lockers does not constitute a search within the purview of the fourth amendment. We hold further that the dogs' sniffing of the childrens' persons does constitute a search within the purview of the fourth amendment, and that in a school setting, individualized reasonable suspicion is required in order for the sniffing to be constitutional.

The school district had contracted with a private security firm. The firm's operations were described in detail.

The defendant [school district], GCISD, adopted the challenged program in response to a growing drug and alcohol abuse problem in the schools. It contracted with a security services firm, Securities Associates International, Inc. (SAI), that provides dogs (generally Doberman pinschers and German shepherds) trained to alert their handlers to the presence of any one of approximately sixty different substances, including alcohol and drugs, both over-the-counter and controlled. The defendant conducted assemblies in the elementary schools to acquaint the children with the dogs and informed students in the junior and senior high schools of the program. On a random and unannounced basis, the dogs are taken to the various schools in the district, where they sniff students' lockers and automobiles. They also go into the classrooms, on leashes, to sniff the students themselves. During their "playtime" at the schools, the dogs are sometimes taken off their leashes. When a dog alerts the handler to the odor of an illicit substance on a student's person, after the sweep of the class is completed and the dog and handler have departed, a school official discreetly asks the student to leave the class and go to the administrator's office, where he is subjected to a search of pockets, purse, and outer garments. When a dog alerts his handler to an automobile, the student driver is asked to open the doors and the trunk. If he refuses, the school notifies the parents. When a dog alerts his handler to a locker, the school searches the locker without the consent of the student to whom it is assigned. If the student is found to possess substances that violate school policy, he may agree to seek outside counseling; otherwise the administrator may recommend to the superintendent that the student be suspended. Second-time violators do not have the option of counseling.

Two of the named plaintiffs in the case triggered alerts by the dogs. One was found to have a small bottle of perfume, which was returned to her. The other student's socks and lower legs were searched, but no contraband was found. The use of large dogs for these sniffs made the interactions with the students more fearsome and more intrusive, but the court said that "as long as the dogs are carefully selected for their nonaggressive character, and the handlers supervise them during their playtime, we do not think that the minimal 'harassment' arising from their mere presence on campus rises to the level of a constitutional violation."[11]

Two students were singled out in a school sniff in a Texas case involving the Latexo Independent School District. The federal district court noted that a flashlight merely enhanced what could be plainly viewed in another light, whereas electronic eavesdropping violated a citizen's individual reliance on personal privacy.

> The dog thus replaced, rather than enhanced, the perceptive abilities of school officials. In that respect, the dog was far more analogous to an electronic "bug" than to a flashlight, which merely augments human sight in particular lighting conditions.
>
> The dog's inspection was virtually equivalent to a physical entry into the students' pockets and personal possessions. In effect, he perceived what the students had secreted and communicated that information to his handler. By way of analogy, if the police approached citizens on the street with a portable x-ray machine to discern what they were carrying in their pockets, purses, and briefcases, surely such a procedure would be a search under the fourth amendment. Yet that was precisely the way in which Merko was employed. Like an x-ray machine, his superhuman sense of smell invaded the students' outer garments and detected the presence of items they were expecting to keep private. All citizens have a reasonable expectation that their privacy will not be intruded upon by electronic surveillance, x-ray machines, or sniffing dogs at the whim of the state. The use of the "sniffer dog" in the Latexo school was thus a search under the fourth amendment.

Thus, the dog was conducting a search, so the next question was whether it was unreasonable.

> The degree of intrusion committed by Merko's sniffing the students and their property was somewhat less extensive than that stemming from a physical search. No laying on of hands was contemplated during the procedure until the dog had completed his tour of each classroom. In that respect, the intrusion more closely resembled electronic bugging or x-rays, which convey private information without a discernible physical intrusion. Moreover, since Merko only signaled his trainer if contraband was detected, this type of search was more limited in nature than other surveillance methods which pick up private information, both incriminating and non-incriminating, in an indiscriminate manner.
>
> On the other hand, the use of an animal such as Merko to conduct a search may offend the sensibilities of those targeted for inspection more seriously than would an electronic gadget. Merko, a German Shepherd, is a large animal who had been trained as an attack dog. Testimony by the school's principal, Mr. Emmons, indicated that the dog "slobbered" on one child in the course of a search. The dog's trainer acknowledged that Merko might physically touch a child during a search if the dog became overly excited. Such a tool of surveillance could prove both intimidating and frightening, particularly to the children, some as young as kindergarten age, enrolled at Latexo. Hence, the degree of intrusion caused by the search was significant, far greater than that which the Fifth Circuit has found unacceptable in the "beeper" cases.

The fact the students knew that a canine search might occur did not diminish their privacy expectations. The court also said that a school sniff was not analogous to a search at an airport, where someone could avoid the search by declining to fly. The students at the school had no way to avoid the searches. The court concluded that the search was in fact unreasonable.

> Just as the police could not lawfully bring Merko into a restaurant, football stadium, or shopping center to sniff-search citizens indiscriminately for hidden drugs, the school officials exceeded the bounds of reasonableness in using Merko to inspect virtually the entire Latexo student body without any facts to raise a reasonable suspicion regarding specific individuals.

The case also involved a parking lot sniff, which the court also found unreasonable.

The sniff-search of plaintiffs' vehicles, isolated from the search of the plaintiffs themselves, also exceeded the bounds of reasonableness. Under school regulations, students had no access to their vehicles while school was in session. Thus, the school's legitimate interest in what students had left in their vehicles was minimal at best.

The court enjoined further use of sniffer dogs.[12] It is not clear that the parking lot sniff would be disapproved of now in the light of *Place* and *Caballes*, both of which the case preceded.

LOCKER AND PARKING LOT SNIFFS

An assistant district attorney of a county in New Mexico contacted two high schools about conducting sweeps of lockers with drug dogs. Although the police and the local district attorney were involved, the actions taken would be decided by the school officials.

Each dog was accompanied by a Principal or Assistant Principal, who walked with them down the halls of the school where there were some 2,000 lockers. When a dog would "key" in on a locker, that locker would be marked, and if the dog keyed three times on any one locker, Worley or Mallory, who had master keys to all lockers, would open it to inspect it. Only school officials opened the lockers.[13]

Marijuana was found in one student's locker. The Tenth Circuit concluded that the search did not violate the plaintiff's Fourth Amendment rights.[14]

A Texas case involving cars in the school parking lot transformed from a school matter to a police matter.[15] Security Associates International (SAI) provided the school district with sniffer-dog services to detect narcotics, marijuana, alcohol, firearms, ammunition, and pyrotechnics. Dogs were walked through the school parking lot.

If a dog was alerted by a scent from a car, the school's policy was to contact the student responsible for the vehicle. If the student refused to consent to a search of the car, school authorities would contact the student's parent. If the parent refused consent, then the authorities would contact law enforcement officials. The hope was that these inspections would discourage students from bringing to school substances and objects banned under school policy.

On March 29, 1985, a trained sniffer dog named King was alerted by an unattended car in the Joshua High School parking lot. William Jennings' daughter Naomi had driven the car to school that day. Naomi Jennings was called out of school and asked to consent to a search of the vehicle. She refused because her father, who had had various jobs as a federal law enforcement official investigating embezzlement and fraud in the United States postal system, had instructed her to refuse consent and call him if a dog ever was alerted by the car.

The father arrived and refused to consent to the search. The county attorney, who was consulted, concluded there was enough evidence to apply for a search warrant, and a county judge, determining there was sufficient probable cause, issued a warrant. The search produced no contraband. Jennings sued under 42 U.S.C. 1983 on behalf of himself and his daughter. The court found that none of the defendants acted outside the scope of his or her authority, and even with probable cause a judgment could not have stood against them. Testimony established that the dog was reliable in detecting "pyrotechnics" and drugs. The dog had been particularly effective on the day in question:

The record shows that of the eight cars actually searched that day, the following was found in each respectively: a 25 caliber pistol, loaded; sixteen 12 gauge shells, beer caps; nine empty beer bottles and four empty beer cans; two 12 gauge shells, two empty beer cans; asthma medication; five empty beer cans and a Primatene inhaler; a cap pistol and caps containing gun powder; the scent of previously vomited beer.

The court did not decide on the issue of probable cause, but said that the officer's belief in the existence of probable cause was not objectively unreasonable. The civil matter was dismissed as to all defendants.[16]

A Georgia case involving a parking lot sniff netted a teacher rather than a student. The dog alerted to the teacher's car and the handler allowed the dog to jump into the car through an open window. The dog alerted to the ashtray. The handler opened the car and found a hand-rolled ciga-rette, which field-tested positive for marijuana. The principal informed the teacher that she would have to take a urinalysis drug test within 2 hours. She refused and was suspended. The school board terminated her after a hearing.

> Merely because a campus police officer was present during the sweep and happened to be the one to find the marijuana does not change the fact that this was a law enforcement event, not bound by any school policy or employment contract. Even if, as Hearn argues, the Board's policy gave employees a heightened expectation of privacy with regard to their personal property at school, that expectation does not bind local law enforcement. They are not parties to the contract. Whatever expectation of privacy Hearn had in her vehicle during a law enforcement event must be located in constitutional law, not local school board policies.

The court concluded that the teacher's constitutional rights were not violated.[17]

IMMUNITY

School sniffs have given rise to lawsuits but state immunity laws have generally protected school officials from money damages, even where dogs alerted to students who were found not to be carry-ing any drugs. Immunity has even applied where courts have specifically found that students were subjected to an unreasonable search.[18]

NOTES

1. L.E. Papet is the president of K9 Resources in Kings Mills, Ohio.
2. Department of Homeland Security, Boy, 12, Arrested in Bomb Threat at Hackensack Private School. Homeland Security: *Daily Open Source Infrastructure Report for 10 December 2010* (p. 15, referencing Hackensack Record).
3. *New Jersey v. T.L.O.,* 469 U.S. 325, 105 S.Ct. 733, 83 L.Ed2d 720 (1985).
4. Ibid. See also *Vernonia School District 471 v. Acton*, 515 U.S. 646, 115 S.Ct. 2386, 132 L.Ed.2d 564 (1995) (citing *New Jersey v. T.L.O.* for the proposition that the state's power over schoolchildren "is cus-todial and tutelary, permitting a degree of supervision and control that could not be exercised over free adults"); see also *DesRoches v. Caprio*, 156 F.3d 571 (4th Cir. 1998); *S.C. v. State*, 583 So.2d 188 (1991) (citing *New Jersey v. T.L.O.* that warrant was not necessary to search school locker when one student told school officials that another student had guns).
5. *New Jersey v. T.L.O.,* n. 7, stating: "We here consider only searches carried out by school authorities act-ing alone and on their own authority. This case does not present the question of the appropriate standard for assessing the legality of searches conducted by school officials in conjunction with or at the behest of law enforcement agencies, and we express no opinion on that question."
6. *Picha v. Wielgos*, 410 F.Supp. 1214 (N.D.Ill. 1976). See *F.P. v. Florida,* 528 So.2d 1253 (Ct.App. 1988) (officer needed probable cause to search student in investigation of auto theft); *Martens v. District No. 220 Board of Education*, 620 F.Supp. 29 (N.D. Ill. 1985) (police officer's limited role in asking student to empty pockets, where no criminal prosecution was contemplated, did not require prob-able cause though "school officials certainly had reasonable suspicions and indeed, probably probable cause to search" student). See *Massachusetts v. Lawrence L.,* 439 Mass. 817, 792 N.E.2d 109 (2003) (memorandum of understanding requiring school officials to notify police if a student was found with a controlled substance did not require school officials to search students and was effectively permitted by *New Jersey v. T.L.O.* to allow search where there was a reasonable basis for believing student was concealing drugs).
7. DeFranco (1999).

8. It is a customary procedure for schools to be under "lockdown" during a sweep. This prevents any unnecessary repetition of sniffs, or any impromptu sniffs at entrances and exits.
9. *Doe v. Renfrow*, 475 F.Supp. 1012 (N.D. Ind. 1979), rev'd on other grounds, 631 F.2d 91 (7th Cir. 1980), cert. denied 451 U.S. 1022, 101 S.Ct. 3015, 69 L.Ed.2d 395 (1981).
10. *City of Indianapolis v. Edmond*, 531 U.S. 32 148 L.Ed.2d 333, 121 S.Ct. 447 (2000).
11. *Horton v. Goose Creek Independent School District*, 690 F.2d 470 (5th Cir. 1982), on motion for rehearing, *Horton v. Goose Creek Independent School District*, 693 F.2d 524 (5th Cir. 1982), cert. denied 463 U.S. 1207 (1983).
12. *Jones v. Latexo Independent School District*, 499 F.Supp. 223 (E.D.Tex. 1980) (emphasis added). See *Washington v. Slattery*, 56 Wash.App. 820, 787 P.2d 932 (1990) ("When the school officials did not find any drugs on Slattery or in his locker, they logically went outside to search his car, which was parked in the school parking lot where the informant had said Slattery had been selling marijuana. The officials found a notebook with names and dollar amounts next to the names and a telephone pager—then the officials found a locked briefcase. ... The school officials' initial search of Slattery's person was justified at its inception. They had reasonable grounds for suspecting that the search of Slattery would turn up evidence that he had violated the law. The searches of Slattery's locker, car, and briefcase were reasonably related in scope to the circumstances which justified the interference in the first place. To limit the school search exception to a search of a student's body or his locker would be anomalous in light of the rationales of [*New Jersey v. T.L.O.*, 469 U.S. 325, 105 S.Ct. 733, 83 L.Ed2d 720 (1985)]").
13. Repetitive alerts may not be meaningful if a second handler and dog are advised to check a locker by the first handler whose dog alerted. This practice could amount to signaling the second dog to alert.
14. *Zamora v. Pomeroy*, 639 F.2d 662 (10th Cir. 1981).
15. It may be argued that the involvement of school officials affects the analysis of the reasonableness of a seizure. See *Illinois v. Kline*, No. 03-CF-786 (Ill.App. 2005) (state arguing "that a different result should follow because Kline's removal from the classroom was primarily carried out by the dean and not by [a police officer]").
16. *Jennings v. Joshua Independent School District*, 877 F.2d 313 (5th Cir. 1989).
17. *Hearn v. The Board of Public Education*, 191 F.3d 1329 (11th Cir. 1999).
18. See *B.C. v. Plumas Unified School District*, 193 F.3d 1260 (9th Cir. 1999).

17 Explosives, Landmine, and Bioweapons Detection

John J. Ensminger, John Grubbs, and L.E. Papet[1]

The Federal Aviation Administration's National Explosive Detection Canine Team Program began in 1972 when a TWA jet bound for Los Angeles from JFK in New York was the subject of a bomb threat. The jet returned to JFK where a bomb-sniffing dog named Brandy found a bomb on the plane just 12 minutes before it was set to detonate. The program began with 40 canine teams at 20 airports in 1973, which grew to nearly 100 teams by the turn of the century. The only police canine known to have died in the World Trade Center on 9/11 was an explosives detection dog named Sirius.[2]

Federal law requires that checked baggage be subjected to a manual or other type of search, which can include a sniff by an explosives detection dog.[3] Explosives detection canine teams now operate in most of the larger airports in the United States. Explosives detection handlers in the Transportation Security Administration (which took over FAA responsibilities in 2001) program are not employees of the federal government but rather work for city, county, and state law enforcement authorities, or for airport authorities. Handlers are trained at the Defense Military Working Dog School at Lackland Air Force Base in San Antonio, Texas.[4] Dogs are trained to search aircrafts, baggage, ground vehicles and transportation structures. Upon finding something with a suspicious smell, the dogs are trained to remain sitting at the location (sometimes called "honoring the odor"), a passive alert.[5]

As of 2000, the Federal Aviation Administration had 126 explosive detection teams in 34 cities.[6] The Department of Defense has about 500 explosives detection dogs worldwide with a proficiency requirement of at least 95% detection rate for targets and 5% or less nonproductive rate (alerts to distracter odors).[7] The Federal Protective Service of the Department of Homeland Security (DHS) assigns explosives detection canine teams to search federal facilities, as well as checking packages, vehicles, and persons in and around such facilities. This program began in 1998 and by 2010 included about 70 teams.[8]

The European Union also provides for the use of explosives detection dogs for screening passengers and employees at checkpoints, including baggage being carried onto airplanes, screening of checked luggage, cargo, and mail being loaded into the hold of an airplane; and for sniffing of vehicles at checkpoints and the insides of airplanes.[9] Dogs are to be single purpose dogs and are to be taught to use a passive response. The dog and handler must both be approved and are to receive both initial and recurrent training. Recurrent training is to be provided at least every 6 weeks in sessions at least 4 hours long. Records are to be kept on both the dog and the handler.[10]

Demand for explosives detection dogs increased as a result of 9/11, unfortunately bringing in a certain amount of fraud, including ineffective dog services sold to the State Department, the Federal Reserve, and the Internal Revenue Service (IRS).[11] Fraud was alleged as to bomb dogs services supplied by an independent contractor to the State Department for sniffing vehicles and packages at the entrance to the presidential compound of Hamid Karzai in Kabul, Afghanistan.[12] See Figure 17.1 for a picture of President Reagan with the Secret Service detail at the "Western White House."

FIGURE 17.1   President Ronald Reagan in 1988 in Santa Barbara with the White House Canine Unit. Dogs were cross-trained for patrol and explosives detection work. (Courtesy of John Grubbs.)

TRAINING

The TSA began a Puppy Program in 1999 and modeled it after the Australian Customs Service National Breeding and Development Centre. The program produces approximately 80 puppies each year to supplement the National Explosives Detection Canine Team Program. Volunteer families in San Antonio and Austin raise puppies between the ages of 9 weeks and 12 months before they can enter explosives detection training. Dogs that are ultimately not used in the program are available for adoption.[13] The DHS Federal Protective Service trains its canine teams at a canine training academy in Anniston, Alabama.[14] Bomb-sniffing dogs may cost up to $20,000 to breed and train along with a handler.[15] It has been reported that the Secret Service runs a 20-week course for bomb-sniffing dogs.[16]

The federal government categorizes explosives in various ways, such as under transportation restrictions,[17] and keeps an annual updated list of explosive materials provided by the Bureau of Alcohol, Tobacco, Firearms, and Explosives (ATF).[18] Requests for bids from private contractors to provide dogs for assignments often contain specific lists of explosives on which the dogs are to be trained. In seeking bids for contract working dogs in Afghanistan, for instance, the U.S. Army sought bidders with dogs trained to recognize the following:

- Commercial dynamite (gelatin and ammonium nitrate)
- Military dynamite
- Water gel (TOVEX)
- TNT (trinitrotoluene)
- Smokeless powder[19]
- C-4 plastic explosives
- Detonating cord
- Potassium chlorate
- Sodium chlorate[20]

Dogs generally alert by sitting or lying down in front of the chemical using a number of training aids.[21] Passive alerts are preferred because of the danger of a dog scratching or biting an explosive device.[22]

A particular problem with explosives detection is that a number of chemicals are used in various explosives, or are found in them by contamination, so that it is not always clear, from a chemical perspective, what the dog is trained to detect. Table 17.1 lists the major chemicals in explosives and explosives mixtures, dividing explosives into five categories, plus the primary explosives. Chemicals, called taggants, may be added to explosives to (1) aid in vapor detection (mononitrotoluenes in plastic explosives) or (2) to trace an explosive to a particular manufacturer.[23]

Many trainers focus on one main explosive from each principal category (e.g., TNT, C-4, detonation cord, dynamite, and a powder explosive).[24] The Scientific Working Group on Dog and Orthogonal Detector Guidelines (SWGDOG) divides the main chemical classes of explosives into those that are mandatory, those dogs must be able to identify to be certified, and those that are elective.[25]

Furton and Myers note that many of the major chemical components in explosive mixtures have very low vapor pressures or limited olfactory receptor response, making them unlikely odor signature chemicals.

For example, single-based smokeless powder contains primarily involatile nitrocellulose but numerous volatile aromatic organic compounds are possible including plasticizers (phthalates), stabilizers (including diphenyl amine, methylcentralite and ethylcentralite) and nitro and nitroso derivatives of diphenylamine formed by its reaction with the degrading nitrocellulose. Some of the other volatile aromatic organic compounds identified in smokeless powder are cresol, nitrotoluene, carbazole, dimethylphthalate, nitroso diphenylamine, N-nitroso-diphenylamine, dinitro cresol, carbanilide, nitrodiphenylamine, diethylphthalate, trinitrotoluene, dinitrodiphenylamine, dibutylphthalate, diphenylphthalate, and triphenyl-phosphoric acid ester. Obviously, the volatile aromatic organic constituents can be complex and isolating the specific chemical(s) used by dogs to detect an explosive is an equally complex task. Double-based smokeless powder contains added nitroglycerin and triple-based smokeless powder also has added nitroguanidine which themselves may serve as target chemicals for detection.

The amount of any particular chemical can also vary considerably, but for training purposes, the chemicals used are often going to be those most commonly encountered or expected.[26]

Negative controls include blanks (nothing present) and representative distracters (non-explosive items commonly encountered under search conditions) which can include acetaminophen, antacids, aspirin, baby powder, bath soap, breath mints, camera film, candy, cereals, coffee, denture tablets, duct tape, electric tape, facial tissues, leather gloves, pet food, plastic bags, polymer gloves, sanitary napkins, shampoo, shaving cream, shoe polish, soda can, soda water bottle, suntan lotion, tampons, tobacco, toothpaste, twine, video tape[27] and vitamins.

Furton and Myers state that the number of negative controls must be limited, with most introduced as part of a detection team's regular maintenance protocols rather than during annual certification testing.

Chemicals composing the scent of an explosive may be vaporized in an unpredictable fashion by evaporation, sublimation, and mechanical disturbances. Plastic food wraps and metal foil are common wrappings found on explosive devices to conceal the scent. Vapor pressures of chemicals in explosives vary considerably. Some explosives, such as PETN, RDX, and HMX, have such low vapor pressures that they might be difficult for a dog to detect, particularly at room temperature. Furton and Myers used solid phase microextraction (SPME) to concentrate headspace odor chemicals. They note the dangers of contamination by human scent or other chemicals, with the possibility that a dog may start to cue on contaminants rather than the parent odor the handler believes the dog is detecting.[28]

In experiments on the detection of nitromethane conducted at the Lawrence Livermore National Laboratory, two researchers tested 41 dogs with various dilutions in water of nitromethane. Samples were placed in ointment tins on a test wheel with four separate stations. With pure nitromethane

TABLE 17.1
Common Major Chemicals in Explosives and Explosive Mixtures

Compound Class	Example	Symbol	Commonly Found In:
Aliphatic nitrates	Nitromethane		
	Hydrazine		Rocket fuel and liquid component of two-part explosive
Aromatic nitrates ($C-NO_2$)	Nitrobenzene	NB	
	Nitrotoluene	NT	
	Dinitrobenzene	DNB	
	Dinitrotoluene	DNT	
	Amino-dinitrotoluene	A-DNT	
	Trinitrobenzene	TNB	
	2,4,6-trinitrotoluene	TNT	Composition B with equal part RDX, Pentolite with equal part PETN
	2,4-dinitrotoluene	DNT	
	Picric acid		
Nitrate esters ($C-O-NO_2$)	Methyl nitrate		
	Nitroglycerin	NG	Certain dynamites, pharmaceuticals
	Ethylene glycol dinitrate	EGDN	Some dynamites
	Diethylene glycol dinitrite	DEGDN	
	Pentaerythitol tetranitrate	PETN	Detonating cord, Detasheet (Flex-X military name), Semtex with RDX
	Nitrocellulose		'Guncotton', main component of single-based smokeless powder
	Nitrocellulose and NG		Double-based smokeless powder
	Nitrocellulose, NG, and nitroguanidine		Triple-based smokeless powder
Nitramines ($C-N-NO_2$)	Methylamine nitrate		
	Tetranitro-N-methyaniline	Tetryl	
	Trinitro-triazacylohexane (cyclonite)	RDX	C-4, tetrytol-military dynamite with TNT
	Tetranitro-tetrazacylooctane (octogen)	HMX	Her Majesty's Explosive
Acid salts	Ammonium nitrate		ANFO with fuel oil, nitro-carbo-nitrates (NCN) with oil
	Ammonium perchlorate		
	Potassium nitrate		Black powder with charcoal and sulfur
Primary explosives	Lead azide		
	Lead styphnate		Blasting caps
	Mercury fulminate		
	Tetramino nitrate		
	Hexamethylene triperoxide diamine	HMTD	
	Triacetone triperoxide	TATP	

Source: Reprinted from *Talanta*, 54, 487–500, Furton, K.G. and Myers, L.J., The Scientific Foundation and Efficacy of the Use of Canines as Chemical Detectors for Explosives, Table 2. (Copyright 2001, with permission from Elsevier.)

and minor dilutions, the researchers scored positive responses from 72% to 94%, but with greater dilutions, results were from 46% to 68%. The researchers concluded that the levels of the substance dogs were trained on affected their performance:

- The levels of the substance to be detected experimentally must also be included in the canines' normal training. A dog not trained to detect very low levels may not do so in an experiment. The dog must be trained at the levels it will be expected to work.
- The presentation order of low levels of a target substance affects the test results. If a relatively high level of a target odor is presented first on a wheel together with a low level of the same substance, the dog may selectively alert to the higher level only.[29]

Research is continuing on isolating compounds released into the air around explosives to see whether dogs trained on the underlying explosive will alert to them.[30] Pseudoscents are being developed for training purposes, in part to avoid complicated Drug Enforcement Administration (DEA) and ATF rules, and from the difficulty of handling explosive materials.[31]

A lack of coordination between the Federal Bureau of Investigation (FBI) and ATF on explosives detection canine training procedures has been noted by the Department of Justice Office of the Inspector General. Part of the disparity in training methods involves the weight of the samples used in training, with the FBI using larger amounts (15–30 grams) and ATF preferring trace amounts (5 milligrams).[32]

TRAINING AIDS

The Army's Military Working Dog Program authorizes as training aids commercial dynamite (gelatin and ammonium nitrate), military dynamite, water gel (TOVEX), TNT, smokeless powder, C-4, detonating cord, potassium chlorate, and sodium chlorate.[33] Training aids are to be used frequently enough to maintain the 95% proficiency level, as well as in day-to-day training.

One research group tested dogs using inert training aids that mimic the odor signatures of explosives, specifically NESTT (nonhazardous explosives for security training and testing). The dogs had difficulty in locating the NESTT aids, but the researchers noted that use of these materials in higher concentrations might still be useful in training.[34]

REQUIREMENTS FOR HANDLERS

Trainers of explosives detection dogs should follow protocols when using explosive substances and must usually maintain an inventory of training aids used. Failure to comply with such requirements has been held grounds for dismissal of a canine trainer.[35] Although most law enforcement agencies prefer the traditional one handler–one dog system, some use secondary handlers. The Army has researched a multiple-handler system[36] but maintains a one dog–one handler policy.[37]

RELIABILITY

Dogs were found in one study to be more accurate for certain chemicals than others, with 88% reliability on C-4 but only 54% reliability for TNT.[38] Another study found a general success rate of 85%.[39] Some training requires the use of very small amounts of the active chemicals because of risks from working with the primary chemical.[40]

Dogs may vary in their reliability over time for a number of reasons. Diseases that are known to temporarily or permanently diminish olfactory function in the dog include canine distemper, canine parainfluenza, Cushing's disease, allergic rhinitis, hypothyroidism, seizure disorders, nasal tumors, head trauma, diabetes mellitus, and chronic renal failure.[41]

One study of the variables affecting the detection by an air-sampling device of concealed RDX and TNT patches on subjects determined that the movement of those wearing the patches enhanced the explosive trace signal above a baseline level. The researches found that clothing blocked some of the movement-generated trace signal and that the signal levels varied from individual to individual, "indicating that human variability is an issue in explosive trace detection."[42] The research was not done for a canine-related project but rather with regard to a chemical trace detection portal that one of the authors of the research has patented.[43]

VISUAL FACTORS IN EXPLOSIVES DETECTION

Researchers in Israel considered whether explosives detection dogs, trained to search for partially visible targets, relied on both sight and scent in detecting the targets, or shifted entirely to olfaction for the work at night.[44] The researchers studied four Belgian Malinois and two Labrador retrievers, placing 30 grams of C-4 explosives in four types of containers:

- Glass salt shakers with metal lids
- Plastic soap holders
- Small metal cans
- Wooden boxes

Identical containers were also filled with substances such as dirt, sugar, coffee, and bread, or left empty. Indoor trials took place in an auditorium, comparing results in bright light and in dim light. Outdoor trials took place on a limestone field track, in daylight and after dark. The dogs wore a tiny wireless microphone and transmitter attached to a head harness. The audio signals were analyzed by computer software that counted the sniffing and panting sounds of the dogs. Dogs searched off leash, with the handler waiting a considerable distance away. Prior to each search, old containers were removed and new containers were hidden in different places. Partially hidden containers could be seen on closer approach.

Upon detecting an explosive, dogs were trained to sit next to it, bark, and point at it with their noses. The handler could ask the dog to point to the target again before approaching the dog and rewarding it with food and praise. The researchers found that the dogs were equally successful in finding the explosives in daylight or low light, found them as quickly, and generated the same amount of sniffing and panting. Insofar as there was a difference between searches in the dark and searches in the light, search duration was shorter in the dark, sniffing frequency increased, and panting frequency decreased. Some of the dogs were more difficult to handle in the dark. The dogs did not identify any negative control containers in tests in the light and made only two mistakes in tests in the dark. Dogs can see in low intensity light better than humans, but the researchers stated that the dogs tested "did not use the visual channel to search for the explosive either in the light or the dim light conditions."[45]

WORKING IN FREEZING TEMPERATURES

In an experiment to look at the effects of temperature, dogs trained to recognize odors of explosives in San Antonio were transported to Colorado to look for explosives in snow and freezing temperatures. They located 96% of buried mines containing dynamite and TNT.[46] Dogs that are panting heavily from excessive exercise have been found not as good at detecting explosives.[47]

CERTIFICATION

The North American Police Work Dog Association requires a minimum of 91.6% pass rate on target odors, including six different odor classes and four of five different search areas.[48] Confidence intervals of 90% to 95% have been argued as being adequate for admissibility in court.[49] The

Army's Military Working Dog Program manual provides that in order to maintain certification, an explosives detection dog must have a 95% or better detection rate.

> Failure to maintain an average that meets or exceeds this minimum standard for three or more consecutive months results in automatic decertification of the EDD team. The team may be recertified only after retraining and consistent demonstration of proficiency to a certification authority.[50]

When a team's proficiency training has been interrupted for 30 or more consecutive days, regardless of the reason, full recertification is required.[51]

The American Working Dog Association specifies that certification tests require vehicle searches, building or residence searches, and parcel searches. Teams are allowed 2 minutes to search a vehicle. Building searches require a space of at least 10,000 square feet, with the team allowed about 3 minutes per 500 square feet. Parcel searches require a lineup of at least 25 pieces, allowing about 15 seconds per item. The overall test involves a total of 20 target odors, 19 of which the dog must alert to in order to pass.[52] The North American Police Work Dog Association does not require but highly recommends that dogs also be tested in aircraft, watercraft, and mass transit vehicles. The recommended aircraft search is described as follows:

> Commuter, commercial and military aircraft capable of carrying a minimum of 16 people may be utilized for this test phase. Inoperable aircraft (used for ground training purposes only but mechanically incapable of flying) are acceptable for certification purposes. The search shall include the interior and exterior of the aircraft along with all ground support equipment. One explosive aid will be placed in the interior of the aircraft. The interior of the aircraft includes the passenger compartment, cockpit, lavatories and cargo compartments. Additional explosive aids may be placed at the discretion of the Master Trainer either inside or outside the aircraft. The exterior of the aircraft includes the landing gear, wings, engines and ground support equipment. There is no time limit during the aircraft search test.[53]

One professional group recommends that dogs be tested by performing searches in four environments: (1) parcels or baggage, (2) buildings and rooms, (3) motor vehicles, and (4) open areas and perimeters.[54] The Army's Military Working Dog Program recommends that in responding to bomb threats, handlers should maintain their dogs' interest by periodically allowing them to find planted explosives:

> During the conduct of the search, training aids such as C-4 plastic explosive, military dynamite, or smokeless powder should be planted periodically so the dog can find them. This helps the dog to maintain interest in the search. Training aids should only be planted in areas that already have been searched by the EDD team. During an actual search, the EDD should be allowed to find a training aid every 15 to 30 minutes to break the search routine and reward the dog for its perseverance. A skilled EDD handler will know the proper interval between training aid finds to maintain the dog's interest. ... All explosive aids used will require the use of a "Barrier" object such as a towel, paper towel, cardboard, etc., to prevent the explosive aid from coming into direct contact with any physical part of the aircraft, causing residue contamination.[55]

In a case arising from a traffic stop in Ohio, defendants attacked the reliability of the dog that had detected 9 kilograms of cocaine, and their expert argued that the dog, although certified by three different agencies, had been insufficiently trained because the dog had not been trained to ignore odors that would normally excite it. The expert also testified that the Ohio certification process for drug sniffing dogs was inherently flawed. The court emphasized the testimony of the dog's handler, who himself had taught more than 100 training sessions with the dog, as establishing reliability.[56]

FIREARMS DETECTION

Some organizations provide separate firearms detection programs and certification. The Eastern States Working Dog Association, for instance, provides a firearms detection test requiring that dogs alert to recently cleaned and fired weapons, magazines (loaded and empty), and shells (brass and shotgun). In addition, dogs must be able to recognize either black and smokeless powders or empty shell casings that have been recently discharged. Dogs are tested in three areas (building, vehicle, open area) and two items (packages, baggage). To be certified, a dog cannot miss any aid in the test.[57]

EXPLOSIVES ALERTS IN CASE LAW

Explosives detection dogs are often used of sweeps of buildings after bomb threats are received.[58] As with narcotics detection, dog sniffs for explosives have been conducted outside storage lockers. In an Arizona case from 1984, an explosives detection dog conducted a sniff of a storage locker of a defendant under surveillance for burglaries involving explosives. The court determined that the alert and other evidence was sufficient for issuing a warrant, under which explosives residue and related tools were discovered. The conviction was affirmed.[59]

A case arising in Florida in 2003 concerned a bomb dog showing interest, but not fully alerting to a vehicle in a parking lot near the site of a summit of the Free Trade Area of the Americas (FTAA), an event that brought many protestors to Miami. The driver of the vehicle had been seen running from the car and hailing a taxi. It turned out the man was a freelance reporter who was in a hurry to get to an FTAA event. A dog was brought but only showed interest. Because of the threat, a decision was made to use a robot and then a man in a bomb suit to search the car. The federal district court found that the absence of a full alert, probable cause was lacking for the warrantless search.[60]

An explosives detection dog in Tulsa alerted to luggage containing drugs, despite not having been trained to alert to narcotics.[61] Such cases may indicate the residual odor of explosives, or the odor of the drugs might have been attractive to the dog.

LANDMINES

In 2002, there were over 600 dogs being used in humanitarian demining programs in 23 countries.[62] Unfortunately, there are over 100 million laid landmines around the world.[63] Dogs are often faster than using metal detection equipment because dogs are not distracted by metal contamination, which can be extensive in battlefield areas and where there is garbage.[64]

CHEMICALS IN LANDMINES

Mine detection dogs are a subset of explosives detection dogs, but their deployment is specific to finding a particular type of device. What dogs detect is not always certain. Trinitrotoluene (TNT) is found in approximately 80% of all mines, but other TNT by-products will be found even in TNT mines, such as dinitrobenzene (DNB) and dinitrotoluene (DNT). Common military explosives, as indicated in Table 17.2, often contain TNT although they are known by other names. Thus, dogs should not be trained solely on TNT or any single explosive.[65]

Some substances or odors are likely to be transported to the soil surface more slowly than others, and these rates are affected by soil composition, temperature, and soil moisture.

> The colder the soil temperature, the less vapour is produced at the soil surface. ... Soil moisture affects the vapor levels of TNT and DNT in three ways. With dry soils, sorption is high and vapor levels are depressed. Upon wetting, the water displaces the TNT or DNT from the soil surfaces, causing much greater vapor levels (up to 10,000 times). However, with continued wetting (rain), the water will wash sorbed TNT or DNT from the soil surface, again decreasing the vapor levels.[66]

The strongest smell of a landmine may not be present directly above the mine. Under certain conditions, molecules will transport laterally. Chemicals inside of landmines do not remain inside the canister, but go up through evaporation and plant root uptake, down with precipitation, and

TABLE 17.2
Chemicals Found in Landmines

Explosive	Main Compositions
C-2	RDX + TNT + DNT + NC + MNT
C-3	RDX + TNT + DNT + Tetryl + NC
C-4	RDX + Polyisobutylene + Fuel oil
Cyclotol	RDX + TNT
DBX	TNT + RDX + AN + Al
HTA-3	HMX + TNT + Al
Pentolite	PETN + TNT
PTX-1	RDX + TNT + Tetryl
PTX-2	RDX + TNT + PETN
Teryol	TNT + Tetryl
Dynamite 3	NG + NC + SN
Red Diamond	NG + EGDN + SN + AN + Chalk + NaCl

Source: Reprinted from *Talanta*, 54, 487–500, Furton, K.G. and Myers, L.J., The Scientific Foundation and Efficacy of the Use of Canines as Chemical Detectors for Explosives, Table 5. (Copyright 2001, with permission from Elsevier.)

sideways with vapor partitioning.[67] By sniffing objects, dogs disturb some particles by exhaled nostril airjets, making some particles airborne where the dog can detect them.[68]

REMOTE MINE DETECTION DOGS

Most mine detection dogs (MDDs) move across minefields, searching for mines directly. A new approach is to obtain air samples from a potential minefield and effectively bring the minefield to the dog. Originally used for drug and explosives detection, the concept was advanced in South Africa, though not through publication in scientific journals.[69] The technique involves vacuuming air from a minefield through a filter and taking the filters to a central location where dogs are allowed to smell them, along with other samples. If a dog alerts to a filter, the section of road or land from which the filter was taken is treated as requiring clearance. If no dog alerts by sitting or lying down before a sample, the area is declared clear. One of the reasons that this approach is not widely used or described is that a training program for dogs to implement it was not developed until recently. After 4½ months of training, the dogs were able to detect TNT reliably at odor concentrations similar to those obtained in an operational situation. The fact that dogs only individually reached 95% to 98% reliability could be dealt with by using several dogs, though whether 100% reliability can be achieved is not certain. This is better than machines that give a clearance reliability of 80%.[70] See Figure 17.2. This approach has been used in cargo sniffs at some airports, particularly in Europe.[71]

IMPROVISED EXPLOSIVE DEVICES

Military dogs used in Afghanistan and Iraq are often required to be trained in the detection of improvised explosive devices (IEDs). The materials used to create IEDs include most of those explosives on which all bomb dogs are trained, but dogs with this specialty must be able to work off-lead and follow a handler's directions in moving along roadways and other locations. Kennel masters and handlers, who must assign teams or participate in operations, must often have military

FIGURE 17.2 Multiple-choice training apparatus for training dogs in remote landmine detection. (From Fjellanger, R., Andersen, E.K., and McLean, I.G. A Training Program for Filter-Search Mine Detection Dogs, *International Journal of Comparative Psychology, 15*, 277–286, 2002. Courtesy of Stan Kuczaj.)

security clearance levels. In 2008, the Federal Claims Court decided a case that involved the largest working dog contract ever awarded to a private canine contractor, reportedly amounting to $44 million.[72]

BIOWEAPONS DETECTION

Using dogs to detect bioweapons presents unique problems. Research conducted for the U.S. Army concluded that using dogs for bioweapons did not seem promising. First, using actual bioweapons would be dangerous to the animals and everyone involved in the training and testing. This meant that training would have to involve finding nonlethal chemicals that are present with the active agents in a bioweapon. There are, however, no common odor elements unique to a broad range of bioweapons. Certain additives are used with anthrax, but they are also added to other bacteria. Nevertheless, training dogs to recognize specific bioweapons may be possible.[73] Some agencies may have shied away from using the program because false alerts, when a dog alerts to a filter but there is no explosive in the region where the air sample was obtained, are very expensive.

TABLE 17.3
Comparing Dogs and Technology-Based Explosives Detection Devices

Aspect	Instrument	Canine
Duty cycle	24-hour day (theoretically)	Approximately 8-hour day (20 min. on/40 min. break, dependent on conditions)[a]
Calibration standards	Can be run simultaneously (i.e., chromatography based)	Run individually
ID of explosive	Presumptive ID possible (limited by selectivity factors)	Not trained to ID with different alerts
Operator/handler influence	Less of a factor	A potential factor
Environmental conditions	Less affected	May adversely affect (i.e., high temperatures)
Instrument lifetime	Generally about 10 years	Generally 6 to 8 years
State of scientific knowledge	Relatively mature	Late emerging
Courtroom acceptance	Generally unchallenged[b]	Sometimes challenged
Selectivity (vs. interferents)	Sometimes problematic	Very good
Overall speed of detection	Generally slower	Generally faster
Mobility	Limited	Very versatile
Integrated sampling system	Problematic/inefficient	Highly efficient
Scent to source	Difficult with present technology	Natural and quick
Intrusiveness	Variable (apprehensiveness not uncommon)	Often innocuous (breed dependent)
Initial cost	Approximately $45,000 (Ionscan 400B)	Approximately $6,000
Annual cost (excluding personnel)	Approximately $4,000	Approximately $2,000 (vet and food bill)
Sensitivity	Very good/well known	Very good/few studies
Target chemical(s)	Parent explosive(s)/well studied	Odorant signatures/mostly unknown
Toxicological considerations	Minimal (operator may be affected at excessive levels)	Minimal (team may be affected at excessive levels)
Downtime	Varies with instrument, operator, and manufacturer	Varies with breed, handler, and medical condition
Instrument components	Varies with manufacturer (variable sampling, separation, detection, ID technology)	Varies with agency (variable breed, training, alert, and reward systems)
Initial calibration	Generally performed by manufacturer (specifications vary by manufacturer)	Generally performed by supplier (specifications vary by supplier, with minimum 6 weeks training)
Operator training	Typically a 40-hour course	Typically 40-hour course minimum[c]
Certifications	Varies, annually to biannually	Annually to biannually
Recalibrations	Daily to weekly	Daily to weekly
Scientific foundations	Electronics, computer science, analytical chemistry	Neurophysiology, behavioral psychology, analytical chemistry
Potential effects on performance	Electronics/ mechanical	Disease conditions

Source: Reprinted from *Talanta*, 54, 487–500, Furton, K.G. and Myers, L.J., The Scientific Foundation and Efficacy of the Use of Canines as Chemical Detectors for Explosives, Table 5. (Copyright 2001, with permission from Elsevier.)

[a] There may, of course, be limitations on the handler as well as the dog.
[b] This is becoming progressively less true, but was accurate when the study was published.
[c] Training programs often go up to 26 weeks.

COMPARING DOGS AND EXPLOSIVES DETECTION TECHNOLOGY

As was previously discussed with regard to narcotics detection dogs, some technologies have been and are being developed for explosives detection. Any comparison is limited by the fact that equipment and technologies are always being refined. Furton and Myers, providing the comparison in Table 17.3 in 2001, concluded that the different factors did not clearly favor either instrumental or detector dog teams.[74]

NOTES

1. John Grubbs is the president of United States Bomb Dogs, Inc., in Etlan, Virginia, and was formerly a member of the U.S. Secret Service. L.E. Papet is the president of K9 Resources in Kings Mills, Ohio.
2. Sirius was told to wait by his human partner, who was helping someone leave the building. The partner, David Lim, survived (http://our.homewithgod.com/mkcathy/sirius.html).
3. 49 U.S.C. 44901(e); 49 CFR 1546.205(g)(2) (screening of cargo loaded inside the United States).
4. *Newsham v. Transportation Security Administration*, 2010 WL 715838 (D.N.J. 2010) (describing training and funding of dog trained by the Transportation Security Administration for the Port Authority of New York and New Jersey).
5. The National Tactical Police Dog Association requires that to be certified explosives detection dogs must use a passive alert. NTPDA Web site (www.tacticalcanine.com/certification.htm).
6. Lawhorn (2000).
7. See Furton and Myer (2001) for a discussion of physiological reasons that dogs may not perform well in detection assignments, particularly involving explosives detection.
8. Department of Homeland Security, Federal Protective Service K9 Program (www.dhs.gov/files/programs/gc_1253814387212.shtm). Many government buildings, and many agencies in their entirety, such as the IRS, rely on civilian contract arrangements. See IRS Solicitation No. TIRNO-09-R-00032; Award NO. TIRNO-10-C-0021 (August 8, 2010) (award to Patriot K-9 Services, Inc. of $8,290,102.57 contract).
9. EC Regulation 272/2009 (April 2, 2009), 185/2010 (March 4, 2010).
10. EC Regulation 573/2010 (June 30, 2010).
11. *U.S. v. Ebersole*, 411 F.3d 517, cert. denied, 126 S.Ct. 1142 (2006), on remand, 2007 WL 219969 (E.D. Va. 2007), aff'd, 189 Fed.Appx. 287 (4th Cir. 2006), motion to vacate denied, 2007 WL 750198 (E.D. Va. 2007).
12. *U.S. ex rel. Cody v. Computer Sciences Corp.*, 246 F.R.D. 22 (D.C. D.C. 2007) (suit brought under the False Claims Act, 31 U.S.C. 3730 et seq. was dismissed on procedural grounds).
13. Transportation Security Administration (www.tsa.gov/lawenforcement/programs/editorial_1886.shtm).
14. Department of Homeland Security, Federal Protective Service K9 Program (www.dhs.gov/files/programs/gc_1253814387212.shtm).
15. Lilly and Puckett (1997).
16. Lawhorn (2000).
17. 49 CFR Part 173, providing an index to hazard class definitions at 49 CFR 173.2.
18. 27 CFR 444.23. In 2010. See Bureau of Alcohol, Tobacco, Firearms, and Explosives, Commerce in Explosives: List of Explosive Materials (2009R-18T), 75 Fed. Reg. 1085 (January 8, 2010).
19. Diphenylamine is a common additive of smokeless powders. Joshi et al. (2009).
20. Department of the Army, Performance Work Statement: Contracted Working Dog (CWD) Services, Kandahar Airfield/Southern Afghanistan (June 5, 2008) (www.fbo.gov/?s=opportunity&mode=form&tab=core&id=bb468fb2256b9c7e99053b543ef9bb88&_cview=0%29). See also Schoon et al. (2006). The American Working Dog Association provides that certification tests may include TNT, C-4, smokeless powder, water gel, commercial dynamite (nitrate and ammonia based), detonation cord, sodium chlorate, potassium chlorate, black powder, Flex X (C-6), RDX, and PETN. Testing weights are to be no less than 20 grams and no more than 1 pound. Searches are to be conducted in vehicles, buildings or residences, and parcels. AWDA Web site (www.americanworkingdog.com/certification_standards.htm). The North American Police Work Dog Association recommends testing for explosives with a hydrogen peroxide base, including triacetone triperoxide (TATP), hexamethylene triperoxide diamine (HMTD), and methel ethyl ketone peroxide (MEKP). NAPWDA Web site (www.napwda.com/pdflib/bylaws_cert_rules.pdf).
21. Mesloh, Wolf, and Henych (2002) (citing Kristofeck, W., *A Study of Attitudes, Knowledge and Utilization of Canine Teams by the Louisville Division of Police*, 1991).

22. Furton and Myers (2001). See also Harper et al. (2004).

23. National Research Council, Existing and Potential Standoff Explosives Detection Techniques, 42 (National Academy of Sciences 2004). The Montreal Convention 1991 requires manufacturers of explosives to introduce taggants into certain products. Detection agents specified in the treaty are ethylene glycol dinitrate (EGDN), 2-3-dimethyl 1-2-3-dinitrobutane (DMNB), para-mononitrotoluene, and orthos-mononitrotoluene (posted at http://dgca.nic.in/int_conv/Chap_XX.pdf). The United States signed the convention January 3, 1991.

24. Harper et al. (2004) (noting "significant odour differences have been highlighted between smokeless powder brands and types," and suggesting "it may be more beneficial to the completeness of the canines' training if significantly more attention was paid to the powder explosives").

25. SWGDOG SC8—Substance Detector Dogs: Explosives Detection (approved August 15, 2007) (available at www.swgdog.org).

26. Prosecutors should be concerned if trainers have not periodically updated their supplies of training materials.

27. A handler described a situation that arose when a network news crew arrived to film a canine event and one of the dogs alerted to one of the crates the crew had brought. The dog may have alerted to video head cleaner containing amyl nitrate, or to degraded videotapes, which release nitrates and nitrites. L.E. Papet, personal communication (December 30, 2010).

28. Furton and Myers (2001).

29. Kury and Strobel (2003).

30. Lorenzo et al. (2004) (listing potential training aids: aliphatic nitro; nitromethane, hydrazine; aromatic nitro ($C-NO_2$): nitrobenzene (NB); nitrotoluene (NT); dinitrobenzene (DNB); dinitrotoluene (DNT); trinitrobenzene (TNB); 2,4,6-trinitrotoluene (TNT); picric acid; nitrate ester ($C-O-NO_2$): methyl nitrate; nitroglycerin (NG); ethylene glycol dinitrate (EGDN); diethylene glycol dinitrate (DEGN); pentaerythritol tetranitrate (PETN); nitrocellulose; nitroguanidine; nitramines ($C-N-NO_2$): methylamine nitrate; tetranitro-N-methyaniline (Tetryl); trinitrotriazacylohexane (cyclonite or RDX); tetranitrotetrazacylooctane (octogen or HMX); hexanitroisowurztitane (CL20). Acid salts ($NH_4 +$, $NO_3–$): ammonium nitrate; ammonium perchlorate; potassium nitrate (in black powder)).

31. Macias et al. (2006).

32. U.S. Dept. of Justice, Office of the Inspector General, Audit Division (October 2009). "Explosives Investigation Coordination Between the Federal Bureau of Investigation and the Bureau of Alcohol, Tobacco, Firearms and Explosives, Audit Report 10-0" ("ATF officials argued that the FBI should not be providing such training, saying that ATF's method is superior because training with trace amounts of peroxides enhances the canines' ability to detect explosives. For example, because these explosives would generally be sealed in containers, the canine must be able to alert based on recognizing a trace amount of explosives left on a container lid or its scent on the potential bomber." The FBI argued in response that trace amounts are susceptible to contamination and dissipate rapidly once exposed.) On August 3, 2010, Acting Deputy Attorney General Gary Grindler directed ATF and the FBI to develop a joint plan for consolidated explosives training of ATF and FBI agents. "Protocol for Assigning Lead Agency Jurisdiction in Explosives Investigations" (internal memo posted at www.scribd.com/doc/36019934/ATF-and-FBI-Final-Memo-080310). The lack of coordination is part of a turf war between the FBI and ATF, which has led to some embarrassing press reports. See Esposito, R. (August 17, 2010). FBI and ATF Turf War Creates 'Confusion' at Bomb Scenes. *ABC News* (http://abcnews.go.com/Blotter/fbi-atf-turf-war-creates-confusion-bomb-scenes/story?id=11410254).

33. MWD Pamphlet 190-12, § 5-2.

34. See Harper et al. (2004). For a description of the Livermore Laboratory's development of NESTT, see Hunter (1997).

35. *Melanson v. Covenant Homeland Security Solutions, Ltd.*, 2009 WL 748345 (E.D. Tex. 2009).

36. Furton and Myers (2001).

37. MWD Pamphlet 190-12, § 1-26.

38. Knauf and Johnston (1974).

39. Williams et al. (1998).

40. Schoon et al. (2006).

41. Furton and Myers (2001), Table 6 (noting the reversibility of many conditions is not known). See MWD Pamphlet, 190-12, § 6-4 for a list of contagious diseases.

42. Gowadia and Settles (2001).

43. U.S. Patent 6073499 (June 13, 2000).

44. Gazit and Terkel (2003).

45. The researchers noted that "even when the container was clearly visible from the position where the dog was standing, rather than approach it directly the animal would continue to search in a typical olfactory search pattern. If the dog had been cueing in on visual cues, one would expect that once it had identified the target it would make a direct approach. Thus, if using visual identification it should have approached the container faster under the light over the dim light intensity conditions, resulting in a shorter duration of search. In fact, however, the duration to finding the target was the same under the two lighting conditions."

46. Dean and Tomlinson (1983) (discussing training techniques in relation to Pavlovian theory). See *Pennsylvania v. McKown*, 2009 WL 2489219, 8 Pa.D. & C.5th 129 (Pa. Ct. of Common Pleas, Centre County 2009) (agent's experience in working with explosives detection dogs was considered in whether his observations [without a dog] provided probable cause).

47. Gazit and Terkel (2003b).

48. North American Police Work Dog Association Certification Rules (N.A.P.W.D.A.), N.A.P.W.D.A., Perry, OH, 1998, 1-23.

49. Aitken (1995).

50. MWD Pamphlet 90-12, § 3-27(c).

51. MWD Pamphlet 90-12, § 2-39b(2).

52. AWDA Web site (www.americanworkingdog.com/certification_standards.htm).

53. NAPWDA Web site (www.napwda.com/pdflib/bylaws_cert_rules.pdf).

54. SWGDOG SC8—Substance Detector Dogs: Explosives Detection (approved August 15, 2007).

55. MWD Pamphlet 190-12, § 2041b(8).

56. *U.S. v. Torres-Ramos*, 536 F.2d 542 (6th Cir. 2008).

57. ESWDA Web site (www.eswda.org/certifications/firearmsdeteciton.html).

58. See Department of Homeland Security, "All Clear Given at Bluffton Grocery Store. Homeland Security Daily Open Source Infrastructure Report for 9 December 2010" (p. 11) (grocery store evacuated, no bomb found by canine unit); "Bomb Threat at Madison County Criminal Justice Center. Daily Open Source Infrastructure Report for 8 December 2010" (p. 16) (bomb threat made to criminal justice complex, no bomb found).

59. *Arizona v. Quatsling*, 536 P.2d 226 (Az.App. 1975).

60. *Lippman v. City of Miami*, 2010 WL 2836713 (S.D.Fla. 2010).

61. *U.S. v. McCranie*, 703 F.2d 1213 (10th Cir. 1983).

62. Goth et al. (2002).

63. Browne et al. (2006).

64. Geneva International Centre for Humanitarian Demining (2005).

65. Landmines produce a bouquet of scents. Uddqvist and Roberthson (2010), 8 (citing personal communication with Schoon).

66. Ibid. (references deleted).

67. Phelan and Barnett (2001).

68. Settles and Kester (2001).

69. See Bach and McLean (2003).

70. Fjellanger et al. (2002, 2003) ("sampling and detection technology need careful tuning if detection success is to achieve acceptable operational levels").

71. See "Canine Remote Explosive Scent Tracing, Long Used in Europe for Screening Air Cargo, Continues to Be Tested in U.S." (November 9, 2010) (www.doglawreporter.blogspot.com).

72. Department of the Army, Solicitation No. W91B4L-08-0025 (June 13, 2008), including Performance Work Statement, Performance Plan, and Responses to Contractor Questions; *EOD Technology, Inc. v. U.S.*, 82 Fed.Cl. 12 (2008); the case led to various protests with the Government Accountability Office (see particularly Protests B-400464, September 11, 2008, B-400464.6, May 5, 2009); Award No. W91B4N-10-C-5001, December 11, 2009). See also Kara M. Sacilotto, Is the Game Worth the Candle? The Fate of the CICA Override, *The Procurement Lawyer*, 45(1), 3 (Fall 2009) (discussing the Federal Claims Court decision).

73. Lawhorn (2000).

74. Furton and Myers (2001), Table 5.

18 Accelerant Detection Dogs

The first arson dog, Mattie, was put into service by the Connecticut State Police in 1986.[1] Mattie was a female black Labrador retriever. By 1988, Mattie had been taught to alert to paint remover, lacquer thinner, charcoal lighter, paint thinner, kerosene, naphtha, acetone, dry gas, heptone, gasoline, No. 2 fuel, diesel fuel, gum terpentine, Heritage Lamp Oil, transmission fluid, octane, and Jet-A-Fuel. Her alert was the sit position, and she was rewarded with food treats. One of Mattie's cases concerned a fire at a manufacturing complex in Branford, Connecticut. Mattie's part in the investigation is described as follows:

> Prior to scene-overhaul, Mattie and her trainer/handler, Trooper First Class James Butterworth examined all entrances to the building for possible accelerants. With approximately six to twelve inches of debris on top of the concrete floor, Mattie alerted in one area adjacent to an entrance door. This area was cleared and pour patterns were evident under the debris. She further alerted at the sill of the door. Samples were taken from these areas. Later that evening, a vehicle was seized from a suspect. Mattie searched the interior of the suspect's car and alerted on the front passenger floor mat. This alert was later corroborated by witnesses who stated that the suspect carried gasoline to the scene of the arson, storing it on the front passenger side floor of his vehicle. The laboratory confirmed gasoline was present on the mat submitted as evidence.

The suspect was convicted of arson in 1987 and sentenced to 15 years in the Connecticut State Prison.[2] In field tests, Mattie alerted to 78 samples, but laboratory analysis by gas chromatography was able to confirm the presence of accelerants in only 49 of those cases.[3]

Mattie's training program became the initial model for the Bureau of Alcohol, Tobacco and Firearms (ATF).[4] By 2000, the bureau had trained 56 accelerant detection canine teams for state and local law enforcement agencies. A significant number of dogs are used by fire services as well. Some insurance companies contract for arson dogs to investigate suspicious claims. Accelerant detection dogs are used in conjunction with laboratory testing to help pinpoint locations from which samples should be taken. By reducing the number of samples, the cost of laboratory work is decreased.[5] For an arson dog working the scene of a suspicious fire, see Figure 18.1. Not all dogs that help solve arson investigations are accelerant detection dogs. Tracking dogs have taken officers from the scene of a fire to the location of the perpetrator.[6]

RESEARCH ON ACCELERANT DETECTION

A test conducted by the Federal Bureau of Investigation (FBI) and the Southern California Bloodhound Handlers Coalition prepared four pipe bombs, each with a different type of explosive, and two containers of gasoline. Six test subjects then handled a bomb or a gas canister for 1 to 2 minutes. After detonating the bombs or igniting the canisters, researchers collected the debris and transferred scents to gauze pads. The pads were stored for 2 to 16 days until the day of the test when 20 bloodhounds each sniffed a scent pad. The bomb and canister handlers walked along trails in a public park. The dogs trailed the bomb handler in 53 of 80 experiments and the arsonist in 31 of 40 experiments, with no false identifications.[7]

A study of dogs from the Illinois State Fire Marshal's Office found that arson dogs could detect residues of gasoline, kerosene, and isopar at levels below what laboratory instruments could detect. Dogs could also be trained to ignore scents from charred carpet and styrene.[8] A wide range of skill levels were found between dogs.

FIGURE 18.1   Arson dog at the scene of a suspicious fire. The arson dog, Charlotte, with her handler, Greg Keller, worked a scene in Lewiston, Idaho. (Courtesy of Greg Keller.)

Dog Outperforms Technology in Detecting Gasoline

A substance developed to absorb suspected accelerants from the scene of a fire, ignitable liquid absorbent (ILA™), was compared to accelerant detection dogs in an experiment reported in 2007. The fires were controlled burns conducted in a wood frame structure. Three rooms were used, each with a different accelerant:

1. Odorless paint thinner (medium petroleum distillate)
2. Camp fuel (light petroleum distillate)
3. Regular gasoline

The accelerant was poured onto flooring panels consisting of oriented strand board and carpet pads. Each flooring panel was nailed to the floor to prevent movement during fire suppression. The three rooms were furnished as, respectively, a bedroom, a kitchen, and a bathroom. Video cameras set up outside the house captured the extent of the burns and recorded the time and progress of the fires. The fires were allowed to burn freely until after about 2 minutes when they began to move into the adjacent hallway, at which point the suppression crews put them out. The dog was a female Labrador retriever trained and certified by the Maine Criminal Justice Academy, State Farm Hydrocarbon Detection Canine program. The dog had worked with the handler for 6 years. In the bedroom, the dog indicated on five of the six flooring panels in the room, but failed to alert to the panel in which the smallest amount of odorless paint thinner had been applied.

After the fire was put out, the ILA was applied to each flooring panel in the bedroom and allowed to absorb for 20 to 30 minutes. The ILA was then scraped off, and put in a clean metal can and sealed for subsequent analysis. The panels were also checked by gas chromatography-mass spectrometry (GC-MS) analysis. The GC-MS analysis correctly found the accelerants on all panels, but the ILA system did not change color (indicating an accelerant) except on the carpeting squares. It did not work on wood. In some of the rooms, the ILA did not work even this well, but the dog correctly alerted to six panels in one room and five of six in the other.[9]

Because of the corroborative nature of two findings in agreement, an accelerant detection dog can justify the additional expense of a chemical detection procedure.

DOGS MAY ALERT FALSELY WHERE CERTAIN PRODUCTS ARE PRESENT

One study found that accelerant detection dogs may alert positively to certain burnt substances, including certain types of carpets, foams, and plastics.[10] Collection of unburned comparison samples is important in determining if accelerants were actually applied.[11] Footwear of investigators has been determined to be unlikely to produce false-positive alerts in fire scene investigations.[12] Forensic testimony has sometimes acknowledged that a positive alert as to a suspect's clothing might be due to products used in manufacturing the clothing.[13]

FOUNDATIONAL ELEMENTS FOR ACCELERANT DETECTION ALERTS

A Delaware court stated that the foundation for admission of a dog's evidence on accelerant detection is analogous to tracking and that in "both cases, there is no requirement of scientific testing to support evidence obtained by a dog if these requirements are met."[14]

A 1994 case of the Iowa Supreme Court involved the work of an accelerant detection dog. In addition to admitting the dog handler's testimony, the court took the opportunity to specifically overrule a prior case, *Grba*, which had rejected dog tracking evidence 70 years earlier.[15] In the context of the decision, it is apparent the court adapted the foundational requirements of tracking to accelerant detection canines. The court noted that *Grba* was decided at a time when courts were "less friendly to expert testimony than they are today." The court determined that the foundation for arson detection dog evidence consisted in establishing:

> (1) the dog handler's expertise; (2) the dog's training; and (3) the general accuracy of the dog's reaction during investigations. This is sufficient foundation. In the present case it is further bolstered by evidence of accuracy in this particular investigation.

The court found the challenge to the foundation without merit.[16]

SCIENTIFIC EVIDENCE STANDARDS APPLIED BY SOME COURTS

In a 2000 Florida case, the defendant was seen near a trailer that was burned by a fire started on a couch outside it. She was seen acting furtively by several neighbors and carrying a cigarette lighter and wearing flip-flops. A fire examiner determined that the fire was started on the couch and that from the burn pattern it was intentionally set. An accelerant detection dog alerted to accelerants on the couch, but samples sent to a laboratory did not test positive for accelerants. The handler testified that the dog had helped investigate over 200 fires and had been between 80% and 90% correct. The defendant argued that a *Frye* hearing on the scientific evidence should have been conducted.[17] The court held that this was not a *Frye* issue, however, "because the use of dogs to detect accelerates is not a new or novel scientific principle."[18] The handler's testimony was "pure opinion" of an expert, which the jury was entitled to evaluate.[19]

In a 2000 Arkansas case, the insurance company declined to pay the insureds because of the suspicious nature of the fire, which the company alleged had been started by the insureds or at their direction. A jury found for the Footes, which was affirmed by the Arkansas Supreme Court. One issue on appeal was whether the trial court erred in refusing to admit evidence of the alert of an accelerant detection dog. The handler testified that the dog had to have an accuracy rate of 100% in order to be certified and described how the dog was more accurate than laboratory tests. The dog had alerted in five places, in two of which a laboratory confirmed the presence of an accelerant. The trial court had applied a *Daubert* analysis in rejecting the evidence.[20] The Arkansas Supreme Court, on the appeal, also referred to its "strikingly similar" analysis of novel scientific evidence from a 1991 case,[21] and concluded that the insurance company had not produced appropriate support for the validity of an accelerant detection canine's alert. Consequently, the court affirmed the decision of the trial court to exclude the evidence.[22] Presumably, a scientific expert would have been adequate.

In a 2002 Utah case, eyewitness evidence suggested that the defendant tried to set fire to a restaurant as well as a nearby van. An accelerant detection dog was brought to the van and alerted in two locations. Samples were taken from those places and sent to the Utah State Crime Lab. The handler testified that the dog was trained by ATF for 6 weeks, where his nose was "calibrated." The defendant was convicted, arguing on appeal that the canine evidence lacked foundation. The court noted that Rule 702 of the Utah Rules of Evidence governs scientific expert testimony, and if novel methods or techniques are involved, a separate threshold on reliability must be met. The court noted that the use of accelerant detection canines is generally accepted in the fire investigation community. Nevertheless, the court held that as proof, the "substantive evidence of canine accelerant detection in the absence of laboratory testing is novel scientific evidence." Despite the prosecution's failure to meet this standard (under the state's version of *Frye*[23]), the court found the error harmless as there was ample other evidence for the conviction.[24]

In a 2008 California case, a car used by a suspect was subjected to a sniff by an "Ignitable, Flammable Liquid Detection Canine" certified by the ATF. The dog, which had worked over 200 fires, had been trained to detect, in the words of a witness, "light, medium, and heavy petroleum distillates: gasoline—pretty common things that are used—alcohol, fuel, white gas, kerosene, paint thinners, pretty much anything that you could start a fire with." The dog alerted to two different areas inside the car and parts of these areas were sent to a crime laboratory to check for ignitable liquid residue, but the tests employed failed to detect any ignitable liquid. The handler characterized a dog as able to detect one part per billion, while the instruments in a crime lab detect only one part per million. The handler admitted, however, that he was only relating what he had heard during the ATF training. The defense counsel did not interpose a *Kelly/Frye* objection, as to which the court expressed some surprise if not a criticism, but the court "was not prepared to assume that such an objection would have ultimately been sustained." Nor was the court prepared to assume that, even in the absence of evidence about the accelerant sniffing dog, it was not reasonably probable that the result would have been different.[25]

TRAINING

In 1994, the Iowa Supreme Court described the handler of the dog whose evidence was admitted at trial as having developed the training system for his dog himself.

> He bought Ty as a seven-week-old puppy in 1985 and trained him in general obedience. In the summer of 1986 Hiles began training Ty to detect and respond to the odor of gasoline, using training techniques adapted from those used by law enforcement officers to train dogs to detect illegal drugs and explosives. Later that year, Hiles began training Ty to detect samples of gasoline that he had placed in actual fire scenes. Hiles then used Ty to detect accelerants at the scene of suspected arsons. Over the next few years Hiles trained Ty to respond to the odor of other flammable liquids, including diesel fuel, kerosene, charcoal lighter fluid, and alcohol. He continued to train Ty regularly, both in and away from fire scenes, and took Ty to many of the fires that he investigated.

The handler was qualified as an expert and his dog "was sufficiently trained to serve in the investigation." The Iowa Supreme Court also discussed the dog's reliability:

> In a large percentage of cases, about three out of four, Ty's location by scent of accelerants was later confirmed by laboratory tests using a gas chromatograph. A seventy-five percent confirmation rate is

perhaps not impressive until it is explained that the twenty-five percent of cases lacking laboratory confirmation can largely be attributed to human error in gathering the material sampled for analysis. It must be remembered too that the accelerant tends to dissipate from the sample while awaiting analysis.

The Iowa Supreme Court then faced the major issue that appears in accelerant detection evidence: the fact that laboratory analysis is often unable to confirm that the dog has detected an accelerant.

In the present case later laboratory tests proved inconclusive, placing this analysis within the twenty-five percent group. But the State offered evidence strongly indicating that the laboratory analysis was considerably less reliable in detecting fire accelerants than trained dogs. There was no evidence that Ty would indicate the existence of an accelerant where no accelerant existed.

Ty's accelerant detection ability was frequently confirmed by visual observation of the dog's selection of its location. Fire investigators have long noted physical characteristics left from the ignition at a fire's source. Investigators, as a part of their expertise, "read patterns" often left by flames and flame residue. Ty of course had no human knowledge of these patterns. But the points he indicated by scent were consistently confirmed independently as the fire source on the basis of patterns. Finally, Ty has a distinguished record of accuracy from many fire investigations where other evidence later confirmed his selection of the fire's source.

The court found that the investigators' reading of the patterns "independently confirmed" the dog's alerts. The conviction was affirmed.[26]

Accelerant detection dogs, also called arson dogs, are often trained on a system where they do not get food rewards unless they correctly detect the desired odor. One study determined that of 42 accelerant detection teams, 60% performed without error.[27] Where errors did exist, missing an accelerant was more common than making a false alert. The researchers concluded (in 1994) that dogs were more accurate than electronic devices.

RELIABILITY

In a 1993 Delaware case, a defendant objected to evidence concerning an accelerant dog's alert because prior alerts by the dog had been corroborated by scientific tests only 17 of 80 times. The court noted, however, that there was no evidence that the dog had incorrectly identified substances as accelerants. In some cases, no chemical conformation was requested. The court also noted that the dog had been certified by the United States Police Canine Association and had been recertified several months before the fire.[28]

GOVERNMENT STANDARD

The Bureau of Alcohol, Tobacco and Firearms in the Department of Treasury was authorized by Congress in 1997 to establish certification standards for explosives detection dogs used by federal agencies.[29] ATF announced the availability of standards to law enforcement and government agencies in 1999.[30] The standards include mandatory testing for six of the most commonly encountered accelerants.[31]

Certification generally involves more than just canine team testing. The North American Police Work Dog Association, for instance, requires that handlers complete courses in crime scene preservation, HAZMAT (hazardous materials) awareness, blood-borne pathogens, and in the Incident Command System and National Incident Management System (FEMA). This organization also provides for testing with a paint-can lineup, a clothing lineup, and interiors of six to ten vehicles.[32]

ALERTING TO SPECIFIC ACCELERANTS

A defendant burned down a trailer home where he resided, and admitted doing so, though he filed a motion to suppress. Canine evidence was also introduced.

Agent Robert Watson of the Bomb and Arson Section testified that he was a certified fire investigator and handler of a hydrocarbon-detection dog. He testified that he had been with his dog since 2000, and he had taken her to "hundreds" of fire scenes. He "works" his dog 365 days a year, and he said, "There are 2,730 some odd distractors that she had been checked off on." Agent Watson testified that he arrived at the scene per Agent Greenwood's request. His dog "alerted in two different areas, indicating ... that there was an ignitable liquid in the floor area." He cut samples from the floor where the dog alerted for later analysis by the TBI [Tennessee Bureau of Investigation]. On cross-examination, Agent Watson clarified that his dog was not trained to alert on "accelerants," but she was trained to alert on "hydrocarbon," which is a component of an ignitable and/or combustible liquid.

Agent Randall Kirk Nelson of the microanalysis unit of the TBI crime laboratory analyzed the fire debris to identify the presence of any ignitable liquids. He stated that the sample provided by Agent Greenwood "revealed the presence of turpenes, which are present in turpentine and occur naturally in some wood products." However, he found that the samples from Agent Watson "revealed the presence of an evaporating gasoline-range product. Products in this range include all brands and grades of automotive fuels, including gasohol." He explained that this "evaporating gasoline-range product" could not be paint thinner, because, although an accelerant, paint thinner is a wholly different classification.

The conviction was affirmed.[33]

NUMBER OF SAMPLES

The federal district court in Massachusetts granted a habeas corpus petition in part because an accelerant detection dog was taken to only one spot in a building that burned down, and only one sample, from the same spot, was subjected to laboratory analysis. The building where the fire occurred was released to the insurance company soon after the fire and demolished, making further testing impossible. The habeas petition was based on ineffective assistance of counsel. In addition to the limited area of the dog's sniff and the lack of sampling of any other area in the building, the judge criticized the defense lawyers for not having sought a *Daubert* hearing, for not having objected to the handler's effusive descriptions of his dog's capabilities (and of other dogs he had used), for not having insisted that the laboratory run further tests on the sample it received to be more precise in its description of the accelerant, which it had labeled a "light petroleum distillate," and for admitting evidence that would not have been sanctioned by the National Fire Protection Association's Guide for Fire and Explosives Investigations (known as NFPA 921). Defense counsel's performance was found to be both deficient and prejudicial and a new trial was ordered.[34]

CORROBORATION

Substantial corroborating evidence has been considered by appellate courts in holding that the trial court did not abuse its discretion in admitting the alert of an accelerant detection dog.[35] One court acknowledged that "dog sniff evidence is not always reliable," but concluded that this meant that "special weight should not be assigned to dog-sniff evidence in the absence of any corroborating evidence," of which there was an ample amount in the case before it.[36]

CANINE ALERTS WITHOUT LABORATORY VERIFICATION

As noted in several of the cases already described, laboratory verification may not always follow a dog's alert, either because no test is performed or because laboratory tests fail to detect an accelerant.[37] Courts have accepted evidence of alerts of accelerant detection dogs where laboratory analysis could not confirm the presence of an accelerant.[38] An Illinois appellate court held that a dog's alert to accelerants at a fire scene that were not confirmed by laboratory analysis did not meet the *Frye* standard.[39] A 1999 Pennsylvania case admitted a canine's alerts when the burn patterns suggested the use of an accelerant.[40] In a 1993 Delaware case, investigators ruled out accidental causes for a fire but performed no laboratory tests on the pour pattern of a fire. A dog's alert, however, was admitted as indicating an accelerant had been used by the arsonist.[41]

In a 2006 New Jersey case,[42] a court held that a defendant could not be convicted of arson in the absence of laboratory confirmation of an accelerant-detection canine's alert, noting there were no "spreadsheets" detailing how many of Blondie's accelerant alerts had been confirmed by laboratories. The court observed that "substantial portions of the contents of defendant's home would qualify as pyrolysis products, which … can cause a canine to give a false alert." The court cited the National Fire Protection Association (NFPA) guide, which states that a canine alert not confirmed by laboratory analysis is not to be considered validated.

> In this matter, evidence uncorroborated by laboratory testing of the accelerant-detection canine's alert to certain locations at the fire scene should be barred under the *Frye* "general acceptance" standard. The scientific theory at issue—that a dog's nose is more accurate than laboratory equipment—is simply *not* supported by experts on fire causation, by scientific literature on the subject, or by judicial opinions. Such a tenuous scientific foundation must be subjected to intense scrutiny in a criminal trial where the liberty interests of the accused are at stake.[43]

A 1996 case concerned an accelerant detection dog's alert inside of a house where a fire had started. Laboratory tests of carpeting in the house did not detect accelerants, though it was not clear whether the dog had alerted to the same areas where the samples were taken. A special agent in the State Fire Marshall's Office and the handler of the dog testified concerning a study where his dog had been able to detect accelerants though chemical analysis had failed to confirm this. The handler acknowledged in testimony that the International Association of Arson Investigators had adopted the position that a canine alert should only be sued where laboratory analysis provided verification. The handler stated that the Canine Accelerant Detection Association took a different position, arguing that canine alerts did not need laboratory verification to be useful. The court concluded that the disagreement among professional organizations indicated there was no "general acceptance" of the reliability of uncorroborated alerts in arson investigations. The appellate court affirmed the trial court's refusal to admit the dog's evidence.[44]

A 1997 Georgia case involved a man who was convicted of murdering his wife by burning their house down. The defendant had escaped but testified that his wife resisted him and he jumped from a window without her. There was circumstantial evidence, including that the defendant had recently verified the insurance on the house if it burned down. He also told their adult son to remove his belongings from the house and to put some items in a safe deposit box. An accelerant detection dog alerted inside the house, but a crime lab test for accelerants was negative.

> Carr [the defendant] argues on appeal that the evidence was inadmissible because there was no evidence at trial that dog-alerts have reached a state of verifiable certainty as required by [state decisional law[45]] and that the error was harmful because it was the only substantive evidence purporting to show the presence of an accelerant.

The court concluded that the dog alert testimony was expert testimony.

> "Expert opinion testimony … is admissible where the conclusion of the expert is one which jurors would not ordinarily be able to draw for themselves; i.e., the conclusion is beyond the ken of the average layman…."[46] Applying that rationale to the evidence involved in this case, it is plain that the dog alert testimony was expert testimony in that the average layperson would not be able to determine from watching the dog lie down, point with his nose, or paw the ground (the methods used by the dog to indicate the presence of hydrocarbons) that chemicals which could accelerate a fire were present. It is only by the dog handler's analysis of the dog's behavior that the conclusion could be reached that an accelerant was present.

The court could find no Georgia case in which a dog alert showed the actual presence of a substance.

> [D]og alerts to accelerants have not been shown, neither at the trial of this case nor in any Georgia appellate decision, to have the scientific reliability necessary to permit their use as substantive evidence of the presence of accelerants. The trial court's ruling to the contrary was error. The State argues that the admission of the evidence, if error, was harmless in light of other evidence of the presence of an accelerant. However, there was no other direct evidence of the presence of an accelerant, and thus, no direct evidence of arson. Notwithstanding the trial court's instruction that the evidence of the dog alert must be considered along with other evidence, we conclude that the potential impact of the evidence admitted was too great for us to conclude that no harm to Carr's right to a fair trial flowed from it. The erroneous admission of that evidence requires a new trial.

The murder conviction was reversed for other reasons as well, but the appellate court cautioned that there might still be enough evidence for a jury to convict.[47]

In a 2010 case arising in West Virginia,[48] an accelerant detection dog owned by the Huntington, West Virginia, fire department alerted, according to the handler, to the defendant's shoes, left pants leg, and jacket sleeve.[49] The dog also alerted to the floor area of the location of the attempted arson. Although the alert occurred on March 23, 2009, laboratory testing of the clothing did not occur until June 14, 2010. A chemist with the West Virginia Police was prepared to testify that the absence of laboratory verification was likely due to the delay in performing the testing. The court noted that the National Fire Protection Association (NFPA) Guide for Fire and Explosion Investigations states that a "canine alert not confirmed by laboratory analysis should not be considered validated."[50] The opinion stated that the prosecution had "provided little on which the Court can base a reasoned and principled application of the *Daubert* factors," and found that "the use of the dog alert as substantive evidence is beyond the accepted scope and application of the technique as described by the NFPA guide." The evidence concerning the dog's alert, and the testimony of the chemist, was excluded.

It is not certain that a hard and fast rule should apply to canine evidence that is not verified by laboratory analysis. If there is substantial other evidence of arson, such as verifiable evidence of a burn pattern or the presence of accelerants in the defendant's possession, it is arguable that the corroborative aspect of the canine's alert should let it into evidence. In any case, prosecutors and insurance companies must be aware of decisions by state courts when dealing with arson canine evidence.

CONSENT

Bringing an accelerant detection dog into a home 2 days after the home was secured from a fire required either a warrant or consent. Alerts by the dog to the presence of accelerants had to be suppressed where they occurred as a result of an illegal entry and before consent was obtained.[51] In a New Jersey case involving a considerable amount of evidence, some of it from an accelerant detection dog, the defendant based her appeal primarily on a lack of consent to a search, arguing that she was too upset to have understood what she was agreeing to, but the appellate court concluded that the consent had been voluntary.[52]

NOTES

1. Lilly and Puckett (1997); Kelly Andersson, "Arson Dogs," *Wildland Firefighter Magazine* (1997) (noting the program was started in conjunction with the Bureau of Alcohol, Tobacco and Firearms); Gialamas (1996).
2. U.S. Treasury Department, Bureau of Alcohol, Tobacco and Firearms, and the Connecticut State Police, *Canine Accelerant Detection Program* (August 23–24, 1988).
3. Lee, H.C. and Messina, D.A. (1988). Evaluation of Arson Canine Testing Program, included in *Canine Accelerant Detection Program*.

4. The name of the agency was changed to add "Explosives" when supervision was transferred to the Department of Justice in 2003 (www.atf.gov/about/history). The acronym generally remains ATF or BATF, however.

5. Gialamas (1996); Browne et al. (2006). A great many factors influence the presence of accelerants after a fire. See Borusiewicz et al. (2006). A 1994 paper estimated there were 200 accelerant detection dogs in the United States. at the time. R. Tindall and K. Lothridge, 1994, An Evaluation of 42 Accelerant Detection Canine Teams, *Journal of Forensic Sciences, 40(4)*, 561–564.

6. *Alsept v. Kentucky*, 240 Ky. 395, 42 S.W.2d 517 (Ct. App. 1931); *Daugherty v. Kentucky*, 293 Ky. 147, 168 S.W.2d 564 (Ct. App. 1943).

7. Stockham et al. (2004b) (also describing scent surviving radiation of papers).

8. Kurz et al. (1994).

9. Nowlan et al. (2007).

10. See Kurz et al. (1996) (dogs were nearly unanimously successful in locating a can containing 50% evaporated gasoline at the 5 microliter level on a burnt carpet matrix or pinpointing a 6-inch carpet sector on a piece of plain carpeting where the same amount of gasoline was applied, but were unsuccessful when lesser amounts (0.05, 0.1, and 0.2 microliters) were applied to a sector; some dogs alerted to samples containing only burnt carpeting material); Kurz et al. (1994) (noting "canines did alert occasionally on background, especially that containing traces of styrene residues, either purposely added in specific amounts or formed upon partial pyrolysis of carpeting material").

11. Tranthim-Fryer and DeHaan (1997) ("canines can respond to pyrolysis products from polymers, such as nylon 616, styrenebutadiene, ethylene-vinylacetate-indene, polypropylene, styrene-butadiene-isoprene, and poly(1-butene)-polyethylene, sourced from carpet pile fibres, adhesives, plastic mesh backing material, rubber underlays and rubber backing materials").

12. Armstrong et al. (2004).

13. *New Jersey v. Keller*, 2010 WL 5346025 (Ct. App. 2010).

14. *Reisch v. Delaware,* 628 A.2d 84, 1993 WL 227264 (1993).

15. *Iowa v. Grba*, 196 Iowa 241, 194 N.W. 250 (1923).

16. *Iowa v. Buller*, 517 N.W.2d 711(1994).

17. *Frye v. U.S.*, 293 F. 1013 (D.C.Cir. 1923).

18. Citing *Florida v. Royer*, 460 U.S. 491, 103 S.Ct. 1319, 75 L.Ed.2d 229 (1983).

19. *Fones v. Florida*, 765 So.2d 849 (Ct. App. 2000).

20. *Daubert v. Merrell Dow Pharmaceuticals, Inc.*, 509 U.S. 579, 113 S.Ct. 2786, 125 L.Ed.2d 469 (1993).

21. *Prater v. Arkansas*, 307 Ark. 180, 820 S.W.2d 429 (1991).

22. *Farm Bureau Mutual Insurance Co. of Arkansas, Inc. v. Foote*, 341 Ark. 105, 14 S.W.3d 512 (2000).

23. *Utah v. Rimmasch*, 775 P.2d 388 (1989).

24. *Utah v. Schultz*, 58 P.3d 879 (Ct. App. 2002). See also *New York v. Dix*, 242 A.D.2d 912, 662 N.Y.S.2d 879 (App. Div. 1997) (no testimony on past performance or effectiveness of dog meant foundation not established, but error was harmless because of other overwhelming evidence).

25. *California v. Adams*, 2008 WL 2115357 (Super. Ct. CC591038, CC466717 2008).

26. *Iowa v. Buller*, 517 N.W.2d (Sup. Ct. 1994).

27. Tindall and Lothridge (1994).

28. *Reisch v. Delaware*, 628 A.2d 84, 1993 WL 227264 (1993).

29. Omnibus Consolidated Appropriations Act of 1997, PL 1004-208, 110 Stat. 3009-369 (September 30, 1996), § 653, providing: "The Secretary of the Treasury is authorized to establish scientific certification standards for explosives detection canines, and shall provide, on a reimbursable basis, for the certification of explosives detection canines employed by Federal agencies, or other agencies providing explosives detection services at airports in the United States." Such sums "as may be necessary to carry out the purposes of this section" were authorized.

30. Notice 878, 64 Fed. Reg. 41487 (July 30, 1999).

31. The American Working Dog Association provides for testing using gasoline, alcohol, diesel fuel, kerosene, and lighter fluid, with substances on burned softwood (pine or fir), burned high density polyethylene (such as a plastic milk jug), burned styrofoam, burned carpet and pad, and weather accelerants on a cotton ball. AWDA Web site (www.americanworkingdog.com/certification_standards.htm). State Department, Office of the Inspector General, *Limited-Scope Review of the Bureau of Diplomatic Security's Oversight of Explosives Detection Canine Programs,* MERO-I-10-14 (September 2010) (finding deficiencies in testing of explosives detection dogs deployed to Iraq and

Afghanistan by military contractors, including inability to test with fresh explosives or training aids; also finding that the Department of State did not have employees who could test contractors' compliance with ATF requirements).

32. NAPWDA Web site (www.napwda.com/pdflib/bylaws_cert_rules.pdf).
33. *Tennessee v. Virga*, 2009 WL 537560 (Ct. Crim. App. 2009).
34. *U.S. v. Hebshie*, 2010 WL 4722040 (D.Mass. 2010). The habeas petition followed affirmance by the First Circuit. *U.S. v. Hebshie*, 549 F.3d 30 (1st Cir. 2008). See also *Babick v. Berghuis*, No. 08-1376 (6th Cir. 2010) (dog's alerts were corroborated by investigators' analyses of burn patterns and positive laboratory result; dissent described dog-sniff evidence as "junk science").
35. *U.S. v. Paccione*, 2000 WL 34251719 (2nd Cir. 2000).
36. *U.S. v. Marji*, 158 F.3d 60 (2nd Cir. 1998).
37. Laboratory verification may not come from finding accelerants at the crime scene but rather on the clothes of the suspect. *Parsons v. Ercole*, 2010 WL 883700 (W.D.N.Y. 2010). See *Jaslar v. Zavada*, 2009 WL 82553 (M.D.Pa. 2009) (dog did not alert to areas where suspect said he used charcoal starter fluid to clean floor but did alert to areas where laboratory analysis failed to confirm presence of accelerants).
38. *Michigan v. Jackson*, 2008 WL 2037805 (Ct. App. 2008) (absence of forensic evidence did not exclude dog's alert when there was corroborative evidence "including but not necessarily limited to the absence of any electrical or other cause to explain the fire, defendant's previous threats coupled with his access and presence in the apartment immediately before detection of the fire"; even if canine testimony was improper, error was harmless). See also *Ohio v. Simpson*, 2002 WL 1625559 (Ct. App. 2002).
39. *Illinois v. Acri*, 277 Ill.App.3d 1030, 662 N.E.2d 115 (Ct. App. 1996).
40. *Pennsylvania v. Gwynn*, 555 Pa. 86, 723 A.2d 143 (1999).
41. *Reisch v. Delaware*, 628 A.2d 84, 1993 WL 227264 (1993).
42. *New Jersey v. Sharp*, 395 N.J.Super. 175, 186, 928 A.2d 165, 172 (2006).
43. NFPA 921: Guide for Fire and Explosion Investigations.
44. *Illinois v. Acri*, 277 Ill.App.3d 1030, 662 N.E.2d 115 (Ct. App. 1996).
45. *Harper v. Georgia*, 249 Ga. 519(1), 292 S.E.2d 389 (1982).
46. Quoting *Smith v. Georgia,* 247 Ga. 612, 619, 277 S.E.2d 678, 683 (1981).
47. *Carr v. Georgia*, 267 Ga. 701, 482 S.E.2d 314 (1997).
48. *U.S. v. Myers*, 2010 WL 2723196 (S.D.W.Va. 2010).
49. In addition to alerting to a suspect's clothing, a dog may alert to a suspect's hands. In the Interest of S.S., Minor Child, 2009 WL 3337667 (Ct. App. Iowa).
50. NFPA 921, § 16.5.3.
51. *U.S. v. Smallwood*, 2010 WL 4008280 (W.D.Ky. 2010).
52. *New Jersey v. Keller*, 2010 WL 5346025 (Ct. App. 2010).

19 Cadaver Dogs

John J. Ensminger and L.E. Papet[1]

Cadaver dogs, used by a wide range of law enforcement agencies,[2] are trained to recognize the scent of human decomposition. Cadaver dogs are also sometimes called human remains detector dogs, forensic search dogs, or decomposition dogs, though these labels are also sometimes described as separate categories of police dogs.[3] The dog may not always alert to a cadaver but perhaps to a scavenged body part, body fluids, or the residual odor of a body. Indeed, no body may ever be found.[4] Nevertheless, the term cadaver dog is widespread and will probably remain the basic term in this type of work. The odors a cadaver dog detects are not certain since there are as many as 424 different volatile chemicals in a cadaver producing odors.[5] Some researchers believe that the presence of a cadaver or remains produces an invisible scent cone of scent-containing molecules.[6] As with other scenting dogs, cadaver dogs may give an aggressive or passive alert, though a passive alert is generally preferable because anxious digging by a dog can disturb a crime scene.[7]

Cadaver dogs have located bodies in hundreds of cases,[8] though they are not always successful.[9] Sometimes they are used to find parts of dismembered bodies[10] or parts of bodies that have been scatted by animal scavenging.[11] Defendants have been known to anticipate the use of cadaver dogs. In one Michigan case, the defendant dug up a body he had buried and, having heard that animal carcasses confuse dogs, put a possum in its place.[12] Cadaver dogs have persuaded law enforcement officials to dig up large areas, sometimes causing damage to property that becomes the subject of a tort action.[13]

There are fewer police dogs trained for cadaver work than other types of police dog work, though many nonpolice agencies also have such dogs. Two officers of the Miami-Dade Police Department Canine Unit argued that many police department assign all aspects of death investigation to crime scene investigation (CSI) and homicide units and do not consider developing human remains detection (HRD) canine teams. Also, large departments with such teams may be willing to lend them out to neighboring departments without the budgets to support all the expenses of a cadaver dog. State-based Federal Bureau of Investigation (FBI) personnel and officers of state law enforcement agencies often keep lists of cadaver dog teams they have used.[14]

Fraud by a cadaver dog handler has led to a prosecution and plea agreement.[15]

SCIENTIFIC ASPECTS OF CADAVER DOG WORK

Cadaver dog work has been the subject of considerable research.[16] A study of eight canine teams simulating search conditions found recovery rates from 57% to 100%.[17] A failure to alert may not be a failure of the cadaver dog since the failure may mean that there was no body at a particular location, perhaps despite the claims of an informant. An alert may also be correct but occur some distance from the body when the odor of a cadaver has been carried by air or water.

MINIMAL CONTACT PERIOD FOR DETECTION

A German team looking at three cadaver dogs of the Hamburg State Police contaminated carpet squares with the scent of two recently deceased bodies.[18] The research was instituted because of a specific case. A married couple went sailing. The wife disappeared on the trip and was reported missing by the husband. The husband came under suspicion of having murdered his wife and a

TABLE 19.1
Carpet Square Test Results for Three Dogs

Test Item/Reaction	B	K	L	Total
Uncontaminated or contaminated by living person/correct negative	26	43	46	115
Uncontaminated or contaminated by living person/false positive	0	3	0	3
2-minute exposure/correct positive	9	27	12	48
2-minute exposure/false positive	0	0	0	0
2-minute exposure/false negative	3	1	4	8
10-minute exposure/correct positive	40	60	76	176
10-minute exposure/false positive	0	1	0	1
10-minute exposure/false negative	0	3	0	3
Total	78	138	138	354

cadaver dog of the Hamburg State Police alerted in the cabin of the yacht. The Hamburg Public Prosecutor's Department wanted to know how long deceased tissue or a deceased body would have to be in contact with material, such as a mattress, for the scent to be detectable by a cadaver dog. The department also wanted to know how long after the item's contact with the body the dog would be able to detect it.

Squares contaminated by being near the bodies of two men in their 60s for 2 minutes were used in tests over 35 days, while tests using carpet squares contaminated for 10 minutes, again without direct contact, were used over 65 days. The men had been dead for about 2 hours and had been wrapped in cotton blankets before the carpet squares were placed under the backs of the men. The cotton blankets simulated a thin layer of clothing covering each individual. Living individuals who had had no contact with deceased tissues served as controls and contaminated carpet squares for the same periods.

The dogs, two Malinois and a herding dog, had been trained on wet materials such as blood, body fluid and muscle tissue. In all, 354 searches were performed, each search consisting of six possible choices, being a carpet square inside of a glass jar. A false positive was alerting to a carpet square of a control and a false negative was failing to alert to a carpet square contaminated by a dead body. The results are contained in Table 19.1, with the dogs labeled B, K, and L.

Searches of squares contaminated with the scent of control (alive) subjects elicited no alerts, and thus no mistakes. The dogs alerted correctly for 2-minute contaminated carpet squares 86% of the time and for 10-minute squares 98% of the time. The researchers acknowledged that "a positive signal by a trained cadaver dog should not be used as the sole evidentiary piece in court." Nevertheless, they noted that the bodies involved here were obtained from dead men in a period when some organs and many cells are still vital and may have had no significant putrefaction.

ODOR OF DECOMPOSITION

Human bodies go through five basic stages of decomposition:

1. Fresh stage—There is little visible change and a dog might even approach the body as though it was alive, but internal decomposition is beginning.
2. Bloated stage—Gas is produced in the body, causing it to swell. An odor of decay is detectible to a human. Entomological activity begins.
3. Decay stage—Gases have escaped and the flesh of the body collapses. Exposed skin color changes to a dark or black appearance, and a strong putrefaction odor is present.

4. Liquefaction stage—The body begins to dry and odor reduces in intensity, but may become musty.

5. Skeletal stage—Most remaining flesh dries to the point of mummification. Musty odor remains but is not as strong. Distance at which a dog can detect the body reduces.[19]

Dogs can detect bodies in all these stages. A group of researchers looking to develop a database of chemical compounds that might be detected by canines and special equipment stated that dogs could "differentiate between odors emitted by a live person and those from recently deceased individuals as well as those in various stages of decomposition, indicating that odor consists of multiple chemical signatures, which change over time." They noted, however, that although dogs may distinguish one complex scent profile from another, this is "difficult to test, validate, calibrate, and most importantly, standardize."[20]

Compounds detected in confined spaces with cadaver samples allowed to decompose for various amounts of time include "1,5-diaminopentane (cadaverine), 1,4-diaminobutane (putrescine), p-cresol, benzopyrrole (indole), 3-methyl-1-indole (skatole), dimethylsulfides, and organic fatty acids."[21] One team found that air samples collected at the soil surface above shallow burial sites contained eight major classes of chemicals with 478 specific volatile compounds associated with burial decomposition.[22] Identifying odor signatures for clandestine burial sites, where human remains are buried in hastily dug, shallow graves, may ultimately necessitate the development of detection devices that can detect bone decomposition better than dogs are able to do.

Distinguishing Cadaver Scent from Waste

In one study, sterile gauze sponges were placed for 20 minutes on the unbroken abdominal skin of cadavers that were from 1 hour to 72 hours postmortem. The gauze sponges were used in line-ups of similar gauze sponges not bearing cadaver scent, but one of which had live human scent. The shortest postmortem duration that resulted in a correct selection was for a sponge placed on a cadaver that was 1 hour 25 minutes. The average overall accurate response was about 50%. The authors concluded:

> Dogs used to develop probable cause based upon residual scent must be negatively conditioned to human urine, feces, and semen in order to ensure that the animal will not alert when encountering these substances during a search. All dogs, no matter what level of training, used in the detection of decomposed human tissue should be negatively conditioned to the scent of decomposed non-human tissue.[23]

Although this caution is well taken, the research was not adequately described to indicate the size of lineups, the training procedures, how dogs were scented, or other key aspects of the study. Nevertheless, handlers are well advised to do such proofing training.

Temperature and Depth of Burial

One study found that a dog's effectiveness declines as temperatures exceed 85°F.[24] Another study in the southeastern United States looked at the abilities of cadaver dogs in high temperatures. The researchers noted that in high heat, dogs are forced to pant, which reduces their ability to locate a scent, though this can still be done if they are within a meter of the item.[25] The study was designed to look at the ability of cadaver dogs to detect human cadaver scent at different buried depths, at different stages of decomposition, and whether dogs could distinguish between animal and human scent at different stages of decomposition. Sterile gauze pads were placed inside a cadaver prepared for autopsy. The pads were left for 20 minutes then placed in plastic Ziploc containers. Samples were stored in a refrigerator until buried. Skeletal remains were also obtained and buried in early May 2001. Animal remains were obtained from the meat department of a grocery store. All samples were enclosed in chicken wire to prevent animal tampering. Disturbances were made in the trial areas with a posthole digger to test the dogs' ability to locate remains by scent, not by soil disturbance. Items were buried at 1 or 2 feet in grass fields and in wooded areas.

Four canine teams participated. The items in each trial were buried 15 feet apart. Each field trial was conducted in an area about 50 by 100 yards. All trial areas were separated by at least a quarter of a mile. The observers did not just look at alerts, failures to alert, and false alerts. They also recorded a "narrowed area" when a dog and handler team correctly concluded that the remains were in a specific area but did not identify the exact location. Observers also recorded "unrecognized alerts" where a dog gave some alerting behavior above the decomposing human remains but the handler did not recognize the signal because it was not the alert the dog was trained to give.[26] Overall, 30% of trials resulted in a correct alert, an unrecognized alert, or a narrowed area. Only 5% of alerts involved locating the remains with the handler recognizing the alert. Dogs ranged from a 20% to 40% alert rate and a 10% to 20% false alert rate. The overall false alert rate was 15%, but 12.5% of these false alerts occurred in the first trial. The researchers found that all of the dogs were able to narrow or give an unrecognized alert for areas that contained skeletal remains at some point in the trials. All teams recognized to some degree human remains buried at one foot depth.

The teams did not distinguish between animal and human remains. The complete failure of the teams to locate either animal or human fresh remains accurately in one trial may have been due to the fact that it was the last trial of the day and the dogs were hot, tired, and distracted.[27] Concerning temperature effects on cadaver dog work, the researchers concluded:

> The optimal conditions for using cadaver dogs are when the ground is moist, the soil is loose, there is a light breeze to circulate the scent, and there is cool air temperature (40 to 60°F). The worst conditions for using cadaver dogs is when it is hot and dry with little or no air movement and when it is raining or snowing heavily.

The results demonstrate that dogs may sometimes be able to detect remains buried at significant depths, though their success will vary depending on the environment, the length of burial, the degree of decomposition, and whether the dog and handler team have been working too long. The researchers noted that some prior studies had focused on remains on the surface,[28] where dogs appear to be more successful.

ELEMENTS OF ADMISSIBILITY

As with other types of dogs, defendants have sometimes objected to the foundation provided for introducing cadaver dog evidence.[29] In a 2004 California case, a cadaver dog, which had previously performed 6 to 12 vehicle lineups as a cadaver dog, alerted to a suspect's car when it was lined up with three other cars. The lineup took place about 2 weeks after the body was discovered. The car had been impounded 2 days after the body was discovered and the windows rolled up and the convertible top closed.

> Scout's handler opened the car doors for him as he went from car to car searching for the scent of a dead human. During the first pass of all the cars, Scout displayed mild interest in King's car. On a second pass, he alerted to the passenger compartment of King's car, indicating a dead human had been there.

The trial court had concluded that because the dog's ability to detect scent was an individual ability, a scientific inquiry was not necessary, finding the situation analogous to tracking.[30]

> First, we are not dealing here with any novel device such as the scent transfer unit. ... Second, we are not concerned with a discriminatory scenting technique (i.e., whether a particular person touched a particular object), but with an *analog of general tracking or trailing*. Here, the dog, Scout, was instructed to find the vehicle that had latent cadaver scent in it. He was not to discriminate whether a particular person had been in the car, nor was he to differentiate between different scents and then find a match.

Rather, he was simply instructed to find what he was generally trained to find—a cadaver. Such a technique is not new or novel. Cadaver dogs are regularly used in reconnaissance and recovery operations and such dogs are certified by both the [California] Office of Emergency Services and the California Rescue Dogs Association.

This, in effect, says that a cadaver dog's work is enough like tracking or trailing that the court did not need to undertake an inquiry as to the scientific validity of results obtained from use of the dog. As will be discussed later, other courts have not agreed. The court then proceeds to apply the tracking rules to cadaver dogs in a lineup:

[T]he dog is simply sniffing to find an "object" rather than discriminating between numerous different scents, prepared by special means (such as scent transferring), in an effort to try to make a positive identification or find a match in a lineup. While we recognize that common sense dictates scenting dogs must be able to discriminate between different scents in conducting ordinary tracking or trailing search operations, nevertheless, such tracking techniques have long been recognized in the law and the appropriate measure of reliability is done, ... on a case-by-case basis. Five elements had to be established as foundation.

The five elements referred to were:

1. The dog's handler was qualified by training and experience to use the dog.
2. The dog was adequately trained in distinguishing the odor of human cadaver scent.
3. The dog has been found to be reliable in alerting on an area where a human cadaver scent has existed.
4. The vehicle line-up wherein defendant's vehicle was placed and wherein the canine, Scout, and his handler participated, was properly and fairly conducted.
5. The defendant's vehicle and the scent within had not become stale or contaminated at the time of the line-up. The staleness requirement is particularly inapposite since cadaver dogs are able to detect the odor of a cadaver years after it has been in a location. The court thought the fact that the handler was blind to the correct car also added to the weight of the evidence and determined that its admission was proper.[31]

In a 2007 Texas case, the court held that the foundational elements of tracking cases had to be adapted to the situation with cadaver dogs. Reliability, as unfortunately happens all too often, was established solely by the handlers. One handler testified "that she had never known Missy to indicate a false positive, such as alerting on animal remains." The other trainer testified that "Chloe had never given an alert that was later proved false."[32] One of the scent lineup requirements is that the dog be given the scent of a participant in the crime. The court said this does not apply to cadaver dog testimony. The court also held that the "period of efficiency" requirement did not apply to a cadaver dog "because the immediacy of the search is not indicative of the efficiency of the scent."[33]

SCIENTIFIC THRESHOLD FOR CADAVER DOG EVIDENCE

Requirements for admission of scientific evidence have been discussed in a number of cadaver dog cases.[34] In a 2007 Texas case,[35] the defendant objected to the admission of evidence concerning cadaver dogs. The court noted that in "areas of soft science and non-traditional sources of expert testimony,"[36] Texas does not rely on a standard scientific threshold.[37] In *Nenno*,[38] the court had stated that in such nontraditional expertise cases, the questions are (1) whether the field of expertise is a legitimate one, (2) whether the subject matter of the expert's testimony is within the scope of the field, and (3) whether the expert's testimony properly relies on or uses the principles involved in the field. *Nenno* had in 2002 previously been applied to a scent lineup in Texas.[39] The defendant's challenge in the 2007 case was to the third prong of this test concerning the expert's testimony. The court held that this third prong required reviewing (1) the qualifications of the trainer, (2) the qualifications of the dog, and (3) the objectivity of the particular search. All three elements were found to be satisfied.[40]

The court was impressed by the handler and made little inquiry regarding his background. As to the qualifications of the dogs, the court cited the five foundational requirements for a dog used in scent lineups as provided in *Risher*.[41] As to the requirement regarding the breed, the court stated:

> [The handler] explained that because a cadaver dog need not distinguish between the scents of different individuals and need only distinguish between the scent of human and animal remains, a breed such as a bloodhound that is traditionally known for its acuteness of scent is not necessary to use as a cadaver dog. [The handler] explained that a bloodhound is typically not a good cadaver search dog because bloodhounds are "not great obedience dogs" and typically must be worked on a lead, or leash. [The handler] testified that in a large area search, a dog that can work off-lead is more credible because it is free to make an independent find, without the possibility that its handler will lead it to a particular area.

The handler testified that dogs other than bloodhounds, such as Rottweilers, mixed breeds, and Labradors, make good cadaver dogs. The court concluded that "the breed of dog characterized by acuteness of scent is not determinative of a cadaver dog's qualification." Thus, even though the court essentially relied on tracking dog requirements, it was willing to accept that a good tracking dog might not be the best cadaver dog.[42]

TRAINING

Cadaver dogs must not have an aversion to the odor of human remains, though being a scavenging animal, this problem is not particularly common. Dogs should have strong drives to search, air scent, retrieve, play, and keep active. Dogs should not attempt to consume or urinate on body parts. Dogs as old as 4 years have begun cadaver dog training.[43] Both training and service records should be maintained on cadaver dog teams.[44]

Some training is done with artificial scents containing putrescine and cadaverine,[45] substances extracted from decaying organic material, though actual cadaver material, such as blood, hair, or skin tissue, may be used. For training purposes, artificial scents sometimes simulate a recently deceased body. Although human flesh is best for training purposes, there is considerable concern about the biological risks to both dogs and handlers. Cadaverine and putrescine, two artificial scents, are produced from the decarboxylation of amino acids, lysine and arginine, respectively. Pigs have also been used to train cadaver dogs, though it has been demonstrated that dogs can distinguish between human and pig remains.[46] Some certifying organizations prohibit the use of pseudoscents. The National Tactical Police Dog Association specifies that aged blood, body fluids, bone, or tissue are acceptable, and testing samples must weigh at least 15 grams.[47]

Dogs must learn to recognize such smells and the handler must be able to interpret the dog's alert, as ideally should a neutral observer. Dogs must be able to search in varied environments, such as in rubble or piles of building materials, in areas of brush where leaves may have covered a body, and so forth. Bodies or body parts might also be placed in vehicles, buildings, or scattered across an area. Dogs are taught to ignore distracting odors from garbage, food, and deceased animals. Dogs will often be asked to search areas where no human remains are present. Searches must be done in a way that will minimize the risk of disturbing crime scene evidence. Passive alerts are preferred for this reason, though some handlers use aggressive alerts as providing a more restricted identification of a location.[48]

Two researchers in San Bernardino looked at whether training dogs to detect both live scent and cadaver scent impeded their performance in detecting one scent or the other as compared to dogs trained to detect only live scent. This is an important question in circumstances, such as a disaster site, where there may be both types of scent and the dogs are being deployed to find survivors. The researchers found that there was no significant difference in the performance of the two types of dogs (the research involved 11 dogs only trained for live scent searches and 12 cross-trained dogs) when only live scent was present, but when both live and cadaver scent was present, the cross-trained dogs did not perform as well as the live scent dogs. The researchers noted that cross-training dogs might be counterproductive for searches of disaster sites where survivors are being sought because this could lead to using rescue resources at locations where only bodies will be found.[49]

Cadaver dogs may be tested in finding bodies (or parts of bodies) above ground and under water.[50] The North American Police Work Dog Association requires certification tests in a rubble area (simulating a collapsed building), an area where the "scent hides" are under dirt, leaves, brush, or tree branches, with some submerged in 2 feet of water, and some in an organic or inorganic rubbish pile.[51]

HANDLER QUALIFICATION

Cadaver dog handlers must not only be trained to work with the dog but are required to have an awareness of human anatomy and a knowledge of rates of decomposition of human bodies when subjected to different disposal methods, including knowledge of soil types, temperature and moisture effects, scavenger activity, search patterns, communications, and evidence preservation. They must have the "field craft" to be able to assess whether changes in the soil, plant life, and insect population indicate the presence of a potential gravesite. The handler must understand how to set the parameters of the search area and must determine which tools may be necessary to work the area. These could include venting rods, power tools, a machete, a boat, and electronic items including video cameras, GPS trackers, two-way radios, and wind sensors.[52]

Cadaver dog handlers are frequently volunteers, so a good deal of dedication is required to reach the appropriate level of expertise with the dog and other aspects of the work.

CIRCUMSTANCES OF A SEARCH

There are not a large number of cases involving disputes about cadaver dogs. This may in part be due to the fact that finding a cadaver or verifying that a cadaver was at a particular location may often be part of a chain of evidence and may not be particularly important in the prosecution of a case in court.[53] In the *Trejos* case previously discussed regarding scientific standards of cadaver dog evidence, two cadaver dog teams were used.

> [The handler] testified that he observed both dog and handler teams used in this case during their searches for Maria's body on November 9, 2001. He stated that both handlers used their dogs in the manner generally employed by cadaver dog teams. Bickel and Spurlock also testified that their dogs followed the practices and procedures that are generally used in searches by cadaver dogs. The two dogs worked independently of one another, so that they would not influence each other. Bickel testified that Missy performed a grid search on three areas on the property, but only alerted on one. Spurlock testified that there were no outside influences on Chloe's search that would have caused her to alert in a designated area. According to Spurlock, Chloe was simply positioned downwind on the property and instructed to start. Each dog performed its search independently from the handlers, working off-lead. Finally, the dogs alerted to the same location that appellant had indicated Maria's body had been placed.[54]

The court concluded that the cadaver search was conducted objectively. The court also concluded that the cadaver dog testimony was not unfairly prejudicial, noting that it was probative.

Flags or other markers can be used to identify sites requiring further investigation. A written record should be made and available to the lead investigators and crime scene specialists on a case.[55]

Helping Get a Confession

A decomposed body of a woman was found in a plastic bag in the trunk of a car. The man who reported the woman missing was a suspect. An interview of his mother led to the information that he had borrowed one of her cars and it had stunk when he returned it. A cadaver dog alerted to the car the suspect had borrowed. After this and other information was explained to the suspect, he confessed.[56] Cadaver dogs may help focus an investigation.[57]

Cold Cases

Cadaver dogs have been useful in solving cold cases. A case from Maryland concerned a 6-year old girl, Michelle Dorr, who disappeared from her father's house in Silver Spring on May 31, 1986. Carl Dorr, Michelle's father, reported her missing at 4 o'clock that afternoon. He told the police that he was not exactly sure when he had last seen his daughter but thought it was shortly after lunch, about 1 o'clock. He seems to have left her unsupervised in the backyard for several hours before noticing that she was no longer there. Carl Dorr was immediately the prime suspect. The police interviewed him aggressively, which did not allay their suspicions. They kept him under surveillance, tapped his phone, reviewed bank and video rental records, questioned his employers, coworkers, friends, neighbors, and family. Dorr had a series of nervous breakdowns. He announced that he was Jesus Christ and said he could bring Michelle back to life. He was hospitalized but suffered another break-down on release. He made incriminating statements, saying once that he had suffocated Michelle and put her body in a sewer. He also said he had buried her near his father's grave. Michelle's mother appeared on *America's Most Wanted* and said her ex-husband had killed their daughter. Carl saw the television program and went to his ex-wife's house. He demanded to be let in and said he knew where Michelle was and that the truth would burn a hole in his wife's soul.

Lost in the police files accumulated after Michelle's disappearance were some other pieces of evidence that did not point to Carl Dorr. Neighbors of Carl Dorr named the Binders had seem something that did not seem so significant at the time. Their neighbor on the other side, Geoffrey Clark, had been allowing a ne'er-do-well brother named Hadden to stay with him. Hadden was moving out of his brother's house the day of Michelle's disappearance, and the Binders, when asked if they had seen anything unusual, said they had seen Hadden loading a duffel bag and a trunk into his white pickup. But this was no later than 12:20, a time fixed by the Binders, because they had left then or before to attend a baptism. Loading a duffel bag was not, however, very suspicious. First, Hadden was moving. Second, this had occurred at least 40 minutes before Carl Dorr said he had last seen his daughter. Hadden was interviewed twice by the police. The first time was 9 days from Michelle's disappearance and was not informative. The second was 3 days after the first interview. In the second interview, Hadden asked to be excused and went into a bathroom where he cried and vomited. When he returned an officer asked him what he had done to Michelle. "I don't know," he replied. "I may have blacked out. I may have done something." Hadden asked to speak to his psychiatrist. He was permitted to leave the police station. Carl Dorr remained the prime suspect.

In October 1992, over 6 years later, a 23-year-old woman named Laura Houghteling disappeared. Hadden, the one who had loaded the duffel bag onto the pickup, had worked as a handyman at Houthteling's family's residence and Hadden became a suspect in this crime, which revived the memory that he had been interviewed in Michelle Dorr's disappearance. On October 31, 1992, Hadden arrived at his sister's home in Rhode Island, where he complained to her that the police were trying to pin a crime on him because he was homeless. That night he went to his family's plot and camped there for the night. When he returned to Maryland, Hadden Clark was interviewed concerning the disappearance of both Laura and Michelle. Officers went to the cemetery where Hadden had spent the night, and found the soil near the family plot had been disturbed. Similar soil was found in Hadden's truck. A cadaver dog named Dan came with his handler, Massachusetts State Trooper Kathleen Barrett, to the cemetery. Dan alerted to an area near the headstone. A second cadaver dog named Panzer also alerted to the same spot. Hadden Clark pled guilty to second-degree murder in Laura's death and was sentenced to 30 years in prison. While in prison, Hadden gave two cellmates a description of how he had killed Michelle 6 years before Laura. He said he had found her playing in his niece's room (the niece and her parents were not home at the time) and cut her up with a butcher knife. He told his cellmates that he had put her in a trash bag and then in a duffel bag that he had loaded in the back of his truck. This was the event noticed by neighbors but initially ignored because it was inconsistent with the time frame of Michelle's disappearance as given by her father. Because of the description of Michelle's death that Hadden gave to his cellmates, the room where he had described killing her was sprayed with luminol, which causes blood to become luminescent. There was a lot of blood, consistent with Hadden's story. Curiously, DNA testing eliminated Michelle as the source of the blood. The police theorized that Hadden had removed the body of Michelle the night he spent at the cemetery after he became a suspect in Laura's death. Although this was not established on the record, Hadden was finally convicted of second-degree murder in Michelle's death. Michelle's body was later found, again alerted to by a dog.[58]

Alerts of cadaver dogs were corroborated by a confession that the murderer later tried to retract.[59] Evidence concerning the alerts of a cadaver dog in an Ohio case was admitted. The dog had alerted to a box that the body may have been in according to other testimony but not to another location that testimony suggested the body had been. Nevertheless, the court determined that there was sufficient corroboration to admit the testimony concerning the cadaver dog.[60]

INTERFERENCE BY A POLICE OFFICER

In a case that received national attention, a local police chief would not let a search team drain a pond where a cadaver dog had alerted. The next day the pond was drained and no body was found, but speculation continued that the police chief notified the suspect and his family of the impending search of the pond.[61] The body was never found, but the evidence of police complicity was sufficient that a jury awarded the victim's family $3.75 million in a civil suit. The police chief was convicted of obstruction of justice.[62]

CORROBORATION

Cadaver dogs have sometimes provided corroboration for eyewitness testimony, such as the descriptions of children of sexual abuse and murder.[63]

SCENT LINEUPS WITH CADAVER DOGS

Cadaver dogs have been used in scent lineups. A California case describing such a lineup stated that the dog had been used in 6 to 12 prior such lineups.[64] In a New York case, a serial killer killed a woman and a blue Cadillac he drove was identified.

On March 22, 1996, Detective White arranged for an officer in the canine unit to check six cars (including the blue Cadillac) parked on this street with the officer's "cadaver dog," a canine certified as having successfully completed various training exercises to detect body fluids or parts or decaying flesh. The canine officer did not know in advance which car was the object of Detective White's suspicions. He walked the dog down the block past the six cars, and back up the block past five cars. He informed Detective White that his dog had reacted positively to one of the cars—the blue Cadillac registered to defendant's brother.

Light blue carpet fibers were found on some of the victims. The conviction was affirmed.[65]

SCENTING TRACKING DOGS FROM CADAVERS

Scenting a tracking dog from a cadaver has also solved crimes, though the dog involved would not fit in the cadaver dog category. A North Carolina case involved tracking from the location of the victim's body to a car in which she had been transported. The scent was prepared using a hemostat and gauze. The gauze was put in a plastic bag that was then held near the tracking dog's nose to key her to the scent of the victim's body.[66]

NOTES

1. L.E. Papet is the president of K-9 Resources in Kings Mills, Ohio.
2. *Hawaii v. Torres*, 122 Hawaii 2, 222 P.2d 409 (2009) (NCIS use of cadaver dogs).
3. Zanoni et al. (1998) (defining a cadaver dog as one that finds bodies; a decomp dog as one that indicates a scent source of human tissue, blood, semen, urine, feces, and items handled by humans; and a forensic search dog as one that alerts to decomposed human tissue but not urine, feces, or semen; alerting to where someone relieved himself can slow an investigation).
4. *California v. Davison* (Ct. App. January 23, 2008) (dogs alerted to area specified by witness but no bodies found).
5. Dorriety (2007).
6. Lasseter et al. (2003).
7. Ibid.
8. See, for example, *Bailey v. Mississippi*, 960 So.2d 583 (Ct. App. 2007) (two cadaver dogs separately alerted to body in defendant's yard); *Banther v. Delaware*, 823 A.2d 467 (2003) (defendant takes detectives to approximate location of body and cadaver dog finds it); *Burns International Security Services Corp. v. Johnson*, 284 Ga.App. 289, 643 S.E.2d 800 (Ct. App. 2007); *Elliott v. Florida*, 2010 WL 4273186 (Ct. App. 2010) (dog taken to area of map drawn by prisoner, found bones near surface): *Frame v. Texas*, 2006 WL 3627155 (Ct. App. 2007) (cadaver dog alerted at trunk of Lexus and on recliner in home); *Gissendanner v. Alabama*, 949 So.2d 956 (2006); *Green v. Texas*, 2004 WL 3094650 (Ct. Crim. App. 2004) (cadaver dog alerted to house, then to recliner behind which was body); *Koenig v. Maryland*, 368 Md. 150, 792 A.2d 1124 (Ct. App. 2002); *New York v. Lifrieri*, 230 A.D.2d 754, 646 N.Y.S.2d 172 (App. Div. 1996); *Richardson v. Indiana*, 912 N.E.2d 915, 2009 WL 2850342 (2009); *Tennessee v. Casteel*, 2004 WL 2138334 (Ct. Crim. App. 2004) (dog started digging beneath a gate and uncovered a pool of blood); *Tennessee v. Cosgrif*, 2010 WL 4238560 (Ct. Crim. App. 2010) (dog found additional bones after searchers found several bones); *Louisiana v. Murray*, 827 So.2d 488 (Ct. App. 2003); *Tennessee v. Myers*, 2009 WL 2503276 (Ct. Crim. App. 2009) (cadaver dogs alerted to garbage bag containing body after defendant drew map of cemetery); *North Carolina v. Petrick*, 186 N.C.App. 597, 652 S.E.2d 688 (Ct. App. 2007); *South Dakota v. Reay*, 762 NW2d 356 (2009) (cadaver dog alerted at place mentioned by defendant in jailhouse conversation); *California v. Stanton*, 2009 WL 4686320 (Ct. App. 2009) (cadaver dogs found body buried under pile of rocks against canyon wall, some rocks so heavy it took two men to move them); *Tennessee v. Wright*, 2008 WL 160243 (Ct. Crim. App. 2008); *Green v. Quarterman*, 2008 WL 442356 (S.D.Tex. 2008) (dog indicated near chair; detective looked behind chair and found human foot in bag); *Maine v. Atwood*, 988 A.2d 981 (2010) (cadaver dogs found body near camp).
9. *California v. Sherman*, 2003 WL 21500301 (Ct. App. 2003) (cadaver dogs did not uncover a body in an area of dense vegetation populated by large and small predators that may have preyed upon the body); *Tennessee v. Bryan*, 2003 WL 23021396 (Ct. Crim. App. 2003) (cadaver dog did not alert to body which was later found in the same place under soil and leaves, above mound of fresh dirt over body); *Thacker v. Kentucky*, 2005 WL 2675001 (2005) (cadaver dogs twice did not confirm presence of body provided by witness); *Richerson v. Indiana*, 912 N.E.2d 915 (Ct. App. 2009) (cadaver dogs did not find body at first site but found grave at second site); *Weinstein v. Texas*, 2010 WL 2967675 (Ct. App. 2010) (cadaver dog alerted in garage; partially decomposed body found in trunk of car).
10. *California v. Nash*, 2010 WL 159356 (Ct. App. 2010) (cadaver dogs find second leg near location where first leg was discovered); *Connecticut V. Eisenbach*, 2010 WL 2748464 (Super. Ct. 2010) (cadaver dogs alerted to clothing in firepit; shallow grave found near firepit).
11. Komar (1999).
12. *Michigan v. Wright*, 2009 WL 4981153 (Ct. App. 2009) (defendant weighted body and put it in lake).
13. *Spangler v. Wenninger*, 2008 WL 4186318, 2008 WL 4218580 (S.D.Oh. 2008), aff'd 2010 WL 3069600 (6th Cir. 2010) (digging up garage resulted in damage that law enforcement officials did not repair; dogs did recover clothing worn by missing person at time of disappearance).
14. Lowy and McAlhany (2000).
15. *48 Hours/Mystery*, An Eagle-Eyed Investigation? (March 12, 2004) (www.cbsnews.com/stories/2004/03/11/48hours/main605483.shtml).
16. Dorriety (2007).
17. Komar (1999). See also Sorg (1998) (finding 83% correct response in training exercises where human remains had previously been found; postmortem intervals varied from about 15 days to 72 months).
18. Oesterhelweg et al. (2008).

19. Dorriety (2007). For a somewhat different description of decomposition stages, see Lasseter et al. (2003), who describe an extreme decomposition stage after the skeletonization stage (which for them is the fourth stage) where the skeleton itself undergoes deterioration and bone exfoliates.
20. Vass et al. (2004); Vass (2001).
21. Lorenzo et al. (2004).
22. Vass et al. (2008).
23. Zanoni et al (1998).
24. France et al. (1997).
25. This may also say something about how the dogs in the study were trained. A properly trained handler would not deploy a canine that was not ready for the task at hand.
26. The possibility that the dog was not alerting but the observer noticed some change in behavior while the dog was near a buried item was not considered. The observers in the trials appear not to have been blind.
27. Lasseter et al. (2003) (citing Killam 1990).
28. Citing Komar (1999).
29. *Lifrieri v. Stinson*, 2009 WL 2413400 (E.D.N.Y. 2009) (appeal based in part on trial court's admission of testimony of witness as expert on use of cadaver dogs; the testimony was not otherwise described).
30. Citing *California v. Craig*, 86 Cal.App.3d 905, 150 Cal.Rptr. 676 (1978); *California v. Malgren*, 139 Cal. App.3d 234, 188 Cal.Rptr. 569 (1983); *California v. Mitchell*, 110 Cal.App.4th 772, 2 Cal.Rptr.3d 49 (2003).
31. *California v. King*, 2004 WL 2012943 (Ct. App. 2004).
32. *Trejos v. Texas*, 243 S.W.3d 30, 53 (Ct. App. 2007).
33. *Trejos*, at 52.
34. *Clark v. Maryland*, 140 Md.App. 540, 781 A.2d 913 (Ct. Spec. App. 2001); *New York v. Shulman*, 6 N.Y.3d 1, 843 N.E.2d 125, 809 N.Y.S.2d 485 (2005) (sufficient evidence regarding serial murders that challenge to dog scent evidence did not need to be addressed).
35. *Trejos v. Texas*, 243 S.W.3d 30 (Ct. App. 2007).
36. *Texas v. Medrano*, 127 S.W.3d 781, 785 (Ct. Crim. App. 2004).
37. *Kelly v. Texas*, 824 S.W.2d 568 (Ct. Crim. App. 1992).
38. *Nenno v. Texas*, 970 S.W.3d 549, 561 (Ct. Crim. App. 1998), overruled on other grounds, *Texas v. Terrazas*, 4 S.W.3d 720 (Ct. Crim. App.1999).
39. *Winston v. Texas*, 78 S.W.3d 522 (Ct. App 2002).
40. *Trejos v. Texas*, 243 S.W.3d 30 (Ct. App. 2007).
41. *Risher v. Texas*, 227 S.W.3d 133 (Ct. App. 2006).
42. *Trejos v. Texas*, 243 S.W.3d 30 (Ct. App. 2007).
43. Dorriety (2007).
44. Lowy and McAlhany (2000).
45. Commercially available artificial scents are popular with cadaver dog trainers (see Web site of Sigma Pseudo™ products [http://www.elitek9.com/Scent_Detection/index.htm#sigma]).
46. Lorenzo et al. (2004). See the Sigma Pseudo™ corpse scents (www.elitek9.com/Scent_Detection/index. htm#sigma).
47. NTPDA Web site (www.tacticalcanine.com/certification.htm); see also the certification standards of the United States Police Canine Association (www.uspcak9.com/certification/USPCARulebook2010.pdf).
48. The National Tactical Police Dog Association specifies, in its certification standards, that the dog "should show a clear change of behavior and make a definite attempt to work to the source of the odor without offering a fringe alert." NTPDA Web site (www.tacticalcanine.com/certification.htm).
49. Lit and Crawford (2006).
50. National Narcotic Detector Dog Association, "Cadaver Search Certification" (www.nndda.org). Human remains for testing purposes includes bone, fluid, and tissue, but not urine.
51. NAPWDA Web site (www.napwda.com/pdflib/bylaws_cert_rules.pdf).
52. Lowy and McAlhany (2000).
53. *Murray v. Warden Louisiana State Penitentiary*, 2009 WL 703297 (W.D.La. 2009) (cadaver dog's alert to truck was part of reason for interrogation of suspect; suspect led investigators to body, claimed self defense).
54. *Trejos v. Texas*, 243 S.W.3d 30, 54 (Ct. App. 2007).
55. Lowy and McAlhany (2000).
56. *New York v. Payne*, 1 Misc.3d 909, 781 N.Y.S. 627 (Sup. Ct. 2004), aff'd 41 A.D.3d 512, 838 N.Y.2d 123 (App. Div. 2007).
57. *U.S. v. Wong*, 334 F.3d 831 (9th Cir. 2003) (cadaver dogs alerted to trunk of car, leading to further investigation).
58. *Clark v. Maryland*, 140 Md.App. 540, 781 A.2d 913 (Md.Ct.Spec.App. 2001).

59. *Trejos v. Texas,* 243 S.W.3d 30 (Ct. App. 2007).
60. *Ohio v. Smith,* 2002 WL 1972931 (Ct. App. 2002).
61. *Culbertson v. Doan,* 65 F.Supp. 701 (S.D.Oh. 1999). See also *Ohio v. Baker,* 137 Ohio App.3d 628, 739 N.E.2d 819 (Ct. App. 2000) (conviction of half-brother of Doan).
62. Several Web sites are devoted to the case (see, e.g., www.charleyproject.org/cases/c/culberson_clarissa.html).
63. See *Kerr v. Lyford,* 171 F.3d 330 (5th Cir. 1999).
64. *California v. King,* 2004 WL 2012943 (Ct. App. 2004).
65. *New York v. Shulman,* 6 N.Y.3d 1, 843 N.E.2d 125, 809 N.Y.S.2d 485 (2005).
66. *North Carolina v. Taylor,* 337 N.C. 597, 447 S.E.2d 360 (Sup. Ct. 1994).

Section IV

Apprehension and Rescue Functions

Suspect apprehension and search and rescue functions involve using dogs to find people, though in apprehension it is a criminal or suspect that is sought, whereas in search and rescue work the dog is looking for someone who is lost or injured. Although both types of dogs will seek to bring attention to the person found so that the handler can take appropriate action, the functions should not be cross-trained because suspect apprehension involves intimidating the subject, whereas search and rescue involves comforting and saving the subject. Search and rescue dogs, sometimes just called SAR dogs, have become a commonplace at disaster sites, as have therapy dogs. Some dogs perform both search and therapy functions.

20 Suspect Apprehension and Bite Issues

One of the most dangerous assignments that can be given to a police dog is apprehending a suspect.[1] Dogs sometimes range beyond sight of their police handlers when directed to find a fleeing or hiding suspect,[2] and thus must deal with the suspect, though usually only for seconds, before being assisted by the handler. They may be shot or stabbed by the suspect in this time. Conversely, the handler may be attacked while the dog is still in the car and may have to come to the handler's assistance, sometimes by being released from a special crate that the officer opens with a remote device.[3] Suspects have been known to use attack dogs to attempt to scare away police dogs.[4] Sometimes dogs accompany police but are not deployed because a suspect becomes so violent that police have to resort to firearms.[5]

Statistics have been gathered in some locations to determine how often bites lead to injuries and hospitalization. An analysis of data from Montgomery County, Maryland, on the outskirts of Washington, D.C., found that 14.1% of suspects apprehended by canines were bitten, 9.1% received medical attention, but only 4.8% received medical attention at a hospital. The canine bite rate was significantly lower for nonwhite suspects than for white suspects.[6] Results in Los Angeles were very different. Between June 1990 and July 1992, LAPD canines apprehended 539 suspects, 239 of which were bitten, a bite rate of 44%. A higher proportion of minority suspects were bitten, but dogs were also deployed more often in nonwhite neighborhoods.[7]

APPREHENSION STYLES

There are specific commands for apprehension work. "Bite and hold" involves the dog getting a secure grip on the subject and holding the grip until directed to release.[8] "Bark and hold," or "circle and hold," involves the dog barking at and intimidating the subject to stay in one place. Critics have argued that the bark-and-hold approach gives the suspect time to arm himself, find a way to injure the dog, or escape, since the dog is being more of an annoyance than an interference. Some police departments prefer the circle and bark approach, seeing this as more in line with the legal concept of reasonable force. Just as a surrendering suspect does not deserve to be struck with a baton, so neither should a suspect be bitten if he is not resisting.[9] Some departments attempt to use a mixture of the approaches, teaching dogs to bark at the suspect, but to bite if the suspect becomes aggressive or attempts to run.[10] The absence of an immediate safety threat may tip the scales of whether the force used was unreasonable.[11]

BREEDS IN APPREHENSION WORK

One study concluded that German shepherds bite only about half as often as the Belgian Malinois, and found that dogs trained to bark and hold actually bite more often than dogs trained in the bite-and-hold approach.

It may be that canine handlers with "*bark and hold*" dogs may be deploying their canines under circumstances where bite and hold dogs are not. In this scenario, the handler is allowing his or her canine to operate freely in a wider variety of conditions and relying on the training to provide a framework for the dog to make decisions. It is unreasonable for a human officer to rely upon the decision-making abilities of a dog, no matter how well trained. Law enforcement agency policy should clearly define the acceptable and non-acceptable deployments for their canines.[12]

It is the responsibility of the handler to control his dog. A 1992 California case held that an order to search and bite was appropriate when an ATM burglary suspect hiding in bushes might have been armed.[13]

Dogs that have been bred for aggression are often inappropriate for police work, and problems have been noted in pit bulls, Rottweilers, and German shepherds crossed with pit bulls. Off duty, police dogs often have normal social interactions, which they often get with the family of the officer or handler.[14]

TRAINING

One national organization, the National Tactical Police Dog Association (NTPDA), provides for certification that tests a dog's ability to follow a bite command, including a bite under gunfire or return gunfire, the dog's ability to release on command (called "the out"), and calling the dog off ("recall" in obedience terms).[15] In a "tactical area search" evaluation, the suspect, in a bite suit, "shall be hidden for at least 15 minutes before the K-9 Team starts" to search the area. The search may be conducted on- or off-lead depending on safety issues. The team can be evaluated under either a bite-and-hold or bark-and-hold approach, depending on the dog's training, which will usually match the protocols established by the police department for which the team works. The following part of the NTPDA's exam describes how an officer is tested on the "call-off" or recall:

> The officer will be directed to apprehend a suspect in hiding. The handler shall call for the suspect to come out of his hiding place. The suspect shall come out, and the handler shall alert his dog on leash. The suspect will be holding a weapon, and initially refuse to give up. The handler will deploy the K9 to apprehend the suspect, based on the suspect's behavior and/or commands from the evaluator. When the subject "gives up" the dog must be stopped from the attack, either by calling off and returning, or being commanded to down, or continuing to the suspect and performing a hold and bark. The suspect shall become passive upon giving up. The call off shall be a maximum of half the distance to the suspect at the time he gives up.

The dog is to remain behind the suspect while he is escorted out of the area.[16]

The effect of gunfire in a suspect apprehension situation is tested by the North American Police Work Dog Association with the following scenario:

> The dog will begin this phase from the heel position. The suspect carrying a handgun loaded with blanks, which at least have the rapport of a .38 cal. live round, will start approximately 30 yards away from the team and run away. The suspect will fire a minimum of two shots as directed by the Master Trainer. The handler sends his dog when the second shot is fired. The suspect must fire the last shot before the dog gets within five yards of him/her. The dog will apprehend and hold the suspect. Upon the handler's arrival at the location of the dog and suspect and at the direction of the Master Trainer, the handler will order the suspect to drop the weapon and then command the dog to release and call off. ... This phase is complete when the dog is returned to the heel position with the handler.[17]

DEADLY FORCE

Just because a dog can kill a person does not mean that releasing a dog to find or subdue a suspect involves deadly force. The Ninth Circuit has held that permitting a dog to bite a suspect does not automatically mean that deadly force was employed.

Appellant contends that any use of a police dog where the dog is allowed to bite the suspect constitutes deadly force. Appellant is incorrect. We have held that whether the use of a dog to apprehend a suspect constitutes the use of deadly force depends on the individual circumstances. Thus, in situations where the dog has remained under the constant control of the handler and the suspect has not suffered life-threatening injuries, use of a dog has been found not to constitute deadly force.[18] … Because the dog's handler was present at all times, the dog released Appellant when ordered to do so, and there was no evidence that Appellant suffered permanent or life-threatening injuries, the district court did not err in refusing to give Appellant's proposed instruction on deadly force.

The grant of judgment in favor of the city was affirmed.[19]

In a case arising in Tennessee, a police dog killed a burglary suspect by biting him on the neck. The alarm had gone off in a car dealership and a canine team arrived. The officer believed the perpetrator might still be in the building and shouted out a warning that they were going to release a dog. They began to check the building. The dog went into a darkened area ahead of the handler. When the officer arrived, his flashlight revealed the dog holding the suspect's neck in his mouth. "The man was lying face down on the floor with half of his body underneath a car. He did not move. A substantial amount of blood had collected around him and more was oozing from his neck." The officer called off the dog but the suspect was dead. The court concluded that the release of a police dog to find a suspect was not deadly force. "There is no indication from the evidence that Barnes intended Briggs to die or suffer serious bodily harm, or that Barnes in any way deviated from the proper procedures for conducting a building search with a police dog." The court described the situation as an extreme aberration:

> More importantly, we find that the use of a properly trained police dog to apprehend a felony suspect does not carry with it a "substantial risk of causing death or serious bodily harm." Although we cannot ignore the fact that, in this case, the use of a police dog did result in a person's death, we also cannot ignore the evidence in the record which indicates that this tragic event was an extreme aberration from the outcome intended or expected. Lieutenant Spain's deposition testimony was unequivocal on the fact that the dogs are trained to seize suspects by the arm and then wait for an officer to secure the arrestee. While it is impossible to know for certain what happened when Casey found Briggs in the bay of the car dealership, the conclusion compelled by the evidence is that when the dog found the suspect, he was hidden underneath a car, his arms were not within the dog's reach and, unfortunately, his neck was. Since the dog had been trained to seize whatever part of anatomy was nearest if an arm was unavailable, the dog acted consistent with its training by seizing Briggs's exposed neck. Given the remote chance that this particular scenario would occur, we cannot conclude that Barnes released the dog with the knowledge that by doing so, he was creating "a substantial risk" that the dog might kill Briggs.

The court noted that there might be liability if Casey was intentionally trained in a manner that was not proper, but no liability would apply if the improper training were due to simple negligence.

> We do not dispute the fact that trained police dogs can appear to be dangerous, threatening animals. The dogs' ability to aid law enforcement would be minimal if they did not possess this trait. However, the mere recognition that a law enforcement tool is dangerous does not suffice as proof that the tool is an instrument of deadly force. As we already have stated, the totality of the factors present in a particular case determine whether deadly force was used to apprehend a suspect. Accordingly, we affirm the district court's conclusion that, although in this particular case the use of a police dog to apprehend a suspected felon resulted in that felon's death, deadly force was not used to seize the felon.

The court noted that the seizure here was not unreasonable even if it did involve deadly force.[20]

In a 1997 California case, Vera Cruz began throwing objects at a fast food restaurant when employees refused to serve him after closing time. A policeman arrived with a K-9 companion.

Escondido Police Officer Eric Distel and his K-9 companion were the first to arrive at the scene. Distel spotted Vera Cruz in a doorway at the rear of the Del Taco throwing objects out of the building. When the officer identified himself, Vera Cruz began walking away. Distel then warned Vera Cruz to stop or he would release the dog; Vera Cruz started running. After giving another warning, Distel released the dog, who bit Vera Cruz on the right arm, bringing him to the ground. After disarming Vera Cruz, Distel ordered the dog to release his bite, and the dog immediately complied. Vera Cruz sustained a large laceration and several puncture wounds on his upper right arm; he required surgery and 8 days of hospitalization.

The trial court declined a deadly force instruction. The Ninth Circuit considered the significance of the term. "Although we have mentioned the 'significant risk of death or serious bodily injury' formulation in three other dog bite cases, we have done so only in dicta." The circuit court noted that Vera Cruz presented no evidence that properly trained police dogs are reasonably capable of causing death, or even that they can kill under any circumstances.

Nevertheless, we will assume that a properly trained police dog could kill a suspect under highly unusual circumstances. The prospect of such an aberration doesn't convert otherwise nondeadly force into deadly force. … In judging whether force is deadly, we do not consider the result in a particular case—be it that the suspect was killed or injured—but whether the force used had a reasonable probability of causing death. … To be entitled to a deadly force instruction, a plaintiff must present evidence that the force used, in the circumstances under which it was used, posed more than a remote possibility of death. Because Vera Cruz presented no such evidence, the district court did not err in refusing to give a deadly force instruction.

The circuit court affirmed the district court's decision not to give a deadly force instruction.[21]

A Ninth Circuit case involved a chase of driver who had been speeding and running red lights. The driver finally drove his car onto the lawn of a restaurant and fled on foot. The court held:

Even assuming that the use of dogs trained to bite and seize constitutes the use of deadly force, we hold that the use of the dog in this case, by officers wishing to prevent harm to themselves and residents in the area, was objectively reasonable.

The police had qualified immunity in any case.[22]

EXCESSIVE FORCE

Courts have acknowledged that releasing a dog may sometimes be the least forceful means of apprehending a fleeing suspect. In a case arising in Illinois, a dog had to be released a second time when the suspect began to try to get something out of his clothing, which was later found to be a gun.[23] Failure to comply with an instruction to remain still justified not recalling a dog once the dog apprehended a suspect.[24] The ability of an officer to call off a dog once the suspect stopped struggling has been enough to deny an excessive force claim.[25]

In a California case from 1994, police Rottweilers bit a bank robber when he came out of some bushes in which he had been hiding. The court stated:

Mendoza did not surrender when warned that he would be bitten if he did not come out of the bushes. He was hiding on private property and the deputies could reasonably have believed he posed a danger not only to themselves but also to the property owners. He had not been subdued when the dog bit him the second time. In fact, once he was out of the bushes, he struggled with the dog, causing the dog to shift its bite. Using a police dog to find Mendoza, and to secure him until he stopped struggling and was handcuffed, was objectively reasonable under these circumstances.

The Ninth Circuit affirmed the district court's dismissal on the grounds of qualified immunity.[26]

In a 1999 case, the Eighth Circuit gave qualified immunity to deputies who were facing a highly armed suspect who killed a police dog.

> The facts of this case, even when viewed in the light most favorable to Ms. Mettler, reveal that Deputies Haltiner and Whitledge fired at Shawn only after Shawn had first shot and killed Bud, the police dog. The two deputies were standing scarcely twenty feet from the shooter, facing a suspect with a high-powered weapon who was hiding in a darkened garage, was concealed by a parked car, and had exhibited a willingness to resist an exercise of police authority through the use of deadly force. Given these circumstances, we find no "clearly established" constitutional right that Deputies Haltiner and Whitledge violated. Therefore, Deputies Haltiner and Whitledge are protected by qualified immunity from [42 U.S.C.] § 1983[27][27] liability for their role in the shooting death of Shawn Michael Mettler.

The circuit court concluded that the district court should have granted the deputies summary judgment on the excessive force claim, and directed that summary judgment be entered on the grounds of qualified immunity.[28] A threatening movement toward the handler, resulting in a dog bite, has provided qualified immunity.[29]

HANDLER'S HISTORY OF EXCESSIVE FORCE CLAIMS

A history of excessive force claims involving the handler and his dog was excluded by a district court in New Mexico even though the suspect had complied with an order to put his hands in the air, the officer had commanded the dog to bite him a second time. The Tenth Circuit found this not to be an abuse of discretion.[30]

A plaintiff in a suit against various officials argued that the handler had a habit and practice of using excessive force with police dogs. The plaintiff had sought a more sharply worded instruction to the jury regarding the use of police dogs. The trial court had instructed the jury as follows:

> A police dog is a tool of law enforcement. Its use constitutes the use of force. The force resulting from the use of a police dog can be proper or excessive, just as a gun, baton or other tool can be.

The appellate court found that this was a correct statement of law. The jury had returned a verdict in favor of the officer and the district court dismissed the action against the city and its officials, concluding that there could be no basis for their liability where the officers had been exonerated by the jury. The circuit court affirmed.[31]

CIRCUMSTANCES OF THE APPREHENSION

A great many cases involve claims of harm that arose from the release of a dog to apprehend a suspect. It is worthwhile to deal with the facts of some of these cases to understand what logic courts may apply. Officers in the field will have to know both departmental policies and applicable judicial decisions in the jurisdictions where they operate.

DEPLOYING DOGS TO FIND SUSPECTS

Police dogs trained in apprehending suspects often have some tracking skills,[32] though some trainers caution against using patrol dogs to track.[33] Let loose in a commercial laundry with a command to find the burglars, a German shepherd searched the building and found a ladder that led to the roof. The suspects were found hiding in an alley nearby. The dog had gone to the ladder that the perpetrators used to exit the building.[34] In a 2002 California case, suspects in a gang murder were tracked from the site where their car crashed into the laundry room in a building. One suspect surrendered on the threat of the dog being turned loose but said no one else was in the laundry room. The dog was released and barked at a door inside the room, where another suspect was found.[35]

In one California case, a dog was deployed after a helicopter unit located a heat source in an abandoned building. The dog found and bit the person hiding in the building, who was identified as the perpetrator.[36]

BITES DURING STRUGGLES

Struggling against a dog and the officer-handler will generally preclude a successful excessive force claim for an ensuing bite. A California case described such a situation:

> Planas and Devey then searched the backyard area and saw Parra attempting to flee. After instructing Parra to stop, the officers released the police dog and gave the dog a "search" command. The dog found Parra, bit him in the foot and pulled Parra off a truck. While Parra struggled with the dog, the dog bit him five times in the arm, leg and foot. At the same time, Planas hit Parra several times on the back and buttocks with his baton. The incident lasted twenty to twenty-five seconds. Once Parra was subdued, Planas commanded the dog to release its bite, and it released Parra.

Parra brought a civil action for deprivation of rights under 42 U.S.C. 1983. The district court dismissed the action and the Ninth Circuit affirmed.[37] Subduing an individual is sometimes required even for traffic stops. In a case from Maine, an individual being arrested for outstanding warrants became sufficiently violent as to justify the use of a dog.[38]

SUBDUING SUSPECT BY DOG AS ARREST

In a 1992 California case, officers pursued two suspects who had attempted to break into an ATM. The suspects fled at first in a car and then on foot. A police dog was released with the command to search and bite, and found a suspect in the bushes. The dog bit the suspect at the top of the scalp because he could not reach anything else. When the officer saw the man was unarmed he called off the dog, which had been biting the man for about 15 seconds. The suspect argued that the use of the dog turned the action into an arrest requiring probable cause. The appellate court found that even if there was an arrest, there was probable cause. The threat was high enough to justify the officer's order to his dog to search and bite, given that the suspect might have been armed.[39]

FAILURE TO USE LEAD

Duluth police officers received a complaint about a party near the University of Minnesota-Duluth. Dennen, a 20-year-old honors student, was very drunk. When instructed to take a preliminary breath test outside the building, Dennen went upstairs instead and attempted to hide under a futon. He was again told to go outside for the test but left the area. Less than an hour later, Dennen was seen several blocks from the party. Dennen saw the patrolling officer and ran away. The officer, Paterson, had a dog and they began to look for the student. The dog was not on a leash when it picked up a scent and ran ahead of the officer. The officer caught up and leashed the dog but the dog may have encountered Dennen before the officer found him. Dennen was lying face down in a creek bed. He was rushed to a hospital with a severe head injury. A toxicology report found barbiturates, amphetamines, and alcohol in his system. There were scratches on his arms that might have been bite marks. He remained in a coma for weeks and spent over a year in rehabilitation. He had no memory of the night but sued for excessive use of force in violation of the Fourth Amendment, creating liability under 42 U.S.C. 1983. The court noted that no case was cited by Dennen, and the court could find none, that it was per se excessive use of force to use a canine without a leash.

Moreover, it would not be practical to require a police officer to always have his canine on a leash. There are a variety of instances when it would not be appropriate to do so. For example, there is no need to have a canine on a leash if an officer is talking to children in a school, or when the dog is sniffing for contraband. Particularly, a leash would not be required in circumstances where officer safety is concerned.

The Eighth Circuit concluded that the officer's actions were objectively reasonable.

Peterson had a concern for his own safety. He was walking at night in a dark area behind houses in a part of town known for some rowdiness and criminal activity. The person that he wanted to question had just disappeared after behaving curiously. He did not know if that person had a weapon or would jump out at him from behind a house.[40]

In a California case, dog bites were held not to be seizures because the attack did not involve the requisite intentional conduct. The officer did not intend to use the dog to subdue the plaintiffs and was not even aware the dog had left the car until one of the girls screamed. The officer did not intentionally deploy the dogs during the investigative stop. Summary judgment of dismissal was affirmed.[41]

SUSPECTS POSSIBLY CARRYING WEAPONS

Officers often direct dogs to bite and hold for fear that the suspect may be armed.[42] This is particularly common when the handler cannot see the hands of the suspect. In a California case, a suspect fled on foot after a high-speed chase and was believed to be hiding in a residential back yard. The officer released the dog, Heros, after shouting a warning. The dog alerted beside a fence and looking over the officer saw the suspect but only the upper part of his body. The testimony of the officer and the suspect diverged at this point. The officer said that he thought the suspect might be reaching for a weapon. The suspect testified that he was trying to surrender when the officer ordered the dog to bite. Once the officer had control of the suspect, he called the dog off. A jury accepted the officer's version of events, and the appellate court affirmed.[43]

SENDING A DOG INTO A HOUSE WITHOUT A WARRANT

Exigent circumstances justifying officers in the decision to send a dog into a house without a warrant include the fact that the person in the house had called a relative to say he was holding a gun and would commit suicide.[44]

RELEASE OF SUSPECT ON COMMAND

An excessive force claim will generally not succeed if the dog involved in an apprehension released its hold on the handler's command. After a high-speed chase in California, a suspect climbed over a fence into a truck yard. The officer announced that if the suspect did not come out, the dog would be sent in to find him:

After receiving no response, Wells released the dog, which almost immediately found Quintanilla hiding between two trucks, beyond the officers' reach. The dog bit Quintanilla's arms and legs. The officers heard the scuffling, ran to the scene, and observed Quintanilla in control of the dog, holding it in a headlock. Wells repeatedly ordered Quintanilla to release the dog and surrender, but he refused. Wells then entered the area between the trucks, dragged Quintanilla out into an open area, where the other officers handcuffed him, and ordered the dog away. The dog immediately complied. The scuffle with the dog lasted approximately 1 minute. Quintanilla required medical treatment but suffered no serious injuries.

The Ninth Circuit noted that the dog was trained to release on command and had done so and affirmed the district court's refusal to give the jury a deadly force instruction.[45]

FAILURE TO SHOUT WARNING

A frequent issue concerns whether a warning was shouted before releasing a dog. The Eighth Circuit has noted that "the presence or absence of a warning is a critical fact in virtually every excessive force case involving a police dog." The facts that brought this issue to the court are described as follows:

> After fleeing a routine traffic stop in the early morning hours, the plaintiff-appellant, Jeffrey M. Kuha, was tracked to a grassy field by two police officers and a police dog. The dog, trained to bite and hold until commanded to release, bit Kuha near his groin, severing his femoral artery.

Kuha brought an excessive force claim based on the use of a dog for a minor traffic violation, failure to give a warning before releasing the dog, and failure to call the dog off. The Eighth Circuit cited a series of cases involving warnings,[46] but determined that the officers were not on notice that a warning was necessary.

> Kuha's right to a verbal warning in this case was not clearly established at the time of the seizure. Officers Anderson and Warosh were not on notice that it arguably was constitutionally impermissible to use a police dog against Kuha without a verbal warning under the circumstances of this case. ... There are no cases from this circuit that mandate such a warning and a review of other circuits offers little guidance on the issue. In most of the published K-9 bite cases, the fighting issue is whether the initial decision to release the dog was objectively reasonable under the circumstances. Where a verbal warning was given, the subsequent release of the dog to locate a hiding suspect has generally met that test. It does not necessarily follow, however, that it was clearly established that the absence of a verbal warning was objectively unreasonable.

The officers were entitled to qualified immunity. The court held that the city, on the other hand, might be liable because of its policy to use the bite and hold method, and its failure to mandate a warning before release of a dog. Whether the city's policy required a warning was a question of fact for the trial court to resolve and the case was remanded.[47]

The Eighth Circuit also considered a case where a homeless person was mistaken for a crash victim in which similar issues were raised. Henry Szabla was sleeping in a shelter for portable toilets, hoping to be first in line for a nearby temporary employment agency the next day. The police found a car rammed into a tree nearby and abandoned. The driver was missing and officers requested a police dog to help them locate him or her. Items in the car suggested it might have been stolen and used for a burglary.

> Baker put on Rafco's tracking harness and took him to the wrecked car to get the scent of the driver. Then Baker gave Rafco the command to "track," which means to find and apprehend a person. The track command focuses on one person and instructs the dog to bite and hold the person until the handler arrives. In contrast, a "search" command would have told the dog to range out over an area and follow any scent that comes up. When told to "search," the dog should not bite. When tracking, the dog is kept on a tracking harness with a lead. Baker testified that because he did not know whether the driver was fleeing because he was involved in a crime or whether the driver had a head injury or needed medical attention, Baker reduced the fifteen-foot lead to less than six feet. Baker testified that the dog was so close his tail was brushing Baker's knees.
>
> Baker and the dog ran through the park. They approached the shelter for the portable toilets. As soon as he came by the wall, Rafco turned in the shelter and bit Henry Szabla, who was lying on the floor of the shelter. Szabla turned over, and grabbed the dog's head; the dog lost his hold and bit Szabla again. Baker ordered Szabla to show his hands. When Szabla put his hands out, Baker called the dog off. Szabla had bites on his legs. The number of actual bites was not clear from the record, but Szabla counted twenty-three tooth punctures on his legs and hip. ...
>
> When the police determined from talking to Szabla that he had no relationship to the car wreck, they took off the cuffs. Szabla himself estimated that he was in handcuffs for about "two minutes, if that."

Szabla heard one of the officers say, "I gave the dog too much leash." Szabla was taken to the hospital by ambulance and treated for the bites.

Szabla understandably sued. The district court granted summary judgment to the defendants.

[T]he officer accompanied the dog, rather than allowing the dog to run loose. Keeping the dog on the lead gave the officer more control over the dog, but it also exposed the officer to greater risk. In both cases, the officer was running with the dog, at night, searching for a person who had fled and whose whereabouts were unknown. Szabla argues that this case is distinguishable from *Kuha* because Baker used a dog to track a person who may have fled because he was injured or ill, not because he wanted to evade the police. This distinction is indeed relevant to the Fourth Amendment reasonableness of Baker's use of the track command, but it does not demonstrate that any reasonable officer would have known on August 17, 2000, that a prior warning was constitutionally required in these circumstances. Baker is therefore entitled to summary judgment on the ground of qualified immunity.

The circuit court determined that given the circumstances there was reason to believe Szabla could have been involved in criminal activity. The court determined that the city that employed the officers might, however, be liable and reversed the trial court's dismissal as to it.[48]

A Fourth Circuit case was reversed and remanded for trial where there was an issue of fact as to whether an officer had issued a warning before releasing a dog. Though other officers said they had heard the warning, a bystander said he had not.[49]

FAILURE TO CALL OFF DOG

In an Eleventh Circuit case, an officer called for canine backup because he saw tracks leading away from a store that had been burglarized. The dog went into nearby woods where, after about 20 minutes, the dog found a suspect hiding in a canal. The suspect said he had been drinking and hid because he was violating parole terms. The canine officer directed the suspect to lie down or he would release the dog on him. Plaintiff testified that the officer ordered the dog to attack him even though he did lie down.

When Plaintiff kicked the dog to stop the dog from biting him, Wheeler let go of the dog's leash, drew his gun, pointed it at Plaintiff's head and said: "You kick him again, I will blow your mother fucking brains out." Although Plaintiff was begging that the dog be called off, both Defendants stood and watched "for an eternity" while the dog continued to attack and to bite Plaintiff on both legs.

The Eleventh Circuit concluded that the evidence was sufficient for the jury to find that the officer was liable for use of excessive force and that the other officer was liable for failing to intervene.[50]

In a Washington case from 2003, an individual had refused to stop for an officer's flashing light and ran into the woods. The use of the dog was neither deadly nor excessive force under the circumstances. In the 45- to 60-second period that the dog bit and held the suspect, the dog had torn through the suspect's biceps all the way to the bone. The court held that even though a police dog can kill a suspect, the possibility is remote and deploying the dog "does not convert otherwise nondeadly force into deadly force." The court emphasized the dog's training and the officer's control:

Deputy Bylsma knew that a trained police dog could be trusted to neutralize the many strategic advantages that Miller had obtained by crouching in the darkness in a remote and unbounded landscape familiar only to Miller and treacherous to others who might enter. Deputy Bylsma knew of the keen nose, acute vision, stealthy speed, natural courage, and lupine strength of the German Shepherd—qualities at the service of the dog's fine instincts and careful training. Deputy Bylsma knew that, despite the darkness, the dog was trained to find, seize, and hold Miller, careful not to hurt Miller more than necessary to disarm, disorient, and restrain him until deputies arrived on the scene seconds later. Deputy Bylsma knew that the dog, trained to obey, would release Miller as soon as Deputy Bylsma determined it was safe and gave the command. He knew that the dog was trained to effect Miller's arrest as safely as possible under the circumstances. In sum, Deputy Bylsma knew that a police dog's excellent canine qualities were well suited to the important task of capturing a fleeing felon in this ominous setting, a threatening landscape that might have filled even staunch human hearts with dread.

The conviction was affirmed.[51]

A case that was much less forgiving of the officer's delay in calling off a dog arose in Oakland, California. The incident was described by the Ninth Circuit:

> On November 20, 1993, Officer Chew and his police canine "Nero" responded to a silent alarm at Hart & Son Auto Body Shop, a commercial warehouse in Oakland. Four other Oakland police officers also responded. Upon arrival, the officers established a perimeter outside the warehouse because they had seen a person running within the building. There was no evidence as to whether the person was armed. Before releasing Nero to search for the person, Officer Chew announced twice: "This is the Oakland Police Department canine unit. Give yourself up or I'll release my dog who is going to find you and he is going to bite you." Watkins did not surrender to the police and claims that he did not hear the announcement. Officer Chew released Nero, a 72 pound German Shepherd, to search. Nero ran out of sight of Officer Chew, located Watkins who was hiding in a car, and bit him. Upon arriving at the scene, Officer Chew did not call Nero off of Watkins; instead, he ordered Watkins to show his hands. Watkins, who was recoiling from the dog's bite, failed to comply. Officer Chew then pulled Watkins out of the car onto the ground. Nero continued to bite until Watkins complied with Officer Chew's orders to show his hands.
>
> Officer Chew and Officer David Walsh, another officer at the scene, testified that ten to fifteen seconds elapsed between the time Officer Chew ordered Watkins to show his hands and the time Watkins complied with that order. The officers both agree that Nero continued to bite Watkins throughout that period. In a later statement to the OPD Internal Affairs Division, Officer Chew stated that the time period was about thirty seconds.
>
> Officer Chew justified his delay in calling off Nero because Watkins, while resisting the dog, failed to show his hands to prove that he was unarmed. Watkins explained that he did not show his hands because he was resisting the dog and recoiling from the pain of Nero's attack. Watkins further claims that Officer Chew continued to allow Nero to bite him even though he was obviously helpless and surrounded by police officers with their guns drawn.

The court held that under the law at the time of the incident, the duration of a bite and encouragement by officers could constitute excessive force. The Ninth Circuit affirmed the district court's denial of the motions for qualified immunity by the two officers involved.[52]

REPEATED BITE COMMANDS

A case that disturbed the Ninth Circuit enough to remand for a trial concerned police response to a domestic violence report. Smith's wife called to say that her husband was beating her. A canine unit, consisting of Officer Aaron Medina and Quando arrived. Smith was outside the house but uncooperative. The court summarized subsequent events:

> Several more officers then moved onto the porch, grabbed Smith from behind, slammed him against the door, and threw him down on the porch; Officer Quinn ordered the canine to attack him. Quando bit Smith on his right shoulder and neck area. At some point, either before or after the order to attack, the dog sank his teeth into Smith's arm and clung to it.
>
> With at least four officers surrounding him and Quando's teeth sunk into his shoulder and neck, Smith agreed to comply with the officers' orders and submit to arrest. Although Smith submitted, he admits that he was "curled up" in a fetal position in an attempt to shield himself from the dog and that one of his hands was "tucked in somewhere," still out of the officers' view. As one of the officers attempted to secure both arms, Quando was instructed by Officer Quinn to bite Smith a second time; this time the dog bit Smith on his left side and shoulder blade. Upon Officer Quinn's order, Quando ultimately retreated, and the officers dragged Smith off the porch, face down. Once off the porch, Smith

continued to shield one of his arms from the dog's attack. Officer Quinn then ordered Quando to bite Smith a third time. This time, the dog bit into Smith's buttock. While all this was transpiring, Smith was pepper-sprayed at least four times, at least two of which sprayings occurred after the police dog had seized him and broken his skin, and at least one after the officers had pinned him to the ground.

Eventually, the officers secured the handcuffs on both of Smith's arms. Officer Reinbolt then washed Smith's eyes out with water from a nearby hose, but did not cleanse the wounds he received as a result of the dog bites. Paramedics arrived shortly thereafter and attended to Smith's injuries.

Smith filed an action for excessive force. The district court granted summary judgment for the officers, but the circuit court held the severity and extent of the force, and the possibility of doing things more peacefully, meant that the matter should not have been received summary judgment. The court also considered whether the use of Quando, the police dog, constituted deadly force.

We need not here determine whether the use of a police dog to subdue a suspect constitutes deadly force generally or the circumstances under which such use might constitute such force. Having announced the definition of "deadly force" we leave to the district court the first opportunity to apply the concept to the facts of this case. We note only that while we have not in any of our prior cases found that the use of police dogs constituted deadly force, we have never stated that the use of such dogs cannot constitute such force.

The case was remanded.[53]

BITES OF BYSTANDERS

A private duty nurse was sleeping after a night shift when a tenant in the basement returned home. The door to the tenant's apartment was open and he suspected a break-in. He called the police, who brought a dog that was commanded to "find him." The dog went upstairs and into the living quarters of the nurse.

The dog bounded to the bed where Vathekan slept and bit into the left side of her skull. She struggled in vain to escape as the dog shook her violently. Suddenly, the dog let go of Vathekan's skull and then clamped its jaws firmly onto the right side of her face. Vathekan was now wide awake and fully conscious of the cracking sound of the bones in her face being crushed under the dog's vise-like grip. From his position across the street, Lopez could distinctly hear Vathekan's screams of terror and pain. ...

Vathekan was carried from the scene in an ambulance, and she would spend the next 6 days in the hospital. Vathekan suffered serious and painful injuries from this attack, including deep lacerations to her head and face, fractured facial bones, and a permanently damaged tear duct in her right eye. She still experiences pain and discomfort from the injuries. And, although she has apparently had some reconstructive surgery, her face remains scarred and disfigured.

The district court dismissed the action, finding that the dog's actions did not shock the conscience as required for a violation of substantive due process. The circuit court disagreed, and reversed and remanded for trial.[54] This case and others eventually led to a Federal Bureau of Investigation (FBI) investigation of the Prince George's Canine Unit.[55]

Bites of bystanders have been considered by courts in other countries.[56]

INNOCENT SUSPECTS ACTING LIKE PERPETRATORS

In a 2005 New Mexico case, a high-speed chase began because the police tried to pull over a car with a broken license plate lamp and the driver did not stop. The police mistakenly believed the car contained burglars. The car hit a wall.

The first officer at the scene was Defendant Lehocky. Lehocky testified that Marquez exited the car from the passenger side door, ignored Lehocky's command to stop and attempted to flee the scene. Lehocky ordered his police service dog, Bart, to apprehend the suspect. Bart complied and latched firmly onto Plaintiff Marquez. Meanwhile, Perkins [the driver], who had briefly exited the car, was now back in the car attempting to drive off. Lehocky then ordered Marquez, with Bart still firmly attached to her, away from the rear of the car. By this time, Officer Heshley had arrived and ordered Perkins out of the vehicle. Perkins complied and was taken into custody by Officer Heshley. Simultaneously, Defendant Lehocky removed Bart from Plaintiff Marquez and took her in custody.

Marquez sued for excessive force, but a jury decided for the defendants. The high-speed chase indicated that Marquez, whom the police reasonably believed had been involved in a burglary (though she had not), was a danger to the public and willing to evade arrest. The circuit court said that the Fourth Amendment does not require the least intrusive means of detention, only a reasonable one.[57]

SADISTIC POLICE OFFICERS

An extreme case arose in Maryland. Two men were seen on the roof of a commercial building and backup was requested, including a police dog. The two men came down from the roof with their hands in the air.

As the suspects stood with their hands up in the air, Delozier approached Bonn and asked: "Sarge, can the dog get a bite?" Bonn "responded with one word, which was yes." Bonn testified that "[a]t that time, [the suspects] still had their hands in the air and they weren't doing anything." Bonn then witnessed Delozier and Mohr have "a very, very brief exchange," followed by Mohr releasing the dog. The dog attacked Mendez, who "still had his hands in the air when ... the dog bit him in the leg. [He] went down screaming and continued to scream." Bonn testified that, prior to Mohr's release of the dog, Mendez did not make "any sudden movement," did not "fail to comply with police command[s]," did not "lower his hands," and did not "attempt to flee in any way." Bonn did not hear any K-9 warning prior to Mohr's release of the dog or at any point during the evening. As a result of the incident, Bonn pled guilty as an accessory-after-the-fact to a civil rights violation and testified for the government pursuant to a plea agreement.

At least one of the bites Mendez suffered was serious. The suspects were homeless and were simply sleeping on the roof. A grand jury indicted the officers on various charges. The first trial resulted in a hung jury, but Mohr was convicted in a second trial, while Delozier was acquitted. Mohr was sentenced to 10 years in prison.[58]

DOGS TRAINED TO APPREHEND SUSPECTS ALERTS TO DRUGS

Sometimes a dog being used for one function begins performing another function in which it has received training. A dog taken to a residence that had been broken into began alerting to drugs that were lying around the house. The Sixth Circuit held that the drugs were covered by the plain-view and plain-sniff doctrines.[59]

CROWD CONTROL

Crowd control includes breaking up gang fights as well as stopping mob activity.[60] Although often depicted as a phenomenon of the civil rights and anti-Vietnam War movements, crowd control now often involves rock concerts. Police took dogs to a Grateful Dead concert, knowing that many fans would try to get in without paying. They were prepared for the "sacrificial lamb" tactic, where one fan would try to run toward the fence and attempt to climb it, thereby occupying a number of officers, while other fans would use the distraction to storm the fence at another point. The sacrificial lamb was bitten by Robo, a police dog, resulting in an excessive force claim. The jury found for the police, and the court denied a motion by the plaintiff for a new trial.[61] Sports events are also places where confrontations between groups of people must be controlled,[62] as are bars.[63]

The Army's Military Working Dog Program manual specifies that a patrol dog should not be used except against a person engaging in readily apparent criminal behavior. Dogs can even escalate violence.

> The crowd often will challenge the MPs to use the patrol dogs as a measure of force, particularly if a situation can be provoked that can later be interpreted or challenged as being an unreasonable use of force by the authorities. According to crowd psychology, the crowd reasons that when authorities act unreasonably, the crowd is then justified in also taking unreasonable actions.[64]

GOVERNMENT POLICIES

A situation that arose in West Palm Beach, Florida, was described by the Eleventh Circuit:

> In the early morning of July 7, 1982, Josh Terrell fell asleep in the front yard of a West Palm Beach home. He was drunk. The sound of police activity and barking subsequently awakened him, and he moved to some bushes at the side of the house, where he again laid down. The police activity was in response to a burglary in the neighborhood. Because the police believed that the suspect might still be in the vicinity, the officers called in Officer Pontieri and his dog, Sultan, to search the area. Sultan picked up a scent and led Pontieri to the side yard of a house, where the dog alerted on Terrell, who was asleep in the bushes. Pontieri told Sultan to "Get 'em," and the dog attacked Terrell, locking onto his arm. Pontieri told the dog to pull back, at which command the dog began to drag Terrell out of the bushes. In so doing, the dog reestablished its grip, biting Terrell again in the arm. Once Terrell was in the open, Pontieri ordered Sultan to release Terrell, who was screaming in pain. Terrell then got up and moved toward Pontieri, who knocked him to the ground by hitting Terrell on the head with a flashlight. Pontieri then handcuffed Terrell, at which point Terrell was again bitten, this time on the thigh. Terrell was then taken to Good Samaritan Hospital, where his wounds were treated. Terrell was not, in fact, the individual the police suspected as having committed the burglary.

Facts involving two other individuals who joined in the suit were also described. The court spent considerable space describing the canine unit of the West Palm Beach Police Department, noting, among other things:

> The Department had no specialized internal procedures for monitoring the performance of the canine unit. Instead, the Department relied on a general system of "force reports," which were prepared by the shift commander upon being notified that an officer had used force to make an apprehension. Under the Department's policy, supervisory personnel—including the chief of police—subsequently reviewed each report to establish that excessive force had not been applied. The force reports were not compiled to keep track of the acceptability of the performance of individual dogs in the canine unit, and were usually discarded after 30 days. The force reports, therefore, were not an effective mechanism for ensuring that misbehaving dogs would be withdrawn from use or given corrective training.

The Eleventh Circuit concluded that a reasonable jury could have found that the city of West Palm Beach and its former police chief knew that the canine unit was operating in an unacceptable manner and that they failed to take remedial action, thus becoming deliberately indifferent to the constitutional rights of the plaintiffs in this case. The circuit court vacated the judgment that had been granted the municipal officials despite the verdict and directed the district court to reinstate the jury's verdict in favor of the plaintiffs against the city and its former police chief. The district court, however, was held not to have erred in declining to certify the action as a class action.[65]

In another California case, the Ninth Circuit held that though the most serious injury to a suspect during an arrest came from the officer, not the dog, the injuries might have come about because the officer was protecting the dog. Therefore, the policies of Los Angeles regarding dog team training could lead to liability, but the plaintiff was already compensated for the injuries and would not be able to obtain punitive damages against the city. Punitive damages against the LAPD Chief Daryl Gates for the city's dog bite policy were possible on remand, however, and on remand the trial court was to determine if Chief Gates had adopted and maintained a policy of training and using police dogs in an unreasonable manner.[66]

The Department of Justice has signed memoranda of agreements with some municipalities regarding use of force, and such provisions often restrict canine off-leash deployments as well as affect training procedures.[67]

APPLICATION OF DOG BITE LAWS TO POLICE DOGS

In a 2005 Minnesota case, the police came to arrest a husband but the wife got in the way. When Andrew Hyatt ran toward the back of the room, Yates released Chips. Instead of pursuing Andrew Hyatt, Chips apprehended Lena Hyatt, taking her to the ground and performing a bite and hold on her left leg and right arm. With the animal holding Lena Hyatt, Yates pursued Andrew Hyatt, who fled through a second-story window. When Yates later reentered the room, he released Chips from Lena Hyatt and instructed Lenzmeier to handcuff and arrest her on suspicion of obstruction of legal process. Lena Hyatt was taken by ambulance to a Coon Rapids hospital and treated for a 2-inch laceration on her right elbow and a 5-inch laceration on her left knee. Hyatt sued on the basis of the Minnesota's dog bite statute, which read:

> If a dog, without provocation, attacks or injures any person who is acting peaceably in any place where the person may lawfully be, the owner of the dog is liable in damages to the person so attacked or injured to the full amount of the injury sustained. The term "owner" includes any person harboring or keeping a dog but the owner shall be primarily liable. The term "dog" includes both male and female of the canine species.[68]

Although the appellate court held that Hyatt could not pursue a claim under the state's dog bite statute, the Minnesota Supreme Court reversed, saying that she could.[69]

A police dog that attacked a neighbor of the officer could be sued in his official capacity despite the fact he was off-duty at the time because departmental policy required that he keep the dog at his home.[70]

Quarantine requirements will generally not apply to police dogs that bite individuals in the line of duty, though they may have to be examined.[71]

IMPORTANCE OF GEAR IN APPREHENSION WORK

Gear is particularly important for dogs assigned to suspect apprehension work. Dogs often wear vests, though some handlers argue that dogs are more likely to be harmed because vests may make the dogs too hot. One officer noted that "the majority of dogs that are shot take a bullet in the head, rather than in the body."[72] A popular technology is a bailout kennel, such as the K-9 Remote System, allowing officers to deploy dogs when they are away from their squad cars. The officer presses a transmitter on his duty belt and the door of the squad car opens, releasing the dog, which can then come to his assistance. The system has a range of 300 yards.[73]

NOTES

1. Apprehending suspects has been a police dog function since formal police dog training began in Ghent, Belgium, in the 1890s. An article in the *New York Times* in 1902 described dogs in Ghent being taught to attack dummies before being muzzled for attacks on real people. Science Siftings, The Police Dogs of Ghent, How They Are Trained to the Duties of Town Constables, *The New York Times* (November 9, 1902).
2. Canine movement and acceleration has been studied. See Walter and Carrier (2009).

3. The American Working Dog Association provides for testing the dog's ability to come to the handler's assistance during vehicle stops. AWDA Web site (www.americanworkingdog.com/certification_standards.htm).

4. Suspected Carjacker Arrested at Gas Station. Elk Grove Citizen Online, March 5–7, 2010, Elk Grove, California (www.egcitizen.com/articles/2010/03/05/news/doc4b913b6b9669d167101530.txt, visited March 7, 2010). The suspect was wanted for parole violations. The article stated that the best chance the pit bull had of not being euthanized would be if the police needed it as evidence in the crimes.

5. *Warren v. Las Vegas Police Department*, 111 F.3d 139 (9th Cir. 1997).

6. Hickey and Hoffman (2003).

7. Campbell et al. (1998).

8. See *Mann v. Yarnell*, 497 F.3d 822 (8th Cir. 2007) (bite and hold for 15 seconds).

9. See Dorriety (2005).

10. Strandberg (1997).

11. *Chew v. Gates*, 27 F.3d 1432 (9th Cir.1994).

12. Mesloh (2006). Arguably, when the officer is relying on the training of the dog, that training governs the dog's decision making in the absence of the officer.

13. *California v. Rivera*, 8 Cal.App.4th 100, 10 Cal.Rptr.2d 785 (Ct. App. 1992).

14. Haverbeke et al. (2009).

15. On the Web site of the National Tactical Police Dog Association (www.tacticalcanine.com/certification.htm). The American Working Dog Association fails a dog that is pursuing a suspect and does not obey a recall but continues after the suspect and bites. AWDA Web site (www.americanworkingdog.com/certification_standards.htm).

16. Biting the suspect during the escort results in a failure in the certification test of the American Working Dog Association. AWDA Web site (www.americanworkingdog.com/certification_standards.htm).

17. NAPWDA Web site (www.napwda.com/pdflib/bylaws_cert_rules.pdf).

18. Citing *Quintanilla v. City of Downey*, 84 F.3d 353 (9th Cir.1996); *Fikes v. Cleghorn*, 47 F.3d 1011 (9th Cir.1995).

19. *Martineau v. City of Cypress*, 95 F.3d 1158 (9th Cir. 1996).

20. *Robinette v. Barnes*, 854 F.2d 909 (6th Cir. 1988). See Dorriety (2005) ("If the dog were considered a weapon, for the purposes of criminal apprehension, it would most likely fit in an area of the continuum under intermediate weapon").

21. *Vera Cruz v. City of Escondido*, 126 F.3d 1214 (9th Cir. 1997).

22. *Shannon v. City of Costa Mesa*, 46 F.3d 1145 (9th Cir. 1995).

23. *U.S. v. Lawshea*, 461 F.3d 857 (7th Cir. 2006).

24. *Matthews v. Jones*, 35 F.3d 1046 (6th Cir. 1994). See also *Jarrett v. Town of Yarmouth*, 309 F.3d 54 (1st Cir. 2002) (describing the situation as similar to that in *Matthew v. Jones* and providing qualified immunity despite jury verdict for plaintiffs).

25. *Fikes v. Cleghorn*, 47 F.3d 1011 (9th Cir. 1995).

26. *Mendoza v. Block*, 27 F.3d 1357 (9th Cir. 1994).

27. 42 U.S.C. 1983 states: "Every person who, under color of any statute, ordinance, regulation, custom, or usage, of any State or Territory or the District of Columbia, subjects, or causes to be subjected, any citizen of the United States or other person within the jurisdiction thereof to the deprivation of any rights, privileges, or immunities secured by the Constitution and laws, shall be liable to the party injured in an action at law, suit in equity, or other proper proceeding for redress, except that in any action brought against a judicial officer for an act or omission taken in such officer's judicial capacity, injunctive relief shall not be granted unless a declaratory decree was violated or declaratory relief was unavailable. For the purposes of this section, any Act of Congress applicable exclusively to the District of Columbia shall be considered to be a statute of the District of Columbia."

28. *Mettler v. Whitlege*, 165 F.3d 1197 (8th Cir. 1999).

29. *Dunigan v. Noble*, 390 F.3d 486 (6th Cir. 2005).

30. *Chavez v. City of Albuquerque*, 402 F.3d 1039 (10th Cir. 2005).

31. *Gilliam v. County of Los Angeles*, 37 F.3d 1505 (9th Cir. 1994).

32. *Dunigan v. Noble*, 390 F.3d 486 (6th Cir. 2005) (dog on tracking leash brought into house to find parole violator; subsequent scuffle with mother of suspect resulted in dog biting her; no excessive force found; qualified immunity applied); *Dodd v. Corbett*, 2004 WL 3046346 (7th Cir. 2005) (dog tracked suspect for several miles before apprehension became possible). See the certification standards of the National Tactical Police Dog Association, which tests basic trailing by the suspect jumping and

running from a vehicle but going no more than 100 yards, followed by a quarter mile trail with at least two turns over two types of surfaces (grass, dirt, gravel, etc.) aged at least 30 minutes. NTPDA Web site (www.tacticalcanine.com/certification.htm).

33. Van Leenen and Staal (2010), 50, warn: "When you do want your patrol dog to track, make sure you put him in the right mode and context for tracking. The patrol dog that is pumped up because he is ready for a bite will never use his nose to track. The drives in him that make him bite are much stronger than the drives that make him track."

34. *Illinois v. Griffin*, 48 Ill.App.2d 148, 198 N.E.2d 115 (Ct. App. 1964).

35. *California v. Sandoval*, 2002 WL 519848 (Ct. App. 2002).

36. *California v. Daniels*, 2010 WL 598611 (Ct. App. 2010).

37. *Parra v. City of Chino*, 141 F.3d 1178 (9th Cir. 1998).

38. *Gill v. Thomas,* 83 F.3d 537 (1st Cir. 1996).

39. *California v. Rivera*, 8 Cal.App.4th 100, 10 Cal.Rptr.2d 785 (Ct. App. 1992).

40. *Dennen v. City of Duluth*, 350 F.3d 786 (8th Cir. 2003).

41. *Marquez v. Andrade*, 79 F.3d 1153 (9th Cir. 1996). See also *Andrade v. City of Burlinga*me, 847 F.Supp. 760 (N.D.Cal. 1994) (The evidence submitted shows that the City had a detailed policy regarding the canine unit. … Plaintiffs have pointed to no evidence to indicate that the City did not follow this policy, nor any evidence to show that the City had any history of problems with the unit. The only evidence plaintiffs present regarding the City's liability on this issue is that the dogs in the canine unit are trained to act on their own initiative in some instances (i.e., if the officer is in danger). This fact alone cannot establish a policy or custom that violates plaintiffs' fourteenth amendment rights.")

42. See Dorriety (2005), 94–95 ("If the dog is trained to bite and hold, this might distract the suspect from the presence of the officer long enough for the officer to tactically approach and take charge of the situation").

43. *Brewer v. City of Napa*, 210 F.3d 1093 (9th Cir. 2000). See also *Baker v. Cohen*, 2010 WL 3385266 (S.D.Fla. 2010) (suspect fled and hid in car; severity of attack before release command was disputed).

44. *Duvall v. City of Santa Monica*, 42 F.3d 1399 (9th Cir. 1994).

45. *Quintanilla v. City of Downey*, 84 F.3d 353 (9th Cir. 1996). See *Jetton v. City of Downey*, 86 F.3d 1162 (9th Cir. 1996) (court directed jury to focus deliberations on whether dog continued to attack suspect once he was prone; jury found for officers and 9th Circuit affirmed). See *Thomson v. Salt Lake County*, 584 F.3d 1304 (10th Cir. 2009) (possibly suicidal person was pointing gun at himself, dog, and officers; no excessive or deadly force in release of police dog or in shooting suspect).

46. *Vathekan v. Prince George's County*, 154 F.3d 173 (4th Cir. 1998) (summary judgment reversed because of failure to give a verbal warning); *Kopf v. Wing*, 942 F.2d 265 (4th Cir. 1991) (reversing summary judgment where factual issue existed on whether there was a verbal warning); *Ruvalcaba v. City of Los Angeles*, 167 F.3d 514 (9th Cir. 1999) (officers gave three warnings in Spanish and English); *Vera Cruz v. City of Escondido*, 139 F.3d 659 (9th Cir. 1998) (two verbal warnings); *Matthews v. Jones*, 35 F.3d 1046 (6th Cir. 1994) (warning issued several times); *Robinette v. Barnes*, 854 F.2d 909. 912 (6th Cir.1988) (attack was objectively reasonable because of three warnings).

47. *Kuha v. City of Minnetonka*, 365 F.3d 590 (8th Cir. 2004).

48. *Szaba v. City of Brooklyn Park*, 429 F.3d 1168 (8th Cir. 2005).

49. *Kopf v. Wing*, 942 F.2d 265 (4th Cir. 1991), 993 F.2d 374 (4th Cir. 1993).

50. *Priester v. City of Riviera Beach, Florida*, 208 F.3d 319 (11th Cir. 2000). See *Trammell v. Thomason*, 2009 WL 1706591 (11th Cir. 2009) (failure to shout warning disputed; dog bit bystander in backyard; failure to intervene was issue for jury and summary judgment should not have been granted; case remanded).

51. *Miller v. Clark County*, 340 F.3d 959 (9th Cir. 2003).

52. *Watkins v. City of Oakland*, 145 F.3d 1087 (9th Cir. 1998).

53. *Smith v. City of Hemet,* 394 F.3d 689 (9th Cir. 2005).

54. *Vathekan v. Prince George's County*, 154 F.3d 173 (4th Cir. 1998). See *Johnson v. Scott*, 576 F.3d 658 (7th Cir. 2009) (distinguishing *Vathekan*, but approving officer taking dog off struggling suspect 5 to 10 seconds after he was handcuffed).

55. FBI Investigating Pr. George's Canine Unit, *Washington Post*, p. A1 (April 4, 1999).

56. In a case from South Auckland, New Zealand, a dog was released to chase a burglar but seriously injured a bystander, who sought exemplary damages of $20,000. The man spent 3 days in the hospital and had two rounds of surgery for bites to his calf. The court found that nothing leading up to the incident indicated the dog had a propensity to bite, and cited the strong public policy argument against imposing a common law duty if it led to defensive policing. "It has to be borne in mind that biting is an inherent risk of using police dogs in the detection of crime and that the tort of negligence is subject to the test of reasonableness." Police Dog Bite Victim Loses Case. *NZHerald,* March 6, 2010 (www.nzherald.co.nz/nz/news/article.cfm?c_id=1&objectid=10630244).

57. *Marquez v. City of Albuquerque*, 399 F.3d 1216 (10th Cir. 2005). The case also involved a bizarre effort on the part of one juror to explain police dog training to other jurors. This is not the only case involving Officer Lehocky and a claim for excessive force. *Chamberlin v. The City of Albuquerque*, 2005 WL 23135 27 (D.N.M. 2005).
58. *U.S. v. Mohr*, 318 F.3d 613 (4th Cir. 2003).
59. *U.S. v. Reed*, 141 F.3d 644 (6th Cir. 1998).
60. *Barton v. Eichelberger*, 311 F.Supp. 1132 (M.D.Pa. 1970) (describing how Canine Division of City of York Police Department participated in 62 episodes of crowd control in 1968, which included stopping gang fights).
61. *Mason v. Hamilton County*, 13 F.Supp.2d 829 (S.D.Ind. 1998).
62. *Ricker v. Weston*, 2000 WL 1728506 (E.D.Pa. 2000).
63. *City of Fairfield v. Suslovic*, 2001 WL 1028404 (Oh. Ct. App. 2001); *Asylum, Inc. v. Liquor Control Commission*, 167 Ohio App. 498, 855 N.E.2d 902 (Ct. App. 2006).
64. MWD Pamphlet 190-12, § 2-17.
65. *Kerr v. City of West Palm Beach*, 875 F.2d 1546 (11th Cir. 1989).
66. *Ruvalcaba v. City of Los Angeles*, 167 F.3d 514 (9th Cir. 1999). See *Goodman v. Harris County*, 571 F.3d 388 (5th Cir. 2009) (damages for excessive force allowed against handler who claimed to have fired to save his dog's life from suspect who was drowning dog; evidence indicated suspect did not have use of arm consistent with handler's description, however; suspect was killed by officer's shot).
67. See Memorandum of Agreement Between the United States Department of Justice and the City of Cincinnati, Ohio and the Cincinnati Police Department, April 12, 2002 (www.cincinnati-oh.gov/police/downloads/police_pdf5112.pdf).
68. Minn. Stat. § 347.22.
69. *Hyatt v. Anoka Police Department*, 691 NW2d 828 (2005).
70. *Kliewer v. Sopata*, 797 F.Supp. 1569 (D.Colo. 1992).
71. See California Health and Safety Code § 121685.
72. DeFranco (1999).
73. Training, *Law Enforcement Technology* (September 2000).

21 Search and Rescue Dogs

Not all police functions involve finding criminals, and not all police dog functions are aspects of criminal law enforcement. Search and rescue work often involves volunteers, who are often provided to police by search and rescue canine organizations. Dogs can be trained by either air-scent or tracking techniques.[1] Search and rescue dogs have been known to perform tracking functions in criminal cases.[2]

SEARCH AND RESCUE WORK

During World War I, Red Cross workers used dogs to find wounded soldiers on the battlefield. The dogs carried saddlebags with medical supplies and canteens of water and spirits. The dogs were trained to ignore the dead and not to bark so as not to draw enemy fire. Some dogs were trained to take a wounded soldier's helmet or cap and bring it to a stretcher station where bearers would follow the dog back to the man.[3]

In a 1991 case, failure to search a field with a canine patrol on the night a person died was dismissed because the officer enjoyed statutory immunity.[4]

TRAINING

Search and rescue dogs are used as part of the National Urban Search and Rescue Response System of the Federal Emergency Management Agency (FEMA). In its *Disaster Search Canine Readiness Evaluation Process* ("Evaluation Process"),[5] FEMA presents a number of testing criteria and policies regarding canine search teams. Most FEMA Urban Search and Rescue handlers are civilians as well as firefighters and police department members. Although most handlers own their dogs, some FEMA Task Forces purchase dogs that are then assigned to Task Force members for rearing and training. The dogs remain the property of FEMA.[6] Most of the dogs are Labrador retrievers, German shepherds, Belgian Malinois, Border collies, and Golden retrievers.[7] FEMA Independent Study Courses are regarded as prerequisites for certification by groups certifying search and rescue dogs.[8]

Barking is important in search and rescue dogs because it alerts rescuers where the dog is. Penetration and digging are desired to help identify the scent source. Focused Bark Indicating Live Human Scent (FBILHS), a term used by FEMA and other organizations, means 30 seconds of barking, which may be interspersed with digging and attempts to penetrate. The dog must stay with the victim after indication of scent. The exercise demonstrating this skill is described as follows:

- The team will have 5 minutes to perform the exercise. The marked starting point will be 25 yards from the victim location. The handler will remove the canine's leash before the exercise begins. The canine may be given a hand signal and voice command to send the canine to the victim location. If the canine does not go directly to the victim location, the handler may use additional commands, as necessary, to direct the canine to the victim location. The handler may not move from the starting position.
- The handler may direct the canine toward the victim location but once the canine has located the victim's scent, the handler may not communicate with the canine in any way. Once the canine has committed to the victim location, it must remain focused, stay at the victim location and demonstrate an "independent of handler" bark alert behavior (FBILHS) for 30 seconds.

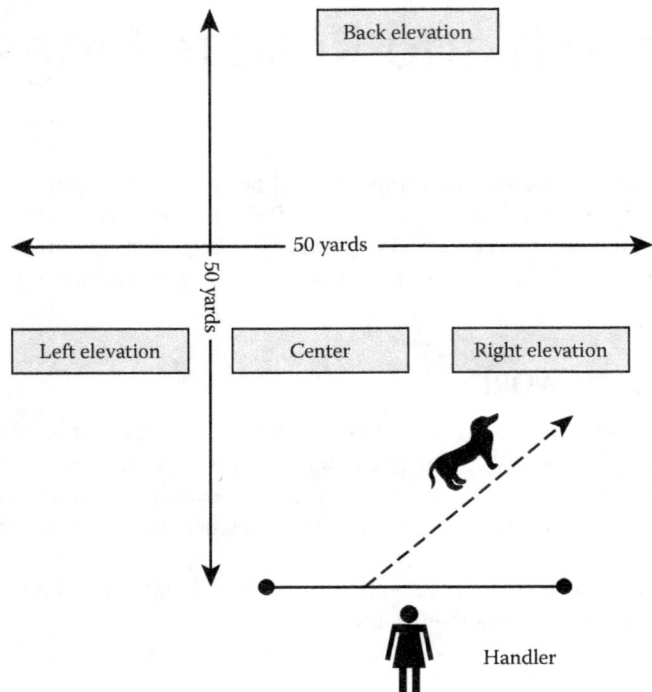

FIGURE 21.1   A handler directing a dog in a FEMA test for responsiveness to the handler's signals.

The Evaluation Process suggests that a "victim" be in a barrel or concrete sewer pipe, beneath a snug-fitting cover with holes for scent to escape. The victim is to be in place for at least 10 minutes before the dog is sent to find him.

When operating in a disaster site, search and rescue dogs should be able to follow visual or auditory cues from the handler. Dog search teams may be sent to different sectors of a search area rather than all being started where the lost individual was last believed to have been.[9] The dog should go to an elevation as directed by the handler, and in a testing situation, FEMA indicates that if the dog goes to the wrong elevation, it is to be recalled and restarted. "The canine will be directed to four or five designated elevations and stay for five seconds on each elevation, ending the exercise with a recall to the handler." A field diagram for testing directional responsiveness is depicted in Figure 21.1.

Dogs are taught to find individuals under various depths of snow. This is time-sensitive work and the "hiders" must be wearing warm clothing and have radio transmitters, and people with shovels should be near.[10] Dogs are also taught to search in rubble with hiding areas constructed for "victims." Dogs can also help find drowned persons.[11]

CLOTHING AS DISTRACTION

One researcher looked at the effect of scent-adsorbing clothing on the tracking ability of dogs. The scent adsorbing clothing was an overgarment lined with activated charcoal and advertised as being capable of concealing human odors from wildlife species. The advantage of such a garment was that observers of wildlife would be less likely to disturb the animals they are watching if the claims for the garments are true. This Scent-Lok® clothing was worn by some subjects, whereas others wore normal clothing. Subjects were driven to assigned stations and crawled directly into a box at the station. After 10 minutes, handlers were instructed to begin a search. Trained search dogs, provided by Search and Rescue Dogs of Colorado, took subjects' scent from a scent article, which were cotton cloths that the subjects handled for 1 minute and placed in a plastic bag. Handlers were directed to follow a normal search procedure following a grid pattern and working from the leeward side of the plot. The same boxes were used for all trials but no two trials occurred within 24 hours of each other. "Detection of the subject was defined as the moment when a dog became alerted to airborne scent, turned, and ran directly toward a box."

Dogs found the subjects within the allotted time in all but one trial. Dogs found the suited subject in 95% of trials and the plain-clothes subject in 100% of trials. The mean time to find subjects wearing a scent-adsorbing suit did not statistically differ from those wearing normal clothing. There was also little difference between detection distances. Thus, the specially designed clothing did not prevent search dogs from finding the hidden subjects. The one case where a dog did not find a subject in the special suit in the allotted time was attributed to changing wind directions.[12]

CERTIFICATION

FEMA provides both basic and advanced certification procedures.[13] The Eastern States Working Dog Association, Inc., offers a search and rescue tracking test resulting in a certification.[14] The Scientific Working Group on Dog and Orthogonal Detector Guidelines (SWGDOG) has a guideline, "Searching for Live People in Disaster Environments."[15] Some states have certification standards for search and rescue dog teams.[16] The International Rescue Dog Organisation provides certification and training of rescue dogs around the world.[17]

USING DOGS TRAINED IN OTHER FUNCTIONS

A case arising in Maryland involved use of a patrol dog trained in the bite-and-hold method to search for a boy on a cold winter night. The boy, 13 years old, went to a party with a friend some 30 minutes' drive from his home. An older youth started serving rum and cola, and the boy, Oscar, got drunk. He went outside with another boy, where the temperature was in the upper 30s or low 40s. The boys intended to circle the block but got lost, getting increasingly intoxicated as the alcohol took effect. The boys saw a man with a dog approaching and Oscar left his friend, walked some distance and went to sleep under a holly bush "so nobody could see me drunk." A couple taking a late night walk saw the boy who was still on the lawn, Brian, and thought they had seen another boy walking away from him. They called 911 and paramedics responded to the call.

The first officer who arrived was told that Brian was suffering from hypothermia and a possible alcohol overdose. The couple told the officer about the boy they had seen. Two officers arrived and circled the neighborhood for about 20 minutes using spotlights mounted on their cars. One officer searched backyards with a flashlight but did not find Oscar. They called a supervisor who suggested bringing a canine unit. Officer John Greene arrived with a patrol dog, Carter, trained in suspect apprehension with the bite-and-hold method. Officer Greene knew that one of the department's bloodhounds would be better for the assignment but that dog had a knee injury and the other bloodhound was at least an hour away. Greene put Carter on a 15 foot lead and began to search.

Greene took Carter to the last point where Oscar was reported seen and commanded Carter to "track." Carter cast about looking for a scent and then began to track down the sidewalk. Greene began to call out to Oscar, saying he was there to help and to take him home. … After tracking a short distance down the sidewalk, Carter turned sharply across a yard and went into a holly bush where Greene could no longer see him. Greene did not interpret the turn as indicating that anyone was close. The lead went slack, and only then did Greene realize that Carter had found Oscar, who was asleep. By the time Greene realized what was happening, the dog had already bitten Oscar's lower right leg.

Greene testified that he did not verbally call Carter off because Oscar was struggling, and Greene was concerned that if the dog released he might re-bite Oscar's face. Instead, Greene walked up the leash and physically removed the dog. While this was happening, the dog pulled Oscar some five or six

feet. .... Oscar suffered two lacerations on his lower right leg just above the ankle, one approximately
4.25 inches and the other 1.5 inches long.

The injuries to Oscar's leg were serious and the court noted that he would have a permanent dis-
ruption in sensation around the scars, and would have to wear a protective ankle brace for athletic
activities indefinitely.

Oscar's father sued on his son's behalf. The Fourth Circuit determined that there were factual
questions that made summary judgment on the excessive force claim inappropriate. Why was the
dog not muzzled? The officer argued that the dog could not follow scent as effectively while muzzled. Why was a long (15 foot) leash used? The officer argued that the dog could not cast properly
without a long lead. Should the officer have recognized from the dog's behavior that it was close to
the boy? A plaintiff's expert testified that a reasonable officer should have realized what was happening when Carter cut across the yard and went under the holly bush.

The trial court noted the policy of the International Association of Chiefs of Police (IACP),
which explicitly allows the use of police canines to track missing persons so long as the dogs
"remain on a leash of sufficient length to provide a reasonable measure of safety to the subject of the
search without compromising the canine's tracking abilities." The Fourth Circuit reversed the trial
court's denial of the motion for qualified immunity and remanded. The determination that qualified
immunity applied did not preclude the plaintiff pursuing certain state law claims, however.[18]

STATE LAWS ON SEARCH AND RESCUE AND EMERGENCY SERVICE DOGS

Dogs trained to deal with emergencies are often grouped with service animals under state access
rules. Kentucky's criminal law, for instance, defines a service animal as including a bomb detection dog, patrol dog, tracking dog, search and rescue dog, accelerant detection dog, cadaver dog, or
assistance dog.[19] Many states criminalize harming search and rescue dogs.

Some states provide public accommodation access to search and rescue dogs similar to that provided
service animals. Pennsylvania law probably provides access only when the police dog is working:

> It shall be unlawful for the proprietor, manager or employee of a theater, hotel, motel, restaurant or other
> place of entertainment, amusement or accommodation to refuse, withhold from or deny to any person, due
> to the *use of a working police dog* used by any State or county or municipal police or sheriff's department or
> agency, either directly or indirectly, any of the accommodations, advantages, facilities or privileges of the
> theater, hotel, motel, restaurant or other place of public entertainment, amusement or accommodation. Any
> person who violates any of the provisions of this subsection commits a misdemeanor of the third degree.[20]

In New Jersey, a member of a police, fire, law enforcement, or other related emergency service
agency, when accompanied by a working dog, "trained by a recognized training agency or school, is
entitled, with the dog, to full and equal access to all public facilities and modes of public transportation," without being charged for the dog but is to keep the dog in custody at all times.[21] The official is
liable for any damages to the premises of a public facility by the dog.[22] In Nevada, it is unlawful for
a place of public accommodation to refuse admittance or service to a person because he is accompanied by a police dog.[23] Nor can an additional fee be charged because a person is accompanied by
a police dog.[24] Connecticut law provides:

> Any individual who is an active member of a volunteer canine search and rescue team ... may travel on
> a train or on any other mode of public transportation, and may enter or visit any other place of public
> accommodation which caters or offers its services or facilities or goods to the general public, including,
> but not limited to, any public building, inn, restaurant, hotel, motel, tourist cabin, place of amusement,
> resort or any facility of any such public accommodation, accompanied by the dog in such team, and such
> individual may keep such dog with him or her at all times in any such public accommodation or facility

thereof at no extra charge, provided such team is engaged in a search or rescue operation and such dog shall be in the direct custody of such individual and shall wear a harness or red or orange-colored identification. No such individual shall be charged any fee not applicable alike to all guests, provided the owner of such dog shall be liable for any damage done to the premises or facilities by such dog.[25]

As a matter of public policy, some access to public accommodations should be assured to police and emergency dogs with government employees and also to private individuals working with their dogs as teams in government-related activities.

New Jersey provides protections as to housing accommodations for officials with working dogs.

A member of a police, fire, law enforcement or other related emergency service agency who possesses a working dog, is entitled to rent, lease or purchase, as other members of the general public, all housing accommodations and business accommodations offered for rent, lease, or compensation in this State, subject to the rights, conditions and limitations established by law. A member of a police, fire, law enforcement or other related emergency service agency who possesses a working dog, or who obtains a working dog, shall be entitled to full and equal access to all housing accommodations and business accommodations and shall not be required to pay extra compensation for the dog, but shall be liable for any damages done to the premises by the dog. Any provision in any lease or rental agreement prohibiting maintenance of a pet or pets on or in the premises shall not be applicable to a working dog owned by a tenant who is a member of a police, fire, law enforcement or other related emergency service agency.[26]

Arkansas provides a tax exemption for sales or services sold to the Arkansas Search Dog Association, Inc.[27]

THERAPY DOGS AT DISASTER SITES

Search and rescue dogs are not the only dogs found at disaster sites. Increasingly, therapy dogs have been seen as providing relief for workers and comfort for survivors or those looking for family members.[28] Both search and rescue and therapy dogs were present at the World Trade Center site after 9/11. One handler explained that his bomb dog also comforted people at the site.[29]

NOTES

1. Lechliter (2008).
2. *Davis v. Cain*, 2005 Wl 5191912 (E.D.La. 2008) ("search and rescue dog … signaled that he detected the defendant's scent on the driver's door handle of the victim's car, on the front left of the victim's car, from the victim's car to the front door of the victim's home, in the front room of the victim's home, and in the back bedroom of the victim's home. The dog was provided the defendant's scent from the defendant's boot after he was in police custody." The dog had been certified by the National Search and Rescue Association but had also received some training from the National Blood Hound Training Institute.)
3. Lemish (1996), 12.
4. *Platacis v. Village of Streamwood*, 224 Ill.App.3d 336, 586 N.E.2d 564, 166 Ill.Dec. 606 (Ct. App. 1991).
5. Posted on the FEMA Web site (www.fema.gov/emergency/usr/canineready.shtm).
6. E-mail from Dean A. Scott, DHS FEMA US&R Branch, Operations Section, Washington, D.C. (May 19, 2009).
7. FEMA, "Canine's Role in Urban Search and Rescue" (www.fema.gov/emergency/usr/canine.shtm).
8. See American Working Dog Association general prerequisites for search and rescue work (www.americanworkingdog.com/certification_standards.htm); American Rescue Dog Association (www.ardainc.org/about_standard.html).
9. Lechliter (2008).
10. Fenton (1992).
11. Browne et al. (2006).
12. Shivik (2002).
13. FEMA, Canine and Handler Certification (www.fema.gov/emergency/usr/caninecert.shtm).

14. Eastern States Working Dog Association, Inc., SAR Tracking Test (www.eswda.org/certifications/search-andrescue.html).

15. SC9 Scent Dogs: Searching for Live People in Disaster Environments (http://swgdog.org).

16. See Maine Association for Search and Rescue, Search Dog Team Certification Standard (2010) (www.emainehosting.com/masar/MASAR_Documents/MASAR%20Search%20Dog%20Standards/Search%20Dog%20Team%20Certification%20Standard%20Rev%207.pdf). (Stating that Maine's standards meet or exceed ASTM F1847-98, "Standard Guide for Demonstrating Minimum Skills for Search and Rescue Dogs and Handlers.") ASTM International provides voluntary consensus standards, for a fee, at www.astm.org. A number of those standards involve canine work.

17. Internationale Rettungshunde Organisation (http://iro-dogs.org).

18. *Melgar v. Greene*, 593 F.3d 348 (4th Cir. 2010).

19. Kentucky Penal Code § 525.010(6).

20. 3 P.S. § 459-602(c) (emphasis added).

21. For this purpose, a working dog is "any dog trained for the purpose of human search and rescue, body recovery, arson detection, bomb detection, narcotics detection, criminal apprehension, police assistance or other related purposes, whether in the performance of such tasks or while traveling to or from such tasks." N.J. Civil Rights Code § 10:5-29.7.1.

22. N.J. Civil Rights Code § 10:5-29.8.

23. Nev. Business Code § 651.075.1(d).

24. Nev. Business Code § 651.075.1(e). A service animal may not be presumed to be dangerous because it is not muzzled. Nev. Business Code § 651.075.3.

25. Conn. Crimes Code § 53-330a(a).

26. N.J. Civil Rights Code § 10:5-29.9.

27. Arkansas Code Annotated 26-52-443.

28. Ensminger (2010), 12, 106.

29. L.E. Papet, personal communication (December 30, 2010).

Afterword

No story about dogs and men ever ends. I said this at the end of my book on service and therapy dogs in American society and it is as true here as well. Yet where service dogs can generally only help individuals and therapy dogs can generally only help society, police dogs are a two-edged sword, capable of helping law enforcement but also capable of doing great damage to the lives of those they encounter. That damage may sometimes be necessary, but police men and women doing canine work know that they have been given a tool as dangerous as the guns in their holsters. That danger is sometimes immediate when a dog is sent to capture a suspect who has run into a darkened building or is hiding in the shrubbery near a crime scene, and sometimes more abstract when a dog is allowed to select a scent from a row of tubes when the selection made may help send a person to prison.

I hope that this book has painted a fair picture of the research that has changed the functions of police dogs in the last 50 years and the law that has put those changes into evidentiary parameters. I also hope that I have painted a fair picture of the courts and the judges that have struggled to interpret the significance of police canine work. Mostly, I hope I have been fair to the tens of thousands of men and women who work day in and day out with a dog that becomes a partner both at work and after work. Their contribution to the safety of society receives far too little recognition.

We continue on our journey with our best friend. He will take us places we never imagined if we but let him.

Appendix A: U.S. Police Canine Associations

Officials of the following associations made themselves available to the author during the research phase of this book. Some officials are cited in footnotes to specific areas discussed, but more than can be listed gave me their time and shared with me their expertise. I realize that such a listing is small thanks for the considerable help I received.

American Rescue Dog Association (www.ardainc.org). Dogs are assessed in various environments including open fields, trails, light brush, dense brush, and night searches. Dogs may also be assessed in human remains detection. This association also provides a mass fatality canine search evaluation.

American Working Dog Association (www.americanworkingdog.com). Certification standards: patrol, narcotics detection, explosives detection, tracking, arson detection, search and rescue ground, personal protection.

Canadian Police Canine Association (www.canadianpolicecanine.com). Membership organization providing educational events regarding police dogs.

Eastern States Working Dog Association (www.eswda.org). Certifications in narcotics, explosives, human remains, firearms, and accelerant detection, search and rescue, and trailing.

International Association of Chiefs of Police (www.theiacp.org). Has issued policy statement on law enforcement canines, as well as concepts and issues paper (1992, revised 2001).

International Rescue Dog Organisation (Internationale Rettungshunde Organisation) (http:// iro-dogs.org). Provides certification and training of rescue dogs around the world.

Law Enforcement Training Specialists International, Inc. (www.letsk9professionals.org). Provides certification standards and testing in narcotics, explosives, patrol, cadaver, and tracking work.

National Narcotic Detector Dog Association (www.nndda.org). Certification in narcotics, explosives, and cadaver detection, and police service dogs.

National Police Bloodhound Association (www.npba.com). Bloodhound training and certification organization.

National Tactical Police Dog Association (www.tacticalcanine.com). Certification of police canine teams as well as proficiency certifications for professional handlers and trainers.

North American Police Work Dog Association (www.napwda.com). Certification in tracking and trailing, narcotics, explosives, accelerant, and cadaver detection, and utility work, including criminal apprehension.

United States Police Canine Association (www.uspcak9.com). Certifications in tracking and accelerant, explosives, narcotics, and cadaver detection.

Appendix B: Bibliography

Ables, E.M., Kay, L.M., and Mateo, J.M. (2007). Rats Assess Degree of Relatedness from Human Odors. *Physiology and Behavior*, 90, 726–732.

Adams, G.J., and Johnson, K.G. (1994a). Behavioural Responses to Barking and Other Auditory Stimuli during Nighttime Sleeping and Waking in the Domestic Dog (*Canis familiaris*). *Applied Animal Behaviour Science,* 39, 151–162.

Adams, G.J. and Johnson, K.G. (1994b). Sleep, Work, and the Effects of Shift Work in Drug Detector Dogs *Canis familiaris. Applied Animal Behaviour Science*, 41, 115–126.

Adams, G.J. and Johnson, K.G. (1995). Guard Dogs: Sleep, Work and the Behavioural Responses to People and Other Stimuli. *Applied Animal Behaviour Science,* 46, 103–115.

Aitken, C.G.C. (1995). *Statistics and the Evaluation of Evidence for Forensic Scientists*. New York: John Wiley & Sons.

Annual Review of Criminal Procedure: Warrantless Searches and Seizures (2008), *Georgetown Law Journal Review of Criminal Procedure,* 37, 39.

Armstrong, A., Babrauskas, V., Holmes, D., Martin, C., Powell, R., and Riggs, S. (2004). Transporting or Tracking Ignitable Liquids in Fire Scenes. *Proceedings of the American Academy of Forensic Sciences,* 10, 50–51.

Bach, H. and McLean, I. (2003). Remote Explosive Scent Training: Genuine or Paper Tiger? *Journal of Mine Action,* 7(1).

Bacon, W.E. and Stanley, W.C. (1968). Avoidance Learning in Neonatal Dogs. *Journal of Comparative and Physiological Psychology*, 71(3), 448–452.

Becker, R. and King, J.E. (1957). Delineation of the Nasal Airstreams in the Living Dog, *Archives of Otolaryngology*, 65(5), 428–436.

Bird, R.C. (1997). An Examination of the Training and Reliability of the Narcotics Detection Dog. *Kentucky Law Journal*, 85, 405.

Bodingbauer, J. (1977). *Das Wunder der Hundenase*. Unsere Hunde: Wien.

Borusiewicz, R. Zieba-Palus, J., and Zadora, J. (2006). The Influence of the Type of Accelerant, Type of Burned Material, Time of Burning and Availability of Air on the Possibility of Detection of Accelerants Traces. *Forensic Science International,* 160, 115–126.

Brisbin, I.L. and Austad, S.N. (1991). Testing the Individual Odour Theory of Canine Olfaction. *Animal Behaviour*, 42, 63–69.

Brisbin, I.L. and Austad, S.N. (1993). The Use of Trained Dogs to Discriminate Human Scent: A Reply. *Animal Behaviour*, 46, 191–192.

Brisbin, I.L., Austad, S., and Jacobson, S.K. (2000). Canine Detectives: The Nose Knows—Or Does It? *Science*, 290(5494), 1093.

Broeders, A.P.A. (2006). Of Earprints, Fingerprints, Scent Dogs, Cot Deaths and Cognitive Contamination—A Brief Look at the Present State of Play in the Forensic Arena. *Forensic Science International*, 159, 148–157.

Browne, C., Stafford, K., and Fordham, R. (2006). The Use of Scent-Detection Dogs. *Irish Veterinary Journal,* 59(2), 97.

Brueggemann, J. and Jeckstadt, S. (1938). Uber Den Weg Des Luftstromes Durch Die Nase Des Hundes (The Direction of the Airstream through the Dog's Nose). *Pflugers Archiv. European Journal of Physiology,* 239, 293–303.

Buck L. and Axel, R. (1991). A Novel Multigene Family May Encode Odorant Receptors: A Molecular Basis for Odor Recognition. *Cell,* 65, 175–187.

Budget, H.M. (1933). *Hunting by Scent*. London: Charles Scribner's Sons.

Buytendijk, F.J.J. (1936). *The Mind of the Dog*. Boston, MA: Houghton Mifflin Co.

Campbell, A., Berk, R.A., and Fyfe, J.J. (1998). Deployment of Violence: The Los Angeles Police Department's Use of Dogs. *Evaluation Review,* 22, 535–561.

Cassidy, B.G. and Gonzales, R.A. (2005). DNA Testing in Animal Forensics. *Journal of Wildlife Management,* 69(4), 1454–1462.

Clark, S.E. (2005). A Re-Examination of the Effects of Biased Lineup Instructions in Eyewitness Identification. *Law and Human Behavior*, 29(5), 575–604.

Comment (1976). *United States v. Solis*: Have the Government's Supersniffers Come Down with a Case of Constitutional Nasal Congestion? *San Diego Law Review,* 13, 410.

Coppinger, R. and Coppinger, L. (2001). *Dogs: A Startling New Understanding of Canine Origin, Behavior, and Evolution.* New York: Scribner.

Craven, B.A. and Settles, G.S. (November 2006). A Computational and Experimental Investigation of the Human Thermal Plume, *Journal of Fluids Engineering,* 128, 1251–1258.

Craven, B.A., Paterson, E.G., and Settles, G.S. (2010). The Fluid Dynamics of Canine Olfaction: Unique Nasal Airflow Patterns as an Explanation of Macrosmia. *Journal of the Royal Society Interface,* 7(47), 933–943.

Curran, A.M. and Furton, K.G. (2006). The Acceptance of Human Scent as Evidence in the U.S. Court System. *Proceedings of the American Academy of Forensic Sciences, 12,* 72–73.

Curran, A.M., Prada, P.A., and Furton, K.G. (2010a). Canine Human Scent Identifications with Post-Blast Debris Collected from Improvised Explosive Devices. *Forensic Science International,* 1999, 103–108.

Curran, A.M., Prada, P.A., and Furton, K.G. (2010b). The Differentiation of the Volatile Organic Signatures of Individuals through SPME-GC/MS of Characteristic Human Scent Compounds. *Journal of Forensic Sciences,* 55(1), 50–57.

Curran, A.M., Rabin, S.I., and Furton, K.G. (2005a). Analysis of the Uniqueness and Persistence of Human Scent. *Forensic Science Communications,* 7(2).

Curran, A.M., Rabin, S.I., Prada, P.A., and Furton, K.G. (2005b). Comparison of the Volatile Organic Compounds Present in Human Odor Using SPME-GC/MS. *Journal of Chemical Ecology,* 31(7), 1607–1619.

Curran, A.M., Rabin, S.I., Prada, P.A., and Furton, K.G. (2006a). On the Definition and Measurement of Human Scent: Response by Curran et al. *Journal of Chemical Ecology,* 32, 1617–1623.

Curran, A.M., Stockham, R.A., Warren, W., and Eckenrode, B. (May 2006b). Human Scent Evidence: Scientific Support of Canine Operations and Teaching an Old Dog New Tricks (Poster and Video Display), Research Partnership Program of 34th Annual Symposium on Crime Laboratory Development.

Curran, A.M., Ramirez, C.F., Schoon, A.A., and Furton, K.G. (2007). The Frequency of Occurrence and Discriminatory Power of Compounds Found in Human Scent across a Population Determined by SPME-GC/MS. *Journal of Chromatography B,* 846, 86–97.

Cutler, B.L., Berman, G.L., Penrod, S.D., and Fisher, R.P. (1994). Conceptual, Practical, and Empirical Issues Associated with Eyewitness Identification Test Media. In *Adult Eyewitness Testimony: Current Trends and Developments,* D.F. Ross, J.D. Read, and M.P. Toglia (eds.), 163–181. New York: Cambridge University Press.

Cutler, B.L., Penrod, S.D., and Martens, T.K. (1987). The Reliability of Eyewitness Identification: the Role of System and Estimator Variables. *Law and Human Behavior,* 11(3), 233–258.

Dawes, J.D.K. (1952). The Course of the Nasal Airstreams. *Journal of Laryngology & Otology,* 66(12), 583–593.

Dean, E.E. and Samuel Tomlinson, S.J. (1983). The Scientific Development of an Efficient Detector Dog Through Olfaction and Behavioral Modification. *Proceedings of the Third International Symposium. on Analysis and Detection of Explosives,* 451–457 (FBI Academy, Quantico).

Dean, S. (2010). Preparing a Young Dog for Operational Police Duty. *Police K-9 Magazine, 6(6),* 68–73.

DeFranco, L.M. (1999). K-9 Partners: Who's Responsible for the Cost of Their Care? *Law Enforcement Technology* (September 1999).

Deffenbacher, K.A., Bornstein, B.H., Penrod, S.D., and McGorty, E.K. (2004). A Meta-Analytic Review of the Effects of High Stress on Eyewitness Memory. *Law and Human Behavior,* 28(6), 687–706.

Doob, A.N. and Kirshenbaum, H.M. (1973). Bias in Police Lineups—Partial Remembering. *Journal of Police Science and Administration,* 1(3), 287–293.

Dorey, N.R., Udell, M.A.R., and Wynne, D.L. (2010). When Do Domestic Dogs, *Canis familiaris,* Start to Understand Human Pointing? The Role of Ontogeny in the Development of Interspecies Communication. *Animal Behaviour,* 79, 37–41.

Dorriety, J.K. (2005). Police Service Dogs in the Use-of-Force Continuum. *Criminal Justice Policy Review,* 16, 88–98.

Dorriety, J.K. (2007). Cadaver Dogs as a Forensic Tool: An Analysis of Prior Studies. *Journal of Forensic Identification, 57(5),* 717–725.

Doyle, C. (1970). The Secret Cloud That Surrounds Us. *Family Health,* 32–35.

Dudek, D. and Srebnik, G. (2000). The Effect of Imposed Contamination with 10% Distilled Vinegar upon Scent Identification by Dogs (in Polish). *Problemy Kryminalistyki* 227, 38–39.

Dysart, J.E., and Lindsay, R.C.L. (2001). A Preidentification Questioning Effect: Serendipitously Increasing Correct Rejections. *Law and Human Behavior,* 25(2), 155–165.

Eckenrode, B.A., Ramsey, S.A., Stockham, R.A., van Berkel, G.J., Asano, K.G., and Wolf, D.A. (2006). Performance Evaluation of the Scent Transfer Unit™ (STU-100) for Organic Compound Collection and Release. *Journal of Forensic Sciences*, 51(4), 780–789.

Edge, B.A., Paterson, E.G., and Settles, G.S. (September 2005). Computational Study of the Wake and Contaminant Transport of a Walking Human. *Journal of Fluids Engineering*, 127, 967–977.

Ensminger, J. (2010). *Service and Therapy Dogs in American Society: Science, Law and the Evolution of Canine Caregivers.* Springfield, IL: Charles C Thomas.

Ensminger, J.J., Jezierski, T., and McCulloch, M.M. (2010). Scent Identification in Criminal Investigations and Prosecutions: New Protocol Designs Improve Forensic Reliability (unpublished manuscript). (Posted at: http://papers.ssrn.com/sol3/papers.cfm?abstract_id=1664766.)

Ensminger, M.E. (1977). *The Complete Book of Dogs.* London: A.S. Barnes & Co./Thomas Yoseloff Ltd.

Fenton, V. (1992). The Use of Dogs in Search, Rescue and Recovery. *Journal of Wilderness Medicine,* 3, 292–300.

Fjellanger, R., Andersen, E.K., and McLean, I.G. (2002). A Training Program for Filter-Search Mine Detection Dogs. *International Journal of Comparative Psychology,* 15, 277–286.

Fjellanger, R., McLean, I.G., and Bach, H. (2003). Vapour Sensing Dogs in Bosnia: A Test of Detection Capacity. *Proceedings of EUDEM2-SCOT,* 1, 162–165.

France, D.L., Griffin, T.J., Swanburg, J.G., Lindemann, J.W., Davenport, G.C., Trammell, V., Travis, C.T., Kondratieff, B., Nelson, A., Castellano, K., Hopkins, D., and Adair, T. (1997). Necroresearch Revisited: Further Multidisciplinary Approaches to the Detection of Clandestine Graves. In W.D. Haglund and M.H. Sorg (eds.), *Forensic Taphonomy: The Postmortem Fate of Human Remains,* 497–509. Boca Raton, FL: CRC Press.

Frijters, J.E.R. (2006). De Geuridentificatieproef in het Licht van het Falsificatiebeginsel [The Dog Scent Lineup in the Light of the Falsification Principle]. *NJB [Nederlands Juristenblad]*, 714, 945–948.

Frijters, J.E.R. and Boksem, J. (2004). Een Positieve Geuridentificatieproef dient vrijwel altijd in een tegenonderzoek te warden herhaald! [A Positive Dog Scent Lineup Nearly Always Has to Be Repeated Through a Countercheck]. *NJB [Nederlands Juristenblad]*, 79, 729–734.

Furton, K.G., Hong, Y.-C., Hsu, Y.-L., Luo, T., Rose, S., and Walton, J. (2002). Identification of Odor Signature Chemicals in Cocaine Using Solid-Phase Microextraction-Gas Chromatography and Detector-Dog Response to Isolated Compounds Spiked on U.S. Paper Currency. *Journal of Chromatographic Science,* 40, 147–155.

Furton, K.G., Hsu, Y.-L., Luo, T.-Y., Alvarez, N., and Lagos, P. (1997a). Novel Sample Preparation Methods and Field Testing Procedures Used to Determine the Chemical Basis of Cocaine Detection by Canines. *Proceedings of the SPIE*, 2951, 56–62.

Furton, K.G., Hsu, Y.-L., Luo, T.-Y., Wang, J., and Rose, S. (1997b). Odor Signature of Cocaine Analyzed by GC/MS and Threshold Levels of Detection for Drug Detection Canines, *Current Topics in Forensic Sciences. Proc. Meet. Int. Assoc. Forensic Sci.*, 14(2), 329–332.

Furton, K.G., Hsu, Y.-L., Luo, T.Y., Norelus, A., and Rose, S. (1999). Field and Laboratory Comparison of the Sensitivity and Reliability of Cocaine Detection on Currency Using Chemical Sensors, Humans, K-9s, and SPME/GC/MS/MS Analysis. *SPIE Proc.* vol. 3576, 41–46.

Furton, K.G. and Myers, L.J. (2001). The Scientific Foundation and Efficacy of the Use of Canines as Chemical Detectors for Explosives. *Talanta*, 54, 487–500.

Garner, K.J., Busbee, L., Cornwell, P., Edmonds, J., Mullins, K., Rader, K., Johnston, J.M., and Williams, J.M. (2001). Duty Cycle of the Detector Dog: A Baseline Study. Institute for Biological Detection Systems, Auburn University.

Gawkowski M. (2000). Identification of Humans on the Basis of Scent Samples [in Polish]. Police Training Center, Legionowo, Poland.

Gawkowski M. (2001). Odor Memory and Effectiveness of the Canine Lineups in Osmological Forensic Investigations [in Polish]. *Problemy Kryminalistyki*, 233, 52–56.

Gazit, I., Goldblatt, A., and Terkel, J. (2005). Formation of Olfactory Search Image for Explosives Odours in Sniffer Dogs. *Ethology,* 111(7), 669–680.

Gazit, I., Lavner, Y., Bloch, G., Azulai, O., Goldblatt, A., and Terkel, J. (2003). A Simple System for the Remote Detection and Analysis of Sniffing in Explosives Detection Dogs. *Behaviour Research Methods, Instruments, and Computers*, 35(1), 82–89.

Gazit, I. and Terkel, J. (2003a). Domination of Olfaction over Vision in Explosives Detection by Dogs. *Applied Animal Behaviour Science*, 82, 65–73.

Gazit, I. and Terkel, J. (2003b). Explosives Detection by Sniffer Dogs Following Strenuous Physical Activity. *Applied Animal Behaviour Science,* 81, 149–161.

Geneva International Centre for Humanitarian Demining. (2005). *Mine Detection Dogs: Operations.* (Geneva GICHD).

Gerritsen, R. and Haak, R. (2001). *K9 Professional Tracking: A Complete Manual for Theory and Training.* Calgary, Alberta, Canada: Detselig Enterprises Ltd.

Gialamas, D.M. (1996). Enhancement of Fire Scene Investigations Using Accelerant Detection Canines. *Science & Justice,* 36(1), 51–54.

Goth, A., McLean, I.G., and Trevelyan, J. (2002). How Do Dogs Detect Landmines? A Review of Research Results. Geneva International Centre for Humanitarian Demining.

Gowadia, H.A. and Settles, G.S. (2001). The Natural Sampling of Airborne Trace Signals from Explosives Concealed upon the Human Body. *Journal of Forensic Sciences,* 46(6), 1324–1331.

Grzybowski, R.A. and Murdock, J.E. (1998). Firearm and Toolmark Identification: Meeting the Daubert Challenge. *AFTE Journal,* 30(1), 3–14.

Hafez, E.S.E. (1969). *The Behavior of Domestic Animals.* London: Bailliere-Tindall.

Hargreaves, G.J. (January 1996). Detection Dog Lineup. *FBI Law Enforcement Bulletin.*

Harper, R.J., Almirall, J.R., and Furton, K.G. (2004). Improving the Scientific Reliability of Biological Detection of Explosives by *Canis familiaris* through Active Odor Signatures and Their Implications. *Proceedings of the 8th International Symposium on the Analysis and Detection of Explosive (ISADE),* Ottawa, Canada.

Harvath, Z., Igyarto, B.-Z., Magyar, A., and Miklosi, A. (2007). Three Different Coping Styles in Police Dogs Exposed to a Short-Term Challenge. *Hormones and Behavior,* 52, 621–630.

Harvey, L.M. and Harvey, J.W. (2003). Reliability of Bloodhounds in Criminal Investigations. *Journal of Forensic Science,* 48(4), 811–816.

Harvey, L.M., Harvey, S.J., Hom, M., Perna, A., and Salib, J. (2006). The Use of Bloodhounds in Determining the Impact of Genetics and the Environment on the Expression of Human Odor Type. *Journal of Forensic Sciences,* 51(4), 1109–1114.

Haverbeke, A., Laporte, B., Depiereux, E., Giffroy, J.-M., and Diederich, C. (2008). Training Methods of Military Dog Handlers and Their Effects on the Team's Performances. *Applied Animal Behaviour Science,* 113, 110–122.

Haverbeke, A., de Smet, A., Depiereux, E., Giffroy, J.-M., and Diederich, C. (2009). Assessing Undesired Aggression in Military Working Dogs. *Applied Animal Behaviour Science,* 117, 55–62.

Hepper, P.G. (1994). Long-Term Retention of Kinship Recognition Established during Infancy in the Domestic Dog. *Behavioural Processes,* 33(1–2), 3–14.

Hepper, P.G. (1998). The Discrimination of Human Odour by the Dog. *Perception,* 17(4), 549–554.

Hepper P.G. and Wells D. (2005). How Many Footsteps Do Dogs Need to Determine the Direction of an Odour Trail? *Chemical Senses,* 30, 291–298.

Hickey, E.R. and Hoffman, P.B. (2003). To Bite or Not to Bite: Canine Apprehensions in a Large Suburban Police Department. *Journal of Criminal Justice,* 31, 147–154.

Honhon, J. (1967). L'Olfaction chez le Chien: Son Rôle Dans le Pistage et la Localisation D'une Source Odorant. *Thèse de doctorat vétérinaire,* Faculté de Médecine, Créteil.

Hudson, D.T., Curran, A.M., and Furton, K.G. (2009). The Stability of Collected Human Scent under Various Environmental Conditions. *Journal of Forensic Sciences,* 54(6), 1270–1277.

Huff, C.R., Rattner, A., and Sagarin, E. (1996). *Convicted But Innocent.* Thousand Oaks, CA: Sage.

Hunt, R. (November 1999). The Benefits of Scent Evidence. *FBI Law Enforcement Bulletin,* 15.

Hunter, D. (2002). Common Scents: Establishing a Presumption of Reliability for Detector Dog Teams Used in Airports in Light of the Current Terrorist Threat. *University of Dayton Law Review,* 28, 89.

Hunter, S. (September 1997). Taming Explosives for Training. *Science and Technology Review,* 24–26.

Jaworski, R. (1999). Identification of Scent or of Emotion [in Polish]. *Problemy Kryminalistyki,* 224, 54–57.

Jesse, G.R. (1866). *Researches into the History of the British Dog, from Ancient Laws, Charters, and Historical Records.* London: Robert Hardwicke.

Jezierski, T. (2002). Ethological Analysis of Mistakes Made during Identification of Humans on the Basis of Scent by Police Dogs [in Polish]. Final Report on Grant No. TOOA 02618 of the Polish State Committee for Scientific Research.

Jezierski, T. (2010). *Scent Lineup Dogs.* Unpublished manuscript.

Jezierski, T., Bednarek, T., Gorecka, A., Gebler, E., and Stawicka, A. (2003). Factors Influencing the Reliability of Canine Identification of Humans on the Basis of Scent [in Polish]. *Problemy Współczesnej Kryminalistyki,* 7(2), 207–215.

Jezierski, T., Sobczynska, M., Walczak, M., Gorecka-Bruzda, A., and Ensminger, J.J. (2012). Do Trained Dogs Discriminate Individual Body Odors of Women Better Than Those of Men? *Journal of Forensic Sciences* (accepted for publication in February 2012 issue).

Jezierski, T., Walczak, M., and Gorecka, A. (2008). Information-Seeking Behavior of Sniffer Dogs during Match-to-Sample Training in the Scent Lineup. *Polish Psychological Bulletin*, 39(2), 71–80.

Johnston, J.M., Myers, L.J., Waggoner, P., and Williams, M. (1994). Determination of Olfactory Thresholds Using Operant Laboratory Methods. *Proceeding of the SPIE*, 2092, 238–243.

Jones, A.C. and Josephs, R.A. (2006). Interspecies Hormonal Interactions between Man and the Domestic Dog (*Canis familiaris*). *Hormones and Behavior*, 50, 393–400.

Joshi, M., Delgado, Y., Guerra, P., Lai, H., and Almirall, J.R. (2009). Detection of Odor Signatures of Smokeless Powders Using Solid Phase Microextraction Coupled to an Ion Mobility Spectrometer. *Forensic Science International*, 188, 112–118.

Julien, M.M. (November 2009). Early Scent Association for the Working Canine: Creating a Narcotics Detection Canine for the Average Canine Handler. *Journal of Veterinary Behavior*, 4(6), 239.

Kaldenbach, J. (1998). *K9 Scent Detection: My Favorite Judge Lives in a Kennel*. Calgary, Alberta, Canada: Detselig Enterprises Ltd.

Kalischer, O. (1909). Weitere Mitteilung uber die Ergebnisse der Drssur als physiologischer Untersuchungsmethode auf den Gebieten des Gehor-, Geurchs-, und Farbensinns. *Archiv für Anatomie und Pysiologie, Abteilung*, 303–322.

Kalmus, H. (1955). The Discrimination by the Nose of the Dog of Individual Human Odours and in Particular the Odours of Twins. *British Journal of Animal Behaviour*, 3(1), 25–31.

Keller, A. and Vosshall, L.B. (2008). Better Smelling through Genetics: Mammalian Odor Reception. *Current Opinion in Neurobiology*, 18, 364–369.

Kemp, T.J., Bachus, K.N., Nairn, J.A., and Carrier, D.R. (2005). Functional Trade-Offs in the Limb Bones of Dogs Selected for Running versus Fighting. *Journal of Experimental Biology*, 208, 3475–3482.

Kerley, L.L. and Salkina, G.P. (2007). Using Scent-Matching Dogs to Identify Individual Amur Tigers from Scats. *Journal of Wildlife Management*, 71(4), 1349–1356.

Killam, W.E. (1990). *The Detection of Human Remains*. Springfield, IL: Charles C Thomas.

King, E., Becker, R.F., and Markee, J.E. (1964). Studies on Olfactory Discrimination in Dogs: Ability to Detect Human Odour Trace. *Animal Behaviour*, 12(2–3), 311–315.

Knauf, H., and Johnston, W.H. (May 1974). Evaluation of Explosives/Narcotics (EXNARC) Detection Dogs. Army Mobility Equipment Research and Development Center, Fort Belvoir, VA, AD0787308, USAMERCDC-2102.

Komar, D. (1999). The Use of Cadaver Dogs in Locating Scattered, Scavenged Human Remains: Preliminary Field Test Results. *Journal of Forensic Sciences*, 44(2), 405–408.

Korting, H.C., Lukacs, A., and Braun-Falco, O. (1988). Microbial Flora and Odor of the Healthy Human Skin (in German). *Der Hautarzt*, 39(9), 564–568.

Kuhn, F. and Natsch, A. (2008). Body Odour of Monozygotic Human Twins: A Common Pattern of Odorant Carboxylic Acids Released by a Bacterial Aminoacylase from Axilla Secretions Contributing to an Inherited Body Odour Type. *Journal of the Royal Society Interface*, 6(33), 377–392.

Kurz, M., Billard, M., Rettig, M., Augustiniak, J., Lange, J., Larsen, M., Warrick, R., Mohns, T., Bora, R., Broadus, K., Hartke, G., Golver, B., Tankersley, D., and Marcouiller, J. (1994). Evaluation of Canines for Accelerant Detection at Fire Scenes. *Journal of Forensic Sciences*, 39(6), 1528–1536.

Kurz, M.E., Schultz, S., Griffith, J., Broadus, K., Sparks, J., Dabdoub, G., and Brock, J. (1996). Effect of Background Interference on Accelerant Detection by Canines. *Journal of Forensic Sciences*, 41(5), 868–873.

Kury, J. and Strobel, R. (2003). Nitromethane K-9 Detection Limit. Lawrence Livermore National Laboratory, UCRL-ID-155191 (www.xm-materials.com/NM%20K-9%20Detection%20Limit.pdf).

Lasseter, R.E., Jacobi, K.P., Farley, R., and Hensel, L. (2003). Cadaver Dog and Handler Team Capabilities in the Recovery of Buried Human Remains in the Southeastern United States. *Journal of Forensic Sciences*, 48(3), 617–621.

Lawhorn, S.J. (January 2000). Feasibility Assessment of the Use of Canines to Detect BW Agents, U.S. Army Soldier and Biological Chemical Command, Edge Chemical Biological Center, ECGC-CR-025.

Lechliter, J. (2008). Best Friends to the Lost. *Forensic Examiner*, 17(2), 12.

Lefebvre, D., Diederich, C., Delcourt, M., and Giffroy, J.-M. (2007). The Quality of the Relation between Handler and Military Dogs Influences Efficiency and Welfare of Dogs. *Applied Animal Behaviour Science*, 104, 49–60.

Lemish, M.G. (1996). *War Dogs: Canines in Combat*. Washington, D.C.: Brassey's.

Lesniak, A., Walczak, M., Jezierski, T., Sacharczuk, M., Gawkowski, M., and Jaszczak, K. (2008). Canine Olfactory Receptor Gene Polymorphism and Its Relation to Odor Detection Performance by Sniffer Dogs, *Journal of Heredity*, 99(5), 518–527.

Lilly, J.R. and Puckett, M.P. (April 1997). Social Control and Dogs: A Sociohistorical Analysis. *Crime & Delinquency,* 43(2), 123–147.

Lindblad-Toh, K., Wade, C.M., Mikkelsen, T.S., Karlsson, E.K., Jaffe, D.B., Kamal, M., Clamp, M. et al. (2005). Genome Sequence, Comparative Analysis, and Haplotype Structure of the Domestic Dog. *Nature,* 438, 803–819.

Lit, L. and Crawford, C.A. (2006). Effects of Training Paradigms on Search Dog Performance. *Applied Animal Behaviour Science,* 98, 277–292.

Lloyd, H.S. (1948). The Dog in War. In D. Vesey-Fitzgerald (ed.). *The Book of the Dog.* London: Nicholas & Watson.

Lorenzo, N., Wan, T.L., Harper, R.J., Hsu, Y.L., Chow, M., Rose, S., and Furton, K.G. (2004). Laboratory and Field Experiments Used to Identify *Canis lupus* var. *familiaris* Active Odor Signature Chemicals from Drugs, Explosives, and Humans. *Analytical and Bioanalytical Chemistry,* 376, 1212–1224.

Low, A.M. (2010) Designing a Constitutional Ruse Drug Checkpoint: What Does the Fourth Amendment Really Protect? *University of San Francisco Law Review,* 44, 955.

Lowy, A. and McAlhany, P. (April–June 2000). Human Remains Detection: The Latest Police Canine Detector Specialty. *FDIAI News,* 6–8.

Lunney, L.A. (2009). Has the Fourth Amendment Gone to the Dogs? Unreasonable Expansion of Canine Sniff Doctrine to Include Sniffs of the Home. *Oregon Law Review,* 88, 829.

Macias, M.S., Guerra-Diaz, P., Almirall, J.R., and Furton, K.G. (2010). Detection of Piperonal Emitted from Polymer Controlled Odor Mimic Permeation Systems Utilizing *Canis familiaris* and Solid Phase Microextraction-Ion Mobility Spectrometry. *Forensic Science International,* 195, 132–138.

Macias, M.S., Harper, R.J., and Furton, K. (February 2006). A Comparison of Real vs. Pseudo Contraband for Reliable Detector Dog Training. *Proceedings of the American Academy of Forensic Sciences,* 12, 43.

Macrakis, K. (2008). *Seduced by Secrets: Inside the Stasi's Spy-Tech World.* Cambridge University Press Cambridge, UK.

MacKenzie, S.A. and Schultz, J.A. (1987). Frequency of Back-Tracking in the Tracking Dog. *Applied Animal Behaviour Science,* 17, 353–359.

Maejima, M., Inoue-Murayama, M., Tonosaki, K., Matsuura, N., Kato, S., Saito, Y., Weiss, A., Murayama, Y., and Ito, S. (2007). Traits and Genotypes May Predict the Successful Training of Drug Detection Dogs. *Applied Animal Behaviour Science,* 107, 287–298.

McGreevy, P.D. and Nicholas, F.W. (1999). Some Practical Solutions to Welfare Problems in Dog Breeding. *Animal Welfare,* 8, 329–341.

McWhorter, J.C. (January/February 1920). The Bloodhound as a Witness. *American Law Review,* 54, 109.

Meserve, J. and King, J. (May 16, 2002). Mental Evaluation Ordered for Philly Bomb Suspect. *CNN* (posted at www.cnn.com/2002/US/05/16/philadelphia.bomb).

Mesloh, C. (2006). Barks or Bites? The Impact of Training on Police Canine Force Outcomes. *Police Practice and Research,* 7(4), 323–335.

Mesloh, C., Henych, M., and Wolf, R. (2002). Sniff Test: Utilization of the Law Enforcement Canine in the Seizure of Paper Currency. *Journal of Forensic Identification,* 52(6), 704.

Mesloh, C. and James-Mesloh, J. (2006). Trained Dogs in the Crime Scene Search. *Journal of Forensic Identification,* 56(4), 534.

Mesloh, C., Wolf, R., and Henych, M. (2002). Scent as Forensic Evidence and Its Relationship to the Law Enforcement Canine. *Journal of Forensic Identification,* 52(2), 169–172.

Meyer, I. and Ladewig, J. (2008). The Relationship between Number of Training Sessions per Week and Learning in Dogs. *Applied Animal Behaviour Science,* 111, 311–320.

Miklósi, Á. (2007). *Dog Behaviour, Evolution, and Cognition.* New York: Oxford University Press.

Miklósi, Á., Polgardi, R., Topál, J., and Csányi, V. (1998). Use of Experimenter-Given Cues in Dogs. *Animal Cognition,* 1, 113–121.

Miklósi, Á., Pongrácz, P., Lakátos, G., Topál, J., and Csányi, V. (2005). A Comparative Study of the Use of Visual Communicative Signals in Interactions between Dogs (*Canis familiaris*) and Humans and Cats (*Felis catus*) and Humans. *Journal of Comparative Psychology,* 119(2), 179–186.

Misiewicz, K. (2000). Influence of Nicotine on Performance of Scent Identification Dogs [in Polish]. *Problemy Kryminalistyki,* 229, 38–40.

Most, K. (1926). Neue Versuche uber Spurfahigkeit. *Z.D. Hund,* 18, 31–35.

Murray, M.K. (1984). The Contributions of the American Military Working Dog in Vietnam. Master's thesis, U.S. Army Command and General Staff College. (Expanded significantly, University Press of the Pacific, 2005).

Myers, R.E., II. (2006a). In the Wake of Caballes, Should We Let Sniffing Dogs Lie? *Criminal Justice,* 20(4), 7.

Myers, R.E., II. (2006b). Detector Dogs and Probable Cause. *George Mason Law Review,* 14, 1.

Nambayah, M. and Quickenden, T.I. (2004). A Quantitative Assessment of Chemical Techniques for Detecting Traces of Explosives at Counter-Terrorist Portals. *Talanta,* 63, 461–467.

Negrusz, A., Perry, J.L., and Moore, C.M. (1998). Detection of Cocaine on Various Denominations of United States Currency. *Journal of Forensic Sciences,* 43(3), 626–629.

Negus, V.E. (1958). *The Comparative Anatomy and Physiology of the Nose and Paranasal Sinuses.* Edinburgh: Livingstone.

Neuhaus, W. (1953). Über die Riechschärfe des Hundes für Fettsäuren. *Zeitschrift für Vergleichende Physiologie,* 35, 527–552.

Neuhaus, W. (1955). Die Unterscheidung von Luftquantitaeten bei Mensch und Hund nach Versuchen Mit Buttersäure. *Zeitschrift für Vergleichende Physiologie,* 37, 234–252.

Neuhaus, W. (1981). The Importance of Sniffing in Canine Olfaction (Die Bedeutung des Schnüffelns für das Riechen des Hundes). *Zeitschrift für Saugetierkunde,* 46, 301–310.

Nowlan, M., Stuart, A.W., Basara, G.J., and Sandercock, M.L. (2007). Use of Solid Absorbent and an Accelerant Detection Canine for the Detection of Ignitable Liquids Burned in a Structure Fire. *Journal of Forensic Sciences,* 52(3), 643–648.

Oesterhelweg, L., Krober, S., Rottmann, K., Willhoft, J., Braun, C., Thies, N., Puschel, K., Sildenath, J., and Gehl, A. (2008). Cadaver Dogs—A Study on Detection of Contaminated Carpet Squares. *Forensic Science International,* 174, 35–39.

Oliver, W.M., Klenowski, P.M., and DiMambro, A. (July 2006). Democratic Reform in Polish Policing. *The Police Chief* (online at http://policechiefmagazine.org/magazine/index.cfm?fuseaction=display&article_id=934&issue_id=72006, accessed August 9, 2010).

Parmeter, J.E., Murray, D.W., and Hannum, D.W. (August 2000). National Institute of Justice, Law Enforcement and Corrections Standards and Testing Program, *Guide for the Selection of Drug Detectors for Law Enforcement Applications* (NLJ Guide 601-00).

Pearsall, M.D. and Verbruggen, H. (1982). *Scent Training to Track, Search and Rescue.* Loveland, CO: Alpine Publications.

Penn, D.J., Oberzaucher, E., Grammer, K., Fischer, G., Soini, H.A., Wiesler, D., Novotny, M.V., Dixon, S.J., Xu, Y., and Brereton, R.G. (2007). Individual and Gender Fingerprints in Human Body Odour. *Journal of the Royal Society Interface,* 4, 331–340.

Peterson, J.L. and Markham, P.N. (1995). Crime Laboratory Proficiency Testing Results, 1978–1991, II: Resolving Questions of Common Origin. *Journal of Forensic Sciences,* 40(6), 1099–1129.

Phelan, J.M. and Barnett, J.L. (February 2001). Phase Partitioning of TNT and DNT in Soils. Sandia National Laboratories Report, SAND2001-0310.

Phillips, M., Cataneo, R.N., Greenberg, J., Gurwardena, R., Naidu, A., and Rahbari-Oskoui, F. (2000a). Effect of Age on the Breath Methylated Alkane Contour, a Display of Apparent New Markers of Oxidative Stress. *Journal of Laboratory and Clinical Medicine,* 136(3), 243–249.

Phillips, M., Greenberg J., and Cataneo, R.N. (2000b). Effect of Age on the Profile of Alkanes in Normal Human Breath. *Free Radical Research,* 33(1), 57–63.

Phillips, R.C. (October 1971). Training Dogs for Explosives Detection. AD-733 469; Contract No. DAAD05-70-C-0347.

Phillips, R.C., Lomax, R., and Krauss, M. (January 1974). Draft Information on Training, Use and Maintenance of Explosives Detector Dogs. AD-777 499/5. Contract No. DAAD04-73-C-0145.

Pongrácz, P., Miklósi, Á., Kubinyi, E., Gurobi, K., Topál, J., and Csányi, V. (2001) Social Learning in Dogs: The Effect of a Human Demonstrator on the Performance of Dogs in a Detour Task. *Animal Behaviour,* 62, 1109–1117.

Porter, J., Craven, B., Khan, R.M., Chang, S.-J., Kang, I., Judkewicz, B., Volpe, J., Settles, G., and Sobel, N. (2006). Mechanisms of Scent-Tracking in Humans. *Nature Neuroscience,* 10(1), 27–29.

Prada, P.A., Curran, A.M., and Furton, K.G. (February 2007). Laboratory Experiments for the Optimization of Non-Contact Human Scent Sampling. *Proceedings of the American Academy of Forensic Sciences,* 13, 45.

Quignon, P., Giraud, M., Rimbault, M., Lavigne, P., Tacher, S., Morin, E., Retout, E., Valin, A.S., Lindblad-Toh, K., Nicolas, J., and Galibert, F. (2005). The Dog and Rat Olfactory Receptor Repertoires. *Genome Biology,* 6(10), R83.

Rattner, A. (1988). Convicted But Innocent: Wrongful Conviction and the Criminal Justice System. *Law and Human Behavior,* 12, 283–293.

Raymond, J.J., Walsh, S.J., van Oorschot, R.A., Gunn, P.R., and Roux, C. (2004). Trace DNA: An Underutilized Resource or Pandora's Box? A Review of the Use of Trace DNA Analysis in the Investigation of Volume Crime. *Journal of Forensic Identification,* 54(6), 668.

Rebmann, A., David, E., and Sorg, M.H. (2000). *Cadaver Dog Handbook: Forensic Training and Tactics for the Recovery of Human Remains*. Boca Raton, FL: CRC Press.

Roberts, S.C., Gosling, L.M., Spector, T.D., Miller, P., Penn, D.J., and Petrie, M. (2005). Body Odor Similarity in Noncohabiting Twins. *Chemical Senses*, 30, 651–656.

Rogowski, M. (2001a). A Case of Two Osmological Expert Reports Compiled Several Years after the Securing of Material Evidence. *Problems of Forensic Sciences*, 48, 127–133.

Rogowski M., (2001b). Influence of Evidence Collection Time on the Result of Osmological Expertise [in Polish]. *Problemy Kryminalistyki* 234, 49–52.

Rogowski, M. (2002). An Attempt to Determine the Possibility of Transfer of a Person's Scent onto a Carrier through the Medium of His or Her Garment Used by Another Person and Infiltration of Scent through the Garment. *Problems of Forensic Sciences*, 50, 64–77.

Rogowski, M. (2003). An Attempt to Determine the Influence of a Female Scent Placed in a Male Selective Sequence on the Indications of Dogs Used for the Identification of Human Olfactory Traces. *Problems of Forensic Sciences*, 53, 74–90.

Rogowski, M. (2004). An Attempt to Determine the Possibility of Penetration of Human Scent through Rubber Gloves. *Problems of Forensic Sciences*, 57, 44–50.

Rogowski M. (2005). An Attempt to Assess the Effect of Scenting One Item by Three Persons on the Results of Osmological Identification [in Polish]. *Problemy Kryminalistyki*, 250, 40–44.

Rogowski M. (2006). An Attempt to Assess the Possibility of Transferring Individual Human Scent on an Item by the Second Person during Shaking Hands [in Polish]. *Problemy Kryminalistyki*, 252, 51–57.

Romanes, G.J. (1887). Experiments on the Sense of Smell in Dogs. *Nature*, 36, 273–274.

Rooney, N.J. and Bradshaw, J.W.S. (2004). Breed and Sex Differences in the Behavioural Attributes of Specialist Search Dogs—A Questionnaire Survey of Trainers and Handlers. *Applied Animal Behaviour Science*, 86, 123–135.

Rooney, N.J., Gaines, S.A., Bradshaw, J.W.S., and Penman, S. (2007). Validation of a Method for Assessing the Ability of Trainee Specialist Search Dogs. *Applied Animal Behaviour Science*, 103, 90–104.

Scheck, B., Neufeld, P., and Dwyer, J. (2000). *Actual Innocence: Five Days to Execution and Other Dispatches*. New York: Doubleday.

Scheiner, C.I. (1999). Statutes with Four Legs to Stand On? An Examination of "Cruelty to Police Dog" Laws. *Animal Law Review*, 5, 177.

Scheiner, C.I. (2001). "Cruelty to Police Dog" Laws Update. *Animal Law Review*, 7, 141.

Schettler, J. (March/April 2010). Trailing versus Tracking: Keys to Success. *Police K-9 Magazine*, 35–38.

Schlegel, S. (September 21, 2005). A Witness to Katrina's Tragedy. *Trenton Times* (www.bearsearchandrescue.org/).

Schoon, G.A.A. (1996). Scent Identification Lineups by Dogs (*Canis familiaris*): Experimental Design and Forensic Application. *Applied Animal Behaviour Science*, 49, 257–267.

Schoon, G.A.A. (1997a). Scent Identifications by Dogs (*Canis familiaris*): A New Experimental Design. *Behaviour*, 134, 531–550.

Schoon, G.A.A. (1997b). The Performance of Dogs in Identifying Humans. Dissertation, University of Leiden, The Netherlands.

Schoon, G.A.A. (1998). A First Assessment of the Reliability of an Improved Scent Identification Lineup. *Journal of Forensic Sciences*, 43(1), 70–75.

Schoon, G.A.A. (1999). *Scent Perception: Theory and Application for Training Search Dogs*. Syllabus.

Schoon, G.A.A. (2001). Scent Identification Lineups Using Trained Dogs in The Netherlands. *Problems in Forensic Sciences*, 47, 175–183.

Schoon, G.A.A. (2002). Influence of Experimental Setup Parameters of Scent Identification Lineups on Their Reliability (in Polish). *Problemy Kryminalistyki*, 236, 43–49.

Schoon, G.A.A. (2003). *Internal Report on the International Workshop for ID-Dog Handlers in Stukenbrock*. September 29–October 2.

Schoon, G.A.A. and de Bruin, J.C. (1994). The Ability of Dogs to Recognize and Cross-Match Human Odours. *Forensic Science International*, 69, 111–118.

Schoon, G.A.A., Curran, A.M., and Furton, K.G. (2009). Odor Biometrics. In *Encyclopedia of Biometrics*, S. Li (ed.). New York: Springer Science & Business Media.

Schoon, G.A.A., Gotz, S., Heuven, M., Vogel, M., and Karst, U. (2006). Training and Testing Explosive Detection Dogs in Detecting Triacetone Triperoxide. *Forensic Science Communications*, 8(4).

Schoon, G.A.A. and Haak, R. (2002). *K-9 Suspect Discrimination: Training and Practicing Scent Identification Line-Ups*. Calgary, Alberta, Canada: Detselig Enterprises.

Schoon, G.A.A. and Massop, A.R.L. (1995). History of Scent Identification Lineups by Tracker Dogs in The Netherlands [in Dutch]. *Delikt en Delikwent*, 25(9), 964–976.

Schreider, J.P. and Raabe, O.G. (1981). Anatomy of the Nasal-Pharyngeal Airway of Experimental Animals. *Anatomical Record*, 200, 195–205.

Schwartz, J. (November 11, 2009). Picked from a Lineup, on a Whiff of Evidence. *New York Times*, A1.

Settle, R.H., Sommerville, B., McCormick, J., and Broom, D. (1994). Human Scent Matching Using Specially Trained Dogs. *Animal Behavior*, 48, 1443–1448.

Settles, G.S. (March 2005). Sniffers: Fluid-Dynamic Sample for Olfactory Trace Detection in Nature and Homeland Security—The 2004 Freeman Scholar Lecture. *Journal of Fluids Engineering*, 127, 189.

Settles, G.S. and Kester, D.A. (April 2001). Aerodynamic Sampling for Landmine Trace Detection. *SPIE Aerosense*, 4394, 108.

Settles, G.S., Kester, D.A., and Dobson-Dreibelbis, L.J. (2003). The External Aerodynamics of Sniffing. In *Sensors and Sensing in Biology and Engineering*, F.G. Barth et al. (eds.), 323–335. New York: Springer.

Shivik, J.A. (2002). Odor-Adsorptive Clothing and Search-Dog Ability. *Wildlife and Habitat Journal*, 1(3),11.

Shutler, G.G, Gagnon, P., Verret, G., Kalyn, H., Korkosh, S., Johnston, E., and Halverson, J. (1999). Removal of a PCR Inhibitor and Resolution of DNA STR Types in Mixed Human–Canine Stains from a Five-Year Old Case. *Journal of Forensic Sciences*, 44(3), 623.

Slabbert, J.M. and Odendaal, J.S.J. (1999). Early Prediction of Adult Police Dog Efficiency—A Longitudinal Study. *Applied Animal Behaviour Science*, 64, 269–288.

Sleeman, R., Burton, F., Carter, J., Robers, D., and Hulmston, P. (2000). Drugs on Money. *Analytical Chemistry*, 72(11), 397A–403A.

Smith, M.E. (2009). Going to the Dogs: Evaluating the Proper Standard for Narcotic Detector Dog Searches of Private Residences. *Houston Law Review*, 46, 103.

Sommerville, B.A., Settle, R.H., Darling, F.M.C., and Broom, D.B. (1993). Short Communications: The Use of Trained Dogs to Discriminate Human Scent. *Animal Behaviour*, 46, 189–190.

Sorg, M.H., David, E., Rebmann, A.J. (1998). Cadaver Dogs, Taphonomy, and Postmortem Interval in the Northeast. In *Forensic Osteology: Advances in the Identification of Human Remains*, 2nd ed., K.J. Reichs (ed.), 120–144. Springfield, IL: Charles C Thomas.

Soproni, K., Miklósi, Á., Topál, J., and Csányi, V. (2002). Dogs' (*Canis familiaris*) Responsiveness to Human Pointing Gestures. *Journal of Comparative Psychology*, 116(1), 27–34.

State Department, Office of the Inspector General (September 2010). *Limited-Scope Review of the Bureau of Diplomatic Security's Oversight of Explosives Detection Canine Programs*, MERO-I-10-14.

Steen, J.B. and Wilson, E. (1990). How Do Dogs Determine the Direction of Tracks? *Acta Physiologica Scandinavica*, 139, 531–534.

Stephanitz, V. (1923). *The German Shepherd Dog in Word and Picture*. Jena, Germany: Anton Kampfe.

Stockham, R.A., Slavin, D.L., and Kift, W. (2004a). Specialized Use of Human Scent in Criminal Investigations. *Forensic Science Communications*, 6(3).

Stockham, R.A. Slavin, D.L., and Kift, K. (2004b). Survivability of Human Scent. *Forensic Science Communications*, 6(4).

Stoddart, D.M. (1980). *The Ecology of Vertebrate Olfaction*. New York: Chapman & Hall.

Strandberg, K.W. (September 1997). Canine Units. *Law Enforcement Technology*.

Stubbs, D.D., Lee, S.-H., and Hunt, W.D. (2005). Vapor Phase Detection of a Narcotic Using Surface Acoustic Wave Immunoassay Sensors. *IEEE Sensors Journal*, 5(3), 335–339.

Svartberg, K. (2002). Shyness–Boldness Predicts Performance in Working Dogs. *Applied Animal Behaviour Science*, 79, 157–174.

Svartberg, K. (2006). Breed-Typical Behaviour in Dogs—Historical Remnants of Recent Constructs? *Applied Animal Behaviour Science*, 96, 293–313.

Svobodová, I., Vápeník, P., Pinc, L., and Bartoš, L. (2008). Testing German Shepherd Puppies to Assess Their Chances of Certification. *Applied Animal Behaviour Science*, 113, 139–149.

Syrotuck, W.G. (1972). *Scent and the Scenting Dog*. Mechanicsburg, PA: Barkleigh Productions, Inc.

Szakacs, N. A. (October 10–13, 2000). *Perspectives on DNA Casework: Unusual Exhibits Mixture Interpretation and Profiles from Inhibited PCR Reactions*. Poster presentation at 11th International Symposium on Human Identification, Biloxi, Mississippi.

Tacher, S., Quignon, P., Rimbault, M., Dreano, S., Andre, C., and Galibert, F. (2005). Olfactory Receptor Sequence Polymorphism Within and Between Breeds of Dogs. *Journal of Heredity*, 96(7), 812–816.

Taslitz, A. (1990). Does the Cold Nose Know? The Unscientific Myth of the Dog Scent Lineup. *Hastings Law Journal*, 42, 15.

Thesen, A., Steen, J.B., and Døving, K.B. (1993). Behaviour of Dogs during Olfactory Tracking. *Journal of Experimental Biology*, 180, 247–251.

Tindall, R. and Lothridge, K. (1994). An Evaluation of 42 Accelerant Detection Canine Teams. *Journal of Forensic Sciences*, 40(4), 561–564.

Tolhurst, W. (1991). *The Police Textbook for Dog Handlers*. Sanborn, NY: Sharp Print.

Tomaszewski, T. and Girdwoyn, P. (2006), Scent Identification Evidence in Jurisdiction (Drawing on Example of Judicial Practice in Poland). *Forensic Science International*, 162, 191–195.

Tranthim-Fryer, D.J. and DeHaan, J.D. (1997). Canine Accelerant Detectors and Problems with Pyrolysis Products. *Science & Justice*, 37(1), 39–46.

Uchida, T. (1956). Fatty Acids and the Olfactory Sense of Dogs. *Proceedings of the Japan Academy*, 32(10), 753–758.

Uddqvist, A. and Roberthson, I. (2010). *Improvement of Sampling System for Remote Explosive Scent Tracing*. Bachelor's Degree Project in Mechanical Engineering, University of Skovde, Sweden.

Van Leenen, D. and Staal, D. (November/December 2010). Hard-Surface Tracking. *Police K-9 Magazine*, 6(6), 48–58.

Vas, J., Topál, J., Gácsi, M., Miklósi, Á., and Csányi, V. (2005). A Friend or an Enemy? Dogs' Reaction to an Unfamiliar Person Showing Behavioural Cues of Threat and Friendliness at Different Times. *Applied Animal Behaviour Science*, 94, 99–115.

Vass, A.A. (2001). Beyond the Grave—Understanding Human Decomposition. *Microbiology Today*, 28, 190–192.

Vass, A.A., Smith, R.R., Thompson, C.V., Burnett, M.N., Wolf, D.A., Synstelien, J.A., Dulgerian, N., and Eckenrode, B.A. (2004). Decompositional Odor Analysis Database. *Journal of Forensic Sciences*, 49(4), 760–769.

Vass, A.A., Smith, R.R., Thompson, C.V., Burnett, M.N., Dulgerian, N., and Eckenrode, B.A. (2008). Odor Analysis of Decomposing Buried Human Remains. *Journal of Forensic Sciences*, 53(2), 384–391.

Wagenaar, W.A. and Veefkind, N. (1992). Comparison of One-Person and Many-Person Lineups: A Warning against Unsafe Practices. In *Psychology and Law: International Perspectives*, F. Losel, D. Bender, and T.H. Bliesenser (eds.), 275–285. Berlin: Walter de Gruyter.

Waggoner, L.P., Johnston, J.M., Williams, Jackson, M.J., Jones, M., Boussom, T., and Petrousky, J.A. (1997). Canine Olfactory Sensitivity to Cocaine Hydrochloride and Methyl Benzoate, *SPIE*, 2937, 216–226.

Waggoner, L.P., Jones, M., Williams, M., Johnston, J.M., Edge, C., and Petrousky, J.A. (1998). Effects of Extraneous Odors on Canine Detection. *SPIE*, 3575, 355–362.

Walter, R.M. and Carrier, D.R. (2009). Rapid Acceleration in Dogs: Ground Forces and Body Posture Dynamics. *Journal of Experimental Biology*, 212, 1930–1939.

Wells, D.L. and Hepper, P.G. (2006). Prenatal Olfactory Learning in the Domestic Dog. *Animal Behaviour*, 72, 681–686.

Wells, G.L. and Seelau, E.P. (1995). Eyewitness Identification: Psychology Research and Legal Policy on Lineups. *Psychology, Public Policy, and Law*, 1(4), 765–791.

Wickenheiser, R.A. (2002). Trace DNA: A Review, Discussion of Theory, and Application of the Transfer of Trace Quantities through Skin Contact. *Journal of Forensic Sciences*, 47(3), 442–450.

Widacki, J. (1999). Neither Randomness Nor Certainty: On One Method for Determination of Diagnostic Value of Osmological Identification [in Polish]. *Problemy Kryminalistyki*, 225, 62–63.

Widacki, J. (2000). Which Image of Scent Identification Examinations is the True One? [in Polish] *Problemy Kryminalistyki*, 229, 46–47.

Williams, M. and Johnston, J.M. (2002). Training and Maintaining the Performance of Dogs (*Canis familiaris*) on an Increasing Number of Odor Discriminations in a Controlled Setting. *Applied Animal Behaviour Science*, 78(1), 55–65.

Williams, M., Johnston, J., Waggoner, L.P., Cicoria, M., Hallowell, S., and Petrousky, J. (1977). *Canine Substance Detection: Operational Capabilities* (Federal Aviation Administration).

Williams, M., Johnston, J.M., Waggoner, L.P., Cicoria, M., Hallowell, S.F., and Petrousky, J.A. (1997). Canine Substance Detection: Operational Capabilities. *Proceedings of the 1999 ONDCP International Technology Symposium*, Washington, D.C.

Williams, M., Johnston, J., Cicoria, E., Paletz, E., Waggoner, L., Edge, C., and Hallowell, S. (1998). Canine Detection Odor Signatures for Explosives. Presentation at SPIE Conference on Enforcement and Security Technologies, Boston.

Wilsson, E. and Sundgren, P.-E. (1997). The Use of a Behaviour Test for the Selection of Dogs for Service and Breeding, I: Method of Testing and Evaluating Test Results in the Adult Dog, Demands on Different Kinds of Service Dogs, Sex and Breed Differences. *Applied Animal Behaviour Science*, 53, 279–295.

Wójcikiewicz, J. (2000). Dog Scent Lineups as Scientific Evidence. Paper presented in 1999 to the International Academy of Forensic Sciences meeting, Los Angeles. (Retrieved from http://www.forensic-evidence. com/site/ID/ID_DogScent.html.)

Wójcikiewicz, J., Bialek, I., Deszynski, K., and Dawidowicz, A.L. (1999). Statistical Interpretation of Eyewitness Testimony Using the Mock Witness Paradigm: A Case Study. *Expert Evidence,* 7, 175–186.

Wright, D.B., Carlucci, M.E., Evans, J.R., and Compo, N.S. (2010). Turning a Blind Eye to Double Blind Line-Ups. *Applied Cognitive Psychology,* 24(6), 849–867.

Wright, D.B. and McDaid, A.T. (1996). Comparing System and Estimator Variables Using Data from Real Line-ups. *Applied Cognitive Psychology,* 10(1), 75–84.

Wright, D.B. and Stroud, J.N. (2002). Age Difference in Lineup Identification Accuracy: People Are Better With Their Own Age. *Law and Human Behavior,* 26(6), 641–654.

Yamazaki, K., Beauchamp, G.K., Curran, M., Bard, J., and Boyse, E. (2001). Parents-progeny recognition as a function of MHC odortype identity. *Proceedings of the National Academy of Sciences of the USA,* 97(19), 10500–10502.

Yamazaki, K., Beauchamp, G.K., Imai, Y., Bard, J., Phelan, S., and Thomas, L. (1990). Odortypes determined by the major histocompatibility complex in germ-free mice. *Proceedings of the National Academy of Sciences of the USA,* 87, 8413–8416.

Yamazaki, K., Singer, A., and Beauchamp, G.K. (1998). Origin, functions and chemistry of H-2 regulated odorants. *Genetica,* 104, 235–240.

Zanghi, B.M., Kerr, W., deRivera, C., Araujo, J., and Milgram, B. (May–June 2010). Sleep and Biorhythms as a Function of Age in the Dog. *Journal of Veterinary Behavior,* 5(3), 159.

Zanoni, M.M., Morris, A., Messer, M., and Martinez, R. (February 1998). Forensic Evidence Canines: Status, Training, and Utilization. *Proceedings of the American Academy of Forensic Sciences,* 106–107.

Zdanowicz, P. and Kaminski, J. (1998). Influence of time on persistence of scent left on gun (in Polish). *Problemy Kryminalistyki,* 222, 43–44.

Zeng, X.N., Leyden, J.J., Lawley, H.J., Sawano, K., Nohara, I., and Preti, G. (1991). Analysis of Characteristic Odors from Human Male Axillae. *Journal of Chemical Ecology,* 17(7), 1469–1492.

Zhang, Z.-M., Cai, J.-J., Ruan, G.-H., and Li, G.-K. (2005). The Study of Fingerprint Characteristics of the Emanations from Human Arm Skin Using the Original Sampling System by SPME-GC/MS. *Journal of Chromatography B,* 822, 244–252.

Zuo, Y., Zhang, K., Wu, J., Rego, C., and Fritz, J. (2008). An Accurate and Nondestructive GC Method for Determination of Cocaine on US Paper Currency. *Journal of Separation Science,* 31, 2444–2450.

Zuschneid, K. (1973). The Olfactory Acuity of the Dog 9Die Riechleistung Des Hundes). PhD thesis, School of Veterinary Medicine, Free University of Berlin, Berlin, Germany.

Zuschneid, K., Bayer, A., and Schaffer, E. (1976). Physiological Observations on Sensory and Behavioural Responses of Hunting Dogs. *Berliner und Munchener Tierarztliche Wochenschrift,* 89(23), 462-465

Appendix C: Federal and State Cases Cited

U.S. SUPREME COURT

City of Indianapolis v. Edmond, 531 U.S. 32 148 L.Ed.2d 333, 121 S.Ct. 447 (2000)

Coolidge v. New Hampshire, 403 U.S. 443, 465, 91 S.Ct. 2022, 2037, 29 L.Ed.2d 564 (1971)

Daubert v. Merrell Dow Pharmaceuticals, Inc., 509 U.S. 579, 113 S.Ct. 2786, 125 L.Ed.2d 469 (1993)

Florida v. Jimeno, 500 U.S. 248, 111 S.Ct. 1801, 114 L.Ed.2d 297 (1991)

Florida v. Royer, 460 U.S. 491, 103 S.Ct. 1319, 75 L.Ed.2d 229 (1983)

Horton v. California, 496 U.S. 128, 110 S.Ct. 2301, 110 L.Ed.2d 112 (1990)

Illinois v. Caballes, 543 U.S. 405, 125 S.Ct. 834, 160 L.Ed.2d 842 (2005)

New Jersey v. T.L.O., 469 U.S. 325, 105 S.Ct. 733, 83 L.Ed2d 720 (1985)

Stoner v. California, 376 U.S. 483, 490, 84 S.Ct. 889, 893-94, 11 L.Ed.2d 856 (1964)

Terry v. Ohio, 392 U.S. 1, 88 S.Ct. 1868, 88 S.Ct. 1868, 20 L.Ed.2d 889 (1968)

Texas v. Brown, 460 U.S. 730, 103 S.Ct. 1535, 1546, 75 L.Ed.2d 502 (1983)

U.S. v. Chadwick, 433 U.S. 1, 97 S.Ct. 2476, 53 L.Ed.2d 538 (1977)

U.S. v. Jacobsen, 466 U.S. 109, 104 S.Ct. 1652, 80 L.Ed.2d 85 (1984)

U.S. v. Kyllo, 533 U.S. 27, 121 S.Ct. 2038, 150 L.Ed.2d 94 (2001)

U.S. v. Montoya de Hernandez, 473 U.S. 531, 105 S.Ct. 3304, 87 L.Ed.2d 381 (1985)

U.S. v. Place, 462 U.S. 696, 103 S.Ct. 2637, 77 L.Ed.2d 110 (1983)

U.S. v. Sokolow, 490 U.S. 1, 109 S.Ct. 1581, 104 L.Ed.2d 1 (1989)

U.S. MILITARY COURTS

U.S. v. Alexander, 34 M.J. 121 (U.S. Court of Military Appeals)

U.S. v. Unrue, 1973 WL 14783 (CMA), 47 C.M.R. 556, 22 USCMA 466 (1973)

U.S. v. Rotramel, 1 M.J. 559 (U.S. Air Force Court of Military Review 1975)

U.S. v. Smith, 68 M.J. 316 (C.A.A.F. 2010)

U.S. v. Thomas, 1975 WL 15554 (NCMR), 40 C.M.R. 114 (U.S. Navy Court of Military Review 1975)

U.S. v. Unrue, 1973 WL 14783 (CMA), 47 C.M.R. 556, 22 USCMA 466 (U.S. Court of Military Appeals 1973)

DISTRICT OF COLUMBIA CIRCUIT

U.S. v. $639,558 , 955 F.2d 712, 293 U.S.App.D.C. 384 (D.C. Cir. 1992)

U.S. v. Battista, 876 F.2d 201, 278 U.S.App.D.C. 16 (D.C. Cir. 1989)

U.S. v. Carrasquillo, 877 F.2d 73, 278 U.S.App.D.C. 128 (D.C. Cir. 1989)

U.S. v. Carter, 985 F.2d 1095, 300 U.S.App.D.C. 36 (D.C. Cir. 1993)

U.S. v. Colyer, 878 F.2d 469, 278 U.S.App. D.C. 367 (D.C. Cir. 1989)

U.S. v. Fulero, 498 F.2d 748, 162 U.S.App.D.C. 206 (D.C. Cir. 1974)

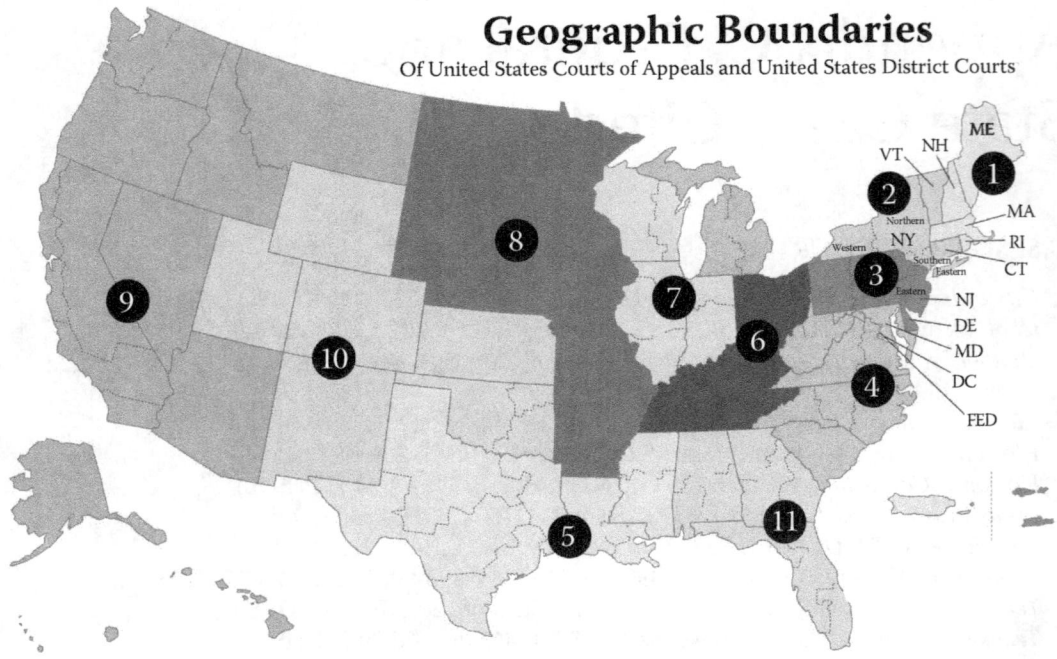

Geographic Boundaries
Of United States Courts of Appeals and United States District Courts

FIGURE C.1   Map of the U.S Circuit Courts of Appeal. Precedential decisions of the federal circuit courts apply to federal districts in the states covered by the circuits.

U.S. v. Maddox, 2010 WL 4352210 (D.C. Cir. 2010)
U.S. v. Nurse, 916 F.2d 20, 286 U.S.App.D.C. 303 (D.C. Cir. 1990)
U.S. v. Smith, 492 F.2d 650, 160 U.S.App.D.C. 384 (D.C. Cir. 1974)
U.S. v. Tartaglia, 864 F.2d 837, 275 U.S.App.D.C. 15 (D.C. Cir. 1989)
U.S. v. Trayer, 898 F.2d 805, 283 U.S.App.D.C. 208 (D.C. Cir. 1990)

FIRST CIRCUIT

Gill v. Thomas, 83 F.3d 537 (1st Cir. 1996)
Jarrett v. Town of Yarmouth, 309 F.3d 54 (1st Cir. 2002)
U.S. v. Allen, 990 F.2d 667 (1st Cir. 1993)
U.S. v. Bizier, 111 F.3d 214 (1st Cir. 1997)
U.S. v. Brown, 500 F.3d 48 (1st Cir. 2007)
U.S. v. de Los Santos Ferrer, 999 F.2d 7 (1st Cir. 1993)
U.S. v. Esquilin, 208 F.3d 315 (1st Cir. 2000)
U.S. v. Hebshie, 549 F.3d 30 (1st Cir. 2008)
U.S. v. Hornbecker, 316 F.3d 40 (1st Cir. 2003)
U.S. v. Jodoin, 672 F.2d 232 (1st Cir. 1982)
U.S. v. Lafrance, 879 F.2d 1 (1st Cir. 1989)
U.S. v. Lerebours, 87 F.3d 582 (1st Cir. 1996)
U.S. v. Meyer, 536 F.2d 963 (1st Cir. 1976)
U.S. v. Lopez, 380 F.3d 538 (1st Cir. 2004)
U.S. v. Maldonado-Espinosa, 968 F.2d 101 (1st Cir. 1992)
U.S. v. Nunez, 19 F.3d 719 (1st Cir. 1994)

U.S. v. Owens, 167 F.3d 739 (1st Cir. 1998)

U.S. v. Quinn, 815 F.2d 153, 158 (1st Cir. 1987)

U.S. v. Race, 529 F.2d 12 (1st Cir. 1976)

U.S. v. Rodriguez-Morales, 929 F.2d. 780 (1st Cir. 1991)

U.S. v. Rosario-Peralta, 199 F.3d 552 (1st Cir. 1999)

U.S. v. Saccoccia, 58 F.3d. 754 (1st Cir. 1995)

U.S. v. West, 731 F.2d 90 (1st Cir. 1984)

SECOND CIRCUIT

Holzapfel v. Town of Newburgh, 145 F.3d 516 (2nd Cir. 1998)

Reich v. New York City Transit Auth., 45 F.3d 646, 651 (2nd Cir. 1995)

U.S. v. Bronstein, 521 F.2d 459 (2nd Cir. 1975)

U.S. v. Hayes, 551 F.3d 138 (2nd Cir. 2008)

U.S. v. Hooper, 935 F.2d 484 (2nd Cir. 1991)

U.S. v. Johnson, 660 F.2d 21 (2nd Cir. 1981)

U.S. v. Marji, 158 F.3d 60 (2nd Cir. 1998)

U.S. v. Paccione, 2000 WL 34251719 (2nd Cir. 2000)

U.S. v. Thomas, 757 F.2d 1359, 1367 (2nd Cir. 1985), cert. denied sub nom. *Wheelings v. U.S.*, 474 U.S. 819, 106 S.Ct. 67, 88 L.Ed.2d 54 (1985)

U.S. v. Waltzer, 682 F.2d 370 (2nd Cir. 1982), cert. denied 463 U.S. 1210 (1983)

U.S. v. Young, 745 F.2d 733 (2d Cir.1984), cert. denied 470 U.S. 1084, 105 S.Ct. 1842, 85 L.Ed.2d 142 (1985)

THIRD CIRCUIT

Karnes v. Skrutski, 62 F.3d 485 (3rd Cir. 1995)

U.S. v. $10,700, 258 F.3d 215 (3rd Cir. 2001)

U.S. v. Brock, 417 F.3d 692 (3rd Cir. 2005)

U.S. v. Burton, 288 F.3d 91 (3rd Cir. 2002)

U.S. v. Cardona-Usquiano, 25 F.3d 1194 (3rd Cir. 1994)

U.S. v. Frost, 999 F.2d 737 (3rd Cir. 1993)

U.S. v. Massac, 867 F.2d 174, 176 (3rd Cir. 1989)

U.S. v. Pierce, Docket No. 1-08-cr-00126-001 (3rd Cir. 2010)

U.S. v. Thame, 846 F.2d 200 (3rd Cir. 1988)

U.S. v. Whitted, 541 F.3d 480 (3rd Cir. 2008)

FOURTH CIRCUIT

CACI Premier Technology, Inc. v. Rhodes, 536 F.3d 280 (4th Cir. 2008)

DesRoches v. Caprio, 156 F.3d 571 (4th Cir. 1998)

Epperly v. Booker, 997 F.2d 1 (4th Cir. 1993)

Kopf v. Wing, 942 F.2d 265 (4th Cir. 1991), 993 F.2d 374 (4th Cir. 1993)

Melgar v. Greene, 593 F.3d 348 (4th Cir. 2010)

Truslow v. Spotsylvania County Sheriff, 993 F.2d 1539 (4th Cir. 1993)

U.S. v. Alpert, 816 F.2d 958 (4th Cir. 1987)

U.S. v. Batts, 21 F.3d 425, 1994 WL 83385 (4th Cir. 1994)

U.S. v. Branch, 537 F.3d 328 (4th Cir. 2008)

U.S. v. Cardona-Usquiano, 25 F.3d 1194 (3rd Cir. 1994)

U.S. v. Carroll, 710 F.2d 164 (4th Cir. 1983)

U.S. v. Carter, 300 F.3d 415 (4th Cir. 2002)

U.S. v. Cofield, 254 Fed.Appx. 971, 2007 WL 3083542 (4th Cir. 2007)

U.S. v. Ebersole, 411 F.3d 517 (4th Cir. 2005), cert. denied, 126 S.Ct. 1142 (2006), on remand, 2007 WL 219969 (E.D. Va. 2007), aff'd, 189 Fed.Appx. 287 (4th Cir. 2006), motion to vacate denied, 2007 WL 750198 (E.D. Va.2007)

U.S. v. Eura, 440 F.3d 625 (4th Cir. 2006)

U.S. v. Farrior, 535 F.3d 210 (4th Cir. 2008)

U.S. v. Jeffus, 22 F.3d 554 (4th Cir. 1994)

U.S. v. Johnson, 256 F.3d 214 (4th Cir. 2001)

U.S. v. Koon Chung Wu, 217 Fed.Appx. 240, 2007 WL 412169 (4th Cir. 2007)

U.S. v. Mohr, 318 F.3d 613 (4th Cir. 2003)

U.S. v. Robinson, 707 F.2d 811 (4th Cir. 1983)

U.S. v. Singh, 363 F.3d 347 (4th Cir. 2004)

U.S. v. Sullivan, 625 F.2d 9 (4th Cir. 1980)

U.S. v. Torres, 65 F.3d 1241 (4th Cir. 1995)

U.S. v. Whitehead, 849 F.2d 849 (4th Cir. 1988)

Vathekan v. Prince George's County, 154 F.3d 173 (4th Cir. 1998)

FIFTH CIRCUIT

Goodman v. Harris County, 571 F.3d 388 (5th Cir. 2009)

Horton v. Goose Creek Independent School District, 690 F.2d 470 (5th Cir. 1982)

Jennings v. Joshua Independent School District, 877 F.2d 313 (5th Cir. 1989)

Kerr v. Lyford, 171 F.3d 330 (5th Cir. 1999)

Resendez v. Miller, 203 F.3d 902 (5th Cir. 2000)

U.S. v. Butler, 988 F.2d 537 (5th Cir. 1993)

U.S. v. Cagle, 849 F.2d 924 (5th Cir. 1988)

U.S. v. Castro, 166 F.3d 728 (5th Cir. 1999)

U.S. v. Cuellar, 478 F.3d 282 (5th Cir. 2007)

U.S. v. Daniel, 982 F.2d 146 (5th Cir. 1993)

U.S. v. Dortch, 199 F.3d 193 (5th Cir. 1999)

U.S. v. Dovali-Avila, 895 F.2d 206 (5th Cir. 1990)

U.S. v. Garcia-Garcia, 319 F.3d 726 (5th Cir. 2003)

U.S. v. Goldstein, 635 F.2d 356 (5th Cir. 1981)

U.S. v. Gonzalez-Basulto, 898 F.2d 1011 (5th Cir. 1990)

U.S. v. Ibarra, 493 F.3d 526 (5th Cir. 2007)

U.S. v. Jackson, 390 F.3d 393 (5th Cir. 2004)

U.S. v. Kelly, 302 F.3d 291 (5th Cir. 2002)

U.S. v. Lovell, 849 F.2d 910 (5th Cir. 1988)

U.S. v. Machuca-Barrera, 261 F.3d 425 (5th Cir. 2001)

U.S. v. Moore, 329 F.3d 399 (5th Cir. 2003)

U.S. v. Moreno-Vargas, 315 F.3d 489 (5th Cir. 2002)

U.S. v. Reyes, 349 F.3d 219 (5th Cir. 2003)

U.S. v. Rivas, 157 F.3d 364 (5th Cir. 1998)

U.S. v. Rozen, 600 F.2d 494 (5th Cir. 1979)

U.S. v. Sanchez-Pina, 336 F.3d 431 (5th Cir. 2003)

U.S. v. Tarazon-Silva, 166 F.3d 341, 1998 WL 912178 (5th Cir. 1998)

U.S. v. Viera, 644 F.2d 509 (5th Cir. 1981)

U.S. v. Williams, 69 F.3d 27 (5th Cir. 1995)

U.S. v. Williams, 365 F.3d 399 (5th Cir. 2004)

SIXTH CIRCUIT

Aiken v. City of Memphis, 190 F.3d 753 (6th Cir. 1999)
Babick v. Berghuis, No. 08-1376 (6th Cir. 2010)
Brock v. City of Cincinnati, 236 F.3d 793 (6th Cir. 2001)
Dunigan v. Noble, 390 F.3d 486 (6th Cir. 2005)
Matthews v. Jones, 35 F.3d 1046 (6th Cir. 1994)
Robinette v. Barnes, 854 F.2d 909 (6th Cir. 1988)
U.S. v. $5,000, 40 F.3d 846 (6th Cir. 1994)
U.S. v. $67,220, 957 F.2d 280 (6th Cir. 1992)
U.S. v. Alvarado, No. 90-6058, 1991 WL 119265 (6th Cir. 1991)
U.S. v. Avery, 137 F.3d 343 (6th Cir. 1997)
U.S. v. Baro, 15 F.3d 563 (6th Cir. 1994)
U.S. v. Bell, III, 555 F.3d 535 (6th Cir. 2009)
U.S. v. Berry, 90 F.3d 148 (6th Cir. 1996)
U.S. v. Boxley, 373 F.3d 759 (6th Cir. 2004)
U.S. v. Buchanon, 72 F.3d 1217 (6th Cir. 1995)
U.S. v. Davis, 430 F.3d 345 (6th Cir. 2005)
U.S. v. Diaz, 25 F.3d 392, 394 (6th Cir. 1994)
U.S. v. Ellis, 497 F.3d 606 (6th Cir. 2007)
U.S. v. Gant, 112 F.3d 239 (6th Cir. 1997)
U.S. v. Garcia, 496 F.3d 495 (6th Cir. 2007)
U.S. v. Gates, 680 F.2d 1117 (6th Cir. 1982)
U.S. v. Guzman, 75 F.3d 1090 (6th Cir. 1996)
U.S. v. Hill, 195 F.3d 258 (6th Cir. 1999)
U.S. v. Howard, No. 08-6143 (6th Cir. 2010)
U.S. v. Huguenin, 154 F.3d 547 (6th Cir. 1998)
U.S. v. Jacob, 377 F.3d 573 (6th Cir. 2004)
U.S. v. Knox, 839 F.2d 285 (6th Cir. 1988)
U.S. v. Lewis, 708 F.2d 1078 (6th Cir. 1983)
U.S. v. Mesa, 62 F.3d 159 (6th Cir. 1995)
U.S. v. Navarro-Camacho, 186 F.3d 701 (6th Cir. 1999)
U.S. v. Reed, 141 F.3d 644 (6th Cir. 1998)
U.S. v. Reid, 67 F.3d 300, 1995 WL 579436 (6th Cir. 1995)
U.S. v. Robinson, 390 F.3d 853 (6th Cir. 2004)
U.S. v. Sanders, 719 F.2d 882 (6th Cir. 1983)
U.S. v. Saperstein, 723 F.2d 1221 (6th Cir. 1983)
U.S. v. Smith, 263 F.3d 571 (6th Cir. 2001)
U.S. v. Torres-Ramos, 536 F.2d 542 (6th Cir. 2008)
U.S. v. Underwood, 97 F.3d 1453, 1996 WL 536796, (6th Cir. 1996)

SEVENTH CIRCUIT

Dodd v. Corbett, 2004 WL 3046346 (7th Cir. 2005)
Howard v. City of Springfield, 274 F.3d 1141 (7th Cir. 2001)
Johnson v. Scott, 576 F.3d 658 (7th Cir. 2009)
Kaniff v. U.S., 351 F.3d 780 (7th Cir. 2003)

Moya v. U.S., 761 F.2d 322 (7th Cir. 1985)
Saffell v. Crews, 183 F.3d 655 (7th Cir. 1999)
U.S. v. $30,670, 403 F.3d 448 (7th Cir. 2005)
U.S. v. $506,231, 125 F.3d 442 (7th Cir. 1997)
U.S. v. Adams, No. 08-4205 (7th Cir. 2010)
U.S. v. Borys, 766 F.2d 304 (7th Cir. 1985)
U.S. v. Dennis, 115 F.3d 524 (7th Cir. 1997)
U.S. v. Edwards, 898 F.2d 1273 (7th Cir. 1990)
U.S. v. Ferguson, 935 F.2d 1518 (7th Cir. 1991)
U.S. v. Fiala, 929 F.2d 285 (7th Cir. 1991)
U.S. v. Finke, 85 F.3d 1275 (7th Cir. 1996)
U.S. v. Ganser, 315 F.3d 819 (7th Cir. 2003)
U.S. v. Goodwin, 449 F.3d 766 (7th Cir. 2006)
U.S. v. Grogg, 534 F.3d 807 (7th Cir. 2008)
U.S. v. Johnson, 323 F.3d 566 (7th Cir. 2003)
U.S. v. Jones, 275 F.3d 648 (7th Cir. 2001)
U.S. v. Klein, 626 F.2d 22 (7th Cir. 1980)
U.S. v. Lawshea, 461 F.3d 857 (7th Cir. 2006)
U.S. v. Limares, 269 F.3d 794 (7th Cir. 2001)
U.S. v. Lozano, 171 F.3d 1129 (7th Cir. 1999)
U.S. v. Marrocco, 578 F.3d 627 (7th Cir. 2009)
U.S. v. Martin, 422 F.3d 597 (7th Cir. 2005)
U.S. v. Mayomi, 873 F.2d 1049 (7th Cir. 1989)
U.S. v. McCarthur, 6 F.3d 1270 (7th Cir. 1993)
U.S. v. Moralez, 964 F.2d 677 (7th Cir. 1992)
U.S. v. Patterson, 65 F.3d 68 (7th Cir. 1995)
U.S. v. Rivera, 825 F.2d 152 (7th Cir. 1987)
U.S. v. Rogers, 387 F.3d 925 (7th Cir. 2004)
U.S. v. de Soto, 885 F.2d 354 (7th Cir. 1989)
U.S. v. Sterling, 909 F.2d 1078 (7th Cir. 1978)
U.S. v. Sullivan, 903 F.2d 1093 (7th Cir. 1990)
U.S. v. Teslim, 869 F.2d 316 (7th Cir. 1989)
U.S. v. Thomas, 87 F.3d 909 (7th Cir. 1996)
U.S. v. Vasquez, 909 F.2d 235 (7th Cir. 1990)
U.S. v. Ward, 144 F.3d 1024 (7th Cir. 1998)
U.S. v. Washburn, 383 F.3d 638 (7th Cir. 2004)
U.S. v. Withers, 972 F.2d 837 (7th Cir. 1992)

EIGHTH CIRCUIT

$404,905 in U.S. Currency, 182 F.3d 643 (8th Cir. 1999)
Conrad v. Davis, 120 F.3d 92 (8th Cir. 1997)
Dennen v. City of Duluth, 350 F.3d 786 (8th Cir. 2003)
Kuha v. City of Minnetonka, 365 F.3d 590 (8th Cir. 2004)
Mann v. Yarnell, 497 F.3d 822 (8th Cir. 2007)
Mettler v. Whitlege, 165 F.3d 1197 (8th Cir. 1999)
Rudolph v. Metropolitan Airports Commission, 103 F.3d 677 (8th Cir. 1996)
Szaba v. City of Brooklyn Park, 429 F.3d 1168 (8th Cir. 2005)
U.S. v. $84,615, 379 F.3d 496 (8th Cir. 2004)
U.S. v. $124,700, 458 F.3d 822 (8th Cir. 2006)

U.S. v. $144,770, 157 F.3d 600 (8th Cir. 1998)

U.S. v. Adams, 110 F.3d 31 (8th Cir. 1997)

U.S. v. Alexander, 448 F.3d 1014 (8th Cir. 2006)

U.S. v. Beck, 140 F.3d 1129 (8th Cir. 1998)

U.S. v. Blaylock, 421 F.3d 758 (8th Cir. 2005)

U.S. v. Bloomfield, 40 F.3d 910 (8th Cir. 1994)

U.S. v. Carpenter, 462 F.3d 891 (8th Cir. 2006)

U.S. v. Carrazco, 91 F.3d 65 (8th Cir. 1996)

U.S. v. Delaney, 52 F.3d 182 (8th Cir. 1995)

U.S. v. DeMoss, 279 F.3d 632 (8th Cir. 2002)

U.S. v. Donnelly, 475 F.3d 946 (8th Cir. 2007)

U.S. v. Escobar, 389 F.3d 781 (8th Cir. 2004)

U.S. v. Foley, 206 F.3d 802 (8th Cir. 2000)

U.S. v. Friend, 50 F.3d 548 (8th Cir. 1995)

U.S. v. Fuse, 391 F.3d 924 (8th Cir. 2005)

U.S. v. Glover, 957 F.2d 1004 (8th Cir. 1992)

U.S. v. Gomez, 312 F.3d 290 (8th Cir. 2002)

U.S. v. Graham, 982 F2d 273 (8th Cir. 1992)

U.S. v. Gray, 369 F.3d 1024 (8th Cir. 2004)

U.S. v. Green, 52 F.3d 194 (8th Cir. 1995)

U.S. v. Gregory, 302 F.3d 805 (8th Cir. 2002)

U.S. v. Gwinn, 191 F.3d 874 (8th Cir. 2000)

U.S. v. Hammons, 152 F.3d 1025 (8th Cir. 1998)

U.S. v. Harvey, 961 F.2d 1361 (8th Cir. 1992)

U.S. v. Hill, 386 F.3d 855 (8th Cir. 2004)

U.S. v. Hogan, 539 F.3d 916 (8th Cir. 2008)

U.S. v. Jacobs, 986 F.2d 1231 (8th Cir. 1993)

U.S. v. Lakoskey, 462 F.3d 965 (8th Cir. 2006)

U.S. v. Large, 729 F.2d 636 (8th Cir. 1984)

U.S. v. Lebrun, 261 F.3d 731 (8th Cir. 2001)

U.S. v. Linkous, 285 F.3d 716 (8th Cir. 2002)

U.S. v. Logan, 362 F.3d 530 (8th Cir. 2004)

U.S. v. Longbehn, 898 F.2d 635 (8th Cir. 1990)

U.S. v. Lyons, 957 F.2d 615 (8th Cir. 1992)

U.S. v. Lyons, 486 F.3d 367 (8th Cir. 2007)

U.S. v. Maejia, 928 F.2d 810 (8th Cir. 1991)

U.S. v. Mahler, 141 F.3d 811 (8th Cir. 1998)

U.S. v. Maltais, 403 F.3d 550 (8th Cir. 2005)

U.S. v. Martinez, 358 F.3d 1005 (8th Cir. 2004)

U.S. v. McGauley, 786 F.2d 888 (8th Cir. 1986)

U.S. v. Morgan, 270 F.3d 625 (8th Cir. 2001)

U.S. v. Morones, 355 F.3d 1108 (8th Cir. 2004)

U.S. v. Munroe, 143 F.3d 1113 (8th Cir. 1998)

U.S. v. O'Neal, 17 F.3d 239 (8th Cir. 1994)

U.S. v. Palacios-Suarez, 149 F.3d 770 (8th Cir. 1998)

U.S. v. Pantazis, 816 F.2d 361 (8th Cir. 1987)

U.S. v. Pulliam, 265 F.3d 736 (8th Cir. 2001)

U.S. v. Riley, 927 F.2d 1045 (8th Cir. 1991)

U.S. v. Rivera, 570 F.3d 1009 (8th Cir. 2009)

U.S. v. Robinson, 984 F.2d 911 (8th Cir. 1993)

U.S. v. Salamasina, No.09-2188 (8th Cir. 2010)

U.S. v. Scott, 610 F.3d 1009 (8th Cir. 2010)
U.S. v. Smith, 383 F.3d 700 (8th Cir. 2004)
U.S. v. Suitt, 569 F.3d 867 (8th Cir. 2009)
U.S. v. Sundby, 186 F.3d 873 (8th Cir. 1999)
U.S. v. Terriques, 319 F.3d 1051 (8th Cir. 2003)
U.S. v. Tugwell, 125 F.3d 600 (8th Cir. 1997)
U.S. v. Valle Cruz, 452 F.3d 698 (8th Cir. 2006)
U.S. v. Vasquez, 213 F.3d 425 (8th Cir. 2000)
U.S. v. Walker, 324 F.3d 1032 (8th Cir. 2003)
U.S. v. White, 42 F.3d 457 (8th Cir. 1994)
U.S. v. Yang, 345 F.3d 650 (8th Cir. 2003)
U.S. v. Zacher, 465 F.3d 336 (8th Cir. 2006)

NINTH CIRCUIT

B.C. v. Plumas Unified School District, 192 F.3d 1260, 1266 (9th Cir. 1999)
Brewer v. City of Napa, 210 F.3d 1093 (9th Cir. 2000)
Chew v. Gates, 27 F.3d 1432 (9th Cir. 1994)
Duvall v. City of Santa Monica, 42 F.3d 1399 (9th Cir. 1994)
Fikes v. Cleghorn, 47 F.3d 1011 (9th Cir. 1995)
Gilliam v. County of Los Angeles, 37 F.3d 1505 (9th Cir. 1994)
Grant v. City of Long Beach, 315 F.3d 1081 (9th Cir. 2002)
In re $102,000, 823 P.2d 468 (9th Cir. 1992)
Jetton v. City of Downey, 86 F.3d 1162 (9th Cir. 1996)
Marquez v. Andrade, 79 F.3d 1153 (9th Cir. 1996)
Martineau v. City of Cypress, 95 F.3d 1158 (9th Cir. 1996)
Mendoza v. Block, 27 F.3d 1357 (9th Cir. 1994)
Miller v. Clark County, 340 F.3d 959 (9th Cir. 2003)
Parra v. City of Chino, 141 F.3d 1178 (9th Cir. 1998)
Quintanilla v. City of Downey, 84 F.3d 353 (9th Cir. 1996)
Ruvalcaba v. City of Los Angeles, 167 F.3d 514 (9th Cir. 1999)
Shannon v. City of Costa Mesa, 46 F.3d 1145 (9th Cir. 1995)
Smith v. City of Hemet, 394 F.3d 689 (9th Cir. 2005)
U.S. v. $22,474, 246 F.3d 1212 (9th Cir. 2001)
U.S. v. $30,060, 39 F.3d 1039 (9th Cir. 1994)
U.S. v. $42,500, 283 F.3d 977 (9th Cir. 2002)
U.S. v. $49,576, 116 F.3d 425 (9th Cir.1997)
U.S. v. $191,910, 16 F.3d 1051 (9th Cir. 1994)
U.S. v. Aldaz, 921 F.2d 227 (9th Cir. 1990)
U.S. v. Attardi, 796 F.2d 257 (9th Cir. 1986)
U.S. v. Ayarza, 874 F.2d 647 (9th Cir. 1989)
U.S. v. Cedano-Arellano, 332 F.3d 568 (9th Cir. 2003)
U.S. v. DiCisare, 765 F.2d 890 (9th Cir. 1985)
U.S. v. Dickerson v. One Cessna 421B Aircraft, 873 F.2d 1181 (9th Cir. 1989)
U.S. v. Erwin, 803 F.2d 1505 (9th Cir. 1986)
U.S. v. Fernandez, 772 F2d 495 (9th Cir. 1985)
U.S. v. Gill, 280 F.3d 923 (9th Cir. 2002)
U.S. v. Golb, 69 F.3d 1417 (9th Cir. 1995)
U.S. v. Guerrera, 554 F.2d 987 (9th Cir. 1977)
U.S. v. Hernandez, 314 F.3d 430 (9th Cir. 2002)

U.S. v. Ibarra, 345 F.3d 711 (9th Cir. 2003)
U.S. v. Jefferson, 566 F.3d 928 (9th Cir. 2009)
U.S. v. Jensen, 425 F.3d 698 (9th Cir. 2005)
U.S. v. Johnson, 990 F.2d 1129 (9th Cir. 1993)
U.S. v. Lozano, No. 09-20151 (9th Cir. 2010)
U.S. v. Lingenfelter, 997 F.2d 632 (9th Cir. 1993)
U.S. v. Low, 887 F.3d 232 (9th Cir. 1989)
U.S. v. Malone, 886 F.2d 1162 (9th Cir. 1989)
U.S. v. Martell, 654 F.2d 1356 (9th Cir. 1981)
U.S. v. Mondello, 927 F.2d 1463 (9th Cir. 1991)
U.S. v. Perez, 37 F.3d 510 (9th Cir. 1994)
U.S. v. Quoc Viet Hoang, 486 F.3d 1156 (9th Cir. 2007)
U.S. v. Ramirez, 473 F.3d 1026 (9th Cir. 2006)
U.S. v. Richards, 500 F.2d 1025 (9th Cir. 1974)
U.S. v. Spetz, 721 F.2d 1457 (9th Cir. 1983)
U.S. v. Stephens, 206 F.3d 914 (9th Cir. 2000)
U.S. v. Taylor, 934 F.2d 218 (9th Cir. 1991)
U.S. v. Todhunter, 297 F.3d 886 (9th Cir. 2002)
U.S. v. Wong, 334 F.3d 831 (9th Cir. 2003)
Vera Cruz v. City of Escondido, 126 F.3d 1214 (9th Cir. 1997)
Vera Cruz v. City of Escondido, 139 F.3d 659 (9th Cir. 1998)
Warren v. Las Vegas Police Department, 111 F.3d 139 (9th Cir. 1997)
Watkins v. City of Oakland, 145 F.3d 1087 (9th Cir. 1998)

TENTH CIRCUIT

Bastible v. Weyerhouser Co., 427 F.3d 999 (10th Cir. 2006)
Chavez v. City of Albuquerque, 402 F.3d 1039 (10th Cir. 2005)
Marquez v. City of Albuquerque, 399 F.3d 1216 (10th Cir. 2005)
Romo v. Champion, 46 F.3d 1013 (10th Cir. 1995)
Thomson v. Salt Lake County, 584 F.3d 1304 (10th Cir. 2009)
U.S. v. $252,300, 484 F.3d 1271 (10th Cir. 2007)
U.S. v. Bell, 892 F.2d 959 (10th Cir. 1989)
U.S. v. Berrelleza, 90 Fed.Appx. 361, 365 (10th Cir. 2004)
U.S. v. Blaze, 143 F.3d 585 (10th Cir. 1998)
U.S. v. Bloom, 975 F.2d 1447 (10th Cir. 1992)
U.S. v. Brown, 24 F.3d 1223 (10th Cir. 1994)
U.S. v. Burns, 624 F.2d 95 (10th Cir. 1980)
U.S. v. Carhee, 27 F.3d 1493 (10th Cir. 1994)
U.S. v. Cervine, 347 F.3d 865 (10th Cir. 2003)
U.S. v. Chavira, 9 F.3d 888 (10th Cir. 1993)
U.S. v. Clarkson, 551 F.3d 1196 (10th Cir. 2009), on remand, 2009 WL 1651043 (D.Utah 2009)
U.S. v. Crabb, 952 F2d 1245 (10th Cir. 1991), cert. denied, 504 U.S. 925 (1992)
U.S. v. DeLuca, 269 F.3d 1128 (10th Cir. 2001)
U.S. v. Forbes, 528 F.3d 1273 (10th Cir. 2008)
U.S. v. Garcia, 42 F.3d 719 (10th Cir. 1994)
U.S. v. Garcia-Zambrano, 530 F.3d 1249 (10th Cir. 2008)
U.S. v. Garzon, 119 F.3d 1446 (10th Cir. 1997)
U.S. v. Gault, 92 F.3d 990 (10th Cir. 1996)
U.S. v. Glover, 104 F.3d 1570 (10th Cir. 1997)

U.S. v Gonzalez-Acosta, 989 F.2d 384 (10th Cir. 1993)

U.S. v. Hall, 978 F.2d 616 (10th Cir. 1992)

U.S. v. Hernandez, 7 F.3d 944 (10th Cir. 1993)

U.S. v. Houston, 21 F.3d 1035 (10th Cir. 1994)

U.S. v. Hunnicutt, 135 F.3d 1345 (10th Cir. 1998)

U.S. v. Kennedy, 131 F.3d 1371 (10th Cir. 1997)

U.S. v. Klinginsmith, 25 F.3d 1507 (10th Cir. 1994)

U.S. v. Ladeaux, 454 F.3d 1107 (10th Cir. 2006)

U.S. v. Ludwig, 10 F.3d 1523, 1528 (10th Cir. 1993)

U.S. v. Ludwig, 2011 WL 1533520 (10th Cir. 2011)

U.S. v. Lux, 905 F.2d 1379 (10th Cir. 1990)

U.S. v. MacDonald, 670 F.2d 910 (10th Cir. 1982)

U.S. v. Manjarrez, 348 F.3d 881 (10th Cir. 2003)

U.S. v. McCranie, 703 F.2d 1213 (10th Cir. 1983)

U.S. v. Mendoza, 468 F.3d 1256 (10th Cir. 2006)

U.S. v. Moore, 22 F.3d 241 (10th Cir. 1994)

U.S. v. Munoz-Nava, 524 F.3d 1137 (10th Cir. 2008)

U.S. v. Nicholson, 144 F.3d 632 (10th Cir. 1998)

U.S. v. Nielsen, 9 F.3d 1487 (10th Cir. 1993)

U.S. v. Oliver, 363 F.3d 1061 (10th Cir. 2004)

U.S. v. Ortega-Jiminez, 232 F.3d 1325 (10th Cir. 2000)

U.S. v. Patten, 183 F.3d 1190 (10th Cir. 1999)

U.S. v. Pinedo-Montoya, 966 F.2d 591 (10th Cir. 1992)

U.S. v. Pinkard, 125 F.3d 865 (10th Cir. 1997)

U.S. v. Place, 462 U.S. 696 (10th Cir. 1983)

U.S. v. Pollard, 466 F.2d 1 (10th Cir. 1972)

U.S. v. Ramirez, 342 F.3d 1210 (10th Cir. 2003)

U.S. v. Romo, 46 F.3d 1013 (10th Cir. 1995)

U.S. v. Rosborough, 366 F.3d 1145 (10th Cir. 2004)

U.S. v. Salas-Torres, 60 F.3d 837, 1995 WL 406937 (10th Cir. 1995)

U.S. v. Scales, 903 F.2d 765 (10th Cir. 1990)

U.S. v. Scarborough, 128 F.3d 1373 (10th Cir. 1997)

U.S. v. Shayesteh, 161 F.3d 19, 1998 WL 694500 (10th Cir. 1998)

U.S. v. Souza, 223 F.3d 1197 (10th Cir. 2000)

U.S. v. Stone, 866 F.2d 359 (10th Cir. 1989)

U.S. v. Sukiz-Grado, 22 F.3d 1006 (10th Cir. 1994)

U.S. v. Valles, 292 F.3d 678 (10th Cir. 2002)

U.S. v. Vazquez, 555 F.3d 923 (10th Cir. 2009)

U.S. v. Venema, 563 F.2d 1003 (10th Cir. 1977)

U.S. v. Villa-Chaparro, 115 F.3d 797 (10th Cir. 1997)

U.S. v. White, 584 F.3d 935 (10th Cir. 2009)

U.S. v. Williams, 726 F.2d 661 (10th Cir. 1984)

U.S. v. Williams, 271 F.3d 1262 (10th Cir. 2001)

U.S. v. Williams, 356 F.3d 1268 (10th Cir. 2004)

U.S. v. Williams, 403 F.3d 1203 (10th Cir. 2005)

U.S. v. Winningham, 140 F.3d 1328 (10th Cir. 1998)

U.S. v. Wood, 105 F.3d 942 (10th Cir. 1997)

Zamora v. Pomeroy, 639 F.2d 662 (10th Cir. 1981)

ELEVENTH CIRCUIT

Hearn v. The Board of Public Education, 191 F.3d 1329 (11th Cir. 1999)
Kerr v. City of West Palm Beach, 875 F.2d 1546 (11th Cir. 1989)
Merrett v. Moore, 58 F.3d 1547 (11th Cir. 1995)
Priester v. City of Riviera Beach, Florida, 208 F.3d 319 (11th Cir. 2000)
Trammell v. Thomason, 2009 WL 1706591 (11th Cir. 2009)
U.S. v. $183,791, 2010 WL 30961 (11th Cir. 2010)
U.S. v. $242,484, 389 F.3d 1149 (11th Cir. 2004)
U.S. v. Anderson, 2010 WL 597230 (11th Cir. 2010)
U.S. v. Banks, 3 F.3d 399 (11th Cir. 1993)
U.S. v. Brown, 731 F.2d 1491 (11th Cir. 1974), modified at 742 F.2d 1505 (11th Cir. 1984)
U.S. v. Campbell, 920 F.2d 973 (11th Cir. 1991)
U.S. v. Cooper, 873 F.2d 269 (11th Cir. 1989)
U.S. v. Dunkley, 911 F.2d 522 (11th Cir. 1990)
U.S. v. Glinton, 154 F.3d 1245 (11th Cir. 1998)
U.S. v. Hardy, 855 F.2d 753 (11th Cir. 1988) cert. denied 109 S.Ct. 1137, 103 L.Ed.2d 198 (1989)
U.S. v. Holloman, 113 F.3d 192 (11th Cir. 1997)
U.S. v. Lavado, 750 F.2d 1527 (11th Cir. 1985)
U.S. v. Ospina, 798 F.2d 1570 (11th Cir. 1986)
U.S. v. Prevo, 435 F.3d 1343 (11th Cir. 2006)
U.S. v. Puglisi, 723 F.2d 779 (11th Cir. 1984)
U.S. v. Rackley, 742 F.2d 1266 (11th Cir. 1984)
U.S. v. Sentovich, 677 F.2d 834 (11th Cir. 1982)
U.S. v. Smith, 459 F.3d 1276 (11th Cir. 2006)
U.S. v. Steed, 548 F.3d 961 (11th Cir. 2008)
U.S. v. Tamari, 454 F.3d 1259 (11th Cir. 2006)
U.S. v. Virden, 488 F.3d 1317 (11th Cir. 2007)
U.S. v. Watts, 329 F.3d 1282 (11th Cir. 2003)

U.S. COURT OF FEDERAL CLAIMS

EOD Technology, Inc. v. U.S., 82 Fed.Cl. 12 (2008)

ALABAMA

State

Aaron v. Alabama, 271 Ala. 70, 122 So.2d 360 (1960)
Allen v. Alabama, 8 Ala.App. 228, 62 So. 971 (1913)
Gallant v. Alabama, 167 Ala. 60, 52 So. 739 (1910)
Gavin v. Alabama, 891 So.2d 907, 971-2 (Ct. Crim. App. 2003)
Gissendanner v. Alabama, 949 So.2d 956 (2006)
Hodge v. Alabama, 98 Ala. 10, 13 So. 385 (1893)
Holcombe v. Alabama, 437 So.2d 663 (Ct. Crim. App. 1983)
Little v. Alabama, 145 Ala. 662, 39 So. 674 (1905)
Loper v. Alabama, 205 Ala. 216, 87 So. 92 (1920)
Richardson v. Alabama, 145 Ala. 46, 41 So. 82 (1906)
Simpson v. Alabama, 111 Ala. 6, 20 So. 572 (1896)
Tariq-Madyun v. Alabama, 2010 WL 2160290 (Ct. Crim. App. 2010)

ALASKA

STATE

McGahan v. Alaska, 807 P.2d 506 (Ct. App. 1991)
Pooley v. Alaska, 705 P.2d 1293 (Ct. App. 1985)
Wilkie v. Alaska, 715 P.2d 1199 (Ct. App. 1986)

ARIZONA

FEDERAL

Bible v. Schriro, 497 F.Supp.2d 991 (D.C.Az. 2007)

STATE

Arizona v. Bible, 175 Ariz. 549, 858 P.2d 1152 (1993)
Arizona v. Box, 205 Ariz. 492, 73 P.3d 623 (Ct. App. 2003)
Arizona v. Coleman, 122 Ariz. 130, 593 P.2d 684 (Ct. App. 1978)
Arizona v. Navarrete, 2008 WL 4287066 (App. Div. 2008)
Arizona v. Roscoe, 145 Ariz. 212, 700 P.2d 1312 (1984), cert. denied, 471 U.S. 1094 (1985)
Arizona v. Wright, 2009 WL 2411298 (Ct. App. 2009)

ARKANSAS

STATE

Adams v. Arkansas, 149 Ark. 669, 235 S.W. 372 (1921)
Cranford v. Arkansas, 130 Ark. 101, 197 S.W. 19 (1917)
Doyle v. Arkansas, 166 Ark. 505, 266 S.W. 459 (1924)
Farm Bureau Mutual Insurance Co. of Arkansas, Inc. v. Foote, 341 Ark. 105, 14 S.W.3d 512 (2000)
Fox v. Arkansas, 156 Ark. 428, 246 S.W. 863 (1923)
Holub v. Arkansas, 116 Ark. 227, 172 S.W. 878 (1915)
Laime v. Arkansas, 347 Ark. 142, 60 S.W. 3d 464 (2001)
Padgett v. Arkansas, 125 Ark. 471, 188 S.W. 1158 (1916)
Prater v. Arkansas, 307 Ark. 180, 820 S.W.2d 429 (1991)
Rolen v. Arkansas, 191 Ark. 1120, 89 S.W.2d 614 (1936)
Sims v. Arkansas, 356 Ark. 507, 157 S.W.3d 530 (2004)
West v. Arkansas, 150 Ark. 555, 234 S.W. 997 (1921)

CALIFORNIA

FEDERAL

Andrade v. City of Burlingame, 847 F.Supp. 760 (N.D. Cal. 1994)
Ochoa v. City of Buena Park, 2008 WL 2003761 (C.D. Cal. 2008)
U.S. v. Solis, 393 F.Supp. 325 (C.D. Cal. 1975), rev'd 536 F.2d 880 (9th Cir. 1976)

STATE

California v. Adams, 2008 WL 21153557 (Super. Ct. 2008)

California v. Aguilar, 2004 WL 2051385 (Ct. App. 2004); habeas, *Aguilar v. Woodford*, 2009 WL 509127 (C.D. Cal. 2009)

California v. Alonzo, 2008 WL 2248628 (Ct. App. 2008)

California v. Barajas, 2002 WL 1722329 (Ct. App. 2002)

California v. Beverford, 2008 WL 1799763 (Ct, App. 2008)

California v. Brown, 709 P.2d 440, 220 Cal.Rptr. 637 (1985)

California v. Chavez, 2004 WL 1173075 (Ct. App. 2004)

California v. Craig, 86 Cal.App.3d 905, 150 Cal.Rptr. 676 (Ct. App. 1978)

California v. Daniels, 2010 WL 598611 (Ct. App. 2010)

California v. Demirdjian, 2003 WL 1963204 (Ct. App 2003); habeas, *Demirdjian v. Sullivan*, 2009 WL 2767673 (C.D. Cal. 2009)

California v. DeSantiago, 2003 WL 21753766 (Ct. App. 2003)

California v. Espinoza, 2008 WL 2908718 (Ct. App. 2008)

California v. Evans, 65 Cal.App.3d 924, 134 Cal.Rptr. 436 (1977)

California v. Furman, 30 Cal.App.3d 454, 106 Cal.Rptr. 366 (Ct. App. 1973)

California v. Gonzales, 218 Cal.App.3d 403, 267 Cal.Rptr. 138 (Ct. App. 1990)

California v. Gutierrez, 2004 WL 723161 (Ct. App. 2004)

California v. Hackett, 2003 WL 463976 (Ct. App. 2003)

California v. Kelly, 17 Cal.3d 24, 549 P.2d. 1240, 130 Cal.Rptr. 144 (1976)

California v. King, 2004 WL 2012943 (Ct. App. 2004)

California v. Lee, 2003 WL 22100843 (Ct. App. 2003)

California v. Loaiza, 2005 WL 237258 (Ct. App. 2005)

California v. Malgren, 139 Cal.App.3d 234, 188 Cal.Rptr. 569 (Ct. App. 1983)

California v. Melara, 2006 WL 164989 (Ct. App. 2006)

California v. Mitchell, 110 Cal.App.4th 772, 2 Cal.Rptr.3d 49 (Ct. App. 2003)

California v. Nash, 2010 WL 159356 (Ct. App. 2010)

California v. Rivera, 8 Cal.App.4th 100, 10 Cal.Rptr.2d 785 (Ct. App. 1992)

California v. Rivera, 2004 WL 2601335 (Ct. App. 2004)

California v. Robinson, 2004 WL 2418068 (Ct. App. 2004)

California v. Rodrick, 2001 WL 1422348 (Cal. App. 2001)

California v. Salcido, GA052057 (Los Angeles Super. Ct., March 11, 2005)

California v. Sanders, 2009 WL 3682460 (Ct. App. 2009)

California v. Sandoval, 2002 WL 519848 (Ct. App. 2002)

California v. Schoppe-Rico, 140 Cal.App.4th 1370 (Ct. App. 2006)

California v. Searcy, 2006 WL 689135 (Ct. App. 2006)

California v. Sherman, 2003 WL 21500301 (Ct. App. 2003)

California v. Smith, 2011 WL 1350762 (Ct. App. 2011)

California v. Sommer, 12 Cal.App.4th 1642, 16 Cal.Rptr.2d 165 (Ct. App. 1993)

California v. Stanton, 2009 WL 4686320 (Ct. App. 2009)

California v. Terrill, 2002 WL 1308297 (Ct. App. 2002)

California v. Valenzuala, 28 Cal.Rptr.4th 817, 33 Cal.Rptr.2d 802 (Ct. App. 1994)

California v. White, 2009 WL 3111677 (Ct. App. 2009)

California v. Willis, 115 Cal.App.4th 379, 9 Cal.Rptr. 3d 235 (Ct. App. 2004)

COLORADO

FEDERAL

Kliewer v. Sopata, 797 F.Supp. 1569 (D.Colo. 1992)

STATE

Colorado v. Boylan, 854 P.2d 807 (1993)
Colorado v. Brooks, 975 P.2d 1105, 81 A.L.R.5th 779 (1999)
Colorado v. Haley, 41 P.3d 666 (2001)
Colorado v. Ortega, 34 P.3d 986 (2001)
Colorado v. Reyes, 956 P.2d 1254 (1998)
Colorado v. Unruh, 713 P.2d 370 (1986)
Colorado v. Wieser, 796 P.2d 982 (1990)

CONNECTICUT

STATE

Connecticut v. Eisenbach, 2010 WL 2748464 (Super. Ct. 2010)
Connecticut v. Esposito, 235 Conn. 802, 670 A.2d 301 (1995)
Connecticut v. Kelly, 2009 WL 323481 (Super. Ct. 2009)
Connecticut v. St. John, 282 Conn. 260, 919 A.2d 452 (2007)
Connecticut v. Wallace, 181 Conn. 237, 435 A.2d 20 (1980)
Connecticut v. Wilson, 180 Conn. 481, 429 A.2d 931 (1980)

DELAWARE

STATE

Banther v. Delaware, 823 A.2d 467 (2003)
Cook v. Delaware, 374 A.2d 264 (1977)
Reisch v. Delaware, 628 A.2d 84, 1993 WL 227264 (1993)

DISTRICT OF COLUMBIA

FEDERAL

Levering v. District of Columbia, 869 F. Supp. 24, 26-27 (D.D.C. 1994)
U.S. v. Broadway, 580 F.Supp.2d 1179 (D.D.C. 2008)
U.S. ex rel. Cody v. Computer Sciences Corp., 246 F.R.D. 22 (D.D.C. 2007)
U.S. v. Computer Sciences Corp., 246 F.R.D. 22 (D.D.C. 2007)
U.S. v. Liberto, 660 F.Supp. 889 (D.D.C. 1987), aff'd 838 F.2d 571 (D.C. Cir. 1988)
U.S. v. Trayer, 701 F.Supp. 250, 256 (D.D.C. 1988)

STATE

Coleman v. U.S., 306 F.2d 751 (Ct. App. 1962)

Edwards v. District of Columbia, 390 So.2d 1239 (D.C. App. 1980)
Frye v. U.S., 54 App.D.C. 46, 293 F. 1013 (Ct. App. 1923)
Starkes v. U.S., 427 A.2d 437 (D.C. App. 1981)

FLORIDA

FEDERAL

Bolick v. Brevard County, Sheriff's Department, 937 F.Supp. 1560 (M.D.Fla. 1996)

STATE

Bain v. Florida, 839 So2d 739 (Ct. App. 2003)
Baker v. Cohen, 2010 WL 3385266 (S.D.Fla. 2010)
Bass v. Florida, 791 So.2d 1124 (Ct. App. 2000)
Cavaluzzi v. Florida, 409 So.2d 1108 (Ct. App. 1982)
Davis v. Florida, 46 Fla. 26, 36 So. 170 (1904)
Dedge v. Florida, 442 So.2d 429 (Ct. App. 1983)
Edwards v. Florida, 390 So.2d 1239 (Ct. App. 1980)
Elliott v. Florida, 2010 WL 4273186 (Ct. App. 2010)
F.P. v. Florida, 528 So.2d 1253 (Ct. App. 1988)
Florida v. Foster, 390 So.2d 469, 470 (Ct. App. 1980)
Florida v. Laveroni, 910 So.2d 333 (Ct. App. 2005)
Florida v. Rabb, 920 So.2d 1175 (Ct. App. 2006), cert. denied, 549 U.S. 1052 (2006)
Fones v. Florida, 765 So.2d 849 (Ct. App. 2000).
Green v. Florida, 641 So.2d 391 (1994)
Green v. Florida, 975 So.2d 1090 (2008)
Jardines v. Florida, 2011 WL 1405080 (2011)
Lippman v. City of Miami, 2010 WL 2836713 (S.D.Fla. 2010)
Matheson v. Florida, 870 So.2d 8 (Ct. App. 2004)
McCray v. Florida, 915 So.2d 239 (Ct. App. 2005)
Nelson v. Florida, 867 So.2d 534 (Ct. App. 2004)
Ramos v. Florida, 496 So.2d 121 (1986)
Stabler v. Florida, 990 So.2d 1258, 1262 (Ct. App. 2008)
Tomlinson v. Florida, 129 Fla. 658, 176 So. 543 (1937)

GEORGIA

STATE

Aiken v. Georgia, 16 Ga.App. 848, 86 S.E. 1076 (Ct. App. 1915)
Bacon v. Georgia, 249 Ga.App. 347, 548 S.E.2d 78 (Ct. App. 2001)
Bogan v. Georgia, 165 Ga.App. 851, 303 S.E.2d 48 (Ct. App. 1983)
Burns International Security Services Corp. v. Johnson, 284 Ga.App. 289, 643 S.E.2d 800 (Ct. App. 2007)
Carr v. Georgia, 267 Ga. 701, 482 S.E.2d 314 (1997), overruled on other grounds, *Clark v. Georgia*, 271 Ga. 5, 515 S.E.2d 155 (1999)
Cole v. Georgia, 254 Ga.App. 424, 562 S.E.2d 720 (Ct. App. 2002)
Dawson v. Georgia, 238 Ga.App. 263, 518 S.E.2d 477 (Ct. App. 1999)

Fife v. Georgia, 16 Ga.App. 22, 84 S.E. 485 (Ct. App. 1915)
Harper v. Georgia, 249 Ga. 519(1), 292 S.E.2d 389 (1982)
Harris v. Georgia, 17 Ga.App. 723, 88 S.E. 121 (Ct. App. 1916)
Johnson v. Georgia, 165 Ga.App. 146, 299 S.E.2d 740 (Ct. App. 1983)
Johnson v. Georgia, 293 Ga.App. 32, 666 S.E.2d 452 (Ct. App. 2008)
Mitchell v. Georgia, 202 Ga. 247, 42 S.E.2d 767 (1947)
Schell v. Georgia, 72 Ga.App. 804, 35 S.E.2d 325 (Ct. App. 1945)
Simmons v. Georgia, 223 Ga.App. 781, 479 S.E.2d 123 (Ct. App. 1996)
Smith v. Georgia, 247 Ga. 612, 619, 277 S.E.2d 678, 683 (1981)
Troup v. Georgia, 26 Ga.App. 623, 107 S.E. 75 (Ct. App. 1921)

HAWAII

STATE

Hawaii v. Torres, 122 Hawaii 2, 222 P.2d 409 (2009)

IDAHO

FEDERAL

U.S. v. Esparza, No. CF-07-14-S-BLW (D.Id. 2007) (memorandum and order)

STATE

Idaho v. Braendle, 124 Idaho 173, 997 P.2d 634 (Ct. App. 2000)
Idaho v. Parkinson, 135 Idaho 357, 17 P.3d 301 (Ct. App. 2000)
Idaho v. Streeper, 113 Idaho 662, 747 P.2d 71 (1987)
Idaho Department of Law Enforcement v. $34,000, 121 Idaho 211, 824 P.2d 142 (Ct. App. 1992)

ILLINOIS

FEDERAL

Graham v. City of Chicago, 828 F.Supp. 576 (N.D.Ill. 1993)
Martens v. District No. 220 Board of Education, 620 F.Supp. 29 (N.D.Ill. 1985)
Picha v. Wielgos, 410 F.Supp. 1214 (N.D.Ill. 1976)
U.S. v. Freymuller, 571 F.Supp. 61 (N.D.Ill. 1983)

STATE

Illinois v. Acri, 277 Ill.App.3d 1030, 662 N.E.2d 115 (Ct. App. 1996)
Illinois v. Bartelt, 384 Ill.App.3d 1028, 894 N.E.2d 482, 323 Ill.Dec. 715 (Ct. App. 2008),
　　aff'd 2011 WL 1049788 (2011)
Illinois v. Caballes, 207 Ill.2d 504, 802 N.E.2d 202 (2003)
Illinois v. Cox, 202 Ill. 2d 462, 782 N. E. 2d 275 (2002), cert. denied 539 U.S. 937, 123 S.Ct.
　　2574, 156 L.Ed.2d 622 (2003)
Illinois v. Cruz, 162 Ill.2d 314, 643 N.E.2d 636 (1994)
Illinois v. Fondja, 317 Ill.App.3d 966, 251 Ill.Dec. 553, 740 N.E.2d 839 (Ct. App. 2000)

Illinois v. Griffin, 48 Ill.App.2d 148, 198 N.E.2d 115 (Ct. App. 1964)
Illinois v. Holmes, 397 Ill.App.3d 737, 922 N.E.2d 1179, 337 Ill.Dec. 602 (Ct. App. 2010)
Illinois v. Lefler, 294 Ill.App.3d 305, 689 N.E.2d 1209, 228 Ill.Dec. 788 (Ct. App. 1998)
Illinois v. McDonald, 322 Ill.App.3d 244, 749 N.E.2d 1066 (Ct. App. 2001)
Illinois v. Pfanschmidt, 262 Ill. 411, 104 N.E. 804 (1914)
Illinois v. Yarber, 279 Ill.App.3d 519, 663 N.E.2d 1131 (Ct. App. 1996)
Platacis v. Village of Streamwood, 224 Ill.App.3d 336, 586 N.E.2d 564, 166 Ill.Dec. 606 (Ct. App. 1991)

INDIANA

FEDERAL

Doe v. Renfrow, 475 F.Supp. 1012 (N.D.Ind. 1979), rev'd on other grounds, 631 F.2d 91 (7th Cir. 1980), cert. denied 451 U.S. 1022, 101 S.Ct. 3015, 69 L.Ed.2d 395 (1981)
Mason v. Hamilton County, 13 F.Supp.2d 829 (S.D.Ind. 1998)
U.S. v. Jackson, 2004 WL 1784756 (S.D.Ind. 2004)

STATE

Bradshaw v. Indiana, 759 N.E.2d 271 (Ct. App. 2001)
Brafford v. Indiana, 516 N.E.2d 45 (1987)
Hoop v. Indiana, 909 N.E.2d 463 (Ct. App. 2009)
Indiana v. McDonald, 322 Ill.App.3d 244, 749 N.E.2d 1066 (Ct. App. 2001)
Neuhoff v. Indiana, 708 N.E.2d 889 (Ct. App. 1999)
Richardson v. Indiana, 912 N.E.2d 915, 2009 WL 2850342 (2009)
Ruse v. Indiana, 186 Ind. 237, 115 N.E. 778 (1917)
Stout v. Indiana, 174 Ind. 395, 92 N.E. 161 (1910)

IOWA

STATE

In the Interest of S.S., Minor Child, 2009 WL 3337667 (Ct. App. Iowa)
Iowa v. Bergmann, III, 633 N.W.2d 328 (2001)
Iowa v. Buller, 517 N.W.2d 711 (1994)
Iowa v. Grba, 196 Iowa 241, 194 N.W. 250 (1923)
McClurg v. Benton, 123 Iowa 368, 65 L.R.A. 519, 98 N.W. 881 (1904)

KANSAS

FEDERAL

U.S. v. Garcia, 52 F.Supp.2d 1239 (D.Kan. 1999)
U.S. v. Germosen-Garcia, 712 F.Supp. 862 (D.Kan. 1989)
U.S. v. Hill, 701 F.Supp. 1522 (D.Kan. 1988)
U.S. v. Lambert, 834 F.Supp. 1318 (D.Kan. 1993)
U.S. v. Meindl, 83 F.Supp.2d 1207 (D.Kan. 1999)
U.S. v. Wood, 915 F.Supp. 1126 (D. Kan. 1996), rev'd, 106 F.3d 942 (10th Cir. 1997)

STATE

Kansas v. Adams, 85 Kan. 435, 116 P. 608 (1911)
Kansas v. Barker, 252 Kan. 949, 850 P.2d 885 (1993)
Kansas v. Evans, 115 Kan. 538, 224 P. 492 (1924)
Kansas v. Fixley, 118 Kan. 1, 233 P. 796 (1925)
Kansas v. Freel, 29 Kan.App.2d 852, 32 P.3d 1219 (Ct. App. 2001)
Kansas v. Netherton, 133 Kan. 685, 3 P.2d 495 (1931)
Kansas v. Schalansky, 112 Kan. 87, 209 P. 816 (1922)
Kansas v. Wainwright, 18 Kan.App.2d 449, 856 P.2d 163 (Ct. App. 1993)

KENTUCKY

FEDERAL

U.S. v. Smallwood, 2010 WL 4008280 (W.D.Ky. 2010)

STATE

Allen v. Kentucky, 26 Ky.L.Rptr. 807, 82 S.W. 589 (Ct. App. 1904)
Alsept v. Kentucky, 240 Ky. 395, 42 S.W.2d 517 (Ct. App. 1931)
Blair v. Kentucky, 171 Ky. 319, 188 S.W. 390 (1916), after remand, 181 Ky. 218, 204 S.W. 67 (1918)
Brummett v. Kentucky, 263 Ky. 460, 92 S.W.2d 787 (Ct. App. 1936)
Bullock v. Kentucky, 249 Ky. 1, 60 S.W.2d 108 (Ct. App. 1933)
Crabtree v. Kentucky, 260 Ky. 575, 86 S.W.2d 301 (Ct. App. 1935)
Daugherty v. Kentucky, 293 Ky. 147, 168 S.W.2d 564 (Ct. App. 1943)
Debruler v. Kentucky, 231 S.W.3d 752 (2007)
Denham v. Kentucky, 27 Ky.L.Rptr. 171, 84 S.W. 538 (Ct. App. 1905)
Hays v. Kentucky, 211 Ky. 716, 277 S.W. 1004 (Ct. App. 1925)
Keaton v. Kentucky, 223 Ky 645, 4 S.W.2d 675 (Ct. App. 1928)
Kelly v. Kentucky, 259 Ky. 770, 83 S.W.2d 489 (Ct. App. 1935)
Meyers v. Kentucky, 194 Ky. 523, 240 S.W. 71 (Ct. App. 1922)
Pedigo v. Kentucky, 103 Ky. 41, 44 S.W. 143, 42 L.R.A. 432 (Ct. App. 1898)
Short v. Kentucky, 251 Ky. 819, 66 S.W.2d 33 (1933)
Sprouse v. Kentucky, 132 Ky. 269, 116 S.W. 344 (Ct. App. 1909)
Stidham v. Kentucky, 221 Ky. 49, 297 S.W. 929 (Ct. App. 1927)
Thacker v. Kentucky, 2005 WL 2675001 (2005)

LOUISIANA

FEDERAL

Davis v. Cain, 2005 Wl 5191912 (E.D.La. 2008)
U.S. v. Cunningham, 1996 WL 665747 (E.D.La. 1996)

STATE

Louisiana v. Davis, 149 La. 1009, 90 So. 385, 154 La. 295, 97 So. 449 (1923)
Louisiana v. Green, 210 La. 157, 26 So.2d 487 (1946)
Louisiana v. Harrison, 149 La. 83, 88 So. 696 (1921)

Louisiana v. Kalie, 699 So.2d 879 (1997)
Louisiana v. King, 144 La. 430, 80 So. 615 (1919)
Louisiana v. Murray, 827 So.2d 488 (Ct. App. 2003)

MAINE

STATE

Maine v. Atwood, 988 A.2d 981 (2010)
Maine v. Cole, 695 A.2d 1180 (1997)

MARYLAND

STATE

Briscoe v. Maryland, 40 Md.App. 120, 388 A.2d 153 (Ct. Spec. App. 1978)
Carter v. Maryland, 143 Md.App. 670, 795 A.2d 790 (Ct. App. 2002), cert. denied 369 Md. 571, 801 A.2d 1032 (2002)
Clark v. Maryland, 140 Md.App. 540, 781 A.2d 913 (Ct. Spec. App. 2001)
Emory v. Maryland, 101 Md.App. 585, 647 A.2d 1243 (Ct. Spec. App. 1994)
Fitzgerald v. Maryland, 153 Md.App. 601, 837 A.2d 989 (Ct. Spec. App. 2003), aff'd 384 Md. 484, 864 A.2d 1006 (2004)
In re Montrail M., 87 Md.App. 420, 589 A.2d 1318 (Ct. Spec. App. 1991), aff'd 325 Md. 527, 601 A.2d 1102 (1992)
Koenig v. Maryland, 368 Md. 150, 792 A.2d 1124 (Ct. App. 2002)
Maryland v. Cabral, 159 Md.App. 354, 381, 859 A.2d 285 (Ct. App. 2004)
Maryland v. Wallace, 372 Md. 137, 142-3, 812 A.2d 291, 294 (Ct. App. 2003), cert. denied 540 U.S. 1140, 124 S.Ct. 1036, 157 L.Ed.2d 951 (2004)
McKay v. Maryland, 149 Md.App. 176, 814 A.2d 592 (Ct. Spec. App. 2002)
Roberts v. Maryland, 53 Md.App. 257, 452 A.2d 1271 (Ct. Spec. App. 1982), aff'd, 298 Md. 261, 469 A.2d 442 (Ct. App. 1983)
Terrell v. Maryland, 3 Md.App. 340, 239 A.2d 128 (Ct. Spec. App. 1968)
Timmons v. Maryland, 114 Md.App. 410, 690 A.2d 530 (Ct. Spec. App. 1997)
Wilkes v. Maryland, 364 Md. 554, 774 A.2d 420 (Ct. App. 2000)

MASSACHUSETTS

FEDERAL

Andrews v. DuBois, 888 F. Supp. 213, 216 (D.Mass. 1995)
U.S. v. Hebshie, 2010 WL 4722040 (D.Mass. 2010)

STATE

Audette v. Massachusetts, 63 Mass.App.Ct. 727, 829 N.E.2d 248 (2005)
Massachusetts v. Feyenord, 62 Mass.App.Ct. 200, 815 N.E.2d 628 (Ct. App. 2004)
Massachusetts v. Lawrence L., 439 Mass. 817, 792 N.E.2d 109 (2003)
Massachusetts v. LePage, 352 Mass. 403, 226 N.E.2d 200 (1967)
Massachusetts v. Smith, 342 Mass. 180, 172 N.E.2d 597 (1961)

MICHIGAN

FEDERAL

Moore v. Howes, 2010 WL 1494764 (E.D.Mich. 2010)

U.S. v. $53,082, 773 F.Supp. 26 (E.D.Mich. 1991), 985 F.2d 245 (6th Cir. 1993)

U.S. v. Lewis, 2005 USDist LEXIS 38142 (W.D.Mich. 2005)

U.S. v. Patty, 96 F.Supp. 703 (E.D.Mich. 2000)

Wade v. Sherry, 2009 WL 5196166 (W.D.Mich. 2009)

STATE

Michigan v. Baker, 2007 WL 600584 (Ct. App. 2007)

Michigan v. Fortin, 2002 WL 77184 (Ct. App. 2002)

Michigan v. Garcia, 2006 WL 1009017 (Ct. App. 2006)

Michigan v. Giles, 2008 WL 2436529 (Ct. App. 2008)

Michigan v. Harper, 43 Mich.App. 500, 204 N.W.2d 263 (Ct. App. 1973)

Michigan v. Hill, 2010 WL 1873105 (Ct. App. 2010)

Michigan v. Jackson, 2008 WL 2037805 (Ct. App. 2008)

Michigan v. Jones, 279 Mich.App. 86, 95, 755 N.W.2d 224, 229 (Ct. App. 2008)

Michigan v. Laidlaw, 169 Mich.App. 84, 96, 425 N.W.2d 738, 743 (Ct. App. 1988)

Michigan v. Martin, 2008 WL 108876 (Ct. App. 2008)

Michigan v. McMillen, 126 Mich.App. 211, 336 N.W.2d 895 (Ct. App. 1983)

Michigan v. McPherson, 85 Mich.App. 341, 271 N.W.2d 228 (Ct. App. 1978)

Michigan v. Norwood, 70 Mich.App. 53, 245 N.W.2d 170 (Ct. App. 1976)

Michigan v. Perryman, 89 Mich.App. 516, 280 NW2d 579 (Ct. App. 1979)

Michigan v. Sands, 280 N.W.2d 579 (Ct. App. 1979)

Michigan v. Stone, 195 Mich.App. 600, 491 N.W.2d 628 (Ct. App. 1992)

Michigan v. Warriner, 461 Mich. 885, 601 N.W.2d 378 (1999)

Michigan v. Wright, 2009 WL 4981153 (Ct. App. 2009)

MINNESOTA

FEDERAL

Shqeirat v. U.S. Airways Group, Inc., 645 F.Supp.2d 765 (D.Minn. 2009)

U.S. v. $90,000 in United States Currency, 2009 WL 6327469 (D.Minn. 2009)

STATE

Crosby v. Moriarity, 148 Minn. 201, 181 N.W. 199 (1921)

Hyatt v. Anoka Police Department, 691 NW2d 828 (2005)

McDuffie v. Minnesota, 482 N.W.2d 234 (Ct. App. 1992)

Minnesota v. Carter, 697 N.W.2d 199 (2005)

Minnesota v. Scharmer, 501 N.W.2d 620 (1993)

MISSISSIPPI

STATE

Bailey v. Mississippi, 960 So.2d 583 (Ct. App. 2007)
Boatwright v. Mississippi, 143 Miss. 676, 109 So. 710 (1926)
Byrom v. Mississippi, 863 So.2d 836 (2003)
Fisher v. Mississippi, 150 Miss. 206, 116 So. 746 (1928)
Harris v. Mississippi, 143 Miss. 102, 108 So. 446 (1926)
Hinton v. Mississippi, 175 Miss. 308, 166 So. 762 (1936)
Millsap v. Mississippi, 767 So.2d 286 (Ct. App. 2000)
Prater v. Mississippi, 18 So.3d 884 (Ct. App. 2009)
S.C. v. Mississippi, 583 So.2d 188 (1991)
Scott v. Mississippi, 108 Miss. 464, 66 So.973 (1915)
Spears v. Mississippi, 92 Miss. 613, 46 So. 166 (1908)

MISSOURI

FEDERAL

U.S. v. $100,000, 761 F.Supp. 672 (E.D.Mo. 1991)

STATE

Missouri v. Barnes, 289 S.W. 562 (Sup. Ct. Div. 2 1926)
Missouri v. Cheatham, 458 S.W.2d 336 (1970)
Missouri v. Dooms, 280 Mo. 84, 217 S.W. 43 (1919)
Missouri v. Fields, 434 S.W.2d 507 (1968)
Missouri v. Freyer, 330 Mo. 62, 48 S.W.2d 894 (Sup. Ct. Div. 2 1932)
Missouri v. Long, 336 Mo. 630, 80 S.W.2d 154 (Sup. Ct. Div. 2 1935)
Missouri v. Rasco, 239 Mo. 535, 144 S.W. 449 (Sup. Ct. Div. 2 1912)
Missouri v. Shawley, 334 Mo. 352, 67 S.W.2d 74 (1933)
Missouri v. White, 195 S.W. 994 (Sup. Ct. Div. 2 1917)

MONTANA

FEDERAL

U.S. v. Neatherlin, 66 F.Supp.2d 1157 (D.Mont. 1999)

STATE

Montana v. Scheetz, 286 Mont. 41, 950 P.2d 722 (1997)
Montana v. Storm, 125 Mont. 346, 238 P.2d 1161 (1951)

NEBRASKA

FEDERAL

U.S. v. Dix, 2007 WL 3046347 (D.Neb. 2007)

U.S. v. Gastelo-Armenta, 2010 WL 1440451 (D.Neb. 2010)

U.S. v. Heir, 107 F.Supp.2d 1088 (D.Neb. 2000)

U.S. v. McGlothen, 2008 WL 4533971 (D.Neb. 2008)

U.S. v. Prokupek, 2009 WL 2634446 (D.Neb. 2009)

STATE

Brott v. Nebraska, 63 L.R.A. 789, 70 Neb. 395, 97 N.W. 593 (1903)

Nebraska v. Ortiz, 257 Neb. 784, 600 N.W.2d 805 (1999)

Nebraska v. Yum, 1998 WL 19484 (Ct. App. 1998)

NEVADA

STATE

Gama v. Nevada, 112 Nev. 833, 920 P.2d 1010 (1996)

NEW HAMPSHIRE

STATE

New Hampshire v. Maya, 126 N.H. 590, 493 A.2d 1139 (1985)

New Hampshire v. Pellicci, 133 N.H. 523, 580 A.2d 710 (1990)

New Hampshire v. Taylor, 118 N.H. 855, 395 A.2d 505 (1978)

NEW JERSEY

FEDERAL

Albanese v. Bergen County, 991 F.Supp. 410 (D.N.J. 1997)

U.S. v. $87,375, 727 F.Supp. 155 (D.N.J. 1989)

STATE

New Jersey v. Keller, 2010 WL 5346025 (Ct. App. 2010)

New Jersey v. Parton, 251 N.J.Super. 230, 597 A.2d 1088 (Ct. App. 1991)

New Jersey v. Sharp, 395 N.J.Super. 175, 186, 928 A.2d 165, 172 (Ct. App. 2006)

New Jersey v. Wanczyk, 196 N.J.Super. 397, 482 A.2d 964 (Super. Ct. 1984)

NEW MEXICO

FEDERAL

Chamberlin v. The City of Albuquerque, 2005 WL 2313527 (D.N.M. 2005)

U.S. v. Florez, 871 F.Supp. 1411 (D.N.M. 1994)

U.S. v. Morales, 489 F.Supp.2d 1250 (D.N.M. 2007)

STATE

New Mexico v. Van Cleave, 131 N.M. 82, 33 P.3d 633 (2001)
New Mexico v. Warsaw, 125 N.M. 8, 956 P.2d 139 (Ct. App. 1998)

NEW YORK

FEDERAL

Hellmers v. Town of Vestal, 969 F. Supp. 837, 842 (N.D.N.Y. 1997)
Holzapfel v. Town of Newburgh, 950 F. Supp. 1267, 1273 (S.D.N.Y. 1997)
Lifrieri v. Stinson, 2009 WL 2413400 (E.D.N.Y. 2009)
Parsons v. Ercole, 2010 WL 883700 (W.D.N.Y. 2010)
U. S. v. $175,260, 741 F.Supp. 45 (E.D.N.Y. 1990)
U.S. v. McNiece, 558 F.Supp. 612, 12 Fed.R.Evid.Serv. 1870 (E.D.N.Y. 1983)
Youngblood v. Conway, 426 F.Supp.2d 107 (W.D.N.Y. 2006)

STATE

New York v. Centolella, 61 Misc.2d 726, 305 N.Y.S.2d 460 (Cty. Ct. 1969)
New York v. Dix, 242 A.D.2d 912, 662 N.Y.S.2d 879 (App. Div. 1997)
New York v. Dunn, 77 N.Y.2d 19, 564 N.E.2d 1054, 563 N.Y.S.2d 388 (1990), cert. den. 501 U.S. 1219, 111 S.Ct. 2830, 115 L.Ed.2d 1000 (1991)
New York v. Gangler, 227 A.D.2d 946, 643 N.Y.S.2d 839 (App. Div. 1996)
New York v. Lifrieri, 230 A.D.2d 754, 646 N.Y.S.2d 172 (App. Div. 1996)
New York v. Muggelberg, 132 A.D.2d 988, 518 N.Y.S.2d 285 (App. Div. 1987)
New York v. Offen, 78 N.Y.2d 1089, 585 N.E.2d 370, 578 N.Y.S.2d 121 (1991)
New York v. Payne, 1 Misc.3d 909, 781 N.Y.S. 627 (Sup. Ct. 2004), aff'd 41 A.D.3d 512, 838 N.Y.2d 123 (App. Div. 2007)
New York v. Price, 54 N.Y.2d 557, 446 N.Y.S.2d 906, 431 N.E.2d 267 (1981)
New York v. Roraback, 242 A.D.2d 400, 405, 662 N.Y.S.2d 327 (App. Div. 1997)
New York v. Shulman, 6 N.Y.3d 1, 843 N.E.2d 125, 809 N.Y.S.2d 485 (2005)
New York v. Tunstall, 278 A.D.2d 585, 717 N.Y.S.2d 685 (App. Div. 2000)
New York v. Vandenbosch, 216 A.D.2d 884 (App. Div. 1995)
New York v. Whitlock, 36 N.Y.Crim.R. 524, 183 A.D. 482, 171 N.Y.S. 109 (App. Div. 1918)

NORTH CAROLINA

STATE

North Carolina v. Bines, 8 N.C.App. 1, 173 S.E.2d 605 (Ct. App. 1970)
North Carolina v. Cross, 681 S.E.2d 566, 2009 WL 2177766 (Ct. App. 2009)
North Carolina v. Davis, 54 N.C. 596, 284 S.E.2d 139 (Ct. App. 1981)
North Carolina v. Dorsett, 245 N.C. 47, 95 S.E.2d 90 (1956)
North Carolina v. Freeman, 146 N.C. 615, 60 S.E. 986 (1908)
North Carolina v. Green, 76 N.C.App. 642, 334 S.E.2d 363 (Ct. App. 1985)
North Carolina v. Hawley, 54 N.C.App 293, 283 S.E.2d 387 (Ct. App. 1981)
North Carolina v. Hunter, 143 N.C. 607, 56 S.E. 547 (1907)
North Carolina v. Irick, 291 N.C. 480, 231 S.E.2d 833 (1977)
North Carolina v. Lanier, 50 N.C.App. 383, 273 S.E.2d 746 (Ct. App. 1981)

North Carolina v. Lee, 211 N.C. 326, 190 S.E. 234 (1937)
North Carolina v. Marze, 22 N.C.App. 628, 207 S.E.2d 359 (Ct. App. 1974)
North Carolina v. McIver, 176 N.C. 718, 96 S.E. 902 (1918)
North Carolina v. McLeod, 196 N.C. 542, 146 S.E. 409 (1929), 198 N.C. 649, 152 S.E. 895 (1930)
North Carolina v. Moore, 55 L.R.A. 96, 129 N.C. 494, 39 S.E. 626 (1901)
North Carolina v. Palmer, 178 N.C. 822, 101 S.E. 506 (1919)
North Carolina v. Petrick, 186 N.C.App. 597, 652 S.E.2d 688 (Ct. App. 2007)
North Carolina v. Porter, 303 N.C. 680, 281 S.E.2d 377 (1981)
North Carolina v. Robinson, 181 N.C. 516, 106 S.E. 155 (1921)
North Carolina v. Rowland, 263 N.C. 353, 139 S.E.2d 661 (1965)
North Carolina v. Spivey, 151 N.C. 676, 65 S.E. 995 (1909)
North Carolina v. Styles, 93 N.C.App. 596, 379 S.E.2d 255 (Ct. App. 1989)
North Carolina v. Taylor, 337 N.C. 597, 447 S.E.2d 360 (1994)
North Carolina v. Walston, 193 N.C.App., 666 S.E.2d 872 (Ct. App. 2008)
North Carolina v. Wiggins, 171 N.C. 813, 89 S.E. 58 (1916)
North Carolina v. Yates, 159 N.C.App. 231, 582 S.E.2d 725 (Ct. App. 2003)

NORTH DAKOTA

STATE

North Dakota v. Iverson, 187 N.W.2d 1 (1971)
North Dakota v. Kesler, 396 N.W.2d 729 (1986)

OHIO

FEDERAL

Cowans v. Bagley, 2002 WL 31370475 (S.D.Oh. 2002)
Culbertson v. Doan, 65 F.Supp. 701 (S.D.Oh. 1999)
Hillman v. Beightler, 2010 WL 2232640 (N.D.Oh. 2010)
Spangler v. Wenninger, 2008 WL 4186318, 2008 WL 4218580 (S.D.Oh. 2008), aff'd 2010 WL 3069600 (6th Cir. 2010)

STATE

Asylum, Inc. v. Liquor Control Commission, 167 Ohio App. 498, 855 N.E.2d 902 (Ct. App. 2006)
Baum v. Ohio, 17 Ohio C.D. 569, 1904 WL 694 (Ohio Cir. 1904)
City of Blue Ash v. Kavanagh, 113 Ohio St.3d 67 (Ct. App. 2007)
City of Fairfield v. Suslovic, 2001 WL 1028404 (Oh. Ct. App. 2001)
Ohio v. Alexander, 141 Ohio App.3d 590, 784 N.E.2d 1225 (Ct. App. 2003)
Ohio v. Baker, 137 Ohio App.3d 628, 739 N.E.2d 819 (Ct. App. 2000)
Ohio v. Bolding, 1999 WL 334494 (Ct. App. 1999)
Ohio v. Bridge, 60 Ohio App.3d 76, 78, 573 N.E.2d 762 (Ct. App. 1989)
Ohio v. Carlson, 102 Ohio App.3d 585, 657 N.E.2d 591 (Ct. App. 1995)
Ohio v. Cowans, 1999 WL 699870 (Ct. App. 1999); 87 Ohio St. 68, 717 N.E.2d 298 (1999); habeas, *Cowans v. Bagley,* 2002 WL 31370475 (S.D.Ohio 2002)
Ohio v. Crowder, 2000 WL 874681 (Ct. App. 2000)

Ohio v. DeWitt, 2007 WL 1934335 (Ct. App. 2007); habeas denied, *DeWitt v. Jackson*, 2009 WL 948903 (S.D.Oh. 2009)

Ohio v. Dickerson, 77 Ohio St. 34, 82 N.E. 969 (1907)

Ohio v. Elkins, 47 Oh.App. 307, 354 N.E.2d 716 (Ct. App. 1976)

Ohio v. Hall, 4 Ohio Dec. 147, 1896 WL 651 (Ct. Com. Pleas 1896)

Ohio v. Knight, 82 Ohio Misc.2d 79, 679 N.E.2d 758 (Ct. Com. Pleas 1997)

Ohio v. Nguyen, 157 Ohio App.3d 482, 811 N.E.2d 1180 (2004)

Ohio v. Palicki, 97 Ohio App.3d 175, 646 N.E.2d 494 (Ct. App. 1994)

Ohio v. Pearson, 2006 WL 3030787 (Ct. App. 2006)

Ohio v. Riley, 88 Ohio App.3d 468, 624 N.E.2d 302 (1993)

Ohio v. Rusnak, 120 Ohio App.3d 24, 696 N.E.2d 633 (Ct. App. 1997)

Ohio v. Serrano, 2004 WL 628970 (Ct. App. 2004)

Ohio v. Simpson, 2002 WL 1625559 (Ct. App. 2002)

Ohio v. Smith, 2002 WL 1972931 (Ct. App. 2002)

OKLAHOMA

FEDERAL

Gilbert v. Franklin, 2008 WL 781863 (E.D.Ok. 2008)

STATE

Buck v. Oklahoma, 77 Okla.Crim. 17, 138 P.2d 115 (Ct. Crim. App. 1943)

OREGON

STATE

Oregon v. Harris, 25 Or.App. 71, 547 P.2d 1394 (Ct. App. 1976)

Oregon v. Slowikowski, 307 Or. 19, 761 P2d 1315 (1988)

Oregon v. Smith, 327 Or. 366, 963 P.2d 642 (1998)

PENNSYLVANIA

FEDERAL

Jaslar v. Zavada, 2009 WL 82553 (M.D. Pa. 2009)

Ricker v. Weston, 2000 WL 1728506 (E.D.Pa. 2000)

U.S. v. Hutchinson, 471 F.Supp.2d 497 (M.D.Pa. 2007)

STATE

Pennsylvania v. Gwynn, 555 Pa. 86, 723 A.2d 143 (1999)

Pennsylvania v. Hoffman, 52 Pa.Super. 272, 1912 WL 4825 (Super. Ct. 1912)

Pennsylvania v. Johnston, 515 Pa. 454, 530 A.2d 74 (1987)

Pennsylvania v. Michaux, 360 Pa.Super 452, 520 A.2d 1177 (Super. Ct. 1987)

Pennsylvania v. Treiber, 582 Pa. 646, 874 A.2d 26 (2005), 970 A.2d. 484 (Table, 2009)

PUERTO RICO

U.S. v. Colon, 845 F.Supp. 923 (D.Puerto Rico 1994)
U.S. v. Maldonado-Espinosa, 767 F.Supp. 1176 (D.Puerto Rico 1991)

SOUTH CAROLINA

FEDERAL

Barton v. Eichelberger, 311 F.Supp. 1132 (M.D.Pa. 1970)

STATE

South Carolina v. Bostick, 253 S.C. 205, 169 S.E.2d 605 (1969)
South Carolina v. Brown, 103 S.C. 437, 88 S.E. 21 (1916)
South Carolina v. Childs, 299 S.C. 471, 385 S.E.2d 839 (1989)
South Carolina v. Johnson, 306 S.C. 119, 410 S.E.2d 547 (1991)
South Carolina v. Jordan, 258 S.C. 340, 188 S.E.2d 780 (1972)
South Carolina v. White, 372 S.C. 364, 384, 642 S.E.2d 607, 617 (Ct. App. 2007), aff'd 382
    S.C. 265, 676 S.E.2d 684 (2009)

SOUTH DAKOTA

STATE

South Dakota v. Guerra, 772 N.W.2d 907 (2009)
South Dakota v. Lockstedt, 695 N.W.2d 718 (2005)
South Dakota v. Nguyen, 726 N.W.2d 871 (2007)
South Dakota v. Reay, 762 NW2d 356 (2009)

TENNESSEE

FEDERAL

Jones v. U.S. Drug Enforcement Administration, 819 F.Supp. 698 (M.D.Tenn. 1993)
U.S. v. Howard, 448 F.Supp.2d 889 (E.D.Tenn. 2006)
U.S. v. Page, 154 F.Supp. 1320 (M.D.Tenn. 2001)

STATE

Copley v. Tennessee, 153 Tenn. 189, 281 S.W. 460 (1926)
Tennessee v. Barger, 612 S.W.2d 485 (Ct. Crim. App. 1981)
Tennessee v. Brewer, 875 S.W.2d 298 (Ct. Crim. App. 1994)
Tennessee v. Bryan, 2003 WL 23021396 (Ct. Crim. App. 2003)
Tennessee v. Casteel, 2004 WL 2138334 (Ct. Crim. App. 2004)
Tennessee v. Cosgrif, 2010 WL 4138560 (Ct. Crim. App. 2010)
Tennessee v. England, 19 S.W.3d 762, 768 (2000)
Tennessee v. Myers, 2009 WL 2503276 (Ct. Crim. App. 2009)
Tennessee v. Shepherd, 902 S.W.2d 895 (1995)

Tennessee v. Virga, 2009 WL 537560 (Ct. Crim. App. 2009)
Tennessee v. Wright, 2008 WL 160243 (Ct. Crim. App. 2008)

TEXAS

FEDERAL

Buchanek v. City of Victoria, 2009 WL 500564, 2010 WL 1268069 (S.D.Tex 2009, 2010)
Green v. Quarterman, 2008 WL 442356 (S.D.Tex. 2008)
Jones v. Latexo Independent School District, 499 F.Supp. 223 (E.D.Tex. 1980)
Karr v. City of Beaumont, 950 F. Supp. 1317, 1322-23 (E.D.Tex. 1997)
U.S. v. $80,760, 781 F.Supp. 462 (N.D.Tex. 1991)
U.S. v. Cota-Lopez, 358 F.Supp. 579 (W.D.Tex. 2002)
U.S. v. Outlaw, 134 F.Supp.2d 807 (W.D.Tex. 2001)

STATE

$217,590 in U.S. Currency v. Texas, 54 S.W.3d 914 (Ct. App. 2001)
Crockett v. Texas, 1991 Westlaw 11999, 803 S.W.2d 803 (Ct. Crim. App. 1991)
Drake v. Texas, 123 S.W.3d 596 (2003)
Frame v. Texas, 2006 WL 3627155 (Ct. App. 2007)
Green v. Texas, 2004 WL 3094650 (Ct. Crim. App. 2004)
Isler v. Texas, 2010 WL 724172 (Ct. App. 2010)
Jennings v. Texas, 2009 WL 167858 (Ct. App. 2009)
Kelly v. Texas, 824 S.W.2d 568 (Tex. Crim. App. 1992)
Martinez v. Texas, 2006 WL 3720136 (Ct. App. 2006)
Miles v. Texas, 2009 WL 4358959 (Ct. App. 2009)
Nenno v. Texas, 970 S.W.2d 549, 561 (Ct. Crim. App.1998), overruled on other grounds sub.
     nom. *Texas v. Terrazas*, 4 S.W.3d 720 (Tex. Crim. App.1999)
Parker v. Texas, 46 Tex.Crim. 461, 80 S.W. 1008 (Ct. Crim. App. 1904)
Perkins v. Texas, 2009 WL 2837356 (Ct. App. 2009)
Porter v. Texas, 93 S.W.3d 342 (Ct. App. 2002)
Ramos v. Texas, 496 So.2d 121 (1986)
Reyes v. Texas, 1997 WL 196356 (Ct. App. 1997)
Risher v. Texas, 227 S.W.3d 133 (Ct. Crim. App. 2006)
Robinson v. Texas, 2006 WL 3438076 (Ct. App. 2006), after remand, 2009 WL 5205361 (Ct.
     App. 2009)
Rodriguez v. Texas, 106 S.W.3d 224 (Ct. App. 2003)
Romo v. Texas, 315 S.W.3d 565 (Ct. App. 2010)
Smith v. Texas, 2004 WL 213395, 2004 Tex.App. LEXIS 1121 (Ct. App. 2004)
Strout v. Texas, 688 SW2d 188 (Ct. App. 1985)
Texas v. $27,877.00, 2010 WL 5187608 (Ct. App. 2010)
Texas v. Medrano, 127 S.W.3d 781, 785 (Ct. Crim. App. 2004)
Thomas v. Texas, 297 S.W.3d 458 (Ct. App. 2009)
Trejos v. Texas, 243 S.W.3d 30 (Ct. App. 2007)
Weinstein v. Texas, 2010 WL 2967675 (Ct. App. 2010)
Wilson v. Texas, 98 SW3d 265 (Ct. App. 2002)
Winfrey v. Texas, 291 S.W.3d 68 (Ct. App. 2009), rev'd 323 S.W.3d 875 (Ct. Crim. App. 2010)
Winston v. Texas, 78 S.W.3d 522 (Ct. App. 2002)

UTAH

STATE

In re $102,000, 823 P.2d 468 (1992)
Utah v. Rimmasch, 775 P.2d 388 (1989)
Utah v. Schultz, 58 P.3d 879 (Ct. App. 2002)

VERMONT

STATE

Vermont v. Bourassa, 137 Vt. 62, 399 A.2d 507 (1979)

VIRGINIA

FEDERAL

Truslow v. Spotsylvania County Sheriff, 783 F. Supp. 274, 277-79 (E.D.Va. 1992)
U.S. v. Watson, 783 F.Supp. 258 (E.D.Va. 1992)

STATE

Epperly v. Virginia, 224 Va. 214, 294 S.E.2d 882 (1982), habeas, *Epperly v. Booker*, 235 Va. 35, 366 S.E.2d 62 (1988)
Hetmeyer v. Virginia, 19 Va.App. 103, 448 S.E.2d 894 (Ct. App. 1994)
Jones v. Virginia, 277 Va. 171, 670 S.E.2d 727 (2009)
Pelletier v. Virginia, 42 Va.App. 406, 592 S.E.2d 382 (Ct. App. 2004)
Virginia v. Patterson, 392 Pa.Super. 331, 572 A.2d 1258 (Super. Ct. 1990)

WASHINGTON

STATE

Washington v. Burnice, 2006 WL 122198 (App., Div. 2006)
Washington v. Dearman, 92 Wash.App. 630, 962 P.2d 850 (Ct. App. 1998)
Washington v. Ellis, 48 Wash.App. 333, 738 P.2d 1085 (Ct. App. 1987)
Washington v. Gross, 57 Wash.App. 549, 552 789 P.2d 317, 319 (Ct. App. 1990)
Washington v. Leuluahialii, 118 Wash.App. 780, 77 P.3d 1192 (Ct. App. 2003), petition for review denied, 154 Wash.2d 1013 (2005); habeas corpus denied, *Leuluaialii v. Sinclair*, 2010 WL 891015 (W.D.Wash. 2010)
Washington v. Lord, 128 Wash.App. 216, 114 P.3d 1241 (Ct. App. 2005)
Washington v. Loucks, 98 Wash.2d 563, 656 P.2d 480 (1983)
Washington v. Nicholas, 34 Wash.App. 775, 663 P.2d 1356 (Ct. App. 1983)
Washington v. Pleadwell, 2010 WL 2994031 (Ct. App. 2010)
Washington v. Salazar-Rodriguez, 1999 WL 780975 (App. Div. 1999)
Washington v. Socolof, 28 Wash.App. 407, 623 P.2d 733 (Ct. App. 1981)
Washington v. Slattery, 56 Wash.App. 820, 787 P.2d 932 (1990)
Washington v. Stanphill, 53 Wash.App. 623, 769 P.2d 861 (Ct. App. 1989)

Washington v. Thein, 138 Wash.2d 133, 977 P.2d 582 (1999)
Washington v. Welker, 37 Wash.App. 628, 683 P.2d 1110 (Ct. App. 1984)
Washington v. Wieting, 1997 WL 88957 (Ct. App. 1997)
Washington v. Wolohan, 24 Wash.App. 813, 698 P.2d 421 (Ct. App. 1979)

WEST VIRGINIA

FEDERAL

U.S. v. Myers, 2010 WL 2723196 (S.D.W.Va. 2010)

STATE

West Virginia v. McKinney, 88 W.Va. 400, 106 S.E. 894 (1921)

WISCONSIN

STATE

Wisconsin v. Garcia, 195 Wis.2d 68, 535 N.W.2d 124 (Ct. App. 1995)
Wisconsin v. Miller, 256 Wis.2d 80, 647 N.W.2d 348 (Ct. App. 2002)

Index